The Horse

A Series of Books in Agricultural Science

Animal Science

Editors: G. W. Salisbury
E. W. Crampton (1957–1970)

 W. H. FREEMAN AND COMPANY · SAN FRANCISCO

J. WARREN EVANS
University of California, Davis

ANTHONY BORTON
University of Massachusetts

HAROLD F. HINTZ
Cornell University

L. DALE VAN VLECK
Cornell University

The Horse

with chapters by

Jay R. Georgi, *Cornell University*
Robert M. Jordan, *University of Minnesota*
John E. Lowe, *Cornell University*
Gary D. Potter, *Texas A & M University*
B. F. Yeates, *Texas A & M University*

Unless otherwise credited, all photographs are by the authors.

Library of Congress Cataloging in Publication Data
Main entry under title:

The Horse.

   Bibliography: p.
   Includes index.
   1. Horses.   I. Evans, James Warren, 1938–
SF285.H748   636.1   76-22686
ISBN 0-7167-0491-9

Printed in the United States of America

Contents

Preface

The horse ceased to be an important source of agricultural power in the United States approximately 30–40 years ago, but popular interest in horses appears to be ever increasing. More people own horses, enjoy watching them, enjoy reading about them, and wish to learn more about them today than at any other time in American history.

Although horses have not received as much attention from scientists as have the other species of livestock, many significant findings about horses have been made in recent years. These findings, combined with the results of early equine studies, information extrapolated from experiments with other species, and observations of experienced horsemen, form the basis of most recommendations for modern horse management. This reference and textbook on the horse represents an attempt to combine these sources of information.

July 1976

J. WARREN EVANS
ANTHONY BORTON
HAROLD F. HINTZ
L. DALE VAN VLECK

The Horse

PART ONE *Introduction*

CHAPTER ONE *The History and Development of the Horse*

The evolution of the horse is one of the most fascinating phenomena in history and is of immense importance to mankind, because the development of most civilizations has been inextricably interwoven with the domestication of the horse. From ancient to modern times, the horse has served man as a beast of burden, a draft animal, and a means of transportation; has helped him wage wars; and has provided him with recreation, companionship, and even food.

> Look over the struggle for freedom
> Trace your present day strength to its source
> You'll find that man's pathway to glory
> Is strewn with the bones of a horse.
>
> ANONYMOUS

According to Charles Russell (1927), the cowboy artist and humorist,

> It was this animal that took 'em from a cave. For thousands of years the hoss and his long-eared cousins furnished all transportation on land for man an' broke all the ground for their farmin'. He has helped build every railroad in the world. Even now he builds the roads for the automobile that has made him nearly useless, an' I'm here to tell these machine-lovers that it will take a million years for the gas wagon to catch up with this hoss in what he's done for man.

Fortunately, the automobile has not rendered the horse useless, and today this sensitive, intelligent, athletic animal is enjoying unprecedented popularity in this country, where its ancestors originated some 50 million years ago. However, modern domesticated horses, because they have evolved relatively recently, represent but a small part of the large and varied group of animals that make up the family Equidae (the horse family), most of which are extinct. This family includes the many breeds, strains, and types of domestic horses, as well as all living "wild" horses, donkeys, zebras, onagers, and their ancestors (also see Chapters 2 and 14).

The horse family is one of the classic examples of evolution for two reasons. First, enormous changes took place in the size and structure of the animal in response to environmental changes, such as changes in climate and food sources. Second, fortunately the fossil remains of the horse were well preserved in the river-valley clays, sands, and sandstones of the rich paleontologic beds of the American West. The association of fossil remains of prehistoric horses with the various geological times furnishes one of the best-documented examples of the evolutionary changes of an animal species.

1.1 Origin

The horse, as we know it today, is descended from a small, primitive, four-toed animal that inhabited the river banks during the early Eocene epoch. This "dawn horse," no larger than a fox and bearing little resemblance to the modern horse, has been named *Eohippus*. (*Eo* is the Greek word for "dawn" and *hippus* is the Greek word for "horse".) From *Eohippus* to the Thoroughbred, dramatic changes occurred in size and shape. There were also remarkable evolutionary changes in the teeth and chewing methods, the size of the skull and brain, and the length of the neck and legs. In addition, the four toes were reduced to a single, sturdy hoof.

Professor O. C. Marsh of Yale University found the first specimen of the prehistoric horse in North America in 1876. Fossil beds in the badlands of Wyoming and New Mexico yielded the first entire specimen to the careful study of E. D. Cope in 1885. The skill, patience, diligence, and enthusiasm of the scientists as they uncovered the mysteries of the prehistoric horse are graphically described by George Gaylord Simpson in *Horses*, an exceptional book on the evolution of the horse.

Eohippus (Dawn Horse): Eocene Epoch

The oldest known ancestor of the modern horse was a tiny, rodentlike, four-toed creature that inhabited the swamps and river beds of North

America during the Eocene epoch. At that time, the climate of the American West was more uniform and milder than at present. The great Rocky Mountains were new, and their base was not much above sea level. The subtropical temperatures and abundant moisture encouraged the growth of lush vegetation and provided an ideal environment for the prehistoric horse. The *Eohippus* was 10–20 inches high and had a flexible, arched back. The hindquarters were higher than the forequarters, much like a rabbit's. The head was not that of a miniature horse but was instead more reptilelike, and contained a small, primitive brain. In fact, the head of *Eohippus* was so unlike that of the modern horse that the first skeletal remains, found near Suffolk, England, in 1838, were wrongly classified on the basis of the rodentlike skull. The British named their discovery *Hyracotherium* (from the Greek *hyrax*, meaning "shrew," and *therion*, meaning "wild beast"). It later proved to be closely related to the North American *Eohippus*.

The evolution of the horse has been traced by detailed studies that have been made of the teeth. An examination of the cheek teeth, the molars, and premolars indicates that a continuous series of evolutionary modifications accompanied the adaptation of the animal to changing food sources and environments. The teeth of *Eohippus* were those of a primitive browser and not of a grazing animal. Their simple structure was adequate for feeding upon lush leaves and soft, fleshy parts of the plants that grew along the fertile river basins of New Mexico and Wyoming where vegetation was copious. The soft, primitive nature of the teeth indicated that *Eohippus* had a short life span.

Evolutionary changes also occurred in the locomotion system, particularly the leg and foot structures. The legs of *Eohippus* were adapted for running. There were four toes in front, each ending in a small hoof. The hind feet had three toes and vestiges of two others. (No five-toed ancestor of the horse has ever been identified.) This primitive animal walked on a pad at the base of the toes, much like a fox, and the hooves were pressed against the ground to grip, but not to support the animal's weight. The *Eohippus* survived as a result of alertness and swiftness of flight. These creatures would hide among the bushes and vegetation and skillfully elude their enemies by fleeing. Their structure indicates that they were "equally well qualified as leapers or as runners" (Riggs, 1932).

Paleontologic records indicate that, beginning with this small, stupid, swift creature, the horse family evolved and flourished on the North American continent during four geological epochs (Figure 1-1). A number of primitive species of horse developed during the Eocene and spread separately across North America and Europe, but the American fossils have been traced as the direct link with modern *Equus*. Interestingly, the early fossil remains found in Great Britain did not develop into an equine dynasty similar to the one in North America.

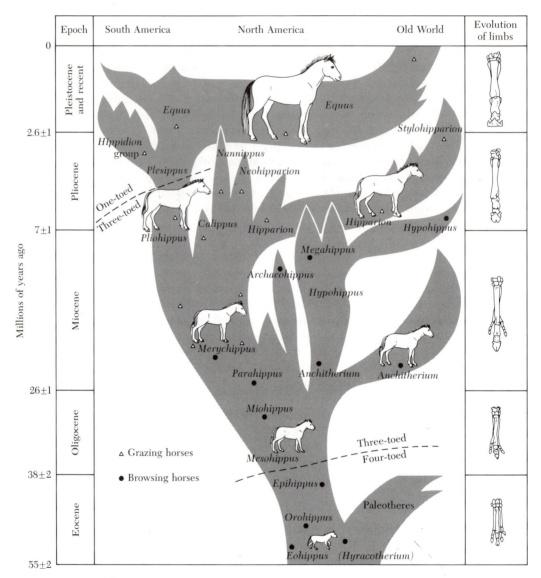

FIGURE 1-1

The evolution of the horse. Modern horses of the genus *Equus* stand as high as 6½ feet, run on one toe on each foot, and have teeth adapted to grazing on grass. *Eohippus*, their earliest known ancestor, was a primitive, 4-toed creature less than 12 inches high, with teeth adapted to browsing on leaves. Note from the ages on the left that the vertical dimension of this figure is out of scale. In a true-scale figure, the Pleistocene and Recent epochs would together account for less than one-twentieth of the height of the figure, leaving insufficient room to include a picture of a modern horse. Adapted from Riggs (1932) and Simpson (1951).

Mesohippus (Middle Horse): Oligocene Epoch

The second piece of the evolutionary puzzle was found in the rich fossil beds from the Oligocene epoch in the Bad Lands of South Dakota. The sediments of the Black Hills and Rocky Mountains covered and preserved fossil remains much more perfectly than the remains of the Eocene epoch. Two distinct kinds of three-toed horses were found, and they numbered more than 30 species. *Mesohippus* was the first three-toed horse and was the most significant link from the Oligocene epoch. The *Mesohippus* was about twice the size (24 inches high) of *Eohippus* and had three toes on the front foot; the middle hoof was noticeably larger than the other two. This creature undoubtedly looked more like a horse than did its primitive ancestor. It had a larger brain, and the skull shape was becoming longer; the face was becoming more slender and the eyes were set further back. The teeth were still primitive and low crowned, and were not those of a grazing animal, although there were some definite "advancements" in the premolars and upper incisors. The legs were long, slender, and elongated below the elbow and the knees.

The second three-toed horse of the Oligocene was *Miohippus*, which was much like *Mesohippus* except that it was larger. Several strains developed from the *Miohippus* in North America and migrated to Europe where they eventually died out.

Merychippus: Miocene Epoch

The "later three-toed horse" of the Miocene Epoch represented a radical change for the horse family. This was a period when the habitat of horses varied: individual species lived in the lowlands, uplands, and desert. During this epoch three important links to the modern horse emerged: *Parahippus*, "the upland horse"; *Merychippus*, "the desert or later three-toed horse"; and *Pliohippus*, "the latest three-toed horse," which spanned the gap into the Pliocene. These horses exhibited dramatic evolutionary changes in size, skeletal structure, and dentition.

During the Miocene epoch grass became more abundant, and the herbivores began to change from browsers to grazers. Grazers need teeth that provide good grinding action because grass is a tough, harsh food. During this period, there was a natural selection in favor of those Miocene horses that developed teeth that were well suited to grazing as opposed to browsing. The crown height of the teeth increased, so that as wear occurred, the tooth continued to grow out and to maintain a good grinding surface. Enamel ridges also appeared in the teeth, providing a heavy cement covering that strengthened and protected the teeth and prolonged their useful

7

life. To adapt to the new, harsher diet and stronger teeth, the motion of the lower jaw changed from an up-and-down crushing action to a side-to-side grinding action of the lower molars against the upper ones. This, of course, is the chewing action of the horse today.

During this time, the skull became more horse-like; the muzzle became elongated and the eyes were placed further apart on the more slender head. The Miocene horses were larger (40 inches high), much more slender, and probably more alert, intelligent, and athletic. They were widely distributed over North America—their fossil remains have been found in such diverse regions as Florida, Texas, Montana, California, and Oregon.

The legs became further modified for speed and efficiency. A loss of rotation resulted from the fusion of the radius and ulna in the forearm into a single bone. A similar fusion occurred between the tibia and fibula of the hind leg. This was an important change because the horse of the Miocene epoch had to run to survive. The joints of the horse work in just one plane, forward and back, and it is this peculiar specialized way of going that has enabled the horse to survive by outdistancing any of its adversaries. "Horses use their legs only for locomotion (or kicking) and not for holding, manipulation, and the like as do men, cats, squirrels and many other animals that retain more flexible limbs" (Simpson, 1951).

There was also a notable change in the toes during this period. The center toe became longer and stronger and able to carry weight. The importance of the foot pad of earlier horses was lost, and the side toes were small although they still ended in small hooves. The side toes no longer made contact with the ground in the standing horse although they may have in the running horse.

Pliohippus: Pliocene Epoch

The *Pliohippus* is often referred to as the first one-toed horse, but in fact it was also the "latest three-toed horse"; the side toes were often weak and small but still present. The *Pliohippus* was the connection between the Miocene and Pliocene, and it was this genus that gave rise to *Equus* with relatively few major evolutionary changes. It was in the *Pliohippus* that toe reduction eventually occurred. However, the loss of the side toes from some of the later species of *Pliohippus* was not of great importance at the time because they had already become nonfunctional. When the toes finally disappeared completely, they left vestiges, the long splint bones that are still present on each side of the cannon of modern *Equus*. The *Pliohippus* was the bridge to *Plesippus*, a very horselike creature of the late Pliocene epoch.

Equus (True Horses): Pleistocene Epoch

Equus, the genus comprising the "true horses," developed during the Pleistocene epoch. It differed little from its immediate ancestors, the major difference being a somewhat more complicated tooth structure. The first true horses spread rapidly throughout the world. The Pleistocene epoch heralded the coming of man and of the Ice Age. It was a period of alternating cold and warmth, and the mammals were forced to migrate to survive the advancing ice sheets. During this time *Equus* developed, flourished, and spread rapidly throughout the world. The animals migrated into South America and the Old World by way of the land bridges that existed then. Fossil remains of *Equus* have been discovered in Asia, Europe, and Africa, as well as throughout North America and South America.

1.2   *Extinction of the Horse in North America*

Thus, *Equus* originated in North America a million years ago and migrated throughout the rest of the world, which was fortunate because there were no horses in the Western Hemisphere when it was discovered by Europeans. The extinction of the horse in North America, after it had flourished for four geological epochs and roughly 50 million years, remains one of the unsolved mysteries of history. The extinction cannot be attributed directly to the effect of glacial cold, because parts of the continent were safe from glaciation, and the horse actually survived the ice ages, only to disappear as the ice was retreating. It should also be noted that companion grazing animals, such as the bison, survived and thrived in the New World. On the other hand, there seems to be no adequate explanation why other specialized mammals of North America also disappeared during the Pleistocene epoch and more recently. The rhinoceros, camel, saber-toothed tiger, elephant, mastodon, and horse all succumbed. No one theory adequately explains the demise of the horse in the Americas. Riggs (1932) concludes that

> the horse, in Pliocene time, had reached a degree of racial old age which, as in the camel of the same time, greatly lowered his adaptability to changed conditions of living. So, in the face of changing climate, changing food, and all the unfavorable conditions which may have gone with them, the horse in America suffered extinction in the Pleistocene while his relatives in Asia and his distant relatives in Africa survived until modern times.

9

Insects, disease, the acts of early man, and the disappearance or depletion of food sources have all been considered and discounted as the sole cause of the extinction of horses throughout North America and South America. This situation caused George Gaylord Simpson (1951) to reflect that "this seems at present one of the situations in which we must be humble and honest and admit that we simply do not know the answer. It must be remembered too that extinction of the horses in the New World is only part of a larger problem. Many other animals became extinct here at about the same time."

In the one million years since the first appearance of *Equus* and its mysterious disappearance from the American continent, man has become civilized and numerous animal species, including the horse, have become domesticated. However, the *Equus* of a million years ago changed remarkably little as a result of its contact with man. The modern *Equus* is still an athletic animal adapted for running and grazing over vast areas of plains, subsisting solely on grasses and escaping its enemies with bursts of speed. The evolutionary process resulted in an animal that was designed for speed, with long, slender legs, and that was permanently up on its toes. Lateral flexion of the joints was lost in favor of one fluid motion forward and backward, without wasted deviation. The neck and head became elongated so that the animal could graze while on its feet; the eyes were placed high on the head so that vision was possible over a long range. The muscles were bunched in the upper legs to allow a maximum of motion with a minimum of contraction. In short, a superb, intelligent, graceful, athletic animal evolved that was to be changed little by man but that was to change the future of all mankind.

1.3   Recent History and Development of the Horse

The tangled web of the recent history of the horse is more obscure and controversial than the horse's evolutionary development. We know that *Equus* spread throughout the world from North America. Various distinct forms of *Equus* then developed in different areas of the world at different times. The horse's development was probably significantly affected by wide variations in altitude, climate, soil, and forages. However, the early wild horses exhibited great adaptability—they flourished in steppes, forests, deserts, and tundra. Some studies of prehistoric horses have classified them by racial groups according to the environment in which they developed.

FIGURE 1-2
Tarpan horses in a corral in winter. Photograph by W. Pruski, courtesy of
Daphne M. Goodall.

Wild Horses

Races of modern horses may have appeared as early as the late glacial
period. Drawings found in caves in southern France show horses with
markedly different characteristics. The heavy, draft type of horse is illustrated next to a smaller, refined, "Arab" type of horse. In Britain, Pleistocene beds have yielded remains of both heavy and light horses. In sum,
the wild horses developed into several forms, all of which still exist: the
"domestic" horse, *Equus caballus*, which was found in northern Asia and
throughout the whole of Europe; the onager and kiang, *Equus hemionus*,
which inhabited central and southern Asia; the ass, *Equus asinus*, of northern Africa; and several species of zebras and quaggas that inhabited Africa
south of the Sahara.

Equus przewalskii presently is the only species of wild horse and is
native to eastern Asia near the Mongolian border. The Tarpan, the European wild horse of eastern Russia (Figure 1-2), probably survived in the
wild until early in this century. Wild species are difficult to find in their
pure form because they interbreed freely with domestic races, thereby
further tangling the threads of their history. *Equus przewalskii* is a small,
compact horse of approximately 13 hands. The head is large and broad, and
the mane is erect and has practically no forelock. The mane and tail are
black, and the lower legs are dark brown or black. *Equus przewalskii* characteristically has a light-colored muzzle. The coat color is variable and

11

ranges from light brown to yellow dun. One of the finest collections of these animals is found at the Catskill Game Farm in Catskill, New York, where these wild horses prefer to remain "wild" and show little interest in even the most elementary domestication.

Domestication

Little is known about either the early development of specific strains of horses or the first domestication of the horse by man. However, modern man and modern horse developed together. Undoubtedly, the earliest association between man and horse was a one-sided one in which man hunted and subsisted on the flesh of horses. The bones of 40,000 horses that existed 25,000 years ago, found outside a rock shelter at Solutré, France, provide evidence of the cave man's dependence on the horse. Perhaps the Paleolithic Indians in North America were partly responsible for the extinction of the horse on that continent, since the appearance of man there closely coincided with the disappearance of the horse.

Early man must have discovered other virtues of the horse even as it was providing him a source of food. Although the precise date of domestication remains unknown, the walls of numerous caves throughout the Old World contain drawings that indicate that man's dependence on the horse dates back to the most ancient times (Figure 1-3).

Charles Russell (1927) has written an entertaining account of man's first domestication of the horse. He describes a cave man who is looking

FIGURE 1-3
Prehistoric cave paintings of horses from the cave gallery at Lascaux, France. Photograph courtesy of Caisse Nationale des Monuments Historiques et des Sites, Paris.

down "from his ledge to the valley below where all these animals is busy eatin' one another, an' notices one species that don't take no part in this feast, but can out-run an' out-dodge all others. This cave man is progressive, an' has learned to think. He sees this animal is small compared to the rest, an' ain't got no horns, tusks or claws, eatin' nothin' but grass." Later, when man has succeeded in capturing a horse, "he finds out that though this beast ain't got horns or claws, he's mighty handy with all four feet, and when Paw sneaks home that evenin' he's got hoof marks all over him an' he ain't had a ride yet. Sore as he is, he goes back the next day an' tries again."

The date and place of the initial domestication of the horse are understandably the subject of considerable disagreement. Simpson (1951) logically suggests that there were probably a variety of races of wild horses and that initial domestication undoubtedly occurred in several parts of the world at approximately the same time. Certainly two of these areas must have been China and Mesopotamia between 4500 and 2500 B.C. In any event, it was in the Near East, the cradle of European civilization, that the horse was rapidly integrated into a way of life that relied upon its use as a draft animal. By 1000 B.C., the domestication of the horse had spread to almost every part of Europe, Asia, and North Africa.

Development of Heavy and Light Horse Types

The cave drawings of western and southern France, Spain, and England were similar in that even at these early times they depicted several types of horses. Horses have been classified as Oriental and Occidental, but these broad descriptions are based on type differences and not necessarily on geographical origin. The Oriental horses, generally termed "hot blooded," had heads that were relatively broader than those of other horses, and developed into the riding horses of the Mediterranean. The Occidental horses, often Roman-nosed, had longer, narrower heads and developed into the "cold-blooded" horses of Europe. In Europe there were actually two types of horses developing: the Celtic pony (44–48 inches high), which was well formed, lightweight, sturdy, and rather short-legged; and the Great Horse of the Middle Ages — the large, slow, and powerful heavy horse.

The Oriental horses were the mounts of the nomadic tribesmen from the Asian steppes who overran the Near East and occupied all of North Africa. Mounted on light, swift, "hot-blooded" horses, the Mongol horsemen traveled west through Europe and introduced the horse culture to Scandinavia, the British Isles, France, and Spain. The Germans and French developed large, heavy horses to carry their armored knights into battle, but the Spanish respected the Arab and Barb blood of the Oriental horses and utilized it to develop their own highly refined *jineta* or jennet. These light and agile Spanish horses were popular in England, and it was from

13

these horses that the English saddle horses were developed. The highly prized Spanish horses were also brought to the New World by the explorers, conquistadors, and early settlers. There had been no horses on the continent for 8,000 years when the white man arrived in the New World, but the rugged Spanish horses were uniquely qualified to thrive in their new environment. Some of the colonists' horses escaped to the western plains of North America and the pampas of South America and became America's "wild horses." These feral horses became the extraordinarily tough and alert American Mustang. Hope Ryden's excellent book, *America's Last Wild Horses* (1970), traces the history of these Mustangs from their origin to their current fight against extinction.

Return of Horses to America

The first horses to reach the North American continent were the well-bred mounts of the Spanish conquistadors. It is a myth that the vast Mustang herds that roamed the West by the 1880s were strays from the expeditions of Cortez, in Mexico in 1519; Coronado, from Arizona to Kansas in 1540; and DeSoto, in Florida and the Southeast, 1541. The exploits of these early Spanish explorers are fascinating and the importance of the horse to them was undeniable, but the evidence does not support the contention that these expeditions brought the horse to the Indians and the continent. Rather, it was the Spanish missions that followed the Spanish explorers into the Rio Grande Valley in the early 1600s that brought with them large numbers of livestock: goats, sheep, cattle, and, of course, horses. More specifically, Juan de Onate established a large settlement in what is now Santa Fe, New Mexico, in 1594. A series of other missions were established (24 in New Mexico) where the Indian children undoubtedly learned farming and were exposed to the breaking, training, and use of the horse. These Indians, thus instructed in horsemanship, probably passed on their knowledge and skills, and even some of the Spanish horses, to other Indians. The century from 1650 to 1750 was a period during which the Spanish horses were dispersed over the plains, and among the Indians a great "horse culture" developed (Figure 1-4). The profound effect that the horse had on the life-style and culture of the Plains Indian in a relative short period resulted in a population and cultural explosion that enabled the Indians to effectively slow the white man's takeover of the West.

It took only 200 years for the great "wild" horse herds of the Plains to become adapted to a region where, 60 million years earlier, the ancestors of the wild horse had begun their development at the dawn of history. The history of the development of the vast horse, bison, and long-horned cattle (also Spanish in origin) herds in the American West is one of the most colorful aspects of the history of the horse in the United States. However, it was the early colonists who settled the East Coast that were

FIGURE 1-4
Plains Indians hunting bison from horseback. This painting by George Catlin, an American ethnologist who studied the Indians of western North America during the 1830s, clearly depicts the impressive riding skill of the Plains Indians. Photograph courtesy of The Mansell Collection, London.

responsible for the development of many of the American breeds of horses.

The East Coast Indians were introduced to horses by the Spanish explorers at about the same time as their western cousins. However, they were farmers and trappers, and their needs for horses were quite different. Their society did not develop around the horse to the same extent that western society did. The horse was used by these Indians primarily as a pack animal to haul hides to the coast. However, their horses were no less fine and were also of Spanish origin, although they were referred to as "Chickasaw" horses. These horses came from a series of Franciscan missions that were established in the Southeast (Georgia) at the same time that Juan de Onate was establishing his mission in the Southwest. Many of the early colonists bought Chickasaw horses from the Indians to use on their farms. These horses then provided a "Spanish" base in the "native" herds that were later used to breed the Quarter Horse, the American Saddle Horse and the Tennessee Walking Horse.

The colonists along the Atlantic seaboard, the English in Virginia, the Dutch in New York, and the French in Quebec brought horses with them. The colonists subsequently imported more horses, but most of them came not from the Old World but from the horse-breeding farms established by the Spanish in the West Indies. The Spanish basis of the light horse stocks of the New World was well established in the Mustangs of the West, the Chickasaw and other Indian horses of the Southeast, and the mounts and farm horses of the colonists.

Horses were little used in colonial New England. The small, hilly, rocky fields were better suited to oxen than to draft horses, and the Puritan ethic militated against the expense and frivolity of keeping riding horses. Horse racing was socially unacceptable because it was too closely associated with the landed gentry in England, whom the colonists had sought to escape by coming to America. However, horse breeding became a popular enterprise later on as the market developed for riding horses, for coach horses, and for work horses in the cities and in the West Indies, where they were used on the sugar plantations. The development of harness racing created a further strain on the colonists' puritanical values, as a demand was created for some of New England's fast strains of harness horses.

As the colonies developed, the farmers in New York and Pennsylvania had need of heavy horses that would not only till the soil but also haul their products to the markets in Philadelphia and New York City. The native horses were a little small and too light for this rugged work, so the colonists naturally turned to the horses of their homelands and imported the Belgian, Percheron, Shire, and Clydesdale breeds. These "draft" stallions were mated to the "native" mares, and although many fine, heavy, coach and wagon horses were produced for use in America's developing cities, no American breed of draft or coach horse was ever developed. A typical tall, rangy, active Conestoga horse was bred in southern Pennsylvania and was highly sought after by the freight haulers, but no breed registry was established, and the Conestoga horse eventually disappeared as imports from the Old World increased.

Development of American Breeds

After the United States was founded and as it began to grow and prosper, the need for horses increased. In the Northeast, there was a need for a versatile draft, light harness, driving, and riding horse, and the versatile Morgan horse developed. In the South, the need for a comfortable, ground-covering, smooth-gaited riding and driving horse resulted in the development of the American Saddle Horse and the Tennessee Walking Horse. The short (approximately 1/4 mile) flat racing of Virginia led to the development of the Quarter Horse, which moved West with the settlers and later was America's premier cow horse. Sporting interests on the East Coast became interested in the harness horse, and the Standardbred breed developed from the best trotting and pacing stock available at the time. In the West, the Nez Percé Indians developed the strong and colorful Appaloosa, a breed that was renowned for its hardiness and endurance.

All breeds have one thing in common: they are not intrinsically pure. There are many interrelationships in the ancestry of the American breeds. Breeds evolved as a result of geographical isolation and selection for a specific purpose. At some point, the desirable characteristics became sufficiently defined that a breed type developed, and finally a breed registry was formed. For example, the registry for the American Quarter Horse, a breed that traces its existence to colonial times, was not formed until 1940. The beautiful American breeds are all light horses that can in some way be traced back to the hardy, refined Spanish horses that populated the Western Hemisphere. It is interesting that no draft breed or pony breeds developed in the United States at the time the light horse breeds were evolving. In the following chapter the breeds of horses that developed in the United States are discussed in more detail.

References

Crowell, Pers. 1951. *Cavalcade of American Horses*. New York: McGraw-Hill.

Denhardt, Robert Moorman. 1948. *The Horse of the Americas*. Norman: University of Oklahoma Press.

Dobie, J. Frank. 1952. *The Mustangs*. Boston: Little, Brown.

Epstein, H. 1971. *The Origin of the Domestic Animals of Africa*. New York: Africana.

Gianoli, Luigi. 1969. *Horses and Horsemanship through the Ages*. New York: Crown.

Haines, Francis. 1971. *Horses in America*. New York: Crowell.

Morris, Pamela MacGregor, and Nereo Lugli. 1973. *Horses of the World*. New York: Crown.

Riggs, Elmer S. 1932. *The Geological History and Evolution of the Horse*. Geology Leaflet 13. Chicago: Field Museum of Natural History.

Russell, Charles U. 1927. *Trails Plowed Under*. Garden City, New York: Doubleday.

Ryden, Hope. 1970. *America's Last Wild Horses*. New York: Dutton.

Simpson, George Gaylord. 1951. *Horses*. New York: Oxford University Press.

Summerhays, R. S. 1961. *Horses and Ponies*. London: Frederick Warne.

Willoughby, David P. 1974. *The Empire of Equus*. Cranbury, New Jersey: A. S. Barnes.

CHAPTER TWO *Breeds in the United States*

Each country has many breeds of horses that it claims as its own. The United States is no exception. Although all foundation stock for American breeds was imported, usually from Europe, American breeders have developed many distinctly American breeds from these stocks. Only a few breeds have been transferred directly to this country.

The usual definition of a breed is that it is a group of animals that have certain distinguishable characteristics, such as function, conformation, and color. Breed registries depend on correct identification to ensure accuracy of ancestry and to establish standards for the fair exchange of horses between buyer and seller. The first Appendix to this chapter gives a brief outline of identification procedures based on color and color pattern (see section 24.2 for a more detailed discussion of other identification methods).

A rather arbitrary distinction exists between horses and ponies. Ponies are less than 14 or 14.2 hands in height (14.2 means 14 hands and 2 inches) measured at the withers, where a hand is 4 inches. Many horse breeds, however, include small members that fall below the dividing line. Most members of some small breeds of horses actually fall into the pony class according to height.

Most of the major breeds of horses, ponies, and asses that maintain registries in the United States are briefly described in this chapter. More detailed accounts are available in the many books that have been written on the history and development of single breeds or that deal specifically with several breeds. The following discussion of breeds follows no particular order except for some consideration of the historical development and recent popularity of each breed.

2.1 The Arabian

No breed of horse has influenced the development of breeds of light horses in America more than has the Thoroughbred, but the Thoroughbred was developed largely from the Arabian. Although the history and origin of the Arabian horse are not always agreed upon even by experts, there is no question that the Arabs have been breeding and selecting for improved Arabian horses for 2,000 years or more. The stock for this selection may have existed for as long as 3,000 years in the Mideast or northern Africa before Arabian horses were first bred on the deserts of the Arabian peninsula.

Some historians believe that the Barb horses of northern Africa (the Barbary States) were ancestors of the Arabian, whereas others believe the Arabians were used in development of the Barb. In any event, the Arabians, Barbs, and Turkmene horses all developed in the same general region of the world. Most of the so-called hot-blooded horses of the world can be traced to these three ancestors.

In spite of the long history of the Arabian horse, the first registry for recording the breed in America was not organized until 1908. The name of the registry, the Arabian Horse Club Registry of America, was changed in 1949 and was shortened in 1969 to the Arabian Horse Registry of America (AHRA). The first Arabians apparently were imported to America shortly before the Revolutionary War, but the major expansion of the breed occurred about 1906 when Homer Davenport imported 27 horses from the deserts of Arabia. Records show that 39 other horses had been imported between 1760 and that year. This stimulus resulted in the organization of the first breed registry. By the end of 1973, 100,000 horses had been registered; approximately 13,000 were registered in that year alone. Before 1908, American Arabs were registered, if at all, by the Jockey Club, which discontinued registration of Arabians and Anglo-Arabs (crosses between registered Thoroughbreds and Arabians) in 1943 and currently registers only Thoroughbreds.

The general rules for registration as given by the AHRA are:

Eligibility (Rule #1, Section 2)

A horse of pure Arabian Blood *may be eligible* for registration in the Arabian Horse Registry of America only if it is within one of the following classifications:

　1. A horse born in the United States, Canada or Mexico whose sire and dam are both registered with the Registry.

　2. A horse imported in utero into the United States, Canada or Mexico whose dam is recorded with the Registry and whose sire is recorded in an approved foreign Stud Book.

19

3. A horse imported into the United States, Canada or Mexico if recorded in an approved foreign Stud Book. Anyone contemplating the importation of an Arabian horse should contact the Registry for a list of approved countries and specific requirements for quality and necessary documents.

In recent years, Polish, or Shagya, Arabians have become popular, and many have been imported (Figure 2-1).

In 1930, the International Arabian Horse Association was formed to promote the Arabian in America. In 1951 that association took over the registration of Half-Arabians and Anglo-Arabs from the American Remount Association. By 1972, 115,000 had been registered; since then there has been an increase of approximately 12,000 per year. Most of these are Half-Arabians, which must have had a registered Arabian either as sire or dam. Thus, the ancestry of the Half-Arabian will be 50 percent or more Arabian.

The Arabian is a general-purpose, light horse with an unsurpassed reputation for endurance. Arabians generally stand 14.1–15.1 hands at the withers and weigh between 800 and 1,000 pounds—somewhat smaller than most general-purpose riding horses. Naturally, some horses do not fall within these limits.

The head of the ideal Arabian is distinctive: relatively small, dished, and triangular with a small muzzle, wide-set eyes, and a chiseled appear-

FIGURE 2-1
A Polish Arabian stallion, *Bask, imported in 1963 by Lasma Arabians, is a Legion of Merit champion that has won several U.S. National Championships. Photograph courtesy of International Arabian Horse Association. (Asterisk preceding horse's name indicates importation.)

ance. The neck is also distinctive; it is long and highly arched, and set high on the shoulder. The back is generally short and straight. The short back of the Arabian has long been attributed to the fact that this breed has one vertebra fewer than other breeds. Nearly 75 percent of the Arabian skeletons, however, are reported to have the usual 6 lumbar vertebrae rather than 5. Of the 7 Arabians studied by Stetcher (1962), 4 had only 17 thoracic vertebrae rather than 18. He found that only 1 of 6 had 5 rather than 6 lumbar vertebrae. The croup is long and comparatively flat to the tail, possibly because some Arabians have 2 fewer caudal (tail) vertebrae than other breeds. The tail is often arched above croup level while the horse is walking or trotting.

The American Horse Show Rule Book lists the following guidelines for judges:

Section 2.   Arabian Type and Conformation

(a) Comparatively small head, profile of head straight or preferably slightly concave below the eyes; small muzzle, large nostrils, extended when in action; large, round, expressive, dark eyes set well apart (glass eyes shall be penalized in breeding classes); comparatively short distance between eye and muzzle; deep jowls, wide between the branches; small ears (smaller in stallions than mares), thin and well-shaped, tips curved slightly inwards; long, arched neck, set on high and running well back into moderately high withers; long sloping shoulder, well laid over with muscle; ribs well sprung; long, broad forearm; short cannon bone with large sinew; short back; loins broad and strong; croup comparatively horizontal; natural high tail carriage. Viewed from rear, tail should be carried straight; hips strong and round; well muscled thigh and gaskin; straight, sound, flat bone; large joints, strong and well defined; sloping pasterns of good length; round feet of proportionate size. Height from 14.1 to 15.1 hands, with an occasional individual over or under.

(b) Dark skin; solid color, except legs and face (white spots on body permissible, but very undesirable in breeding classes); fine coat.

(c) Stallions especially should have an abundance of natural vitality, animation, spirit, suppleness and balance.

The colors for Arabians preferred by most breeders are generally solid: bay, brown, chestnut, gray, and black. Bays (Figure 2-2) and grays (Figure 2-3) have been particularly popular. White Arabians are grays that have turned white with age. Official publications of the AHRA state that "One

21

FIGURE 2-2
The 1973 National Champion Arabian stallion, Khemosabi, owned by Haifa Arabian Horses. Photograph by Polly Knoll, courtesy of Dr. and Mrs. B. P. Husband.

FIGURE 2-3
*Dornaba, a Legion of Merit Champion Arabian mare that won the 1966 U.S. National and Canadian Championship. Owned by Dr. Howard F. Kale. Photograph courtesy of International Arabian Horse Association.

never sees duns, piebalds or palominos, . . ." However, a noted student of the Arabian, Gladys Brown Edwards (1971), disagrees somewhat:

> The Arabian is not a color breed, so markings and color are not all that important, except that the body spot has been discriminated against in the judging rules—though recently modified—and accordingly, has been considered "unclean" by novices. Some of the more naive—unfamiliar with the breed's tradition of plentiful markings—have considered it a "sign of admixture." Instead, it is more likely a sign of the breed's antiquity. In the first place, the reason for this "anti-white" clause was to discourage production of pintos in the breed, and after decades of teaching that "Arabians are never parti-color," it is embarrassing to admit that they are.

On the other hand, Half-Arabians resulting from crosses with Appaloosas, Paints, or Palominos, as shown in Figure 2-4, may be variable in

FIGURE 2-4
Half-Arabians: *a*, Candyhorse Kachina, Appaloosa-Arabian of Candyhorse Farm (Alexander photo); *b*, Shoshone's Fancy, Pinto-Arabian, Richard and Sherrie Koehler, owners; *c*, My Mystic Mirage, Palomino-Arabian gelding owned by Mr. and Mrs. George Albin. Photographs courtesy of International Arabian Horse Association.

a

b

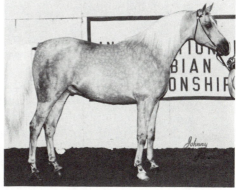

c

23

color while maintaining some desired Arabian characteristics. Naturally, Half-Arabians vary greatly also in size and type as well as color, depending on the cross.

2.2   The Thoroughbred

The Thoroughbred has been developed for speed at intermediate distances. No other breed can match the Thoroughbred at racing distances of 6 furlongs (¾ mile) to 1½ miles. In addition, Thoroughbreds have been popular as polo ponies, hunters, and jumpers, as well as for pleasure riding. For many years, Thoroughbreds and Half-Thoroughbreds were popular with the United States Cavalry. In fact, General George A. Custer was mounted on a Thoroughbred, Vic, by Austerlitz, at the Little Big Horn River on June 25, 1876.

The Thoroughbred provided foundation stock for many of the light horse breeds of the United States, including the Standardbred, the American Saddle Horse, the Morgan, and the Quarter Horse, which still accepts Half-Thoroughbreds.

Many states receive substantial revenues as their share of parimutuel betting. In 1972, the 28 states with legalized parimutuel betting shared more than $326 million from betting on Thoroughbred races. In addition, $1.5 million of unclaimed winnings of bettors was also turned over to the state treasuries. Total attendance exceeded 45 million persons.

The history of the Thoroughbred as a breed began in England. Native horses had been crossed with light horse mares imported from Spain, Turkey, and Italy. Then, from the late 1600s until 1750, Arabians, Turks, and Barbs (Oriental sires as they were called) were imported for the purpose of increasing the speed of horses used for the popular sport of racing. Three of these 174 stallions became most famous and eventually became the basis of the three stallion lines to which nearly all Thoroughbreds can be traced.

A horse known as the Byerly Turk (foaled in 1679) was taken to England by Captain Byerly in 1689; Herod, a great-great-grandson (1758), was a founder of one of the three stallion lines. The Godolphin Barb (some claim that he was an Arabian), foaled about 1724 on the Barbary Coast, found his way to France and later to England, where he was the property of Lord Godolphin. His grandson was Matchem (1748), another foundation sire. Nearly 90 percent of all Thoroughbreds trace to Eclipse (1764), who was unbeaten in 26 starts. This foundation sire was the great-great-grandson of the Darley Arabian, who was foaled in Syria in 1700 and imported to England in 1704. Bulle Rock is traditionally regarded to be the first Thoroughbred imported to America (in 1730 at the age of 21 years).

The first recording of Thoroughbreds in England was in 1791 by James Weatherby, Jr., in his *Introduction to a General Stud Book*. Volume 1 of the *General Stud Book* appeared in 1793, and revisions were published in 1803, 1808, 1827, 1858, and 1891. All English Thoroughbreds must trace to animals included in the *General Stud Book*. This requirement naturally excluded many Thoroughbreds in America. Volumes 1 and 2 of *The American Stud Book* were published in 1873. The rights to this registry were purchased in 1894 by The Jockey Club, which continues to publish *The American Stud Book* and to register American Thoroughbreds. *The American Stud Book* is also closed. Only horses whose sire and dam are registered in *The American Stud Book* or similar stud books of other countries are eligible to be registered:

> ii. 64. Only those horses are eligible for registry which authentically trace, in all of their lines to animals recorded in *The American Stud Book* or in a Stud Book of another country recognized by The Jockey Club, and which are eligible under the rules and regulations from time to time adopted by the Stewards of The Jockey Club. A horse born in the United States or its possessions, Canada or Cuba may not be registered unless both its sire and dam have been previously registered in *The American Stud Book* after importation, and whose sire was not imported but is properly recorded in the Stud Book of a country recognized by The Jockey Club.

The imported stallion *Petrone is shown in Figure 2-5.

Approximately 650,000 Thoroughbreds were registered by The Jockey Club through 1974, and more than 20,000 were registered in 1974 alone. They have only recently been surpassed by the Quarter Horse in total number registered.

FIGURE 2-5
An imported Thoroughbred stallion, *Petrone. Photograph courtesy of A. C. Asbury for Hastings Harcourt, Santa Ynez, California.

25

The ideal Thoroughbred is difficult to describe. The oldest axiom in racing is "They run in all shapes and sizes." The most complete measure of the racing Thoroughbred is the stopwatch. Performance under racing conditions is the essence of racing. A superior racer will have acceptable conformation, but superior conformation does not necessarily lead to even adequate speed. Most Thoroughbreds, however, tend to have a long fore-arm and gaskin and display considerable length from the hip to the hock. They are noted for long, smooth muscling. The rear, or propelling, quarters are especially powerful. Thoroughbreds excel at the run or extended gallop but may seem awkward at the walk or trot. The usual range in size at racing condition is 15.1–16.2 hands and 900–1,150 pounds. The modern Thoroughbred (Figure 2-6) is nearly 2 hands taller than the foundation Thoroughbreds of about 1750.

The world record of 1:32⅕ seconds for the mile around one turn was set by Dr. Fager (Figure 2-7) in 1968 at Chicago's Arlington Park while

FIGURE 2-6
Boldwood, a Thoroughbred son of Bold Ruler and grandson of Bull Lea, at stud at Matron Farm. Photograph courtesy of James K. Thomas, Lexington, Kentucky.

FIGURE 2-7
Dr. Fager, Champion American Racehorse of 1968 and holder of the record for one mile, 1:32⅕ seconds carrying 134 pounds at Arlington Park, Illinois, on August 24, 1968. Photograph by Jim Raftery Turfotos, courtesy of the owners, Tartan Farms.

FIGURE 2-8
The 1973 Triple Crown winner, Secretariat, owned by Meadow Stables. NYRA photograph by Bob Coglianese, courtesy of Penny Tweedy, Doswell, Virginia.

carrying a heavy weight of 134 pounds. In 1956, Swaps at Hollywood Park ran the mile around 2 turns faster than any other Thoroughbred, in 1:33⅕ seconds. In 1973, Secretariat (Figure 2-8) became the first horse in 25 years to win all the Triple Crown races for 3-year-olds. His amazing performance was climaxed in the final race at Belmont, where he broke the track record of 2:26⅗ by 2⅗ seconds. (The nine Triple Crown winners are listed in Table 2-1). His feats, however, only slightly dull the performance of the original Big Red, Man-O-War, who was a winner in 21 of 22 starts but was not entered in the Kentucky Derby.

Thoroughbreds are performance horses, so their color is not important. Colors and markings are recorded at registration, however, for purposes of identification. The Jockey Club recognizes black, dark bay or brown, bay, chestnut, gray, and roan. The description of roan is really a nonblack gray, not a true roan. White Thoroughbreds are generally gray early in

TABLE 2-1
Triple Crown winners (winners in three major races for 3-year-olds: Kentucky Derby, Preakness Stakes, Belmont Stakes)

Year	Horse	Owner
1919	Sir Barton	J. K. L. Ross
1930	Gallant Fox	William Woodward
1935	Omaha	William Woodward
1937	War Admiral	Samuel D. Riddle
1941	Whirlaway	Warren Wright
1943	Count Fleet	Mrs. John Hertz
1946	Assault	R. J. Kleberg, Jr.
1948	Citation	Warren Wright
1973	Secretariat	Mrs. Penny Tweedy

FIGURE 2-9
Native Dancer (*left*) retiring at Belmont with E. Guerin up, on November 2, 1954. Photograph courtesy of Keeneland-Morgan, Keeneland Library, Lexington, Kentucky.

life, and with age may turn white. Native Dancer, shown in Figure 2-9 at his retirement, was dark gray when he excited television fans but later turned snow white. Dun is a rare color, but white at birth is even rarer. The first white United States Thoroughbred, a filly named White Beauty, was registered in 1963. Another was born in France in the same year, and yet another had been foaled in Germany more than 100 years earlier. The American Racing Manual for 1955 reports the following percentages for the different colors: 46 percent bay, 30 percent chestnut, 18 percent brown, 3 percent black, 2 percent gray, and 1 percent roan.

In colonial America, raising and racing racehorses was centered in Virginia. The center of Thoroughbred racing then moved to the bluegrass country of Kentucky and Tennessee. In 1969, 17 percent of the foals in the United States were born in Kentucky; 16 percent were born in California; and 7 percent were born in Florida. These percentages indicate the spread of the Thoroughbred industry.

2.3   The American Quarter Horse

Admirers of the Quarter Horse claim it was the first breed developed in the United States, even before the Thoroughbred was developed and long before Paul Revere made his historic ride—on, it is said, a Quarter Horse. The quarter running horse (quarter of a mile) is said to have run in colonial America on the short, flat stretches of towns and villages. These horses probably would have developed from crosses with horses that had been brought to Florida earlier by the Spaniards. Whether this is accepted history or whether the development of the cow horse in the southwest range country during the middle and late 1800s should be considered the beginning of the breed does not really matter to the many proud owners of the modern Quarter Horse. More Quarter Horses were registered in 1972 (115,000) than all other breeds combined. In 1974, it was estimated that more than 1 million had been registered in the 34 years since the American Quarter Horse Association was formed in 1940.

Even if this version is not accepted by all historians, there is general agreement that a Thoroughbred imported in 1752 had a lasting influence on the development of the Quarter Horse type. Most of the foundation sire lines trace to him. Janus, a grandson of Godolphin Barb, was noted for speed at distances of 4 miles. Yet he sired many quarter running horses that had exceptional short distance speeds. He also sired many famous Thoroughbred stallions and mares. In fact, more than one winner of the Kentucky Derby traces to Janus. Thus, he truly represented the meaning of his name—to look in opposite directions.

29

Many stallions were bred during the movement west and were mated to horses of Spanish ancestry in the Southwest during the development of the working Quarter Horse. Their names are colorful and evoke memories of times past. Steeldust, foaled in Illinois in 1843 and moved to Texas in 1846, was perhaps the most famous horse of the early Quarter Horse type. Until about 1938, horses of the quarter type were called Steeldusts. Copper Bottom and Old Shiloh were two of his contemporaries.

In 1895, Peter McCue was foaled in Illinois and became the most important of all sires in the development of the breed. More than 20 percent of the Quarter Horses registered prior to 1948 traced on the male side to Peter McCue. The next most important horse, Traveler, had only one-third as many similar descendants.

Old Sorrel, foaled in 1915, a grandson of Peter McCue, deserves special mention. The King Ranch of Texas decided that he most nearly fit their ideal of the working cow horse. A linebreeding program that had hardly ever been used with any other kind of livestock was initiated to fix his type (Rhoad and Kleberg, 1946). Figure 16-6 is a diagram of the breeding plan.

The American Quarter Horse Association was the first organization formed to register Quarter Horses. The bases for registration were type, pedigree, and performance. This and rival organizations were merged in 1950 and issued a more nearly closed stud book. Today the stud book is closed to all except crosses with Thoroughbreds and is essentially divided into two parts, the *Numbered Stud Book* and the *Appendix*.

The *Numbered Stud Book* registers progeny of registered parents and animals recorded in the new *Appendix* that have excelled, according to a Register of Merit rating, in either racing or performance. Animals advanced from the new *Appendix* to the *Numbered Stud Book* also must pass a conformation inspection. The new *Appendix* records progeny of a cross between registered Quarter Horses and Thoroughbreds. Animals in the new *Appendix* may compete in horse shows in Quarter Horse classes with some age restrictions.

Breeders of the Quarter Horse are somewhat divided as to the performance objectives of that breed. The increasing demand for and stakes in Quarter Horse racing have directed some to breed primarily for speed by increased introduction of Thoroughbred breeding. Go Man Go, a leading sire with regard to earnings and register of merit winners, shown in Figure 2-10, was sired by Top Deck, a Thoroughbred. For many years Three Bars, a Thoroughbred, was also a leading sire. Other breeders are more interested in maintaining the image of the shorter-coupled, more muscular front and rear-ended cow horse, which has the dexterity and tenacity the rancher needs. This type of horse is illustrated by Wimpy P-1, shown in Figure 2-11 in retirement at the King Ranch. Wimpy was awarded the first permanent registration number by virtue of being named the grand champion stallion at the 1941 Fort Worth Exposition. Wimpy is a grandson

FIGURE 2-10
A head study of Go Man Go, a son of the Thoroughbred Top Deck, whose Quarter Horse get have earned more than $4.5 million. Photograph by Bob Taylor, courtesy of Jack McReynolds, Purcell, Oklahoma.

FIGURE 2-11
Wimpy P-1. The holder of the first permanent registration number in the American Quarter Horse Association is shown in retirement at the King Ranch. Photograph courtesy of King Ranch, Incorporated, Kingsville, Texas.

of Old Sorrel, a grandson of Peter McCue. Whether both groups can be maintained under one registry is debatable, but the breed may be numerous enough to allow the luxury of two distinct types of Quarter Horses. Some horses combine ability in racing and excellence in other areas of performance (Figure 2-12), although such general ability is not always found.

31

FIGURE 2-12
Deck Jack, a Supreme Champion
Quarter Horse stallion, owned by
Robert Kowalewski, East Aurora,
New York. A Supreme Champion
must combine a high speed rating
as well as two Grand Championships
and points in halter and performance
classes. Photograph by Darol Dickinson,
courtesy of Robert Kowalewski.

The Quarter Horse Division of the American Horse Shows Association lists the following as a guide to judging Quarter Horses.

Rule XXIX. Quarter Horse Division

Sec. 2. Registration. Horses shown in performance classes in this division must be registered with the American Quarter Horse Association in the Permanent, Tentative, N.Q.H.B.A., new Appendix or Appendix. In halter classes, weanlings and yearlings must be registered or be eligible to be registered in the numbered registry or in the new Appendix, two-year-old stallions and mares must have been issued a registration certificate by the AQHA; stallions and mares three years old and older must be registered with a number; geldings may show at any age if registered in the numbered registry or in either Appendix. All horses must be entered under their full registered names.

Sec. 3. Type and Conformation. Head relatively short and wide with small muzzle and shallow firm mouth; nostrils full and sensitive; ears, short and active, set wide apart; large eyes, set wide; well-developed jaws with width between lower edges, neck of sufficient length, with a trim throatlatch and not too much thickness or depth joining the head at a 45° angle and blending into sloping shoulders which are long and relatively heavy muscled; medium-high and well defined withers the same height as croup; deep and broad chest with wide set forelegs and well muscled forearm; back, short close coupled and powerful across loin; deep girth with well sprung ribs; broad, deep, heavy, well muscled quarters that are full through the thigh, stifle and gaskin; cannon bones short with broad, flat, clean strong low set knees and hocks; firm ankles and medium length sloping pasterns; tough textured feet with wide open heel. Any color without spots acceptable. The generally accepted height limits for mature horses are 14.3 to 15.1 hands and the generally accepted weight limits are 1,100 to 1,300 pounds. Some animals, however, may be over or under these limits.

The stopwatch is the measure of the racing Quarter Horse. The increase in popular interest in Quarter Horse racing is illustrated by Figure 2-13, which shows an increase in racing purses from $776,000 in 1953 to $16,482,000 in 1973. The number of races and amount of parimutuel betting followed a similar pattern. The richest purse in racing, more than $1 million in 1972, is the All American Futurity run for Quarter Horses at Ruidoso

FIGURE 2-13

Total purse distribution in recognized races for Quarter Horses during 1953–1973. From *Quarter Horse Journal*, April 1974, p. 242.

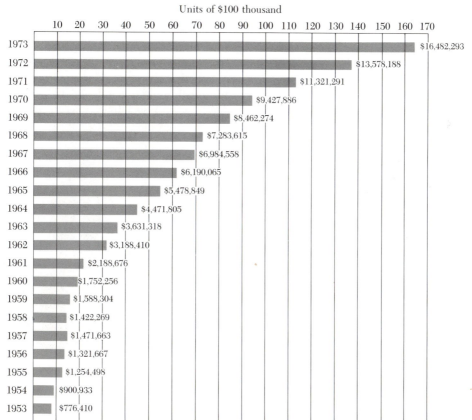

Units of $100 thousand

1973 $16,482,293
1972 $13,578,188
1971 $11,321,291
1970 $9,427,886
1969 $8,462,274
1968 $7,283,615
1967 $6,984,558
1966 $6,190,065
1965 $5,478,849
1964 $4,471,805
1963 $3,631,318
1962 $3,188,410
1961 $2,188,676
1960 $1,752,256
1959 $1,588,304
1958 $1,422,269
1957 $1,471,663
1956 $1,321,667
1955 $1,254,498
1954 $900,933
1953 $776,410

Downs in New Mexico. In 1973 the winner, Timeto Thinkrich (Figure 2-14a), earned approximately one-third of the total purse for a winning effort of 21.58 seconds for 440 yards. Before 1973 the race was run at 400 yards. Most (99 percent) Quarter Horse races are at distances of 440 yards or less. Although records vary according to track conditions, Truckle Feature (Figure 2.14b) set a world record for 440 yards in 21.02 seconds and for 400 yards in 19.38 seconds.

Color of the Quarter Horse is stated to be of no particular importance except for personal preference, but animals with spots or markings that indicate Paint, Pinto, Appaloosa, or American Albino breeding are not eligible for registration. Dun, buckskin, and palomino are acceptable.

2.4 The Standardbred

The Standardbred, once called the American Trotting Horse, was developed from Thoroughbred, Norfolk Trotter, Barb, Morgan, and Canadian

FIGURE 2-14
Timeto Thinkrich (a), owned and bred by Frank Vessels, Jr., winner of the richest race in horse racing, the All American Futurity, in 1973, was the champion quarter running 2-year-old colt in 1973 and running horse in 1974. Truckle Feature (b), owned by Gordon B. Howell, was the world champion quarter running horse in 1973 and the world record holder at 440 and 400 yards. Photographs courtesy of the American Quarter Horse Association, Amarillo, Texas.

a

b

FIGURE 2-15
Nearly all Standardbred horses trace
to this stallion, Hambletonian 10,
which was owned by Bill Rysdyk.
Rysdyk bought the bay as a foal for
$125 and eventually collected
$300,000 in breeding fees. Photograph
of a painting courtesy of United States
Trotting Association, Columbus, Ohio.

pacing ancestors. The name Standardbred comes from the practice that began in the 1800s of registering horses that trotted or paced the mile in less than a "standard" time. Over the years, since Yankee first trotted the mile under saddle in less than 3 minutes at the Harlem racetrack in 1806, the standard has been lowered. The standards first officially set in 1879 were 2:30 for trotters and 2:25 for pacers. The current standard is 2:20 for 2-year-olds and 2:15 for older horses, although horses are now only rarely registered on the basis of these standards.

Many breeders trace the Standardbred to Messenger, a gray Thoroughbred imported to Philadelphia from England in 1788. Messenger traces to all three foundation sires of the Thoroughbred breed. Although neither Messenger nor any of his sons trotted or paced, he traces to a stallion, Blaze, that sired the foundation horse of the Norfolk-Hackney Trotters, Old Shales. Messenger appears three times in the pedigree of his great-grandson, Hambletonian 10 (Figure 2-15), foaled in 1849. Hambletonian, number 10 in the first numbered stud book, is perhaps the greatest name in the history of the breed; approximately 99 percent of all Standardbreds trace to him. Part of his predominance may be due to his prolificacy—1,331 living foals. His sons founded the four predominant sire lines of the present-day breed—The Direct and The Abbe lines of pacers and The Axworthy and Peter the Great lines of trotters—although Hambletonian himself never raced. The imported Bellfounder, which had Norfolk Trotting ancestry, was the maternal grandsire of Hambletonian. Tom Hal was the founder of a Canadian pacing line that, along with other Thoroughbreds, Morgans, and native horses, contributed to the development of the breed.

The official stud registry of the breed is the *American Trotting Sires and Dams Book*, now administered by the United States Trotting Association. J. H. Wallace prepared the forerunner of this book in 1871. The stud book is now closed to all horses except those sired by registered sires and dams. Horses that have a registered sire and that meet the current standards of performance may also be registered, but few such applications have been approved recently. Approximately 400,000 Standardbreds were registered between 1871 and 1974; approximately 12,000 have been registered annually in the last 5 years.

More than 25 million people watch harness racing at parimutuel tracks each year. In 1972 betting on these races returned about $166 million to state treasuries. These figures are augmented by racing at county and state fairs, the only places where harness racing was done for many years.

The measure of performance is speed, usually for the one-mile distance. Parimutuel racing has changed the original format of racing. The classic harness race was originally to win 3 heats; it later became the best 2 out of 3 heats. Winners would occasionally need to race 11 or 12 heats that emphasized endurance as well as speed for the mile. Many major races, such as the Hambletonian Classic and the Little Brown Jug, still require the winner to win 2 heats. Now most races are decided by a single one-mile "dash," which furnishes better entertainment for race fans.

The record for a one-mile track for trotters is held by Nevele Pride (Figure 2-16) in a time trial of 1:54⁴/₅ in 1969; for pacers, the record is held by Steady Star (Figure 2-17) in a time trial of 1:52 in 1971, which lowered the previous record by nearly 2 seconds. Time trials are races against time, not against other horses. Records made in time trials are denoted by TT; for example, TT 1:54⁴/₅.

Dan Patch was the most famous and most enduring star of pacers. He held the record from 1903 until 1938, when Billy Direct lowered the record by only ¼ of a second—and that record lasted for another 22 years. Dan Patch was literally 4 or 5 generations ahead of his time. His best time was 1:55¼ in 1905. He is shown with the equipment of that era in Figure 2-18.

FIGURE 2-16
Nevele Pride broke the trotting record of Greyhound in 1969 with a 1:54⁴/₅ mile. Stanley Dancer is shown driving the 1968 Hambletonian winner and Harness Horse of the Year for 1967, 1968, and 1969. Photograph courtesy of *Horseman and Fair World*, Lexington, Kentucky.

FIGURE 2-17
Steady Star shown with Joe O'Brien after breaking the pacing record of
Bret Hanover by nearly 2 seconds—the pacing mile in 1:52. Photograph
courtesy of *Horseman and Fair World*, Lexington, Kentucky.

Greyhound (Figure 2-19) held the trotting crown for nearly as long, from
1937 until 1969, when Nevele Pride bettered Greyhound's time of 1:55¼
by less than half a second. Greyhound was also the holder of records for
trotting under saddle and for the mixed pair.

The greatest modern stallion is probably the pacer Adios, whose offspring are the measure of his greatness: 50 of them have records of less
than 2 minutes for the mile, and their lifetime earnings total $20 million.

Most of the major increases in speed have come with changes in equipment or track procedures. Little progress appears to have been made in
increasing the speed of the racers, although a slightly higher fraction of
starters now run the mile in 2:00 minutes or less: .49 percent in 1972 compared with .13 percent in 1948.

Early breeders favored trotters and did not appreciate pacers. Now, however, except for some of the classic races, pacers predominate at most

FIGURE 2-18
Dan Patch, considered by many
to be the greatest harness horse
of all time, shown with driver
H. C. Hersey. Dan Patch held
the pacing record for 35 years.
His fastest time of 1:55¼ was
beaten by only 1/4 second 33
years later by Billy Direct,
whose record stood for 22 years
thereafter. Photograph courtesy
of the United States Trotting
Association, Columbus, Ohio.

37

FIGURE 2-19
Greyhound, shown with trainer-driver Sep Palin, helped increase the popularity of harness racing. His trotting record of 1:55¼ in 1938 stood for 31 years. He still holds the world trotting record for geldings. Photograph courtesy of the United States Trotting Association, Columbus, Ohio.

parimutuel betting tracks. Usually 8 of 9 races on the card are for pacers, which are, on the average, only marginally faster but do not race with trotters. Genetic factors and, more importantly, training and shoeing methods, are used to determine or to change the gait. A few horses have the ability to race well at either the trot or the pace—in separate races, of course. The trot is a two-beat diagonal gait. As illustrated in Figure 2-20a, the opposite front and rear feet push off and land at the same time. The pace is a two-beat lateral gait, as shown in Figure 2-20b—the front and hind feet on the same side start and land together.

Some breeders believe the tendency to trot is inherited as a single dominant trait, but Harrison (1968) asserts that the tendency to pace is dominant. He has observed that pacers mated to pacers produce pacers 99 percent of the time, whereas pacers mated to trotters usually produce pacers, and trotters mated to trotters frequently produce pacers. Actually, his observation also supports the theory that the gene for trotting is dominant over the gene for pacing. Probably neither view is completely correct since the traits are undoubtedly affected by more than one genetic factor.

The measure of performance of the Standardbred is speed. Conformation may contribute to freedom from injury and breakdown, but it is not primarily important. The body conformation of the Standardbred is similar to that of the Thoroughbred, although the Standardbred is generally smaller. The range in height is often 14.2–16.2 hands; the range in weight is 850 to 1,150 pounds when the horse is in racing condition. Early breeders tended to favor horses whose length exceeded their height. However,

Greyhound may have changed the minds of many breeders because he was taller than he was long.

Bay is the predominant color, but chestnut, brown, black, and, of course gray, are also seen. There seems to be no color discrimination if the horse is fast.

Another notable breed of trotter is the Orlov trotter of Russia. These horses have been crossed with the American Standardbred in an attempt to introduce more speed. The French are also proud of their trotters, which do well in international competitions.

2.5   The Appaloosa

The Palouse River country of the northwestern United States has given its name to a distinctive breed of horse. The name "Appaloosa" was derived from the slurring of "A Palouse" to form Apaloose, which later became Apaloosie and is now Appaloosa (ap-pah-*loose*-ah).

Horses with the colorful characteristics of the Appaloosa appear in Chinese art dating from 500 B.C. and in Persian and European art of the fourteenth century.

Spanish horses that were brought to Mexico about 1600 apparently have formed the basis for the present-day Appaloosa. The Spanish horses

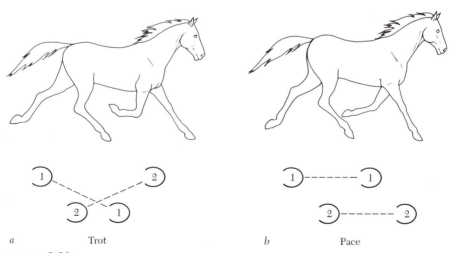

a Trot *b* Pace

FIGURE 2-20
Illustration of the trot (a two-beat diagonal gait) and of the pace (a two-beat lateral gait).

and their descendants spread northward and, by 1730, had been acquired by the Nez Percé tribe in the Palouse country. Because of their colorful markings and riding characteristics (endurance, surefootedness), the Nez Percé bred the Appaloosa for rugged mountain traveling for the next 100 years. As a type, the Appaloosa nearly disappeared after the surrender of Chief Joseph and the Nez Percé to the United States Army in the Bear Paw Mountains of Montana in 1877.

The Appaloosa Horse Club was formed in 1938 to preserve, improve, and standardize the spotted horse of the Nez Percé. Since the few foundation descendants of the Nez Percé horses were registered in that year, the registry of the Appaloosa has grown rapidly. More than 200,000 had been registered through 1973; 20,000 were registered in 1973 alone.

Three distinctive characteristics are required of all Appaloosas: (1) the eye is encircled with white like the human eye (Figure 2-21); (2) the skin is mottled irregularly with black and white (parti-colored), particularly around the nostrils (Figure 2-21) and genitalia; and (3) the hooves are narrowly striped vertically in black and white (Figure 2-22). The color patterns vary widely, as shown by the 8 different patterns in Figure 2-23. Any combination and many variations of these patterns may occur. Because the genetics of the color patterns is not well understood, standardizing the breed and even predicting the results of particular matings are difficult. The color patterns may not be apparent at birth and may change with age. The mane and tail of most Appaloosas are usually sparse. This is called the rat-tailed condition.

A definite effort has been made to standardize the breed to a general-purpose riding horse that can be used for pleasure, parade, rodeo, western show, and racing. Appaloosas must exceed 14 hands in height by the time

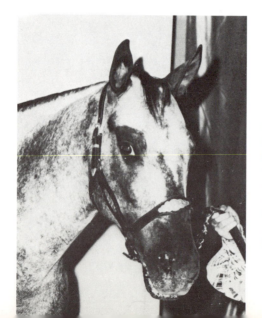

FIGURE 2-21
Photograph of Joker's Starlight. Registered Appaloosas must have white encircling the eye, and the skin must be mottled, which usually shows on the muzzle or genitalia. Photograph by Johnny Johnston, courtesy of Howard C. Hanson, Jr., Blair, Nebraska.

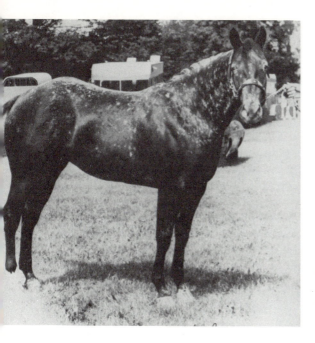

FIGURE 2-22
The hooves of registered
Appaloosas must show vertical
stripes of black and white, as
shown in this photograph of
Hands Up Cowgirl. Photograph
courtesy of Ken Friday,
Jefferson, Iowa.

they are 5 years of age. Horses with pony or draft horse breeding are not eligible for registration. In an attempt to protect the distinctive color pattern, horses with Albino, Pinto, or Paint breeding or markings are also excluded, as are horses with excessive white or misplaced spots.

The Appaloosa Horse Club maintains an open registry with 3 sections. All registered Appaloosas must meet the eye, skin, and hoof requirements and must be of riding-horse breeding, type, and conformation.

Permanent registration is possible for horses whose parents are registered or identified with the Appaloosa Horse Club or with approved breed associations (Canadian, Mexican, and Australian Appaloosas, Thoroughbreds, Quarter Horses, Arabians, Morgans, Standardbreds, and American Saddle Horses). Geldings and spayed mares are excepted. A hardship clause permits registration of stallions and mares of above-average merit that do not meet the registration requirement.

Outstanding Appaloosas not out of a registered sire and dam receive *tentative registration.* They are eligible for showing and racing. An animal may advance from tentative registration if its sire and dam are both advanced to permanent registration.

The *breeding stock only* provision is for horses that have Appaloosa breeding and basic characteristics but that do not show, in photographs, easily recognizable Appaloosa coat patterns. They are not eligible for show, race, or exhibition.

The production requirement for permanent registration is met when a stallion sires 12 registered foals or a dam has produced 3 registered foals. Foals registered under the breeding stock provision count toward this requirement.

41

a

b

c

d

FIGURE 2-23

Illustrations of eight different patterns of Appaloosa markings. There are many variations and other combinations of these patterns. *a.* Most typical is the colored pattern with white blanket and spots over loin and hips (Stud Spider; photograph courtesy of Jane Brolin, Los Angeles, California). *b.* The leopard pattern—white with colored spots over the body. There is much possible variation in size of spots (Joker's John E.; photograph courtesy of Mr. and Mrs. E. D. Pollard, Caldwell, Idaho). *c.* White blanket over back and hips, no spots in blanket (Domino's Le Don; photograph courtesy of Darrel Steenblock, Fremont, Nebraska). *d.* Colored body with white spots over loin and hips (Dash's Charm;

2.6   The Morgan Horse

Morgan is the only breed named after a horse. No other horse has such a distinction as Justin Morgan, the foundation sire of the Morgan Horse. Actually, the stallion was called Figure as a foal, and took his adult name from his owner (a Massachusetts schoolteacher), as was the custom in the

e

f

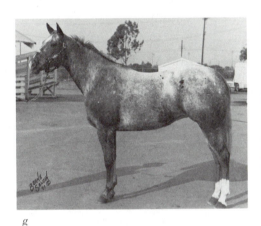

g

h

photograph by Johnny Johnston, courtesy of Howard C. Hanson, Jr., Blair, Nebraska). *e.* Colored body, speckled white over entire body (Spots Souviner; photograph courtesy of Kent E. Ellsworth, Ontario, California). *f.* Colored body, slight roaning with dark spots over loin and hips, no blanket (Good John; photograph courtesy of L. J. and Zora Estes, Milton-Freewater, Oregon). *g.* Roan body, light over loin and hips (Bar My Hart; photograph by Berne Salvin, courtesy of Don F. Craib, Jr., Lake Forest, Illinois. *h.* Roan body, white blanket with spots over loin and hips (War Reed's Echo; photograph by Ric Robinson, courtesy of Ray Jensen, Manager, Windswept Acres, Woodstock, Illinois).

late 1700s. He followed Justin Morgan from Massachusetts (where the stallion was foaled) through and around Vermont.

Justin Morgan, the horse, became famous because of his outstanding progeny and because of his ability, according to stories that still persist, to outrun, outpull, outwalk, and outtrot all competition. Horses with Morgan blood became popular before 1850 for their all-purpose ability — on the farm, at the trot, and under the saddle. After 1850, the developing Standard-

43

bred breed, to which Morgan Horses contributed substantially, replaced the Morgan on the race tracks. Later, motor vehicles replaced the Morgan on the farms and roads. Since then the Morgan has been used primarily for pleasure riding and more recently as a show horse.

The ancestry of Justin Morgan is not clear, although Colonel Joseph Battell, who became a prime benefactor of the Morgan breed, came to believe that the horse was sired by a Thoroughbred called True Briton (also called Beautiful Bay) and out of a mare of Arabian breeding. Since Thoroughbreds of that time were closely related to Arabians, Justin Morgan had and passed on many characteristics of the Arabian—especially the refined head and raised tail when on the move.

Justin Morgan's progeny and grandprogeny were used in establishing the Standardbred and American Saddle Horse breeds. Many Quarter Horses also trace to Morgan breeding.

Colonel Battell founded the Morgan Horse Register in 1894. The Register was taken over by the Morgan Horse Club in 1930, some 21 years after the Club was organized. Colonel Battell also gave a large farm near Middlebury, Vermont, to the United States Department of Agriculture to be used to preserve and improve the breed. The farm was turned over to the University of Vermont in 1951.

The Morgan today is popular for riding (Figure 2-24) and for shows (Figure 2-25). The size has increased, from Justin Morgan's 14 hands and less than 1,000 pounds to a usual range of 14.1 to 15.1 hands and 1,000–1,200 pounds. Approximately 46,000 Morgans were registered through 1972; the annual increase was approximately 2,000.

The American Morgan Horse Association, as it is now named, registers only horses that have registered sires and dams. There must be no white above the knee or hock except on the face. Horses with no pigment in the iris are also ineligible. All colors are acceptable except white, and spotted horses and those with Appaloosa patterns are ineligible. Palominos, duns, and buckskins are acceptable. The dark liver or black chestnut color is found more often in the Morgan than in any other breed. The suggested type of the Morgan is described by the American Horse Shows Association as:

> Sec. 2. Type and Conformation. A Morgan is distinctive for its stamina and vigor, personality and eagerness and strong natural way of moving. The head is made up of a straight or slightly dished face; big, prominent eyes set wide apart; small ears set rather wide apart carried alertly; small muzzle with firm lips and large nostrils; prominent jaw. In body conformation the Morgan gives the appearance of a very strong powerful horse with great shoulder angulation and depth, short back, broad loins, muscular and well developed croup and with tail set in high and carried gracefully. Head is carried proudly and neck slightly crested, meeting the head at a

FIGURE 2-24
Tara's Delight, a Morgan mare shown in an English pleasure class. Photograph by Paul Quinn, courtesy of Dr. and Mrs. V. Watson Pugh, Raleigh, North Carolina.

FIGURE 2-25
A seal brown Morgan stallion, Royalton Hubert, in show position. Photograph by Warren E. Patriquin, courtesy of Mrs. Pat Harvey, North Stonington, Connecticut.

well defined throttle. Legs are straight and sound with short cannons, flat bone, medium length pasterns and an appearance of overall substance with refinement. The Morgan ranges from 14.1 to 15.1 hands with occasional entries over or under.

2.7   The American Saddle Horse

The American Saddle Horse was first bred in the United States, and the type evolved as the needs of the country changed. The residents of the bluegrass region of Kentucky and areas of Tennessee, Virginia, West Virginia, and (later) Missouri desired an easy-riding, general-purpose type of horse for the plantations and hilly grazing areas. The first name given to horses of this type was the Kentucky Saddle Horse. This easy-gaited saddle horse developed from Thoroughbred, Canadian pacer, American trotter, Morgan, Arabian, and other ancestors. In 1901 the American Saddle Horse Association listed 10 foundation sires, but in 1908 the list was reduced to the Thoroughbred stallion, Denmark — undoubtedly the most important. The others were given registration numbers and the status of Noted Deceased Sire. Another famous family is the Chief Family, which traces to Mambrino Chief, a trotter, which in turn traces to the imported Thoroughbred, Messenger. Early development of the breed preceded Denmark, although the era of its popularity was after Denmark and the Civil War. The Saddlebred horse is not highly inbred, although Steele (1944) found more inbreeding among Saddlebreds than among Thoroughbreds and Standardbreds.

As needs changed, the American Saddle Horse developed into what has been called the peacock of the horse world. Breeding has been largely for horse show purposes (Figure 2-26). The Saddlebred is in demand for three- and five-gaited classes, for fine harness, and for combination saddle and harness classes, although many of these horses are also used for pleasure riding.

The show class Saddlebred has emphasized the flashy and exaggerated but controlled gaits, high carriage of the head, and distinctive set of the tail (Figures 2-27, 2-28). The angle of the tail is partly determined by the trainer, who "sets" the tail.

The American Saddle Horse Breeders Association has given the following short description of the ideal American Saddlebred:

> The ideal American Saddlebred has a well-shaped head, small alert ears, large eyes set well apart, a good muzzle, wide nostrils. His long neck is nicely arched with a fine small throttle. He has sharp withers, sloping shoulders and a short back. The croup is level, with the tail coming out high. The hind quarters are well

FIGURE 2-26
Plainview's Julia, a three-time winner of the $10,000, five-gaited American
Saddle Horse Championship. Photograph by Paulette, courtesy of the American
Saddle Horse Breeders Association.

muscled to the hocks. Legs are straight with long sloping pasterns
providing the springiness so necessary for a smooth comfortable
easy ride. He has good sound hoofs, open at the heels.

The average height is 15 to 16 hands and the weight from 1,000 to
1,200 pounds.

Dark colors are preferred but the coloring can be bay, brown, black,
chestnut, gray, or roan. Large, white markings are avoided by many
breeders and trainers, although the Pinto Horse Association also registers
spotted horses of the Saddlebred type.

47

FIGURE 2-27
Wing Commander, six-time winner of the $10,000, five-gaited championship at
the Kentucky State Fair. Photograph by John R. Horst, courtesy of the American
Saddle Horse Breeders Association.

The American Saddlebred can be three- or five-gaited. The Saddlebred
is trained to perform each gait distinctly with considerable action, to go
without hesitation from one gait to the other, and to change lead at the
canter from left to right on command. The basic three gaits are the walk,
trot, and canter. The three-gaited horse must go from the trot, a high-action,

FIGURE 2-28
Lisa Hampton on Denmark's Sir
Bonaventure, a five-gaited American
Saddle Horse owned by Mr. and Mrs.
Harold N. Hampton, Conover, North
Carolina. Photograph by Curtie
Vaughn, courtesy of trainer, Lewis P.
Eckard, Hildebran, North Carolina.

two-beat diagonal gait, to the slow, flat-footed, springy four-beat walk, and then to the slow, rhythmic, smooth canter, a three-beat gait. Additional training and ability are required for the unnatural gaits of the five-gaited horse. The slow gait is a rich, high-stepping four-beat gait. Any of several gaits, such as the amble, slow pace, stepping pace, running walk, or fox trot meet the slow gait requirement. The rack is a fast, flashy, four-beat gait (sometimes called the single foot) that is free from any pacing motion. This gait is easy on the rider but tiring for the horse and receives much emphasis in the judging of five-gaited horses.

Saddlebred pleasure classes for mares and geldings, including three- and five-gaited horses utilizing both western and English equipment, are judged 75 percent on performance and manners and 25 percent on conformation and neatness of attire. Most other performance classes are judged on performance, quality, and manners. Championship classes are also judged on conformation.

The American Saddle Horse Breeders Association, formed in 1891 (this, the current name, was adopted in 1899), registered 150,000 horses from its founding through 1973. Registrations in 1973 totaled approximately 4,000. To be eligible for registration, the horses must have both a registered sire and a registered dam. Geldings may also be registered if sired by a registered stallion and out of a mare tracing to registered Saddlebred stock. Only registered American Saddle Horses are eligible for the three-gaited, five-gaited, fine harness, and pleasure horse classes of the American Saddle Horse sections. Saddle-type classes with western equipment do not have the same restriction.

2.8 The Tennessee Walking Horse

Like the Saddlebred and the Morgan, the Tennessee Walking Horse was developed as a general-purpose breed for riding, driving, and farm work. The history of the breed, which originated in the Middle Basin of Tennessee, traces to contributions of Thoroughbreds, Standardbreds, American Saddle Horses, Morgans, and Narraganset and Canadian pacers, as well as less well-recorded stock.

The uniqueness of the Tennessee Walking Horse is described by the breed registry as follows:

> The Tennessee Walking Horse is the only horse in the world which is capable of naturally overstriding. When performing the running walk, a good show horse of the breed will overstride; that is, he will place the back hoof ahead of the print of his fore hoof. Some of the great Tennessee Walking Horses have been known to overstride fifty inches or more.

49

The flat-foot walk is the slowest of the three gaits and is a diagonally opposed movement of the feet. It is a bold, even gait and is gentle on the rider.

The natural gait is the running walk. A bit faster than the flat-foot walk, this gait is smooth and gentle and combines the nod of the head with each step.

The performance of the running walk is natural and should not require weighting or boots or soring. These methods, however, do accentuate and exaggerate the gait. Unfortunately, many exhibitors have sored the horses to obtain the best performance. The Tennessee Walking Horse Breeders' Association has cooperated with the federal government to eliminate the practice of soring. Soring is defined in Section 2 of the Horse Protection Act of 1970 as:

A horse shall be considered to be sored if for the purpose of affecting its gait—

1. A blistering agent has been applied . . . internally or externally to any of the legs, ankles, feet, or other parts of the horse;

2. burns, cuts, or lacerations have been inflicted . . . on the horse;

3. a chemical agent, or tacks or nails have been used . . . on the horse; or

4. any other cruel or inhumane method or device has been used . . . on the horse, including, but not limited to, chains or boots;

which may reasonably be expected (A) to result in physical pain to the horse when walking, trotting, or otherwise moving, (B) to cause extreme physical distress to the horse, or (C) to cause inflammation.

Examination by veterinarians to ensure conformance with these federal regulations will eliminate this practice and may lead to new winners in the show ring. The Horse Protection Act applies to all classes in all horse shows.

When the Tennessee Walking Horse Breeders' Association was formed in 1935, Allan F-1 (also known as Black Allan) was designated as the official foundation sire. Allan F-1, foaled in 1886 of mixed Standardbred, Morgan, and Naragansett pacers, sired several sons that were bred to other saddle breeds. One of the more famous sons was Roan Allen F-38, who was reportedly able to trot in harness and win, then do five gaits and win, then return and win the walking classes. The influence of Allan F-1 was nearly as great in establishing the Walking Horse type as the influence of Justin

Morgan was in establishing the Morgan breed. Interestingly, the Tennessee Walking Horse (at one time more popularly known as the Plantation Walking Horse) developed naturally, as did the Morgan, to meet the work needs of its region and not the desires of fanciers, although more recent demands of the show ring have not been as natural.

The Walking Horse type is similar to the American Saddlebred but is heavier, more powerful, and coarser. The neck is shorter and the head is carried lower.

The first Saturday night in September climaxes the most exciting week of the year for Tennessee Walking Horse breeders, for it is then that approximately 25,000 people gather to see the Grand Champion Walking Horse of the world crowned at The Tennessee Walking Horse National Celebration at Shelbyville (Figure 2-29). The best of the Tennessee Walkers compete at this horse show, which began in 1939 shortly after the breed registry was chartered in Tennessee.

Walking Horses come in all solid colors. White markings are common. Gray and roan are not undesirable. In the 1940s and 1950s, roan was very popular, but since the 1960s and 1970s blacks and dark colors have been most popular.

Because of its open registry, the breed expanded very quickly, and by 1948 more than 30,000 horses had been registered—more than 5,000 in that year alone. Now only horses with registered sires and dams can be registered. By 1974, approximately 165,000 had been registered; in recent years, 8,000 to 10,000 have been registered annually.

FIGURE 2-29
Delight Bumin Around, the 1973 Grand Champion Walking Horse of the World, owned by Mr. and Mrs. John C. Miller, Anchorage, Alaska. Official stud photograph courtesy of Voice Publishing Company, Chattanooga, Tennessee.

2.9   The Fox Trotting Horse

The Fox Trotting Horse of the Ozark Mountains of southern Missouri and northern Arkansas developed to meet the need of that area in the nineteenth century for a riding horse that could travel long distances with a comfortable gait at a speed of 5–8 miles per hour. With the resurgence of the popularity of riding in the 1960s, these horses were well suited for pleasure and cross-country trail riding.

The characteristic gait that developed, the fox trot, is a major requirement for registration in the Missouri Fox Trotting Horse Breed Association (incorporated in 1948) or in the rival, nationally oriented, American Fox Trotting Horse Breed Association, which was organized in 1970. Many horses are double registered with both associations and with other breed groups.

Melvin Bradley, a Missouri extension horse specialist, has described the fox trotting gait as one that

> starts out as a simple trot; that is, diagonal feet leave the ground at the same time. The back diagonal foot, however, comes down later than the front foot. This makes a four-beat gait instead of the hard two-beat square trot. The back foot does not come down in a hard step, but actually appears to slide a little bit or contact the ground softly. The body is rising in front and lowering behind in unison. This keeps the rider hinged in the middle with a very soft ride.

Fox Trotters are shown with western equipment at the flatfoot walk (20 percent), fox trot (40 percent), and canter (20 percent), and are shown without set tails. Conformation is allowed 20 percent in the official judging standards. Two-year-olds are, however, not required to canter. Judges are to disqualify horses shown with artificial appliances and with raw sores around the coronet or legs. A time-keeping head motion is allowed at the walk, although exaggerated nodding like that displayed by the Tennessee Walker is penalized. At both the walk and fox trot, the hind feet may overreach the front feet by up to one foot instead of the hind foot "capping" (stepping on the same spot as) the front track as earlier required.

Many Fox Trotters have a "fox walk" for distance traveling, which is intermediate in speed between the walk and fox trot. The back end jogs rather than trots.

The Fox Trotting Horse traces first to Arabians, Morgans, and plantation horses. There was a subsequent infusion of the American Saddlebreds, Tennessee Walkers, and Standardbreds. The names of early Fox Trotting families (Copper Bottoms, Diamonds, Chiefs, Steel Dusts, Cold Decks, and others) suggest strong ties to the early Quarter Horses.

The Missouri Fox Trotting Horse Breed Association had registered 7,500 horses between 1948 and 1974, including more than 1,000 in 1972. Nearly all colors are common, but palominos, blacks, sorrels, and blue and red roans are the most popular. A full mane and long, flowing tail are desirable. The ideal height is between 14.2 and 15.3 hands, and the range in weight is 950–1,200 pounds. The preferred body type is essentially western pleasure, which is somewhat intermediate between the American Quarter Horse and the American Saddlebred or Tennessee Walking Horse. A World Champion Fox Trotter at the 1967 Annual Fox Trotting Horse Show and Celebration is shown in Figure 2-30.

2.10   The Pasos: Paso Fino and Peruvian Paso

Most of the light horse breeds in the United States have developed in the United States from varied ancestral breeds. In the middle 1960s, however, two breed registries were incorporated that register somewhat similar horses: Pasos imported from Peru (the Peruvian Paso) and Pasos imported from Puerto Rico, Cuba, and Columbia (the Paso Fino). Both groups trace to similar ancestors and are noted for the smoothness of their natural gait, called the *paso* gait. This gait has five forms, of which the most important are: the *paso fino*, a slow show ring gait; the *paso corto*, a more relaxed form; and the *paso largo*, a speed gait that may exceed the speed of the canter. The same rhythm is maintained for all speeds of the gait.

The paso gait is essentially a broken pace, that is, a lateral rather than a diagonal gait. The sequence of movement of the hooves is: right rear, right fore, left rear, left fore. The hind foot touches the ground a fraction of a second ahead of the front foot, and this helps to eliminate the jarring effect of the true pace so that the rider has little up and down movement. Many Pasos also trot, canter, and gallop.

FIGURE 2-30
Danney Joe W., the 1967 World Champion Fox Trotter at the 1967 Annual Fox Trotting Horse Show and Celebration. Photograph courtesy of the owner, Dale Wood, Nebo, Missouri.

The Pasos are descendants of the Spanish horses of Andalusian, Barb, and Friesian breeding brought to Santo Domingo (capital of the Dominican Republic) in 1493 on Columbus' second voyage to America. These horses, and similar ones that were imported later, became the foundation stock for the remount stations of the Conquistadores. Salazar took some of them to Puerto Rico in 1509, and when Velasquez invaded Cuba in 1511, he took others. Pizzaro used Dominican horses when he seized Peru in 1533.

The size of modern Pasos ranges from large pony to small horse. Their height ranges from 13 to 15 hands and their weight ranges from 700 to 1,200 pounds. The Paso Fino tends to be somewhat smaller and more variable than the Peruvian Paso. Breeders in the United States have tended to increase the size by selective importing and breeding and by improved nutrition.

The American Paso Fino

The American Paso Fino Pleasure Horse Association, Inc., registered more than 1,800 Paso Fino horses between 1964, when the registry opened, and 1972. The rules state that to be registered, a horse must be a purebred Paso Fino:

A. The progeny of registered APFPHA stallions and mares will be eligible.

B. Paso Finos with *acceptable* registration from the country of origin will be eligible and the progeny of two parents with acceptable registration from the country of origin will be eligible.

C. Paso Fino horses other than the above may be accepted for registration upon review of all background information submitted on the horse and possible personal inspection by the Registrar or Inspector designated by the Association.

No color restrictions are imposed by the Paso Fino registry. Paso Finos show all solid colors and roans, as well as spotted, creme, buckskin, and palomino patterns. Solid colors, grays, and roans are preferred by breeders of Peruvian Pasos.

Most imported Paso Fino Horses registered by APFPHA have come from Puerto Rico (Figure 2-31) or Colombia. The association does not register half-breeds and does not encourage crosses with other breeds.

The Paso Fino Owners and Breeders Association also promotes and registers Paso Fino Horses.

The Peruvian Paso

The Peruvians are proud that their Paso developed solely from Andalusian, Barb, and Friesian Horses brought to Peru by the Spanish Conquistadores. Two groups in the United States register these horses, which have been imported from Peru (Figure 2-32). Horses imported to the United States must be registered in Peru to be eligible for registration.

The American Association of Owners and Breeders of Peruvian Paso Horses registered approximately 800 horses from 1967, when it was incorporated, through 1972. The association imposes no color restrictions. Between 60 and 100 horses are imported to the United States from Peru each year.

The Peruvian Paso Horse Registry of North America also registers Peruvian Pasos. It restricts registration to horses of a single color; paints, pintos, and albinos are not eligible.

2.11   The Galiceño

The Galiceño (gal-i-*sehn*-yo) is a small, sturdy horse of 12 to 13.2 hands—the size of a pony but in all other ways a horse. These horses have been imported from Mexico since 1959. The breed probably originated in sixteenth-century Spain in the ancient province of Galicia, of Spanish Jennet and Barb breeding.

The Galiceño Horse Breeders Association was formed in 1959 and had registered approximately 2,500 horses by 1972.

The Galiceño was a contemporary of the Paso Fino stock of Central and South America but has not been crossed with larger breeds, so the Galiceño is now much smaller—600 to 700 pounds (Figure 2-33). The Galiceño

FIGURE 2-31
Faetón, an American Paso Fino stallion (Sire of the Year in 1971 and 1973) imported from Puerto Rico in 1964. Photograph courtesy of the owners, John and Carolyn Ziegler, Marysville, Ohio.

55

FIGURE 2-32
Rizado, the 1972–1973 National
Champion Peruvian Paso gelding.
Photograph by Foucher Equine
Photography, courtesy of Hacienda
de la Solana, Guerneville, California.

comes in all solid colors; albinos, pintos, and crosses are not eligible for
registration. Unique among pony-size horses, the Galiceño has a running
walk similar to that of the Tennessee Walking Horse and the Pasos. The
other standard gaits—walk, trot, and canter—are also natural.

The Galiceño has competed against larger, western-type horses. Western
equipment is used and showing is Quarter Horse style. Most owners have
thought the Galiceño to be ideal for children or for young adults who
want something larger than a pony.

FIGURE 2-33
A registered Galiceño mare, dun with
black dorsal stripe. Photograph
courtesy of the owners, Mr. and Mrs.
Robert I. Kinsel, Jr., Hamilton, Texas.

2.12   The Gotland

The first Gotlands were brought to the United States in 1957 from Sweden where their ancestors had existed since the Stone Age, as evidenced by excavations from a cave on the Swedish Island of Gotland. The Gotland, a small horse called Skogsruss by the Swedes, served as mounts for the Goths, Vikings, and other Swedish warriors and falls into the pony-size category of less than 14 hands. They are of good temperament and uniform type because of selective breeding by the Gotland Pony Club, which acted to preserve this historic breed from possible extinction by wholesale exportation to the mines of England, Germany, and Poland. Naturally, they share some of the characteristics of the wild Tarpan horses of northern Europe because they have descended from them without much crossing, except for a few matings to Oriental blood that were made about 1850 to provide a strong genetic base.

The American Gotland Horse Association maintains a closed herdbook to prevent further dilution of the breed. Approximately 250 had been registered by 1972. The association plans to open a Half-Gotland registry for foals crossbred with registered Gotland stallions.

These small horses are used as children's mounts (Figure 2-34) and have been shown in halter, equitation, harness, and hunter classes. Gotlands also compete in trotting races as well as endurance and competitive trail rides.

FIGURE 2-34
Kronas Kometen II, a sorrel Gotland gelding ridden by Marsha Price in a trail class. Photograph by William Stinson, courtesy of the owner, Marsha Price, Bonner Springs, Kansas.

2.13   Paint, Pinto, and Spotted Horses

Many of the traditional breed registeries will not register horses with body spots. Since color is not related to function, several registries whose function is to register spotted horses have developed.

The words *paint* and *pinto* are used by two associations and the word *spotted* is used by another. Since "pinto" is derived from a Spanish word that means "paint or painted or spotted," the terms are synonymous; all can be used to describe horses with body markings of white and another color.

The English have two other words to describe the spotted horse. *Piebald* refers to a horse that is black with white spots; *skewbald* denotes a spotted horse of white and any color other than black.

Two types of spotting are the Overo (o-*ver*-o) and Tobiano (toe-be-*an*-o) patterns. These patterns describe the general location of white on the horse and not the amount of white.

The *Overo* pattern (Figure 2-35) is basically colored with white spots. The usual guidelines are:

1. White does not cross the back.
2. One or more legs are dark.
3. The head is often bald, apron-, or bonnet-faced.
4. The white body markings are irregularly spotted or splashy.
5. The tail is usually one color.

The *Tobiano* pattern (Figure 2-36) is basically white with colored spots. Other guidelines are:

1. White crosses the back.
2. The head is marked like that of a solid-color horse—solid or having blaze, strip, star, or snip white markings.
3. All legs are white, at least below hocks and knees.
4. Body spots are regular, oval-shaped, and distinct.
5. One or both flanks are usually dark.

Either pattern may be mainly colored or mainly white, but the ideal for both is approximately equal parts white and colored. Tobiano is thought to be a dominant genetic trait and Overo is thought to be a recessive genetic trait (see Chapter 15), but these hypotheses have not been well tested; many genes probably operate to develop both patterns. Crosses between horses with Overo and Tobiano patterns add to the variation in spotting.

FIGURE 2-35
Yellow Mount, the first American
Paint Horse Association Champion,
showing the Overo pattern on a red
dun background. Photograph courtesy
of the owner, Stanley Williamson,
Iowa Park, Texas.

FIGURE 2-36
A Tobiano Paint Horse mare, Flicker's
Miss Cody. Photograph courtesy of
owners, Trienta Stock Farm,
Arlington, Texas.

59

None of the three associations registers spotted horses of pony or draft breeding or characteristics. Glass eyes are acceptable because this is a common characteristic of horses with spotted breeding—especially when the white spotting extends over the area of the eye.

The American Paint Horse Association

The American Paint Horse Association formed in 1965, registered approximately 27,000 horses through 1973; approximately 4,300 were registered in 1973 alone. This association was organized partly as the result of the failure of the Quarter Horse Association to register spotted horses. The APHA registers primarily stock and Quarter Horse-type horses that are taller than 14 hands. Certain registration rules apply to animals foaled before 1964 and will not be listed here. Some of the more important requirements of the American Paint Horse Association for the regular registry are similar to those of the American Quarter Horse Association. They are:

104. A. All horses must be sired by a stallion with a registration number in the APHA, the American Quarter Horse Association or The Jockey Club of New York to be eligible for registration in this Association.

105. A. All horses in the Regular Registry will be identified by a registration number. The Regular Registry shall include:

B. All Paint mares and geldings under two years of age which have both sire and dam registered in the APHA, AQHA or The Jockey Club or a combination of any two of these associations. These horses do not have to be inspected. AQHA Appendix mares and AQHA numbered mares will have the same status for registration of Paint foals.

C. All Paint mares and geldings which are *over* two years of age and which meet the bloodline requirements and the height requirement of 14 hands.

D. All Paint stallions over two years of age which have passed inspection.

There is also an appendix registry, essentially for animals under 2 years of age including mares and geldings with unregistered dams that can be advanced to the regular registry. A breeding stock registry is maintained for solid-color foals from registered sires and dams.

The basic color requirements are also listed:

60

112. A. For a horse to be entered in the Regular or Appendix Registry, it must be a recognizable Paint Horse. A Paint Horse may be

have some definite Paint body markings (visible from a normal standing position) to be eligible for the Regular Registry. However, if only one or small minimal white body markings are evident, then two additional characteristics must be present in order for the horse to qualify for the Regular Registry. Paint Horse characteristics include:

1. White on legs above knees and hocks.

2. Glass, blue or watch eyes.

3. Apron face.

4. White on the jaws.

5. Pink skin under white hair and/or a blue zone between white hair and other color present.

6. Two-colored mane and/or tail as characterized by the tobiano type (excluding flaxen).

C. Horses with Appaloosa characteristics or known Appaloosa breeding are not eligible for registration in this Association.

Gaited horses that single-foot or pace are not eligible for registration, but horses that fox-trot or have a running walk are eligible.

The registry is open to outstanding horses under a hardship clause that requires a special inspection.

The Pinto Horse Association of America

Horses registered in the Pinto Horse Association of America, Inc., founded in 1956, generally belong to three conformation types: the stock horse with Quarter Horse and Thoroughbred breeding (Figure 2-37), the pleasure type with Arabian bloodlines, and the saddle-type, which traces to the American Saddlebred (Figure 2-38). The PHAA also recognizes outcrosses with Quarter Horses, Arabians, and American Saddlebreds. Approximately 22,000 were registered through 1973; approximately 2,300 were registered in 1973 alone. All horses registered are personally inspected to meet the requirements, which are similar to those of the APHA except that there is no discrimination against Appaloosa breeding and patterns.

A tentative registry is provided for foals under 2 years of age. These horses are eligible for permanent registration when they are 2 years old.

Horses taller than 14.1 hands, having at least 3 body spots, and dark or blue eyes are eligible for the permanent registry. An approved breed registry is open to permanent registry Pintos, stallions with 4 foals in the permanent or tentative registry, and mares with 3 foals registered.

61

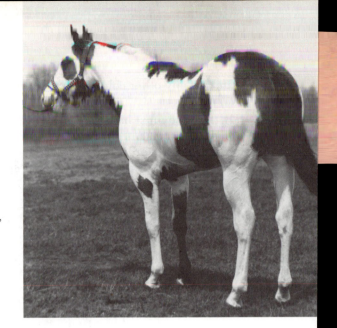

FIGURE 2-37
A Pinto stallion, Country Flyer, showing the Medicine Hat pattern. Photograph by Bruce Peasley, courtesy of Terry and Judy Mosley, Jonesville, Michigan.

Morocco Spotted Horse Cooperative Association of America

This association was formed in 1935 and was originally named the Iowa Spotted Horse Association. It was chartered in 1939 as the Morocco Spotted Horse Cooperative Association of America. After a period of inactivity, the association was reactivated in 1971. Approximately 2,000 horses were registered between 1935 and 1972.

FIGURE 2-38
Mr. O. S. U., a Tobiano Pinto, shown with western equipment in a three-gaited Saddle Horse class. Photograph by Leslie Howard, courtesy of the owners, Jef-Lyn Stables, Hartville, Ohio.

The history of these horses is somewhat different from that of the horses in the Pinto and Paint registries. The breed was formed from crosses of piebald and skewbald English Hackney general-purpose horses and French coach horses with Morocco Barb Horses. American Saddle-breds and Arabians as well as horses without known ancestry have also been used.

The Morocco Spotted Horse is similar to the Arabian but is larger, averaging as an ideal 1,000 pounds and 15 hands. Mature weights must be between 850 and 1,300 pounds and the minimum height must be 14.2 hands (Figure 2-39).

Horses with pony, draft, or Appaloosa breeding are not eligible for registration. Similarly, horses with stock and Quarter Horse breeding and conformation are not registered. Gaited horses are registered, and this registration is encouraged. The association has listed 6 breed or breed-type divisions in an attempt to fill the gaps in the registration of spotted horses left by the Paint and Pinto associations. These divisions are: American Saddle Horse, Tennessee Walking Horse, Thoroughbred, Arabian, Hackney Horse, and Morgan. A premium Morocco division is maintained for horses tracing to 4 foundation sires.

Inspection for color and conformation at about 2 years of age is required for permanent registration of mares and geldings. An additional inspection at 3 years of age is required for stallions.

2.14   The Palomino

The Palomino is truly the golden horse. Palominos are registered according to color and not as to type except that pony and draft breeds are excluded. The color (within 3 shades) is approximately that of an untarnished United

FIGURE 2-39
Chief's Paint, a triple-registered, Overo Morocco Spotted Horse stallion. Photograph courtesy of Morocco Spotted Horse Association, Ridott, Illinois.

63

horse, trotting and pacing, harness classes, three- and five-gaited classes, and Tennessee Walking Horse contests (Figure 2-40). In fact, many Palominos are double-registered with their appropriate breed associations (Figure 2-41), and this practice will be described more fully in the discussion of registration requirements that follows.

The earliest myths and legends of both Eastern and Western cultures referred to the golden horses with silver manes and tails. In the Spain of Queen Isabella, such horses became known as Golden Isabellas (see the next section). One version of the origin of the American name Palomino is that it is derived from the color of the golden grape of California, the Palomino grape. The ancestors of the American Palomino, which developed primarily in Mexico and California, were undoubtedly introduced from Spain by Cortez and the early Spanish explorers.

The first registry of Palominos was private and began in 1932. In 1941, the Palomino Horse Breeders of America became the primary registry for the Palomino. The Palomino Horse Association, Inc., was formed in 1936. The requirements for registration of the PHBA and PHA are similar except that horses of either light or dark skin can be registered in the PHA but only those with dark skin can be registered in the PHBA. Current registration statistics are unavailable, but approximately 38,000 Palominos were registered by the PHBA from 1941 until 1972, and in recent years 1,000–1,500 have been added annually.

Two registries for Palominos over one year of age are maintained by the Palomino Horse Breeders of America. All horses must meet the color, conformation, and breeding requirements of the PHBA. Each horse registered must be inspected by an approved inspector as a prerequisite to registration. There are restrictions on how much white is allowed on the legs and head. The general color rules of the PHBA are as follows:

Section 3. *Color:*

a. The body coat color must approximate that of a United States gold coin. The body coat shall be free of the following faults: a dorsal stripe of brown or black along the spine, Zebra stripes of lighter or darker color running around the legs or transversely across the shoulders or withers, and patches of white hair except if caused by injury.

b. The skin must be black, dark, or mouse-colored without pink spots wherever it shows, . . . except that skin on the face may be pink where it is a continuation of a white marking. The eyes must

64

FIGURE 2-40
Mack's Wonder Boy, Palomino
stallion of Saddle Horse type.
Photograph by Jean Whitesell,
courtesy of owner, Franklin L.
Hersom, Curlew, Iowa.

be the same color and have black, brown, or hazel irises. "Glass"
eyes will disqualify.

c. The mane and tail must be white with not more than 15 percent dark, sorrel, or chestnut hair in either.

Section 4. *Conformation:*

To be eligible for registration, a Palomino must show refinement
of head, bone, and general structure, appropriate to the breeds
recognized, . . . [and] . . . be between 14 and 17 hands when
full grown and show no draft horse characteristics.

FIGURE 2-41
Hoppy's Own, a Palomino Horse
Breeders Association Champion and
double-registered American Quarter
Horse. Photograph courtesy of owner,
Don Scroggins, Pearl River, Louisiana.

The additional requirements for the regular registry and the Palomino breed registry after one year of age are:

Regular registry

1. No Palomino, except a gelding, is eligible for registration in the Regular Registry unless its sire or dam is registered in PHBA, or unless the animal itself, or its sire or dam is registered in one of the following recognized breed associations:

American Remount Association; Arabian Horse Club; American Quarter Horse Association; American Saddle Horse Breeders Association; Jockey Club; Morgan Horse Club; Tennessee Walking Horse Breeders Association; United States Trotting Association.

2. A gelding is acceptable for registration strictly on color and conformation, regardless of whether or not it has a registered sire or dam.

3. No Palomino is eligible for registration in this Association if its sire or its dam is a draft horse or pony, or if its sire or dam is a piebald (having a body coat made up of patches of different color) or an Albino (lacking pigment in skin, hair and iris).

Palomino breed registry

1. No Palomino is eligible for registration in the Palomino Breed Registry unless the animal qualifies either by pedigree or by its progeny.

2. To qualify by pedigree, both the sire and the dam must be registered, one of which must be registered in the records of Palomino Horse Breeders of America. The other parent, either the sire or the dam, not registered in PHBA shall then qualify as to bloodline, such bloodline to be registered American Quarter Horse, Arabian, Thoroughbred, or American Saddlebred.

3. To qualify by its progeny, a Palomino stallion must be registered in Palomino Horse Breeders of America and must also have five of his get registered in PHBA. A mare to qualify, must herself be registered in Palomino Horse Breeders of America and must also have three of her produce registered in PHBA.

Since eligibility of a horse to be registered as a Palomino depends on obtaining the correct golden color, some mention of the difficulties should be made even before the discussion of genetics in Chapter 15. Research has shown that a simple genetic factor for dilution of chestnut color results in the palomino color. Animals carrying two dilution genes will be diluted to a near-white or off-white called cremello. Thus, the expected results from various matings to produce palominos are:

palomino by palomino = 1/4 chestnut + 1/2 palomino + 1/4 cremello
chestnut by palomino = 1/2 chestnut + palomino
palomino by cremello = 1/2 palomino + 1/2 cremello
chestnut by cremello = all palomino

Thus, there is no way palominos can breed true or produce more than half palominos from matings among themselves. The mating of chestnut with cremello should give all palominos, but if cremellos are classified as albinos, then that is not a legal mating. In fact, true albinos are not known in the horse since all white horses have colored rather than pink eyes.

Ysabella

The Ysabella (pronounced Isabella) breed is also a palomino-color breed except that the two-color types of horses that produce the palomino color are also registered. L. D. McKinzie (Figure 2-42), of Williamsport, Indiana, began in 1920 to breed these horses, which are named after Queen Isabella of Spain. The colors of the Ysabella are those proposed by Gremmels (1939)

FIGURE 2-42
L. D. McKinzie, the founder of the Ysabella Saddle Horse Association, mounted on a Ysabella Horse of golden palomino color. Photograph courtesy of the owner, L. D. McKinzie, Williamsport, Indiana.

67

to belong to the Ysabella group—a group having flaxen or silver manes and tails. The Ysabella Saddle Horse Association registers sorrels and chestnuts as well as the golden palomino—all with silver mane and tail—under the Gold Seal Registry. The cremello or pseudo-albino with silver mane and tail is registered under the Silver Seal. A total of approximately 2,100 Ysabella horses have been registered since 1920.

The major differences between the practices of the Palomino and Ysabella breeders are the use of the pseudo-albino to produce the palomino, the insistence that the chestnuts that are registered have light mane and tail, and the registering of chestnuts and cremellos by the Ysabella association. The latter has no strict conformation rules except that the height should be between 11 and 16 hands. This requirement differs from that of the Palomino Horse Breeders of America, which requires Palominos to meet the conformation standards appropriate to the breeds recognized by them.

2.15   Buckskins

Since 1963, two registeries have developed for Saddle Horses with buckskin, dun, and grulla colors: the American Buckskin Registry Association, Inc., and the International Buckskin Horse Association. Both registries have nearly the same description of these colors. Following is an abridged classification of eligible colors of the International Buckskin Horse Association:

Buckskin. The body coat of the Buckskin is predominantly a shade of yellow, ranging from gold to nearly brown. Points (mane, tail, legs, and so on) are black or dark brown. On the true Buckskin the dorsal stripe, shoulder stripe, and barring on the legs is always present. However, the dorsal stripe is *not necessary* for registration of the Buckskin.

Dun. The Dun differs from the "Buckskin" only in the respect that the body color is of a lighter shade. [Genetics journals and dictionaries, however, refer to buckskin as a light, clear shade of dun.]

Grulla. Smokey blue or mouse colored, with black points. The Grulla (*grew*-yah) has no white hair mixed in with darker hair, as is seen in the roan or grey. The name "Grulla" comes from the Spanish, meaning "Blue Crane." Grulla hair is a solid mousy blue or slate color.

68   *Red Dun.* The Red Dun is just that—red. Body coat may vary

FIGURE 2-43
Nicky Dean, a Buckskin mare, registered with the American Buckskin Registry Association and the American Quarter Horse Association, showing the black dorsal stripe, black points, mane, tail, and shoulder stripe. Owned by Clayton E. Gillette, Wessington Springs, South Dakota. Photograph courtesy of the American Buckskin Registry Association, Anderson, California.

from a yellow to a nearly flesh color. Points are dark red. Dorsal stripe must be present.

NOTE: The Grulla, Red Dun and some shades of Dun must have the dorsal stripe to be eligible for registration. Dorsal stripe is not a requirement for the Buckskin.

White Markings. White markings on the face and lower legs are permissible. Horses having white markings on the body elsewhere than on the face or lower legs will not be accepted. White markings on the legs may not go above the knees or hocks.

A Buckskin mare with the dorsal stripe and shoulder striping is shown in Figure 2-43. A golden Buckskin is shown in Figure 2-44.

FIGURE 2-44
Hank's Billy Van, a golden Buckskin, registered with the International Buckskin Horse Association. Photograph courtesy of IBHA, St. John, Indiana.

Buckskin breeders trace the ancestry of their horses to a true breeding Buckskin of Spain, the Sorraia, and to the Norwegian Dun. These were crossed with Barb and Arabian horses in Spain. During the following 700-year period, Spain developed many fine horses, many with buckskin and grulla patterns. Some of these were introduced by the Spanish explorers to Mexico and the United States early in the sixteenth century. Many of the modern western Buckskins probably trace to these animals. The buckskin pattern, however, appears in most breeds.

The dun or buckskin pattern, with lighter body and dark points and dorsal stripe, is similar to that of the Tarpan, a wild horse of central Europe, and of Przewalski's horse which represent nearly true breeding for color.

The genetics of buckskin or grulla color is not clear. The Buckskin registries claim that their horses breed true 70 percent to 80 percent of the time. However, one form of buckskin and dun results from a dilution of bay. A double dilution gives a so-called perlino (near white with darker mane and tail). The dilution type of dun would not breed true. Perhaps data from these new registries will be used to unravel some of the mystery of buckskin and dun inheritance. The hair shaft of the Buckskin appears to have pigment on only one side, as contrasted with both sides for most colors. Further discussion of this inheritance of buckskin, dun, and grulla pattern is found in Chapter 15.

The American Buckskin Registry Association, Inc., was formed in 1963 and registered approximately 2,200 animals through 1972—usually 200–300 each year.

The International Buckskin Horse Association began registering horses late in 1971 and registered 1,000 during the first year.

The requirements for registry are similar for both registries. Conformation can vary in each, although draft-type animals are not eligible. The ABRA will register ponies; the IBHA will not. Blue or glass eyes are not allowed by ABRA but are allowed by IBHA.

Both groups have the same registration classifications: appendix, tentative, and permanent. The Appendix is for foals registered before one year of age. If eligible, they can be then advanced to permanent or tentative status. The IBHA rules for tentative and permanent registration are:

Tentative Registration

All stallions and mares are first registered in the Tentative Book, unless both parents are already Permanent. Stallions are held in the Tentative Registry until they have sired twelve (12) foals which are registered. Mares are held in the Tentative Book until they have produced three (3) foals which are registered. Once this requirement is met, horses in the Tentative Book are eligible for advancement into Permanent Registry.

Permanent Registry

Geldings are eligible for direct registration into the Permanent Registry. Stallions and mares are advanced to Permanent from Tentative when they have met requirements. Foals registered to prove the breeding ability of stallions and mares may be of any age and may have been registered prior to stallion or mare.

All Buckskin, Grulla or Dun foals with both sire and dam registered in the Permanent Registry are eligible for direct Permanent registration.

Registered Buckskins are eligible for many shows and contests. There appears to be no restriction on double registration with other breeds for horses meeting the color standards of both registries. The IHBA is one of the few breed organizations whose rules permit artificial insemination and use of frozen semen when supervised by approved artificial insemination organizations.

2.16   Whites and Cremes: The American Albino

The white horse is the horse of heroes, history, art, and fiction. Children who grew up during the 1940s remember the Long Ranger's horse, Silver. Fewer people, however, remember Old Whitey, the mount of General Zachary Taylor, who pastured the horse on the White House lawn after he became President.

The Thompsons of Naper, Nebraska, contributed to the history of the white horse when in 1918 they purchased Old King, a white stallion of Arabian and Morgan breeding. He was the foundation sire of the American Albino registry set up by the Thompsons in 1937. Many of his white foals were from solid-colored Morgan mares.

Although albino is a synonym for white, the choice of name was probably unfortunate because in many species the true albino has serious problems because of lack of pigment in the eye. As previously mentioned, no true albino is known in the horse. The horses of the Thompson's White Horse Ranch had eyes with blue, brown, or hazel pigment. The skin is pink and the hair is clear white, but some small, colored spots occasionally occur.

The dominant white of the American Albino Horse is also apparently lethal when both gene units are the dominant white (see Chapter 15). Thus, no dominant white horse can breed true. Since one-fourth of foals are resorbed and never seen, 2/3 of the foals will be white and 1/3 will be colored when a dominant white is mated to a dominant white. Matings of dominant whites to colored horses produce 1/2 white and 1/2 colored (see Chapter 15).

71

Only dominant white horses and ponies (ponies if less than 14.2 hands) were registered until 1949. Then the cremellos and perlinos (near-white horses), which result from a double dose of the dilution gene that produces palominos and buckskins, were also registered as albino types A and B. In 1970, a separate section for *American Creme Horses* was formed for the creme horses. The classifications are:

A — Body ivory white, mane white (lighter than body), eyes blue, skin pink.

B — Body cream, mane darker than body, cinnamon buff to ridgeway, eyes dark.

C — Body and mane of the same color, pale cream, eyes blue, skin pink.

D — Body and mane of the same color, sooty cream, eyes blue, skin pink.

Combinations of the above classifications are also acceptable.

The distinctions between classes A and C and between classes B and D are not clear genetically. Type A bred among themselves should breed true.

The dominant white horse is now classified either as the American White Horse or as the American Albino Horse, depending on the wish of the owner.

There are no conformation standards because this is a color registry. All types are accepted. Approximately 2,500 have been registered since 1937. Many are used in troupes and in parades (Figure 2-45). The dominant white has appeared in most breeds of horses including, for the first time in 100 years, the Thoroughbred breed — one in Kentucky and one in France, both in 1963.

2.17   The "Native" Horses

Many of the horses of the early Spanish explorers escaped or were captured by Indians. Some of these were bred and selected by Indian tribes to form such types as the Appaloosa Horse in the Northwest and the Chickasaw Horse in the Southeast. Others ran free, especially in the Southwest and West, and became feral and semiferal in the harsh world of the survival of the fittest.

Chickasaw Horse

72   The first horses of the Chickasaw Indians of Tennessee and North Carolina were captured from the members of the 1539 expedition of DeSoto. These

FIGURE 2-45
R. R. Snow King, an American White
Horse in parade equipment, ridden
by Rose Simmering. S & E photo
courtesy of American Albino
Association and Ruth White.

small, short-coupled, well-muscled horses were popular with early colonists for general-purpose use although not for distance running. The Chickasaw Horse was utilized in cross-breeding to develop the early colonial quarter-mile horse, and it is one of the ancestors of the modern Quarter Horse. The Chickasaw Horse Association of Love Valley, North Carolina, was organized to register horses of the early Chickasaw type with a height range of 13.1 to 14.3 hands.

Spanish Mustangs

Robert Brislawn, Sr., and his brother, Ferdinand Brislawn, are given credit for forming the first and oldest mustang registry in 1957 in Sundance, Wyoming—the Spanish Mustang Registry. Since the 1920s the Brislawn brothers had been collecting a foundation stock of the purest wild and semiwild Spanish Mustangs. These last remnants of the naturally selected wild horses of Spanish-Barb and Andalusian ancestry were to be preserved and perpetuated for posterity as a living heritage of frontier America. To ensure the authenticity of future registered animals, the rules state that

> if at any time . . . any or all of the directors of the registry attempt to improve or in any way change the genotypes of the registered mustangs by hybridization with any other breed or breeds of horses or hybrids thereof, then the registry and its name should become null, void, and defunct.

Only horses that can reasonably be shown to be authentic are registered, and only after inspection. The typical mustang is approximately 13.2

73

hands, shortbacked, and wiry, and weighs 800 to 900 pounds. They have developed in the many colors and patterns of duns, solids, whites, palominos, appaloosas, and pintos. One of the most unusual is the Medicine Hat pattern, which was especially favored by the Cheyenne Indians who thought the Medicine Hat had supernatural powers of protection and invincibility. The Pinto stallion shown in Figure 2-37 exhibits the pattern—particularly about the head.

The Spanish-Barb

The Spanish-Barb Breeders Association was formed in 1972—also to promote and perpetuate the mustang as a breed but with emphasis on breeding for, and breeding back for, the ideal of the original Spanish-Barb Horses. Only authentic horses may be registered, and crossbreeding is not practiced. A Spanish-Barb gelding is shown in Figure 2-46. A future goal is to re-establish the Spanish-Barb in a sanctuary in the western plains—to allow them again to run wild without interference from man.

The American Mustang

The American Mustang Association, Inc., registered nearly 1,000 horses from 1957 through 1974 and has been dedicated to preserving and con-

FIGURE 2-46
Taw-ka Chi Who-ya, a Spanish-Barb gelding in action. Photograph by Susan Banner, courtesy of the Spanish-Barb Breeders Association, Colorado Springs, Colorado.

FIGURE 2-47
Taric, the 1973 National Merit American
Mustang stallion and the 1974 National
Grand Champion Get of Sire Award
winner. His dam was carrying him when
captured from a wild herd in Utah.
Photograph by Robin Bock, courtesy of
Diane and Robin Bock, Mustang Manor,
Costa Mesa, California.

tinuing the best specimens of the American Mustang, which descended
from the early Spanish horses. The association has begun a stud book and,
unlike many mustang registries, holds a national and several local mustang
shows (Figure 2-47). Inspection for suitable conformation by an authorized
inspector or a licensed veterinarian is required before registration. To be
registered, a mustang must be between 13.2 and 15 hands. Any color is
acceptable. Crossbred mustangs are not eligible, but such mares and geldings may be registered in the associated Half-Mustang Registry along with
other horses that show mustang characteristics but that do not meet all
requirements.

2.18   The Shetland

When most people think of a pony, they have in mind the Shetland. The
technical dividing line between horses and ponies is at 14 or 14.2 hands.
However, the Shetland is much smaller. Their maximum height is 46
inches (11.2 hands), and most are approximately 40 inches tall. As is well
known, these ponies developed in the Shetland Islands approximately
100 miles north of Scotland and 350 miles from the Arctic Circle. The
name "Shetland" derives from an old Norse word meaning "highland."
These small islands provided a harsh, rugged environment for the development of a hardy breed of ponies, which began before the Norsemen settled
the islands about 850. The shaggy, furry coat worn by Shetlands in winter
months and by some foals until they are 2 years of age must have developed
to withstand the rigors of the North Sea winters and storms. The native
pony of the Shetland Islands was a miniature draft horse, as contrasted

FIGURE 2-48
A 2-year-old Shetland pony mare,
Fernwood Frisco Caroline II. Photo-
graph by Carlin H. Brearley, courtesy
of the owner, Harry K. Megson,
Chazy River Farms, Champlain,
New York.

with the refined American Shetland (Figure 2-48). They became popular
in England and Scotland for work in the mines because of their strength
and small size.

The Shetland came with the English settlers to the United States, as
did the Thoroughbred. The Arabian and Barb breeding, by way of the
Hackney, as evidenced in the modern American Shetland, apparently
resulted from crosses that were made in the 1880s. Other than those
crosses, the Shetland has been a relatively true-breeding breed—at first
because of the isolation of its native islands, and later because of the
desire to maintain a small children's pony.

The modern American type of Shetland is the result of selection from
the draft or "Island" types that were imported to America. The types have
diverged so much that today the native Shetland can no longer be registered in the American Stud Book. Many nonregistered Shetlands, however,
show more of their ancestral type than do the registered show class Shetlands (Figure 2-49).

The American Shetland Pony Club was organized in 1888. Through
1972, more than 130,000 ponies were registered. Recently the annual

FIGURE 2-49
A boy and his nonregistered
pony of Shetland heritage.

average has been approximately 2,000. In a recent step to increase the popularity of the cyclically popular breed, a new Division B for registration of crossbred Shetlands having at least 50 percent registered Shetland breeding was approved. Division A is retained for animals with registered Shetland parents. The application for registration includes the following instructions:

> Effective November 14, 1970, the American Shetland Pony Club will accept for entry in the Stud Book an animal that is the result of crossing registered Hackney blood, or registered Welsh blood, with registered Shetland blood, providing that said animal carries no less than 50% Shetland blood. Said animals will be entered in Division B of the Stud Book, as compared to Division A, which will designate those animals that are the offspring of a registered Shetland sire and dam. Also recognized as acceptable parents of Division B ponies are registered Harness Show Ponies and registered Americana ponies, providing matings of these animals produce offspring that carry no less than 50% Shetland blood.

The ASPC registers also the Harness Show Pony, a type of miniature, fine harness horse that results from crosses between registered Shetlands and registered Welsh or Hackneys.

In 1972, the ASPC opened a registry for miniature horses (animals 34 inches or less at maturity)—the American Miniature Horse Registry.

Harness racing for ponies is governed by the United States Pony Trotting Association, which became affiliated with the ASPC in 1964.

The standard of perfection for the Shetland is stated in the Official Show Rules of the ASPC:

> Conformation should be that of a strong, attractive, versatile pony, blending the original Shetland type with refinement and quality resulting from American care and selective breeding. The barrel should be well rounded, back short and level, with flat croup. The head should be carried high and on a well-arched neck, and should be symmetrical and proportionate to the body, with width between prominent eyes, a fine jaw, short, sharp and erect ears, small muzzle with flaring nostrils and a refined throat latch. The pony shall have a full mane and tail. The pony's structure should be strong with refinement, with high withers, sloping shoulders, flat bonded, muscular legs (not cow or sickle hocked), strong springy pasterns and good strong serviceable feet.

Ponies with convex face or Roman nose are unacceptable and are disqualified by judges.

Ponies come in all colors. Black, dark brown, bay, and chestnut pre-

FIGURE 2-50
A Shetland pony in action in a fine harness class. Photograph by Morris, courtesy of the American Shetland Pony Club, Fowler, Indiana.

dominate, especially for the show ring, where white markings have not recently been preferred although color fads change. Spotted ponies are popular for children's mounts. A color unique to Shetlands is the silver dapple—a dappled chestnut with silver or white mane and tail. Another unique color is the light bay with only a few black hairs intermingled in a flaxen mane and tail. Black points on the legs are nearly absent.

The show ring accommodates the versatile Shetland in breeding and harness classes (Figure 2-50). As with most pony breeds, the classes are divided according to height. The dividing line of 43 inches appears to nearly equalize the number in the "over" and "under" classes.

2.19 The Pony of the Americas

Black Hand No. 1, born in 1954, the foundation sire of the Pony of the Americas, was the result of a mating of an Appaloosa mare and a Shetland pony stallion (Figure 2-51). The characteristics of Black Hand served as an inspiration for his owner, Leslie L. Boomhower of Mason City, Iowa, to establish a breed association for an "in-between" size, western-type pony that would be small enough for children, yet large enough for adults to break and train. This registry, the Pony of the Americas Club (POAC), was organized in 1955 with 23 members and 12 ponies. The foremost purpose of the organization was to establish and promote a children's working pony.

The size limits of 46 inches–54 inches were met by the crossing of pony breeds with Appaloosas, the crossing of Quarter Horses and Arabians with ponies having Appaloosa markings, and the importation from Mexico and Central and South America of small horses of the required size and Appaloosa colors. The registry was open until 1970, when the POAC required that at least one parent had to be registered except for hardship cases.

The ideal for the Pony of the Americas (POA) has been described as a cross between a Quarter Horse and an Arabian in miniature and having the Appaloosa color patterns. The eligibility requirements for color are essentially those for the Appaloosa. The white sclera is required but does not have to encircle the eye. Striped hooves are desirable but are not required. All registrations are tentative until inspection between 5 and 6 years of age determines eligibility for permanent registration. If eligibility requirements are not met for size, an identification (I.D.) certificate may be issued, with foals eligible for registration subject to the other requirements. Some of the more important rules are:

Eligible

1. Pony must have Appaloosa characteristics (sclera and mottled skin) and color. One parent must be a registered POA, unless hardship clause is satisfied.

2. At maturity pony must be 46″ and not over 54″. (If pony matures under 46″ or over 54″, its pedigree will be voided, and the registration fee forfeited. If pony is a stallion or mare, it will be issued an I.D. Certificate with Full Breeding Rights. . . .

Not Eligible

3. Ponies with pinto color, or pinto sire and/or dam.
4. Ponies with albino color, or albino sire and/or dam.

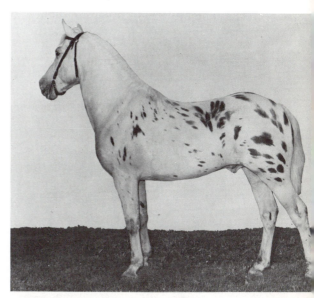

FIGURE 2-51
Black Hand No. 1, the foundation sire of the Pony of the Americas, was the result of mating an Appaloosa mare and a Shetland stallion. Photograph courtesy of the U.S. Department of Agriculture.

5. Ponies with white stockings above either knee and/or either hock, or white on the face behind a line from the center of each ear to the corner of the mouth, and from the corner of the mouth underneath the lower jaw directly to the other corner of the mouth.

6. Roan ponies, unless they are the approved Appaloosa color and are strong in Appaloosa characteristics.

General

10. Marginal registration is available for ponies with Appaloosa characteristics and white frost or Appaloosa color, not clearly visible at 40 feet. These ponies are ineligible to show and a notation to this effect is included on their pedigrees. If these ponies develop easily recognizable Appaloosa color at 40 feet as they mature . . . , the marginal restriction will be removed and they will be eligible to show.

The performance classes are for youths of 17 years and younger and include most western-type classes (Figure 2-52). There are additional costume classes. Adults often show halter-class entries. Naturalness is emphasized. POA classes are divided by size into two divisions: 46 inches–50 inches and 50 inches–54 inches. The Appaloosa minimum height of 56 inches is 2 inches more than the maximum for the POA, although the POAC has discussed changing their maximum to 56 inches.

The POAC registry has grown quickly. More than 18,000 horses were registered from 1955 to 1973. An additional 3,600 I.D. Certificates were also issued.

The National Appaloosa Pony, Inc., which began in 1963, registers Appaloosa-type ponies whose height falls below 46 inches, as well as

FIGURE 2-52
A Pony of the Americas and its young rider. Photograph by Paulsen, courtesy of the Pony of the Americas Club, Inc., Mason City, Iowa.

those whose height is above 46 inches. Class A includes Appaloosa ponies whose size is 40 inches–48 inches; the class B size is 48 inches–56 inches. All ponies are inspected to ensure that all requirements for registration are met. Nearly 1,500 ponies were registered during the first 2 years.

As with most new breeds, much selection will need to be done. Rules and regulations will no doubt receive minor changes, but the enthusiasm of owners and the need for a western-style children's working pony seem to guarantee a long future for the Appaloosa-type pony.

2.20 The Welsh Pony

The ancestors of the Welsh Mountain Pony developed in the severe terrain of Wales even before the Roman legions invaded the British Isles. In the early 1800s, Throughbred, Arabian, and Hackney blood was incorporated. In the late 1800s, some Welsh Ponies were imported to the United States, where the Welsh Pony and Cob Society was incorporated in 1906. (The Welsh Cob is a larger version of the Welsh Pony.) The breed expanded for some time, then declined. There were virtually no registrations during the depression of the 1930s. A renaming and reorganization took place in 1946, and "Cob" was dropped from the society's name, because no Cobs had been registered in the United States. Most Welsh Ponies trace to importation from England after 1947. Approximately 30,000 were registered between 1906 and 1972. There was an increase of 1,100 in 1973 alone.

The Welsh Pony is intermediate between a Shetland and most riding horses and is useful for children who have outgrown ponies of Shetland size (Figure 2-53). Welsh Ponies are also used as hunters for children. Welsh Ponies registered in division A cannot exceed 50 inches; taller ponies are registered in division B but cannot exceed 58 inches.

FIGURE 2-53
Liseter Shooting Star, a Welsh Pony champion and sire of champions. Photograph courtesy of the owner, Mrs. J. A. duPont, Newton Square, Pennsylvania.

Rather than show the Welsh Pony as a "fitted," high-stepping pony, as are the Shetland and Hackney, Welsh breeders have adopted a more natural way of presentation. In the formal driving classes, fine harness equipment is used but without artificial appliances.

Some special rules for showing, as described by the American Horse Shows Association for both Section A and Section B Welsh Ponies, are:

Sec. 4. Artificial Appliances and Irritants. Any pony wearing turnbuckles, equipment or devices other than those permitted in specific classes and any pony showing evidence of the use of ginger or other irritants to produce a higher tail carriage than the natural position shall be disqualified from the class in which it is showing.

Sec. 5. Shoeing Regulations. Ponies may be shown barefoot. Foals and Yearlings must be shown barefoot. In Breeding Classes when Two-Year-Olds are shod the shoes must be unweighted and the foot natural with frog close to ground; pads and additional weight of any description shall disqualify.

A frequent color of the Welsh is gray, especially in England (Figure 2-54). Any color is acceptable, but spotted patterns are not.

The Welsh has been frequently crossed with larger riding-horse breeds to produce ponies whose height ranges between 13 and 14 hands. The Halfbred and Crossbred Welsh Registry was formed in 1959 to record animals and to protect buyers and sellers. A Halfbred Welsh has one registered Welsh parent and an unregistered parent of any other breed or combination of breeds. A Crossbred Welsh has registered parents,

FIGURE 2-54
A gray Welsh stallion and Section B champion, Cusop Sheriff, was imported from England. Photograph by Tarrance Photos, courtesy of the owner, Mrs. Karl D. Butler, Ithaca, New York.

one Welsh and the other of another breed. There are no color or height limitations.

2.21   The Hackney Pony

The elegant, fiery Hackney has been called the Prince of Ponies. Used almost exclusively for showing in harness classes, this aristocrat of the pony world is an adult's pony—too small to be ridden by an adult but too spirited and frisky for most children.

The Hackney Pony derives from the same ancestors as his bigger brother, the Hackney Horse. The ancestors of the Hackneys were bred for riding and driving in England. The terms "Hackney" and "Roadster" were applied to them. The Norfolk trotters were the most famous. Crosses of these horses with the Thoroughbred led to the Hackney that pulled the British Hackney coaches of the eighteenth century. They were selected to show flashy action at the trot. Their hallmark was, and remains, extreme flexion of knees and hocks at the trot. The Hackney Horse was not large—14.2–15.2 hands and 900–1,100 pounds. A pony version of the Hackney was made up of the small Hackneys and resulted also from crosses with the Welsh Pony. Selection for a smaller size completed the establishment of the Hackney Pony. There are no major differences between the Hackney Pony and the Hackney Horse except size. The pony may more closely approach the Hackney ideal in exaggerated action and flash. The Hackney Pony is, indeed, a horse in a small package.

Hackneys were imported to America, particularly in the late nineteenth century, mainly for show and fancy driving. Today both are registered in the United States by the American Hackney Horse Society. Only in shows are they separated; the pony is classified as having a height of 14.2 hands and under.

At horse shows, Hackney Ponies are divided into Cob-Tail (Hackney) and Long-Tail (harness) classes. The name "Cob-Tail" derives from the English custom of docking the tail to a 6-inch length for carriage style (Figure 2-55). Manes are tightly braided for these classes, which are for registered American and Canadian Hackneys only. The Hackney classes also may be divided by size: 13 hands and under, or 13 hands and over but under 14.2 hands. Harness classes are open to ponies of all breeding that are 12.2 hands or under. These are shown with long manes and tail (Figure 2-56). The harness classes were originally meant for Shetland crosses, but the small Hackneys, when shown with natural manes and tails, have completely dominated these open classes (Figure 2-57) with long mane and tail.

83

FIGURE 2-55
Whyworry Lobelia, shown in Hackney (Cob-Tail) pony class. Photograph by
Fallow, courtesy of Mrs. W. P. Roth, San Mateo, California.

Most Hackney Ponies are dark. They are predominantly bay, but there
are also some blacks, browns, and chestnuts. White socks and stockings
as well as white face markings are allowed. Spotted ponies seldom exist.

FIGURE 2-56
An international champion harness (Long-Tail) pony, Johnny Dollar, shown by
Mrs. David LaSalle. Photograph by Tarrance Photos, courtesy of David LaSalle,
North Scituate, Rhode Island.

FIGURE 2-57
Batman, a world champion roadster pony (Hackney) owned and driven by
Chris Good, Hickory, North Carolina. Photograph courtesy of the trainer,
Lewis P. Eckard, Hildebran, North Carolina.

Approximately 95 percent of the 600–1,000 Hackneys registered each
year are ponies. Some 19,000 Hackney Horses and Hackney Ponies have
been registered since the American Hackney Horse Society was founded
in 1891. Only ponies with dams and sires registered in the American,
English, and Canadian Hackney Stud Books are eligible for registration.

The unique action of the Hackney Pony that so fascinates and excites
spectators and exhibitors is the reason for its dominance of the show ring.
The extreme action of the front legs—the "rainbow" arch that they form
on the way to the ground—and the matching high hock action, together
with the well-flexed neck holding the head high and proud, have maintained the status of the Hackney as the Prince of Ponies.

2.22   The Connemara

The Connemara Pony is famed for its ability as a jumper (Figure 2-58).
Although a large pony, officially standing 13–14.2 hands, the Connemara
has outjumped horses 8–12 inches taller. This pony originated in the
Connemara region in County Galway, Ireland.

The ancestry of the breed includes Spanish-Barbs, Jennets, and Anda-
lusians of the sixteenth century that were crossed with native ponies. Later,
Arabians were crossed with the descendants of these horses. During the

85

last half of the nineteenth century, there was much crossing of native Connemara Ponies with other breeds. The best crossbreds resulted from using Welsh Cob stallions. To prevent the breed from being crossed out of existence, the Connemara Pony Breeders' Society was formed in 1923. It selected the finest of the available stock on which to base the breed.

The first Connemaras were imported to America for breeding purposes 28 years later in 1951. The owners, although few, were spread across the country. The American Connemara Pony Society was founded late in 1956. Some 3,000 had been registered by 1972 — an average of 300–400 each year. All colors are permitted except that neither spotted nor blue-eyed cream ponies may be registered. Animals under 14.2 hands are registered as ponies; animals over 14.2 hands are registered as horses that are often referred to as oversize ponies. There is some tendency to breed for the larger type of Connemara. The Irish Connemara remains pony size. A supplemental registry is maintained for Halfbred Connemara Ponies — one parent must be registered. After five generations of crosses with registered Connemara Ponies, the Halfbred Connemara is eligible for entry to the Purebred Stud Book.

Connemara Ponies are shown in jumping and hunting pony classes. Long toes are reason for disqualification, as are artificial devices. Ponies are not to be parked in a stretched position. These ponies can be ridden by an adult in jumping events but are said to be gentle enough for a young child and also suitable as a driving pony.

2.23   Synthetic, Gaited, and Quarter Ponies

A synthetic breed is started by crossing two or more breeds and then mating among the first generations of crossbred animals. The first cross may give the desired result with considerable uniformity as dictated by the laws of genetics. Matings among crossbreds, however, also follow the laws of genetics and result in considerable variability ranging in extremes between the parent breeds. Continued *inter se* mating of future generations of crossbreds and selection is required to develop a desirable and reasonably uniform breed.

The Americana

The Americana is a synthetic breed that was begun in 1962 by crossing Shetland and Hackney Ponies to produce a miniature Saddlebred type of show pony. The disposition and conformation were to come from the Shetland; the action, animation, style, and slightly larger size were to come

FIGURE 2-58

A gray Connemara mare, R. H. F. O'Harazan, in action. Photograph by Paul A. Quinn, courtesy of the owner, Gilnocky Farm, Windsor, Vermont.

from the Hackney. This same cross was used to produce harness ponies, but as explained in section 2.18, they failed to be competitive with small Hackneys.

The Americana Club registers only foals of registered Americanas, foals of crosses between registered Shetlands and registered Hackneys, and foals of crossbreds with registered Shetlands to further reduce the size. Maximum height at maturity is 46 inches. All the variation of Shetland coloring is seen, including the silver dapples, palominos, and pintos, as well as the more nearly true-breeding solid dark colors. More than 1,000 Americana Ponies had been registered by 1966.

The Americana are shown as miniature American Saddlebreds; classes include halter, riding, harness, and roadster. The harness classes use the same equipment as American Saddlebred Horses.

The American Walking Pony

The American Walking Pony originated in the 1950s at Browntree Stables in Macon, Georgia. The owner, Mrs. Joan Brown, chose to cross the Tennessee Walking Horse and the Welsh Pony to form a breed of walking pony to be used as a pleasure and show pony. The size requirement is a minimum of 13 hands and a maximum of 14.1 hands. These ponies have been shown in open and Walking Pony halter classes (Figure 2-59).

The American Saddlebred Pony

The American Saddlebred Horse Association has no minimum height requirement, and thus the smaller American Saddlebreds fall into the pony class. Saddlebred Pony classes are sanctioned by the American Horse Shows Association. Saddlebred Ponies are prepared and shown just as are the larger Saddlebred Horses and perform in three- and five-gaited classes as well as in fine harness classes. These ponies (13–14.2 hands) are ponies in name only; they are horses in conformation and temperament, although in miniature.

The Walking Pony

Just as the American Saddlebred comes in pony size, so does the Tennessee Walking Horse. The pony-size Walking Horse has the same colors, conformation, and gaits as do larger Walking Horses. Walking Pony classes are for those under 14.2 hands. Walkers under 13 hands are rare. Training and showing are the same as for their big brothers, although many of the classes are divided also by age of rider: 15–18 years and 14 years and younger.

FIGURE 2-59
An American Walking Pony, BT Summer Magic, bred by Browntree Stables, Macon, Georgia, and owned by Miss Faye Collins of Macon, Georgia. Photograph by Allen Zebell, courtesy of the American Walking Pony Association, Macon, Georgia.

FIGURE 2-60
Cowboy's Super, 55 inches tall and
twice National Champion American
Quarter Pony halter mare. Photograph
by W. A. Campbell, courtesy of
owner, Ed Ufferman, Marengo, Ohio.

The American Quarter Pony

Quarter Horse types that could not be registered because of lack of height led to the establishment in 1964 of the American Quarter Pony Association, whose function was to register riding and show ponies of the Quarter Horse type that measured 46 inches to, but not including, 58 inches (Figure 2-60). Ponies with Appaloosa, albino, or spotted characteristics are not eligible for registration. Several hundred have been registered in the United States and Canada.

2.24 Miniature Horses

Miniature horses are rare. Only about one in several thousand horses qualifies as a miniature. The maximum height of a miniature horse is usually defined as 32 inches, although some assert it to be 36 inches. Miniatures are used as pets, in circuses, and even as curiosity pieces. The true miniature is simply a small pony or horse and is not a malformed dwarf. Miniatures are just as healthy as regular horses, although because of their size they are much more susceptible to accidents and to attacks by packs of dogs.

There are no miniature breeds, but the American Shetland Pony Club does maintain a registry for horses under 34 inches—the American Miniature Horse Registry. If successful, a breed may develop from this effort.

Another group that may be considered a private breed is the Falabella Horses of Argentina. The Falabella family began in 1868 to breed for miniature size. The present herd consists of some 400 head, which is larger than some breed registries. Falabellas are derived from Shetland as well as larger stock. Many have been imported into the United States since 1962. The Falabella Horses are noted for the excellence of their conformation, which is often faulted in many miniatures. The smallest Falabella is 15 inches tall and weighs only 27 pounds.

Several breeders in the United States have collected and developed herds of miniature horses (Figure 2-61). Some of these horses are as small as 20 inches and weigh only 40 pounds. Colors generally cover the same broad range as the colors of the Shetland, from which most miniature herds have developed.

Tom Thumb was a rather famous small horse that was 23 inches tall and weighed 45 pounds at 8 years of age. He was exhibited in sideshows with a small mare, Cactus, that measured 26 inches. Both, however, were dwarf horses, not miniature horses. Both were from full-size parents and were found to be sterile.

2.25 The Draft Breeds

Descendants of the "Great Horse," the horse of knights in armor of the Middle Ages, make up the five major draft breeds in the United States. These breeds all developed in northern Europe—Scotland, England, France, and Belgium. All are named for their regions of origin: the Percheron from La Perche, an ancient district south of Normandy, France; the Belgian, a descendant of the great horse of Flanders; the Clydesdale from the Clyde River area known as Clydesdale in Scotland; the Shire, named for the English areas of Lincolnshire and Cambridgeshire; and the Suffolk from the agricultural county of Suffolk, also in England.

These horses, so frequently described in history and legend, developed into heavy-carriage, draft, and farming horses. Although their early history is obscure, the Percheron is thought to be the only one of these so-called cold-blooded horses to have had an infusion of Arab and Barb (hot-blooded) ancestry, a legacy of the Moorish invasion of Spain and western France in the early eighth century.

Nearly all the draft breeds are large and heavily muscled; they stand approximately 16–17 hands and weigh 1,600–2,200 pounds depending on sex, age, and condition.

FIGURE 2-61
Joel R. Bridges, surrounded by part of a band of miniature horses—the smallest 26½ inches tall and the largest 30 inches tall as adults. Photograph by Pat Canova, courtesy of the owner, Kokomo Ranch, Newberry, Florida.

The Percheron

Percherons are known to have been imported to the United States in 1839. After 1851, imports were numerous as the Percheron became the most popular among the draft breeds.

The forerunner of the Percheron Horse Association of America was first organized in 1876. Since then approximately 250,000 Percherons have been registered—more than all the other draft breeds combined. More Percherons were registered annually than any other draft breed until the Belgian became popular in the 1920s. In 1973, 250 Percherons were registered—second only to the Belgians among the draft horses.

The Percheron is known as the breed of blacks and grays because approximately half are black and half are gray (Figure 2-62). Other colors are known, and white markings are common although not extensive.

Despite its immense size, the Percheron is active and light on its feet. It displays considerable knee action and a bold trot, both of which make it a popular horse in draft horse shows. Its popularity as a draft horse was due to its speed at the walk and the lack of feathering about the fetlock.

a

FIGURE 2-62
The Percherons are known as the
breed of the blacks and grays.
a, A black gelding with long mane
and tail. Photograph by Howard O.
Merry, courtesy of E. S. Rickard,
Cobleskill, New York. *b*, A black
stallion, Don-A-Tation, with braided
mane and tail, in a halter class.
Photograph by John M. Briggs, Ithaca,
New York. *c*, A gray stallion, Shady
Creek Carnot, with braided tail.
Photograph by James M. Barnhart,
Butler, Missouri.

b

c

The Belgian

From 1910 through the 1930s, the Belgian—the sorrels and roans—surpassed the blacks and grays of the Percheron in popularity among American farmers. The predominant color soon became sorrel (many light horse breeders call it chestnut) with white mane and tail (Figure 2-63). The lighter shades are known as blonde sorrels. The characteristics of the Belgian suited the needs of the American farmer, and thus Belgian stallions were much in demand for crossing with native draft-type horses and particularly for crossing with Percheron mares. The uniformity of color of Belgians was popular and they were known for ease of management. The Belgian has been distinguished in pulling contests and is very quiet and docile, but is somewhat slow-motioned and does not show much high-leg action. The influence of the imported roan stallion, Farceur, provided more action and quality (that is, better body and leg conformation).

The origin of the Belgian Draft Horse Corporation of America traces back to 1887. The current name was adopted in 1937. In recent years, more Belgians have been registered each year than all other draft breeds combined. Approximately 73,000 had been registered through 1973; nearly 1,000 were registered in 1973 alone.

The Clydesdale

The advertising (including television commercials) of the Budweiser brewery (Figure 2-64) and other companies having six- and eight-horse hitches make the Clydesdale one of the most well known of American draft

FIGURE 2-63
Sunny Lane Tamara, a champion Belgian mare. Photograph by Leonard C. Novak, courtesy of the owner, Leo J. Fox, David City, Nebraska.

FIGURE 2-64
The Budweiser Clydesdale eight-horse hitch showing the noted action and
dramatic feathering of the breed. Photograph courtesy of the owner,
Anheuser-Busch, Inc., St. Louis, Missouri.

horses. The extensive white face and leg markings, together with the
"feather" (long, silky hair on the lower legs), which creates a bell-bottomed
effect, give the Clydesdale a unique appearance to go with the noted action
of the breed—long, springy strides with extreme flexion of the knees
and hocks.

The Clyde is somewhat lighter on the average than the other breeds
although it is just as tall. The bones of these horses are cleaner and flatter
than those of other breeds. Clydes are considered more nervous than the
other draft breeds and are too difficult for most American farmers to handle.

The Clydesdale Breeders Association of the United States registered
95 in 1973, and the breed trails only the Belgian and Percheron in popularity.

The Shire

The Shire, like its ancestral cousin, the Clydesdale, developed from the
English Great Horse. Robert Bakewell (1726–1795), who developed many
improved breeds of livestock, also initiated the improvement of the Shire
as a draft horse. The Shire is known as the biggest of the draft horses, but
there are so few in the United States that such comparisons are not very
meaningful. Approximately 30 or more Shires have been imported in recent
years. Earlier imports to Canada date from 1836, although most activity
occurred during the 1880s.

Black is the dominant color of Shires, although the related colors of bay
and dark brown are known (Figure 2-65). White markings on the face and
legs are common. Like the Clydesdale, the Shire has feathering on its
legs, although the feather is finer and silkier now than when it retarded

94

FIGURE 2-65
Jim's Chieftain, a black Shire stallion, showing the feathering and extensive white markings of the breed. Photograph courtesy of the owner, Arlin Wareing, Blackfoot, Idaho.

the acceptance of the Shire in America. The American Shire Horse Association registers the few Shires that are registered.

The other draft breed of English origin is the Suffolk.

The Suffolk

This chestnut breed of draft horse was developed primarily for farm use. Due to their rather rounded, punched-up appearance, they were originally called Suffolk-Punches. The Suffolk differs from the other two British breeds in that the leg is not feathered. The color has been standardized to a true-breeding dusty chestnut or sorrel; the mane and tail are often lighter (Figure 2-66). Like the Percheron, the white markings of the Suffolks, if present at all, are unobtrusive on both face and legs.

FIGURE 2-66
A six-horse hitch of Suffolks at the trot. Photograph by Edward T. Gray, courtesy of the owner and driver, D. F. Neal, Slippery Rock, Pennsylvania.

95

Very few Suffolk horses were ever imported or bred in the United States because they were too small to produce draft animals that would be large enough when crossed with the lighter breeds found in America. The American Suffolk Horse Association has registered fewer than 3,000 horses. Registration through the 1960s averaged less than 10 per year.

2.26 The Long Ears: Burros, Donkeys, and Mammoth Jacks

A close relative of the horse (*Equus caballus*) is the ass (*Equus assinus*). Just as horses come in all sizes and colors, so do asses. The male ass is known as a *jack* and the female is known as a *jennet.* The most noticeable differences between an ass and a horse are that an ass has longer, larger ears, a sparser mane and tail, a more brushlike tail, and smaller hooves. The muzzle and underbelly area are light in color, and there are no chestnuts on the inner sides of the legs. The characteristic bray contrasts with the whinny of the horse. The gestation period of the jennet is approximately 30 days longer than the 11 months of the mare.

During the early history of the United States, jacks were bred to use on horse mares to produce *mules* (Figure 2-67). Mules were very popular as work animals. The reverse cross between the jennet and the stallion is known as a *hinny* (Figure 2-68). The mule is said to be somewhat more like the horse and the hinny is a little more like the ass. Mules and hinnys of both sexes are sterile, but their sexual instincts are normal.

Donkeys are small asses. The name derives from a diminutive of the English word "dun," which describes the usual color. The Spanish translation of "donkey" is "burro," so donkey and burro are synonymous.

The popularity of asses declined in the United States as the demand for draft animals declined, until the 1960s when they became more popular as pets and curiosities. There are now several registries for different types of asses.

The American, Mammoth, or Standard Jack and Jennet

The American Jack, also known as the Mammoth Jack or the Standard Jack, was bred for crossing with mares to produce mules. The American Jack is a blend of various stocks imported from southern Europe and the Mediterranean. Some of these stocks are listed in Table 2-2.

George Washington was one of the first breeders of Jacks; he crossed strains of asses received as gifts from the King of Spain and General

FIGURE 2-67
Mr. Tips of Oregon, an unusual
leopard Appaloosa mule from the
cross of a jack and an Appaloosa
mare. Photograph courtesy of Urban
J. Woida, Veneta, Oregon.

Lafayette of France. Henry Clay imported Maltese stock. The famous jack,
Imported Mammoth, imported from Catalonia in 1819, was crossed with
the Clay imports. Since most Jack stock traces to Mammoth, it is natural
that one of the alternate names for American Jacks is the Mammoth Jack.

The Standard Jack and Jennet Registry and the newly formed (1969)
American Donkey and Mule Society register American Jacks and Jennets.
In the 31 years from 1941 to 1972, the Standard Registry registered approximately 3,000 jacks and jennets, but few have been registered since
1970. The ADMS registers all breeds and types of asses and was formed
to promote interest in the long-eared species.

FIGURE 2-68
A saddle hinny from a cross of a
Morgan stallion and a burro jennet.
Owned by E. C. Porter, Safford,
Arizona. Photograph courtesy of
American Donkey and Mule Society,
Indianapolis, Indiana.

97

TABLE 2-2
The foundation stocks of the American Jack

Name of Stock	Native Province	Approximate Height (hands)	Characteristics
Catalonian	Catalonia, Spain	14–15.2	Black, brown, white points, good heads, stylish
Adalusian	Andalusia, Spain	13.2–15	Gray, large, good heads
Majorca	Majorca Island	14.2–15.2	Black, large, sluggish
Maltese	Malta Island	13–14.2	Black or brown, very refined, small
Poitou	Poitou, France	15–16	Black or brown, very drafty, long hair
Italian	Italy	13–14	Black, small, inferior

SOURCE: Briggs, H. M. 1969. *Modern Breeds of Livestock*, p. 688.

The requirement for registration in the Standard Registry is that the animals must have registered sires and dams. Other animals are registered if certain physical requirements are met:

Jacks must measure not less than 14 hands, standard, in height; at least 60 inches around the heart girth, and at least 7½ inches around the front leg at the smallest place between the ankle and the knee, the leg to be normal.

Jennets must measure not less than 13½ hands, standard, in height; at least 58 inches around the heart girth, and at least 7 inches around the front leg at the smallest place between the ankle and the knee, the leg to be normal.

Any color is permitted although most Jacks are dark with white points.

The Burro

The Burro is the small, so-called native, ass of North America and South America. Most are 40–50 inches in height. The burro or donkey of the Americas is a blend of many breeds of European and Middle Eastern countries. The ancestors of the burro were probably brought to the Americas with the Spanish expeditions. Burros come in all sizes and colors (Figure (Figure 2-69). They can be registered in the stud book of the American Donkey and Mule Society.

FIGURE 2-69
An unusual dappled gray
American Burro jennet owned
by Carl A. Wilson, Indianapolis,
Indiana. Photograph by D.
Bennett, courtesy of Paul and
Betsy Hutchins, Denton, Texas.

The American Spotted Ass

The American Council of Spotted Asses was formed in about 1967 to register spotted or pinto asses of primarily burro size. All animals must be inspected and approved before registration. The color pattern may be white with colored spots or colored with white spots (Figure 2-70). The qualifying spots must be above the knees and hocks and behind the throat latch. Stockings and face markings do not qualify as spots. The council plans to close its stud book after an initial period of registering foundation animals.

FIGURE 2-70
Shenandoah, a young American
Spotted Ass jennet owned by E. Diane
Hunter. Photograph courtesy of
American Donkey and Mule Society,
Indianapolis, Indiana.

The Miniature Donkey

A Miniature Donkey Registry was formed in the Midwest in 1958 to provide an imported strain of miniature donkeys less than 38 inches high. The organizers included the owners of the St. Louis Cardinals and the Cincinnati Reds, and Daniel Langfeld, Jr., and Daniel Langfeld, Sr., of Omaha. The original animals were imported from the Mediterranean (chiefly Sicily and Sardinia), and were 28–38 inches in height. Import restrictions have curtailed further importation.

The characteristics of the Miniature Donkey make it an attractive pet (Figure 2-71). Colors range from a light gray to a dark, almost black, brown. The cross on the back, their well-known trademark, is formed by a dorsal stripe running from the mane to the tail that is intersected by the arms of the cross at the withers. The cross is said by legend to be the reward for carrying Mary to Bethlehem and Jesus to Jerusalem.

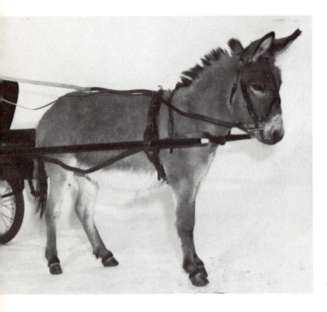

FIGURE 2-71
A registered Sicilian Miniature Donkey owned by Danby Farm, Omaha, Nebraska. Photograph courtesy of American Donkey and Mule Society, Indianapolis, Indiana.

Appendixes

Identification

The purposes of breed associations can be satisfied only by reliable identification of animals and their sires and dams. Nearly all breeds require a written description of colors and color patterns together with a sketch or picture of the animal. Even more positive identification (see section 24.2) is required by some registries: lip tattoos and photographs of a horse's "fingerprints"—unique patterns of the chestnuts (night eyes) that are found on the insides of the legs. Muscular dimples, cowlicks (hair swirls), scars, or brands should also be described and located on the sketch.

Color is an obvious characteristic of a horse although many horses have the same color. Color terms may also have different meanings for different people. Colors are discussed and illustrated in Chapter 15. There are five basic colors together with variations that result from graying, roaning, spotting, and dilution.

Basic Colors

All colors described are in addition to white markings on the head and legs.

1. *Black.* The entire coat is black, including the muzzle, flanks, and legs. Some black horses will fade or have a smoky appearance.

2. *Brown.* Many brown horses are dark enough to appear black except that close examination will reveal brown or tan hairs about the muzzle or flanks. The mane, tail, and legs are always black. A dark brown horse is sometimes called a seal brown, and sometimes a lighter brown horse is called a dark bay.

3. *Bay.* The body color may range from a light golden red to a dark mahogany color. The body color is similar to that of chestnuts except that the lower legs, mane, and tail of a bay horse are always black.

4. *Chestnut.* The range of chestnut runs from light golden red, sometimes called sorrel, to a very dark chocolate shade called liver or black chestnut. The legs never have black hairs, and often a lighter shade appears on the lower legs. The shade of the mane or tail may be the same as the body, lighter or darker than the body, but never black.

5. *White*. A true white horse is born white. Most white-appearing horses are grays that become progressively whiter with age. Some near-white horses are light ivory or cream, and these horses are difficult to distinguish from the whites.

Modification of Basic Colors

The major variations simply modify the basic color in some way.

1. *Gray*. The foal coat of a gray horse will be solid color. Each new coat adds more and more white hairs until the horse appears white. The gray pattern (intermixture of white hairs with colored hair) may occur with any background color or pattern. Gray on black, liver chestnut, or seal brown will be a blue or steel gray; gray on bay or chestnut will be a shade of rose gray. Dappling occurs within any color pattern but is more obvious on a gray background.

2. *Roan*. Roan and gray are often confused. The roan horse, however, is born with the same proportion of white hairs as will be present in each successive coat. As with gray, the roan pattern may be present on any background of colored hair. Often patches of roan will not be uniform over the body. The head, neck, and lower legs in particular may be more solid-colored than the remainder of the body. Red roan comes on a bay background, strawberry roan comes on chestnut, and blue roan comes on a dark (black, brown, or liver chestnut) background.

3. *Dilutions*. The dilution colors come from a lessening of the intensity of the basic color in each hair, not from mixing with white hairs. Chestnut dilutes to palomino of various shades—from bright copper to light yellow with lighter-to-white mane and tail. Double dilution causes the chestnut to go to a cream. Bay dilutes to buckskin or dun of shades similar to the palomino, but the mane, tail, and points are black whereas a Palomino has no black hair. Duns often have a black dorsal stripe (a coyote dun) and sometimes have black stripes on legs and withers (a zebra dun). A double-dilute bay is called a perlino and is ivory white with slightly darker, rusty-appearing points.

A red or claybank dun has a dorsal stripe that is a darker red (not black) on a chestnut background. It is not clear whether red dun is a dilution. A dilute black is known as grulla (*grew*-yah), which is also described as a mouse color. The coat has no white hairs and appears to have a blue or yellowish tone. The points are always black, and most duns have the dark back stripe; many also have zebra stripes.

4. *Pinto-Paint-Calico*. The body is spotted—either color on white or white on color. The spots are larger than 2 inches. This spotting is in addition to the usual white markings on the head and lower legs. White spotting of any size should be indicated. True white areas are present at birth, grow out of pink skin, and do not change with age.

Head and Points

Head markings may consist of some combination of a star, strip, snip, or blaze, as shown in Figure 2-72.

1. *Star*—a white mark on the forehead.

2. *Strip*—a narrow patch of white down the face from the forehead to the muzzle.

3. *Snip*—a narrow patch of white down over the muzzle.

4. *Blaze*—a wider patch of white down the face covering the full width of the nasal bones.

5. *Bald face*—a white marking covering the front of the face and extending over the sides of the face.

FIGURE 2-72
White head markings: *a*, star; *b*, stripe; *c*, snip; *d*, star and stripe; *e*, star, stripe, and snip; *f*, blaze; *g*, bald face.

a   b   c   d

e   f   g

6. *Wall-eye* (watch eye, glass eye)—a light blue or hazel iris resulting from a lack of brown pigment. (Horses' eyes are usually brown with no white around the edge.) In some areas the term "wall-eye" indicates a defective eye, and in other regions a horse that has white spotting covering the eye is called a wall-eye. A requirement for Appaloosas is the white ring of sclera around the iris, which is rare in most breeds.

Leg Markings

Hooves are usually white at birth but attain their adult color as growth occurs. The nomenclature of white on the feet and legs refers to the area covered by white as shown in Figure 2-73.

1. *Coronet*—a white strip covering the coronet band.
2. *Pastern*—white from the coronet to the pastern.
3. *Ankle*—white from the coronet to the fetlock.
4. *Sock* or *half-stocking*—white from the coronet to the middle of the cannon.
5. *Stocking*—white from the coronet to the knee.
6. *White marks* or *spots*—white about the front of the coronet or the heel.
7. *Distal spots*—dark spots on a white coronet band.

Variations and extensions of these should be indicated.

FIGURE 2-73
Description of white on the feet and legs: *a*, coronet; *b*, pastern; *c*, ankle; *d*, sock or half-stocking; *e*, stocking; *f*, white spots on coronet; *g*, white spots on heel; *h*, distal spots (dark on white coronet band).

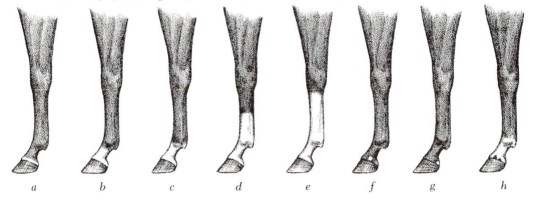

a	*b*	*c*	*d*	*e*	*f*	*g*	*h*

Mane and Tail

The mane and tail of many horses is the same color as the body, although sometimes a lighter or darker shade occurs. Bays and seal browns have black manes and tails. Flax or flaxen refers to a straw yellow or off-white color caused by a mixture of dark and white hairs in the mane and tail. A silver mane or tail is mostly white with a few dark hairs. True white manes and tails include only white hairs. A heavy, coarse, full tail is referred to as a broom or bang tail. The tail of a rat-tailed horse is sparsely furnished with hair, and is commonly found in Appaloosas.

The careful reporting of these characteristics as part of positive identification is important in establishing sound breeding programs and in maintaining integrity in the buying and selling of horses.

Breed Associations and Registries

(Asterisk indicates related associations)

American Albino Association, Inc. Ruth White, Secretary. P.O. Box 79, Crabtree, Oregon 97335.

American Andalusian Horse Association. Glenn O. Smith, Registrar. P.O. Box 1290, Silver City, New Mexico 88061.

American Association of Owners and Breeders of Peruvian Paso Horses. P.O. Box 371L, Calabasas, California 91302.

American Bashkir Curly Registry. Sunny Martin, Secretary. Box 453, Ely, Nevada 89301.

American Buckskin Registry Association, Inc. Marilyn Johnston, Executive Secretary. P.O. Box 1125, Anderson, California 96007.

American Connemara Pony Society. Mrs. John E. O'Brien, Secretary. Hoshiekon Farm, R.D. #1, Goshen, Connecticut 06756.

The American Council of Spotted Asses. Box 21, Fishtail, Montana 59028.

American Cream Draft Horse Association. Hubbard, Iowa 50122.

The American Donkey and Mule Society. Carl A. Wilson III, President. 2410 Executive Drive, Indianapolis, Indiana 46241.

American Fox Trotting Horse Breed Association, Inc. Wanda Chapman, Secretary. 100½ South Crittenden, Marshfield, Missouri 65706.

American Gotland Horse Association. Bob Lee, President. R.R. #2, Box 181, Elkland, Missouri 65644.

American Hackney Horse Society. Paul E. Bolton, Jr., Executive Secretary. P.O. Box 630, Peekskill, New York 10566.

American Horse Council, Inc. 1776 K Street Northwest, Washington, D.C. 20006.*

The American Horse Shows Association. 527 Madison Avenue, New York, New York 10022.*

American Indian Horse Registry, Inc. Rocking LJK Ranch, Box 127, Apache Junction, Arizona 85220.

American Miniature Horse Registry. P.O. Box 468, Fowler, Indiana 47944.

American Morgan Horse Association, Inc. Box 1, Oneida County Airport, Westmoreland, New York 14390.

American Mustang Association, Inc. P.O. Box 338, Yucaipa, California 92399.

The American Paint Horse Association. Sam Ed Spence, Executive Secretary. P.O. Box 13486, Fort Worth, Texas 76116.

American Part-Blooded (APB) Horse Registry. Mrs. Barbara J. Bell, Secretary. 4120 South East River Drive, Portland, Oregon 97222.

American Paso Fino Horse Association, Inc. Mellon Bank Building, Room 3018, 525 William Penn Place, Pittsburgh, Pennsylvania 15219.

American Performance Horse Association, Inc. P.O. Box 203, Huron, South Dakota 57350.*

American Quarter Horse Association. Don Jones, Secretary. 2736 West Tenth, P.O. Box 200, Amarillo, Texas 79168.

American Quarter Pony Association. Harold Wymore, Secretary. New Sharon, Iowa 50207.

American Remount Association. 20560 Perris Boulevard, Perris, California 92370. [Half-Thoroughbred Registry.]

American Saddle Horse Breeders' Association, Inc. Charles J. Cronan, Jr., Secretary. 929 South Fourth Street, Louisville, Kentucky 40203.

American Saddlebred Pleasure Horse Association. Irene Zane, Executive Secretary. 801 South Court Street, Scott City, Kansas 67871.*

American Shetland Pony Club. P.O. Box 468, Fowler, Indiana 47944.

American Shire Horse Association. Edwin R. Henken, Secretary. 6960 Northwest Drive, Ferndale, Washington 98248.

American Suffolk Horse Association. Jerry Coughlon, Secretary. 672 Polk Boulevard, Des Moines, Iowa 50312.

American Thoroughbred Breeders and Owners Association. 36 Ozone Park, Jamaica, New York 11417.*

The American Walking Pony Association. Mrs. Joan H. Brown, Executive Secretary. Route 5, Box 88, Upper River Road, Macon, Georgia 31201.

The Americana Pony, Inc. Vern Brewer. 926 Summit Avenue, Gainesville, Texas 76240.

106

Appaloosa Horse Club, Inc. George B. Hatley, Executive Secretary. P.O. Box 8403, Moscos, Idaho 83843.

The Arabian Horse Registry of America, Ind. One Executive Park, 7801 Belleview Avenue, Englewood, Colorado 80110.

Arabian Horse Racing Association of America. 66 South Riverside Drive, Batavia, Ohio 45103.*

Belgian Draft Horse Corporation of America. Blanche A. Schmalzried, Secretary-Treasurer. P.O. Box 335, Wabash, Indiana 46992.

Capitol Quarter Horse Association. 25302 Edison Road, Box 594, South Bend, Indiana 46624.

The Chickasaw Horse Association, Inc. Mrs. J. A. Barker, Jr., Secretary. Love Valley, Statesville, North Carolina 28677.

Cleveland Bay Society of America. A. MacKay-Smith, Secretary. White Post, Virginia 22663.

Clydesdale Breeders Association of the United States. Maurice Telleen, Secretary. Route 3, Waverly, Iowa 50677.

Colorado Ranger Horse Association, Inc. John E. Morris, President. 7023 Eden Mill Road, Woodbine, Maryland 21797.

Cross-Bred Pony Registry. Beatrice Langfeld, Secretary. 1108 Jackson Road, Omaha, Nebraska 68102.

The Galiceño Horse Breeders Association. Mary E. Bradley, Secretary. 111 East Elm Street, Tyler, Texas 75701.

Hungarian Horse Association. Bitterroot Stock Farm, Hamilton, Montana 59840.

The Hunter Club of America. Box 274, Washington, Michigan 48094.

Icelandic Pony Club and Registry, Inc. Mrs. Judith Hassed, Secretary. 56 Alles Acres, Greeley, Colorado 80631.

The International Arabian Horse Association. Ralph E. Goodall, Jr., Executive Secretary. 224 East Olive Avenue, Burbank, California 91503. [Half-Arab and Anglo-Arab Registries.]

International Buckskin Horse Association, Inc. Richard E. Kurzeja, Executive Secretary. P.O. Box 357, St. John, Indiana 64373.

International Society for the Protection of Mustangs and Burros. Helen A. Reilly. Badger, California 93603.*

The Jockey Club. 300 Park Avenue, New York, New York 10022. [Thoroughbred horses.]

Miniature Donkey Registry of the United States, Inc. Beatrice Langfeld, Secretary. 1108 Jackson Street, Omaha, Nebraska 68102.

Missouri Fox Trotting Horse Breed Association, Inc. L. Barnes, Secretary. P.O. Box 637, Ava, Missouri 65608.

Model Quarter Horse Association. Mrs. Lavonne Foster. P.O. Box 127, Monument, Oregon 97864.

Morab Horse Registry of America. P.O. Box 143, Clovis, California 93612. [Morgan-Arabian crosses.]

Morgan Horse Club, Inc. Seth P. Holcombe, Secretary. P.O. Box 2157, Bishop's Corner Branch, West Hartford, Connecticut 06117.

Morocco Spotted Horse Cooperative Association of America, Inc. Lowell H. Rott, Secretary-Treasurer. Route 1, Ridott, Illinois 61067.

National Appaloosa Pony, Inc. Ray Smiley, Executive Secretary. 112 East Eighth Street, Box 297, Rochester, Indiana 46975.

National Association of Paso Fino Horses of Puerto Rico. Aptdo. 253, Guaynabo, Puerto Rico 00657.

National Chickasaw Horse Association, Inc. Mrs. Duane Sunderman, Secretary. R.R. #2, Clarinda, Iowa 51632.

National Cutting Horse Association. P.O. Box 12155, Fort Worth, Texas 76116.*

National Mustang Association, Inc. Newcastle, Utah 84756.*

National Palomino Breeders Association, Inc. Mrs. Nora Lee Howard, Secretary. P.O. Box 146, London, Kentucky 40741.

National Quarter Horse Registry, Inc. Cecilia Connell, Secretary. Box 235, Raywood, Texas 77582.

National Reining Horse Association. William E. Garvey. R.R. #2, Greenville, Ohio 45331.*

National Trotting & Pacing Association. Ronald R. Moul, Executive Secretary. 575 Broadway, Hanover, Pennsylvania 17331.*

National Trotting Pony Association, Inc. Ronald R. Moul, Executive Secretary. 575 Broadway, Hanover, Pennsylvania 17331.*

Original Half Quarter Horse Registry. I. M. Hunt, Secretary. Hubbard, Oregon 97032.

The Palomino Horse Association, Inc. P.O. Box 324, Jefferson City, Missouri 65101.

Palomino Horse Breeders of America. Mrs. Melba Lee Spivey, Secretary. P.O. Box 249, Mineral Wells, Texas 76067.

Paso Fino Owners and Breeders Association, Inc. P.O. Box 2725, Valdosta, Georgia 31601.

Percheron Horse Association of America, Inc. Dale Gossett, Secretary. Rural Route 1, Belmont, Ohio 43718.

The Peruvian Paso Horse Registry of North America. P.O. Box 816, Guerneville, California 95446.

The Pinto Horse Association of America, Inc. P.O. Box 3984, San Diego, California 92103.

Pony of the Americas Club, Inc. George A. Lalonde, Executive Secretary. 1452 North Federal Street, P.O. Box 1447, Mason City, Iowa 50401.

Racking Horse Breeders Association of America. Helena, Alabama 35080.

Shetland Pony Identification Bureau, Inc. 1108 Jackson Street, Omaha, Nebraska 68102.

Spanish-Barb Breeders Association. Peggie Cash, Secretary. Box 7479, Colorado Springs, Colorado 80907.

The Spanish Mustang Registry, Inc. Mrs. Leana Rideout, Secretary-Treasurer. Route 2, Box 74, Marshall, Texas 75670.

The Standard Jack and Jennet Registry of America. Mrs. F. Gerald Johns, Secretary. Route 7, Todds Road, Lexington, Kentucky 40502.

Standard Quarter Horse Association. 4390 Fenton Street, Denver, Colorado 80212.

Tennessee Walking Horse Breeders' Association of America. Emmet Guy, Executive Secretary. P.O. Box 286, Lewisburg, Tennessee 37091.

Thoroughbred Racing Associations of the United States, Inc. Five Dakota Drive, Lake Success, Hyde Park, New York 12538.*

United States Pony Clubs, Inc. Mrs. John Reidy, Secretary. Pleasant Street, Dover, Massachusetts 02030.*

The United States Trotting Association. Edward F. Hackett, Secretary. 750 Michigan Avenue, Columbus, Ohio 43215. [Standardbred horses.]

United States Trotting Pony Association. P.O. Box 468, Fowler, Indiana 47944.*

The Welsh Pony Society of America, Inc. Gail Headley, Secretary. P.O. Drawer A, White Post, Virginia 22663.

Ysabella Saddle Horse Association, Inc. L. D. McKenzie, Secretary. McKenzie Rancho, R.R. #2, Williamsport, Indiana 47993.

Horse Magazines

A.B.R.A. Newsletter. American Buckskin Registry Association, Inc. P.O. Box 1125, Anderson, California 96007.

American Connemara Pony Society News. American Connemara Pony Society. Hoshiekon Farm, R.E. #1, Goshen, Connecticut 06756.

The American Fox Trotting Horse. American Fox Trotting Horse Breed Association, Inc. Route 2, Box 200, Marshfield, Missouri 65706.

American Horseman. Countrywide Communications, Inc. 257 Park Avenue South, New York, New York 10010.

American Shetland Pony Journal. American Shetland Pony Club. 218 East Fifth Street, P.O. Box 468, Fowler, Indiana 47944.

Appaloosa News. Appaloosa Horse Club, Inc. P.O. Box 8403, Moscow, Idaho 83843.

The Arabian Horse. 1777 Wynkoop Street, Suite 1, Denver, Colorado 80202.

109

The Arabian Horse News. P.O. Box 2264, Fort Collins, Colorado 80522.

Arabian Horse World. 2650 East Bayshore, Palo Alto, California 94303.

The Arizona Horseman. 2517 North Central Avenue, Phoenix, Arizona 85004.

Arizona Thoroughbred. 3223 Pueblo Way, Scottsdale, Arizona 85251.

The Backstretch. 19363 James Couzens Highway, Detroit, Michigan 48235.

The Belgian Review. Belgian Draft Horse Corporation of America. P.O. Box 335, Wabash, Indiana 46992.

The Blood-Horse. P.O. Box 4038, Lexington, Kentucky 40504.

The British Columbia Thoroughbred. 4023 East Hastings Street, North Burnaby, British Columbia, Canada.

The Chronicle of the Horse. Middleburg, Virginia 22117.

Equestrian Trails. 10723 Riverside Drive, North Hollywood, California 91602.

Florida Horse. P.O. Box 699, Ocala, Florida 32670.

The Hackney Horse. Peekskill Towers, Peekskill, New York 10566.

The Harness Horse. Telegraph Press Building, P.O. Box 1831, Harrisburg, Pennsylvania 17105.

Hoofbeats. United States Trotting Association. 750 Michigan Avenue, Columbus, Ohio 43215.

Hoofs and Horns. 1750 Humboldt Street, Suite 21, Denver, Colorado 80218.

Horse and Horseman. 34249 Camino Capistrano, Capistrano Beach, California 92624.

Horse and Rider. Gallant Publishing Co. 116 East Badillo, Covina, California 91722.

Horse and Show. Box 386, Northfield, Ohio 44067.

The Horse Lover's Magazine. P.O. Box 914, El Cerrito, California 94530.

Horse Show. The American Horse Shows Association. 527 Madison Avenue, New York, New York 10022.

Horse Show World. P.O. Box 39848, Los Angeles, California 90039.

Horse World. P.O. Box 588, Lexington, Kentucky 40501.

Horseman. 5314 Bingle Road, Houston, Texas 77018.

Horseman & Fair World. 904 North Broadway, P.O. Box 11688, Lexington, Kentucky 40511.

The Horseman's Journal. 138 South Fitzhugh Street, Rochester, New York 14608.

The Horseman's Gazette. R.R. #1, Badger, Minnesota 56714.

Horseman's Journal. Suite 1038, 425 13th Street N.W., Washington, D.C. 20004.

Horseman's Review. P.O. Box 116, Roscoe, Illinois 61073.

Horsemen's Yankee Pedlar. Wilbraham, Massachusetts 01095.

I.B.H.A. News Report. International Buckskin Horse Association, Inc. P.O. Box 357, St. John, Indiana 46373.

The Lariat. Route 6, 14239 Northeast Salmon Creek Avenue, Vancouver, Washington 98665.

The Maryland Horse. P.O. Box 4, Timonium, Maryland 21093.

The Morgan Horse. The American Morgan Horse Association, Inc. Box 29, West Lake Moraine Road, Hamilton, New York 13346.

Mr. Longears. The Noteworthy Company. Amsterdam, New York 12010.

The National Horseman. 933 Baxter Avenue, Louisville, Kentucky 40204.

Northeast Horseman. P.O. Box 47, Summer Street, Hampden Highlands, Maine 04445.

Oregon Thoroughbred Review. 1001 North Schmeer Road, Portland, Oregon 97217.

The Owners and Breeders Registry. Drawer XX, Livingston, Alabama 35470.

The Paint Horse Journal. The American Paint Horse Association. P.O. Box 13846, Fort Worth, Texas 76116.

Palomino Horses. Palomino Horse Breeders Association, Inc. P.O. Box 249, Mineral Wells, Texas 76067.

The Peruvian Horse Review. P.O. Box 816, Guerneville, California 95446.

The Peruvian Horse World. Doug Hart, Editor. 11101 Orange Park Boulevard, Orange, California 92669.

The Pinto Horse. P.O. Box 3984, San Diego, California 92103.

Pony of the Americas. Pony of the Americas Club, Inc. 1452 North Federal Street, P.O. Box 1447, Mason City, Iowa 50401.

Practical Horseman. Pennsylvania Horse, Inc. 19 Wilmont News, West Chester, Pennsylvania 19380.

Quarter Horse Digest. Gann Valley, South Dakota 57341.

The Quarter Horse Journal. P.O. Box 9105, Amarillo, Texas 79105.

Quarter Horse Racing World. P.O. Box 1597, Roswell, New Mexico 88201.

¿Que Pasó? American Association of Owners and Breeders of Peruvian Paso Horses. P.O. Box 371, Calabasas, California 92302.

The Rangerbred News. Colorado Ranger Horse Association, Inc. 7023 Eden Mill Road, Woodbine, Maryland 50677.

Rodeo News. 703 North Cedar, P.O. Box 587, Pauls Valley, Oklahoma 73075.

Saddle and Bridle. 2333 Brentwood Boulevard, St. Louis, Missouri 63144.

Side-Saddle News. R.D. #2, Box 2096, Mt. Holly, New Jersey 08060.

The Southern Horseman. P.O. Box 5735, Meridian, Mississippi 39301.

The Spanish-Barb Quarterly. Box 7479, Colorado Springs, Colorado 80907.

111

The Spanish Mustang News. 2005 Ridgeway, Colorado Springs, Colorado 80906.

Tack 'N Togs. The Miller Publishing Co. P.O. Box 67, Minneapolis, Minnesota 55440.

The Thoroughbred of California. 201 Colorado Place, Arcadia, California 91006.

Thoroughbred Record. P.O. Box 580, Lexington, Kentucky 40501.

The Trail Rider. Trail Rider Publications. Chatsworth, Georgia 30705.

The Trottingbred. 525 Broadway, Hanover, Pennsylvania 17331.

Turf and Sport Digest. 511–513 Oakland Avenue, Baltimore, Maryland 21212.

Voice of the Tennessee Walking Horse. Voice Publishing Co. 3710 Calhoun Avenue, P.O. Box 6009, Chattanooga, Tennessee 37401.

The Washington Horse. 13470 Empire Way South, Seattle, Washington 98178.

Welsh News. The Welsh Pony Society of America, Inc. P.O. Drawer A, White Post, Virginia 22663.

The Western Horseman. P.O. Box 7980, Colorado Springs, Colorado 80933.

The Whip. The American Driving Society. Robert G. Heath, Secretary. 1230 Nepperhan Avenue, Yonkers, New York 10703.

Your Pony. Box 125, Barboo, Wisconsin 53913.

References

American Horse Shows Association Rule Book. New York: The American Horse Shows Association, Inc. [Annual.]

American Racing Manual. Chicago: Triangle Publications. [Annual.]

American Stud Book. New York: Jockey Club. [Every 4 years.]

Bailey, L. H., editor. 1908. *Cyclopedia of American Agriculture.* New York: Macmillan. [Contains articles on many pre-1905 breeds.]

Briggs, H. M. 1969. *Modern Breeds of Livestock.* 3rd ed. New York: Macmillan.

Castle, W. E., and J. L. King. 1947. The Albino in Palomino Breeding. *Western Horseman* 12:24 (December).

Davenport, Homer. 1909. [Republished 1947.] My Quest of the Arabian Horse. *Arabian Horse Registry of America.*

Denhardt, R. M. 1948. *The Horse of the Americas.* Norman: University of Oklahoma Press.

Deutschbein, Liz. 1971. Albino horses: A horse of history. *American Horseman* 39 (September).

Dinsmore, Wayne, and John Hervey. 1944. *Our Equine Friends.* Horse and Mule Association of America, Inc. Chicago: Drivers Journal Press.

Edwards, Gladys Brown. 1971. *Know the Arabian Horse.* Omaha, Nebraska: Farnam Horse Library.

Estes, J. A., and Joe H. Palmer. 1942. *An Introduction to the Thoroughbred Horse.* First revision, 1949, by Alex Bower; second revision, 1972, by Charles H. Stone. Lexington, Kentucky: *The Blood-Horse.*

Fletcher, J. Lane. 1945. A genetic analysis of the American Quarter Horse. *J. Heredity* 36:346.

Fletcher, J. Lane. 1946. A study of the first fifty years of Tennessee Walking Horse breeding. *J. Heredity* 37:369.

Gazder, P. J. 1954. The genetic history of the Arabian horse in the United States. *J. Heredity* 45:95.

Gilbey, Sir Walter. 1900. *Ponies, Past and Present.* London: Vinton.

Glyn, Richard. 1971. *The World's Finest Horses and Ponies.* Garden City, New York: Doubleday.

Goodall, D. M. 1965. *Horses of the World.* London: Country Lite Ltd.

Gremmels, Fred. 1939. Coat color in horses. *J. Heredity* 30:437.

Griffen, Jeff. 1966. *The Pony Book.* Garden City, New York: Doubleday.

Haines, Francis. 1963. *Appaloosa, The Spotted Horse in Art and History.* Fort Worth, Texas: Amon Carter Museum of Western Art.

Haines, Francis, Robert L. Peckinpah, and George B. Hatley. 1957. *The Appaloosa Horse.* Lewiston, Idaho: R. G. Bailey Printing Co.

Harrison, James C. 1968. *Care and Training of the Trotter and Pacer.* Columbus, Ohio: U.S. Trotting Association.

Hayes, M. H. 1904. *Points of the Horse.* London: Hurst and Blackett, Ltd.

Hervey, John. 1947. *The American Trotter.* New York: Coward-McCann.

Houser, Helen B., and Leslie L. Boomhower. The heritage of POA. *Pony of the Americas:* 32.

Jones, W. E. 1965. *The phenotypic effects of the D gene in the American Quarter Horse.* Master's thesis. Colorado State College, Greeley.

Knight, L. W. 1902. *The Breeding and Rearing of Jacks, Jennets, and Mules.* Nashville, Tennessee: Cumberland Press.

Mellin, J. 1961. *The Morgan Horse.* Brattleboro, Vermont: Stephen Greene Press.

Miller, Robert W. *Appaloosa Coat Color Inheritance.* Bozeman: Montana State University.

113

Nye, Nelson. 1964. *The Complete Book of the Quarter Horse.* New York: A. S. Barnes.

Osborne, W. D. 1967. *The Quarter Horse.* New York: Grosset & Dunlap.

Patten, John W. 1960. *The Light Horse Breeds.* New York: A. S. Barnes.

Reese, H. H. 1956. *Horses of Today, Their History, Breeds, and Qualifications.* Pasadena, California: Wood and Jones.

Rhoad, A. O. 1961. The American Quarter Horse. *Quarter Horse Journal* (March).

Rhoad, A. O., and R. J. Kleberg, Jr. 1946. The development of a superior family in the modern Quarter Horse. *J. Heredity* 37:227.

Robertson, W. H. P. 1965. *The History of Thoroughbred Racing in America.* Englewood Cliffs, New Jersey: Prentice-Hall.

Salisbury, G. W., and J. W. Britton. 1941. The inheritance of equine coat color. II. The dilutes with special reference to the Palomino. *J. Heredity* 32:255.

Sanders, A. H., and Wayne Dinsmore. 1917. A history of the Percheron horse. Chicago: *The Breeders' Gazette.*

Savory, Theodore H. 1970. The Mule. *Scientific American* 223:102 (December).

Savitt, Sam. 1966. *American Horses.* Garden City, New York: Doubleday.

Sires and Dams Book. Columbus, Ohio: U.S. Trotting Association. [Annual.]

Speelman, S. R. 1941. Breeds of light horses. *U.S.D.A. Farmers' Bulletin* 952.

Steele, D. G. 1944. A genetic analysis of the recent Thoroughbreds, Standardbreds, and American Saddle Horses. *Kentucky Agricultural Experiment Station Bulletin* 462.

Stetcher, R. M. 1962. Anatomical variations of the spine of the horse. *J. Mamm.* 43:205.

Taylor, Louis. 1961. *The Horse America Made: The Story of the American Saddle Horse.* New York: Harper & Row.

Telleen, Maurice. 1972. The draft breeds. *Western Horseman* 37:80 (October).

Trotting and Pacing Guide. Columbus, Ohio: U.S. Trotting Association. [Annual.]

The Welsh Pony. West Chester, Pennsylvania: The Welsh Pony Society of America, Inc.

Wentworth, Lady. 1945. *The Authentic Arabian Horse and His Descendants.* London: George, Allan, and Unwin, Ltd.

Widmer, Jack. 1959. *The American Quarter Horse.* New York: Scribner's.

Zaher, A. 1948. *The genetic history of the Arabian horse in America.* Unpublished Ph.D. thesis. Michigan State University, East Lansing.

CHAPTER THREE *Horse Racing*

3.1 Historical Introduction

Although our knowledge of horse racing in antiquity is scanty, we do know that horse racing antedates the Christian era by many centuries. As early as the fifteenth century B.C., horses and riders participated in the competitions of the Olympiads. From earliest times, when man first domesticated the horse, he recognized that the speed and the endurance of individual horses vary, and consequently he pitted one horse against another, often with the fortune or the life of the riders dependent upon the outcome.

England

It was not until the era of modern England—particularly during the reigns of the Tudor and Stuart kings—that the nobility developed horse racing into the sport we know today. Henry VIII (1509–1547) was so inordinately fond of horses and horse racing that he promulgated legislation prohibiting the grazing of stallions on the public lands of England ("the age of the gelding") in order to ensure the improvement of the horse population through the controlled use of well-bred stallions. To further encourage this upgrading, he urged that the noble families maintain, and make available at stud, high-quality, saddle-type stallions for mating with the mares of England. Under the Stuart kings, James I (1603–1625) and particularly Charles II (1660–1685), the sport continued to thrive. During the years of the Commonwealth (1649–1660), however, there was a hiatus during which both kings and horse racing were banished from the islands. Although Cromwell, the Lord Protector, had a great love for horses, his supporters, the Puritans, were so rigid in their opposition to worldly pleasures that the racetracks were closed. They did not reopen until the restoration of the Stuarts to the throne (1660) under Charles II.

The racing stock of this time, which was descended from the primitive strains of horses in early England with heavy infusions of blood from the horses brought by the Romans and later by the Norman French, possessed great stamina but lacked the combination of speed and endurance that makes for great racehorses. To remedy this major defect, English breeders, during the early part of the eighteenth century, brought in horses of Oriental breeding—Barbs, Turks, and Arabians—to cross with the native stock. Although many of these Oriental stallions were used, only three left their mark, and it is to them that all modern Thoroughbreds (the most famous of the racing breeds) trace their lineage in the male line. They were the Byerly Turk (the Herod line), the Godolphin Barb (the Matchem line), and the most influential of all, the Darley Arabian (the Eclipse line; see Figures 3-1 and 3-2).

During this period, the Jockey Club of Newmarket (founded c. 1750) established the rules under which English racing has been governed ever since. Initially the races were run over any convenient open space, and it was not until the mid-seventeenth century that the Jockey Club laid out a circular track at Newmarket and appointed racing stewards (then called tryers) to supervise and conduct the meets. To this day the English have not adopted the regular oval track so common throughout the United States; rather, their horses may run through an undulating and wooded area that can at times take the contestants out of the sight of the viewer. Although racing at this time was a bit primitive, these early enthusiasts did recognize differences in the ability of horses and used weight handicaps to minimize some of the advantage of the superior horse.

FIGURE 3-1
The Darley Arabian, foaled about 1700. Photograph courtesy of Historical Pictures Service, Chicago.

FIGURE 3-2

Eclipse, by Marske out of Spiletta (1764), continuing the line of the Darley
Arabian. Photograph courtesy of Historical Pictures Service, Chicago.

America

Because the eastern seaboard of North America was colonized by people of
English descent, many English customs with regard to horse racing have
prevailed—including wagering on the outcome.

Shortly after Peter Stuyvesant surrendered the Dutch colony of New
Amsterdam to the British (August 1664) and it became New York, Richard
Nicolls, now the colony's governor, laid out America's first racetrack (New
Market) at Hempstead Plains—an open area on Long Island not far from
the present-day courses of Aqueduct and Belmont. This track continued
to be used for some 100 years. A silver cup inscribed "Wunn at Hempstead
Plains, March 25, 1668" is America's oldest horse-racing trophy.

Horse racing soon spread to the other colonies and achieved an instant
popularity in the more populated settlements of the South—Baltimore,
Richmond, Williamsburg, and Charleston, South Carolina, where a Jockey
Club was formed in 1734, some years before the founding of the English
club.

Strong rivalries soon developed not only between horsemen of the
colonies and England but among enthusiasts of various colonies—particularly the North and the South. This early enthusiasm of Americans for
horse racing has continued unabated throughout three centuries, despite
depressions and wars, thus making horse racing America's oldest major
sport.

Changes Since the Civil War

There have been some notable changes in racing since the Civil War. Among them are the following.

1. The 3- and 4-mile heats (in which the best performer in 2 out of 3 heats was declared the winner) have been largely replaced by a single dash or heat.

2. Match races between 2 horses where the winner "takes all" are rare. There have been only 74 since 1900; they simply do not lend themselves to pari-mutuel wagering.

3. The universal birth date (the day all horses born in a certain year are given as their official birthday) has been changed from May 1 to January 1, thus accentuating the problems of breeding mares in mid-winter.

4. Illegal gambling and bookmaking are still gigantic illegal operations in many states, but legislative bodies have acquired increased control of racing during the past 40 years in order to ensure honest conduct of racing, which, in turn, encourages pari-mutuel wagering and results in increased tax revenue.

5. Horses today are raced at younger ages; the greatest opportunity for racing is given to the 2- and 3-year-olds.

6. Average purses, although still inadequate to compensate for the high costs of training and racing, have skyrocketed (Figure 3-3). The top money horse in 1933 won $88,050, whereas in the early 1970s the sums brought by winning horses exceeded $500,000.

7. Stud fees for the top stallions in the 1940s were $1,000; they are now 10–20 times that figure.

8. The major change has been that racing is no longer merely a sport and a hobby but is now a major national industry. Pari-mutuel wagering gained a foothold in the early 1930s and provided a total tax revenue of $6 million in 1934, $178 million in 1954, and $502 million in 1972.

Horses and Horsemen

Racing history is an account of the accomplishments of horses and horsemen who have left their mark on the industry. Numerous men have contributed greatly to the development of racing in America by breeding great horses and by providing leadership and exerting political influence with regard to the laws affecting racing. Their contributions are many, but unfortunately few are inscrolled on racing's roll of honor. More avail-

FIGURE 3-3
Fresh Yankee, shown with trainer-driver Joe O'Brien, ranks as the greatest bargain in harness horse history. Purchased as a yearling for only $900 in 1964, by the 1972 season she had won $1,294,252, to rank as top money-winning Standard-bred in North America. Photograph courtesy of the United States Trotting Association, Columbus, Ohio.

able to the public is information concerning the leading owners, trainers, jockeys, and sires and dams of the horses that won the most money and/or the most races.

Famous Horses. Few horses have captured the public's interest and promoted horse racing more than Thoroughbreds Man O'War (Figure 17-8), Kelso, and Secretariat (Figure 2-8), and Standardbred Dan Patch (Figure 2-18). They were all truly the "peoples' horse." Man O'War, winner of 21 of 22 starts in the 1920s, has been and still is considered by many to be the greatest horse that ever lived. The gelding Kelso, horse of the year for 5 years and winner of almost $2 million during the 1950s, set a record that will not soon be beaten. Secretariat, Triple Crown winner and everyone's "Horse of the Year" in 1973, perhaps made more friends for racing than any horse since Man O'War. He had the charisma that is needed by the racing industry.

Dan Patch, pacer nonpareil, raced at all the major tracks in the Midwest at the turn of the century. Livestock producers thronged to the Midwest fairs and agricultural events in hopes of witnessing him set another pacing record. He set a record of 1:55¼ and paced a mile 31 times in less than 2:00 minutes. Both accomplishments have been surpassed by few horses.

America's racing fraternity measures the stature of a racehorse by the amount of money or number of races won, or by the accomplishments of the horse's progeny. Some of the "Big Horses" that have left their mark as sires are listed in Table 3-1. Table 3-2 lists some horses that have won in excess of $1.0 million. Time antiquates any ranking; however, it may be a long time before another Kelso or Secretariat appears on the track. The Daily Racing Form's Twentieth-Century Hall of Fame (Table 3-3) lists the most impressive thoroughbreds since 1900.

Famous Owners and Trainers.   To single out one or two outstanding horse breeders or trainers obviously slights others who are equally deserving, but the intention in doing so is to pay tribute to all. The staff of Calumet Farm, under the direction of Warren Wright, was truly outstanding, not only for the horses that they brought to the tracks but for the horses that they bred, not all of which they raced. Harry P. Whitney and C. V. Whitney were both leading owners for 5 years during the 1920s and 1930s. Two men stand out as owners and trainers. Samuel C. Hildreth led the list of owners (based on money won) during the years 1909–1911, and as a trainer he was the leading money winner for 9 years. H. Guy Bedwell, another owner and trainer, led the list of owners (based on races) for 6 years (1912–1917 and 1924) and was the leading trainer for 7 years (1909 and 1912–1917).

Racing has truly had some outstanding jockeys, and the top 6, as listed in Table 3-4, are literally household names. Willy Shoemaker leads the list as to the percentage of winners, the number of starters that won, and the amount of money won by the horses he has ridden. Johnny Longden had a remarkable racing career that spanned 4 decades.

Some unusual records have been set by jockeys. For example, the English jockey Sir Gordon Richards rode 12 consecutive winners, and Albert Adams of the United States had 9 winners on 9 starters in a row. Only 7 jockeys have had perfect days—that is, all mounts were winners. Willy Shoemaker, along with 31 other jockeys, has had three 6-out-of-7 winners in one day.

3.2   Modern Racing in the United States

A mammoth industry such as racing requires many organizations to administer and regulate its conduct, look after the welfare of its participants, and preserve its rich tradition. These organizations are listed briefly in this section. For those students unfamiliar with racing, Table 3-5 is an abbreviated listing of some of the leading racetracks; Table 3-6 is a list of famous stake races.

TABLE 3-1
Leading racehorse sires

Thoroughbreds	Quarter Horses	Standardbreds	
		Trotters	Pacers
Bold Ruler	Jet Deck	Speedy Scot	Race Time
T. V. Lark	Go Man Go	Stars Pride	Meadow Skipper
Herbager	Rocket Bar	Ayres	Bret Hanover
Intentionally	Three Bars	Hickory Pride	Shadow Wave
Chieftain	(registered Thoroughbred)	B F Coaltown	Baron Hanover
Quadrangle	Top Deck	Hickory Smoke	Tar Heel
Round Table	(registered Thoroughbred)	Speedster	Adios Vic
Olden Times	Top Moon	Speedy Count	Bye Bye Byrd
Graustark	Double Bid	Noble Victory	Overtrick
Tom Rolfe	Tiny Charger		Best of All
	Moon Deck		
	Little Request		
	(registered Thoroughbred)		

Bodies Governing Racing in the United States

Following is a brief list of the organizations that govern and influence the racing industry in the United States.

  1. The state racing commissions and their commissioners administer the basic governing policies and rules enacted into law by the state legislative bodies.

TABLE 3-2
Leading Thoroughbred money earners

Horse and Year Foaled	Starts	1st	2nd	3rd	Earnings
Kelso, 1957	63	39	12	2	$1,977,896
Round Table, 1954	66	43	8	5	1,749,869
Buckpasser, 1963	31	25	4	1	1,462,014
Secretariat, 1970	21	16	3	1	1,316,808
Nashua, 1952	30	22	4	1	1,288,565
Carry Back, 1958	62	21	11	11	1,241,165
Damascus, 1964	32	21	7	3	1,176,781
Cougar II, 1966	48	20	7	15	1,119,741
Fort Marcy, 1964	75	21	18	14	1,109,791
Citation, 1945	45	32	10	2	1,085,760
Native Diver, 1959	81	37	7	12	1,026,500
Riva Ridge, 1969	27	16	2	1	1,022,027
Dr. Fager, 1964	22	18	2	1	1,002,642

TABLE 3-3
Horses nominated to the Daily Racing Forms
Twentieth-Century Hall of Fame

Horse	Year	Horse	Year
Citation	1945	Man O'War	1917
Colin	1905	Nashua	1952
Count Fleet	1940	Native Dancer	1950
Equipoise	1928	Swaps	1952
Exterminator	1915	Sysonby	1902
Kelso	1957	Tom Fool	1949

SOURCE: *The American Racing Manual.* 1972.

NOTE: These nominations were made before Secretariat raced.

2. The National Association of State Racing Commissioners encourages uniformity of racing rules throughout the United States.

3. The Jockey Club is the registry association for Thoroughbred horses and, through its stewards, is responsible for the day-to-day operations of the racing meet.

4. The Thoroughbred Racing Association.

5. The Thoroughbred Owners and Breeders Association.

6. The Horseman's Benevolent and Protective Association.

7. The American Trainers Association.

8. The Jockey Guild, Inc.

9. The Jockeys Association, Inc.

10. The Thoroughbred Racing Protective Bureau is responsible for policing the races.

TABLE 3-4
The six leading American jockeys: lifetime record

Name	Years Riding	No. of Mounts	No. of Times First	Percentage of Wins	Amount Won
W. Shoemaker	23	25,542	6,267	24.5	$46,731,086
J. Longden	40	32,406	6,026	18.5	24,665,800
E. Arcaro	31	24,092	4,779	19.8	30,039,543
S. Brooks	32	30,264	4,447	14.7	18,214,947
W. Hartack	19	20,179	4,093	20.3	25,216,892
T. Atkinson	22	23,661	3,795	16.0	17,449,360

SOURCE: *The American Racing Manual.* 1972.

TABLE 3-5
Leading racetracks in the United States, based on daily average purse distribution

	Year								
	1972			1969			1966		
Track	Rank	Racing Days	Daily Average Purses	Rank	Racing Days	Daily Average Purses	Rank	Racing Days	Daily Average Purses
Hollywood Park	1	75	$102,593	3	75	$84,627	1	55	$79,596
Saratoga	2	24	102,479	1	24	89,786	4	24	68,970
Belmont Park	3	72	101,842	2	72	88,088	3	50	70,952
Santa Anita	4	75	99,593	5	71	72,373	2	56	77,048
Oak Tree	5	20	88,600	8	20	65,075	–	–	
Aqueduct	6	136	85,514	4	136	79,360	6	160	62,401
Gulfstream Park	7	40	83,170	13	43	51,674	17	46	45,387
Monmouth Park	8	60	65,740	9	59	62,315	16	56	46,250
Del Mar	9	43	64,675	20	42	42,890	24	42	35,260
Hialeah Park	10	49	64,592	7	40	66,275	7	40	62,113
Average, all tracks in U.S.			$ 30,593			$27,890			$23,846

SOURCE: *The Blood-Horse*, April 23, 1973.

TABLE 3-6
Famous stake races

Year	Name of Race	Track	1971 Purse (thousands of dollars)	Conditions
1860	Queen's Plate	Woodbine, Ontario	50	1¼ mile, 3-yr-olds, Canadian foaled
1864	Travers	Saratoga, N.Y.	110	1¼ mile, 3-yr-olds
1867	Belmont Stakes	Belmont Park, N.Y.	163	1½ mile, 3-yr-olds
	Champagne Stakes	Belmont Park, N.Y.	195	1 mile, 2-yr-olds
1868	Ladies Handicap	Aqueduct, N.Y.	58	1¼ mile, fillies and mares, 3 yrs old and over
1871	Monmouth Oaks	Monmouth Park, N.J.	58	1⅛ mile, 3-yr-old fillies
1873	California Derby	Golden Gate Field, Calif.	125	1⅛ mile, 3-yr-olds
	Preakness	Pimlico, Md.	190	1³/₁₆ mile, 3-yr-olds
1875	Kentucky Derby	Churchill Downs, Ky.	188	1¼ mile, 3-yr-olds
	Kentucky Oaks	Churchill Downs, Ky.	65	1¹/₁₆ mile, 3-yr-old fillies
1881	Spinaway Stakes	Saratoga, N.Y.	88	¾ mile, 2-yr-old fillies
1884	Am. Derby	Arlington Park, Ill.	138	1⅛ mile, turf, 3-yr-olds
	Suburban Handicap	Aqueduct, N.Y.	115	1¼ mile, 3-yr-olds
1889	Breeders Stake	Woodbine, Ontario	46	1½ mile, turf, 3-yr-olds, Canadian foaled
1899	Grand National Steeplechase Handicap	Saratoga, N.Y.	40	2½ mile, 4-yr-olds

11. The National Steeplechase and Hunt Association encourages the conduct of and administers steeplechase meets.

12. The American Horse Council is composed of all groups interested in horses. Its purpose is to consolidate efforts relative to federal and state legislative bills that affect the horse industry.

Centers of Racing

Racing and pari-mutuel betting are conducted in 30 states. Approximately half the total attendance occurs in New York, California, Illinois, and Pennsylvania. West Virginia has a sizable racing industry because it is in close proximity to densely populated areas in which betting on horses is not permitted. New Hampshire has a tremendous tourist business, and thus more racing is conducted there than the population of the state would suggest. New York, New Jersey, Maryland, Delaware, Massachusetts, and California support the majority of the tracks. Table 3-5 lists the 10 leading tracks in America based on the daily average purse distribution.

FIGURE 3-4
Flat racing: *The Jockey*, by
Henri Toulouse-Lautrec, 1899.

Types of Racing and Races

The following are the most common types of racing in the United States:

1. Flat racing—conventional racing around an oval track by Thoroughbreds. Quarter Horses, Arabians, and Appaloosas are popular in the West and Southwest for straightaway racing.

2. Steeplechase—a race over obstacles (hurdles, water jumps) conducted on either dirt or grass turf.

3. Hunt clubs—organizations in the Carolinas, Virginia, and other Southern states that conduct combination meetings—both steeplechase and flat races.

4. Harness racing—trotters and pacers pull sulkies.

Classification of Races in Order of Importance. Races can be classified in the following order of importance: stake races; handicap races; overnight races (which would include allowances, weight for age, and special weights); graded allowance and graded handicap races; maiden and maiden allowance races; combination races; claiming races; and match

125

races. There have been only 74 matched races since 1900, but on occasion they take precedence over other race meets.

Literally hundreds of stake races have been named after famous horses, people, or places. Table 3-6 is a very abbreviated listing of some of the older and more prestigious stake races.

3.3 The Modern Race Industry

Racing is in fact an industry, but one that is little understood and often maligned. The members of the general public have not been informed about the virtues and vices of pari-mutuel wagering. They are anxious as to whether pari-mutuel wagering increases crime or welfare problems and whether racing is honestly conducted. Most people have little conception of the magnitude of the racing industry, including the horse-breeding establishments, or of the employment within that industry.

The purpose of this section is to (1) analyze the impact of racing on the economy of states where pari-mutuel wagering is allowed; (2) determine the reasons for the success or failure of the various segments of the industry (owners, breeders, track owners, and state government); and (3) characterize the typical stable or breeding farm with regard to size, expenditures, share of winnings, and prices received for sale of yearlings. It is hoped that the reader will realize that the race horse industry is a business—a risky business—and that only to the "swift" (bought, bred, or trained) horses go the riches (Figure 3-5). It is a business spurred on by the anticipation, dreams, and hopes that can be summed up by the expression "waiting for the big horse"—a horse like Secretariat or Bret Hanover (Figure 17-6), a horse whose offspring sell in the $50,000–$75,000 bracket rather than the $5,000–$7,000 bracket.

FIGURE 3-5
Albatross, shown with trainer-driver Stanley Dancer, won 59 of 71 starts from 1970 through 1972 and became the top money-earning pacer in history with $1,201,470. At the close of his career, he held the pacing record in actual race competition on mile, five-eighths, and half-mile tracks. Photograph courtesy of *Horseman and Fair World*, Lexington, Kentucky.

Racing

The racing industry has four major costs and sources of income: (1) pari-mutuel take, which goes to the state, the track, and the local government; (2) the purses, which go to the racehorse owner; (3) the training fees and expenses of the grooms and jockey; and (4) income earned by the brood farms from the sale of yearlings and stallion breeding awards.

For the businessman, racing requires the investment in horses and payment of the recurring annual expenses in order to keep his horses racing or producing racing prospects. For racetrack managers, owners, and breeders, the financial concerns include an understanding of racetrack attendance, pari-mutuel handle, purses, and taxes.

In 1972, the total number of race days for Thoroughbreds in the United States, Canada, and parts of Mexico was 6,624; there were 52,561 starters and 59,416 race programs. Novick (1973) estimates that an additional 112,000 Thoroughbred horses (mares, stallions, yearlings, foals, and horses unsuited or ill prepared for racing) were maintained. Novick also estimates that the owners and breeders spent $625 million to support the approximately 52,000 starters and invested another $550 million in Thoroughbred horses that were not racing. If 7 percent interest is charged against this $550 million and another 7 percent is spent for amortization, these owners spent $77 million for capital charges, or a total of approximately $700 million to collect the $210 million available in purses in 1972. Some of this "loss" may be recouped in the form of tax deductions.

Thoroughbred racing constitutes the bulk of racing in the United States. However, harness racing is particularly popular in some of the Eastern states and Quarter Horse racing is much in vogue in the West and Southwest. For example, harness racing attracts as many or more fans than Thoroughbred racing in Delaware, Illinois, New Hampshire, New York, Ohio, and Pennsylvania (Figure 3-6). In 1972, 70,807,226 people attended all races in the United States. Of this total, 42,812,452 people attended Thoroughbred races, 25,118,519 attended harness races, and 2,876,255 attended Quarter Horse races and fair racing.

In an attempt to bolster track income and state taxes on pari-mutuel wagering, the number of racing days has been increased (from 3,900 in 1958 to 6,600 in 1972), but total attendance at Thoroughbred races has not increased since 1970. The amount wagered on Thoroughbreds in 1972 ($4.5 billion) was up from $4.3 billion in 1970, but the states' revenue, $322 million in 1972, was down for the first time in 20 years. By some measurements, the racing industry is in the doldrums and is seeking ways to encourage attendance.

In contrast to this trend, Quarter Horse racing is booming, particularly in the West and Southwest (Figure 3-7). The big race, the All-American Futurity, run at Ruidoso Downs, New Mexico, attracts the top horses, and the big crowds. During the past few years wagering has steadily increased.

FIGURE 3-6
Nevele Pride, with Stanley Dancer driving, as usual at the front of the pack, is history's fastest trotter on a one-mile track (1:54-4/5), a five-eighths-mile oval (1:58), and a half-mile track (1:56-4/5). He retired with 57 victories in 67 starts and 16 world records. Photograph courtesy of the United States Trotting Association, Columbus, Ohio.

FIGURE 3 7
Quarter Horse races are characterized by close finishes and the necessity of a good start. Photograph by McNabb, Hopkins Photography, courtesy of the American Quarter Horse Association, Amarillo, Texas.

FIGURE 3-8
Easy Jet by Jet Deck, bred and owned by Joe McDermott and Walter Merrick, was the 1969 winner of the All-American Futurity and 1969 world champion quarter running horse. With earnings of $445,721 on 27 firsts, 7 seconds, and 2 thirds in 38 starts, he was the leading money-earning horse up to 1974. Photograph courtesy of the American Quarter Horse Association, Amarillo, Texas.

In 1973, total purses for Quarter Horses exceeded $16 million, pari-mutuel handle (total amount bet legally at the tracks) exceeded $164 million, and more than 9,000 Quarter Horse races were run (Figure 3-8).

The National Association of State Racing Commissioners' statistical report for all types of racing in the United States during 1972 makes available the following data: total racing days, 11,478; total attendance, 70,807,226; total pari-mutuel turnover, $6,401,582,132; total revenue to the 30 states, $502,706,070; and total purses distributed $281,551,208. Revenue to the states from taxes on monies wagered has increased from approximately $6 million in 1934 (when few states permitted pari-mutuel wagering) to $55.9 million in 1944, $178.0 million in 1954, $350 million in 1964, and more than $502 million in 1972.

Owners

Has racing been profitable for the horse owner? One would think so, if one considers that the purses for Thoroughbred racing alone exceeded $210 million in 1972. Actually, such an assumption is far from the truth. Approximately 5 percent more purse money was available in 1972 than in 1971, but 5 percent more horses raced and competed for that money. Furthermore, averages can be misleading. Of the horses that started, 848 won stake races and earned almost $30 million in added money (money added by track to money collected from bettors, to attract top horses and increase track attendance). This number of horses represented 1.6 percent of the total that went to the gate, yet they won 14 percent of the money. Approximately 18 percent of the horses that raced in 1972 earned $6,000 or more per year, approximately 68 percent earned less than $6,000, and approximately 14 percent earned nothing (Table 3-7). Thus, in general, more than 80 percent of the horses that go the gate earn less than the costs of campaigning a horse.

An additional racing cost is the cost of purchasing and maintaining horses that have short and disappointing racing careers. To determine a

129

TABLE 3-7
Distribution of purses among Thoroughbred starters, 1970–1972

Distribution of Starters	1970		1971		1972	
	No.	Percent	No.	Percent	No.	Percent
Total starters	47,769	100	50,189	100	52,561	100
Earned nothing	6,782	14.2	7,195	14.3	7,511	14.3
Earned less than $6,000	32,913	68.9	34,038	67.8	35,570	67.7
Earned $6,000 or more	8,057	16.9	8,949	17.9	9,480	18.0

SOURCE: Data from *Thoroughbred Record*, March 31, 1973.

depreciation schedule for the Internal Revenue Service in 1971, the Thoroughbred Owners and Breeders Association conducted a study that revealed some interesting information (Hollingsworth, 1972). Of the 19,124 foals born between 1939 and 1941, only 49.4 percent earned purse money as racehorses. The average racehorse earned $10,310 in 4 years of racing. A realistic annual depreciation of a yearling racing prospect was approximately 20 percent. Of the 9,614 fillies born, 4,140 (43.1 percent) earned an average of $6,559 during 3.4 years of racing. Of the 9,510 colts born, 1,391 (14.6 percent) earned an average of $15,312 during 3.6 years of racing. The 3,923 geldings (41.2 percent of all males born) earned an average of $12,496 during 5.0 years of racing.

The tax study of these 1939–1941 foals revealed that productive life as a breeding animal is also short. Of all the fillies dropped in this period (9,614), 55.1 percent produced at least one foal. But of the total, only 46.4 percent produced more than one foal, and these fillies averaged 5.5 foals over 7.9 years. Of the productive stallions (499), 5.2 percent of the 9,510 colts had a lifetime average of 40 foals during an 8-year period. Even the most successful stallions produced only 104.6 foals during an average of 12 years. Thus, the maximum useful breeding period of a Thoroughbred is approximately 10 years.

Of the horses that race, approximately 45 percent of the Thoroughbreds and approximately 23 percent of the Standardbreds start racing as 2-year-olds. Racing at the age of 2 is not necessarily advantageous for a horse over the long run, but if a person has a $20,000 investment in a colt, the sooner that colt starts paying his way the better the business proposition. Approximately 63 percent of the Thoroughbreds are on the track as 3-year-olds, compared with only 50 percent of the Standardbreds. From 3 years of age on, the percentage of Thoroughbreds that race declines appreciably; only about 33 percent are still racing as 5-year-olds.

Horse Breeders

Kentucky and California produce the most foals and the greatest number of stake winners (Table 3-8). Income to breeders is primarily from the sale of yearlings. The year 1972 was a "vintage year," and 1973 brought even higher auction prices for yearlings. The 4,108 yearlings (16 percent of the record yearling crop of 1972) that were sold at auction realized a record $37,880,275 ($9,221 per head). Again, however, averages can be very misleading. In 1972, three of every four yearlings sold at public auction brought less than $9,221. Since 1968, approximately 20 percent of the auctioned yearlings brought more than $25,000 but the balance sold for less than $4,000, which was less than the cost of rearing and selling them.

There are many things besides the general condition of the national economy that influence the auction price of a yearling. The current racing success of the sire's older progeny, the sire's record, the popularity of the pedigree, and the conformation and excellence of the yearling himself are all important. Not all yearlings rate highly on all of these counts, but the $225,000 price for the top yearlings at Saratoga in 1973 and the average price of $42,718 in that same sale are examples of the incentive that keeps people investing and trying to breed or buy the "Big Horse."

Another factor affecting prices for yearlings sold at auction is the specific sale at which the yearlings are sold. Keeneland and Saratoga are prestigious sales. Unquestionably, the caliber of yearlings offered at these two sales has much to do with prices, but the pageantry of the auctions and the wealth of the buyers attracted to them also contribute to the average prices.

TABLE 3-8
Distribution of foals and stake winners by state, 1961–1970

Registered Foals		Stake Winners	
State	Percentage of Total	State	Percentage of Total
Kentucky	18.6	Kentucky	32.8
California	15.4	California	14.3
Canada	7.1	Canada	9.6
Florida	6.1	Florida	9.2
Maryland	5.1	Washington state	3.6
Virginia	4.8	Maryland	3.4
Texas	3.9	Virginia	3.2
Illinois	3.6	Illinois	2.4
Washington state	3.0	Nebraska	2.3
Oklahoma	3.0	Ohio	1.9

SOURCE: *The Blood-Horse*, March 5, 1973.

3.4   Two Economic Case Stories of Horse Racing

Maryland and Arizona have conducted economic studies of the impact of racing in their states that reveal some interesting data. The data were gathered from interviews, questionnaires, and track and government attendance and wagering figures.

Maryland's Racing Industry

The economic impact of horse racing is 10 times more important to Maryland than the state's share of pari-mutuel wagering suggests. In 1970, the pari-mutuel taxes paid to the state exceeded $14 million. However, those taxes were only 8.6 percent of the $163 million cash flow generated by Maryland's Thoroughbred industry.

In the period 1968–1970, racing's annual in-state expenditures in Maryland were estimated to be $163,000,300. This included a payroll of $29.7 million for an estimated 5,600 employees and an annual investment of more than $9 million, which was added to the total investment of just under $200 million.

However, there are economic problems confronting racing in Maryland. While population, income, and operating cost have been rising, average daily attendance and wagering have been either constant or declining. Even though racing is still very much of a sport, one of the goals of the industry must continue to be a reasonable economic return to its participants, because few horsemen can tolerate continuous losses.

According to the Maryland study, every group in racing receives some return on its investment, except the owner of the horses that are racing

TABLE 3-9
Source of racing's annual cash flow: Maryland, 1968–1970

Group	Millions of Dollars Spent	Percentage
Tracks	15.4	9.4
Horseman (owners, breeders)	59.3	36.4
Professionals	2.0	1.3
Industry-related businesses	17.5	10.7
Other businesses	11.7	7.2
Racing patrons (spectators)	47.8	29.3
Racing commission	.1	.1
New investment	9.2	5.6
	163.0	100.0

SOURCE: Lawrence, Robert G. 1972. *Maryland's Racing Industry.*

and the horse breeders. An analysis of Maryland's race industry as a whole indicates that the total purse and receipts from sales of yearlings or other horses is less than the total expenditures of the owners and breeders. For example, $11 million was paid out in purses at Thoroughbred races and almost $1.5 million was paid at harness tracks, for a total of $12.5 million. However, the expenses of Maryland owners and of out-of-state owners racing in Maryland exceeded $15 million. Although owners and breeders, in the aggregate, lost money, this does not mean that all owners and breeders lose or that they lose every year. Some do show a profit, but the distribution of the income is skewed, with the majority making very little.

As an indication of the scope and magnitude of these expenditures, the basic money transactions in 1968–1970 are presented in Table 3-9.

Arizona's Thoroughbred Industry

The Department of Agricultural Economics of the University of Arizona has compiled data on the Thoroughbred industry in that state in 1970. The capital investment required to breed horses and the financial budget of the racing industry should be particularly interesting to those contemplating investing in that industry.

The value of Arizona breeding stock varies widely. Approximately two-thirds of the stallions were valued at $5,000 or less; more than 50 percent of the mares and yearlings were valued at less than $2,000, and 68 percent of the foals were valued at $1,500 or less. Approximately 45 percent of the racing stock was valued at $3,000 or less and approximately 12 percent was valued at more than $10,000.

Interestingly, capital investment in land, buildings, and equipment was about the same whether the operation comprised more than 20 head or less than 10 head. The average investment was approximately $4,500 per head (Table 3-10). The farm budget, on a per-horse basis (Table 3-11),

TABLE 3-10
Capital investment in Arizona horse establishments, 1970

Size of Stable	Value per Horse Maintained (dollars)			Total
	Land	Equipment	Buildings	
Large (20 head and more)	2,720	762	1,403	4,885
Medium (10–19 head)	2,690	769	998	4,457
Small (less than 10 head)	2,850	1,180	704	4,734

SOURCE: Data from Angus and Hanckamp. 1970. *Arizona Thoroughbred Industry.*

133

TABLE 3-11

Thoroughbred broodmare and stallion budgets per head in Arizona, 1970

Budget Item	Mare	Stallion
Farm maintenance		
Labor	$ 240	$ 240
Repairs, operating expenses, insurance	199	199
Depreciation	180	180
Taxes	63	63
Subtotal	$ 682	$ 682
Horse upkeep		
Feed	313	313
Veterinary	106	106
Blacksmith	48	48
Miscellaneous	25	25
Subtotal	$ 492	$ 492
Depreciation	233	
$5,124 stallion(A)		472
$35,000 stallion(B)		2,917
Stud fee	338	
Total	$1,745	$1,601(A)
		$4,091(B)

SOURCE: Angus and Hanckamp. 1970. *Arizona Thoroughbred Industry.*

indicates that the cost per horse to maintain the farm exceeded that of maintaining the horse itself. Admittedly, not all the expenses were out-of-pocket expenses (depreciation), but the yearly cost of $1,745 to keep a brood mare is sizable. Obviously, if this budget was used for a truly top mare bred to a popular stallion, both the depreciation and stud fee would increase that figure considerably.

The training fee, which includes feed, care, and stabling, was the largest expenditure for the horse at the track (Table 3-12). One item omitted from this budget is vanning costs, which can be expensive if a horse is moved from track to track with any frequency. The total of $433 for one start per month is a sizable expenditure that the owner usually hopes will be covered by his share of the purse.

Although the racing industry of Arizona is small in comparison with that of Maryland, approximately $10.6 million is invested each year in land, horses, buildings, and equipment. In order to conduct the race meets, approximately $2 million is injected into Arizona's economy annually.

No economic study in which average values are present will exactly fit a specific brood farm or racing stable. Furthermore, changes in the national economy (such as inflation) may distort the validity of the figures used. However, both the Maryland and Arizona studies provide some long-needed bench marks that the Thoroughbred industry, racing commissions, state governments, and others can afford to consider.

3.5 Racing and the Spectator

The opportunity to wager on the outcome of the race encourages millions of people to attend race meets. Therefore, a discussion of pari-mutuel betting and off-track betting is in order.

Pari-mutuel Betting and Establishing the Odds

Pari-mutuel wagering is based on odds established by the total amount of money bet on a horse rather than odds set by a bookmaker. A totalizator

TABLE 3-12
Average expenditures per horse to race at Turf Paradise
in Phoenix, 1970

Expenditure	Cost per Month
General upkeep costs	
Training fee	$300.00
Veterinary fees	38.00
Blacksmith fees	14.00
Miscellaneous	11.00
Total per month	$363.00
Costs to start per race	
Jockey fees (including commission)	$ 28.00
Commission paid to trainer	42.00
	$ 70.00
Total costs per month for one start	$433.00

SOURCE: Angus and Hanckamp. 1970. *Arizona Thoroughbred Industry.*

(electronic machine) registers and totals each ticket as it is issued; keeps a running total of all money bet on each horse in the win, place, and show pools; and calculates the betting odds on each horse.

A $2.00 wager "bet to win" is calculated as follows. Assume that $10,000 was bet on all the horses in the win pool and $8,000 was bet on the favorite and eventual winner. To determine the mutuel payoff price for a $2.00 win ticket, the calculators first deduct the combined state and track percentage from the gross amount bet in the win pool. In this example, 15 percent or $1,500 would be deducted, leaving $8,500 in the win pool.

The next step is to deduct from the total win pool ($8,500) the amount wagered on the horse that won ($8,000), leaving a balance of $500. This $500 is divided among the holders of the winning tickets, plus the original $8,000 bet. The odds are then calculated by dividing the $500 by the $8,000 bet to give odds of $500/$8,000 = 6.25¢. Since the payoff is calculated to the next lowest nickel (sometimes dime), the 1.25¢ (2.5¢ on each $2.00 bet) is the breakage per dollar bet, kept by the state and track. Since all wagering is based on a $2.00 bet, the dollar odds are multiplied by 2 (5¢ × 2 = 10¢), so the winning $2.00 ticket returns $2.10.

The place bet (the horse will finish at least second) and show bet (the horse will finish at least third) work similarly except that 2 or 3 horses are involved. The gross place pool bet on all the horses to place first or second, less the state and track percentage take, is divided by 2 because half the money in the net place pool goes to the holder of the place ticket on the winner and half goes to the ticket holders on the second horse. The same procedure is followed to compute the show mutuel except that 3 horses share in the show pool.

Off-Track Betting

Off-track betting allows the bettor an opportunity to wager on a horse race without attending the race. The purpose is to increase the state's revenue.

The Delafield Commission Report (published in *Hoofbeats*, May 1973) concluded that off-track betting has been financially damaging to horse racing. The report states that the horse-racing industry in New York State directly employs 20,000 people and indirectly employs many more (the payroll of those directly employed exceeds $90 million a year); that the industry is the largest corporate taxpayer in the state, producing some $200 million a year in various forms of revenue for the government; and that it draws more spectators than all other professional sports combined. The commission concluded that the net effect of off-track betting has been a redistribution of earnings (resulting in more revenue for New York City and less revenue for New York State). Track business has suffered; tracks are not adequately compensated for the reduced attendance and the consequent adverse effect of off-track betting on track revenue. Surprisingly, the cost of operating off-track betting in New York State was 10 percent of each dollar bet. The comparable figure for on-track betting was 1.66 percent. Off-track betting produced 8¢ revenue to the state for each dollar bet, whereas on-track betting produced 16.3¢ for every dollar bet. The state and track split the 16.3¢ take from each dollar bet.

Proposed federal legislation would make it a federal offense to take bets on out-of-state races. If this legislation is passed, states where racetracks do not exist could not offer off-track betting on races in another state. The concern of the National Association of State Racing Commissioners, Owners, and Breeders is that if bets can be taken in one state on races run in another state, the industry will need to breed fewer horses because all the betting can be done on races run at one or two major tracks.

Illegal Wagering

How much illegal wagering is conducted is a moot question. Some argue that if there is no pari-mutuel betting, there will be little or no gambling. Others cite *Scarne's Complete Guide to Gambling*. Scarne concluded that for every legal $1.00 bet at the track, $16.50 was wagered illegally. Scarne estimated that there are 40,000–60,000 bookmakers operating in the United States. Applying even a fraction of $16.50, it is evident that the states miss a tremendous amount of tax money.

The report of the Committee for Economic Development (1972) indicates that illicit gambling is the main source of funds for criminal syndicates and police corruption. The committee estimates the annual revenue from illicit gambling (races, athletic contests, and numbers) to be $20–$50 billion.

Originally, antigambling laws were adopted in conformity with the Puritan moral code. Times have changed, and probably the majority of people reject the traditional code. The committee's report states that half of the television football fans make token bets and that as much as 90 percent of the bookmaker's business stems from team sports.

The solutions suggested by the committee to control illegal gambling include: (1) stern government suppression; (2) simple legalization; (3) regulation through licensing as practiced in Nevada; and (4) gambling under governmental auspices, such as off-track betting as now allowed in New York State and lotteries as allowed in New Hampshire, New York, New Jersey, and Pennsylvania.

Seemingly, the committee is grasping for a system that can run illicit gambling out of business. The committee recognizes that if such a system is to be successful, convenience to bet, pay off, and tax on winnings must be as attractive for a legal wager as it now is for an illegal wager.

137

Integrity of Racing

The mention of pari-mutuel wagering on races always raises the question of the integrity of the race. Racing has evolved into a giant industry, and in some instances crime has been associated with it. However, it is unlikely that any other sport makes as great an effort to maintain the integrity of wagering and the security of contestants as does organized racing in America.

Each state has a racing commission with policing powers and also has the ability to grant or deny a license for the privilege of participating in racing. The day-to-day security related to the operation of a racing event is also strictly supervised. The racing commission has at its disposal, for those tracks that are members of the Thoroughbred Racing Association (and most tracks are), the services of the Thoroughbred Racing Protective Bureau (TRPB). This organization is extremely meticulous and monitors every phase of the operation of a racetrack, including examination and fingerprinting of track employees, examination of identification marks of the horses, inspection by veterinarians of each horse before each race and administering of chemical tests following the race, control of telephones during racing hours, and filming of each race from various positions on the track to ensure enforcement of rules.

Appendix

Racing Terms

ALLOWANCE RACE   A race where there are both allowances and penalties, with regard to the conditions of the race, monies won or races won, or the date the last race or races were won.

BACKSTRETCH   The stable area of a racetrack.

BLOW OUT   To work a horse fast over a short distance in order to put an "edge on him" for a race.

BREAKAGE   In pari-mutuel betting, the odd cents left over, after paying the successful bettors to the nearest 10¢.

138   BREEDER   Owner of the dam at time foal is dropped.

BREEZE   To exercise a horse at moderate speed.

CLAIMING PRICE   The predetermined price at which a horse in a claiming race must be sold, if it is claimed.

CLAIMING RACE   The conditions for this race provide that each entry may be bought at a predetermined price by an owner who meets certain track qualifications; for example, one who has started a horse at the meeting.

CHUTE   Straight part of the track behind the barrier.

CONDITION RACE   A race in which certain conditions are specified (usually number of wins up to a certain date, weights carried, distance, and so on). A calendar of races that includes the stipulations and provisions under which each race is to be run is published in the condition book.

COUPLED   Two or more horses are grouped in the betting, and bets upon them are decided by the position of the foremost horse.

DRIVER   Individual who guides harness horses from the seat of a sulky.

ENTRY   Two or more horses belonging to same owner or trainer that compete in the same race. A bet on one is a bet on the other.

EXERCISE BOY   A jockey or other rider who gallops horses in workouts.

A FIELD   When more horses are entered in a race than there are positions on the odds board. If there are 10 starters and only 8 positions on the board, then horses 8–10 may be grouped as a field. Thus, a wager on one in the field is a wager on all. They can be considered one entry as far as wagering is concerned.

FILM PATROL   Moving pictures are taken of the races by a number of cameras, set strategically at various points around the track. Films of the races are developed immediately after each race and are viewed by the stewards within a few minutes after the finish of a race for possible rule infractions during the race.

FLAT RACING   Racing on a flat surface, as opposed to racing over steeplechase jumps and hurdles.

FURLONG   One-eighth of a mile or 220 yards.

FUTURITY   Nominations for a specific race are made a long time before the race is run. Usually portions of the total nomination money are called for at specific times.

HANDICAP RACE   A race in which the competing horses are assigned weights to carry that will, ideally, equalize their chances of winning.

HANDLE   In pari-mutuel betting, the total amount of money bet on a race, on the day's racing, on the races at a meeting, or during the entire racing season.

HARNESS RACING   Racing with Standardbred horses that either trot or pace in harness pulling a driver riding a sulky.

139

HOT WALKER   A groom or exercise boy who walks a horse after a race or workout. (The process is called cooling out.) Also a mechanical device to which horses are fastened that rotates and assures exercise.

JOCKEY   A professional race rider.

JOCKEY AGENT   A person employed by a jockey to secure mounts for him.

JOCKEY'S VALET   A jockey's assistant, whose duty it is to take care of the rider's tack, assist him in dressing, carry the tack to and from the scales, and generally help the jockey through a day's racing.

JUDGE   A steward, placing judge, paddock judge, or patrol judge.

LAPPED   To be one full length behind another horse during the race.

MAIDEN   A horse that has never won a race.

MARK   A horse's best winning time. A horse may have been second in a photo finish with the winner clocked in 2:01; yet his best winning time may be 2:04.

MATCH RACE   A race between two horses owned by different parties on terms agreed upon with no money added.

MUTUEL POOL   The total amount bet on any race, on any day, or at any meeting.

NOMINATION   The naming of a horse for a stakes race on a specific date well in advance of the race. A set fee is paid on the nomination of a horse, and other fees are paid at stated intervals.

OUTRIDER   The mounted track employee whose duty it is to keep the horses in order during the parade from paddock to post before a race, to catch runaways, and to assist jockeys thrown from their mounts.

OVERNIGHT RACE   Race entries close 72 hours (exclusive of Sundays) or less before the first race of the day on which the specific race is to be run.

OWNER   A person or stable that has property rights in a horse or horses or that has leased the racing qualities of a horse or horses.

PACER   A Standardbred horse that races by moving with a lateral gait (both left legs in unison, then both right legs).

PADDOCK JUDGE   A racetrack official whose duty it is to get the jockeys or drivers and their horses on the racing strip on time.

PARI-MUTUEL   The system of racetrack betting that returns to successful bettors the precise amount of money wagered by unsuccessful bettors after deduction of commission and breakage.

PATROL JUDGE   A racing association official who watches a race from a certain part of a racetrack and reports what he has seen to the stewards. There are usually 3 or 4 patrol judges.

PENALTIES   Extra weight a horse must carry in a given race due to winnings collected after a certain date.

PLACING JUDGE   A racing association official who, with the other placing judges, decides the placement of the horses in their order of finish.

PONY BOY   The rider of a horse who accompanies and aids the jockey in controlling his mount in the post parade, or the rider of a horse who leads a riderless horse in a workout.

POOL   Total money bet on horses in a race.

RACE MEETING   The period of days during which races are run at any specified racetrack.

RACETRACK   The place where races are run; the racing strip.

RACING CHEMIST   An analytical chemist whose duty it is to analyze saliva, urine, and blood samples of horses that have just completed a race (usually the winners) to ensure that such samples are free from forbidden substances, such as narcotics and stimulants.

RACING COMMISSION   A state-appointed body charged with the duty of regulating and supervising the conduct of racing in its jurisdiction.

RACING SECRETARY   The racetrack official whose duty it is to write the races (that is, to make up the conditions for the races and assign weights in handicap races.)

ROUTE   A distance race, usually 1⅛ mile or longer.

SET DOWN   To be deprived of all racing privileges.

SHED ROW   The stables.

SHORT HORSE   A horse inept in distance races (sprinter).

SHUT OFF   The situation that exists when a horse is forced back by another horse pulling over in front of him.

STABLE   In addition to its conventional meaning, the term also means a number of horses owned by an individual or group of individuals.

STAKES RACE   A race in which the owners nominate their horse for participation and pay subscriptions, entrance, and starting fees, whether money or any added prize is added or not (unless it is a private sweepstakes).

STANDARDBRED   A pedigreed horse whose ancestry must have been standard and registered for generations. "Standard" originally meant that the horse had to race up to a certain set "standard" of speed.

STARTER   The racetrack official whose duty it is to get the horses away to a fair start in a race.

STEEPLECHASE   A race over actual or artificial obstacles, such as fences, hedges, and water jumps.

STEWARD OF THE RACE MEETING   Usually there are 3, and it is their duty to see that the race meeting is run according to the rules of racing. They are judges of all matters with respect to the conduct of a race meeting, but their decisions are subject to appeal to the state racing commission.

141

SULKY   Light, 2-wheel racing rig used in harness racing.

TACK   The equipment used, such as saddle, bridle, blinkers, bits, shadow roll, harness, boots, and harness bags. The term is also applied to stable gear, such as tubs, pails, bandages, and brushes.

TAKE OUT   The total amount deducted from the amount bet on a race, to be paid to the taxing authority and the racetrack.

THOROUGHBRED   A breed of running racehorses whose lineage is traceable to the 1700s and to one of three foundation sires.

TOTALIZATOR   A refinement of the pari-mutuel system of racetrack betting. Tickets are printed as purchased and are automatically recorded at a central place, so that the approximate odds may be quickly determined at any particular time, flashed on the odds board for public view, and correctly determined and flashed again when the race is over.

TOUT   One who sells racing tips.

TRAINER   An individual who supervises and cares for the racehorses in his charge. It is his duty to enter the horses in races that suit them. In most jurisdictions, a trainer is licensed by the racing commission or governing body of racing.

TROTTER   A Standardbred horse that races with a diagonal gait.

WALK OVER   An event in which only one horse starts.

WEIGHT FOR AGE   All horses carry weights according to scale (age, sex, distance) without penalties or allowances based on previous performances.

WELL-IN-HAND   A horse running at a fraction of his best speed.

WRAPS   A turn of the reins around the jockey's hands to restrain a horse.

References

The American Racing Manual. 1972. Lexington, Kentucky: Triangle Publications.

Angus, Robert C., and William J. Hanckamp. 1970. *Arizona Thoroughbred Industry.* Tucson: University of Arizona, Department of Agricultural Economics.

Committee for Economic Development. 1972. *Reducing Crime and Assuring Justice.* A statement by the Research and Policy Committee.

Hollingsworth, Kent. 1972. So what is the economic useful life of a Thoroughbred? *The Blood-Horse* (March 13).

Hoofbeats. 1973

Lawrence, Robert G. 1972. *Maryland's Racing Industry.* College Park: University of Maryland.

Novick, David. 1973. Economic outlook of the racing industry. *The Blood-Horse* (July 23).

President's Commission on Law Enforcement and Administration of Justice. 1967. *The Challenge of Crime in a Free Society.*

The Quarter Horse Journal. 1976. Vol. 26 (April).

The Quarter Racing World. 1974. Roswell, New Mexico.

Report of the Pari-mutuel Betting Study Commission to the Governor and General Assembly of Virginia. House Document No. 2. 1972.

Robertson, William H. P. 1964. *The History of Thoroughbred Racing in America.* New York: Bonanza Books.

Scarne, John. 1965. *Scarne's Complete Guide to Gambling.* New York: Simon and Schuster.

Statistical Report on Horse Racing in the United States for the Year 1972. Lexington, Kentucky: The National Association of State Racing Commissioners.

CHAPTER FOUR *Recreational Use of the Horse*

The early 1960s marked the beginning of a dramatic increase in the horse population. Americans were seeking relaxation from the pressures of their occupations. The horse, an animal that is able to give and receive affection, offered an emotional outlet for many. Approximately 75 percent of the horses in the United States are used primarily for pleasure. More than one-half of all horse owners live in rural areas or cities with populations of less than 50,000. Contrary to popular opinion, approximately 60 percent of all horse owners earn, or belong to families that earn, a less-than-average income.

The number of events sanctioned by the American Horse Shows Association increased about threefold during the 1960s. In addition to AHSA shows, each breed association sponsors shows. In 1971 the American Quarter Horse Association sponsored 1,480 adult shows and 1,361 youth shows, for which there was a total of 244,207 entries. Many horse clubs and organizations also sponsor unsanctioned shows so that their members can have a "play day." Competitive events, such as endurance rides, polo, and rodeo, have also contributed to the horse's popularity.

4.1   Horse Shows

The American Horse Shows Association was founded in New York City in 1917 under the name of the Association of American Horse Shows, Inc. In 1933, the name of the organization was changed to the American Horse Show Association, and was changed again shortly thereafter to its present form. The AHSA has grown steadily since its inception, but in recent years its growth has been phenomenal. In 1959 there were 425 sanctioned shows,

144

which distributed $1,453,322 in prize money. These shows put on 15,055 classes. The total membership numbered 5,253. Twelve years later in 1971, 1,000 shows distributed $3,421,000. Total membership in that year jumped to 14,000.

In addition to sanctioning shows, the AHSA keeps all records, licenses judges and stewards, handles disciplinary matters, awards annual prizes, and compiles the annual rule book, which is the "Bible" of the horse show world.

The AHSA is a member of the *Fédération Equestre Internationale,* the world governing body of equestrian sports. It is the certifying agency for equestrian athletes for the Olympic Games and any other international competition.

Horses are shown in many divisions under the auspices of the AHSA: Appaloosa, Arabian, Combined Training, Dressage, Equitation, Gymkhana, Hackney and Harness Pony, Hunter, Hunter and Jumper Pony, Jumper, Junior Hunter and Jumper, Morgan, Palomino, Parade, Pinto, Paint, Pony of the Americas, Quarter Horse, Roadster, Saddle Horse, Shetland Pony, Tennessee Walking Horse, Welsh Pony, and Western. Each breed has specific classes and there are open shows where the horse can be of any breed or nonregistered. Some of the most popular classes are the equitation, hunter, jumper, Western, gaited, roadster, and halter.

Halter Classes

Most halter classes are judged on type, conformation, quality, substance, and soundness. Each breed organization has specific guidelines that are used by the judge. There are classes for weanlings, yearlings, fillies, and mature stallions (Figure 4-1), mares, and geldings. Horses are also shown in breeding classes, such as produce of dam (2 animals from same dam), get of sire (3 animals by same sire, as in Figure 4-2), and sire and get (sire and 2 of get).

Equitation Division

The equitation division is divided into 3 classes: hunt, saddle, and stock seat. Only the rider is judged in equitation classes. Therefore, any horse that is suitable for a particular style of riding and is capable of performing the class routine is acceptable.

In hunt seat equitation, the rider uses a forward saddle with knee rolls (Figure 4-3). At horse shows, the class may or may not be over obstacles. In nonjumping classes, the entries are required to perform at the walk, trot, canter, and hand gallop, and to execute individual figures. Competitors in the saddle seat division ride a park saddle (Figure 4-4). They are

145

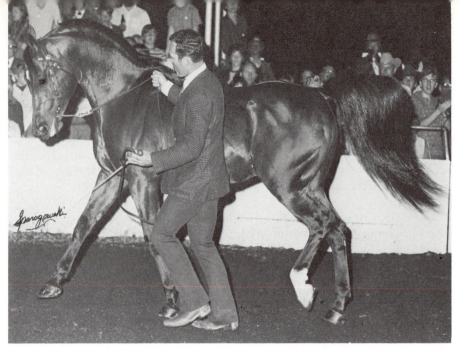

FIGURE 4-1
Halter class. The Arabian stallion Fadjur, being shown by Paul Polk at Houston, Texas. Photo by Sparagowski, courtesy of Jack Tone Ranch.

FIGURE 4-2
Get of sire class. The Arabian horses Sa-Fadjur, Fadzana, and Bint Ferneyna were sired by Fadjur owned by the Jack Tone Ranch in Stockton, California. Photo by Johnny Johnston, courtesy of Jack Tone Ranch.

146

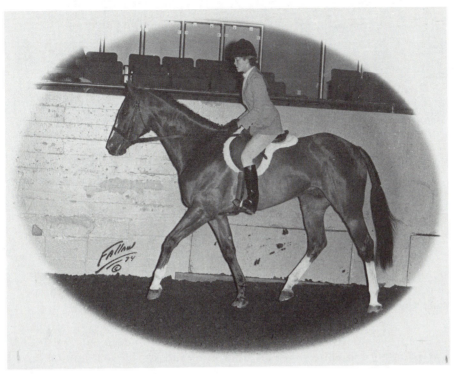

FIGURE 4-3
Hunt seat class. Jani Chambers showing Common Cause in a hunt seat class.
Photo by June Fallaw, courtesy of Connie Chambers.

FIGURE 4-4
Saddle seat equitation. Kathleen
Daly, 1974 National Saddle
Seat Equitation Association
Hi-Point Award winner for
riders age 17 and under, is
shown riding Abu Pzazz, 1974
Champion Saddle-Type Pleasure
Horse. Photo by June Fallaw,
courtesy of Kathleen Daly.

147

FIGURE 4-5
Stock seat equitation. Marie Graver riding College Vixen while winning a stock seat equitation class. Photo by June Fallaw, courtesy of M. Graver.

required to demonstrate the walk, trot, canter, and individual tests. Stock seat equitation is quite different from hunt and saddle seat equitation in that the rider uses a western stock saddle (Figure 4-5). In competitive events, the horse and rider are scored as a team.

Western Division

The Western division is composed of stock, trail, and pleasure horse classes. Horses may be of any breed or combination of breeds as long as they are at least 14.1 hands, serviceably sound, and of stock horse type. Riders must be dressed as for the stock seat equitation class and carry a lariat or reata. A rain slicker may be required in trail and pleasure classes.

Stock Horse. The stock horse is judged on its rein work, conformation, manners, and appointments. Some classes also require the horse to work cattle. A good AHSA stock horse will have the following characteristics. (1) The horse should have a good manner. (2) The horse should be shifty, smooth, and have its feet under it at all times. (The hind feet should be well under the animal when it stops.) (3) The horse should possess a soft mouth so that it stops easily and has a light rein. (4) The horse's head should be kept in its natural position. (5) The horse must remain under the rider's control but still work at a reasonable speed. Horses are faulted for the following: switching tail, exaggerated opening of mouth, hard mouth, nervousness, and anticipation of maneuvers—particularly stopping.

The AHSA has suggested that when stock horses are not worked on cattle, the working pattern in Figure 4-6 be followed.

Jacquima. The Jacquima class (Figure 4-7) is similar to the stock horse class except that the horses are up to 5 years of age and have never been shown in a bridle other than a snaffle bit. The rider uses both hands on the mecate while showing the horse. Jacquima horses work equally as fast as stock horses. They are not required to work cattle in most shows.

Trail. Trail horses (Figure 4-8) are shown at walk, trot, and lope both ways in the ring. They must work on a loose rein and without undue restraint. They are also required to work through and over obstacles that might be found on the trail. These tests include crossing bridges, mounting and dismounting, backing through or around obstacles, and riding through water or over other types of obstacles. Trail horses are always required to allow the rider to open a gate, pass through it, and close it while maintaining control. Performance and manners are scored 60 percent; appointments, equipment, and neatness are scored 20 percent; and conformation is scored 20 percent.

Pleasure. The Western pleasure horse class is popular. In this class, the horses are required to be shown at walk, trot, and lope. They must work both ways in the ring on a reasonably loose rein and be able to extend the gaits. The horses are also required to back in a straight line. Finalists in a

FIGURE 4-6
American Horse Show Association suggested working pattern for stock horse class.

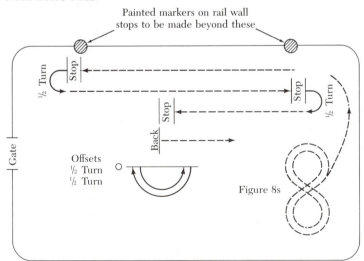

class may be required to do further ring work. They are judged on performance (60 percent), conformation (30 percent), and appointments (10 percent).

Jumper Division

The Jumper division of the AHSA is a popular division. Jumping horses may be of any breed, height, or sex. In this division, unsoundness does not penalize an entry unless it severely affects the horse's performance. Each horse is classified as preliminary, intermediate, or open depending upon the amount of money or points that horse has won. An amateur-owner jumper is any horse that is ridden by an amateur-owner or an amateur member of the owner's immediate family. The horses are required to go over a course that should allow the exhibitor a fair opportunity to demonstrate his horse's capabilities and training. Each course must be carefully designed to fit the capabilities of the horses to be exhibited. Ideally, the faults should be evenly distributed over the course after the first or second jump, which is a single jump. A reasonable percentage of the horses should be able to negotiate the courses without faults, and if no horse has a "clean round" (no faults), the course is too severe a test. Variation of

FIGURE 4-7
Jacquima class. Chex of Chex being shown by Les Vogt of Clovis, California. Photo by June Fallaw, courtesy of Les Vogt.

150

FIGURE 4-8
Trail horse class. Horse going through a gate obstacle in a trail horse class. Photo by June Fallaw, courtesy of George Cardinet.

obstacles on the course is important; however, they must be fair, "jump-able" tests for a horse's ability. The jumper is scored on a mathematical basis according to the number of penalty faults. Disobediences, falls, knockdowns, touches, and time penalties are considered *penalty faults. Refusals, run-outs, loss of gait, and circling are disobediences.* A *refusal* is when a horse stops in front of an obstacle to be jumped, whether or not the horse knocks it down or displaces it. When a horse evades or passes an obstacle to be jumped or jumps the obstacle outside its limiting markers, the horse is penalized for a *run-out*. A *loss of gait* fault occurs when there is loss of forward movement after the horse crosses the starting line. A penalty is also given the horse if it crosses its original track between two consecutive obstacles anywhere on the course. A horse is penalized if it falls on the course. *Knockdown faults* are given when any part of an obstacle that establishes the height of the obstacle is lowered, whereas touching any part of the obstacle is considered a *touch fault.* The horse with the best score wins the class.

Hunter Division

The hunter division of the AHSA is open to all horses of either sex (Figure 4-9). The division is usually divided into breeding, conformation, and working classes. In each class, a green hunter is a horse in its first or second year of showing, whereas a regular hunter is a horse of any age that is not restricted by the number of years showed previously in any division. Breeding classes are judged on conformation, quality, substance, and suitability to become or, in the case of sires and dams, apparent ability to produce and beget, hunters. Conformation classes are judged on conformation and performance. Depending upon the class, conformation

151

FIGURE 4-9
Hunter division. Emerald Bay being shown over an obstacle by Gerth
Christensen of the Happy Horse Riding School. Photo by June Fallaw, courtesy
of Dee Littrel.

may count toward 25–60 percent of the total score. Working hunters are
judged on performance and soundness. Conformation and working hunters
are exhibited over a course with obstacles that are between 3 feet 6 inches
and 4 feet 6 inches high. The fences usually simulate obstacles found in
the hunting field, such as natural post and rail, stone wall, white board
fence or gate, chicken coop, aiken (parallel bars with brush in the middle),
and hedge. Hunters should keep an even hunting pace and have good
manners and jumping style. They are also scored on faults and way of
moving over the course, as well as soundness. Faults include falls, touches,
knockdowns, and disobediences.

Saddle Horse Division

Classes for three-gaited and five-gaited horses are offered within the
Saddle Horse division (Figure 4-10). The horses must be registered with
the American Saddle Horse Breeders Association. Three-gaited horses

FIGURE 4-10
Annabelle, a 9-year-old, five-gaited American Saddlebred, is being shown at the trot by Bob Robinson. Annabelle has been champion five-gaited horse at many of the large horse shows on the West Coast. Photo by June Fallaw, courtesy of S. Dodson.

are required to be shown at the walk, trot, and canter. Five-gaited horses must also be shown at a slow gait (slow pace or trot) and the rack. Horses are worked both ways in the ring at all gaits. Finalists are usually requested to do further work as directed by the judge. Gaited horses are shown in any bridle that suits the horse and with a flat, English-type saddle. The exhibitor wears informal dress during morning and afternoon classes and dark-colored riding habit with accessories during the evening classes. For formal wear, women usually wear a tuxedo-style jacket with matching jodhpurs, whereas men usually wear a dark suit. Both wear a saddle derby or silk top hat.

Roadster Division

Horses shown in the roadster division of AHSA may be of any breed (Figure 4-11). The only qualifications for the horse shown in this division are an attractive appearance, good conformation, and good manners that make the horse a safe risk in the ring. The horse must also be serviceably sound. Horses are shown as bike roadsters or road wagon roadsters. Some horses can be shown in either class, but the road wagon roadster is larger than the bike roadster. Roadsters are shown at a walk, slow jog trot, fast road gait (also a trot), and full speed trot. When working in the show ring, the roadster has animation and brilliance. When asked for speed, this horse maintains form and shows full speed. Their gaits must be even and smooth at all times, particularly in the turns. The exhibitor in the bike class wears his stable colors and a cap and jacket that match. In the road class, the exhibitor wears a business suit and hat.

153

FIGURE 4-11
Roadster division. Emerald's Big
John, owned by Emerald Acres
Morgan Farm, is being shown in the
roadster division. Photo courtesy
of *Morgan Horse Magazine*.

Three-Day Event

The three-day event is the competition that demands extensive training
and devotion to horsemanship (Figure 4-12). Originally a trial for cavalry
patrol mounts, it became a recognized form of equestrian competition in
1912, when it was included in the Olympic Games. It is now defined as
"the most complete combined competition, demanding of the rider considerable experience in all branches of equitation and a precise knowledge

FIGURE 4-12
Catherine Mill taking a water
jump on Basque Bay during a
three-day event. Photo courtesy
of Catherine Mill.

of his horse's ability, and of his horse a degree of general competence resulting from intelligent and rational training."

On the first day of the three-day event, the Dressage test is given. The Dressage test consists of a series of movements that are designed to show the horse's fitness, suppleness, and sensitive obedience. Each movement is marked by judges. The Speed Endurance and Cross-Country test is held on the second day. The aim of this test is to prove the speed, endurance and jumping ability of the true cross-country horse. At the same time it demonstrates the rider's knowledge of pace and the coordination of effort between horse and rider. The test given on the third day is stadium jumping. Its object is to prove that on the day after a severe test of endurance, the horse has retained the suppleness, energy, and obedience necessary to continue in service.

Gymkhana

Gymkhana events or games on horseback are held by many riding clubs, 4-H clubs, and other interested horsemen. They are very popular with children but are also enjoyed by many adults because they are competitive and require harmony between rider and horse. The rules of gymkhana events may be established by the contestants or they may be closely governed by breed or horse show organizations.

Barrel Racing. Barrel racing is a standard gymkhana event. The rules vary depending upon the organization that sanctions the gymkhana. The standard positioning of the 3 barrels and the distance between them are illustrated in Figure 4-13. The event is sometimes called clover-leaf

FIGURE 4-13
Clover-leaf barrel racing pattern.

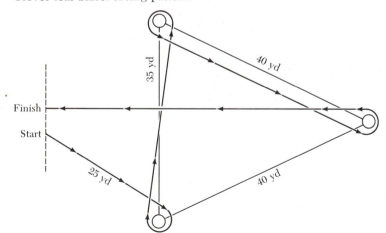

155

barrel racing because the race pattern resembles a cloverleaf. The rider has a running start when he crosses the starting line. Knocking over a barrel or failing to follow the prescribed course results in a time penalty or disqualification. The horse and rider with the fastest time win the race.

Pole Bending. Pole bending is a timed event in which the horse must travel a pattern around 6 poles (Figure 4-14). The 6-foot-high poles are set on top of the ground, and if a horse knocks down a pole, it is disqualified. There are two types of patterns that can be used. In one pattern (Figure 4-15), the 6 poles are placed 20 feet apart in a straight line. The timing line is perpendicular to the line of poles and located even with pole 1. The horse crosses the timing line, bends between the poles, circles pole 6, returns through the course by bending between the poles, and crosses the timing line. In the other pattern (Figure 4-16), the poles are

FIGURE 4-14
Pole bending. Horse turning the sixth pole in pole bending competition. Photo by June Fallaw, courtesy of George Cardinet.

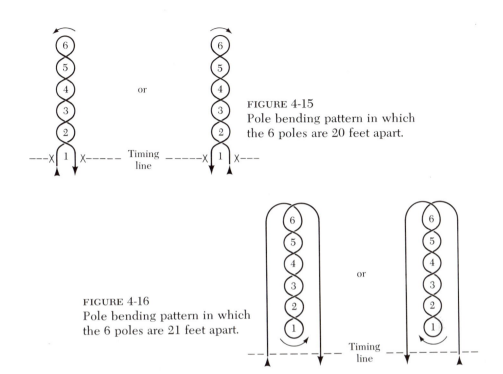

FIGURE 4-15
Pole bending pattern in which the 6 poles are 20 feet apart.

FIGURE 4-16
Pole bending pattern in which the 6 poles are 21 feet apart.

21 feet apart and the timing line is 21 feet from pole 1. The horse crosses the timing line, moves parallel to the line of poles, makes a 180° turn around pole 6, passes between poles 6 and 5, bends through the poles to pole 1, circles pole 1, bends through the poles to pole 6, makes a 180° turn around pole 6, and moves parallel to line of poles to cross the finish line.

Keyhole Race. The keyhole race is run over a course that is laid out with a limed keyhole on the ground. The throat of the keyhole is perpendicular to and faces the timing line. The center of the keyhole (20 feet in diameter) is 100 feet from the timing line. The horse crosses the timing line, enters the throat of the keyhole, goes to the center of the keyhole, makes a 180° turn in either direction, and returns across the timing line. The entry is disqualified if the horse steps on or over the limed keyhole at any point or if it fails to turn around in the center of the keyhole.

Stake Race. Young riders find the stake race a challenge during their early stages of learning horsemanship. The rider has to run a figure-eight pattern around 2 upright markers that are 80 feet apart (Figure 4-17). If an upright marker is knocked down, the entry is disqualified.

Other events, such as figure-eight stake, quadrangle stake, scurry, figure-eight relay, rescue, speed barrel, and potato race competitions are exciting, and a successful competitor requires a well-schooled horse.

157

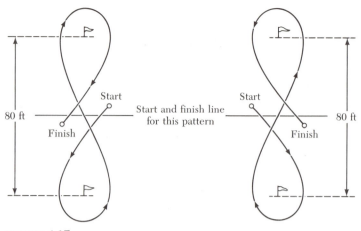

FIGURE 4-17
Pattern for a figure-eight stake race.

Foxhunting

Foxhunting was a popular sport in Great Britain and the United States during the eighteenth and nineteenth centuries (Figure 4-18). The sport was firmly established in colonial America by 1775. Hounds were imported to this country as early as 1650 by Robert Brooke of Maryland. The first hunt club, the Gloucester Foxhunting Club, was organized near Philadelphia in 1776. Packs of hounds may be owned by one individual, but subscription packs, in which a group of people support the hunt, introduced the sport to many people and are responsible for continuation of the sport. During the period 1781–1861, the sport was enjoyed mainly by

FIGURE 4-18
An early foxhunting scene: *A Kill at Ashdown Park,* by James Seymour.
Photograph courtesy of the Tate Gallery.

158

FIGURE 4-19
Piedmont Hunt in Virginia. Photo courtesy of Douglas Lees.

the wealthy landowners of Pennsylvania, Maryland, and Virginia. A pack of hounds was one of their prized possessions. From 1865 to 1906, many organized hunts and clubs were founded. In 1907, the Masters of the Foxhounds Association of America (112 Water Street, Boston, Massachusetts) was founded. Since then, the sport has been closely regulated and has grown steadily in popularity despite urbanization and modern farming methods. Several hundred packs of hounds are kept by hunt clubs throughout the world so that horsemen can enjoy a fast cross-country ride behind them when they so desire (see Figure 4-19).

Foxhunting adheres to strict rules of protocol that were established in the 1900s. Most hunting clubs have a similar type of organization. The Master of the Foxhounds is in direct command of the field (members of the hunt). He determines if a hunt will be held and where it will be held, and makes the necessary arrangements with the farmers. The huntsman maintains the pack and kennels and is responsible for the hounds in the field. He is also responsible for giving various signals to the hounds and the field with the horn. The huntsman is assisted by the whippers-in, who go to the woods where a fox is supposed to be. They watch for the fox "to go away" and signal the fox's escape. The hunt then begins. Once the chase starts, the hounds are in front, followed by the Master of the Foxhounds and the field. The hunt usually ends when the fox "goes to earth" (disappears in his hole).

Because foxes are getting scarce and because available land is difficult to find, drag hunts are held. Instead of chasing a live animal, the pursuers and hounds follow a scented trail laid out by touching the ground with a fox's brush or litter from the fox's den.

4.2 Social, Endurance, and Competitive Trail Riding

Some horsemen enjoy the competition of endurance and competitive trail riding, whereas others enjoy social trail riding. Social rides take many forms. Small groups of friends may ride together to discuss common interests and to enjoy the scenery along a trail. Horseback trips are made into the wilderness areas in and around the national parks. At pack stations, which are either privately owned or a service of the Forest Service, one may rent guides, horses, and all the necessary gear to travel into the wilderness. Many riding clubs sponsor well-organized rides; one such group is Equestrian Trails, Inc., a California organization made up of many local corrals whose goal is to preserve and develop riding trails. Each corral has many activities, including rides, tack and tog swaps, tours, and educational meetings. Social rides, such as the Desert Caballeros, Old Spanish Trail Riders, Rancheros Visitadores, and Sonoma County Trail Blazers, are becoming increasingly popular. These rides last for several days and cover 100–200 miles.

Competitive trail riding (Figure 4-20) is rapidly becoming one of the nation's most popular horse activities. Far from being a new sport, it is gaining in popularity, primarily because of the efforts of the North American Trail Ride Conference (NATRC). This body was organized in 1961 for the purpose of sanctioning competitive trail rides under a uniform judging system. The NATRC annually publishes a Rule Book, Judges Manual, and Management Manual that are available to interested horsemen. The objectives of the NATRC are:

1. To stimulate greater interest in the breeding and use of good horses possessed of stamina and hardiness as qualified mounts for trail use.

2. To demonstrate the value of type and soundness and the proper selection of horses for a long ride.

3. To learn and demonstrate the proper methods of training and conditioning horses for a long ride.

4. To encourage horsemanship in competitive trail riding.

5. To demonstrate the best methods of caring for horses during and after long rides without the aid of artificial methods or stimulants.

The NATRC sponsors both one-day (Class B) and two-day (Class A) rides. Appropriate points are given toward the annual championships, which are awarded to the finishing horses. Daily mileage in the open division is 25–40 miles (depending upon the steepness of the terrain), to be covered in 6½–7 hours riding time. Novice riders cover a shortened course of approximately 20 miles. The main object is to work all of the

FIGURE 4-20
Ruth Waltenspiel riding Kandar,
12-year-old Arabian gelding, in a
competitive trail ride. Kandar was 1973
National Heavyweight and National
NATRC champion. Photo by Hughes,
courtesy of NATRC.

horses over an identical trail in the same length of time, thereby establishing a basis of fair comparison for determining the horses' soundness, condition, and manners. Although this is not a race, judgment in timing and pacing is important, because the winner is usually the one who rode his horse at a consistent pace throughout the ride rather than "hurrying up and waiting."

One of the attractions of competitive trail riding is that no special type or breed of horse is necessary or favored. The prime requisite is a well-conditioned, calm horse. Riders condition their horses by following a well-planned training schedule that includes careful work over all types of terrain. Straight-away trotting, walking up and down progressively steeper hills, and working in soft sand are a few of the methods used to maximize development of the muscles, heart, and lungs.

The rides are judged by a team of at least 2 judges, one of whom must be a practicing veterinarian. The open division, for horses over 5 years of age, is divided into Junior (riders age 10–17) and Lightweight (rider and tack weighing less than 190 pounds) categories. The Novice division is primarily for young horses (age 4–5) and for newcomers to the sport.

For purposes of judging, each horse starts the ride with a score of 100, evaluated as follows: soundness, 40 percent; condition, 40 percent; manners, 15 percent; way of going, 5 percent. Although only the horses are judged, the riders also compete for horsemanship awards and are judged on the care and handling of their mounts during the entire weekend.

One of the older competitive trail rides is sponsored by the Green Mountain Horse Association. It is a 100-mile ride that is ridden for 3 days. During the first and second days, 40 miles are ridden between 6½ and 7 hours. During the third day, 20 miles are ridden between 2¾ and 3 hours. Riders are penalized if they do not finish within the time limits.

Competitive trail riding should not be confused with endurance riding. In contrast to competitive trail riding, where the horse must travel a fixed distance within a fixed period and is judged mainly on its soundness, condition, and manners, the endurance ride is primarily a race. The endurance ride is usually 50–100 miles long and must be completed within a maximum period. The horses are examined to determine that they are sound and are willing to proceed on the trail. There are 3 one-hour mandatory rest stops. During the rest stops, each horse is given a thorough veterinary check, which eliminates approximately 40 percent of the entries (Figure 4-21). Awards are made to all horses that complete the ride, to the first horse to finish the ride, and to the horse that finishes in best condition.

Several 50- to 100-mile endurance rides are held annually. The "Granddaddy" of them all is the Tevis Cup ride, which covers 100 miles in less than 24 hours. The Tevis Cup ride runs over the old Pony Express route from Lake Tahoe across the Sierra Nevada to Auburn, California. Horse and rider encounter temperature extremes, ranging from almost freezing in the snow-covered heights to 120 degrees in the canyons, as well as altitude extremes. The trail is rough, dusty, and rocky and includes steep inclines.

4.3 Polo

Polo developed in Persia, although it was first played in some form in China and Mongolia (Figure 4-22). The earliest references to polo are in connection with Alexander the Great and Darius, King of Persia. The oldest polo club, the Silchar Club, was founded in 1859. The Silchar

FIGURE 4-21
Endurance horse receiving a veterinary examination at a mandatory rest stop. Photo courtesy of NATRC.

FIGURE 4-22
Chinese polo. Watercolor on silk. Photograph courtesy of the Victoria and Albert Museum.

Club rules of play were the foundation for the modern rules. International matches between Great Britain and the United States were begun in 1886. The game was played widely throughout the United States until the mid-1930s (Figure 4-23). Recently, there has been a revival of interest in polo in this country.

The game requires excellent horsemanship and balance (Figure 4-24). A successful player must have complete control of his horse, be aware of the position of every other player on the field, relate the ball to the position of his teammates, and be able to hit the ball accurately at full speed while competing with his counterpart on the opposite team.

The game is played on a regulation field that is 300 yards long by 200 yards wide. The sidelines of the field have wooden boards to deflect the ball back into play, but these boards are never more than 11 inches high. The other essential pieces of equipment include the goal posts, which must be at least 10 feet high and are located 24 feet apart at the center of the backlines, a ball made of willow or bamboo root, polo sticks or mallets, and the rider's personal equipment and horses. Personal equipment includes blunt spurs, protective headgear, brown boots, whip, and polo saddle.

The objective of polo is to get the ball in the opposing team's goal. It is a team effort with established plans and maneuvers. A team consists of 4 players of which 2 are forwards, one is a half-back, and one is a back. The game is played in chukkers of 7½ minutes each. There may be 4 to 8 chukkers, depending on the nature of the competition. There is a 3-minute break between chukkers and there is a 5-minute break at half time.

A variation of polo known as cowboy polo is currently enjoying increased popularity. It differs from polo in several respects. It is a faster game that

FIGURE 4-23
Modern polo depicted in a magazine advertisement from the early 1900s. Courtesy of The Bettmann Archive.

is easier to watch and does not require uniforms or "select" facilities. Cowboy polo can be played both indoors and outdoors. The game is played on a dirt-sand field. The field is 260 feet long and is divided into 4 zones each 50 feet long and a fifth zone 60 feet long. A guard and a forward play in every zone except the 60-foot-long zone, which is patrolled by 2 centers. Four chukkers of 15 minutes each are played. The ball is 11 inches in diameter. Cowboy polo is a more aggressive game and involves considerably more contact than polo (Figure 4-25).

4.4 Rodeo

Organizations

Professional Rodeo Cowboys Association (PRCA). In the early days of the rodeo, it was largely unorganized and there were no standard rules. A ring of cars often formed the arena. In 1936, a group of cowboys formed

FIGURE 4-24
Polo. William Linfoot (*right*) playing off a 9-goal handicap polo match. Photo by Charles White, courtesy of William Linfoot.

FIGURE 4-25
Cowboy polo. Paul Dutton (*left*) riding Suzy, an Arabian mare, in hot competition for the ball in a cowboy polo match. Photo courtesy of Paul Dutton.

the Cowboys Turtle Association at the Boston Garden Rodeo when they realized that there was only enough prize money at stake for the top money winners barely to pay their expenses to get home. After waging a successful strike for more purse money, the CTA grew rapidly. In 1945, the group reorganized to form the Rodeo Cowboys Association. The PRCA has a membership of approximately 3,000 members who spend in excess of $25 million each year to compete for a payoff of approximately $5 million. Approximately 10 million spectators attend PRCA rodeos annually.

At the end of each year, an all-around champion is selected. The choice is based upon total money won from 2 or more events (Table 4-1). World champions for each event are determined by total dollars won in that event during a given year.

Girls Rodeo Association (GRA). The Girls Rodeo Association, closely patterned after the PRCA, was organized in 1948 with 76 members. There are no restrictions as to age. These women compete in the same contests as the men with the exception of the clover-leaf barrel race (Figure 4-26). Because of the popularity of the barrel race, PRCA rodeos added it to their program. In slightly more than two decades, the GRA has become a professional organization that awards more than $50,000 in prize money annually.

High School. The National High School Rodeo Association, Inc., sanctions rodeos for high school students of both sexes. The program encompasses 24 states and one province of Canada. Claude Millins, the father of high school rodeo, has said, "It is the inherent desire of every American youth to play cowboy. They want to be good cowboys, for the good cowboys made America. It is our responsibility to provide them the chance to participate in a good clean American Sport."

Intercollegiate. The National Intercollegiate Rodeo Association was formed in August of 1949. The NIRA establishes the rules for competition in each event and the standards for academic eligibility. It also maintains records of national standings. A cumulative grade index of "C" or better is required of all contestants.

The NIRA is organized in regions that include Southwestern, Southern, West Coast, Rocky Mountain, Central Rocky Mountains, Great Plains, Northwest, Ozark, Big Sky and Central Plains. These regions have a total individual membership of more than 2,000 athletes representing approximately 200 colleges and universities. Men compete in bareback riding, saddle bronc, bull riding, ribbon roping, steer wrestling, and calf roping events. Women participate in barrel racing, goat tying, and breakaway roping.

166

The team records for the national championship from 1949 to 1975 are given in Table 4-2. Several of the national all-around champions, such as

TABLE 4-1
All-around rodeo champions, 1929–1975

Year	Champion
1929	Earl Thode, Belvedere, S. Dak.
1930	Clay Carr, Visalia, Calif.
1931	Johnie Schneider, Livermore, Calif.
1932	Don Nesbitt, Snowflake, Ariz.
1933	Clay Carr, Visalia, Calif.
1934	Leonard Ward, Talent, Ore.
1935	Everett Bowman, Hillside, Ariz.
1936	John Bowman, Oakdale, Calif.
1937	Everett Bowman, Hillside, Ariz.
1938	Burel Mulkey, Salmon, Idaho
1939	Paul Carney, Galeton, Colo.
1940	Fritz Truan, Long Beach, Calif.
1941	Homer Pettigrew, Grady, N. Mex.
1942	Gerald Roberts, Strong City, Kans.
1943	Louis Brooks, Pittsburg, Okla.
1944	Louis Brooks, Pittsburg, Okla.
1945	Bill Linderman, Red Lodge, Mont.
1946	Gene Rambo, Shandon, Calif.
1947	Todd Whatley, Hugo, Okla.
1948	Gerald Roberts, Strong City, Kans.
1949	Jim Shoulders, Henryetta, Okla.
1950	Bill Linderman, Red Lodge, Mont.
1951	Casey Tibbs, Fort Pierre, S. Dak.
1952	Harry Tompkins, Dublin, Tex.
1953	Bill Linderman, Red Lodge, Mont.
1954	Buck Rutherford, Lenapah, Okla.
1955	Casey Tibbs, Fort Pierre, S. Dak.
1956	Jim Shoulders, Henryetta, Okla.
1957	Jim Shoulders, Henryetta, Okla.
1958	Jim Shoulders, Henryetta, Okla.
1959	Jim Shoulders, Henryetta, Okla.
1960	Harry Tompkins, Dublin, Tex.
1961	Benny Reynolds, Melrose, Mont.
1962	Tom Nesmith, Bethel, Okla.
1963	Dean Oliver, Boise, Idaho
1964	Dean Oliver, Boise, Idaho
1965	Dean Oliver, Boise, Idaho
1966	Larry Mahan, Brooks, Ore.
1967	Larry Mahan, Brooks, Ore.
1968	Larry Mahan, Brooks, Ore.
1969	Larry Mahan, Frisco, Tex.
1970	Larry Mahan, Frisco, Tex.
1971	Phil Lyne, George West, Tex.
1972	Phil Lyne, George West, Tex.
1973	Larry Mahan, Frisco, Tex.
1974	Larry Mahan, Frisco, Tex.
1975	Leo Camarillo, Donald, Ore., and Tom Ferguson, Miami, Okla.

TABLE 4-2
National Intercollegiate Rodeo Association Championships: 1949–1975

Year	Location	Team	All-Around Champion
1949	Cow Palace, San Francisco, California	Sul Ross State	Harley May, Sul Ross State
1950	Cow Palace, San Francisco, California	Sul Ross State	Harley May, Sul Ross State
1951	Will Rogers Coliseum, Fort Worth, Texas	Sul Ross State	Dick Barrett, Oklahoma A & M
	(Rodeo did not have national representation so points were based on season totals)		
1952	Rose Festival, Portland, Oregon	Colorado A & M	Dick Barrett, Oklahoma A & M
1953	Abilene, Texas	Hardin-Simmons University	Tex Martin, Sul Ross State
1954	(National Finals Rodeo not held – points based on season totals)	Colorado A & M	Howard Harris, University of Idaho
1955	Lake Charles, Louisiana	Texas Tech, Lubbock	Ira Akers, Sam Houston State
1956	Colorado Springs, Colorado	Sam Houston State	Ira Akers, Sam Houston State
	(1st year, All-Around Girl)		Kathlyn Younger, Colorado A & M
1957	Colorado Springs, Colorado	McNeese State	Clyde May, McNeese State
1958	Colorado Springs, Colorado	McNeese State	Jack Burkholder, Texas A & I
1959	Klamath, Oregon	(Unknown)	Jack Roddy, California State Polytechnic, San Luis Obispo
	(All-Around Girl)		Pat Dunigan, New Mexico State University
1960	Clayton, New Mexico	California State Polytechnic, San Luis Obispo	Ed Workman, Lubbock Christian College
	(All-Around Girl)		Karen Mangum, Sam Houston State
1961	Sacramento, California	University of Wyoming	Ed Workman, Lubbock Christian College
	(Girls' Team)	Sam Houston State	Sue Burgraff, Montana State College
1962	Littleton, Colorado	Sul Ross State	Ed Workman, Lubbock Christian College
	(Girls' Team)	Sul Ross State	Donna Jean Saul, Sul Ross State
1963	Littleton, Colorado	Casper College	Shawn Davis, Western Montana College
	(Girls' Team)	Colorado State University	Leota Hielscher, Colorado State University
1964	Douglas, Wyoming	Casper College	Pink Peterson, Casper College
	(Girls' Team)	Colorado State University	Marie Mass, Southern Colorado State College

Year	Location	Team Champions	Individual Champions
1965	Laramie, Wyoming (Girls' Team)	Casper College; Sam Houston State	Pink Peterson, Casper College; Becky Bergren, Sam Houston State
1966	Vermillion, South Dakota (Girls' Team)	Casper College; Arizona State University	Dave Hart, Idaho State University; Carol O'Rourke, Montana State University
1967	St. George, Utah (Girls' Team)	Tarleton State College; Eastern New Mexico University	A. C. Ekker, University of Utah; Barbara Socolsfsky, Kansas State University
1968	Sacramento, California (Girls' Team)	Sam Houston State; Sam Houston State	Phil Lyne, Sam Houston State; Donna Kinkead, Eastern New Mexico University
1969	Deadwood, South Dakota (Girls' Team)	Eastern New Mexico University; Tarleton State College	Phil Lyne, Sam Houston State; Nancy Robinson, California Polytechnic Institute at San Luis Obispo
1970	Bozeman, Montana (Girls' Team)	California Polytechnic Institute at San Luis Obispo; Tarleton State College	Tom Miller, Black Hills State College; Linda Sultemeir, Eastern New Mexico University
1971	Bozeman, Montana (Girls' Team)	California Polytechnic Institute at San Luis Obispo; Montana State University	Tom Miller, Black Hills State College; Jan Wagner, Montana State University
1972	Bozeman, Montana (Girls' Team)	Eastern New Mexico University	Dave Brock, Southern Colorado State College; Linda Munns, Utah State University
1973	Bozeman, Montana (Girls' Team)	California Polytechnic Institute at San Luis Obispo; University of Arizona	Dave Brock, Southern Colorado State College; Lou Ann Herstead, University of Wyoming
1974	Bozeman, Montana (Girls' Team)	Eastern New Mexico University; Sam Houston State	Dudley Little, Florida State University; Pam Simon, University of Arizona
1975	Bozeman, Montana (Girls' Team)	Montana State University; New Mexico State University	Skip Emmett, University of Tennessee; Jennifer Haynes, New Mexico State University

FIGURE 4-26
Barrel racing. Barrel racer Jeana Day is turning a barrel in a barrel race in the National Finals Rodeo. Jeana has been competing in professional rodeo since she was 15 years old. Photo by Al Long, courtesy of the Golden State Rodeo Company.

Harley May, Jack Roddy, Shawn Davis, and Phil Lyne, have subsequently been quite successful in the PRCA.

Saddle Bronc Riding

This is one of the classic events of rodeo (Figure 4-27). The rules of competition are strictly in favor of the horse, and few contestants become top saddle bronc riders unless they have had a solid foundation of riding rank, unbroken horses. The PRCA rules state that the rider, to qualify, must have the spurs over the break of the shoulders and touching the horse when the front feet hit the ground on the first jump out of the chute. The rider is disqualified for being bucked off, changing hands on the rein, losing a stirrup, or touching the horse, saddle, or rein with his free hand. The rider must ride the horse for 8 seconds and use a saddle that conforms with the design specified by the PRCA. A 6-foot rein is used and is attached to the halter. The rider wears short-shanked spurs with dull rowels and lightweight chaps. The total score is based upon how difficult the horse is to ride, the amount of control exercised by the rider, and how he spurs. The rider should maintain a smooth spurring stroke from the horse's neck to the rear of the saddle. This stroke resembles an arc, and the longer the arc, the more points the rider earns. The rider is given from 1 to 25 points and the animal is given from 1 to 25 points by each of 2 judges. A combined score in the high 60s is considered a good ride.

FIGURE 4-27
Saddle bronc riding. Bill Nelson of
San Francisco, California, riding
Rawhide, owned by the Golden State
Rodeo Company. Photo courtesy of
the Golden State Rodeo Company.

Bareback Riding

This is the youngest of rodeo's three standard riding contests (Figure 4-28).
This event bears no relationship to ranch work. However, it is one of the
most popular events for cowboys as well as for spectators. The bareback
rigging consists of a leather pad with a handhold that is cinched to the
bronc's back. There are no stirrups or reins, so that the rider must stay on
by gripping the handhold on top of the rigging. Judging is based upon the
extent to which the horse bucks and the rider's ability to stay in command,
maintain his balance, and spur properly. The horse must be ridden for
8 seconds and the contestant is disqualified if he touches the horse with
his free hand or fails to have his spurs over the break of the horse's shoulders
when the horse's feet touch the ground on the first jump out of the chute.

Bull Riding

Bull riding has more entries than the other two riding events, even though
serious injury occurs more often in bull riding than in any other rodeo

FIGURE 4-28
Bareback riding. Butch Cody of Cedar Vale, Kansas, riding Bones. Photo courtesy of the Golden State Rodeo Company.

event (Figure 4-29). A bull rider uses a rope that is looped around the animal's middle. The rider puts his gloved hand in a loop in the rope and another cowboy pulls the slack out of the rope. When the rope's tightness feels correct to the rider, he takes the free end and lays it across his palm, wraps it once again behind his riding hand, lays it across his palm again, and clenches it with all his strength. The only rules are that the bull must be ridden 8 seconds, the rope must have a bell, and the free hand cannot touch the animal. Brahman bulls were introduced into the rodeo arena in 1921. They are difficult to ride because they have a very loose hide and add injury to insult by trying to gore or trample a fallen rider. The judges look for the bull's ability to jump and kick high and to change directions very quickly. The rider's ability to assume control of the bull by staying reasonably erect and to use his legs and spurs to help him in his ride are judged to form a composite score for bull and rider.

Calf Roping

Calf roping is one of two events that originated on the early ranches. Calves had to be roped on the range to be doctored or branded. The arena event is a race against time requiring the coordinated effort of horse and rider (Figure 4-30). At the beginning of the contest, the rider and his horse are behind a rope barrier. The barrier is released when the calf crosses a measured distance. If the roper breaks the barrier he is given a 10-second

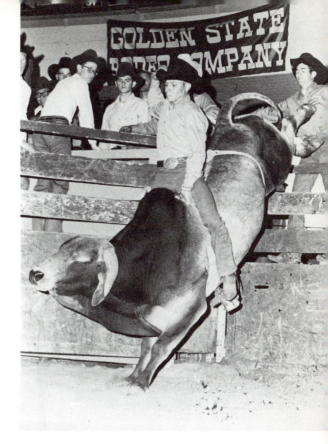

FIGURE 4-29
Bull riding. Larry Smith of San José,
California, riding Lippy Leo, owned
by Golden State Rodeo Company.
Photo courtesy of the Golden State
Rodeo Company.

FIGURE 4-30
Calf roping. Bob Kreiger of
Novato, California, roping a calf.
Photo courtesy of the Golden
State Rodeo Company.

penalty. After the calf is roped with a manila rope that is approximately 25 feet long, the horse stops abruptly, thus propelling the rider toward the calf as he dismounts. The roper must then throw the calf by hand. The horse keeps the rope tight to aid the roper in throwing the calf. Three legs of the calf must be tied with a 6-foot length of rope called a piggin' string. Time is completed when the roper raises his hands. The calf must remain tied for at least 6 seconds before the time is official. Ten seconds is considered an excellent time.

Steer Wrestling

Commonly called bull dogging, this event was developed in the rodeo arena by Bill Pickett, a black cowboy, as a part of a Wild West show. The event starts with 2 cowboys mounted on horses on opposite sides of a chute containing a horned steer. The cowboy on the right of the steer is called a hazer and it is his responsibility to keep the steer running straight. The cowboy on the left side of the steer is the "dogger." The dogger starts from behind a barrier, and if he breaks the barrier before the steer crosses a designated score line, a 10-second penalty is added to the time. As the dogger catches up to the steer, he reaches out with his right hand and grabs the right horn (Figure 4-31). The dogger's horse speeds by the steer as the dogger snugs the right horn in the crook of his right elbow. Simultaneously, his left hand pushes down on the other horn while his horse veers off to the left. As the dogger leaves his horse, he drops his heels ahead of his body and at a 45° angle to the path the steer is taking. The dogger tips the steer's head and pulls it toward the center of a left-hand turn. As the steer slows down, the dogger's left hand catches the steer's upturned nose. The steer is then thrown on its side. Times of 4 and 5 seconds are considered excellent.

Team Roping

Team roping is a popular event that is a rodeo version of cattle work in which one cowboy ropes a steer around the horns and another cowboy then ropes the steer's heels (Figure 4-32). There are two styles of team roping. Dally team roping, in which the roper must take a turn around the saddle horn with his rope after he catches the steer, is the standard pattern on the West Coast. The Arizona style calls for the lariat rope to be tied to the saddle horn. If the heeler only catches one hind foot, the team is assessed a 5-second penalty. A variation of Arizona style of team roping is team tying. After the steer is roped, the roper who roped the horns must dismount and tie a short rope around the steer's hind legs.

FIGURE 4-31
Steer wrestling. Bob Ragsdale, President of the PRCA, getting down on a steer. Photo courtesy of the Golden State Rodeo Company.

FIGURE 4-32
Team roping. Ted Ashworth, former PRCA Champion Team Roper, coming in to rope the heels of a steer. Photo courtesy of the Golden State Rodeo Company.

175

Other Events

At some rodeos, such as Cheyenne Frontier Days and the Pendleton Roundup, single-steer roping is held. A mounted roper ropes a running steer by the horns and lays the slack in the rope over the steer's right hip. By turning his horse off to the left, the steer is "tripped" to the ground. The roper dismounts and ties 3 legs while the horse leans into the rope and keeps the steer prone.

In the wild horse race, teams of 3 cowboys, on foot, try to saddle unbroken mustangs in the arena. After the mustang is saddled, one member of the team rides the horse across a given score line.

The wild cow milking event requires a team of 2 cowboys. One cowboy ropes a wild cow released from a chute. The second cowboy mugs or holds the roped cow so that the roper can milk her into a bottle. After milking the cow, the roper must run across a designated score line.

4.5   Cutting Horses

The cutting horse event developed out of a need for cowboys to separate an individual animal from a herd with minimal disturbance. Cutting horses are still used to work cattle and also participate in cutting horse contests (Figure 4-33). Cutting horse contests were started between neighboring ranches in about 1850. Money undoubtedly changed hands during the early contests, but the first recorded "money event" was held in Haskell,

FIGURE 4-33
Sugar Vaquero, a world champion cutting horse of 1975 ridden by Bobby Sikes, is shown working a cow in competition. Photo by Dalco, courtesy of the National Cutting Horse Association.

Texas, on July 22, 1898, at the Cowboy Reunion. In March 1946, the event was placed under a uniform set of rules when the National Cutting Horse Association was formed. The NCHA approves more than 750 open and championship shows each year and compiles the results from more than 400 contestants.

In a contest, the horse moves into a herd of 15–20 head of cattle that are held at one end of an arena by 2 men called herd holders. One cow is cut out of the herd and driven to the center of the arena. The cow is turned back toward the herd by 2 riders known as turn back men. As the cow attempts to return to the herd, the cutting horse makes counter moves to prevent its return to the herd. In making the counter moves, the horse must be able to turn around quickly, roll out quickly to the left and right, and stay head to head with the cow. The horse is judged on how hard it was challenged by the cow, how it met the challenge, and what mistakes, if any, were made.

Appendix

Addresses of Riding Associations

Professional Rodeo Cowboys Association, 2929 West 19th Avenue, Denver, Colorado 80204.

Cowboy Polo Association Inc., 8295 Ralston Road, Arvada, Colorado 80002

National Intercollegiate Rodeo Association, P.O. Box 2088, Huntsville, Texas 77340

National High School Rodeo Association, Inc., 2018 West Prospect Avenue, Visalia, California 93277

Girls Rodeo Association, 8909 North East 25th, Spencer, Oklahoma 73084

North American Trail Ride Conference, 1995 Day Road, Gilroy, California 95020

United States Polo Association, 1301 West 22nd Street, Oak Brook, Illinois 60521

Masters of Foxhounds Association of America, 112 Water Street, Boston, Massachusetts 02109

United States Equestrian Team, Gladstone, New Jersey 07934

177

United States Combined Training Association, 50 Congress Street, Boston, Massachusetts 02109

National Cutting Horse Association, P.O. Box 12155, Fort Worth, Texas 76116

American Horse Shows Association, 527 Madison Avenue, New York, New York 10022

References

American Horse Show Association Rule Book. 1974. New York: AHSA. [Annual.]

Barsaleau, R. B., and S. Saare. 1973. Endurance riding and competitive trail riding. *The Western Horseman* 37:64–67.

Jones, Caroline. Fox hunting in America. 1973. *American Heritage* 14(1): 62, 68, and 101.

Horseback trips into the wilderness. 1972. *Sunset Magazine* 148(2):52–56 and 84–90.

Hope, C. E. G., and G. N. Jackson. 1973. *The Encyclopedia of the Horse.* London: Rainbird Reference Books, Ltd.

Albright, V. R. 1971. *The Tevis Cup.* Los Gatos, California: Forge Valley Books.

Gorman, J. A., 1967. *The Western Horse.* Danville, Illinois: The Interstate Printers and Publishers, Inc.

PART TWO *Biology of the Horse*

CHAPTER FIVE *The Anatomy and Physiology of the Horse*

5.1 Introduction

The horse's body is a complex mechanism, and an understanding of its structure and function will result in more intelligent care and management of the animal. Anatomy and physiology are the sciences of the relationship of form to function, and knowledge of these subjects separates the true horseman from the horse lover.

The body of the horse is made up of the following systems:

1. Skeletal (the bones and joints).
2. Muscular (the muscles).
3. Respiratory (the lungs and air passages).
4. Circulatory (the heart and vessels).
5. Digestive (the gastro-intestinal tract and urinary system).
6. Nervous (the brain, spinal cord, associated nerves, and special senses).
7. Endocrine (the ductless glands, responsible for the chemical control of the body).
8. Reproductive (the ovaries, testicles, and associated organs).
9. Integumentary (the skin and associated structures).

5.2 Skeletal System

The skeleton of the horse (Figure 5-1) consists of the trunk (skull, spinal column, ribs, and breastbone) and limbs. The skeletal system includes the bones and ligaments, which bind the bones together to form joints. It provides the framework that gives the body form, supports the soft parts, and protects the vital organs. The bones act as levers, store minerals, and are the site of blood cell formation.

The skeleton of the horse is made up of 205 bones as follows: vertebral column, 54; ribs, 36; sternum, 1; skull, 34; thoracic limbs, 40; pelvic limbs, 40.

Bones are classified as long, short, flat, and irregular. The *long bones* function chiefly as levers and aid in support of weight and locomotion. The *short bones* absorb concussion. They are found in the complex joints such as the carpus (knee), tarsus (hock), and fetlock (ankle). The *flat bones* enclose the cavities containing vital organs: skull (brain) and ribs (heart and lungs). The flat bones also provide large areas for the attachment of muscles. The *irregular bones* are the bones of the spinal column; they protect the central nervous system.

The periosteum is a tough membrane that covers the bones throughout the body except at their points of articulation. The periosteum protects the bone and is the site of healing should there be a fracture. Abnormal growth in the periosteum is termed *exostosis*. In the horse, the response of the periosteum to injury may result in undesirable bone growths, such as splints, spavins, and ringbone (see Chapter 6). The articulating surface of the bone is covered with a thick, smooth cartilage that diminishes concussion and friction.

Bones are held together by *ligaments*, whereas muscles are attached to the bones by *tendons*. The layer within the joint capsule is sealed by a delicate layer of synovial membrane, and the joint is lubricated by a secretion termed *synovial fluid*.

Skull

The bony framework of the head consists of 34 irregularly shaped flat bones joined by immovable joints. The *cranial cavity* encloses and protects the brain and supports many sense organs. The facial portion of the skull consists of orbital, nasal, and oral passages. The *orbital cavity* is the bony socket that surrounds and protects the eye. The *nasal cavity* is the passageway to the respiratory system. It contains scroll-shaped turbinate bones that serve as baffles to deflect and warm inspired air as it passes over the vascular, mucous membrane that lines the entire cavity. This mucous membrane also contains the sensory nerve endings of the olfactory nerve,

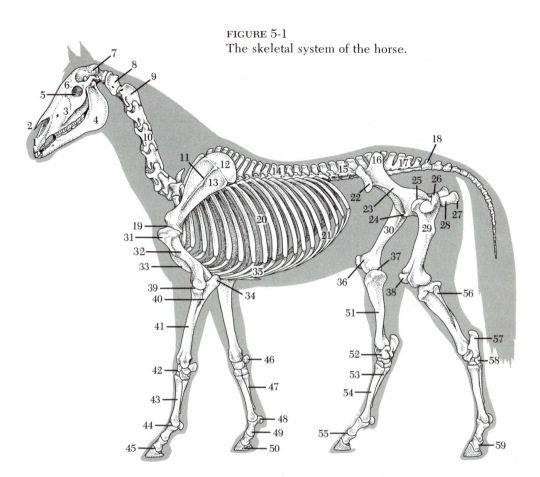

FIGURE 5-1
The skeletal system of the horse.

1	Incisive bone (premaxillary)	20	Ribs (forming wall of thorax: there are usually 18 ribs)	42	Carpus
2	Nasal bone			43	Metacarpus
3	Maxillary bone			44	Fetlock joint
4	Mandible	21	Costal arch (line of last rib and costal cartilages)	45	Coffin joint
5	Orbit			46	Accessory carpal bone (pisiform)
6	Frontal bone	22	Tuber coxae		
7	Temporal fossa	23	Ilium	47	Small metacarpal bone (splint bone)
8	Atlas (first cervical vertebra)	24	Pubis		
9	Axis (second cervical vertebra)	25	Hip joint	48	Proximal sesamoid bone
10	Cervical vertebra (there are 7 of these, including the atlas and axis)	26	Femur, greater trochanter	49	First phalanx
		27	Tuber ischii	50	Distal phalanx (third phalanx)
		28	Ischium		
11	Scapular spine	29	Femur, third trochanter	51	Tibia
12	Scapular cartilage	30	Femur	52	Talus (tibial tarsal bone) (astragalus)
13	Scapula	31	Humeral tuberosity, lateral		
14	Thoracic vertebrae (there are usually 18 of these)	32	Humerus	53	Small metatarsal bone (splint bone)
		33	Sternum		
15	Lumbar vertebrae (there are usually 6 of these)	34	Olecranon	54	Metatarsus
		35	Costal cartilages	55	Pastern joint
16	Tuber sacrale	36	Femoral trochlea	56	Fibula
17	Sacral vertebrae (sacrum) (there are usually 5 vertebrae fused together)	37	Stifle joint	57	Calcaneus (fibular tarsal bone)
		38	Patella		
		39	Elbow joint	58	Tarsus
18	Coccygeal vertebrae	40	Ulna	59	Middle phalanx (second phalanx)
19	Shoulder joint	41	Radius		

183

which is responsible for conveying the sense of smell. The *oral passage,* buccal cavity, or mouth is the passageway to the digestive tract. The maxillae are the bones of the upper jaw that carry the upper cheek teeth (pre-molars and molars). The mandible is the hinged lower jaw.

The age of a horse can be determined with considerable accuracy up to 9 years of age by examining the incisors (Figure 5-2). There is a total of 6 incisors in the upper jaw and 6 incisors in the lower jaw. In the male horse, canine teeth (tushes) erupt in the interdental spaces, but these 4 extra teeth are usually missing in the mare. There are 6 pre-molars and 6 molars in each jaw of both sexes. Small pointed teeth that sometimes appear at the base of the first pre-molar tooth are termed *wolf teeth.*

The dental formula of a mature horse is:

$$\text{Male:} \quad 2\left(I\,\frac{3}{3}\;C\,\frac{1}{1}\;P\,\frac{3 \text{ or } 4}{3}\;M\,\frac{3}{3}\right) = 40 \text{ or } 42$$

$$\text{Female:} \quad 2\left(I\,\frac{3}{3}\;C\,\frac{0}{0}\;P\,\frac{3 \text{ or } 4}{3}\;M\,\frac{3}{3}\right) = 36 \text{ or } 38$$

The foal often does not have any incisors visible at birth, but they erupt at regular intervals during the first 6–10 weeks. The young horse has 24 deciduous or temporary milk teeth. The 12 incisors are all replaced by the time an animal is 4½ years old. The eruption and wear of the permanent incisors are utilized as a method of determining age of the horse as follows:

Permanent Incisor	Age at Eruption	Years of Wear
1st incisor	2½ years	3
2nd incisor	3½ years	4
3rd incisor	4½ years	5
Canine	4 to 5 years	

The permanent pre-molars and molars are also erupting during this period but they are not used to determine the age of a horse because of their inaccessibility. The age at eruption of pre-molars and molars is as follows:

Pre-molars and Molars	Age at Eruption
1st pre-molar	5–6 months
2nd pre-molar	2½ years
3rd pre-molar	3 years
4th pre-molar	4 years
1st molar	9–12 months
2nd molar	2 years
3rd molar	3½–4 years

With experience, one can determine age from 6–9 years using the wear or smoothness of the indentations (cups) in the incisors as a guide. Between 9 and 12 years of age, some subtle changes occur in the incisors. After 12 years all teeth are smooth (the horse is then referred to as "smooth mouthed") and it is extremely difficult to determine age by examining the teeth (mouthing a horse). Some experienced horsemen can determine age with fair accuracy until the horse is 30 years of age, but this began to become a lost art with the advent of the era of the purebred and the recording of the birthdate on the registration papers. The majority of horse owners find it difficult to determine age from the teeth much past 9 years of age, and consequently any horse over this age is classified as "aged."

Abnormalities in the jawbone can result in the overshot jaw (parrot mouth) or undershot jaw (monkey mouth) condition. These conditions are congenital and may be inherited (see section 6.3). Because they can interfere with successful grazing, they are undesirable traits.

The upper lip is a sensitive, strong, mobile organ of prehension. In grazing action, the lip places the food between the incisor teeth by which it is cut. In the manger, the lip and the tongue aid in collecting loose food.

Simple up and down movement of the pre-molars and molars is inadequate to grind tough, coarse feed, and therefore the horse is capable of lateral grinding movements of the jaw. The upper jaw is wider than the lower jaw, and consequently mastication can occur in only one side at a time. The tooth of the horse is composed of veins of enamel that keep the surfaces rough. The lateral grinding movement of the jaws develops chisel-sharp surfaces that can cause damage to the soft tissues of the mouth. The inner edges of the lower teeth can injure the tongue, and the outer edges of the upper teeth can lacerate the cheek. Consequently, it is sometimes necessary to file the sharp edges of molars and pre-molars. This process is termed *floating the teeth.*

There are 3 pairs of salivary glands in the horse: the parotid gland located below the ear, which is the largest; the submaxillary gland located primarily between the jaws; and the sublingual gland located in the mucous membranes beneath the tongue. These glands can become the site for an acute contagious bacterial infection termed *equine distemper* or *strangles* (see Chapter 18). This infection causes a fever (104°–106°F) and an intense swelling of the submaxillary and parotid lymph nodes, which may abcess and rupture. If untreated, the infection may spread to the abdominal lymph system and the disease may become fatal.

The lateral portion of the skull articulates with the atlas joint of the cervical vertebrae.

FIGURE 5-2
Guide to determining the age of a horse by its teeth.

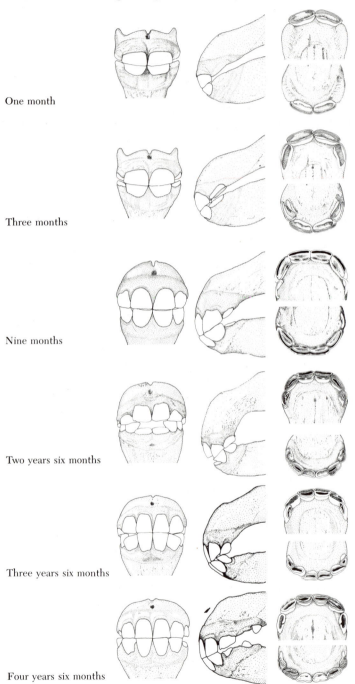

One month

Three months

Nine months

Two years six months

Three years six months

186

Four years six months

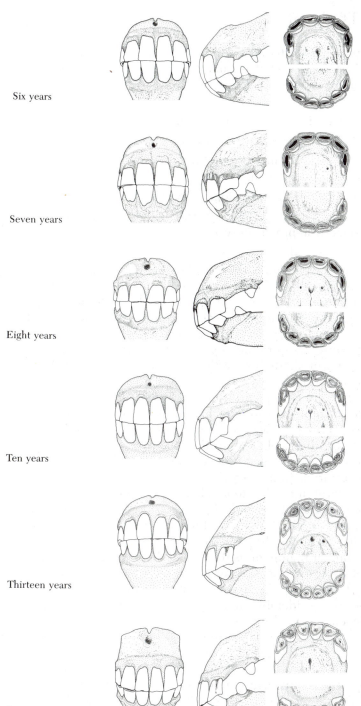

Six years

Seven years

Eight years

Ten years

Thirteen years

Seventeen years

187

Spinal Column

The spinal or vertebral column is comprised of a series of irregularly shaped bones that stretch from the base of the head to the tip of the tail. The regions of the spinal column are:

1. Cervical (neck): 7 vertebrae.

2. Thoracic (back): 18 vertebrae usually, but sometimes 19 or 17.

3. Lumbar (loin): 6 vertebrae usually, but are sometimes fused; 5 are not uncommon.

4. Sacral (croup): fusion of 5 vertebrae.

5. Coccygeal (caudal or tail): varies considerably in number; average is approximately 18.

The cervical region is the most flexible portion of the vertebral column. The initial vertebra of the cervical region is the *atlas;* it is attached to the skull to permit extension and flexion of the head and neck. The second vertebra is the *axis;* it permits side-to-side articulation with the atlas. The atlas-axis joint is commonly referred to as the "yes-no" joint. The remaining cervical vertebrae form an S shape when viewed from the side, and the lengthening or shortening of the neck can be accomplished by changing the amount of this curvature.

The 18 vertebrae of the thoracic region have articulating surfaces on their dorsal processes for attachment of the 18 pairs of ribs. The spinous processes (upper surface of the spine) is of increased height in the third, fourth and fifth vertebrae, and these form the withers, the highest part of the horse. There is very little movement of the thoracic vertebrae. The thoracic cavity is formed by the vertebrae on the top, the ribs on the side, and the sternum on the floor. This cavity contains the vital organs of the respiratory, circulatory, and digestive systems. The first 8 pairs of the 18 pairs of ribs are the *true* ribs, which are attached to the sternum by means of cartilage. The last 10 pairs are *false* ribs.

The lumbar region forms the loin of the horse and sometimes is missing a vertebra. Horses of Arabian breeding often have only 5 lumbar vertebrae, but a number of purebred Arabians also have 6.

There is considerably more movement in the lumbar vertebrae than in the thoracic or sacral regions.

The sacrum contains 5 vertebrae that are fused together and underlie the croup of the horse. The sacrum is jointed securely to the hip bones (pelvis) on either side.

The tail region is made up of a varying number of coccygeal vertebrae. They become reduced in size as they proceed caudally, and the last one is pointed. The spinal canal is very narrow in this portion of the spinal column. The tail of driving and work horses was often cut off (docked) to prevent its interference with the reins.

Limbs

The front limb of the horse is not attached directly to the vertebral column. The *scapula* (shoulder blade) is attached by a muscular sling that supports the thorax and reduces concussion. The slope of the scapula, and therefore the angle formed by its junction with the humerous (arm), provides additional shock absorption and has much to do with the smoothness of gait of a riding horse. The *radius* is the main bone of the forearm, and the *ulna* is fused to the upper part. The *carpus* is the knee and consists of 8 carpal bones arranged in 2 rows. Therefore, the carpus joint or knee joint actually consists of 3 articulating surfaces. The *metacarpal* bones are 3 in number. The large middle metacarpal (cannon bone) extends from the carpus to the fetlock joint. The 2 smaller metacarpals on each side of the cannon are termed *splint bones* and are vestiges of additional toes.

The hind limb is attached to the vertebral column at the sacrum by the pelvic girdle that is formed by the union of the hip bones. The *femur* is the bone of the thigh, and the patella is a small bone of the stifle joint corresponding to the knee cap in man. The *tibia* is the main bone of the gaskin, and the *fibula,* a small rudimentary bone, is fused to it. The *tarsus* or hock contains 7 bones and corresponds to the ankle and heel in man. The 3 bones of the cannon on the hind limb are the *metatarsals.* As in front, there are a large middle metatarsal and 2 splint bones.

The structures of the front and hind foot of the horse are basically the same (Figure 22-2). At the base of the cannon bone, there are 2 small bones called the *proximal sesamoids,* which form the back part of the fetlock joint. These bones are completely surrounded by connective tissue and provide a bearing surface for the flexor tendons.

Below the fetlock joint is the *first phalanx* (long pastern), *second phalanx* (short pastern), and *third phalanx* (coffin or pedal bone), which is surrounded by the hoof. In back of the coffin bone is the *distal sesamoid* or *navicular bone,* which provides an articulating surface for the pedal bone and an important bearing surface for the flexor tendons. An inflammation of the distal sesamoid results in *navicular disease* (see Chapter 6). The coffin, navicular, and short pastern bones are the 3 bones of the foot. The coffin bone is attached to the hoof wall by the sensitive laminae (see Chapter 22 for more information about the hoof).

Joints of the Leg

Movement of the horse is dependent upon the contraction of muscles and the corresponding articulation of the joints. In the front leg, there are 6

189

joints: the shoulder, elbow, carpus, fetlock, pastern, and coffin joints. The hind limb has 7 joints: the sacro-iliac, hip, stifle, hock, fetlock, pastern, and coffin. These numerous articulations are the source of many of the unsoundnesses in the horse. The joint capsule is a fluid-filled sac (synovia). If an excess of this fluid is produced, a puffy, soft swelling such as a bog spavin occurs. Ligaments hold the joints together (attach bone to bone) and have a limited blood supply. If there is an injury to a ligament such as a sprain, it tends to heal slowly and often incorrectly. Sesamoiditis is an example of such an injury to the suspensory ligament, and a curb is an example in the plantar ligament, which holds the back of the hock together. Muscles are attached to bone by tendons. The horse has no muscle below the knee or hock, and consequently many leg muscles have long tendons that pass down the leg over joints where there are protective tendon sheaths or "tendon bursa." Chronic irritation of these bursa can result in excess fluid production and soft swellings. When they appear above the fetlock, these swellings are called wind puffs or wind galls. They rarely result in a distinct lameness but they do result in short, stiff strides. Distinct lameness can result when the tendons bear against bones that are roughened from fracture or exostosis as in navicular disease. Abuse of the legs can result in the contraction, rupture, or bowing (straining) of tendons.

5.3   Muscular System

The muscles are the largest tissue mass in the horse's body (Figure 5-3). They perform their work by contracting to allow for locomotion and the performance of vital functions. The muscles are classified as *smooth muscle, cardiac muscle,* and *skeletal muscle.* The smooth and cardiac muscles are involuntary or automatic in their contraction and are active in the digestive tract, respiratory, circulatory, and urogenital systems. The skeletal muscle is voluntary and functions in the movement of the horse.

The activities of the multitude of muscles in the body are complex. A comparison of a horse grazing with a horse performing in a Grand National racing competition emphasizes the diversity of muscular activity that is possible. However, the basic principle of muscular activity is the same for all muscles: a period of contraction (shortening of muscle fibers) followed by a period of relaxation (lengthening of muscle fibers). The muscle fibers are bound together by fibrous connective tissue to form bundles, and the bundles are arranged in parallel bands or sheets to form muscles.

Muscles are attached to bone by *tendons,* composed of dense connective tissue. The tendons may be short, as at the shoulder blade, or long as in the legs. The action of bone levers, joint hinges, and tendon cables, and the contraction of muscles make motion possible. Skeletal muscles have

FIGURE 5-3
The muscular system of the horse.

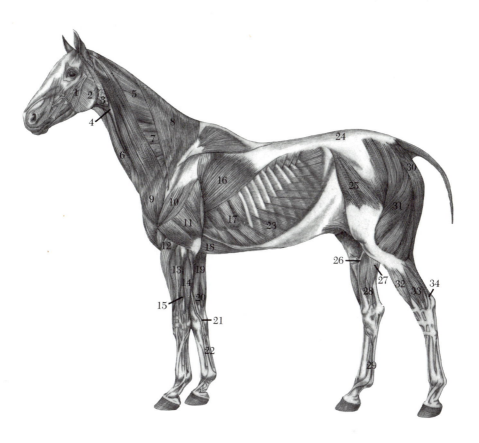

1 Facial nerve	20 Ulnar carpal flexor muscle
2 Masseter muscle	(flexor carpi ulnaris muscle)
3 Parotid salivary gland	21 Cephalic vein
4 Jugular vein	22 Digital flexor tendons
5 Splenius muscle	23 External abdominal oblique muscle
6 Sternocephalic muscle	24 Gluteal muscles
7 Serratus ventralis muscle	25 Tensor fasciae latae muscle
8 Trapezius muscle	26 Saphenous vein
9 Brachiocephalic muscle	27 Gastrocnemius muscle
10 Deltoid muscle	28 Long digital flexor muscle
11 Triceps muscle	29 Digital flexor tendons
12 Radial carpal extensor muscle	30 Semitendinosus muscle
(extensor carpi radialis muscle)	31 Biceps femoris muscle
13 Common digital extensor muscle	32 Long digital extensor muscle
14 Ulnaris lateralis muscle	33 Lateral digital extensor muscle
15 Lateral digital extensor muscle	34 Achilles' tendon
16 Latissimus dorsi muscle	(also called the hamstring: consists
17 Serratus ventralis muscle	of tendons of gastrocnemius, biceps
18 Pectoral muscle	femoris and superficial digital
19 Radial carpal flexor muscle	flexor muscles attaching to calcaneus)
(flexor carpi radialis muscle)	

counterparts that produce opposite effects. Thus, in the leg of the horse there is a group of muscles that cause flexion of a joint (*flexor muscles*), and there is an opposing group that extend or straighten a joint (*extensor muscles*).

The contractive process is a chemical reaction within the muscle that produces heat in addition to performing work. The heat of contraction and recovery is important in body temperature regulation. In cold weather, *shivering* is a spasmatic muscle contraction that produces heat to help maintain body temperature. In hot weather, the heat of exertion must be dissipated by sweating and radiation.

Overexertion of a muscle without adequate conditioning can lead to muscle fatigue because of the depletion of muscle stores of glycogen and the accumulation of metabolic waste products (lactic acid). Paralytic myoglobinuria (Azoturia, Monday Morning disease, Blackwater) and the tying-up syndrome are complex metabolic disorders called exertional myopathics that affect the muscles of the horse. A careful conditioning program combined with a sound nutritional regime will prevent these muscle disorders. There are also myopathics that result from muscle disuse. Muscle atrophy can have a variety of causes but often denervation of the muscle tissue is a main cause. For example, trauma to the supra-scapular nerve can result in disuse and atrophy of several shoulder muscles, resulting in a *shoulder sweeney* (see Chapter 6).

5.4   Respiratory System

Oxygen is the element that is most vital to life. Without sufficient oxygen the horse will expire within minutes. The major function of the respiratory system is to supply oxygen to the tissues and to remove carbon dioxide. The respiratory system is also important in temperature regulation, elimination of water, and phonation. The respiratory system consists of a series of air passages that connect the lungs to the external air. The organs of respiration are the nasal cavity, pharynx, larynx, trachea, bronchi, and lungs.

The entrance to the *nasal cavity* is protected by the nostrils, which in the horse are vascular, soft, pliable, and capable of great dilation. The muzzle contains tactile hairs and is a sensitive organ of touch and prehension. The nasal cavity is lined with a mucous membrane capable of warming the inspired air. The *pharynx* is a common opening between the nasal passages and the mouth. The *larynx* guards the entrance of the trachea against the inspiration of foreign objects and regulates the flow of air. A cartilage trap called the *epiglottis* closes the air passage when food is swallowed. The larynx is also the chief voice organ and contains the vocal cords. Occasionally paralysis of the laryngeal muscles occurs, and the horse is unable to control the vocal cords on inspiration. The resulting sound is called roaring. The *trachea* is a long, noncollapsible tube that connects the throat to the lungs at the point where they branch to form the bronchi, which in turn further branch to form bronchioles. The *lungs* are paired and contain numerous air sacs where gaseous exchange occurs between the air and the pulmonary capillaries.

The movement of air in and out of the lungs (respiration) is achieved by the contraction and relaxation of the diaphragm and intercostal muscles. The rate of respiration is dependent on the tissues' need for oxygen. The nervous system has an elaborate system to control the respiration rate. Normally, at rest a horse breathes 8–16 times per minute. This rate increases tremendously during activity.

Bacterial infection of the lungs results in pneumonia. Pulmonary alveolar emphysema (more commonly termed "broken wind" or "heaves") is another respiratory problem of horses. This condition results from a breakdown of the elasticity of the air sacs, which reduces inspiratory volume. The pronounced breathing difficulties that result are aggravated by dusty or moldy feed.

5.5   Circulatory System

A homeostatic internal environment is maintained in the horse by the circulation of blood. Blood has been called the seat of the soul because it bathes the body's tissues with fluids necessary for the support of life. Some of the functions of blood are:

1. Transport of nutrients from the alimentary tract to tissues.
2. Removal of waste products of metabolism.
3. Transport of oxygen to the tissues.
4. Transport of endocrine secretions.
5. Equalization of water content.
6. Temperature regulation.
7. Regulation of acidity of body.
8. Defense against microorganisms.
9. Immunity to disease.
10. Allergenic reactions.

The circulatory system consists of the heart (the pump) and a system of vessels throughout the body. *Arteries* are thick-walled, muscular vessels that carry the blood away from the heart. These vessels branch, decrease in size, and proliferate to become *arterioles* (small arteries) and, finally, the *capillary bed.* The capillary bed is the tissue site of fluid and nutrient exchange. The *capillaries* unite to form small *veins,* and these veins combine to form the large veins that return the blood to the heart. The *pulmonary artery* carries the oxygen-poor blood from the heart to the lungs, and the enriched blood is returned to the heart via the *pulmonary veins.*

The lymphatic system is an adjunct to the circulatory system. The capillary blood pressure is sufficient to force nutrients and fluid into the tissues but not all the fluid returns via the venous system; the remainder is picked up through the thin-walled lymph vessels. This clear, colorless fluid (*lymph*) is propelled by gravity and muscle action through the system of lymph vessels or ducts until it is dumped into the venous system. A series of filters (*lymph nodes*) prevent tissue bacteria and foreign matter from re-entering the blood stream. *Leg edema* in stabled horses is often a result of an insufficiency of the muscular activity needed to "pump" excess tissue fluid back into the circulation. The edematous condition is called stocked up or filled in horses and usually disappears following mild exercise.

Edematous swellings also occur as a result of injury, infection, or other interference with lymphatic drainage. For example, swelling of the abdomen of the mare late in pregnancy is common but quickly subsides after foaling. Strangles is a bacterial infection of the lymph glands.

The *heart,* a large, massive, muscular organ in the horse, serves as a magnificent pump for the circulatory system. It is a 4-chambered double pump; the right side pumps into the pulmonary circulatory system and the left (larger) side sends the blood throughout the systemic circulation. The heart contracts rhythmically with an intrinsic heartbeat. However, there is a complex nervous control of the heart that can greatly alter the heart rate under varying physiological conditions. In the mature, normal, resting horse, the heart beats 36–40 times a minute. This rate is somewhat slower in draft (cold-blooded) horses and somewhat faster in Thoroughbred (hot-blooded) horses. The heart rate is influenced by a number of physiological factors, such as excitement, muscular exercise, environmental temperature, digestion, sleep, and a variety of pathological conditions. Table 5-1 indicates the influence of age on the heartbeat (pulse rate) of the horse.

5.6   Digestive System

The gastrointestinal tract is a musculo-membranous tube that extends from the mouth to the anus. In the horse, this mucous-membrane-lined tube is approximately 100 feet long and functions in ingestion, grinding, mixing, digestion, and absorption of food, and elimination of solid waste.

TABLE 5-1
Age and corresponding pulse rate of the horse

Age	Pulse Rate (beats per minute)
8–10 weeks	60–79
6 months	60–71
10–12 months	50–68
2 years	44–65
3 years	39–62
4 years	36–59
5 years	36–57

The digestive organs of the horse are the mouth, pharynx, esophagus, stomach, small intestine, cecum, large intestine, and anus (Figure 7-1). The digestive system is discussed more fully in section 7.1.

5.7 Urinary System

The urinary system consists of a pair of kidneys, the ureters, the bladder, and the urethra. The kidneys provide a blood-filtering system that is responsible for the excretion of many waste products from the body. The kidneys control water balance, pH, and the levels of many electrolytes. They cleanse the blood and are responsible for the stabilization of blood composition. The kidneys are located in the loin region of the horse, and many stiff and sore backs have been falsely attributed to kidney disease. In fact, the horse suffers very few diseases of the urinary system, and renal (kidney) diseases are extremely rare. Azoturia is a metabolic disease, severe cases of which can result in renal failure, but it is not primarily a kidney disease (see Chapter 18).

The kidney filtrate is urine. It is conveyed to the bladder by two muscular tubes, the ureters. The bladder is a flexible, distensible, muscular storage organ for urine. At the time of micturition or urination, the muscular walls of the bladder contract and urine is carried to the exterior by the urethra. The external organ of the urinary system is the penis in the stallion and gelding and the vulva in the mare.

5.8 Nervous System

The nervous system is an extensive control mechanism that can perceive and immediately react to changes in the external and internal environment of an animal. The nervous system also stores and associates sensations in the memory for future use. The equine nervous system is highly sophisticated, as evidenced by the outstanding coordination of motor activities.

The horse is unusually sensitive, and its acute tactile perception, coupled with an unusual learning ability, have enabled it to be domesticated and utilized by mankind. Its superb athletic ability is fortunately combined with a willingness and desire to please, but it is the sensitivity of the horse to touch and pressure, its low tolerance for pain, and its outstanding memory that make the horse the most tractable of the large domestic animals.

The functional divisions of the nervous system are the central nervous system, the peripheral nervous system, and the specialized sensory organs. The *central nervous system* consists of the brain, brain stem, and spinal cord. The brain is enclosed and protected by the cranial cavity, and it is not unusually large for an animal of its size. As a result the reasoning intelligence of the horse is somewhat limited, but the horse is amazingly trainable and possesses a remarkable memory. The central nervous system coordinates the activities of the peripheral nervous system, as it is the brain that processes, integrates, and stores sensory information. The lower brain (brain stem) subconsciously coordinates and controls many of the life processes (respiration, blood pressure, and so on).

The spinal cord connects the brain with the peripheral nerves, and at this level many of the simpler motor responses occur as "spinal reflexes" without directly involving the higher "conscious" levels of the nervous system. For example, the basic patterns of locomotion appear to occur as a spinal reflex and do not require conscious coordination on the part of the horse. The panniculus muscle of the horse underlies the skin and is capable of shaking off a fly that lands on the skin. This reflex action exemplifies the tactile sensitivity of the horse and the action of the nervous system below the conscious level.

The *peripheral nervous system* provides a network of communication between the internal or external environment and the central nervous system. The peripheral nervous system consists of the spinal and cranial nerves and their sensory or motor endings. Pain is an example of an internal stimulus. A horse is extremely sensitive to pain and appears to have a low tolerance for internal pain. As an example of an external stimulus, the horse has the ability to detect vibrations on the ground long before the cause can be seen or heard. This stimulus from the external environment is transmitted by the peripheral nervous system to the central nervous system. In this instance, there is no unconscious spinal reflex. Rather, the impulse is transmitted to the brain. The animal then becomes aware of approaching danger and makes the appropriate response.

The autonomic nervous system is the involuntary portion of the peripheral system that is associated with control of the glands, blood vessels, heart, sweating, body temperature, gastrointestinal motility, urinary output, and smooth muscle activity. The autonomic system provides involuntary control of body actions below the level of consciousness, particularly in time of stress.

The horse has survived throughout history because of its ability to perceive its environment and respond accordingly. Because the horse had to run away from danger rather than fight its enemies, survival was often based on its perception of sight, sound, or smell. The eyes, ears, and nose are *specialized sensory organs* of the nervous system that are little studied and often misunderstood in the equine.

The horse has a highly developed sense of hearing and is capable of detecting sounds unperceivable to man. There are apparently breed differences in hearing sensitivity; the light breeds are much more sensitive and responsive than the heavy breeds. The active ears of the horse are the most mobile of any of the domestic animals and greatly aid in the detection of sound. The ear movement does much to express the disposition and attentiveness of the animal. The rider is impressed by an alert horse that cocks one ear to listen for a command while the other ear remains forward and attentive to the surroundings. The sense of hearing in the horse has been the subject of little research despite the fact that it appears to be a more highly refined sense than vision. The flexibility of the neck and the mobility of the ears enable the horse to perceive sounds and locate their source with great precision. The horse often reacts to a sound before it sees its source.

The eyes of the horse are unique, but the horse's vision is probably much more limited than would be expected. The attentive expression of the horse, ears pricked forward as it examines some object, gives the impression that the horse possesses exceptional eyesight. In fact, the eyes of the horse are capable of discerning detail to a much lesser extent than the eyes of man, but the equine's unique combination of monocular and binocular vision provides a remarkably broad field of vision.

In man and most mammals, light rays enter the lens of the eye and are focused on the retina. The shape of the lens is altered by the ciliary muscle so that the eye can accommodate or focus on objects regardless of their distance. The horse may not be capable of focusing an image as sharply as can man. Instead of being uniformly round, the equine retina is irregularly concave. Until recently, the focal length was believed to vary depending on the angle at which light rays enter the eye, and accommodation by the equine lens was thought to be limited. Consequently, the horse would obtain a clear image by moving its head up or down to the optimal angle for the light rays from the object to strike the retina. This type of vision seems impractical, and it has been demonstrated that the ramp-shaped

197

retina cannot serve accommodation. The existence of an area centralis (area for acute resolution) also seems to contradict the ramped retina concept of accommodation in the horse. The optical advantage obtained by placing the image at a more appropriate distance from the lens would be negated by the fact that the image position would no longer coincide with an area of retinal organization necessary for good resolution. Some dynamic accommodative ability in the living eye has been observed.

The horse possesses binocular vision when both eyes are focused on an object in front; however, because of irregularities in the retina, the image often is not sharp and clear. The eyes of the horse cannot focus clearly closer than 4 feet, and most detail is apparently lost in the distance although movement is readily discerned. The extent to which a horse is capable of experiencing color vision has not been determined.

In addition to binocular vision, the horse possesses the ability to see separately from each eye at the same time. This enables the horse to have a large field of lateral and rear monocular vision. The field of monocular vision is limited only by the position of the eye on the head and of the animal's own body. Unquestionably, monocular vision is limited, but objects and movement are readily detected. When an object is spotted in the monocular field of view, the horse will turn its head, whenever possible, and "focus" on the object with both eyes. The change from monocular to binocular vision can cause a stationary object to "jump," and the horse may therefore unexplainably "spook" at some unexpected object.

Horses are not capable of focusing with binocular and monocular vision at the same time, and this is why it is important to have their attention when working around them. Most grooms and experienced horsemen talk to their horses constantly as they work around them because the ears of the horse are better suited to pinpointing location than are the eyes.

Little is known about a horse's sense of smell, but undoubtedly food is located as much by smell as by sight. The sense of smell is also highly developed; some horses develop panic at the smell of smoke or blood. The medicinal smell may arouse a horse's attention before the veterinarian or medicine is in sight. The horse often nuzzles and smells a person probably because its limited focal length makes visual recognition difficult. The uninitiated horseman sometimes mistakes this peculiar behavior for either viciousness or friendliness when in fact it is the horse's way of identifying an object at close range, particularly when there was no sound or the voice was unfamiliar.

The horse has always relied on its special senses for survival. An early warning system was important to a species that took flight from its enemies. Vibrations, movement, sound, and smell were the stimuli for action. The horse is a sensitive, powerful, athletic animal capable of magnificent reflexes. Because man has adopted the horse to his purposes, it behooves him to understand the unique nature of the equine nervous system.

5.9   Endocrine System

Whereas the nervous system provides immediate response to the environment, the endocrine system exercises long-range control over the body systems. The endocrine system is the name applied to a number of ductless glands of the body that produce chemical substances called *hormones,* which are transported by the circulatory system and can influence a variety of body functions. The endocrine system, in combination with the nervous system, is important in maintaining internal body stability or homeostasis.

Endocrinology is a sophisticated science whose detailed analysis is beyond the scope of this book. However, it should be recognized that the endocrine glands control such important functions as growth, reproduction, metabolism, and digestion. The endocrine tissues, the hormones secreted, and their major physiological actions are listed in Table 5-2.

5.10   Reproductive System

The male reproductive system consists of the testicles, the accessory glands and ducts, and the external genital organ (see Chapter 12). The female reproductive system consists of the ovaries, oviducts, uterus, vagina, and external genitalia (see Chapter 11).

The primary sex organs, the testicles and ovaries, produce the germinal or sex cells (ova and spermatozoa) as well as the sex hormones. The sex cells contain the genetic material that unites during fertilization to form a new individual. The mare's ovaries produce ova or eggs and the female sex hormones estrogen and progesterone. The testicles of the stallion produce spermatozoa as well as the male sex hormone testosterone. Because of the complexity and importance of the reproductive process, Chapters 11, 12, and 13 of this book are devoted specifically to that topic.

5.11   The Integument

The integument is the skin and hair that covers the horse's body and forms the boundary between the animal and its environment. The integument provides protection from mechanical, chemical, and physical agents. The skin is important in thermoregulation and in the sensation of heat, cold,

TABLE 5-2
Endocrine tissues in the horse: The hormones and their action

Endocrine Tissue	Hormone Secreted	Tissues Influenced	Action
Hypothalamus (brain)	Releasing factors	Anterior pituitary Posterior pituitary	Releases specific tropic hormones. Releases oxytocin, vasopression.
Pituitary Anterior	Growth hormone (GH)	All	Promotes increase in protein and fat in body. Promotes growth of muscle and bone.
	Thyrotropin (TSH)	Thyroid gland	Maintenance of the secretion of the thyroid gland.
	Adrenocorticotropin (ACTH)	Adrenal cortex	Maintenance of the secretion of the adrenal cortex.
	Follicle Stimulating Hormone (FSH)	Ovary	Stimulates follicle development.
	Luteinizing Hormone (LH)	Ovary	Ovulation and formation of corpus luteum.
	Luteotropin (LTH)	Ovary	Maintenance of corpus luteum; progesterone secretion.
		Mammary gland	Milk formation in alveoli.
Posterior	Oxytocin	Smooth muscle	Stimulates smooth muscle contraction in uterus and mammary gland.
	Vasopressin	Blood vessels	Vasoconstrictor; antidiuretic.

Gland	Hormone	Target	Function
Pancreas	Insulin	All	Controls sugar level in body.
Thyroid	Thyroxine	All	Controls metabolic rate.
Parathyroid	Parathyroid hormone	Kidney, bone	Maintains calcium and phosphorus levels.
Adrenal Glands			
Cortex	Corticoids	All	Controls salt, sugar, and water levels of body.
Medulla	Epinephrine	Skeletal muscle	Controls blood flow and strength of muscular contraction. Mobilizes energy stores.
Ovaries			
Follicle	Estrogens	Mammary gland Genital tract	Duct development. Estrus behavior. Prepares for fertilized ova.
Corpus luteum	Progesterone	Mammary gland Genital tract	Alveolar development. Diestrus. Maintains pregnancy.
Testes	Androgens	Sex organs Body	Sperm production, sex drive. Secondary male characteristics.
Uterus	Pregnant Mare's Serum Gonadotropin (PMSG)	Ovary, uterus	Complements other gonadotropin action.
	Prostaglandin ($PGF_{2\alpha}$)	All, corpus luteum	Numerous functions. Inhibits corpus luteum action.

pain, and touch. The mane, tail, and body hair provide effective protection against insects and play a prominent role in temperature regulation.

The skin of the horse is remarkably strong and highly sensitive. The skin consists of two layers, the *epidermis* or outer layer and the underlying *dermis*. The epidermis consists of stratified squamous eipthelium cells and is divided into a deep, growing layer and a hard, tough, cornified surface layer. The surface has no blood supply, and as a result these flat, dry cells are continuously being shed.

The hair and hooves of the horse grow directly from the epidermal layer, and the epidermis is modified to form hornlike growths on the inside of the legs (chestnuts) and at the back of the fetlock (ergots). The chestnuts are located on the front legs above the knees and on the rear legs below the hocks. The chestnut is a modification of only the epidermal layer and there is no evidence for the theory that they represent vestiges of missing digits from extinct species of horses.

The ergots are located at the back of the fetlocks, and their size differs between breeds. The ergot is hidden in the fetlock hair (feathers) and often goes undetected.

The *dermis* is the deep connective tissue portion of the skin that attaches to the panniculus carnosus, a sheet of skeletal muscle that separates the rest of the body tissues from the skin. The dermis contains arteries, veins, capillaries, lymph veins, sensory nerve endings and fibers, hair follicles, and sweat and sebaceous glands. It is the active portion of the skin that is vital for a healthy, pliable, elastic skin and rich, bright hair coat. The skin of the horse is highly sensitive because it contains many sensory endings. There are also sensory nerve connections in the hair follicles and on the tactile hairs of the muzzle.

The sweat glands are located over the entire body of the horse except the legs. The evaporation of sweat and the pilo-erection of the hair are the primary means of temperature regulation of the horse. A horse sweats more readily than any other farm animal. The sweat glands produce a salty, alkaline, watery fluid that is discharged directly on the skin surface and imparts a characteristic "horsey" odor. A horse sweats most readily at the base of the ears and on the neck, chest, and flanks. The evaporation of sweat from the body has a cooling effect on the surface of the body.

Hair covers most of the skin area except underneath the tail, around the genitals, and on the inside of the thighs. The fibrous and bulky nature of the hair provides excellent protection against cuts and abrasions and is an effective insulator against the elements. In the dermis there are bundles of smooth muscle fibers called *errectores pilorum* that attach to the hair follicle and the surface of the skin in such a manner that their contraction causes an erection of the hair. The pilo-erection of the hair increases the insulating effect by reducing air convection currents across the skin as well as heat loss in cold weather.

There are two types of body hair, the dense undercoat and the less prevalent long "guard" hairs. The mane, tail, eyelashes, and tactile hair of the muzzle are permanent but the general body hair is shed twice a year, in the spring and fall. Hair color is due to pigmented *melanin* granules. The variation in the hair color of different horses is due to differences in the amounts and location of the melanin granules. These color differences are under genetic control (The inheritance of coat color is explained in Chapter 15). The skin is pigmented in all coat colors except under some white markings or spots.

The sebaceous glands are located in the same places as the hair follicles and open directly on the surface of the skin. They produce *sebum*, an oily, waxy secretion that coats the hair, protects it from overwetting, and increases its insulating ability. The sebum adds sleekness and luster to a horse's coat; vigorous brushing and rubbing can increase secretion and make the coat "bloom."

References

Bone, J. F., ed. 1963. *Equine Medicine and Surgery*. 1st ed. Wheaton, Illinois: American Veterinary Publications.

Catcott, E. J., and J. F. Smithcors, eds. 1972. *Equine Medicine and Surgery*. 2d ed. Wheaton, Illinois: American Veterinary Publications.

Cavalry School. 1935. Horsemanship and horsemastership. *Animal Management*. Vol. 2, Part 3. Fort Riley, Kansas.

Dukes, H. H. 1955. *The Physiology of Domestic Animals*. Ithaca, New York: Cornell University Press.

Edwards, Gladys Brown. 1973. *Anatomy and Conformation of the Horse*. Croton-on-Hudson, New York: Dreenan Press.

Frandson, R. D. 1965. *Anatomy and Physiology of Farm Animals*. Philadelphia: Lea and Febiger.

Kays, D. J. 1969. *The Horse*. Rev. ed. New York: A. S. Barnes.

Rossdale, Peter D. 1972. *The Horse*. Arcadia, California: California Thoroughbred Breeders Association.

Sivak, J. G., and D. B. Allen. 1975. An evaluation of the "ramp" retina of the horse eye. *Vision Research* 15:1353–1356.

Swenson, Melvin J. 1970. *Duke's Physiology of Domestic Animals*. 8th ed. Ithaca, New York: Cornell University Press.

Way, Robert F., and Donald G. Lee. 1965. *The Anatomy of the Horse*. Philadelphia: Lippincott.

CHAPTER SIX *Selection of the Horse*

The purpose for which a horse is to be used is the single most important consideration in selecting a horse. The use dictates the breed, training, soundness, disposition, and conformation. Selecting a potential racehorse at one of the yearling sales is an entirely different process from selecting the first horse for a youngster. Selection is a process of analyzing and evaluating—balancing the good against the bad—for the purpose intended. Because horses are used for such a variety of purposes, there are few universal rules for judging horses, but some general considerations should be borne in mind, regardless of the intended use of the horse.

6.1 General Considerations

General Appearance

The general appearance of a horse is less important to many horsemen than its training or athletic potential, but all appreciate a horse that is balanced and possesses symmetry. The length of the legs should be in relation to the height and length of the body. The head, neck, and body should be in proportion to each other. All saddle horses should be agile, athletic, and tractable. Beauty in conformation of the horse should reflect those traits which enable a horse to give years of service.

A horse should be attractive in appearance. The majority of horses in this country are kept for pleasure. Since the reason for having a pleasure horse is personal enjoyment, the owner should be satisfied with his investment. Consequently the color, age, sex, and breed are matters of individual preference that should be considered with the intended use.

Temperament

The disposition of a horse is of paramount importance. A common mistake made in selecting one's first horse is placing insufficient emphasis on temperament. Experience is required to determine whether a horse is too spirited or too phlegmatic for the purpose intended. A horse is a product of its environment, and abuse or incompetence in handling the horse can result in undesirable and dangerous behavior. A spoiled horse can create problems in its handling, whether the horse be a pleasure, race, or performance animal, but fortunately most horses are readily receptive to training and handling and possess a tremendous desire to please. A few horses are mentally deficient; a very few are vicious.

The temperament is expressed by the eyes and ears of the horse and implemented by the feet and teeth. With experience, one can recognize a horse's mood by observing the horse's ears. A "mean" or "sour" horse is unpredictable and is a potential danger that should not be tolerated. A mean horse is equally dangerous at both ends. A horse can inflict as much damage by biting or striking out with the front feet as it can from a kick.

Training

When selecting a horse, the extent of its training must be considered. The less experience one has with a horse the better trained the horse should be. No beginner should undertake the training of a young horse. On the other hand, most experienced horsemen prefer an untrained horse. The disposition, athletic ability, and mental capacity of a horse are reflected in its training.

Breed Type

There is no "best" breed of horse; some are better suited for one purpose than another and there is considerable variation in type and ability within all breeds. A breed is a group of horses possessing distinctive characteristics not common to other horses. These characteristics determine "breed type" if they are sufficiently well fixed to be uniformly transmitted. Breed type is an important consideration for the purebred market breeder. The selection of a breed should be determined by the intended use of the horse. The various breeds of horses are discussed in detail in Chapter 2.

Pedigree and Performance Records

Purebred horses are often selected and priced on the basis of their pedigree. The individual conformation or ability should be important criteria in selecting a horse, but the pedigree can be a useful tool, particularly when a horse is selected at an early age or is being considered as a breeding animal. The best test of a breeding animal is the type of offspring it produces, but because this information is often unavailable before purchase or selection, the pedigree is the next best guide for making an enlightened choice. The quality and reputation of the ancestors in the pedigree can both greatly enhance the value of an animal and detract from it. Pedigree "fads" develop in all breeds from time to time when a particular strain gains temporary popularity, usually based on the performance of the offspring of that breeding. Good breeders develop their own ideals and stick to them regardless of temporary changes in the popularity of particular strains.

Performance records on horses can be of particular usefulness in the selection of horses for some specific purposes. Racing records are the classic example when value is placed on racing ability or potential and the actual racing records of the sire or dam can be the definitive factor in selection. Performance records of traits other than speed can also be useful. Records of show ring performance, cutting horse ability, and cow sense are examples of records that are often considered by horse breeders. Produce records of broodmares are valuable in selecting animals for the breeding herd. Unfortunately, performance testing is seldom used with horses, but it is hoped that performance records will become more available and useful in the future. Use of records of relatives in selection is considered in section 17.3.

Selection of a horse is a series of enlightened compromises based on all the information that is available. Pedigree, performance, and produce records provide valuable information for consideration when selecting a horse.

Quality

Quality refers to refinement of hair, hide, bones, and joints. Refinement of hair is evidenced by a fine, silky mane and tail. The hair coat should be fine and should have a "bloom" or luster. The chin, throat, ears, and legs should be free of excess hair, which indicates coarseness. Refinement of hide is exemplified by a thin, pliable hide that clearly defines the blood vessels underneath. A thin, pliable hide assures rapid cooling and quick return of the body to its normal state.

There is no reliable measure of bone texture in the live animal. However, since there is no muscling below the knees and hocks of the horse, the lower legs are used to estimate bone quality. The cannons should be strong, flat, and clean, with good definition of the tendons. Coarseness is expressed by meatiness and roundness of the cannons and pasterns. The joints of the leg should be well defined, clean-cut, lean, and free from swellings and other unnatural development.

206

Size

Generally, the size of a horse is expressed in height at the withers. The measurement is expressed in hands. (A hand represents 4 inches.) Fractions of a hand are expressed in inches.

The size of the horse should be adequate for the desired purpose and should be appropriate to the task. A rule of thumb is that other things being equal, size is an asset.

6.2 Basic Conformation

The horse is an athlete and its conformation determines its ability to perform. When all the horse's parts are so constructed and proportioned one to another that it is perfectly adapted to its work, then it has good conformation (Figure 6-1). Type is a personal preference, but certain conformation characteristics are common to all types. Thus the following description of desirable conformation applies to all horses regardless of breed.

Head and Neck

The head and neck play an important role in determining the athletic ability of the horse. A supple horse uses his head and neck as a rudder and a stabilizer. Freedom of motion in the head and neck has a profound influence on the horse's way of going. For a horse to be well balanced, the neck should be long and lean with the head in proportion.

Head. The head of the horse should follow the type of the breed. It is usually the first part of the horse to be seen and should be attractive, refined, and in proportion to the size of the body. It should be finely chiseled with good definition of the bony framework. The skin should be thin and the underlying blood vessels clearly defined. The mane should be fine and silky and the chin and jaw should be free from excess long, coarse hair. Such a head gives an appearance of intelligence and refinement and is much more acceptable than a heavy, dull, plain head. The head is important because it is the sensory center for the horse and its structure indicates much about disposition and intelligence. The head should be triangular as viewed from the side; it should have large, powerful jaws and adequate brain capacity; and it should taper to large nostrils capable of great dilation. The profile of the face varies considerably, but a straight or slightly dished face is generally preferred to an arched face or Roman

207

FIGURE 6-1

General conformation and points of the horse.

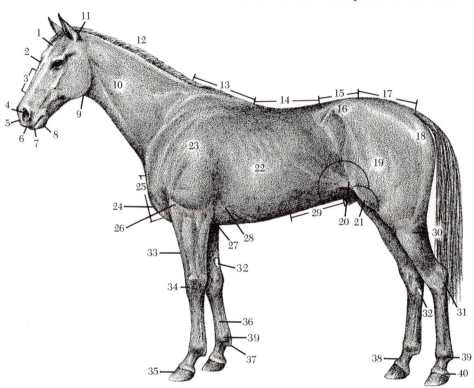

1	Forehead	11	Poll	21	Stifle	31	Hock
2	Face	12	Crest	22	Barrel	32	Chestnut
3	Bridge of nose	13	Withers	23	Shoulder	33	Forearm
4	Nostril	14	Back	24	Point of shoulder	34	Knee
5	Muzzle	15	Loin	25	Chest	35	Hoof
6	Upper lip	16	Point of hip	26	Arm	36	Cannon
7	Lower lip	17	Croup	27	Elbow	37	Ergot
8	Under lip	18	Buttock	28	Girth	38	Pastern
9	Throat latch	19	Thigh	29	Abdomen	39	Fetlock
10	Neck	20	Flank	30	Gaskin	40	Coronet

nose. As viewed from the front, there should be width of forehead between the eyes, and they should be placed between the poll and nostrils in such a position to make the head proportionate. Long, narrow heads indicate plainness and are undesirable.

The size of the head varies among breeds, but it should be in proportion with the rest of the body. A long, large head or a short, small head can be unbalanced with the rest of the body and give the undesirable impression of draftiness or poniness in the riding horse. Disproportionate heads are often accompanied by plainness in the other features of the head.

The eyes should be alert, brilliant, friendly, and widely spaced. They should be prominent without giving the bulging or "Popeyed" appearance called *bovine eyes.* Similarly, they should be large and clear with a deep hazel color. Small *pig eyes* placed close together on the head limit the field of vision, are unattractive, and give an expression of laziness and stubbornness.

Blindness is a serious unsoundness that renders the horse unsafe and reduces its market value. Any cloudiness or milkiness in the eye may indicate a sight problem and should be avoided, as should a partially closed eye or one that is secreting excessively. The eyes of most horses are dark, but occasionally blue eyes are seen, and are often associated with white spots as in the Pinto. Blue eyes have been traditionally discriminated against, but there is no evidence to support the theory that they are in any way inferior or weaker. The deep coloration of the eye is usually all that is visible, but there is a white sclera that encircles the eye. Sometimes this white ring is visible in a horse and gives it a wild-eyed appearance that is undesirable in some breeds. On the other hand, the Appaloosa has mottled skin around the eye, and the visible white sclera is considered a breed characteristic.

The ears should be light, slender, alert, and delicately formed. Their position or set on the head can have as profound an effect on the appearance of the horse as can their size and shape. The ears of mares are often a little larger and not so pricked as those of stallions. Long, thick, and heavy ears (mule ears) and ears carried horizontally to the side (lop ears) are undesirable and coarse. An alert, pricked, active ear indicates alertness, whereas an inactive, droopy ear reflects dullness. An overactive ear may suggest a nervous disposition or difficulty in perceiving sight or sound.

The horse must have adequate exchange of air for breathing during exertion. The nostrils should be large but thin and delicate and capable of great dilation. A large nostril is indicative of capacity in other parts of the respiratory system. The nostrils will flare after exercise but should return quickly to normal following rest. Respiratory infections are one of the most common ailments of horses and can be diagnosed by raspy or labored breathing and colored or thickened discharge from the nostrils. The normal discharge is colorless, odorless, and slight.

The mouth of the horse should be such that the incisor teeth and the lips meet evenly. The lips should be pliable yet quite muscular and capable of prehension. They aid the horse in collecting food and moving it into the mouth. If the lower jaw of the horse recedes so that the upper incisors are prominent and "buck-toothed," the horse is said to be parrot-mouthed. The opposite condition, in which the lower jaw protrudes in front of the upper jaw, is known as the undershot jaw or the monkey mouth condition. Both conditions can interfere with eating, particularly grazing, and since they may be inherited traits, they are seriously discriminated against in the show ring and breeding herd. The dental pattern and characteristics of the horse's teeth are discussed in Chapter 5.

209

Neck. The head should attach to the neck in such a manner as to provide ample movement and flexion without impairment of the air passages. Therefore, a clean, trim, well-defined throat latch capable of great flexion is desired. A short, thick neck is often correlated with a thick, unyielding throat latch. There should be adequate width between the lower jaws to provide ample space for the windpipe. The head should attach to the end of the neck and not appear to be imbedded into it. The attachment of the head to the neck has a direct relationship to beauty and usefulness.

The neck of all saddle horses should be long, imparting the appearance of elegance and grace. It should also be functionally flexible to enhance balance and length of stride. The neck should be slender, clean in the throat, and swan-shaped at the poll.

The neck of the saddle horse should be supple and mobile for the best performance. These characteristics are associated with adequate length, whereas short, thick necks are often associated with lack of suppleness, balance, and mobility. In some breeds, a slight arch or crest on the top of the neck is pleasing and desirable, but an excessive crest, thick upper neck, or *broken crest* (lop neck) are undesirable because they can interfere with flexibility. The stallion should naturally carry more crest than the mare. A thick, "studdy" neck in the mare is usually associated with a lack of femininity. The underline of the neck should be straight and come high out of the shoulder region. A concave neck accompanied by a depression in front of the withers and often a thickened, rounded underline is termed *ewe neck*. Such necks usually result in high-headed horses that have minimal flexion at the poll and are therefore limited athletically. The ewe-necked condition is awkward and unsightly.

Forequarters

The forequarters provide propulsion in front, serve as a base of support, and contain shock-absorbing mechanisms that alleviate the concussion of motion. The majority of the weight (60–65 percent) is carried on the front legs, and consequently most unsoundnesses from concussion and trauma occur in the front legs of riding horses. The length of the stride, smoothness of gait, soundness of legs, and power of propulsion are dependent upon the architecture of the forequarters.

The two most critical aspects of ideal conformation of the forelimbs are the slope and angles of the bones, to ensure absorption of concussion, and the straightness and trueness of the limbs, so that no one segment receives unusual or abusive wear. Concussion in the forequarters is absorbed by the unique muscular attachment of the forelimb to the body; the sloping shoulder and consequently the angle formed between the scapula and humerus; the angle formed between the humerus and forearm; the small bones and surrounding bursa of the carpus; the sloping, springly pastern; and the expansion and absorption mechanism of the hoof.

Shoulder. The shoulder of the horse should be long, sloping, and muscular, and should extend well into the back. The scapula or shoulder blade is the primary point of attachment of the forelimbs to the rest of the body. The longer the shoulder the greater the area for attachment of the many muscles that tie the forelimb to the vertebral column with a muscular sling that supports the animal's weight, providing an excellent shock-absorbing mechanism. The shoulder should slope well into the back. This decreases the angle between the scapula and humerus, and therefore reduces concussion. A sloping shoulder also provides for free forward motion of the limb by allowing the humerus to move forward and the forearm to extend, thereby allowing maximum length of stride. Short, straight shoulders reduce stride and increase impact so that a horse strikes the ground harder. A straight shoulder is often associated with a short, straight pastern that further shortens the stride and increases concussion.

Arm. The humerus or arm should be of moderate length and well muscled. The arm extends from the point of the shoulder, its articulation with the scapula, to the elbow joint, its junction with the forearm. Since the scapula and the humerus are not outwardly distinguishable one from the other, the arm is often overlooked as a part of the shoulder. However, the importance of the humerus in the antishock mechanism has already been discussed. In addition, the length of the humerus is integral to the length of stride. An excessively short arm, with its accompanying short muscles, will not advance the forearm sufficiently and the stride will be shortened. On the other hand, a long arm causes excessive wear to the shoulder muscles and the stride is likewise diminished. The important point is that the length of the arm is relative to the length of the shoulder and forearm. Kays (1969), in his outstanding discussion of the relation of form to function, concludes that "a long shoulder, a short arm, plus a long forearm makes possible maximum extension of stride and speed." The length of the arm determines whether the legs are set forward or back under the body. The legs should be set well forward.

The plane of the arm is important in determining the set of the feet on the ground. The arm should be in a parallel plane with the spinal column. If the elbow is set in too close to the body, the feet will toe out. The elbow should be clear of the body, but if it is inclined outward too much, the horse will toe in and will stand pigeon-toed.

Foreleg. Length of leg in the horse is supplied primarily by the forearm and cannon regions. The forelegs should be straight and perpendicular when viewed from all directions. The forearm is formed by the fusion of two bones, the radius and the ulna, and extends from the elbow to the knee. It should be long and well muscled. The length of the forearm in large part determines the length of stride. The cannon, on the other hand, should be short and flat as viewed from the side, and should have tight, fluted,

211

well-defined tendons set well back to give the appearance of abundant support below the knees. When viewed from the front, the cannon should be centered in a straight, wide, clean knee. Round-appearing cannons and tendons tied in behind the knee are undesirable as they indicate small tendons and lack of support.

The knee is a vital junction between the forearm and the cannon because it must be capable of bearing weight and supporting the body. Some racehorse trainers consider the knees one of the most critical areas of all. The knee should be straight from both front and side views—thick, wide, deep, and squarely placed on the leg. A horse that is sprung forward in its knees is termed *buck-kneed*, but this is a much less serious fault than being *calf-kneed*, or back at the knees. A calf-kneed horse is considered weak because tremendous additional strain is placed on the tendons, ligaments, and bones. Such a horse is a prime candidate for unsoundness when heavy work is required. The knee should also be straight as viewed from the front. A break inward or *knock-kneed* condition and an outward *bow-legged* condition are both considered defects. Sometimes the cannon is not centered in the knee as viewed from the front; this offset knee or *bench knee* is considered a congenital weakness. Such a condition places additional stress on the medial splint bones and predisposes the development of front leg splints. William Haughton (1968), the famous harness horse driver, tests the knee by picking up the foot and folding the leg back until the foot touches the elbow. "If they don't fold up, if they're tight and can't get up to the elbow, then trouble is quite apt to develop. If you can't make the fold, it means the knee isn't functioning properly, its conformation is preventing it from folding completely."

Foot. The fetlock joint, located as it is between the cannon and pastern bones, connects the leg with the foot. The fetlock should be set well back on pasterns of medium length that are strong and sloping. The fetlock and pastern together provide springiness to the gait and also disperse concussion. Roughened hair, nicks, and scars on the fetlock are evidence that a horse may interfere (hit part of one leg with another leg) when in motion, and the joint should be examined carefully to see that it is strong, clean, and free from stiffness. Both the slope and length of the pastern are important. They help to determine the smoothness, spring, and strength of stride. The pastern, with its 2 bones, 3 articulating surfaces, and suspensory ligament sling, is capable of tremendous flexion and shock absorption. Too long and sloping a pastern (coon foot) causes weakness because it puts undue strain on the tendons, sesamoid bones, and suspensory ligament. On the other hand, a short, upright pastern increases concussion and trauma to foot and fetlock; lameness and unsoundnesses can result.

The old adage "no foot, no horse" has basis in fact because no matter how fine the conformation of the horse, if the feet will not support it, the animal is worthless. Horses vary greatly in size, shape, and strength of feet, and many farriers feel that horse breeders pay too little attention to foot structure.

The foot should be sized in proportion to the horse. It should be more rounded in front than behind, and wide and deep at the heel. The hooves should be clean, straight, and free from rings and cracks. The angle of the foot should be the same as the angle of the pastern. The specific anatomy and care of the foot are discussed in Chapters 5 and 22, but it should be recognized that the foot itself serves as a shock absorber by yielding at the sole and the pedal joint and expanding and cushioning at the frog and the plantar cushion upon impact.

The set of the forelegs is important for the normal functioning of the limbs. The legs should be square under the corners in parallel planes. When viewed from the front, the legs should be straight; the feet should be flat on the ground and should point directly ahead. A line dropped from the point of the shoulder should bisect the forearm, knee, cannon, fetlock, pastern, and foot equally. When viewed from the side, the forearm, knee, and cannon should be in straight line with the shoulder, the pastern, and the slope of the foot.

Defects in the set of the legs take many forms. The feet may be base wide or base narrow, they may toe-in or toe-out, or they may be a combination of these conditions. Figure 6-2 illustrates the types of conformational defects that can be observed from the front, rear, and side.

When the horse is in motion, these conformational faults are usually manifest in faulty flight of the foot, which places undue strain on various parts of the limb. A toed-in condition usually accompanies the base narrow condition; the foot has a tendency to "paddle" to the outside when in motion. The toed-out condition is the more serious, particularly when accompanied by a narrow chest or a base narrow condition, because the foot "wings" in and has a greater chance of striking the supporting leg.

The ideal horse stands square and has legs that are straight and feet that in flight move true with no deviation from a straight line.

Body

The body contains the vital organs (heart, lungs, digestive tract), supports the rider's weight, and transmits the propulsion of the rear quarters. The body should be deep, short, and have well-sprung ribs.

Withers. The withers are the high point of the horse's back, located at the base of the neck, between the shoulder blades. The height of a horse is

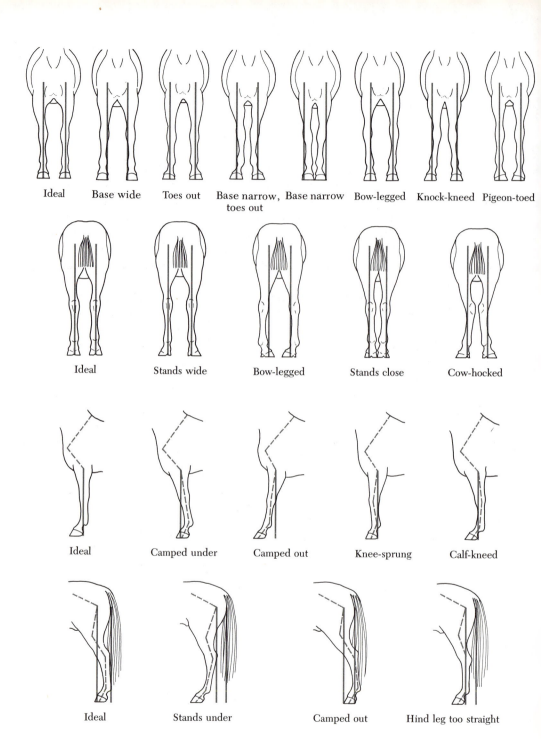

FIGURE 6-2
Conformation defects in the front and rear legs as viewed from the front, rear, and side. From *4-H Horse Judging Guide,* Cooperative Extension, Cornell University, Ithaca, New York.

measured at the withers because this distance is the tallest constant part of the horse. The withers should be prominent and capable of holding a saddle. They should be muscular and well defined at the top, and should extend well into the back. Horses with low, round, thick withers often have rolling gaits and heavy front ends, and move poorly. These flat, mutton withers are particularly objectionable in a riding horse because the saddle does not stay in place and the horse may be predisposed to forge. When the withers are prominent, the ligaments and muscles that attach the neck to the thorax are much freer to move, and the horse exhibits greater flexibility, coordination, and energy in its movement. High, sloping withers are usually associated with long, sloping shoulders, and the increased length of the muscles in the front end result in a lighter, freer action. It should be emphasized that prominent withers should be accompanied by muscling because thin, overprominent withers are often rubbed by the saddle and result in stiffness and soreness.

Thorax. The thorax is bounded by the back on the top, the ribs on the side, and the sternum at the base. When viewed from the front, the chest should be wide and deep. A narrow chest indicates lack of muscling and vital capacity. An excessively wide chest forces the legs out so that the gait may be rolling and labored. The thorax, when viewed from the side, should be deep and strong in the heartgirth. This region contains the vital lungs and heart and must be well developed for optimal performance. The chest should be deep, with long and well-sprung ribs that project far backward. The rib cage provides a base of attachment for the muscles of the forelimb as well as protection for the vital organs. When the ribs are well arched and project backward, it is possible for the horse to have a long, deep chest and still have a short, straight, strong back. Short, flat, straight ribs decrease the vital capacity of the horse and correspondingly reduce its athletic potential.

The back carries the weight of the rider and must be short, straight, strong, and muscular. The back extends from the withers to the last rib or loin region. A concave or sagging back is termed *swayback* and is undesirable because it denotes weakness. Many long-backed horses become "easy in their topline" (swaybacked) with age. A convex, or *roach back*, is also undesirable because it lacks flexibility of movement, results in leg interference and shortness of stride, and is uncomfortable, inefficient, and unsightly. The loin, which connects the thorax with the powerful propulsion muscles of the hind limbs, is sometimes called the *coupling*. It transmits power to the forequarters and therefore must be short, wide, strong, and heavily muscled. A horse weak in its coupling and shallow in and flank may be termed *hound gutted* or wasp-waisted. Such horses lack drive in the hindquarters and make undesirable mounts. A fit horse is often acceptably tight in its middle and cut up in its flank because of its outstanding condition. On the other hand, shallow-bodied horses are undesirable, and depth of flank and strength of loin are the desired norm.

215

Hindquarters

The main role of the hindquarters is to provide the force for propulsion, and everything about their structure should reflect speed, power, endurance, and athletic ability. They should be long and well muscled; the legs should move in parallel planes and the hocks should be clean and well placed to allow maximum efficiency of forward motion. The hips should be smooth, should be level when viewed from behind, and should extend well forward. Uneven or knocked-down hips often result in lameness with work. The hips should show definition, but excessive prominence is undesirable because it indicates lack of condition, strength, and endurance. The croup or rump should be long, uniform in width, muscular, and evenly turned over the top. The length and width of the croup are important conformational considerations because long muscles are associated with speed and endurance, and width of muscling is related to strength and power. The length of the croup is measured from the hip to the buttocks; the slope is the inclination of this line to horizontal. The desired slope of the croup is determined by breed preferences and intended use. Long-distance runners should have long, level croups, whereas horses that run short distances and are mobile do well with slightly sloping croups. In either case, the extremes should be avoided, and the intermediate long, muscular, rounding yet fairly level croup is preferred. The short, steep croup is faulted because it is often associated with sickle hocks and places undue strain on the hind legs. A croup that slopes and tapers from the hips to the buttocks is *goose-rumped.* A deeply creased croup is preferred because it indicates a well-muscled horse.

Hind Leg. The hind leg propels the horse forward and should have long, heavy muscling through the thigh, stifle, and gaskin. The muscles of the thigh are the most massive and powerful in the horse's body. The femur (thigh bone) should be relatively short and should be inclined forward, downward, and slightly outward. The location of the femur should be such that the legs are set well under the horse with the stifle slightly outward so that there will be a full range of movement for the hind leg. If the femur is carried too far backward, the legs are carried too far to the rear; if it is carried too far forward, the legs are brought too much under the body. The outward inclination of this region is necessary so that the stifle can move freely without striking the belly; at the same time, this outward inclination directs the hocks inward under the body where they can work closely together. The stifle should be muscled to the point of being the widest point in the hindquarter. The gaskin (tibia) should be long and well muscled. A long gaskin increases the length from the hip to the hock, a distance long associated with speed and desirability in form. A long gaskin

216

ensures a maximum range of action and provides a maximum area for attachment of the drive muscles of the hindquarters. A short gaskin decreases the length of stride and is therefore undesirable. The gaskin should have well-defined muscling; it should be broad, wide, and deep toward the hock.

The hock joint is the hardest-working joint in the horse's body. It is the pivot of action that propels the horse forward simultaneously with the contraction of the powerful hindquarter muscles. The hock should be clean, well defined, deep, strong, wide, and flat across, and not rough, puffy, rounded, or fleshy. The lower hock should attach strongly to a short cannon with flat, well-defined tendons that are set well back to give the hock strong support.

The set or angle of the hock when viewed from the side should be neither too straight nor too acute (see Figure 6-2). The line connecting the back hock and fetlock should be straight and vertical. A horse's hocks are crooked when there is excessive angulation. Such a horse is said to be set in its hocks or *sickle-hocked,* the most common conformational fault of the hind limbs when viewed from the side. The stride of a horse set in its hocks is reduced and the horse will often stand too far under, placing extensive strain on the plantar ligament at the rear of the hock. If this area becomes inflamed, a curb may result, and therefore sickle hocks are termed "curby" conformation. A hock that is too straight receives excessive concussion and trauma.

When hocks are viewed from the rear, they should be set relatively close together under the horse with the cannons parallel. If the points of the hock turn inward, the horse is *cow-hocked;* if the horse is also base wide, it is likely to interfere behind. If the points of the hock turn outward, the horse is said to be *open in its hocks* and predisposed to a rotating action behind that puts great strain on the rear leg. A horse should "use its hocks" or "work off its hocks" when in motion, and this is best accomplished when the hocks move in parallel planes with the cannons and fetlocks with no deviation from a straight line.

The fetlock, pastern, and foot of the hind limb are similar in structure to those of the front limb. The fetlocks should be strong and clean. The pasterns should be strong, well defined, and of medium length. The rear pastern may be shorter and less sloping than the front pastern.

The set of the hind legs when viewed from the side should be such that a plumb line dropped from the point of the buttocks touches or almost touches the rear border of the hock, runs parallel to the cannon, and strikes the ground 3–4 inches behind the heel. When the hind legs are viewed from the rear, a line dropped from the point of the buttocks should fall upon the center of the hock, cannon, pastern, and heel. The toes may turn out slightly so long as the cannons remain parallel.

6.3 Unsoundnesses and Blemishes

The horse is an athlete, and anything that interferes with its performance reduces its value. Desirable conformation has little value unless the horse is able to perform. Consequently, it is important to be able to recognize and evaluate the common defects that occur in horses. There is no universal classification of defects as unsoundnesses and blemishes. A splint, for example, can be considered either an unsoundness or a blemish depending on its location and whether it is accompanied by lameness. Determination of the seriousness of a defect requires experience and judgment. Unsoundnesses that are a result of faulty conformation are the most serious because they will continue to recur and may be inherited. Very few horses are completely sound, and most examining veterinarians prefer to use the phrase "serviceably sound for the use intended."

Unsoundnesses are defects in form or function that interfere with the usefulness of the horse. They include defects in conformation, feet, legs, eyes, wind, health, and reproductive functions. They may be congenital or acquired. Horses with congenital unsoundnesses should not be used for breeding. Soundness is sometimes classified as working soundness or breeding soundness since a horse can be used for one purpose even if it is unsound for another. A blemish is an acquired physical defect that does not interfere with the usefulness of the horse but may diminish its value. Some unsoundnesses and blemishes are illustrated in Figures 6-3 and 6-4.

Blemishes and Unsoundnesses of the Forelimb

The forelimbs support the major part of the horse's weight and consequently receive the majority of those injuries that result from concussion and trauma. Most of the forelimb unsoundnesses occur below the knee, and many are accompanied by inflammation of joints and bones. Inflammations that affect the bones and articulation of joints (arthritis) can be generally classified as more serious than injuries to soft tissues such as muscles, tendons, or ligaments.

Splints. A splint is a calcification or bony growth, usually occurring on the inside of the cannon or splint bone area (medial and small metacarpal bones) of the front leg. A splint is usually the result of a tear of the interosseous ligament that binds the splint bones to the cannon, but it can result from any inflammation of the periosteum (periostitis). Splints are a result of trauma but can also have many other causes, such as slipping, running and jumping, or getting kicked or receiving a concussion from hard surfaces. Occasionally a fracture of the splint bones is possible. A developing splint (green splint) can cause pain and lameness, but once a bony callus

218

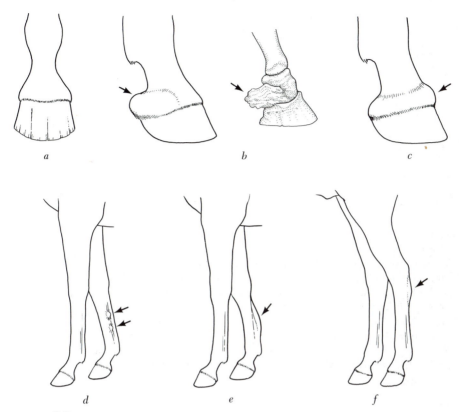

FIGURE 6-3

Some unsoundnesses and blemishes of the foot, pastern, and cannon. *a: Toe crack*, a split in the front part of the hoof wall—may be partial, complete, high, or low; *quarter crack*, a split in the quarter area of the hoof wall that runs toward the heel; and *seedy toe*, a separation of the wall of the hoof near the toe. *b: Side bones*, ossification of the lateral cartilages resulting from injuries that cause calcium to accumulate and harden. *c: Ringbone*, a bony enlargement surrounding the bones of the pastern. *d: Splint*, a bony enlargement in the groove formed by the splint and cannon bone—may be high or low, forward, or back. *e: Bowed tendon*, an extension backward of the flexor tendons, caused by tearing or stretching. *f: Curb*, an enlargement of the ligament, tendon sheath, or skin below the point of the hock. From *4-H Horse Judging Guide*, Cooperative Extension, Cornell University, Ithaca, New York.

is formed the splint rarely causes trouble unless the exostosis encroaches on the flexor tendons, suspensory ligament, or carpal joint. In the majority of cases a splint will "set" with rest, and the inflammation resolves itself naturally to a bony blemish. If lameness persists, a more rigorous treatment, such as blistering or surgery, is possible, and is successful approximately half the time. Splints usually occur on the inside of the leg because this

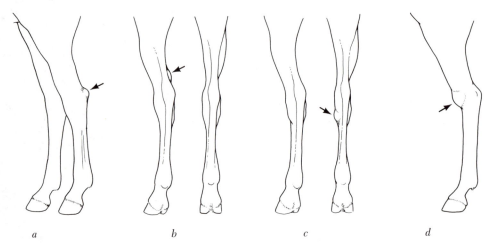

a   b   c   d

FIGURE 6-4

Some unsoundnesses of the hock area. *a: Capped hock*, an enlargement on the point of the hock, usually caused by bruising. *b: Thoroughpin*, a puffy condition in the hollows of the hock that can be identified by movement of the puff, when pressed, to the opposite side of the leg. *c: Bog spavin*, any inflammation or swelling of the soft tissues of the hock. *d: Bone spavin* or *Jack spavin*, a bony enlargement that appears on the inside and front of the hock at the point where the base of the hock tapers into the cannon bone. From *4-H Horse Judging Guide*, Cooperative Extension, Cornell University, Ithaca, New York.

area receives the greatest weight. Poor nutrition or faulty conformation, such as over at the knees or bench knees, can be predisposing causes. Occasionally splints occur on the outside of the cannon or on the hind legs. The splint is one of the most common defects of the front limbs and usually occurs in young horses, almost always before 6 years of age.

Sore or Bucked Shins. A bucked shin is an enlargement on the front of the cannon between the knee and the fetlock joints. This enlargement, which usually occurs in the front limb, is due to trauma to the periosteum that is most often caused by concussion. The condition may be confined to soreness, but if periostitis occurs, new bone growth (exostosis) can result in a "bucked" appearance of the shin. This condition often occurs in young horses in rigorous training. Bucked shins can result in lameness that can be corrected by rest and treatment.

Bowed Tendons or Tendonitis. A bowed tendon is an inflammation and enlargement of the flexor tendons at the back of the front cannon. The general cause of bowed tendons is severe strain. In some instances the condition also results from actual rupture of the tendon caused by stress from galloping, jumping, or other strenuous use. Predisposing causes may

220

be calf knees; long, weak pasterns; a long toe and low heel; improper shoeing; being tied in at the knees; and legs that are too fine for the size of the horse. When injury occurs, it is accompanied by soreness to the touch, heat, swelling, and a tendency to flex the knee in order to raise the heel and relieve pressure. In mild cases, the superficial flexor tendon is affected, but in more serious cases the deep flexor tendon and the suspensory ligament may also be injured. The bowed appearance is a result of formation of fibrinous tissue. The bow may occur anywhere along the cannon and is classified as low, medium, or high depending on its location. Surgical procedures have had only limited success because excessive scar tissue usually develops, and healing is slow because of poor circulation to the region. Treatment requires a long period of convalescence—sometimes more than a year. Prognosis is not good if actual tendon rupture has occurred or if faulty conformation is a predisposing cause.

Sidebones. These are calcifications of the lateral cartilages of the third phalanx or coffin bone. This condition is rarely found in ponies and is less common in the light breeds than in the draft breeds. Lameness may occur during the period of ossification, but after the condition is "set" the animal is usually serviceably sound. The condition is more common in horses that toe in or toe out. Sidebones are considered an unsoundness in the young horse because the premature ossification of the lateral cartilages will result in contracted heels and abnormal foot growth. Rest to eliminate the inflammation and, later, special shoeing to prevent recurrence is the prescribed treatment.

Ringbone. Ringbone is an exostosis of the pastern bone in the form of a raised bony ridge usually parallel to the coronary band. The classification of ringbone as high or low describes the location of the new bone growth, according to whether it occurs on the lower part of the first phalanx above the pastern joint (high) or the lower part of the second phalanx at the coronary band (low). Bone growth in the proximity of the joint (articular periostitis) is much more serious than if there is no joint involvement (periarticular periostitis). The name "ringbone" was given to this condition because the exostosis can encircle or ring the pastern bone, but more commonly the enlargement occurs on the front of the pastern, on the sides, or on the front and sides but not the back. Ringbone commonly occurs on the front pasterns but is also found behind. The usual cause is strain on the ligaments or tendons where they attach to the phalanges. The tearing of the fibers at the point of insertion into the bone causes disturbances of the periosteum, and the resulting inflammation is resolved as exostosis. Faulty conformation that increases concussion is a predisposing cause, but ringbone can also be the result of a direct blow or an injury, such as a wire cut that inflames the periosteum. Lameness, heat, and swelling are results of the periostitis, and treatment is not always effective. Ringbone is a trouble-

221

some condition; because of its location, it is subjected to continued trauma and therefore the prognosis is not generally favorable. By the time the exostosis is visible, the condition is chronic and permanent lameness can result; so early diagnosis, treatment, and elimination of the cause are desirable.

Osselets. An inflammation of the periosteum on the anterior surface of the fetlock joint may lead to periostitis and subsequently bony outgrowths termed osselets. A sprain or pulling of the joint capsule at its point of insertion in the cannon and long pastern bones initiates the inflammation. Heat will be present, and pain will result in a short, choppy stride and definite lameness. Any conformational fault such as straight pasterns that increases concussion is considered contributory. Osselets are easy to detect and are a common ailment of racehorses. They usually occur in young horses that are under too much strain from training. As long as no new bone growth occurs on the articulating surfaces of the joint, the prognosis is good because, with rest and treatment, the osselets will solidify and become dormant. The ankles of older horses can be enlarged and the flexibility of the joint will thus be impaired.

Sesamoiditis. This is an inflammation of the proximal sesamoid bones that is serious because it usually results in chronic lameness. The initial cause is trauma or strain to the fetlock region and injury to the sesamoid bones. Sesamoiditis is another example of inflammation of the bone surface due to tearing of the insertion of a ligament, the suspensory ligament. Swelling and enlargement of the area occur and lameness results. Because the sesamoids provide support for the suspensory ligament, any fracture, exostosis, or roughness of the sesamoids is often a predisposing factor for suspensory lameness.

Suspensory Ligament Unsoundness. This type of lameness is common in racehorses. The suspensory ligament attaches to the back of the cannon bone just below the knee, travels downward, and splits above the sesamoid bones into two parts, each attaching to a sesamoid bone. A smaller part continues downward and forward and attaches to the long pastern bone. The suspensory ligament is one of the main supporting structures of the horse's leg and is important in absorbing shock. It is subjected to great stress, and injury can occur to it in any one of a number of sites. Ligament tears high at the point of attachment on the cannon are commonly referred to as check ligament lameness, although it is the suspensory ligament that is affected. Injuries to the middle portion of the ligament usually occur with splints, whereas injuries to the fetlock region of the ligament occur when there is injury to the sesamoid bones. A sprain at the point where the suspensory ligament splits is the most serious because it is extremely painful and because the weight of the horse constantly exerts pressure that prevents proper healing. Suspensory trouble can occur in any of the legs, but it is more likely to occur in the front legs. Treatment and prognosis are variable depending on the severity and location of the injury.

Navicular Disease. Navicular disease is any injury of the navicular bone of the front foot. Faulty conformation and injuries are the most important causes of navicular disease, although nutritional and hormonal imbalances are also possible. A straight pastern and shoulder or a small foot will increase the concussion on the navicular bone, thus forcing it against the flexor tendon and causing excess friction and possible damage. Horses worked repeatedly on hard surfaces are predisposed to the disease, which often affects horses during their prime years (ages 6–10). The disease usually begins as an inflammation of the navicular bursa, but it is often complicated by inflammation, ulceration, and partial degeneration of the navicular bone itself, and may progress to exostosis of the bone and calcification of the associated ligaments and cartilage. The term "navicular disease" is also applied to the chipping or fracture of the navicular bone, which may or may not be caused by earlier navicular disease damage. An afflicted horse shortens its stride and tends to go up on its toes and to have an increased tendency to stumble. The shoes or foot typically are worn more in the toes than in the heels. When standing, the horse points the toe of the most seriously affected foot, a behavior that has been accepted as typical of a navicular problem. The disease causes varying degrees of lameness, and there is no permanent cure. Corrective shoes that keep the toe short and the heels elevated decrease pressure on the frog and often permit the horse to travel sound. Pain-killers may restore afflicted horses to usefulness for short periods. As a last resort, permanent relief from pain can be accomplished by a posterior digital neurectomy (nerving), but other complications can then arise. A horse that has had a neurectomy is considered unsound even if there are no outward signs of pain or lameness.

Carpitis or Popped Knee. An enlargement of the knee joint as a result of inflammation to the joint capsule, the bones of the carpus, or the associated ligaments is known as carpitis. Carpitis usually results from concussion and trauma, which may cause chip fractures, increased joint fluid, and arthritic modification. The knee is a complex joint composed of 8 small bones connected in 2 rows. Consequently, there are numerous areas where inflammation can occur, and the seriousness of the condition depends on the degree of inflammation, its location, the extent of exostosis, and the amount of articular surface that is affected. Faulty conformation, particularly calf knees and bench knees, can predispose but trauma from kicks and banging of knees on jumps, against stall walls, and in trailers can also cause carpitis. This condition is considered an unsoundness if lameness or altered function of the knee joint occurs; otherwise it is considered a blemish.

223

Capped Elbow or Shoe Boil. A capped elbow is a bursitis or swelling at the point of the elbow and is usually caused when the horse irritates the elbow bursa with the shoe or hoof of the front foot when lying down. The swelling may be extensive, but serious lameness rarely develops. If the elbow is protected by a shoe boot and fibrosis has not developed the results of treatment should be favorable. A scar may be created by a capped elbow and is considered a blemish.

Sweeney. Atrophy of the muscles of the shoulder due to paralysis of the suprascapular nerve is called a sweeney. The condition is usually caused by direct injury to the point of the shoulder and subsequent damage to the nerve. No successful treatment is currently available. Occasionally the nerves regenerate. The horse may be sound with limited use, but often lameness results or the horse becomes lame with extensive use.

Blemishes and Unsoundnesses of the Hind Limb

The hind limb is the main propulsive force for the horse, and therefore the blemishes and unsoundnesses of this region are primarily a result of strains, sprains, and twists rather than injuries from concussion. This is not to imply that traumatic injuries do not occur behind, as many front-leg unsoundnesses, such as splints, ringbone, and sesamoiditis, also occur occasionally in the hind legs.

Knocked-down Hip. When one hip is lower than the other (viewed from the rear) because of the fracture of the point of the hip on one side, it is termed the hip-down condition. The fracture is usually the result of a direct blow. Horses with a hip down are a poor risk for racing because they inevitably develop lameness behind and have a crooked, hitching gait.

Stifle Lameness or Gonitis. The stifle is a large, muscular joint that is held together by a number of long ligaments. This structure is subject to a number of different types of inflammation that can affect the patella, ligaments, or joint capsule and that can result in stifle lameness or gonitis. The degree of lameness, the seriousness of the injury, and the prospects for recovery depend on the location, type, and severity of the inflammation. If ligaments have been strained, the prognosis is favorable, but if chronic synovitis or arthritis have occurred, the possibility of recovery is limited.

Stifled or Upward Fixation of the Patella. A particular type of stifle inflammation, in which the patella locks and causes the leg to remain in the extended position, is referred to as the stifled condition. The stifle and the hock are unable to flex and the foot is dragged, but the patella can be released by manipulating the leg forward or backing the horse several steps.

224

A young horse may outgrow this condition, and surgical correction is possible when the condition affects an older animal. The prognosis is favorable so long as gonitis is not severe and arthritis has not developed. There is some evidence that the tendency toward the stifled condition may be inherited.

Stringhalt. Stringhalt is a sudden, spasmodic, involuntary jerking and an excessive flexion of one or both hocks. The cause is not completely understood, but nerve damage to the region may be contributory. Some horses with stringhalt will not exhibit the characteristic flexion after warming up, and the severity of the affliction may be intermittent. Stringhalt is particularly obvious when an animal is backed or turned sharply.

Capped Hock. A capped hock is one of the most common defects of the hind limbs. It is a firm enlargement at the point of the hock that reflects an inflammation of the bursa. Capped hock is caused by trauma to the hock, usually as a result of kicking a wall, trailer gate, or some solid object. Extensive fibrosis can occur and a permanent blemish can result, but a capped hock rarely causes serious lameness. A severe injury can cause extensive swelling, but corticoid injections have successfully reduced the inflammation.

Curb. A curb is a hard enlargement on the rear of the cannon immediately below the hock that develops in response to stress. It develops as an inflammation and subsequent thickening of the plantar ligament on the posterior of the hock. Occasionally a curb will also affect the bone, but it is usually confined to the plantar ligament. The condition is associated with faulty conformation, particularly sickle or cow hocks. Kicking or a direct blow may also cause a curb. A curb may result in temporary lameness, but with rest it abates, although the thickened scar tissue remains as a permanent blemish. If periostitis has occurred, then the condition is more serious and a chronic lameness may persist, particularly if there are predisposing conformational faults.

Thoroughpins. A thoroughpin is a soft, fluid-filled enlargement in the hollow on the outside of the hock. The swelling can be pushed freely from the outside to the inside of the hock by palpation. It is caused by strain on the flexor tendon, which causes synovial fluid to escape into the hock hollow. Fortunately, the condition rarely causes lameness and is usually considered a blemish.

Bog Spavin. A soft distension on the inside front portion of the hock joint caused by an inflammation of the synovial membrane of the hock is known as a bog spavin. Faulty conformation (such as straight hocks), strain (resulting from quick stops), and rickets (caused by a nutritional deficiency)

225

may be predisposing causes that result in inflammation of the bursa and an increased production of synovial fluid. A bog spavin, although unsightly, rarely interferes with the usefulness of the horse. In young horses, bog spavins may appear and disappear spontaneously. They may be treated with some success by draining, corticoid therapy, firing, or blistering, but if the cause persists, the condition tends to recur, although it is rarely accompanied by lameness.

Bone Spavin or Jack Spavin. A bone spavin is a bony enlargement on the lower interior surface of the hock joint that may result in limited flexion of the hock. Spavin lameness typically results in an irregularity of gait. Faulty hock conformation, excessive concussion, nutritional deficiencies, and hereditary predisposition are considered causes of the bone spavin, but a traumatic event, such as jumping or vigorous training, is usually required to cause its development. A bone spavin will result in lameness of varying degrees of severity, but prognosis is favorable because as many as two-thirds of those afflicted become serviceably sound, albeit blemished. Lameness may persist as a result of tendon irritation over the point of exostosis, but in some instances an effective treatment is to cut the cunean tendon to relieve tension and pressure over the jack. This operation is relatively safe and simple and often results in immediate relief and soundness for the horse. Horsemen refer to this procedure as "having the jacks cut."

Occult Spavin. Hock lameness without visible exostosis is termed an occult or "blind" spavin. The occult spavin occurs on the articulating surface of the hock joint and is not generally recognized unless accompanied by lameness. Prognosis is unfavorable for blind spavins because they tend to lead to chronic discomfort and further lameness.

Wind Galls or Wind Puffs. Wind puffs are soft, fluid-filled enlargements that occur around a joint capsule, tendon sheath, or bursa. They are the result of excess synovia and are commonly found on the knees, cannons, and fetlocks as a result of trauma. They rarely cause lameness and are considered common blemishes although they impart a "used" look to the horse.

Blemishes and Unsoundnesses of the Hooves

Laminitis or Founder. Laminitis is a noninfectious inflammation of the sensitive laminae of one or more hooves. Severe pain can result from circulatory congestion within the foot. A variety of causes have been recognized, including overeating (grain founder), digestive disturbances (enterotoxemia), retained afterbirth (foal founder), lush pastures (grass founder), and concussion (road founder).

When the sensitive laminae become inflamed in a founder attack, the fragile union between the hoof and laminae weakens and the pull of the deep flexor tendon may actually create a separation of the laminae and the hoof wall. A foundered horse often has a distorted hoof with characteristic irregular "founder rings," a long toe that curls if neglected, a dished hoof, and a dropped sole caused by the downward rotation of the pedal bone. In severe cases, the pedal bone can protrude through the sole of the foot. There are many treatments for founder, but the prognosis is guarded depending on the extent of alteration of the foot. A new procedure that temporarily replaces the damaged part of the hoof with acrylic resin, combined with therapeutic shoeing, has had encouraging results. If the pedal bone has penetrated the sole, the prognosis is unfavorable (see Chapter 10 for a more complete discussion).

Cracked Hooves or Sand Cracks.   Cracked hooves, usually found on the feet of unshod horses, indicate neglect in the care of the foot. They may be called quarter crack, toe crack, or heel crack, depending upon their location on the hoof. Hoof cracks vary in length and depth. When a crack reaches the coronet or the sensitive laminae, lameness usually results. The problem with cracked hooves is that once they begin, the constant pressure from the horse's weight during motion forces the crack to persist. Treatment usually includes special shoeing, a clinch, or special grooving of the hoof. Severe cracks have been successfully repaired with acrylic.

Contracted Heels.   Contracted heels is a condition in which the frog is narrow and shrunken and the heels of the foot are pulled together. The foot may become smaller at the ground surface than at the coronary band. This condition tends to be a problem in show horses because hoof growth and improper shoeing, which prevents sufficient pressure against the frog, may cause contracted heels. Lameness can eventually result if the contraction is not corrected by special shoeing.

Quittor.   A chronic, purulent, inflammatory swelling of the lateral carti-lage resulting in intermittent subcoronary abscesses is called quittor. Heat and pain are usually followed by suppurative tracts that periodically heal and reopen. The condition may be caused by a trauma, puncture, bruise, or laceration near the coronary band. Intermittent lameness continues as the condition persists, and permanent lameness can result if the foot is permanently damaged or deformed.

227

Other Unsoundnesses

The majority of the unsoundnesses in the horse result in lameness; however, there are a number of other abnormal conditions that can interfere with the usefulness of the horse. These conditions are briefly mentioned here and are covered more fully in other sections.

Head.
Eyes: blindness, cloudy eyes, cataracts, and conjunctivitis (an irritation of the eye).

Mouth: improper meeting of incisors, overshot jaw (parrot mouth), undershot jaw (monkey mouth).

Nostrils: discharge, reflecting respiratory infection.

Poll: poll evil, an inflammation of the bursa at the poll that often becomes infected.

Body.
Fistula of withers: an inflammation similar to poll evil except that it affects the bursa at the withers.

Saddle and girth sores.

Hernias: umbilical hernias occur in both sexes; inguinal or scrotal hernias occur only in the male.

Systemic Unsoundnesses.
Contagious diseases of any type.

Heaves: chronic pulmonary emphysema (a respiratory disorder).

Azoturia: a paralytic metabolic disorder of horses.

Roaring: paralysis of the intrinsic muscle of the larynx.

Colic: a general term used to describe a variety of digestive disorders.

Other Foot Unsoundnesses.
Thrush: a bacterial infection resulting in degeneration of the foot.

Corns: a bruising of the sole that may become infected.

Scratches: dermatitis of the back of the fetlock and pastern—also called grease heel.

Seedy toe: separation of the wall of the hoof from the sensitive laminae in the toe.

Breeding Unsoundnesses.
Genital abnormalities: occur in both sexes.

228   Tipped vulva: "windsuckers"—aspiration of air into vagina that causes chronic infection.

Infertility: occurs in both sexes, has a variety of causes.

Cryptorchidism: retained testicle in male—a congenital condition. The cryptorchid horse is sometimes referred to as a ridgling.

6.4 Way of Going

The way of going refers to the nature of the movement of the horse; the gait describes a specific way of going. There are differences in the gaits performed by the various breeds and their method of execution. The term "action" is used to describe the amount of flexion of the knees and the hocks. The essentials of a satisfactory way of going are:

1. Straight-line action. Any deviation from the straight is wasted motion.

2. Long stride. Essential for ground-covering performance.

3. Regularity of gait. Athletic movement should be free, fluid, and regular. Lameness is often manifested in irregularity of gait.

4. Briskness of gait. Preferable to lethargy in all horses; the extent of the desired action is dependent upon the use of the horse. A Saddlebred should exhibit more action than a Quarter Horse, but the gaits of both should be executed with a briskness.

The gaits of the horse are classified as natural and artificial or acquired. The natural gaits are the walk, trot, and gallop and, in some horses, the pace and the running walk. The canter is a collected or restrained gallop and occurs both naturally and with training. The artificial gaits are taught and include the running walk, slow gait, rack, and, in some instances, the pace. The artificial gaits are all modifications of the walk (four beat); the walking horses learn their gait most easily.

The Natural Gaits

The walk (Figure 6-5a) is the horse's most useful gait and is the "mother of all gaits." The walk is a slow, flat-footed, four-beat gait that should be executed with "snap and animation." There should be a regular 1-2-3-4 cadence to the beat of the walk.

The trot (Figure 6-5b) is a rapid, two-beat gait in which the diagonal forelegs and hind legs move together. There can be a tremendous variation in the height, length, and speed of the trot. A Standardbred may take rapid, long, ground-covering strides (extended trot) during which the horse

229

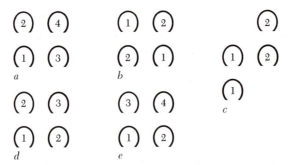

FIGURE 6-5

a: The walk. *b:* The trot. *c:* The pace. *d:* The canter. *e:* The gallop.

may be completely suspended in air or "floating." On the other hand, a Hackney takes shorter strides (collected trot) and exhibits much higher action with no period of suspension. There should be a regular 1-2-1-2 beat to the trot.

The pace (Figure 6-5*c*) is a rapid, two-beat gait in which the lateral fore-legs and hind legs move together. Because of the lateral base of support, the pacer tends to throw its body from side to side and thus the pace is an uncomfortable gait to ride. However, the pace is faster than the trot and is a popular gait for harness racing, when speed is preferred to action. There are natural or free-legged pacers, but the majority of horses must be trained to the pace. The pace should have a regular 1-2-1-2 cadence like the trot.

The canter (Figure 6-5*d*) is a fast, three-beat gait done under restraint. Two of the diagonal legs are paired to make one beat while the remaining hind leg and foreleg act independently and are called the leading legs. Consequently, at the canter (and gallop), the horse can be in either the left or right lead. The three beats of the right lead illustrated in Figure 6-5*d* are: (1) left hind, (2) right hind and left fore, (3) right fore. There is then a moment of suspension and the beat repeats itself in a regular 1-2-3 cadence. When cantering in a straight line, the horse will occasionally switch leads to keep from tiring. However, when the horse turns to the left, it will be more stable in the left lead; when the horse turns to the right, the right lead is the "correct" lead.

The gallop (Figure 6-5*e*) is the fastest gait of the horse. It is an extended canter that results in a four-beat gait; the middle diagonal beat of the canter is extended to two beats because the hind foot hits slightly before the diagonal fore foot. The cadence of the gallop is 1-2·3-4. As with the canter there are left and right leads to the gallop and there is a period of complete suspension in the air.

The Artificial Gaits

The artificial gaits are a group of related gaits that collectively are four-beat gaits with a sequence similar to that of the walk (left hind, left fore, right hind, right fore). These gaits include the amble, rack, stepping pace, pacing walk, slow gait, running walk, paso, and single foot. Hildebrand (1965) justifiably uses "single-foot" to classify all of them.

The running walk (Figure 6-6a) is the fast, four-beat, ground-covering walk characteristic of the Tennessee Walking Horse. It is the smoothest gait of this horse and made this breed popular as a ground-covering riding horse in the South; hence the name "plantation gait." The running walk is characterized by a smooth, fluid motion; the hind foot overstrides the print of the front, and there is a typical nodding of the head. The running walk should not be confused with the stepping pace. In the running walk the feet on the same side leave the ground at different times. There is an even 1-2-3-4 cadence to the running walk.

The slow gait and the rack are the two artificial, taught gaits performed by the "five-gaited" American Saddle Horse. Since these are slow gaits, extreme action is preferred to ground-covering ability. The slow gait (Figure 6-6b) is often called the stepping pace because it resembles the pace. There is lateral movement of the legs; the fore foot and the hind foot leave the ground at the same time. However, the slow gait is not a true pace because as a result of the higher action of the front limb, the hind foot hits the ground before the front foot on the same side. There is a break in cadence in the slow gait; the foot beats $1 \cdot 2 - 3 \cdot 4$. The slow gait is tiring for the horse and uncomfortable for the rider.

The rack (Figure 6-6c) is the fastest four-beat gait. It should be performed with animation and in a regular four-beat cadence, 1-2-3-4. The rack is a distinct gait; each foot leaves and strikes the ground at regular intervals. The rack is difficult and extremely tiring for the horse, but easy on the rider. The rack differs from the running walk in that there is much more up and down motion of the limbs (action) and the hind foot does not overreach the forefoot to such an extent.

FIGURE 6-6
a: The running walk. b: The slow gait. c: The rack.

Defects in Way of Going

A horse's gait is examined in terms of length, height, spring, promptness, power, balance, directness, and regularity. Any deviation in the flight of the foot wastes energy and places stress on the limbs. There are a number of conformational faults that can predispose the horse to faulty action. Many defects in way of going can be corrected by proper trimming or shoeing (see Chapter 22).

The most common defects in way of going are deviation in the flight of the foot and interference of one leg with another. There are basically two types of interference: *striding leg interference,* in which one moving leg makes contact with another, and *supporting leg interference,* in which the striding leg strikes a supporting leg.

Striding Leg Interference. At the trotting gait, striding leg interference occurs when the hind limb hits the folding forelimb on the same side; at the pacing gait, the interference is between the diagonal forelegs and hind legs. Different descriptive terms are used, depending on the point of contact.

Forging is the hitting of the sole or shoe of the forefoot with the toe of the hind foot on the same side. Forging usually occurs at the slow trot and causes a characteristic "click, click, click" at this gait that usually disappears at a faster trot.

Cross-firing, a term confined to pacers, is when the hind foot on one side strikes the diagonal forefoot. In other words, cross-firing is forging in the pacer.

Scalping is hitting the hind leg at the coronet with the toe of the fore-foot.

Speedycutting is hitting the hind leg at the pastern or fetlock with the toe of the forefoot.

Shin hitting is hitting the cannon or shin of the hind leg with the front toe.

Supporting Leg Interference. At the trotting or pacing gaits, supporting leg interference is the result of hitting one front leg with the other or one hind leg with the other as it strides past the supporting leg. The inter-ference can occur at the coronet, pastern, ankle, shin, knee, or forearm. The term *brushing* is used when contact is slight; the term *striking* is used when interference results in an open wound. Interference is common in racehorses, particularly as they tire during a race, and many are forced to wear protective boots and pads.

Deviation in Flight of the Foot. The flight of the foot should be perfectly straight, but commonly it will be deviated outward or inward. Such deviation from normal can place additional stress on the limbs and cause a myriad of unsoundnesses.

Paddling is throwing the front feet outward while in flight. This action is associated with the toe-in or pigeon-toed position.

Winging out is an exaggerated paddling observed in high-stepping harness horses and saddle horses.

Dishing or winging is throwing the front feet inward while in flight. Dishing is associated with toe-out or splay-foot conformation and is considered serious because it can lead to knee-knocking or other supporting leg interference.

Rolling is a defect of wide-fronted horses in which they roll from side to side as they stride. This is a laboring, unpleasant, inefficient type of action.

Winding or *rope walking* is the twisting of the striding leg around the supporting leg in such a manner that the horse appears to be tightrope walking.

Trappy is the term used to describe a short, quick, high, and often choppy stride.

Pounding is a hard contact with the ground that causes excessive concussion, often associated with straight shoulders and pasterns and typical of a "heavy-going" horse.

6.5 Vices

A vice is a bad habit that may affect a horse's usefulness, dependability, or health. It is often a reflection of the animal's personality, as vices can be the result of nervousness, viciousness, fear, curiosity, excessive energy, nutritional deficiencies, or boredom. By nature the horse is an athletic animal that is used to roaming and running at will over large areas but with domestication it has become increasingly restricted. "The idle mind is the devil's playground," and the stall is the birthplace of most vices—they are much more common in stabled than pastured horses. Vices that seem to result from boredom and inactivity often disappear with regular exercise. However, a vice is a habit, and once established it is extremely difficult to eliminate. Vices try man's patience and tax his ingenuity while confirming the horse's inventiveness. Vices can be classified as dangerous to the handler, dangerous to the horse, and nuisance habits. Vices dangerous to both the handler and the horse require vigorous correction to prevent tragedy.

233

Vices Dangerous to Man

Biting and *nipping* are two of the most dangerous vices because a horse can do severe damage to a handler with its powerful jaws. Stallions are particularly apt to bite and should always be watched carefully. Young horses and bored mature horses sometimes get nippy (a much less dangerous habit), but neither vice should be tolerated.

Striking is a natural defense reaction of the horse to fear or confinement, but it is an extremely dangerous habit for the handler. A striking horse can do serious bodily harm to someone in front of it, so it is best to handle the horse from the side and remain alert to its use of its front legs. A horse is most apt to strike when in nose-to-nose contact with another horse. A stallion will often strike when teasing or breeding a mare. A good horseman anticipates these situations and prevents striking so that it does not develop into a habit or vice.

Rearing is another of the defensive behaviors of the horse and is also dangerous for the handler because the flailing forelegs can come dangerously close to the head. Again, rearing should be anticipated and prevented by firm and drastic handling if necessary. An experienced handler can usually use a lead shank to prevent a horse from striking or rearing. There are situations in which a whip should be used vigorously, as a striking or rearing horse is a potential killer.

Kicking deliberately at a handler is an act of meanness or fear on the part of the horse and must be corrected immediately. A cowkick is a forward and sideward kicking action that can catch a handler at the horse's side. Kicking stall walls or trailer gates is a nuisance habit but creates the possibility of trauma and injury to the legs as well as expensive damage to the facilities. Many capped hocks and curbs had their origin in needless kicking.

Charging is when a horse attacks or savages an unsuspecting attendant in a stall or paddock. This vicious vice is most common among stallions but is occasionally observed in mares or geldings. The most serious injury I have ever received from a horse was from a charging gelding that was distraught after a day of having hay bales unloaded in the loft directly above his stall. The best correction is prevention by maintaining control of such a horse when in its stall or paddock.

Crowding is when a horse consciously crowds or squeezes the handler against the wall of the stall with its body. Correction requires alertness and anticipation.

Vices Dangerous to Horses

234   *Cribbing* is a habit of force-swallowing gulps of air. It usually requires that the cribber grasp an object with its incisor teeth and then pull its

neck back in a rigid arch as it swallows air. The condition is considered a habit of boredom but is dangerous to horses because the swallowed air can create gastric upsets or colic. Cribbing is a vice that is frequently copied by other horses.

Wood chewing is a habit that is costly and can be injurious to the horse. Wood chewing is sometimes incorrectly referred to as cribbing but it is a separate vice that does not entail swallowing air. Wood chewers do not usually ingest the wood they chew, but some splinters can cause buccal infections, colic, or excessive tooth wear. Wood chewing is an acquired habit, and an entire herd may pick it up from one horse. Application of creosote to the chewed boards will help decrease the habit but must be repeated annually because with weathering the horse will renew the vice. Wood chewing is a vice rather than a nutrient deficiency, although some horsemen claim that the horses are "going after the grain in the wood" (see section 10.3).

Eating bedding, manure, or *dirt* is an unpleasant habit. Dirt and sand eaters are susceptible to colic, and eating of any nonnutritious foreign material can cause digestive disorders (see section 10.3).

Bolting food is the habit of some horses of eating their grain without adequate chewing. This condition can also result in digestive upsets and decreases the nutrient efficiency of the feed. If several large, round rocks are placed in the feeder, the bolting of the grain will be decreased (see section 10.3).

Fighting is a perennial problem because some horses are constantly aggressive toward other horses. On the other hand, a group of horses running together will establish a certain hierarchy or "pecking order." An incessant fighter may have to be separated from a herd because it can cause considerable injury to the other horses by biting, kicking, and chasing. Young horses play at fighting but rarely exhibit true aggressive behavior.

Shying is a habit that may reflect poor vision or immaturity and lack of experience. Shying is usually a response to fear and can be dangerous to both horse and handler, as a shying horse is unpredictable and may shy away from one object only to face more serious trouble.

Nuisance Habits

Weaving is a vice of a high-strung, nervous horse. The horse stands in place but rocks back and forth or weaves from side to side. Weaving can be considered a nuisance, but it can have more serious consequences. Some weavers will stress the legs in such a manner that lameness occurs, whereas others will lose weight and become physically exhausted. Weaving is another vice that is easily learned by stablemates.

Stall walking is another vice resulting from nervousness and excessive energy. The horse constantly paces or circles around the stall. This habit can have the same detrimental effect on the horse as weaving.

235

Pawing is a nuisance and creates additional work for the horseman. The horse continually paws at the floor and, if possible, digs holes that constantly need repair. Pawing creates the possibility of leg injury.

Tail rubbing is considered a vice, but it may be a sign of fungus, lice, or worms. However, some horses rub their tails without any external causes, and this creates a nuisance problem for the owner.

Halter pulling is a vice that is usually a result of poor or inadequate training in tying when young. Some horses can never be cured of the habit of pulling back when tied, and a horse that will not tie is a nuisance that is sometimes dangerous.

References

Adams, O. R. 1966. *Lameness in Horses.* Philadelphia: Lea and Febiger.

Albert, W. W. 1972. *Suggestions for Buying and Judging Horses.* Extension Circular 1057. University of Illinois.

Beeman, Marvin. 1973. Conformation: The Relationship of Form to Function. *Quarter Horse Journal* (January).

Beeson, W. M., R. E. Hunsley, and J. E. Nordby. 1970. *Stock Horses, Livestock Judging and Evaluation.* Part 5. Danville, Illinois: The Interstate Printers and Publishers, Inc.

Catcott, E. J., and J. F. Smithcors, eds. 1966. *Progress in Equine Practice.* Wheaton, Illinois: American Veterinary Publications.

Cavalry School. 1935. Horsemanship and Horsemastership. *Animal Management.* Vol. 11. Fort Riley, Kansas.

Churchill, E. A. 1968. Lameness in the Standardbred. *Care and Training of the Trotter and Pacer.* Chap. 16. Columbus, Ohio: U.S. Trotting Association.

Cresswell, H., and R. H. Smythe. 1963. Lamenesses. In *Equine Medicine and Surgery.* 1st ed. Wheaton, Illinois: American Veterinary Publications.

Ensminger, M. E. 1969. *Horses and Horsemanship.* Danville, Illinois: The Interstate Printers and Publishers, Inc.

Hanauer, Elsie. 1973. *Disorders of the Horse.* New York: A. S. Barnes.

Haughton, W. R. 1968. Selecting the Yearling. *Care and Training of the Trotter and Pacer.* Chap. 2. Columbus, Ohio: U.S. Trotting Association.

Hildebrand, Milton. 1965. Symmetrical Gaits of Horses. *Science* 150:701.

Hipsley, W. G. 1970. *Judging the Halter and Pleasure Horse in Individual and Team Competition*. Extension Publication No. 65. University of Massachusetts.

Kays, D. J. 1969. *The Horse*. Rev. ed. New York: A. S. Barnes.

Moxley, H. F., and B. H. Good. 1955. *The Sound Horse*. Extension Bulletin 330, Michigan State University.

Reeves, Richard Stone. 1970. The Perfect Horse. *The Thoroughbred Record* (July 18).

Rooney, J. R. 1972. The Muscoskeletal System. In *Equine Medicine and Surgery*. 2d ed. Wheaton, Illinois: American Veterinary Publications.

Rooney, James R. 1974. *The Lame Horse: Causes, Symptoms, and Treatment*. Cranbury, New Jersey: A. S. Barnes.

Rossdale, Peter D. 1972. *The Horse*. Arcadia, California: California Thoroughbred Breeders Association.

Smythe, R. H. 1964. *Horses in Action*. Springfield, Illinois: Charles C. Thomas.

Smythe, R. H. 1972. *The Horse, Structure and Movement*. London: J. A. Allen.

Straiton, E. C. 1973. *The Horse Owner's Vet Book*. Philadelphia: Lippincott.

Wakeman, D. L. 1965. Selecting and Judging Light Horses. *Light Horse Production in Florida*. Florida Department of Agriculture Bulletin 188:31.

Wakeman, D. L. 1965. Blemishes and Unsoundnesses. *Light Horse Production in Florida*. Florida Department of Agriculture Bulletin 188:43.

Wentworth, Lady. 1957. *The Swift Runner*. London: George Allen, Ltd.

Willis, Larryann C. 1973. *The Horse Breeding Farm*. Cranbury, New Jersey: A. S. Barnes.

237

PART THREE *Nutrition of the Horse*

CHAPTER SEVEN

Digestive Physiology

Now, good digestion wait on appetite, and health on both.
Macbeth, Act III, Scene IV.

7.1 The Digestive Tract

Horses are nonruminant herbivores. They eat fibrous feeds (roughages) but do not have a rumen with bacteria to help utilize the fiber. In ruminants, such as cattle and sheep, bacteria in the rumen produce enzymes such as cellulases that digest the fiber.

Nonruminant herbivores, such as the horse, rabbit, and guinea pig, utilize roughages because they have a relatively large cecum and/or colon that contains the necessary bacterial population for fiber digestion.

Many animals, such as man, rat, and pig, have relatively simple digestive tracts and cannot effectively digest large amounts of roughage. Figure 7-1 is a diagram of the digestive tract of the horse.

Mouth. The mouth is the first part of the digestive system. The teeth should be examined periodically by a veterinarian. (The dental pattern was discussed in section 5.2.) Horses do not normally have dental cavities comparable to those of humans, but other difficulties can occur. For example, the cheek teeth may develop sharp edges that interfere with chewing or that may even injure the tongue and cheeks. This problem can be corrected by "floating the teeth," that is, filing down the projections with a rasp. Some of the teeth may be missing. For example, a 31-year-old donkey in a Japanese zoo was a favorite of the children, but

241

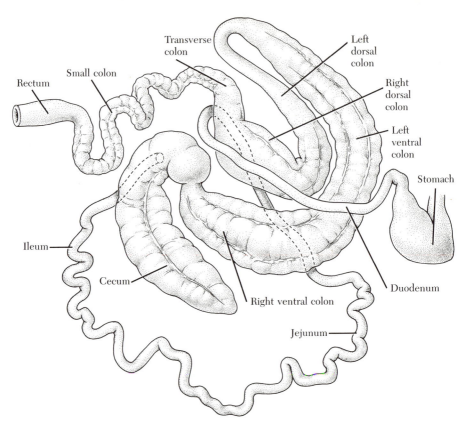

FIGURE 7-1
Digestive tract of the horse.

gradually became very thin. Upon examination it was found that the animal had lost several of its incisor teeth in both jaws and thus had difficulty chewing food and biting off grass. Dentures were attached to the remaining incisors by metal bridges. The donkey could then chew food and returned to good health; however, the false teeth cost approximately $2,200. Obviously, most horse owners cannot afford dentures for their horses, but horses with worn or missing teeth should be fed crushed or rolled grains rather than whole grains. Hay can be softened if it is coarsely chopped and then soaked in water. Complete pelleted rations are also useful for horses with poor teeth.

The two main functions of the mouth are to masticate feed and to wet it with saliva. The saliva is produced by three pairs of glands— parotid, submaxillary, and sublingual. The parotid is the largest of these glands and has received most attention from scientists. There is profuse secretion of parotid saliva during eating, but unlike the dog, the horse does not secrete saliva at the sight of food. The quantity of saliva is quite large. Ponies may secrete as much as 12 liters per day (Alexander and

Hickson, 1970). The ion composition of parotid saliva is shown in Table 7-1. Saliva contains a very low concentration of amylase, and this enzyme is probably of minor significance in the process of digestion.

Esophagus. The esophagus in the mature horse is approximately 50–60 inches long. Because of the tonus of the muscle of the lower esophagus, vomiting is rare in the horse. The horse is the only species in which distension of the stomach can be so severe that it will rupture before vomiting occurs.

Stomach. The stomach of the horse is relatively small. It provides approximately 10 percent of the capacity of the gastrointestinal tract. Alexander (1963) suggested that limited bacterial digestion takes place in the stomach and that the primary product of digestion is lactic acid and not volatile fatty acids. He found the ratio of lactic acid to volatile fatty acids in the stomach of the horse to be 1.7:1, compared with 0.15:1 and 0.12:1 in the pig and rabbit, respectively. Although the horse's stomach is seldom completely empty, emptying of the stomach starts soon after feeding, and there is rapid movement of a meal through the stomach and small intestine into the large intestine. Feed that passes rapidly through the stomach has only limited contact with the gastric secretions. Thus, because of the small capacity of the stomach and the potentially rapid movement of digesta, it is usually recommended that the horse be fed 2 or more meals daily.

Small Intestine. The small intestine provides approximately 30 percent of the capacity of the gastrointestinal tract and has about the same capacity as that of the small intestine of a cow of a similar weight. Carbohydrases and proteases, enzymes that digest carbohydrates and protein, respectively, are present in secretions of the intestinal cells and pan-

TABLE 7-1
Composition of 24-hour samples of parotid saliva from the horse

Constituent	Concentration (mEq/1)
Na^+	55.0 ± 7.0
K^+	15.0 ± 2.0
Ca^{2+}	13.6 ± 1.7
Cl^-	50.0 ± 13.0
HCO_3^-	52.0 ± 5.6
HPO_4^{2-}	0.25 ± 0.00

SOURCE: Adapted from Alexander and Hickson. 1970.

243

creas. The volume of pancreatic juice secretion may be greater than the volume of saliva produced by the parotid glands.

Horses do not have a gallbladder to store bile. Therefore, bile salts that promote emulsification of lipids and are thus important in lipid digestion are secreted constantly into the small intestine. The rate of bile secretion in a horse is estimated to be approximately 300 ml per hour. The contents of the small intestine are quite fluid; they contain only 5–8 percent dry matter.

Large Intestine. The large intestine is approximately 25 feet long and is divided into cecum, right ventral colon, left ventral colon, left dorsal colon, right dorsal colon, transverse colon, small colon, and rectum (Figure 7-1). The cecum is a pouch at the junction of the small intestine and colon. The contents of the cecum usually contain 6–10 percent dry matter. The colon has the greatest capacity of any segment of the digestive tract and provides 40–50 percent of the total capacity of the intestinal tract. The dry matter content of the ingesta increases as the material travels from the cecum to rectum. The ingesta in the first part of the ventral colon, dorsal colon, and rectum contains 12–15 percent, 15–19 percent, and 19–24 percent dry matter, respectively.

The microbial populations of the cecum of the horse and of the rumen of the sheep and cow are qualitatively similar; that is, in general, they consist of the same types of organisms (Smith, 1965). Kern *et al.*[3] (1973) fed steers and ponies hay with or without oats and found that the numbers of bacteria per volume of cecal ingesta increased when oats were fed to the ponies but not when oats were fed to the steers. Rods, both gram-negative and gram-positive, predominated in the gram-smear counts of both ponies and steers. Cellulolytic bacteria numbers per gram of ingesta were similar in the ponies' cecum and steers' rumen whether or not oats were included in the diet.

Kern *et al.* (1974) compared the microbial population of steers and ponies that were fed timothy hay. The total bacterial, viable bacterial, and ammonia concentrations and pH were higher in the rumen of steers than in the cecum of ponies (Table 7-2).

7.2 Rate of Passage

Approximately 95 percent of the food particles destined to appear in the feces pass through the digestive tract within 65–75 hours after ingestion, when horses are fed a hay-grain ration. A slightly faster rate of passage may be expected when only grain or a pelleted diet or fresh grass is fed. The length of the time that food remains in the stomach is

244

TABLE 7-2
Chemical and microbial characteristics of ingesta from intestines of ponies and steers fed timothy hay

Characteristic	Pony Gut Regions			Steer Gut Regions			
	Ileum	Cecum	Colon, Terminal	Rumen	Ileum	Cecum	Colon, Terminal
Ingesta pH	7.4^w	6.6^w	6.6^w	6.9^{ax}	7.3^{aw}	7.0^{aw}	7.2^{ax}
Viable bacteria/gm 10^{-7}	36.0^b	492.0^{cw}	363.0^d	1658.0^{ax}	5.4^b	230.0^c	12.7^d
Rods (percent)							
Gram-negative	9.2^a	63.8^{bw}	54.3^b	33.1^x	20.3	29.9^x	25.7
Gram-positive	38.9	6.4	11.2	2.4	0.9	2.7	5.5
Cocci (percent)							
Gram-negative	6.4	33.1	22.6	44.1	33.9	46.9	45.9
Gram-positive	36.2^a	5.6^a	11.2^b	19.4^a	44.7^c	22.7^b	25.3^b
DNA, $\mu g/g$	9.9^b	8.4^{cw}	6.2^c	51.6^x	25.5^b	24.8^{bx}	16.0^c
NH$_3$–N, mg/100 ml	5.2^w	2.9^w	5.4	10.6^x	15.5^x	18.2^x	13.1

SOURCE: Kern *et al.* 1974.

[a,b,c,d]Means on the same line (within species), bearing different superscript letters, differ significantly ($P > .01$).

[w,x]Comparison: fundic *vs.* abomasum; pyloric *vs.* abomasum; small intestine *vs.* cecum; colon *vs.* cecum; cecum *vs.* rumen. Means (between species) on the same line bearing different superscript letters for each comparison differ significantly ($P > .01$).

245

variable. Solid particles may reach the cecum within 45 to 60 minutes after eating; however, some particles remain in the stomach for 4 to 7 hours. Fluids may reach the cecum within 30 minutes after ingestion. The stomach empties more slowly in the young foal than in older animals. When barium meals were fed to suckling foals and to weaned foals and the rate of passage followed by radiographing the animals, most of the barium was found to reach the cecum of the weaned foals within 3 hours, whereas after 6 hours there was still barium in the stomach and small intestine of the suckling foal (Alexander, 1946).

The size and digestibility of the feed particles may also influence rate of passage. Inert particles 2 cm × 2 mm were retained in the intestinal tract much longer than particles 2 mm × 2 mm (Argenzio *et al.*, 1974).

7.3   Digestibility

Knowledge of digestive physiology of the horse is essential to the development of sound nutritional practices. There is a need to know not only how the digestive tract of the horse works, but how efficiently it works. One method of measuring efficiency is to determine digestion coefficients for various feeds. Digestibility is calculated according to the following formula:

$$\text{Digestibility} = 100 \times \frac{\text{Nutrient intake} - \text{Nutrient in feces}}{\text{Nutrient intake}}$$

Animals can be housed in metabolism stalls (Figure 7-2) or fitted with collection harnesses (Figure 7-3) so that feces and urine can be collected separately and analyzed. Digestibility can also be determined indirectly by using an indigestible indicator in the ration. By determining the ratio of the concentration of indicator to that of a given nutrient in the feed and the same ratio in the feces, the digestibility of the nutrient can be obtained without measuring either food intake or feces output. The formula is:

$$\text{Digestibility} = 100 \times \left(1 - \frac{\%\ \text{indicator in feed}}{\%\ \text{indicator in feces}} \times \frac{\%\ \text{nutrient in feces}}{\%\ \text{nutrient in feed}}\right)$$

The values determined by these formulas are really only apparent digestion coefficients because not all the material in feces is residue from the diet. Feces also contain cells sloughed from the lining of the intestine and material that was secreted or excreted into the intestine. The

FIGURE 7-2
Metabolism stall used for complete collection of feces and urine in nutrition trials.

nondietary fraction is called the endogenous fraction. True digestibility or true digestion coefficients are calculated by subtracting the amount of endogenous material from the total amount present in the feces to determine the actual amount of dietary residue. For example, endogenous losses of calcium can be determined by using radioactive calcium, and then the true digestibility of dietary calcium can be calculated (Schryver *et al.*, 1970).

FIGURE 7-3
The use of harnesses and bags permits complete collection of feces and urine.

The study of digestive physiology in the horse has been advanced by the use of surgically prepared animals. Fistulas or windows can be placed in various parts of the digestive tract. For example, the pony in Figure 7-4a has a small fistula into the cecum. Horses have been fistulated in the cecum and the dorsal and ventral colon at the same time. Other techniques, such as the re-entrant cannula, have also been developed. The pony in Figure 7-5 has a tube in the small intestine that is brought to the outside of the animal and then returned to the small intestine. Such a technique allows measurement of the various nutrients passing from the small intestine into the cecum.

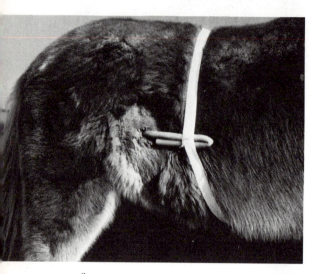

a

b

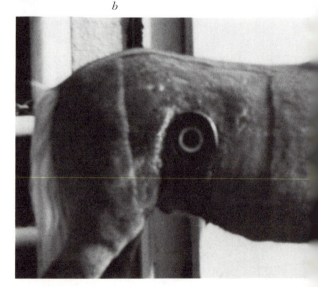

FIGURE 7-4
Small (*a*) and large (*b*) fistula or window in the cecum of the pony. Such fistulas are not harmful to the animal and have helped greatly in the study of horse nutrition.

248

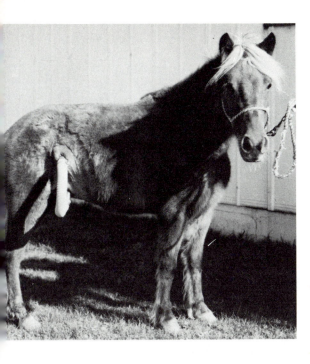

FIGURE 7-5
Pony with surgical preparation
that allows collection of ingesta
coming from the small intestine.

7.4 Site of Digestion

Estimates of the site of digestion and absorption of various nutrients are
summarized in Table 7-3.

Protein. The primary site of protein digestion is the small intestine.
Dietary protein is broken down by acid hydrolysis and by protein-
splitting enzymes (such as trypsin, chymotrypsin, and carboxypeptidases)
into amino acids, which are actively absorbed. The proteolytic activity
per mg of ingesta in the ileum of the small intestine is 500 times greater
than the activity of ingesta in the cecum or colon (Kern *et al.*, 1974).
Thus, in the horse, the amino acids that are absorbed are supplied by
the amino acids in the diet. In contrast, in the ruminant the bacteria of
the rumen may alter the amino acid makeup of the diet so that the amino
acids that are absorbed are determined by the amino acid content of
bacterial protein.

There also appears to be some absorption of amino acids of bacterial
origin from the large intestine of the horse. The total contribution of such
amino acids to the nutrition of the horse is not known, but in one study
in which bacterial protein containing N^{15} was placed in the cecum of
ponies via a cecal fistula, amino acids containing N^{15} were found in the

TABLE 7-3
Estimates of site of digestion and net absorption

Dietary Fraction	Small Intestine (percent)	Cecum and Colon (percent)
Protein	60–70	30–40
Soluble carbohydrates	65–75	25–35
Fiber	15–25	75–85
Fats	Primary[a]	—
Calcium	95–99	1–5
Magnesium	90–95	5–10
Phosphorus	20–50	50–80
Vitamins	Primary[a]	—

[a]Estimates of percentage absorbed in various segments are not available, but the small intestine is probably the primary site of absorption of dietary sources of these nutrients.

portal blood of the ponies (Slade *et al.*, 1971). However, other studies have reported that the bacterial amino acids synthesized in the large intestine are not efficiently utilized by the horse (Wysocki and Baker, 1975; Reitnour and Salsbury, 1975).

Young foals can absorb intact proteins such as antibodies up to 36 hours after birth. It is important for the foal to receive the mare's colostrum, which contains antibodies, as soon as possible after birth, because there is no transmission of antibodies across the placenta to the foal.

Carbohydrates. The soluble carbohydrates are digested and absorbed primarily in the small intestine. The carbohydrases of the pancreatic secretions and intestinal mucosa break down the soluble carbohydrates such as starch to glucose and other 5- or 6- carbon sugars, which are readily absorbed. Several carbohydrases, such as sucrase, maltase, trehalase, and β-galactosidase, are present in the small intestine, but activity depends on the age of the horse. Horses at birth have very little maltase or sucrase activity, but the levels gradually increase to a peak at 6–7 months. Lactase activity is high at birth but drops off sharply at 3–4 years of age (Roberts, 1975). Thus, feeding high levels of sucrose to young foals or feeding high levels of lactose to horses older than 3 years of age could result in digestive upsets and diarrhea because of the enzyme deficiency. Some of the soluble carbohydrates reach the large intestine, where they are fermented by bacteria. The end product of that digestion or fermentation is volatile fatty acids (VFA). The major volatile fatty acids are acetate (2 carbons), propionate (3 carbons), and butyrate (4 carbons). The volatile fatty acids are absorbed from the large intestine and utilized as sources of energy by the tissues of the horse. Propionate can be used by the tissues to synthesize glucose.

The fibrous fraction of the diet is digested primarily in the large intestine. The principal end products of digestion are VFA. The ratios of VFA produced are quite similar to the ratios produced by ruminant microflora (Table 7-4). Increasing the proportion of grain to hay in the diet of both horses and ruminants decreases the relative amount of acetate and increases the relative amount of propionate produced. Such findings also demonstrate that not all of the soluble carbohydrates are digested in the small intestine but that some are digested in the large intestine of the horse. Feeding of pelleted roughages may also increase the percentage of propionate in the cecal fluid, presumably because the rate of passage of pelleted roughages through the digestive tract is faster, and thus more of the soluble carbohydrates reach the lower gut.

Fat. Relatively little is known about lipid digestion in the horse. The dietary lipids apparently are digested and absorbed in the small intestine. The composition of the body fat is influenced by the composition of dietary fat because the fatty acids are absorbed from the small intestine before they can be altered by the bacteria in the large intestine. As mentioned earlier, the horse does not have a gallbladder. However, the lack of a gallbladder does not appear to hinder the digestion of fat. Several species, such as rats, deer, camels, elk, whales, porpoises, and pigeons, also do not have gallbladders, but they all secrete bile from the liver. Mature horses can tolerate diets containing high levels of fat. For example, the fat in diets containing 15 percent beef tallow and 85 percent alfalfa pellets has been found to be highly digestible (Table 7-5).

Vitamins. The fat-soluble vitamins (A, D, E, and K) are apparently absorbed in the small intestine. The horse also absorbs carotene from the small intestine. Carotene, a yellow compound obtained from plant material, can be converted by the tissues of the horse into vitamin A. Not all of the carotene is converted immediately into vitamin A; some is stored in fat deposits. Thus, horses fed diets containing carotene have yellow blood plasma and yellow fat. Cattle, man, and chickens also

TABLE 7-4
Comparison of ratios of volatile fatty acids in rumen fluid and cecal fluid of cattle and ponies fed rations with varying hay-to-grain ratios (percent)

Hay-to-Grain Ratio	Species	Acetate	Propionate	Butyrate
1:0	Pony	73	17	8
	Cattle	74	18	8
1:4	Pony	59	25	11
	Cattle	62	22	16

SOURCE: Hintz *et al.* 1971. Also Templeton and Dyer. 1967.

TABLE 7-5
Apparent digestibility of alfalfa pellets and
alfalfa plus animal fat (percent)

Fraction	Alfalfa	Alfalfa + 15 Percent Fat
Dry matter	56.0[a]	59.5
Ether extract	−6.4[b]	88.1
Calcium	70.0	72.5
Phosphorus	21.0	21.0
Magnesium	61.0	58.3

SOURCE: Monroe and Hintz, unpublished data.

[a]Average of 4 values.

[b]Negative apparent digestibility because of metabolic
fat in feces.

absorb and store carotene, but many species, such as sheep, rabbits,
rats, guinea pigs, water buffalo, swine, camels, and dogs do not store
appreciable amounts of carotene in the fat and hence have white fat.
However, these animals are also able to convert carotene into vitamin A.
It is interesting that two other members of the equine family, the donkey
and the zebra, do not absorb carotene and hence have white fat, in contrast to the horse.

Dietary B vitamins are absorbed from the small intestine. Considerable amounts of B vitamins are synthesized by the microflora in the large
intestine of the horse (Table 7-6), and some of these vitamins are absorbed (Linerode, 1967). Further studies are needed to quantitate the
amounts accurately.

Minerals. Calcium, phosphorus, magnesium, and zinc have been shown
to be absorbed from the small intestine, and other minerals are probably
also absorbed from that section of the gut. Calcium is actively absorbed;

TABLE 7-6
Vitamin content of samples from hay, cecum, colon, and
feces of ponies (micrograms per gram of dry matter)

Vitamin	Source			
	Hay	Cecum	Colon	Feces
Niacin	31	92	143	206
Pantothenate	4	20	31	40
Riboflavin	17	14	15	100
Thiamin	0.4	4	17	9

SOURCE: Adapted from P. A. Linerode. 1967.

the mucosal cells of the small intestine contain a calcium-binding protein that facilitates calcium absorption. Vitamin D is necessary for the synthesis of the calcium-binding protein. Thus, when there is a deficiency of vitamin D, calcium absorption is decreased. Phosphorus, but not calcium and magnesium, may also be absorbed from the large intestine. Alexander and Hickson (1970) have suggested that phosphate may be an important buffer to maintain bacterial activity in the large intestine.

Water. The cecum is the primary site of net water absorption, although significant amounts of water are also absorbed from the colon (Argenzio *et al.*, 1974b). The cecum effectively passes dry material into the colon. The amount of water in the digestive tract and feces (that is, the efficiency of water recovery) depends on the diet. The feces usually contain 66–76 percent water. The feces of horses fed high-grain diets have a lower water content than the feces of horses fed a hay diet. If a horse is fed only oats, the water content of the feces is 50 percent. Alfalfa hay may cause a temporary increase in the water content. However, Fonnesbeck *et al.* (1967) found little difference in the fecal water content of horses that were fed and had adjusted to a wide variety of grass and legume hays. Feeding of pelleted feeds increases the fecal water content. Ponies and donkeys may have a slightly drier fecal content than horses fed the same diet. Contrary to popular opinion, feeding horses a wet wheat bran mash does not produce feces with greater water content than feeding a dry wheat bran, assuming, of course, that the horse has access to drinking water.

7.5 Factors Affecting Digestion

Processing of Feeds. The method of processing may influence digestion. For example, the pelleting of roughage decreases fiber digestion approximately 9–15 percent. Rolling or breaking the kernel is important in the digestion of small grains, such as wheat and milo. Processing of larger grains, such as corn and oats, does not seem to greatly improve digestibility (Table 7-7). All grains should be cracked, crimped, or rolled for foals and horses with poor teeth. There is no advantage in cooking, fermenting, or predigesting feed for horses with good teeth. Steeping of wheat bran in warm water (50° C) for one hour does not affect the digestibility of dry matter, protein, or phosphorus.

Level of Intake. The level of intake does not appear to greatly affect the digestibility of all-roughage diets. However, the digestibility of diets containing forage and grain may be decreased with increased dietary intake.

253

TABLE 7-7
Comparison of digestibility of whole and crimped oats (percent)

Type of Oats	Digestibility[a]		
	Dry Matter	Crude Protein	Neutral Detergent Fiber
Whole	73.2 ± 4.4	85.6 ± 2.7	36.4 ± 4.0
Crimped	75.8 ± 2.2	84.7 ± 3.0	39.2 ± 4.5

SOURCE: Graves *et al.*, unpublished data.
[a]Means are average of 6 values.

Frequency of Feeding. Frequent feedings (2 or 3 times a day) are usually recommended for horses. Because the horse has a relatively small stomach, severe overeating at one time can produce colic or even a ruptured stomach. Of course, overeating may also produce founder. Therefore, the policy of feeding grain at least 2 times a day seems reasonable. Frequency of feeding, however, does not appear to affect digestibility, at least of complete pelleted diets. For example, when the daily feed of ponies was divided into 1, 2, or 6 feedings, digestibility was found not to be influenced by frequency of feeding, as shown in Table 7-8.

Work. Early studies indicated that activity may have some influence on the digestion of the horse. Olsson and Ruudvere (1955) suggested that light exercise might improve digestibility but heavy work may inhibit it. They cited the data of Grandeau and LeClere shown in Table 7-9.

Individuality. The individuality of the horse is sometimes thought to affect feed digestibility. For example, Fonnesbeck *et al.* (1967) reported that horses differ significantly in their ability to digest crude protein and nitrogen-free extract. This suggests that some of the hard keepers may have an impaired ability to digest feeds.

Associative Effects. No associative effects or interactions were observed when ponies were fed diets containing all hay, 50 percent hay and 50 percent grain, or 20 percent hay and 80 percent grain; that is, the addition of the grain did not appear to influence the digestion of the hay (Hintz *et al.*, 1971). There may be special associative effects. For example, the addition of wheat bran may decrease the absorption of calcium, but the bran does not appear to influence the digestion of fiber or protein.

Time of Watering. It is often stated that horses should be watered only before feeding because if they are watered after feeding, the digestibility of the diet will be decreased; that is, the water will wash the material

254

TABLE 7-8
Effect of feeding frequency on digestibility of complete pelleted horse feed
(percent)

Feeding Frequency	Digestibility[a]			
	Dry Matter	Crude Protein	Neutral Detergent Fiber	Acid Detergent Fiber
1 time/day	71.5	82.3	45.9	28.2
2 times/day	71.0	80.6	44.6	27.6
6 times/day	72.0	79.5	44.2	28.1

SOURCE: Butler and Hintz. 1971.

[a]Means are average of 3 values.

out of the digestive tract. There is no evidence to support such a theory.
In fact, several studies have demonstrated that time of watering does
not affect digestibility. However, watering before feeding is still a good
practice, because many horses will not eat unless they are first watered.

7.6 Comparative Digestion

Horses and ponies appear to be quite similar in their ability to digest
feedstuffs. Several studies have shown that the horse can digest protein
as efficiently or perhaps slightly more efficiently than ruminants. However, ruminants digest fiber more efficiently than horses. The differences
between equine and bovine species vary with the type and amount of
fiber (that is, the differences increase as the quality of roughage decreases), but in general, horses are approximately 2/3 as efficient in the
digestion of fiber as ruminants. The decreased efficiency of horses is
usually attributed to faster rate of passage of digesta. The bacteria in

TABLE 7-9
Effect of work on digestibility of horse

Amount of Activity	Relative Digestibility
Rest	100
Walking without load	106
Walking with load	101
Trotting without load	98
Trotting with load	97

SOURCE: Cited by Olsson and Ruudvere. 1955.

255

the large intestine of the horse do not have as much time to digest the fiber as the bacteria in the rumen. However, there may be other reasons. Ground roughages in nylon bags were placed in the cecum of ponies and the rumen of cattle via a fistula for the same length of time. A greater percentage of dry matter and fiber disappeared from the bags in the rumen than from the bags in the cecum (Koller, 1976). Comparison of fiber digestion of horses with that of other species is shown in Table 7-10. The horse is much more efficient in the digestion of fiber than the rabbit, even though the rabbit practices coprophagy (eating of feces) and has a large cecum. Some horses, particularly young foals and confined animals, also practice coprophagy. The effect of coprophagy on the digestion of the horse is not known, but it probably is so slight that it can be ignored. As mentioned earlier, the digestion coefficients obtained for horses and for ponies are similar. Further studies comparing other equidae are needed. Some preliminary reports suggest that the mule, donkey, and onager may be more efficient in the digestion of fiber than the horse.

Ruminants are more efficient than horses in the utilization of phytic acid phosphorus. Bacteria in the rumen produce an enzyme called phytase, which breaks down the phytate molecule and renders the phosphorus available for absorption. Phytase is also present in the intestinal tract of the horse but is not as effective as in the rumen, perhaps because of the faster rate of passage of digesta in the horse.

TABLE 7-10
Estimates of relative ability of various species to digest fiber

Species	Relative Value	Species	Relative Value
Llama	115–120	Mule	66–75
Water buffalo	100–110	Donkey	66–75
Cattle	100	Horse	66–70
Sheep	100	Zebra	66–70
Deer	100	Elephant	66–70
Bison	100	Guinea pig	62–70
Gazelle	100	Pig	50–55
Kangaroo	75–80	Hamster	40–45
Chinchilla	75–80	Rabbit	40–45
Onager	70–75	Vole	40–45
		Tortoise	40–45

References

Alexander, F. A. 1946. The rate of passage of food residues through the digestive tract of the horse. *J. Comp. Path.* 56:266.

Alexander, F. 1962. The concentration of certain electrolytes in the digestive tract of the horse and pig. *Res. Vet. Sci.* 3:78.

Alexander, F. 1963. Digestion in the horse. In *Progress in Nutrition and Allied Sciences,* D. P. Cuthbertson, ed. Chap. 23, p. 259. London: Oliver and Boyd.

Alexander, F., and J. C. D. Hickson. 1970. The salivary and pancreatic secretions of the horse. In *Physiology of Digestion and Metabolism in the Ruminant,* A. T. Phillipson, ed. Newcastle: Oriel Press.

Argenzio, R. A., J. E. Lowe, D. W. Pickard, and C. E. Stevens. 1974a. Digesta passage and water exchange in the equine large intestine. *Am. J. Physiol.* 226:1035.

Argenzio, R. A., M. Southworth, and C. E. Stevens. 1974b. Sites of organic acid production and absorption in the equine gastrointestinal tract. *Am. J. Physiol.* 226:1043.

Argenzio, R. A. 1975. Functions of the equine large intestine and their interrelationship in disease. *Cornell Vet.* 65:303.

Butler, D., and H. F. Hintz. 1971. *Animal Science Memo,* Cornell University.

Fonnesbeck, P. V., R. K. Lydman, G. W. VanderNoot, and L. D. Symons. 1967. Digestibility of the proximate nutrients of forage by horses. *J. Animal Sci.* 26:1039.

Fonnesbeck, P. V. 1968. Consumption and excretion of water by horses receiving all hay and hay-grain diets. *J. Animal Sci.* 27:1350.

Hintz, H. F., R. A. Argenzio, and H. F. Schryver. 1971. Digestion coefficients, blood glucose levels, and molar percentage of volatile acids in intestinal fluid of ponies fed varying forage-grain ratios. *J. Animal Sci.* 33:992.

Hintz, H. F., H. F. Schryver, and J. E. Lowe. 1973. Digestion in the horse—a review. *Feedstuffs* (July 2), p. 25.

Kern, D. L., L. L. Slyter, J. M. Weaver, E. C. Leffel, and G. Samuelson. 1973. Pony cecum vs. steer rumen: The effect of oats and hay on the microbial ecosystem. *J. Animal Sci.* 37:463.

Kern, K. L., L. L. Slyter, E. C. Leffel, J. M. Weaver, and R. R. Oltjen. 1974. Ponies vs. steers: Microbial and chemical characteristics of intestinal ingesta. *J. Animal Sci.* 38:559.

Koller, B. 1976. "Comparative cell wall and dry matter digestion in the cecum of the pony and rumen of the cow using in vitro and nylon bag techniques." Master's thesis, Cornell University, Ithaca, New York.

Linerode, P. A. 1967. Studies on synthesis and absorption of B-complex vitamins in the horse. *Am. Assoc. Equine Pract.* 23:283.

Olsson, N., and A. Ruudvere. 1955. Nutrition of the horse. *Nutr. Abst. Rev.* 25:1.

Reitnour, C. M., and R. L. Salsbury. 1975. Effects of oral or cecal administration of protein supplements on equine plasma amino acids. *Brit. Vet. J.* 131:466.

Roberts, M. C. 1975. Carbohydrate digestion and absorption studies in the horse. *Res. Vet. Sci.* 18:64.

Robinson, D. W., and L. M. Slade. 1974. Current status of knowledge on the nutrition of equines. *J. Animal Sci.* 39:1045.

Schryver, H. F., P. H. Craig, and H. F. Hintz. 1970. Calcium metabolism in ponies fed varying levels of calcium. *J. Nutr.* 100:955.

Slade, L. M., R. Bishop, J. G. Morris, and D. W. Robinson. 1971. Digestion and absorption of ^{15}N-labeled microbial protein in the large intestine of the horse. *Brit. Vet. J.* 127:xi.

Smith, H. W. 1965. Observations on the flora of the alimentary tract of animals and factors affecting its composition. *J. Path. Bact.* 89:89.

Templeton, J. A., and I. A. Dyer. 1967. Diet and supplemental enzyme effects on volatile fatty acids of bovine rumen fluid. *J. Animal Sci.* 26:1374.

Tyznik, W. J. 1973. The digestive system of the horse. *Stud Managers Handbook* 9:55. Clovis, California: Agriservices Foundation.

Wysocki, A. A., and J. P. Baker. 1975. Utilization of bacterial protein from the lower gut of the equine. *Proc. Fourth Equine Nutr. Phys. Symp.* (January), Pomona, California, p. 21.

CHAPTER EIGHT *Nutrients*

On examining the animal's head, I was particularly struck with the enlarged and roundish appearance of the facial region. . . . He stepped short, flexed his limbs with difficulty and apparently with much pain. . . . Bran formed the greater part of the diet. Thinking that perhaps the kind of food the horses had been eating had had something to do in producing the disease, I advised that the bran should be given occasionally, and that some other food should be made the basis of the support.

G. VARNELL. 1860. *The Veterinarian* 33:493.

8.1 Energy

Several methods are commonly used to determine the energy content of feeds. The gross energy is determined by igniting the feed in a bomb calorimeter and recording the amount of heat produced. The digestible energy content is determined in a digestion trial (see section 7-3), in which the energy content of the feed and feces is determined. Digestible energy is gross energy in feed minus energy lost in feces. Metabolizable energy is determined by correcting digestible energy for energy lost in the gaseous products of digestion, such as methane, and the energy lost in urine. Net energy is the term used to refer to the energy that is actually used by the animal. These methods commonly express the energy content as calories per unit of weight.

Another method of energy evaluation is to calculate total digestible nutrients (TDN). This is the sum of all the digestible organic nutrients (protein, fiber, nitrogen free extract, and fat). The digestible fat content is multiplied by 2.25 because the energy content of fat per unit of weight is 2.25 times that of carbohydrates. TDN is determined in digestion trials and is similar to digestible energy (DE). Values for TDN can be converted to approximate DE by assuming that 2,000 kilocalories is equal to one pound of TDN. (4,400 kilocalories would equal one kilogram of TDN.) TDN and DE are the two most commonly used methods of evaluating the energy content of horse feeds.

Metabolism. The carbohydrate fraction of the diet is the primary source of energy, although protein and fat are also used as energy sources. When high levels of soluble carbohydrates are fed, glucose is the primary product of digestion and is the primary energy source. The importance of volatile fatty acids (VFA), which are the end products of bacteria fermentation, increases as the amount of roughage in the diet increases (see Table 7-4).

The nature of endocrine response to glucose and VFA in the horse differs from the response in ruminants; in horses, VFA does not stimulate the release of insulin. The endocrine response to glucose infusion in horses is more similar to the response obtained in nonruminants such as the dog than to the response obtained in ruminants. Fasted horses are much less sensitive to insulin action than are fed horses (Argenzio and Hintz, 1970; Evans, 1971).

Requirements. The maintenance requirement for DE (kcal/day) = 155 $W^{.75}$, where W equals weight of the horse in kilograms. This is approximately 0.75 lb of TDN per 100 lb of body weight for horses weighing 1,000–1,100 lb. Pregnancy does not increase the energy requirement until the last third of the gestation period. At that time, energy intake should be increased approximately 5 percent above maintenance. Intake should be gradually increased throughout the last third until it is approximately 20 percent above maintenance at time of foaling. Lactation may greatly increase the energy needs, but the amount will, of course, depend on the level of milk production. Peak lactation usually occurs 8–12 weeks after foaling. At peak lactation milk production may be as high as 50–60 lb per day, but it is usually much less. In general, lactation usually increases the energy requirement 50–70 percent above maintenance.

Estimates of the energy requirements for work are shown in Table 8-1. However, more research is needed to refine these estimates. Few studies have been conducted on the energy requirements of working light horses or the factors affecting energy requirements, such as sources of energy.

The requirements for growing animals depend on the growth rate that is desired. The optimal growth rate for maximum performance and productivity including longevity is yet to be defined. The National Research

260

TABLE 8-1
Estimates of energy requirements for various
activities

Activity	Requirement (kcal/hr/kg body wt)[a]
Walking	0.5
Slow trotting, some cantering	5.1
Fast trotting, cantering, some jumping	12.5
Cantering, galloping, jumping	24.0
Strenuous effort	39.0

SOURCE: National Research Council, 1973.
[a]Requirement above maintenance.

Council (1973) estimates of energy requirements of growing horses are given in Table 8-2.

Deficiency. A deficiency of energy in the young horse results in a poor rate of growth and a generally unthrifty appearance. In mature horses there is loss of weight, poor performance, and generally poor condition.

Toxicity. An excess of energy results in obese horses. The excess fat may decrease performance and reproductive efficiency. Obesity is often considered the most common form of malnutrition in horses in the United States. Also, excess energy makes horses "high" and more difficult to handle. Grain is not usually fed during initial breaking for this reason.

8.2 Protein

Protein is composed of a chain of smaller units called amino acids, which contain nitrogen. These amino acids are the building blocks the body uses to synthesize body tissues. Some of these amino acids can be synthesized by the body but others, called the essential amino acids, cannot and must be supplied in the diet. Table 8-3 lists the essential amino acids and some of the nonessential amino acids.

Metabolism. The small intestine is the primary site of protein digestion in the horse, although significant amounts of nitrogen are absorbed from the large intestine. The nutritional value of nitrogen absorbed from the large intestine is currently the subject of considerable debate. Some

261

TABLE 8-2
Energy requirements of growing foals

Age (Months)	Body Weight (kg)	Percentage of Mature Weight	Daily Gain (kg)	Daily Feed (kg)[a]	Digestible Energy (Mcal)
		200 kg Mature Weight			
3	50	25.0	0.70	2.94	7.43
6	90	45.0	0.50	3.10	8.53
12	135	67.5	0.20	2.89	7.95
18	165	82.5	0.10	2.94	8.08
42	200	100.0	0	3.00	8.24
		400 kg Mature Weight			
3	85	21.3	1.00	3.80	10.44
6	170	42.5	0.65	4.51	12.41
12	260	65.0	0.40	4.96	13.63
18	330	82.5	0.25	5.13	14.10
42	400	100.0	0	5.04	13.86
		500 kg Mature Weight			
3	110	22.0	1.10	4.39	12.07
6	225	45.0	0.80	5.60	15.40
12	325	65.0	0.55	6.11	16.81
18	400	80.0	0.35	6.24	17.16
42	500	100.0	0	5.96	16.39
		600 kg Mature Weight			
3	140	23.3	1.25	5.15	14.15
6	265	44.2	0.85	6.26	17.21
12	385	64.1	0.60	6.86	18.86
18	480	80.0	0.35	6.98	19.20
42	600	100.0	0	6.83	18.79

SOURCE: National Research Council. 1973.

[a]Assuming 2.75 Mcal of digestible energy per kg of 100 percent dry feed.

reports indicate that bacteria use nitrogen in the digesta to synthesize amino acids and that the bacterial amino acids are subsequently absorbed from the large intestine, but other reports suggest that the primary products absorbed from the large intestine are not amino acids but ammonia and other nonamino acid nitrogen compounds (see section 7.4). These latter compounds can be used by the tissues in the synthesis of the nonessential amino acids but cannot be used in the synthesis of the essential amino acids.

TABLE 8-3
Amino acids generally considered dietary essentials for most nonruminants and some of the nonessential amino acids

Essential Amino Acids	Nonessential Amino Acids	Essential Amino Acids	Nonessential Amino Acids
Threonine	Glycine	Leucine	Aspartic acid
Valine	Alanine	Methionine	Glutamic acid
Phenylalanine	Serine	Isoleucine	Proline
Arginine	Cystine	Tryptophan	Hydroxyproline
Lysine	Tyrosine	Histidine	Citrulline

Significant quantities of urea are recycled and hydrolyzed in the gastrointestinal tract of the horse under normal feeding conditions, that is, even when the dietary nitrogen is primarily protein and the protein is not fed at an excessively high level.

Mature horses can use limited amounts of nonprotein nitrogen compounds such as urea in the diet to increase nitrogen retention, but such compounds are not utilized as efficiently as dietary protein.

Requirements. The quality of the protein (the amino acid content) included in the diet is very important for the growth of young foals. For example, young horses fed a diet in which milk products were the primary protein source grew much faster and more efficiently than horses fed a diet in which linseed meal was the primary protein source (Hintz *et al.*, 1971). The milk products contained a higher level of the amino acid lysine than linseed meal, and the addition of lysine to the linseed diet greatly improved the growth rate (Table 8-4). Weanlings appear to require 0.65–0.7 percent lysine in the daily diet. Other amino acids that have been demonstrated to be required for nonruminants such as rat and man are probably also required in the diet of the young horse, but no estimates of the actual requirements are available.

The protein requirement depends on the amino acid content. However, estimates of the total protein required can be made if the diet is assumed to contain a high-quality protein (good mixture of essential amino acids), including an adequate lysine level. Lysine is often the limiting amino acid in vegetable proteins (that is, it limits the growth of the animal because it is not present in adequate amounts). The protein and lysine content of some common feedstuffs is shown in Table 9-4. Soybean meal contains the highest lysine content of the commonly used vegetable proteins. The percentage of protein in the form of lysine is higher in animal products, such as dried skim milk and fish meal, but these products are usually much more expensive than soybean meal. Of course, not only the amount of protein or amino acids, but also their

263

TABLE 8-4

Weight gain and feed-to-gain ratio of growing horses fed diets containing milk protein (MP) or linseed meal (LSM)

Diet	No. of Animals	Average Daily Weight Gain (kg)	Average Daily Intake (kg)	Feed-to-Gain Ratio
Trial 1 (1–76 days): Part 1				
MP	6	0.95[a]	5.24[a]	5.52[a]
LSM	6	0.60[b]	4.58[b]	7.63[b]
Trial 1 (77–111 days): Part 2				
MP	6	0.91[a]	5.77[a]	6.34[a]
LSM	3	0.50[b]	4.25[b]	8.49[b]
LSM + 0.4% lysine	3	0.91[a]	4.88[a,b]	5.36[a]
Trial 2 (117 days)				
MP	5	0.49[a]	5.05	10.32[a]
MP	5	0.41[a,b]	4.69	11.44[a,b]
LSM	5	0.37[b]	4.67	12.61[b]
LSM + 0.4% lysine	5	0.42[a,b]	5.05	12.03[a,b]

SOURCE: Adapted from Hintz *et al.* 1971. *J. Animal Sci.* 33:1274.

[a,b]Comparable values with unlike superscripts are significantly different ($P < .05$).

availability or digestibility, is important. The values in the last column in Table 9-4 indicate that most common protein sources are readily digested by the horse. Excessive heating of the protein supplement during processing greatly decreases the digestibility of the protein by the horse.

In general, foals weaned at 4 months should be fed a diet containing 16 percent protein. Foals at 6 months of age should be fed at least 14 percent protein, assuming that the diet contains high-quality proteins. Yearlings require 12 percent protein, mature horses require 8 percent, pregnant mares require 11–12 percent, and lactating mares require 13–15 percent. Work does not increase the protein requirement when expressed as a fraction of the diet. The increased food intake as a result of the increased energy needs for work compensate for any nitrogen lost in sweat. The National Research Council's estimates of protein requirements, as well as requirements of calcium, phosphorus, and vitamin A are given in Appendix Tables 8-1 through 8-4.

Deficiency. Signs of protein deficiency are general rather than specific. In young animals, poor growth, a high feed-to-gain ratio, and general unthriftiness can result because of protein deficiency. In mature animals, there may be a loss of weight. Pregnant mares fed protein-deficient diets will have small, weak foals.

Toxicity.   Protein toxicity is not a problem. When excessive amounts of protein are fed, the carbon chain of the amino acid is utilized for energy and the nitrogen is excreted via the urine by the kidneys. Excessive ingestion of nitrogen-rich compounds such as urea, however, can be toxic. Urea is converted into ammonia and carbon dioxide by an enzyme, urease, that is produced by the intestinal bacteria. The resulting increase in ammonia absorption can be lethal. One of the clinical effects of ammonia toxicosis is severe central nervous system derangement (Hintz *et al.,* 1970). The earliest signs are aimless wandering and incoordination followed by pressing of the head against fixed objects (Figure 8-1). Once head pressing begins, it is usually continued until the animal falls, and remains at this site until death. Death usually occurs 30–90 minutes after the onset of the first signs of nervous system derangement. The first signs of derangement may occur 2–10 hours after animals ingest a toxic dose of urea. Although high levels of urea are toxic to horses, horses are more tolerant of dietary urea than cattle. Thus, there is no danger in feeding horses a ration containing urea if the ration is safe for cattle. In the horse, much of the dietary urea is absorbed from the small intestine and excreted via the kidneys. Thus the bacteria in the large intestine do not have an opportunity to convert urea into ammonia and carbon dioxide.

FIGURE 8-1
Head pressing in a pony caused by brain damage due to a high level of ammonia in the blood.

265

8.3 Minerals

Calcium

Metabolism. Calcium has many important functions in the body. It is necessary for bone formation; approximately 99 percent of the total body calcium is contained in the skeleton. It is also necessary for normal muscular activity, blood clotting, and enzyme activation. Animals have a regulatory system that tries to ensure that the blood always contains adequate levels of calcium. Whenever the blood calcium level decreases, the parathyroid gland releases a hormone, parathormone, that causes calcium to be released from the bone and thus increases the amount of calcium in the blood. Calcitonin, a hormone produced in the thyroid gland, is activated when the blood calcium level is too high. This hormone decreases the amount of calcium that is removed from the bone. Excessive intakes of calcium result in increased kidney excretion of calcium.

Calcium is absorbed from the small intestine, and the amount absorbed is influenced by many factors. Vitamin D apparently stimulates calcium absorption by inducing the formation of a calcium-binding protein in the cells of the intestine. This calcium-binding protein is important in the absorption of calcium. The level of calcium in the diet also influences the efficiency of calcium absorption, because high levels of dietary calcium decrease the digestibility of calcium. A high level of dietary phosphorus relative to the dietary calcium also decreases calcium absorption. Therefore, the diet should always contain at least as much calcium as phosphorus; that is, the calcium-to-phosphorus ratio should be at least 1:1. Lactose, particularly in the diet of the young animal, may increase calcium absorption.

Requirements. Young animals that are rapidly synthesizing bone and lactating mares have the greatest calcium needs.

Mineral requirements for growth are more difficult to determine than those for maintenance because the criteria of adequacy are not well defined. The rate of body gain, although sometimes used, is not a good criterion because dietary mineral levels that are adequate for optimum weight gain may not be adequate for proper bone formation. In one experiment, ponies fed a low calcium diet for 12 weeks were found to be in negative calcium balance but gained in height and weight at the same rate as those fed higher levels of calcium (Schryver *et al.*, 1974). The criteria for the mineral requirements for growth that were used to obtain the estimated values that follow included mineral retention, bone ash per unit volume of bone, calcium and phosphorus content of bone and of the total body, and specific gravity of bone.

266

Weanlings require 150–180 mg of calcium per kilogram of body weight per day and yearlings require 110 mg of calcium per kilogram of body weight per day. Thus diets for weanlings that contain 0.7 percent calcium and diets for yearlings that contain 0.6 percent calcium are adequate.

Diets containing 0.35 percent calcium are adequate for maintenance. The mineral requirement of the mare is increased during the last third of pregnancy to provide calcium and phosphorus for mineralization of the developing fetal skeleton. However, the calcium demands of pregnancy are relatively small and can be met by diets containing 0.4 percent calcium.

The mineral requirements of lactation are much greater than those of pregnancy and increase as lactation progresses, reaching a peak at 8–12 weeks. During peak lactation, a 450-kilogram mare may produce 20 kg of milk daily containing 800–1,000 mg of calcium per kg. Lactation calcium requirements can be met by diets containing 0.5 percent calcium. These estimates are summarized in Table 8-5.

Deficiency. Bone is formed by a complicated series of events. A simplified explanation is that cells called osteoblasts produce a protein matrix called osteoid tissue. The tissue is calcified when the proper amounts of calcium, phosphorus, magnesium, and other minerals are present. However, bone is not static; it is continually being reformed. Calcium and phosphorus are constantly being released by the action of cells called osteocytes and osteoclasts. If the young, growing animal does not have enough calcium to adequately calcify the bone, the bone becomes weak and may be deformed. This condition, *in extremis,* is called rickets. (Rickets occurs only in young animals and can be caused by a deficiency of calcium, phosphorus, or vitamin D.)

Nutritional secondary hyperparathyroidism is a bone disease that may occur in horses if their diet contains a low level of calcium and a high level of phosphorus. A high level of phosphorus interferes with calcium

TABLE 8-5

Estimates of requirements of calcium and phosphorus for horses with mature weight of 1,100 lb

Class	Grams/day		Percentage in diet	
	Ca	P	Ca	P
Weanlings	38	25	0.70	0.45
Yearlings	35	21	0.60	0.35
Mature horses	22	14	0.35	0.25
Pregnant mares	30	23	0.40	0.30
Lactating mares	50	36	0.50	0.35

SOURCE: Schryver, H. F., *et al.* 1974.

267

absorption. As discussed earlier in this section, a normal level of blood calcium is required for many functions. Whenever the blood calcium level drops, the parathyroid hormone increases the release of calcium from the bone to maintain the blood level of calcium. Lameness and enlarged facial bones may result (Figure 8-2). The enlarged facial bones result because fibrous connective tissue invades the area from which calcium was resorbed. The bones are lacking in density and sound hollow when tapped. This condition is often called big head disease, brain disease, or miller's disease. It is called bran disease because feeding high levels of wheat bran, which is very high in phosphorus and low in calcium, produces the condition. The name "miller's disease" was given to the condition because in the past it was common among horses owned by grain millers. The miller often fed his horses the by-products of the milling industry such as wheat bran.

Toxicity. It has been proposed that when animals are fed high levels of calcium for prolonged periods, their bones become very brittle and dense because of an overproduction of the hormone calcitonin (Krook *et al.*, 1969). Whitlock (1970) reported that young horses fed high levels of calcium for long periods had levels of calcitonin that were above normal and evidenced decreased bone resorption. However, calcium excess does not appear to be a prevalent problem. High dietary levels of

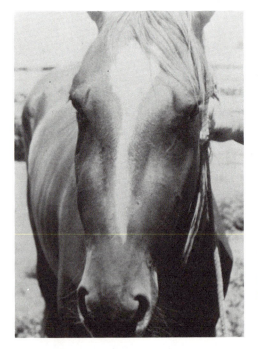

FIGURE 8-2
"Big head" disease in a horse caused by excessive phosphorus and a low level of calcium. Photo courtesy of Texas A & M University.

calcium may reduce the availability of other minerals such as phosphorus, magnesium, and manganese.

Phosphorus

Metabolism. Approximately 80 percent of the body's phosphorus is contained in the skeleton. Phosphorus is a component of many compounds, such as phospho-proteins, nucleoproteins, phospholipids, and the energy-rich adenosine phosphate compounds. The feces are the primary pathway for phosphorus excretion, but the kidneys also excrete some phosphorus when large amounts of phosphorus are fed. Inorganic phosphate compounds are readily digested by the horse, but some organic compounds, such as phytin phosphorus, are less available. Horses do not utilize phytin phosphorus as efficiently as ruminants but they are more efficient than pigs and chicks, probably because the enzyme phytase, produced by the intestinal bacteria, renders some of the phytin phosphorus available for absorption. Fortunately, the horse can absorb phosphorus from the large intestine, which is the primary site of phytase activity. Although a high phosphorus-low calcium ratio greatly hinders calcium digestibility, the opposite effect is much less dramatic. The data shown in Table 8-6 demonstrate that although high levels of calcium inhibit phosphorus absorption, the effect is not so great as the effect of phosphorus on calcium absorption. This may be because much of the calcium is absorbed from the small intestine. Thus, the actual calcium-to-phosphorus

TABLE 8-6
Effect of calcium and phosphorus on digestibility

Percentage in Diet		Ca:P Ratio	Estimated True Digestibility (percent)	
Ca	P		Ca	P
Trial 1				
0.40	0.20	2.0:1.0	68.1	40.0
0.35	1.19	0.3:1.0	43.5	47.0
Trial 2				
0.15	0.35	0.4:1.0	70.0	53.2
1.50	0.35	4.3:1.0	46.0	47.2
Trial 3				
0.80	0.25	3.2:1.0	75.1	57.4
3.40	0.25	13.6:1.0	52.7	40.7

SOURCE: Schryver, H. F., *et al.* 1974.

ratio of the digesta in the large intestine, a primary site of phosphorus absorption, is much different than the calcium-to-phosphorus ratio in the diet.

Requirements. Dietary requirements for phosphorus are as follows: weanlings require 0.45 percent of the ration, yearlings need 0.35 percent, mature horses need 0.25 percent, pregnant mares require 0.30 percent, and lactating mares need 0.35 percent.

Deficiency. A phosphorus deficiency will result in rickets in the young animal. In a mature animal, deficiency results in osteomalacia (soft bones). Depraved appetite and reduced productive performance are also signs of possible phosphorus deficiency.

Toxicity. The feeding of diets containing high levels of phosphorus, such as wheat bran diets, may be toxic because of the induced calcium deficiency. However, the situation can easily be remedied by the addition of calcium to the diet or removal of the wheat bran.

Magnesium

Metabolism. Magnesium is an essential constituent of bones and teeth and is required for many body processes as an activator of enzymes. The endogenous losses of magnesium, in contrast to the losses of calcium and phosphorus, are greater in the urine than in the feces. Magnesium digestibility is decreased when excessive amounts of either phosphorus or calcium are present in the diet.

Requirements. Few studies have been conducted on the magnesium requirement, but mature horses apparently require 13 milligrams per kilogram of body weight per day (Meyer, 1960; Hintz and Schryver, 1973).

Deficiency. The signs of magnesium deficiency are hyperirritability, glazed eyes, tetany, and eventual collapse. The condition is often precipitated by some form of stress. Some veterinarians have reported that some horses at sales exhibit these signs and seem to respond to a magnesium-calcium injection. Years ago, it was reported that when mountain ponies or ponies that worked in mines were transported, they suffered from a "transit tetany" that responded to magnesium and calcium injection (Green et al., 1935). Harrington (1971) reported that magnesium deficiency in young foals resulted in calcification of the blood vessels.

Toxicity. There have been no reports that magnesium toxicity in the horse can be attributed to the diet. However, prolonged breathing of magnesium fumes could be toxic.

Potassium

Metabolism. Potassium is readily absorbed from feeds, and the primary path of excretion is the urine.

Requirements. It has been suggested that the diets of early weaned foals should contain at least 1 percent potassium per day (Stowe, 1971). Recent studies indicate that mature horses need approximately 0.5–0.6 percent potassium in the diet to maintain positive potassium balance (Hintz and Schryver, 1976).

Deficiency. Reduced appetite is an early sign of potassium deficiency.

Toxicity. There have been no reports of potassium toxicity in the horse.

Iodine

Metabolism. Iodine is a component of thyroxine, a product of the thyroid gland that contains 75 percent of the iodine present in the body and controls the metabolic rate. Little research has been conducted on iodine metabolism in the horse, but the element is probably readily absorbed from the small intestine. The urine is the primary path of excretion.

Requirements. The National Research Council (1973) suggests that the iodine requirement is 0.1 ppm daily.

Deficiency. When mares are fed iodine-deficient diets, their foals may have an enlarged thryoid (goiter) and be stillborn or weak and hairless.

Toxicity. Feeding excessive levels of iodine to the mare (more than 40 mg per day) may result in weak foals with goiters (Figure 8-3) (Baker and Lindsay, 1968; Drew *et al.*, 1975). Such foals often have leg weaknesses and may die shortly after birth. Some types of kelp, a seaweed, contain high levels of iodine.

Iron

Metabolism. Iron is an essential component of the hemoglobin of the red blood cells. Iron is primarily absorbed from the small intestine. Presumably, iron absorption in the horse is similar to that reported for other species in that the efficiency of absorption is determined by the body's need. Iron is efficiently conserved by the body because the endogenous losses

271

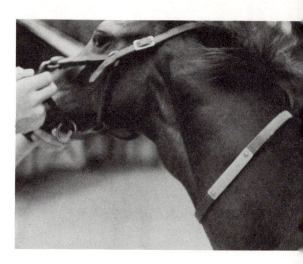

FIGURE 8-3
Enlarged thyroid in foal caused by feeding excess iodine to the mare. Photo courtesy of William Sippel and Florida Department of Agriculture.

are small. Loss of blood because of heavy parasite loads or wounds is the primary cause of iron loss.

Requirements. The National Research Council (1973) suggests that 40 ppm of iron daily is adequate for mature animals but that rapidly growing foals may require 50 ppm.

Deficiency. Anemia is the primary sign of iron deficiency.

Toxicity. Iron toxicity has been produced in several species but there have been no reports of dietary iron toxicity in the horse and it does not appear to be a problem of practical concern. Several cases have been reported in which horses died shortly after being given an intramuscular injection of iron dextran (Wagenaar, 1975). Thus iron dextran injections should not be used.

Zinc

Requirements. The daily zinc requirement is probably less than 50 ppm.

Deficiency. The signs of deficiency are decreased zinc blood levels, poor growth, and skin lesions (parakeratosis) (Harrington *et al.*, 1973).

Toxicity. Growing horses fed diets containing 0.54 percent zinc developed anemia, swelling at the epiphyseal region of the long bones, stiffness, and lameness (Willoughby *et al.*, 1973) (Figure 8-4). In some areas the forage may contain high levels of zinc because of fumes from nearby smelters.

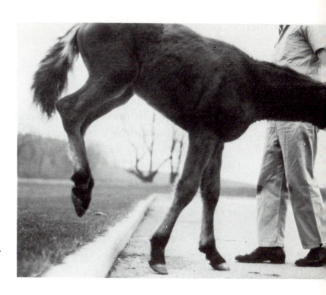

FIGURE 8-4
Zinc toxicity in this foal caused pain and stiffness, and the animal had difficulty stepping over an 8-inch curb. Photo courtesy of R. Willoughby.

Selenium

Requirements. The selenium requirement appears to be 0.1 ppm daily. The requirement depends on the vitamin E content of the diet because vitamin E and selenium act synergistically.

Deficiency. Selenium deficiency results in muscle degeneration in the young foal. The muscles become very pale, hence the name "white muscle disease" (Figure 8-5). The affected foals often die of starvation because they are too weak to nurse. The condition occurs in areas where the soil has a low selenium content. The incidence of selenium deficiency appears to be increasing in some areas. Several cases of white muscle disease have recently been diagnosed in foals raised in New York State. Several foals in the central Kentucky area were found to have low blood selenium levels, and it was concluded that subclinical selenium-responsive muscular diseases exist in horses in the central Kentucky area, even though gross lesions may be rare (Stowe, 1967).

FIGURE 8-5
White muscle disease in a foal. Note the striations or pale areas in the intracostal muscles. Photo courtesy of R. Whitlock.

273

Toxicity. Chronic selenium toxicity can result in sloughing of hooves, loss of manes and tails, and eventually death. The condition is called alkali disease. Acute toxicity results in respiratory failure, blindness, and death. The condition is called blind staggers. The soil in areas of Wyoming, South Dakota, and Nebraska has a high selenium content, and plants raised in these areas may be toxic to horses. Commercial mineral mixes do not contain significant amounts of selenium, and thus free-choice feeding of mineral mixes does not produce selenium toxicity. Selenium injections are often used for various muscle disorders, and improper use could result in excess selenium, but few such cases have been reported.

Sodium Chloride (Salt)

Requirements. The requirement for sodium chloride depends on the amount lost in sweat. The National Research Council (1973) suggests that 50–60 g of supplemental salt daily will meet the needs of most horses but that additional salt is required in hot climates.

Deficiency. The signs of deficiency are depraved appetite, rough hair coat, and reduced growth.

Toxicity. There is little danger of excess sodium chloride unless water is not available. However, there have been some reports of fatalities caused by the drinking of salt brine, or the feeding of salt to salt-hungry horses when adequate water was not available. Salt poisoning signs are colic, diarrhea, frequent urination, weakness, staggering, and paralysis of the hind limbs (Friedberger and Frohner, 1908).

Copper

Requirements. The copper requirement is estimated to be 5–8 ppm daily (Cupps and Howell, 1949).

Deficiency. The first sign of copper deficiency would probably be anemia. The activity of the osteoclasts (bone-forming cells) would be decreased and the bones would be thin and weak.

Toxicity. The level of copper that is toxic to horses has not been established. Sheep are less tolerant of high dietary levels of copper than any other species that has been studied. Liver damage has been reported in sheep fed diets containing 50–60 ppm copper, whereas rats can tolerate diets containing 500 ppm copper. Horses are also more tolerant of copper than sheep. For example, in recent studies horses were fed 800 ppm copper as $CuCo_3$ for 180 days with no apparent harmful effects (Smith *et al.*, 1975).

274

Fluorine

Deficiency. A fluorine deficiency has not been demonstrated in the horse.

Toxicity. Horses are apparently more tolerant of fluorine than cattle and sheep, but the lesions resulting from toxicity are similar to those observed in other species. Teeth and bones are the parts of the body most severely affected. The severity of the lesion depends on the level of fluoride. Teeth may be mottled and stained. Higher levels cause the enamel to be pitted and off-colored and may also cause severe abrasion and loss of teeth. The bones may become thicker and have abnormal patterns. A "Roman nose" appearance may result because of the thickening of the nasal and maxillary bones (Shupe and Olson, 1971).

Lead

Deficiency. Lead is not an essential nutrient.

Toxicity. An excess of lead in young horses causes pharyngeal and laryngeal paralysis, bone lesions, poor growth, muscular weakness, and anemia (Willoughby *et al.*, 1972). Lead poisoning has been reported in horses located near smelters in Germany, the United States, and Ireland. The pastures contained a high level of lead because of a lead emission from the smelters. Excessive chewing of wood coated with lead paint can also result in lead poisoning.

8.4 Vitamins

Vitamin A

Requirements. The National Research Council (1973) suggests that 25 IU of vitamin A per kilogram of body weight daily is adequate for maintenance; 40 IU per kilogram daily is adequate for growing animals; and 50 IU per kilogram daily is adequate for pregnancy and lactation.

Deficiency. There are many signs of vitamin A deficiency. Anorexia (loss of appetite), night blindness, lacrimation (excessive tearing or watering of the eyes, shown in Figure 8-6), keratinization of the cornea and skin, respiratory difficulties, reproductive failure, convulsive seizures, blindness caused by pinching of the optic nerve, bone lesions, and impaired resistance to disease can result from a deficiency of vitamin A. One of the

275

FIGURE 8-6
Chronic lacrimation (tearing) in a foal
deficient in vitamin A. Note matted
hair below the medial canthus of the
eye. Narrowing of the nasolacrimal
duct, the result of squamous
metaplasia, may have caused some
of the flowing tears.

earliest reports of a probable vitamin A deficiency in the equine is found
in Jeremiah 14:6. The wild asses had trouble seeing and breathing possibly
because a drought had killed all the grass, and dried grass has no vitamin
A value.

Toxicity. There have been no reports of vitamin A toxicity in the horse.
The signs would probably be similar to those reported for other species.
Decreased growth and deformed, shortened bones have been reported in
pigs, calves, and dogs fed several hundred times the vitamin A requirement.

Vitamin D

Requirements. The daily requirement for vitamin D has not been established, but 6.6 IU per kilogram of body weight is known to be adequate.
Horses are not likely to need vitamin D supplements when they are fed
sun-cured roughages or are exposed to sunlight. Sun-cured hay contains
significant amounts of vitamin D, and the ultraviolet rays of sunlight convert the dehydrocholesterol produced by the animal's body into vitamin D.

Deficiency. Vitamin D deficiency has not been demonstrated in horses,
but presumably a deficiency would result in rickets in young horses.

Toxicity. Levels of 14,000 IU per kilogram of body weight per day result
in acute toxicity and calcification of lungs, heart, kidneys, and other organs

within 10 days (Figure 8-7). Levels of 3,500 IU per kilogram of body weight per day resulted in chronic toxicity. The signs were elevated serum phosphorus, calcification of kidneys, rarefication of bones, severe loss of weight, and death after 3–4 months. Levels of 700 IU per kilogram of body weight per day were fed to young ponies for 9 months and no lesions were observed (Hintz *et al.*, 1973).

Vitamin E

Requirements.   The requirement for vitamin E has not been established, but foals deficient in vitamin E have been shown to require 27 µg of parenteral tocopherol or 233 µg of oral tocopherol per kilogram of body weight per day to maintain erythrocyte stability (Stowe, 1968). Vitamin E combined with selenium has also been effective in the treatment of white muscle disease.

Toxicity.   There have been no reports of vitamin E toxicity.

B Vitamins

The National Research Council (1973) has stated that B vitamins need not be added to rations of most horses, because good-quality hay is an excellent source of B vitamins and significant amounts of B vitamins are produced in the large intestine of the horse. However, the National Research Council (1973) further suggested that additional vitamins might

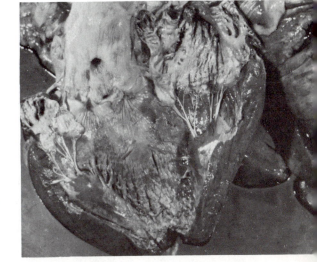

FIGURE 8-7
Calcification of the heart muscles of a
growing foal because of excessive
intake of vitamin D.

be needed if the horse is under heavy stress, or used for performance such as racing or show, or if very poor-quality hay is fed for prolonged periods. Presumably the recommendation for stressed horses was made because the B vitamins play a role in energy metabolism. The greater the energy intake, the greater the B vitamin requirement. However, no information is available as to whether a greater ratio of B vitamins to energy is needed for exercised horses than for horses fed maintenance diets.

Thiamin

Requirements. The requirement for thiamin has not been established, but 3 mg per kilogram of feed appears to be adequate. Although some thiamin appears to be absorbed from the large intestine (Linerode, 1967), Carroll (1950) demonstrated that horses fed poor-quality hay may develop a thiamin deficiency.

Deficiency. Horses fed thiamin-deficient diets exhibited anorexia, nervousness, incoordination in the hindquarters, loss of weight, and general weakness (Carroll, 1950). Thiamin deficiency may be induced in horses by the ingestion of plants such as bracken fern and "mare's tail," which contain compounds that destroy thiamin (Figure 8-8).

Toxicity. There have been no reports of thiamin toxicity in horses.

Riboflavin

Requirements. The riboflavin requirement is not known, but 2.2 mg of riboflavin per kilogram of feed is adequate.

Deficiency. Early reports indicated that riboflavin deficiency may produce periodic ophthalmia or moonblindness (recurrent equine uveitis–

FIGURE 8-8
Bracken fern contains an antithiamin compound and may induce thiamin deficiency in horses. Horses seldom eat the plant but will do so when other feeds are not available.

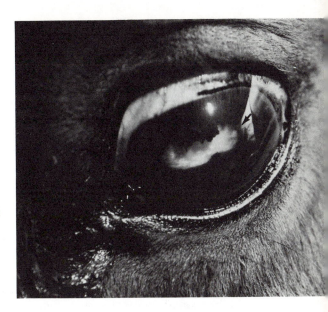

FIGURE 8-9
Recurrent equine uveitis (periodic ophthalmia, or moonblindness) is often thought to be caused by riboflavin deficiency. However, most recent studies indicate that the condition is an immunological response to other diseases. The cataract (*at arrow*) in the eye is the result of several episodes of recurrent uveitis. Sequelae of this disease can cause severe internal architectural damage, cataracts, and blindness. Photo courtesy of R. Riis.

see Figure 8-9) in the horse (Jones, 1942). However, most veterinarians today do not accept the theory that riboflavin deficiency causes the condition. Recurrent equine uveitis is probably an immunological response to other disease conditions.

Toxicity. There have been no reports of riboflavin toxicity in horses.

Vitamin B_{12}

Requirements. Mature horses that received 6 mg of vitamin B_{12} per day for 11 months failed to show any signs of B_{12} deficiency (Stillions *et al.*, 1971a). Significant amounts of B_{12} are produced by the bacteria in the digestive tract (Davies, 1968), and it has recently been suggested that some B_{12} can be absorbed from the large intestine (Salminen, 1975).

Deficiency. Vitamin B_{12} deficiency has not been produced experimentally in animals; however, severely debilitated, anemic, heavily parasitized animals appear to respond to B_{12} injections.

Toxicity. No information is presently available on the toxic levels of B_{12} or signs of vitamin B_{12} toxicity.

Other B Vitamins

Few studies have been made of the other B vitamins. Horses fed a low level of niacin excreted more niacin than they consumed, which suggests that niacin is not a dietary essential for horses (National Research Council, 1973). No differences in growth rate were observed when horses consumed 38 mg or 150 mg of pantothenic acid per kilogram of body weight. Thus, diets containing lower levels of pantothenic acid must be fed in order to determine if it is a dietary essential. Pyridoxine, folic acid, and biotin are synthesized in the lower digestive tract but there is presently no information as to their dietary requirements.

Ascorbic Acid

Requirements. Ascorbic acid (vitamin C) is not considered a dietary essential for horses. Adequate amounts of ascorbic acid are synthesized in the liver of the horse (Stillions *et al.*, 1971b). One early report of a study done with small numbers of animals indicated an increase in the fertility of stallions and mares that were fed vitamin C, but the experiment has never been repeated (Davis and Cole, 1943). Johnson *et al.* (1973) reported that vitamin C is often used in the treatment of epistaxis (bleeding from the nose) and sometimes seems to alleviate this condition, but the vitamin C levels in the blood of horses with epistaxis were not found to differ from those of horses without epistaxis.

8.5 Water

Metabolism. In addition to drinking water, horses also obtain water contained in feeds and water from metabolic water formed during the oxidation of protein, carbohydrates, and fats within the body. The oxidation of 100 g of glucose, protein, and fats results in 60, 42, and 100 g of metabolic water, respectively. The primary paths of water loss from the body are urine, feces, sweat, and respiration. During periods of water deprivation, the amount of water lost in the feces decreases. Diarrhea results in great water loss and can lead to severe dehydration.

Requirements. Water requirements are difficult to discuss without discussing the many factors that influence the water needs of the horse.

1. Temperature. An increase in the environmental temperature increases the water requirement. Studies in Russia demonstrated that increasing the temperature from 55° to 70°F increased the water requirement of horses by 15–20 percent (Caljuk, 1961).

2. Activity. Moderate work may increase the water requirement by 60–80 percent above the amount required by the resting animal and hard

work may increase it 120 percent. There may be interactions between factors. For example, hard work in a hot environment may increase the water requirement more than one might expect to obtain by simply adding the effect of temperature and the effect of work.

3. Function. Mares in the last third of gestation drink approximately 8–10 percent more water than nonpregnant mares. Lactating mares may increase their water intake from 50 percent to 70 percent. Of course, the intake will vary according to milk production as milk is approximately 90 percent water.

4. Food intake and type of food. Several studies have shown that the total water intake is related to the dry matter intake. Thus, the amount of drinking water needed depends on the water content of the food and the total dry matter intake. The water content of feeds can vary greatly. For example, fresh young grass contains 70–80 percent water, whereas hay and most stored grains contain approximately 10 percent water. Several estimates of water requirements are available, but most of them indicate that the horse requires approximately 1–2 quarts of water per pound of dry matter consumed. Thus, a 1,000-lb horse that consumed 16 pounds of hay per day would need approximately 4–8 gallons of water per day.

Other dietary variables also influence water needs. The greater the fiber content, the greater the fecal excretion of water. An increased ash or mineral intake increases the amount of water needed. Water contains varying levels of minerals, depending on the source. In some areas drinking water may supply significant amounts of calcium, copper, magnesium, zinc, and manganese. Of course, water may also contain toxic amounts of minerals such as fluorine, lead, nickel, and selenium. Estimates of water intake are shown in Table 8-7.

Deficiency. It has often been stated that there is no one most important nutrient; that is, all the essential nutrients must be supplied, and a diet is limited if any one of these nutrients is missing or deficient. However, water is the nutrient that man or animal will miss first. For example, ponies

TABLE 8-7
Estimated water intake of
1,000-lb horse (environmental
temperature = 60–70°F)

Activity	Gal/day
Nonworking	4–8
Gestation	7–9
Peak lactation	9–11
Medium work	9–15
Heavy work	12–15

deprived of water ate slowly and had decreased their feed intake by the second day. By the third day they were not eating anything, and by the fourth day they were so restless that the experiment was stopped. Each pony lost approximately 40 lb during the experiment, but within 3 days after the end of the experiment, the weight losses were recovered (Turancic and Tvoric, 1971). Donkeys and mules are more tolerant of water deprivation and dehydration than horses (Macfarlane, 1964).

Toxicity. Hot horses or horses that have been deprived of water should not be given large amounts of water at one time or else founder or colic may result.

8.6 Other Equine Species

The requirements previously discussed pertained to the horse. Ponies are generally regarded as "easier keepers" than horses; however, the National Research Council (1973) assumes that the requirements for ponies and horses are similar when corrected for body size. The efficiency of digestion is similar for ponies and horses, and recent studies have indicated that the maintenance requirements of minerals such as calcium and phosphorus are similar for ponies and horses when expressed on a body weight basis.

The qualitative requirements for nutrients required are probably the same for all equidae—horses, ponies, donkeys, mules, zebras, and onagers. Whether the amount of nutrients required per unit of body weight is the same for all is a matter of some controversy. Traditionally, the donkey also has a reputation of being an easy keeper. There is an old saying that thistles and straw are sufficient feed for a donkey. The animal is often fed poor-quality hay yet manages to survive. Unfortunately, few studies have been made on the nutrient requirements of the donkey. Southern farmers claimed that mules required less feed to do the same amount of work as a horse. In fact, it was often stated that "the mule will not require half the feed necessary to sustain a horse. Mules can thrive on hay while horses need grain." (Anon., 1892). Such statements appear to be exaggerations. Lamb (1963) reviewed some early experiments. One experiment in Ohio indicated that mules and horses that were doing the same work ate similar amounts of feed proportionate to their weights. Another experiment in Illinois indicated that the mules ate 0.94 lb of feed per 100 lb of live weight, whereas the horse ate 1.07 lb. Thus, a 1,600-lb mule would eat approximately 2 lb less feed per day than the 1,600-lb horse. Another experiment cited by Lamb indicated that mules are just as expensive to maintain as horses. The report stated, "it is probably true that the mule is more cheaply maintained but the mule has not been consulted."

Morrison (1957) concluded that mules may require slightly less feed than horses to do a given amount of work. But he also pointed out that although mules will endure more neglect than horses, good care and feed will prove to be profitable. He suggested that the same feeds may be used for both mules and horses and that the same principles apply in adjusting the amount of feed to the size of the aminal and to the severity of the work performed. Many zoos have satisfactorily fed rations formulated for domestic horses to wild equidae.

Mules and donkeys are generally considered to be more sensible in eating and less likely to overeat than horses. The mechanism of feed intake control is not known, but several reports suggest that the mule and donkey can be self-fed without the great risk of colic, founder, and obesity that is present when mature horses are self-fed.

References

Anon. 1892. In Defense of the Mule. *Weekly Horse World* (November 4), p. 377.

Argenzio, R. A., and H. F. Hintz. 1970. Glucose tolerance and effect of volatile fatty acid on plasma glucose concentration in ponies. *J. Animal Sci.* 30:514.

Baker, H. J., and J. R. Lindsey. 1968. Equine goiter due to excess dietary iodide. *J. An. Vet. Med. Assoc.* 153:1618.

Caljuk, E. A. 1961. Water metabolism and water requirements of horses. *Trudy Vses. Inst. Konevodstra.* 23:295. [As abstracted in *Nutr. Abs. Rev.* 32:574 (1962).]

Carroll, F. D. 1950. B vitamin content in the skeletal muscles of the horse fed a B vitamin low diet. *J. Animal Sci.* 8:290.

Cupps, P. T., and C. E. Howell. 1949. The effects of feeding supplemental copper to foals. *J. Animal Sci.* 8:286.

Davies, M. E. 1971. The production of vitamin B_{12} in the horse. *Brit. Vet. J.* 127:34.

Davis, G. K., and C. L. Cole. 1943. The relation of ascorbic acid to breeding performance in horses. *J. Animal Sci.* 26:1030.

Drew, B., W. P. Barber, and D. G. Williams. 1975. The effect of excess dietary iodine on pregnant mares and foals. *Vet Rec.* 97:93.

Evans, J. W. 1971. Effect of fasting, gestation, lactation and exercise on glucose turnover in horses. *J. Animal Sci.* 33:1001.

Friedberger, F., and E. Frohner. 1908. *Veterinary Pathology.* Trans. by M. H. Hayes. London: Keener and Co.

Green, H. H., W. M. Allcroft, and R. F. Montgomerie. 1935. Hypomagnesaemia in equine transit tetany. *J. Comp. Pathol.* 48:74.

Harrington, D. D., C. Marroguin, and V. White. 1971. Experimental magnesium deficiency in horses. *J. Animal Sci.* 33:231.

Harrington, D. D., J. Walsh, and V. White. 1973. Clinical and pathological findings in horses fed zinc deficient diets. *Proc. Third Equine Nutrition and Physiology Symposium* (January), Gainesville, Florida.

Hintz, H. F., J. E. Lowe, A. J. Clifford, and W. J. Visek. 1970. Ammonia intoxication resulting from urea ingestion by ponies. *J. Am. Vet. Med. Assoc.* 157:963.

Hintz, H. F., and H. F. Schryver. 1973. Magnesium, calcium and phosphorus metabolism in ponies fed varying levels of magnesium. *J. Animal Sci.* 37:927.

Hintz, H. F., and H. F. Schryver. 1976. Potassium metabolism in ponies. *J. Animal Sci.* 42:637.

Hintz, H. F., H. F. Schryver, and J. E. Lowe. 1971. Comparison of a blend of milk products and linseed meal as protein supplements for young growing horses. *J. Animal Sci.* 33:1274.

Hintz, H. F., H. F. Schryver, and J. E. Lowe. 1973. Effect of vitamin D on calcium and phosphorus metabolism in ponies. *J. Animal Sci.* 37:282.

Johnson, J. H., H. E. Gainer, D. P. Hutcheson, and J. G. Merriam. 1973. Epistaxis. *Proc. Am. Assoc. Equine Prac.*, p. 115.

Jones, T. C. 1942. Equine periodic ophthalmia. *Am. J. Vet. Res.* 3:45.

Krook, L., L. Lutwak, and K. McEntee. 1969. Dietary calcium, ultimobrachael tumors and osteopetrosis in the bull. *Am. J. Clin. Nutr.* 22:115.

Lamb, R. B. 1963. *The Mule in Southern Agriculture.* Los Angeles: University of California Press.

Linerode, P. A. 1967. Studies on synthesis and absorption of B-complex vitamins in the horse. *Am. Assoc. Equine Pract.*, p. 283.

Macfarlane, W. V. 1964. Terrestrial animals in dry heat: Ungulates. American Physiological Society, *Handbook of Physiology*, Section 4: *Adaptation to the Environment*, p. 509. Baltimore: Williams & Wilkins.

Morrison, F. B. 1957. *Feeds and Feeding.* Ithaca, New York: Morrison.

Meyer, H. 1960. *Magnesiumstoffwechsel, Magnesiumbedarf und Magnesiumversorgung.* Hanover: Schaper.

National Research Council. 1973. *Nutrient Requirements of Horses*. Publication No. 6. Washington, D.C.

Robinson, D. W., and L. M. Slade. 1974. Current status of knowledge in the nutrition of equines. *J. Animal Sci.* 39:1045.

Salminen, K. 1975. Cobalt metabolism in horses. *Acta. Vet. Scand.* 16:84.

Schryver, H. F., H. F. Hintz, and J. E. Lowe. 1974. Calcium and phosphorus in the nutrition·of the horse. *Cornell Vet.* 64:494.

Shupe, J. L., and A. E. Olson. 1971. Clinical aspects of fluorosis in horses. *J. Am. Vet. Med. Assoc.* 158:167.

Smith, J. D., R. M. Jordan, and M. L. Nelson. 1975. Tolerance of ponies to high levels of dietary copper. *J. Animal Sci.* 41:1645.

Stillions, M. C., S. M. Teeter, and W. E. Nelson. 1971a. Utilization of dietary vitamin B_{12} and cobalt by mature horses. *J. Animal Sci.* 32:252.

Stillions, M. C., S. M. Teeter, and W. E. Nelson. 1971b. Ascorbic acid requirements of mature horses. *J. Animal Sci.* 32:249.

Stowe, H. D. 1967. Serum selenium and related parameters of naturally and experimentally fed horses. *J. Nutr.* 93:60.

Stowe, H. D. 1968. Alpha-tocopherol requirements for equine erythrocyte stability. *Am. J. Clin. Nutr.* 21:135.

Stowe, H. D. 1971. Effects of potassium in a purified equine diet. *J. Nutr.* 101:629.

Turancic, V., and S. Tvoric. 1971. Effect of water deprivation on horses. *Veterinaria Yugoslavia* 20:179. [As abstracted in *Nutr. Abs. Rev.* 42: 1593, 1972.]

Wagenaar, G., 1975. Iron dextran administered to horses. *Tijdschr. Diergeneesk.* 100:562.

Whitlock, R. H. 1970. The effects of high dietary calcium in horses. Ph.D. thesis, Cornell University, Ithaca, New York.

Willoughby, R. A., E. MacDonald, B. J. McSherry, and G. Brown. 1972. Lead and zinc poisoning and the interaction between Pb and Zn poisoning in the foal. *Can. J. Comp. Med.* 36:348.

See overleaf for Appendixes to Chapter Eight

Appendixes

Nutrient requirements of mature horses, pregnant mares, and lactating mares (daily nutrients per animal)

Body Weight (kg)	Daily Feed[a] (kg)	Digestible Energy (Mcal)	Protein (g)	Digestible Protein (g)	Vitamin A (thousands IU)[b]	Ca (g)	P (g)
			Mature Horses at Rest (maintenance)				
200	3.00	8.24	300	160	5.0	8.0	6.0
400	5.04	13.86	505	268	10.0	16.0	12.0
500	5.96	16.39	597	317	12.5	20.0	15.0
600	6.83	18.79	684	364	15.0	24.0	18.0
			Mature Horses at Light Work (2 hr/day)				
200	3.80	10.44	383	202	5.0	8.0	6.0
400	6.68	18.36	672	355	10.0	16.0	12.0
500	7.96	21.89	803	424	12.5	20.0	15.0
600	9.23	25.39	930	491	15.0	24.0	18.0
			Mature Horses at Medium Work (2 hr/day)				
200	4.79	13.16	483	255	5.0	9.2	7.0
400	8.65	23.80	871	460	10.0	17.2	13.0
500	10.43	28.69	1,047	553	12.5	21.2	16.0
600	12.22	33.55	1,229	649	15.0	25.2	19.0
			Mares, Last 90 Days of Pregnancy				
200	3.16	8.70	364	216	10.0	10.4	8.0
400	5.41	14.88	613	375	20.0	19.5	15.0
500	6.31	17.35	725	434	25.0	24.0	18.0
600	7.25	19.95	837	502	30.0	28.0	21.0
			Mares, Peak of Lactation				
200	5.54	15.24	750	480	10.0	34.0	23.4
400	8.91	24.39	1,181	748	20.0	42.0	35.6
500	10.04	27.62	1,317	829	25.0	47.0	38.6
600	10.92	30.02	1,404	876	30.0	51.0	39.0

SOURCE: National Research Council. 1973.

[a]Assume 2.75 Mcal of digestible energy per kg of 100 percent dry feed.

[b]One mg of beta-carotene equals 400 IU of vitamin A.

APPENDIX TABLE 8-2

Nutrient requirements of growing horses (daily nutrients per animal)

Age (months)	Body Weight (kg)	Digestible Energy (Mcal)	Protein (g)	Digestible Protein (g)	Vitamin A (thousands IU)[b]	Ca (g)	P (g)
			200-kg Mature Weight				
3	50	7.43	526	383	2.0	17.4	10.9
6	90	8.53	462	315	3.6	16.6	10.4
12	135	7.95	338	206	5.4	12.0	7.5
18	165	8.08	314	181	6.6	10.4	6.5
42	200	8.24	300	160	5.0	8.0	6.0
			400-kg Mature Weight				
3	85	10.44	741	553	3.4	26.1	16.4
6	170	12.41	640	430	6.8	35.0	21.9
12	260	13.63	600	370	10.4	22.0	14.8
18	330	14.10	575	339	14.2	19.0	13.8
42	400	13.86	505	268	10.0	16.0	12.0
			500-kg Mature Weight				
3	110	12.07	834	618	4.4	30.5	19.1
6	225	15.40	800	536	9.0	46.0	28.7
12	325	16.81	750	472	11.0	26.0	17.4
18	400	17.16	700	418	16.0	23.0	16.1
42	500	16.39	597	317	12.5	20.0	15.0
			600-kg Mature Weight				
3	140	14.15	958	705	5.6	52.0	32.2
6	265	17.21	870	582	10.6	51.2	32.0
12	385	18.86	837	524	15.4	32.9	20.6
18	480	19.20	775	458	19.2	31.3	19.6
42	600	18.79	684	364	15.0	24.0	18.0

SOURCE: National Research Council. 1973.

[a]Assume 2.75 Mcal of digestible energy per kg of 100 percent dry feed.

[b]One mg of beta-carotene equals 400 IU of vitamin A.

APPENDIX TABLE 8-3
Nutrient requirements of mature horses, pregnant mares, and lactating mares
(nutrient concentration in ration dry matter)

Body Weight (kg)	Per Animal (kg)	Percentage of Live Weight	Digestible Energy (Mcal)	Protein (percent)	Digestible Protein (percent)	Ca (percent)	P (percent)
	Daily Feed		Percentage of Ration or Amount per kg of Feed				
Mature Horses at Rest (maintenance)							
200	3.00	1.5	2.75	10.0	5.3	0.26	0.20
400	5.04	1.3	2.75	10.0	5.3	0.31	0.24
500	5.96	1.2	2.75	10.0	5.3	0.33	0.25
600	6.83	1.1	2.75	10.0	5.3	0.35	0.26
Mature Horses at Light Work (2 hr/day)							
200	3.80	1.9	2.75	10.0	5.3	0.21	0.15
400	6.68	1.7	2.75	10.0	5.3	0.24	0.18
500	7.96	1.6	2.75	10.0	5.3	0.25	0.18
600	9.23	1.5	2.75	10.0	5.3	0.26	0.19
Mature Horses at Medium Work (2 hr/day)							
200	4.79	2.4	2.75	10.0	5.3	0.19	0.14
400	8.65	2.2	2.75	10.0	5.3	0.20	0.15
500	10.43	2.1	2.75	10.0	5.3	0.20	0.15
600	12.22	2.0	2.75	10.0	5.3	0.20	0.15
Mares, Last 90 Days of Pregnancy							
200	3.16	1.6	2.75	11.5	6.9	0.33	0.25
400	5.41	1.4	2.75	11.5	6.9	0.36	0.28
500	5.31	1.3	2.75	11.5	6.9	0.38	0.29
600	7.25	1.2	2.75	11.5	6.9	0.39	0.29
Mares, Peak of Lactation							
200	5.54	2.8	2.75	13.5	8.7	0.61	0.41
400	8.91	2.2	2.75	13.3	8.4	0.47	0.40
500	10.04	2.0	2.75	13.1	8.3	0.47	0.37
600	10.92	1.8	2.75	12.9	8.0	0.47	0.36

SOURCE: National Research Council. 1973.

APPENDIX TABLE 8-4
Nutrient requirements of growing horses (nutrient concentration in ration dry matter)

Age (months)	Body Weight (kg)	Percentage of Mature Weight	Daily Gain (kg)	Daily Feed[a] Per Animal (kg)	Daily Feed[a] Percentage of Live Weight	Digestible Energy (Mcal)[a]	Percentage of Ration or Amount per kg of Feed Protein (percent)	Digestible Protein (percent)	Ca (percent)	P (percent)
					200-kg Mature Weight					
3	60	25.0	0.70	2.94	5.9	7.43	17.9	13.0	0.59	0.37
6	90	45.0	0.50	3.10	3.4	8.53	14.9	10.2	0.53	0.34
12	135	67.5	0.20	2.89	2.1	7.95	11.7	7.1	0.41	0.25
18	165	82.5	0.10	2.94	1.8	8.08	10.7	6.2	0.35	0.22
42	200	100.0	0	3.00	1.5	8.24	10.0	5.3	0.29	0.20
					400-kg Mature Weight					
3	85	21.3	1.00	3.80	4.5	10.44	19.5	14.6	0.68	0.43
6	170	42.5	0.65	4.51	2.7	12.41	14.2	9.5	0.78	0.48
12	260	65.0	0.40	4.96	1.9	13.63	12.1	7.5	0.45	0.30
18	330	82.5	0.25	5.13	1.6	14.10	11.2	6.6	0.37	0.27
42	400	100.0	0	5.04	1.3	13.86	10.0	5.3	0.32	0.24
					500-kg Mature Weight					
3	110	22.0	1.10	4.39	4.0	12.07	19.0	14.1	0.69	0.44
6	225	45.0	0.80	5.60	2.5	15.40	14.3	9.6	0.82	0.51
12	324	65.0	0.55	6.11	1.9	16.81	12.3	7.7	0.43	0.28
18	400	80.0	0.35	6.24	1.6	17.16	11.3	6.7	0.37	0.26
42	500	100.0	0	5.96	1.2	16.39	10.0	5.3	0.34	0.25
					600-kg Mature Weight					
3	140	23.3	1.25	5.15	3.7	14.16	18.6	13.7	1.01	0.63
6	265	44.2	0.85	6.26	2.4	17.21	13.9	9.2	0.81	0.51
12	385	64.1	0.60	6.86	1.8	18.86	12.2	7.6	0.48	0.30
18	480	80.0	0.35	6.98	1.5	19.20	11.1	6.6	0.45	0.28
42	600	100.0	0	6.83	1.1	18.79	10.0	5.3	0.35	0.26

SOURCE: National Research Council. 1973.

[a]Assume 2.75 Mcal of digestible energy per kg of 100 percent dry feed.

CHAPTER NINE *Feeds and Feeding*

Go through the land to all the springs of water and to all the valleys; perhaps we may find grass and save the horses and mules alive and not lose some of the animals.

1 Kings 18:5.

9.1 Sources of Nutrients

Energy

Grains. Any of the grains can be used for energy sources if the characteristics of the grain are considered when balancing the diet. Oats is the grain most preferred by horsemen. It is an excellent feed, but it usually is more expensive per unit of energy than corn. One advantage of oats is that it is a safer feed because it is more difficult to overfeed oats than the other grains. The reasons are that oats are not as digestible and hence are lower in total digestible nutrients (TDN) (Table 9-1), and the density or weight per volume is less for oats than for the other grains (Table 9-2). Thus, there may be twice as much digestible energy in a quart of corn as in a quart of oats (Figure 9-1); see also Appendix Table 9-1 at the end of this chapter). Oats do not have to be processed for horses with sound mouths. Oats also contain slightly more protein and minerals than the other grains.

Corn is often used as an energy source and is usually quite economical. It can be fed whole or cracked or as ear corn.

290

FIGURE 9-1
Feed by weight, not volume.
There may be twice as much
digestible energy in a quart of
corn as in a quart of oats because
of the greater density and
digestibility of corn.

Barley is commonly fed in the western United States. The energy concentration of barley is greater than oats but less than corn.

Milo must be ground, crimped, or rolled because the grains are so small and hard that the horse can not efficiently digest the whole kernel. Wheat must also be processed, but fine grinding should be avoided because of dust problems.

Rye is usually not as palatable as the other grains and should be limited to one-third of the grain mixture. It also must be processed.

Dried brewer's grains are by-products of the brewing industry. In the production of beer, barley is soaked in warm water and allowed to sprout. The germinated kernels form a product called malt. The malt is crushed and heated and the starch is converted enzymatically to sugar. Sugar and other soluble material are removed for further processing. The material

TABLE 9-1
Estimates of energy content of grains and hays (dry matter basis)

Feed	TDN (percent)	Digestible Energy (Mcal/kg)
Barley	83	3.66
Corn	91	4.01
Oats	70	3.09
Wheat	88	3.88
Alfalfa, early bloom	59	2.33
Midbloom	57	2.25
Full bloom	53	2.10
Mature	49	1.94
Timothy, prebloom	53	2.10
Midbloom	49	1.93
Late bloom	44	1.90

SOURCE: National Research Council. 1973.

TABLE 9-2

Comparison of weights and volumes of various feeds

Feed	Weight of One Quart (lb)	Volume of One Pound (qt)
Alfalfa meal	0.6	1.7
Barley, whole	1.5	0.7
Beet pulp, dried	0.6	1.7
Corn, dent, whole	1.7	0.6
Corn, dent, ground	1.5	0.7
Cottonseed meal	1.5	0.7
Linseed meal, old process	1.1	0.9
Linseed meal, new process	0.9	1.1
Molasses, cane	3.0	0.3
Oats	1.0	1.0
Rye, whole	1.7	0.6
Soybeans	1.8	0.6
Wheat, whole	1.9	0.5
Wheat bran	0.5	2.0

SOURCE: Adapted from Morrison, F. B. 1959.

remaining after the sugar and soluble material are removed is called brewer's grains. The soluble material is boiled with hops, and yeast is added to convert the sugar to alcohol. The yeast that grows during the fermentation procedure can be harvested and sold as brewer's yeast. Brewer's yeast is an excellent source of B vitamins. Dried brewer's grains are higher in protein but lower in energy than whole grains such as barley and oats. Early research conducted with draft horses indicated that brewer's grains are a wholesome, nutritious, and palatable feed for horses. Because of their high fiber and high protein content, they are useful in the manufacture of complete pelleted feeds for horses.

Molasses. Molasses is a good source of energy but it is quite low in protein and phosphorus. Molasses is often added to horse rations to reduce dust and thus to improve palatability.

Vegetables. Fresh vegetables such as carrots and turnips are often used as treats for horses but they are not rich energy sources because they contain almost 90 percent water. Morrison (1959) states that horses and mules may be fed potatoes, cooked or raw, in amounts up to 15 or 20 lb per head daily.

Beet Pulp. Dried beet pulp can be used as a source of energy and roughage for horses. It contains more digestible energy than hay but provides more bulk than grains. Beet pulp contains significant amounts of calcium but has a very low level of phosphorus and B vitamins and contains no carotene or vitamin D.

Citrus Pulp.   Citrus pulp is a by-product of the processing of oranges and grapefruit for juice. It consists of the peel and residue from the inside portion. Citrus pulp contains very little protein, phosphorus, or carotene. It contains a high level of calcium because lime is added during the drying process. The palatability of citrus pulp varies with the processing conditions. Care should be taken to feed high-quality pulp. One of the best methods of feeding the dry pulp is to incorporate it in a pellet.

Forages

Hay.   Hay provides energy but the energy concentration is much lower than that in grains. Thus, hay cannot supply all the energy needs of animals with a high energy requirement. For example, hard-working horses, lactating mares, and rapidly growing foals need grain in addition to hay.

The key to simplified horse feeding is to have good-quality hay. Any of the common hays can be fed to horses. The important thing to consider when buying hay is not the kind of hay but rather the nutritive value in relation to the cost. A high-quality hay that costs more per ton may be a better buy than cheaper, poor-quality hay. One important consideration when evaluating the quality of the hay is age at harvesting. Young plants contain more digestible energy and nutrients per pound than older plants. As the hay matures, the lignin content increases. Lignin is a structural component and is not digested by horses (Figure 9-2). The effect of the maturity and digestibility of hay is shown in Table 9-1.

Other criteria of good-quality hay are (1) freedom from mold, dust, and weeds; (2) lack of excessive weathering; (3) leafiness and lack of stems; (4) species (legume or grass).

There are two general classes of hay: legume and grass. Legume hay contains a higher content of digestible energy, calcium, protein, and vita-

FIGURE 9-2
Mature timothy hay. Hay made from such plants contains a high content of lignin and a low content of digestible nutrients.

min A than grass hay harvested at the same stage of maturity. Alfalfa is one of the legume hays commonly fed to horses (Table 9-3). However, many horse owners are prejudiced against feeding it to horses. This prejudice is traditional and is probably based on the fact that unless good harvesting methods are used, alfalfa hay often is more moldy and dustier than grass. However, in the last 10–20 years many horsemen have realized the advantage of alfalfa hay, particularly for the broodmare, and thus the use of alfalfa hay has been increasing. Horses should be gradually changed to alfalfa hay because an abrupt change from grass hay to legume hay could cause digestive upsets. Horses fed alfalfa hay may urinate more and there may be a stronger smell of ammonia in the barn because alfalfa hay contains a higher level of nitrogen than grass hay. However, this is not harmful to the horse. The urine will also contain more sediment because of the high calcium content of alfalfa hay; the excess calcium is excreted via the kidneys.

Clover and birdsfoot trefoil, when properly harvested, have nutritional characteristics similar to those of alfalfa hay. Moldy red clover hay may cause an extensive amount of saliva excretion (slobbering disease). Moldy sweet clover can induce vitamin K deficiency because of the presence of an antivitamin K factor in the mold. Some producers feel that horses are not particularly fond of birdsfoot trefoil hay and will select other hay when given a choice.

Timothy hay is the favorite of many horsemen. Good-quality timothy hay is an excellent hay for horses, but of course, the grain mixture must contain higher levels of protein and calcium than when legume hay is fed. Other grass hay, such as bromegrass, orchard grass, coastal Bermuda grass, and bluegrass, are also good horse hays.

TABLE 9-3
Examples of legume and grass hays

Legume Hay	Grass Hay
Alfalfa	Barley hay
Birdsfoot trefoil	Bermuda grass
Clover	
Alsike	Bluegrass
Crimson	Bluestem
Red	Bromegrass
Ladino	Fescue
Sweet	Oat hay
Cowpea	Orchard grass
Lespedeza	Prairie grass
Soybeans	Reed canary grass
	Rye grass
	Sudan grass
	Timothy

Silage. Either legume grass silage or corn silage can be fed to horses and can be a very economical source of nutrients. But the silage must be as free of mold as possible because spoiled silage can be poisonous to horses. (It is difficult to have completely mold-free silage.) Silage is not often fed to horses, but Morrison (1959) states that silage can replace from one-third to one-half of the hay usually fed on a dry matter basis.

Protein

Protein Supplements. Protein supplements that contain a good mixture of essential amino acids are preferred for young growing horses and may also be of benefit to mature horses that require additional protein. Soybean meal contains more lysine than most vegetable proteins and is an excellent protein supplement for horses (Table 9-4).

Two common types of soybean meal contain 44 percent protein and 50 percent protein. The 50 percent protein meal is prepared by removing the hulls, which are high in fiber but low in protein; the resulting product is relatively richer in protein content. Fish meal, dried skim milk, and meat and bone meal are also excellent sources of amino acids but are usually more expensive than soybean meal. Vegetable proteins, such as linseed meal and cottonseed meal, should not be the primary protein source for young horses unless they are fed at higher levels (which may be uneco-

TABLE 9-4
Protein and lysine content of horse feeds and supplements (percent)

Feeds	Protein	Lysine	Lysine/ Protein	Protein Digestibility
Alfalfa meal	18	1.20	6.8	75
Alfalfa hay	16	0.90	5.6	74
Clover hay	14	0.90	6.0	75
Corn	9	0.24	2.7	80
Oats	12	0.34	2.8	75
Linseed meal	36	1.20	3.3	70
Soybean meal (44 percent)	44	3.0	6.5	78
Soybean meal (50 percent)	50	3.2	6.6	78
Dried skim milk	34	2.60	7.7	85
Timothy hay	7	0.31	4.4	70
Barley	12	0.39	3.3	76
Peanut meal	45	2.30	5.1	75
Beet pulp	9	0.60	6.5	70
Fish meal	6	4.40	7.2	76

SOURCE: Values for protein and lysine content obtained from National Academy of Sciences, 1971. Values for protein digestibility estimated from several sources; major source was Schneider, B. H. 1947.

nomical) or combined with additional lysine sources. Cottonseed meal contains a compound, gossypol, which is toxic to pigs, but mature horses can be fed at least 1.5 lb of cottonseed meal per day per 1,000-lb live weight without experiencing any gossypol-caused problems (Morrison, 1959).

Urea or other nonprotein nitrogen compounds may be used by the horse in limited amounts under certain conditions, but such compounds are utilized much less efficiently than dietary protein (see section 7.4).

Legume hays or pellets are also excellent sources of protein for horses.

Minerals

The calcium and phosphorus content and true digestibility of several sources of calcium and phosphorus are shown in Table 9-5. The inorganic sources that are listed are excellent sources of minerals. Grains are poor sources of calcium. The phosphorus in wheat bran is in the form of phytin and is therefore less available than inorganic forms. Legume hays are excellent sources of calcium.

Roughages are good sources of potassium and, usually, magnesium, whereas grains are low in both potassium and magnesium.

Sodium chloride (salt) should be provided free choice. The trace-

TABLE 9-5
Calcium and phosphorus content and true digestibility of some common horse feeds and supplements (percent)

Feed/Supplement	Content		True Digestibility	
	Ca	P	Ca	P
Organic				
Beet pulp	0.60	0.10	60	—
Corn	0.02	0.28	—	32
Linseed meal	0.40	0.85	—	30
Milk products	1.30	1.00	79	64
Oats	0.09	0.35	—	40
Wheat bran	0.14	1.15	—	29
Alfalfa hay	1.40	0.20	77	44
Timothy hay	0.32	0.20	70	46
Inorganic				
Bone meal	29.0	14.0	71	58
Dicalcium phosphate	27.0	21.0	74	58
Limestone	35.0	—	69	—
Monosodium phosphate	0.0	22.0	—	58

mineralized form should be used because it supplies such trace minerals as iodine, copper, manganese, and iron. Either loose or block salt can be used. Waste is minimized when block salt is used, but loose salt permits greater intake.

Vitamins

Vitamin A. The requirement for vitamin A is approximately 5–6 mg of carotene per kilogram. Thus, the vitamin A or carotene content of good-quality hay (Table 9-6) is usually adequate for horses, although Fonnesbeck and Symons (1967) suggest that horses are not particularly efficient in converting carotene to vitamin A. Hay that has been severely weathered or stored for more than 2 years has a much lower carotene content. Such grains as barley, oats, and wheat do not provide any carotene but yellow corn provides a small amount. Synthetic vitamin A compounds, such as vitamin A palmitate, are inexpensive and stable and can easily be added to feeds containing low levels of vitamin A.

TABLE 9-6
Vitamin content of several feeds and feed by-products (mg/kg of dry matter)

Feed/By-Product	Carotene	Thiamin	Riboflavin	Niacin	Pantothenic Acid
Requirement[a] (mg/kg of dry matter)	6	3	2.2	0.8	2
Alfalfa pellets	100	6	14	40	30
Alfalfa hay	20	3	14	34	18
Timothy hay	14	3	15	30	?
Alfalfa pasture	200	6	11	42	34
Bluegrass pasture	180	5	11	?	?
Dried skim milk	—	4	20	11	36
Brewer's yeast	—	120	34	502	120
Torula yeast	—	7	48	540	73
Corn	3	4	2	20	6
Oats	—	6	1	14	15
Linseed meal	—	9	3	30	12
Soybean meal	—	7	3	25	13
Wheat bran	2	8	3	33	25

SOURCE: Requirements taken from National Research Council. 1973. (Minimum requirements have not been established, but these levels are known to be adequate.) Other values from National Academy of Sciences. 1971. Also from Morrison, F. B. 1959.

Vitamin D. Sun-cured hay contains approximately 2,000 IU per kilogram of feed. A mature horse does not need more than 3,300 units per day; thus a vitamin D deficiency does not appear likely when horses receive sun-cured hay. The horses also obtain vitamin D from the action of ultraviolet light on compounds in the skin. Grains and grain by-products contain almost no vitamin D. Supplements that provide high levels of vitamin D include irradiated yeast (9,000–140,000 IU per gram depending on the type of yeast), cod-liver oil (85 IU per gram), and cod-liver oil meal (40 IU per gram).

Vitamin E. Alfalfa pellets and most good-growing pastures contain approximately 400 mg of vitamin E per kilogram of dry matter and are excellent sources of the vitamin for horses. Grains contain low levels of vitamin E (5–10 mg per kilogram).

B Vitamins. The B vitamin content of several feeds is shown in Table 9-6. Brewer's yeast is an economical supplement to use if additional thiamin is needed. Riboflavin deficiency does not occur when the ration contains good-quality hay. Deficiencies of niacin or pantothenic acid are very unlikely to occur in the horse.

The composition of many feeds used in horse rations is shown in Appendix Table 9-1, at the end of this chapter.

9.2 Balancing Rations

Ration balancing is often a tiresome chore and a source of confusion. Several methods can be used but the important principle is that first the horse's requirements must be determined and then the diet must be formulated to satisfy these requirements. Regardless of the method used, a considerable amount of mathematical calculation is necessary. One method is to set up a series of equations with several unknowns and then to solve them by using a calculator or computer. Another method is the trial and error method, illustrated by the following example taken from a publication of the National Research Council (1973).

For purposes of illustration, assume that a ration is to be formulated for a 6-month-old colt weighing 225 kg with an expected mature weight of 500 kg. Timothy hay (midbloom) is the roughage to be fed, at the rate of 1 kg per 100 kg (1 percent) of body weight. Seven steps are required. These steps and the results of the calculations are as follows.

1. *Determine daily nutrient requirements.*

The requirements for the colt in the example given in Appendix Table 8-2 are as follows:

Digestible energy	15.40	Mcal
Digestible protein	536	g
Total protein	800	g
Calcium	46	g
Phosphorus	28.7	g
Vitamin A	9,000	IU

2. *Determine digestible energy and digestible protein supplied by roughage.*

Appendix Table 9-5 gives the following values for timothy hay (mid-bloom):

Digestible energy	1.94 Mcal/kg
Digestible protein	3.6 percent

3. *Calculate the concentrate needed to supplement the forage.*

A 225-kg colt fed roughage at a rate of 1 kg per 100 kg of body weight will receive 2.25 kg of hay per day.

a. Calculate the digestible energy (DE) and digestible protein (DP) supplied by the roughage.

$$2.25 \text{ kg} \times 1.94 \text{ Mcal/kg} = 4.3 \text{ Mcal/day}$$
$$2.25 \text{ kg} \times 3.6 \text{ percent DP} = 0.081 \text{ kg or } 81 \text{ g/day}$$

b. Subtract the amount of DE and DP supplied by the roughage from the DE requirement of the horse.

$$15.40 - 4.36 = 11.04 \text{ Mcal/day needed from the concentrate}$$
$$536 - 81 = 455 \text{ g/day of DP needed from the concentrate}$$

The amount of oats needed to supply the needed energy may be calculated by dividing the DE of oats (3.09 Mcal/kg) (Appendix Table 9-1) into the needed DE.

$$11.04 \div 3.09 \text{ Mcal/kg} = 3.57 \text{ kg of oats}$$

This level of oats will not meet the DP needs:

$$3.57 \text{ kg} \times 3.6 \text{ percent} = 0.128 \text{ kg or } 128 \text{ g of DP}$$

A high-protein ingredient must be fed with oats to meet both the DE and DP needs. The amounts of soybean meal and oats needed to meet both the DE and DP needs can be calculated by selecting a proportion of soybean meal to oats, calculating the resulting DE and DP content, and adjusting the levels by trial and error to achieve the desired results.

$$(3.08 \text{ kg oats} \times 3.09 \text{ Mcal/kg}) + (0.44 \text{ kg soybean meal} \times 3.53 \text{ Mcal/kg})$$
$$= 11.070 \text{ Mcal}$$

(3.08 kg oats × 1,000 g/kg × 8.4 percent)
$$+ \text{(0.44 kg soybean meal} \times 1{,}000 \text{ g/kg} \times 3.6 \text{ percent)}$$
$$= 455 \text{ g DP}$$

4. *Calculate the amounts of supplemental sources of other nutrients.*
After energy and protein, the major nutrients to be considered in horse rations are phosphorus, calcium, and vitamin A. For the colt in the example, the phosphorus requirement is 28.7 g per day.

a. Find in Appendix Table 9-1 the phosphorus content of the ingredients included thus far and multiply it by the amounts of the ingredients to be fed.

$$2.25 \text{ kg of timothy hay} \times 0.19 \text{ percent} = \quad 4.28 \text{ g}$$
$$3.08 \text{ kg of oats} \times 0.33 \text{ percent} = 10.16 \text{ g}$$
$$0.44 \text{ kg of soybean meal} \times 0.75 \text{ percent} = \quad \underline{3.30 \text{ g}}$$
$$17.74 \text{ g}$$

b. Subtract the amount of phosphorus supplied by these ingredients from the phosphorus requirement of the horse.

$$28.7 - 17.7 = 11 \text{ g of phosphorus needed}$$

This requirement may be met by feeding dicalcium phosphate, which has a phosphorus content of 18.65 percent (Appendix Table 9-1):

11 g of phosphorus ÷ 18.65 percent phosphorus/g of dicalcium phosphate
$$= 59 \text{ g or } 0.059 \text{ kg dicalcium phosphate}$$

In the same way, calculate the amounts of calcium, vitamin A, and other nutrients that should be added to the ration.

5. *Adjust the ration to an as-fed basis.*
Most ingredients in horse rations contain water. The ration must therefore be adjusted to an as-fed basis. To do this, divide the dry weight by the dry matter (DM) content of the ingredient (Appendix Table 9-1) and multiply by 100. Example:

(2.25 kg of timothy hay ÷ 88.4) × 100 = 2.55 kg on an as-fed basis

Similar calculations can be made for each ingredient.

6. *Convert the ration formula to a percentage basis.*
Divide the amount of ingredient fed (on an as-fed basis) by the total feed on an as-fed basis and multiply by 100. Example:

(2.545 kg of timothy hay ÷ 6.54 kg) × 100
$$= 38.87 \text{ percent of timothy hay in total ration}$$

Similar calculations can be made for each ingredient.

7. *Calculate the amount of concentrate that is to be fed separately from the roughage.*

a. Subtract the roughage from the total feed (as-fed basis). Example:

6.54 kg (total feed) − 2.54 kg (roughage) = 4.00 kg of concentrate

b. To obtain a percentage formula for the concentrate, divide each ingredient in the concentrate by the level of concentrate fed (on an as-fed basis) and multiply by 100. Example:

(3.39 kg of oats ÷ 4.00 kg of concentrate) × 100
= 87.7 percent of oats in concentrate

Similar calculations can be made for each ingredient in the concentrate.

Calculating Nutrient Composition of the Total Ration and Concentrate

The daily intake of each nutrient may be calculated by multiplying the daily intake of each ingredient by its nutrient content and adding the results. The digestible energy consumption is calculated as follows:

(2.25 kg hay × 1.94 Mcal/kg) + (3.08 kg oats × 3.09 Mcal/kg)
+ (0.44 kg soybean meal × 3.53 Mcal/kg)
+ (0.059 kg dicalcium phosphate × 0)
+ (0.056 kg limestone × 0) = 15.43 Mcal

Similar calculations may be made for the other nutrients.

In the following table the nutrient requirements for a 6-month-old colt whose expected mature weight is 500 kg are compared with the nutrients supplied by the ration formulated previously.

Nutrient	Nutrient Requirements	Nutrients Supplied
Digestible energy (Mcal)	15.40	15.43
Digestible protein (g)	536	536.4
Total protein (g)	800	823
Calcium (g)	46	46
Phosphorus (g)	28.7	28.7

Short-cut Method. A short cut to ration balancing is to use guidelines. This method is not as exact as ration balancing but it does have some merit for making preliminary evaluations of diets and rough approximations of reasonable rations. Table 9-7 gives estimates of feed intake and Table 9-8 lists the protein content that is required in the grain mixture of various classes of horse fed legume hay or grass hay. Table 9-9 gives an estimate of the amount of the various protein supplements needed in

301

TABLE 9-7
Estimated feed intake (pounds/100 lb
body weight) required for various classes
of activity

Activity	Hay	Grain
Maintenance	$1\frac{1}{2}$	—
Late gestation	$1–1\frac{1}{2}$	$\frac{1}{4}–\frac{3}{4}$
Lactation	$1–1\frac{1}{2}$	$1–1\frac{1}{2}$
Heavy work	$1–1\frac{1}{4}$	$\frac{3}{4}–1\frac{1}{2}$
Weanlings	$\frac{3}{4}–1\frac{1}{4}$	$1\frac{3}{4}–2\frac{1}{2}$

TABLE 9-8
Required protein content of grain mix when feeding
legume hay or grass hay (percent)

Class	Legume Hay	Grass Hay
Weanlings	14–16	18–20
Yearlings	12–14	15–18
Mature (maintenance)	8–10	8–10
Gestation	10–12	12–14
Lactation	12–14	15–18

TABLE 9-9
Estimated protein supplement needed to provide various levels of protein
in total grain mixture (percent)

Supplement	Pounds of Supplement/100 lb Total Grain Mixture						
	10	12	14	16	18	20	22
Dried skim milk (34 percent protein)	None	9	17	24	32	40	50
Linseed meal (36 percent protein)	None	8	16	22	30	39	48
Soybean meal (44 percent protein)	None	6	12	18	24	30	36
Soybean meal (50 percent protein)	None	5	10	15	20	25	30

302

NOTE: Grains are assumed to contain approximately 10 percent protein.

the grain mixture to provide the necessary level of protein. Table 9-10 lists estimates of the amount of calcium and phosphorus supplements needed for the various classes of horse.

An example of the short-cut method is the formulation of a ration for a 1,000-lb lactating mare. From Table 8-7, the mare is estimated to eat approximately 10–15 lb of hay and 10–15 lb of grain. In this example, the mare is fed timothy hay. According to Table 9-8, the mare's grain mixture should contain 15–18 percent protein. In order to provide this level of protein when using soybean meal (50 percent), the grain mixture should contain 15 lb of soybean meal per 100 lb of grain mixture. According to Table 9-10, 100 lb of dicalcium phosphate and 20 lb of limestone should be added per ton of grain mixture when a grass hay is fed to lactating mares. Of course, trace-mineralized salt should be fed free choice. A commercial vitamin could be added if the grass hay was of poor quality.

The kind of grain would depend on its cost and availability. To repeat, obviously the short-cut method is not as precise as the trial and error method, but it can be helpful in certain situations.

9.3 Feeding

The following sections list example diets but it must be remembered that these diets are only *examples*. Many feeds or combinations of feeds can be used. The selection of feeds should be based on nutrient content, cost, availability, and acceptability to the horses. It may not be econom-

TABLE 9-10
Estimated amount of calcium and phosphorus supplement needed per ton of grain mixture

Class	Legume Hay	Grass Hay
Weanlings	20 lb dicalcium phosphate	20 lb dicalcium phosphate 30 lb limestone
Yearlings	10 lb dicalcium phosphate	10 lb dicalcium phosphate 20 lb limestone
Gestation	10 lb dicalcium phosphate	10 lb dicalcium phosphate 20 lb limestone
Lactation	10 lb dicalcium phosphate	10 lb dicalcium phosphate 20 lb limestone

NOTE: Amount of supplement can be more accurately calculated when actual intakes of hay and grain are known. Other supplements, such as treated rock phosphate and bone meal, can be used in place of dicalcium phosphate.

ical or convenient to use several rations, particularly on small farms. When a single ration is desired, it is usually most economical to formulate that ration for the types of animals with the lowest requirements. The extra nutrients (such as protein and minerals) needed by the other animals (such as weanlings and lactating mares) can be provided by the addition of supplements. Trace-mineralized salt should be fed free choice.

The three classes of horse that are of the greatest concern to the nutritionist are the young foal, the lactating mare, and the hard-working horse. Feeding programs for the various classes are discussed in the following section.

Young Foal. Creep feeding (providing an area where the foal can eat without interference from the mare) is important in the rearing of foals (Figure 9-3). Feed should be made available within 2 weeks after birth. The foal will not eat significant amounts of feed at this time, but it gradually increases its intake. The creep ration should be highly digestible and palatable. It should contain 18–20 percent protein, 0.8 percent calcium, and 0.6 percent phosphorus. Several good creep rations can be obtained commercially, or the ration can be prepared on the farm. Tyznik (1972) suggests a ration containing 42.5 percent cracked corn, 31 percent soybean meal, 23 percent heavy rolled oats, 0.5 percent brewer's yeast, 3 percent molasses, 1 percent dicalcium phosphate, 1 percent limestone, and 1 percent trace-mineralized salt.

An important consideration in the growth of young foals is the rate of gain desired. Further research is needed to determine the optimal rate of gain for maximum productivity. Some horsemen feel that a foal that grows too fast may be more likely to become unsound. However, if horses are to be worked hard as 2- and 3-year-olds, a reasonable rate of gain during the period from birth to yearling is essential.

FIGURE 9-3
Creep feeding is important for the fast growth of young foals. The foals can eat without interference by the mare.

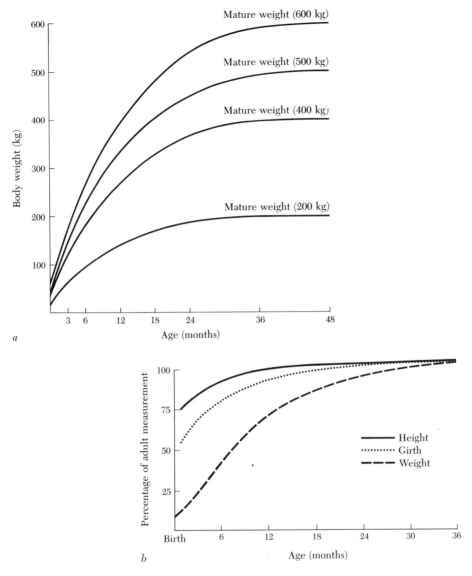

FIGURE 9-4
Growth curves for horses with four different mature weights. These are examples
rather than models. Further work is necessary to determine optimal growth
weight.

Some weight gains and changes in height are shown in Figure 9-4. The
curves are presented as examples rather than models because they were
derived from limited observations. However, they can be used as values
that might be reasonably expected by the average horse owner.

The horse's weight at 6 months is approximately 70 percent of its
weight at 12 months and 50 percent of its weight at 24 months. Thus, the

305

first six months is the period of most intensive weight gain. The weight at 12 months is 60 percent of the mature weight.

Height at the withers at birth is approximately 70 percent of the height at 12 months of age. However, height at birth has a relatively low correlation with mature height. Height at 6 months is approximately 90–95 percent and 80–85 percent of height at 12 months and 24 months, respectively. Height at 12 months is approximately 85–90 percent of mature height, whereas weight at 12 months is only 60 percent of mature size. Thus, the skeleton grows relatively more rapidly than the rest of the body. Thus, the inclusion of calcium, phosphorus, and protein (nutrients that are very important for bone building) in the diet is critical during the first 12 months of the horse's life.

Other data indicate that the size of the heart girth at birth is approximately 50–55 percent of the size at 12 months of age. The size of the heart girth at 6 months is approximately 80 percent and 75 percent of the size of the heart girth at 12 and 24 months, respectively.

The total ration for weanlings should contain 14–16 percent protein, 0.7 percent calcium, and 0.45 percent phosphorus. The protein should contain proper amounts of the essential amino acids (see section 8.2). Examples of rations that should be adequate for weanlings when fed with good-quality legume or grass hay are shown in Table 9-11.

Yearlings. The requirements of protein, calcium, and phosphorus (when expressed as a percentage of the diet) for yearlings are less than those for weanlings because the rate of muscle and bone development has decreased. The yearling ration should contain 12–14 percent protein, 0.6 percent calcium, and 0.35 percent phosphorus. Examples of grain mixtures adequate for yearlings are shown in Table 9-11.

TABLE 9-11
Examples of rations for yearlings and weanlings fed grass or legume hay

Ingredient	Grass Hay		Legume Hay	
	Weanling Ration (lb/100 lb)	Yearling Ration (lb/100 lb)	Weanling Ration (lb/100 lb)	Yearling Ration (lb/100 lb)
Corn	39	42	45	46
Oats	30	35½	39	42½
Soybean meal (50 percent protein)	25	15	12	8
Molasses	3	3	3	3
Limestone	2	1	–	–
Dicalcium phosphate	1	½	1	½

Mature Horses. The horse that is of least concern to the nutritionist is the nonpregnant, nonlactating horse that is not worked very hard. Of course, proper nutrition is just as important for this class of horse, but the absolute amount of the various nutrients that are required is much less. In fact, good pasture or good-quality hay plus trace-mineralized salt can supply all the nutrients needed by this class of horse. Feeding grain to a horse that is seldom worked is not necessary unless the weather is very cold. Cold weather increases energy requirements because the energy is used to keep the animals warm.

Breeding Animals. The effect of nutrition on horse breeding has long been a controversial topic. Some authorities feel that nutrition is very critical, whereas others feel that even if the diet is barely adequate for maintenance, the animals will still be able to reproduce.

The energy intake, and hence the body condition at breeding time, is considered very important by many authorities. For example, Fallon (1971) states that the most common form of malnutrition in horses is obesity. Obesity in Thoroughbreds, according to Fallon, occurs primarily in sale horses and barren mares. He suggests that fat mares should be fed a limited amount of feed and exercised so that by January 1, they will be down to the desired weight. The feed should then be increased so that the mare is in a gaining state at the beginning of the breeding season. Ott (1972) also suggests that the mare should be in a good body condition but not fat. He suggests that an increased plane of nutrition should be started 30–45 days before the start of the breeding season and continued until the mare is diagnosed in foal. Other studies have also suggested that an increased plane of nutrition in mares could be helpful during breeding season.

It is often stated that excess fat can be detrimental to the libido of stallions. Certainly regulating the body condition of stallions by supervising their diet and exercise appears to be a very important husbandry practice.

Very little research has been conducted on the effect of protein on the breeding performance of horses. Studies of other species indicate that very low levels of protein cause cessation of estrus or fetal deaths, but that very high levels of protein during the breeding season are neither beneficial nor harmful.

A severe phosphorus deficiency causes irregularity or cessation of estrus in cattle and rats and, therefore, presumably in horses. Deficiencies of many other minerals, such as manganese, iron, and iodine, could also result in failure of the mare to settle. However, the requirements for these minerals during the breeding season do not seem to be much, if any, greater than the requirements for maintenance; that is, there is no evidence that supplementing an adequate diet with minerals at this time increases the conception rate. One mineral that may receive greater attention in the future because of its effect on reproduction in horses is selenium. There is increasing evidence that selenium is deficient in the diets of the livestock, including horses, in many areas of the United States (see section 8.3). Muscle degeneration is frequently observed in young calves, foals, and lambs raised in selenium-deficient areas. However, studies conducted in New Zealand indicate that selenium deficiency may also cause reproductive failure in sheep. For example, the percentage of barren ewes in flocks treated with selenium averaged approximately 8 percent, compared with 45 percent in untreated flocks. Therefore, the effect of selenium on reproduction in the horse merits further study.

Stowe (1967) has suggested that combined vitamin A and E supplementation, either by mouth or by injection, significantly improved the reproductive performance of barren mares. In one trial, one group of 9 mares was not fed a supplement and one group of 9 mares was fed 100,000 IU of vitamin A and 100 IU of vitamin E per day for 3 months starting approximately one month before the beginning of the breeding season. Only one of the 9 mares that were not given a supplement had a live foal, whereas 6 of the 9 mares that were given the supplement had live foals. Supplements of only vitamin A or vitamin E were less effective. Similar results were obtained in a subsequent trial in which the vitamins were injected rather than fed. The control group of 9 mares had 2 live foals and the group of 9 mares injected with vitamin A and E had 7 live foals. Studies conducted in Europe showed that mares given vitamin E had a 5 percent increase in conception rate and 7 percent increase in the number of live foals. Several large breeding farms in the United States have administered a high-level supplementation of vitamin A and E to mares but the responses have varied. Further studies to determine the effectiveness or perhaps the conditions under which the vitamins might be effective are necessary before the practice can be routinely recommended.

Few experiments have been conducted on the effect of B vitamins on reproduction. It is usually assumed that unless the utilization of B vitamins synthesized in the intestine is impaired, or the animals are fed very poor-quality hay, B-vitamin supplementation is not necessary during the breeding season. Vitamin C is often given to stallions on breeding farms to improve semen quality. Davis and Cole (1943) reported that administration of 1 gram of ascorbic acid per day improved the semen quality and libido of one Belgian stallion. Further studies are necessary if an accurate assessment is to be made of the value of such a practice, as other workers have reported that low fertility does not appear to be associated with a low level of ascorbic acid in equine semen or serum (Dimock and Errington, 1942).

Pregnant Mares. During the first two-thirds of the gestation period, the fetus is not very large and the nutrient requirements of the mare are not greatly increased, but during the last third of gestation the fetus rapidly increases in size and nutrient requirements are greatly increased. During

308

this time, the intake of bulky feeds such as hay decreases. Thus, more concentrated feeds and grains need to be added to the mare's ration. The mare will still probably eat about 1 lb of hay per 100 lb of body weight and she will need about ¼ to ½ lb of grain per 100 lb of body weight in addition to the hay. Legume hay, such as alfalfa or clover, contains more protein and calcium than grass hays. If a grass hay is fed, the grain mix should contain 14 percent protein, 0.5 percent calcium, and 0.4 percent phosphorus. A ration containing 42 percent oats, 34 percent corn, 10 percent soybean meal, 10 percent wheat bran, 3 percent molasses, and 1 percent limestone would be adequate. If a legume hay is fed, the grain mix does not need to contain any protein or calcium supplements. A mixture of 45 percent oats, 42 percent corn, 10 percent wheat bran, and 3 percent molasses would be adequate.

Lactating Mares. During peak lactation, which usually occurs 8–12 weeks after parturition, nutrient requirements are greatly increased (Figure 9-5). A high-producing mare may need as much as 1 to 1½ lb of grain per 100 lb of body weight. Of course, mares vary considerably in their ability to produce milk, and the best rule is to observe the mare and feed accordingly. For example, if she is too thin, increase her grain ration. The grain mix should contain at least 16 percent protein, 0.7 percent calcium, and 0.5 percent phosphorus when a grass hay is fed and 12 percent protein and 0.5 percent phosphorus when a legume hay is fed. A ration containing 40 percent corn, 35 percent oats, 15 percent soybean meal, 5 percent wheat bran, 3 percent molasses, 1.5 percent limestone, and 0.5 percent dicalcium phosphate could be used with the grass hay. A ration containing 46 percent corn, 44.5 percent oats, 5 percent soybean meal, 5 percent wheat bran, and 0.5 percent dicalcium phosphate could be used with the legume hay.

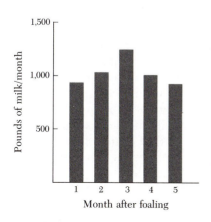

FIGURE 9-5
Milk production varies greatly among mares, but peak lactation might be expected 8–12 weeks after parturition.

Stallions. More information is needed about the effect of nutrition on stallion performance, but most studies indicate that the nutritional requirements of the stallion are not significantly greater than the requirements for maintenance. For example, the National Research Council (1973) has established specific requirements for pregnant mares and lactating mares but not for stallions. The amount of feed necessary varies with the individual, but ¼ to ¾ lb of grain and 1 to 1½ lb of hay per 100 lb of body weight might be a reasonable amount. The most important rule is to keep the stallion in a trim condition. Exercise by riding or lounging not only helps to keep the stallion in good physical condition but also minimizes boredom and keeps him more alert. The stallion should not be allowed to become too thin or run down. In fact, one of the earliest references to the relation between nutrition and reproduction in horses is found in the Bible (Jeremiah 5:8), where it is implied that the libido of well-fed stallions is greater than that of poorly fed stallions. However, the stallion should not be too fat.

The grain mixture described for the pregnant mare should be adequate for the stallion.

As stated previously, these grain ration formulations are only examples. Many different combinations of feeds can be used. The important point is that the nutrients must be present in adequate amounts. Other examples of ration formulations can be found in books by Morrison (1959), Ensminger (1969), and Harper (1969), as well as various experiment station publications.

Hard-working Horses. Exercise increases the need for energy. Sustained work may increase the energy requirement threefold or more above that of maintenance. Thus, hard-working horses require more feed and, just as importantly, the feed should contain a high concentration of digestible energy. If diets that consist only of such feed as poor-quality hay, which contains a low amount of digestible energy, are fed, the horse's performance will suffer because of the energy shortage and the horse will probably develop a "hay belly"—that is, it will eat more feed in an attempt to obtain the needed energy but the extra bulk in the diet will distend the intestinal tract. Thus, working horses fed high-quality hay often look trimmer and more attractive than horses fed poor-quality hay.

Work does not greatly increase the protein requirement. Contrary to popular opinion, muscle is not broken down during work. Some nitrogen is lost in the sweat, but the protein concentration required in the feed of working horses is not greater (in fact, it can be less) than that required for the maintenance of horses in general because the working horse has a greater total feed intake and thus obtains the necessary total protein intake.

310

Work does not greatly increase the requirement for calcium and phosphorus. As with protein, some calcium and phosphorus are lost in the sweat, but the increased feed intake easily compensates for the slightly increased needs. However, work increases the stress on the skeleton and increases the rate of calcium and phosphorus turnover and bone remodeling. Therefore, a working horse fed a marginal level of calcium or phosphorus in the diet will be more likely to develop lameness than a nonworking horse fed a marginal level of these nutrients. It is particularly important that young horses that are being worked receive adequate minerals because their bones are still growing.

Further controlled studies are needed to evaluate the requirements of other minerals, but it has been reported that the blood level of electrolytes, such as potassium, sodium, and chloride, may be decreased during extreme prolonged work such as endurance rides (Carlson and Mansmann, 1974). Furthermore, the decreased blood level of potassium may be related to thumps (synchronous diaphragmatic flutter) (Mansmann et al., 1974). Thumps, which in some respects is similar to the hiccoughs of man, often occurs in horses during endurance rides. A decreased level of blood calcium may also produce thumps.

The requirement for B vitamins increases as the amount of energy intake increases because B vitamins are necessary cofactors for energy utilization. Some authorities feel that the decreased feed intake observed in some racehorses may be related to thiamin deficiency. The feeding of one or two tablespoons of brewer's yeast daily to hard-working horses to supply additional thiamin has been recommended (Tyznik, 1972).

In summary, the requirement that is increased most for working horses is the requirement for calories, which are provided by increasing the grain intake. There may be small increases in the protein, vitamin, and mineral requirements; however, the increase in feed intake will generally provide the additional nutrients needed if the feed is of good quality and well balanced.

9.4   Pasture

Pasture is very important in any horse-feeding program. Good pasture, water, and trace-mineralized salt can provide complete nutrition for many classes of horse, such as mature, nonworking animals, yearlings, and pregnant mares (at least in the first part of the gestation period—see Figure 9-6). Hard-working horses, lactating mares, and weanlings may require nutrient intakes greater than that provided by pasture. However, several factors, such as pasture management, species of plant, and amount of land determine the amount of nutrition obtained from pastures.

311

FIGURE 9-6
Good-quality pasture, trace mineral salt, and water provide adequate nutrition for most classes of horse. Weanlings, lactating mares, and hard-working horses usually require some additional grain.

Management.   Some features of good pasture management are:

1. Be sure not to overgraze. Too many pastures are simply exercise lots. Rotating pastures is also beneficial to the parasite prevention program.

2. Clipping pastures prevents plant material from becoming too mature, helps maintain a balance of legumes and grasses, and controls weeds.

3. Spread manure droppings with a chain harrow.

4. Keep pasture free of mechanical hazards such as wire and nails.

5. Keep pasture free of weeds, particularly poisonous weeds such as nightshade, yellowstar thistle, horse nettle, and ragwort.

6. Keep horses out of the pasture during extreme wet weather to avoid damage to the turf.

Species of Plant.   The species of plant used in the pasture depends on local soil and climate conditions. Many different plant species can be used in horse pastures, and the local extension agent can provide appropriate information concerning species and planting and fertilizing procedures.

Bluegrass, bluestem, bromegrass, fescue, orchard grass, and cereal grasses are examples of grasses that are frequently used for horse pastures. In warmer climates, such as that of Florida, pangola grass, bahia grass, carpet grass, or para grass are often used in horse pastures. Legumes used include alfalfa, red clover, white clover, and birdsfoot trefoil. However, red clover does not provide a long-lasting pasture.

Mixtures of grasses and legumes are usually the most satisfactory because they provide a greater total amount of nutrients and longer grazing seasons (Figure 9-7).

For example, Jordan and Marten (1975) reported that reed canary grass was a good pasture grass for horses early in the grazing season but that in the latter part of the season its palatability greatly decreased because of an increased alkaloid content. Thus, reed canary grass should not be used as the only pasture. Kentucky blue grass withstands close grazing and is most productive during hot dry summer periods. On the other hand, orchard grass grows well under high summer temperatures, has some drought and shade tolerance but is relatively unpalatable at maturity and cannot tolerate close grazing. Birdsfoot trefoil is productive even when grown on poorly drained soil but is more difficult to establish than some of the other legumes. Sorghum-sudangrass hybrids should be avoided because they may produce the cystitis syndrome, which is an irritation of the urethra caused by the presence of a sticky granular fluid in the bladder. Death may occur if kidney infection results. Thus a mixture of grasses and legumes could blend the advantages of the individual species and therefore, help alleviate their disadvantages.

Amount of Land.   The amount of land required per horse to provide adequate nutrition depends on many factors, such as type or class of horse, rainfall, soil fertility, plant species, shade, and pasture management. One acre of renovated legume grass pasture that was properly managed and enjoyed good growing conditions could provide enough feed for a horse during the grazing season. However, under most common conditions, it is recommended that there be at least 2–3 acres of pasture per horse.

FIGURE 9-7
A mixture of grass and legumes
makes an excellent pasture.

9.5 Commercial Feeds

Sales of commercial horse feeds have greatly increased in the past 20 years. For example, in 1956 11,252 tons of horse and mule feed were sold in Kentucky. Sales in that state increased to 15,443 tons in 1966 and 29,794 tons in 1973. Other areas of the United States have had even more spectacular gains. In Arizona only 1,989 tons of horse feed were reported to have been sold in 1958, compared with 15,215 tons in 1966 and 41,483 in 1973.

Unfortunately, reliable statistics are not available to allow an accurate estimation of how much of the increased tonnage of commercial feeds is due to the increased number of horses and how much is due to changes in feeding practices. However, it appears likely that the latter is a significant factor.

The history and development of commercial horse feeds in the United States is quite interesting. Commercial horse feeds were not used by many horse owners before 1900. However, many expensive tonic feeds were sold. In 1860 Thorley's Feed cost $14 per 100 lb. It was shipped from London and contained beans, barley, flaxseed, Peruvian bark, and quinine tonics. At that time, oats were selling for about $1.40 per 100 lb. The tonic feed in the advertisement shown in Figure 9-8 cost $20 per 100 lb in 1893, when the price of oats was about $1 per 100 lb. In 1901 tonic feeds cost about $15–$20 per 100 lb, while the ingredients cost about $1.00–$1.50 per 100 lb.

The tonic feeds usually had linseed meal or grain as a base and contained compounds such as gentian, fennel, fenugreek, charcoal, sulfate, anise, asafoetida, licorice root, mandrake root, walnut bark, iron oxide,

FIGURE 9-8
Advertisement from *The Ohio Practical Farmer* (1893).

Blatchford's Royal Stock Food.

THE MOST COMPLETE FEEDING CAKE
EVER MADE.

A Perfect Milk Substitute or Calf Meal,
—AND—

Unequaled for All Kinds of Young Stock!

INVALUABLE FOR CATTLE, HORSES, SWINE, AND SHEEP.

☞ **For Directions and Testimonials send for PAMPHLET ON FEEDING, issued and mailed free by**
E. W. BLATCHFORD & CO., Sole Manufacturerers, Chicago, Ill.

FIGURE 9-9
Advertisement from *Breeder's Gazette* (1886).

and rosin. Exotic names were sometimes used for common materials, such as capsicum for black pepper, frumentum powder for cornmeal, and princess metallic for dried paint. The claims for some tonic feeds were all-inclusive. One tonic claimed to increase endurance, keep colts healthy, make horses fat and their coats glossy, minimize the need for corn and oats in the diet, and cure heaves, coughs, colic, distemper, dropsey, colds, and dyspepsia.

The tonic with the most interesting advertisement was the International Stock Food Tonic. M. W. Savage, the owner of the company, owned one of the most famous horses of all times, Dan Patch (section 2.4). An advertisement published in 1915 claimed that Dan Patch had been given the tonic every day for more than 14 years. Advertisements for the tonic showing a picture of Dan Patch that was suitable for framing were distributed free of charge, and a Dan Patch Gold Stop Watch was given to everyone who purchased 3 pails of the tonic.

In the early 1900s many universities warned farmers against buying tonics. In spite of these warnings, tonic feeds were still commonly used in the 1920s and 1930s. Many states eventually made the sale of such feeds illegal.

An early advertisement that did not claim a tonic effect for a feed appeared in the *Breeder's Gazette* in 1886 (Figure 9-9). However, other advertisements for Blatchford's meal indicate that it contained locust beans, wheat, linseed meal, cottonseed meal, and fenugreek. Some high-quality feeds were available before 1900. In 1893 a New Jersey Experiment Station report stated, "A farmer who intelligently exchanges farm products for commercial feeds even at the same price per ton may secure not only an increase in feeding value but also a gain in fertility."

In the late 1890s and early 1900s many states initiated control programs. Massachusetts started analyzing commercial feedstuffs and publishing the results in special bulletins in 1897. Only one horse feed (H. O. Horse Feed) was listed in the 1898 bulletin. The feed contained oat feed

315

and corn. Oat feed was defined as the refuse from factories that manufactured oatmeal for human consumption.

Three horse feeds were listed in the 1903 bulletin. One of them, Blomo, contained dried blood, molasses, and ground corn stalks, and provided 15 percent protein. The 5 feeds listed in the 1906 bulletin contained mostly oat by-products.

Nine feeds were listed in 1907 and several, such as Molac, Sucrene, and Alfalmo, contained molasses. The molasses was frequently added to increase palatability and to disguise some of the other ingredients.

By 1914, 20 different horse feeds were tested in Massachusetts. It was concluded that "some of them [horse feeds] make very satisfactory grain rations and these, if the feeder is willing to pay the price and does not care to go to the trouble of home mixing, will be found very acceptable providing they do not contain inferior by-products. It is believed, however, that it is possible to home-mix fully as good rations at a lower cost." There were some high-protein feeds but most contained only 9–10 percent protein. Some brand names were Iroquois, Algrane, Schumacher Special, O.K., and Very Best. Feeds containing alfalfa and molasses were Clover Leaf, Kornfalfa Kandy, Peerless, Arab Horse, and June Pasture. Molassine and X-tra Vim contained 75 percent molasses and 25 percent sphagnum moss. The moss was considered to have little value except as a carrier for the molasses.

The 1916 bulletin included such names as Eat-al Horse Feed, King Falfa, Mo-Lene, and Quaker Green Cross. The 1917 bulletin mentioned Alfacorn, King Cotton, Tip-Top, Blue Seal, Peters Re-Peter, Purina O-Molene, Tom Boy, and Good Luck.

In 1921 the bulletin reported, "Mix 500–600 lb of oat feed [oat hulls, shorts, and middlings] with enough corn and hominy meal to form one ton and the result will be a typical horse feed. Oat feed is only slightly superior to mixed hay and should be classed as a roughage." However, the sale of molasses feeds, such as Nu-Life, Badger Prancer, O-Keh, Vim-O-Lene, Your Choice, and Farmer Jones, continued to increase.

By 1928, more than 35 horse feeds were being analyzed by the Massachusetts station. The ingredients were no longer reported in the bulletins, but most of the feeds still contained 9–10 percent protein, which suggests that no radical changes were made in formulation. Interesting brand names included Vigor, Bull Brand, Best Ever, Amco Arabs, Domino, and Chelsea.

Although the horse population started to decline about 1915, the number of brands of horse feed (at least according to the Massachusetts sample) continued to increase. In 1935 approximately 50 horse feeds were analyzed. Changes in formulation were evident, as most of the feeds analyzed contained 12 percent or more protein and many contained molasses. In 1933 the Kentucky Department of Agriculture had reported that the horse and mule feeds registered in that state usually consisted of corn, oats, barley, alfalfa, and wheat bran. Molasses was also often included.

In the 1920s some companies added by-products containing high quantities of B vitamins, and vitamin-rich mixtures were added to several feeds in the 1930s. Salt was already being added to rations before 1900.

One of the most common nutritional problems of horses was calcium deficiency, or "big head disease." The first suggestion that the condition was caused by feeding high levels of wheat bran was made in 1860, but the relation between the high phosphorus content of the wheat bran and impaired calcium nutrition was not established until much later. Calcium was first routinely added to commercial horse feeds in the mid-1930s. However, it had been added to general stock rations and fitting rations before that time.

The next important change in feed composition occurred in the early 1960s, when pelleted grains and pelleted complete diets were first extensively manufactured. Of course, pelleting of horse feeds was not a new concept, even in 1950. Pellets or biscuits had been used to feed horses in the Franco-Prussian War of 1870–1871. The Russians fed horses small biscuits composed of oatmeal, pea flour, rye, and ground linseed in 1877. The biscuits were said to provide approximately 1/5 the bulk of oats. The German armies used compressed feeds in World Wars I and II.

The use of pellets has several advantages, such as decreased feed waste, economy of space in storage and transportation, and reduced dust. These advantages appealed to horse owners, and sales of pelleted feeds increased rapidly. Complete pelleted diets also permit the use of properly supplemented by-products and feeds or ingredients that might not normally be accepted by horses. For example, pelleted feeds containing cereal by-products, corn cobs, peanut hulls, or a high level of fat are currently being marketed. Such formulations may become even more important in the future as the competition among feeds and foods increases. Other possible ingredients in pelleted diets include corrugated paper and computer paper. The disadvantages of the complete pelleted feed may include increased cost and usually result in an increase in such bad habits as wood chewing and tail biting if the pellets are fed without any other roughage. There is also a slight decline in fiber digestion, but the decrease is not of great practical concern.

Many companies manufacture horse feeds and most companies have different mixtures for the various classes of horse. There are many factors to consider when determining which feeds to buy. One factor is the reputation of the company. Most companies are reliable and make every effort to consistently produce a high-quality product. Quality control is very important to such companies and they closely monitor their products. Of course, some companies are not so conscientious. The company's reputation can be evaluated by asking other horsemen about their experi-

317

ences with the company's feed and by checking with the agency that enforces feed laws to determine if the product meets the guarantee on the feed tag. Most feeds meet the guarantee, but there are exceptions. For example, the 1974 report of the Office of the State Chemist of Arizona analyzed 30 different brands of horse feed. Only 4 brands did not meet the guarantee in all categories. Twelve feeds were complete feeds; that is, they were designed to be fed without hay. The average minimum guarantees were 11.3 percent protein and 1.5 percent fat. The average maximum fiber guaranteed was 26.6 percent. The feeds contained an average of 13.4 percent protein, 2.0 percent fat, and 22.6 percent fiber. The 18 grain mixtures were guaranteed to have minimums of 11.3 percent protein and 2.3 percent fat and a maximum of 6.6 percent fiber. The average analyses were 12.3 percent protein, 3.2 percent fat, and 6.4 percent fiber.

Another factor is that the feed selected should meet the needs of the horses but should not be provided in excess, which is costly. Most companies clearly indicate the class of horse for which the feed is intended, but the feed tag should be scrutinized to ensure that the feed is adequate. The feed tag requirements vary from state to state but the minimum amount of information should include minimum crude protein and crude fat and maximum fiber level. Some companies will also provide information about the calcium and phosphorus levels. If information about calcium and phosphorus is not on the tag, the feed dealer might be able to provide it.

The feed should also be selected according to the type of forage that is being fed. The information in Table 9-12 can be used as a rough guide in determining whether the nutrient content of the commercial mixture is adequate for various feeding situations. The table indicates that the advantage of feeding a mixed or legume hay to weanlings is that the grain mixture does not need as much protein. Protein is usually one of the most expensive ingredients in a commercial grain mixture.

The feed tag also lists the ingredients. The wording is often ambiguous so that changes in formulation can be made to take advantage of price changes of the basic ingredients. With such adjustments, the feed can be sold at a lower cost and the nutrient content will still meet the guarantee. However, radical changes may influence the palatability. Of course, factors other than nutrient content determine the value of the feed. The palatability must be satisfactory and the feed must be accepted by the horse. The feed should not be moldy or dusty. Pelleted feeds should not contain a lot of fines (small, dusty particles) or broken pellets.

The services provided by the dealer and the company should also be considered. Will the feed be available when it is needed? Be wary of companies that make outrageous claims and imply that their feed has "magic" qualities.

TABLE 9-12
Estimates of nutrient content needed in commercial feeds in order to meet
nutrient requirements for various classes of horses

Class of Horse	Nutrient (percent)	Type of Forage Feed			
		Legume Hay	Mixed Hay	Grass Hay	None[a]
Weanlings	Crude protein[b]	14	16	18	14
	Calcium	0.2[c]	0.6	0.9	0.7
	Phosphorus (%)	0.6	0.6	0.6	0.45
Yearlings	Crude protein	10	12	14	12
Mares					
Late gestation	Calcium	0.1[c]	0.3[c]	0.7	0.55
Lactation	Phosphorus	0.5	0.5	0.5	0.35
Mature horse	Crude protein	8	8	10	10
	Calcium	—[d]	—[d]	0.2[c]	0.30
	Phosphorus	0.3	0.3	0.3	0.25

[a]Feeding small amounts of hay even when using complete feeds will help alleviate such vices as wood chewing.

[b]The protein should be of good quality—that is, it should supply the essential amino acids. Soybean meal, milk proteins, and meat meal are examples of reasonable protein sources.

[c]Many mixtures will contain calcium levels greater than 0.3 percent, but the extra calcium is not harmful when an adequate level of phosphorus is provided.

[d]The forage will normally provide all the calcium needed.

9.6   Supplements and Conditioners

There are many supplements and conditioners on the market. When should they be used and of what value are they? Many manufacturers make unrealistic claims and their products are really of little or no value. For example, one company claims that its product will so greatly enhance digestion that there will be almost no fecal material, but in fact, the product has little value as an aid to digestion. Some products are of nutritional value but are sold in a very expensive form. Other supplements are worthwhile only under certain conditions. A vitamin supplement might be very appropriate when animals are under stress such as heavy lactation or hard work and are being fed a very poor-quality hay. But some vitamin supplements have a lot of additional material that is of no known value and are overpriced. Thus, there is no easy answer to questions of the value of supplements and when they should be used. Common sense and ex-

319

perience are the best guides. Do not expect miracle compounds to change the old gray mare into a champion.

9.7   General Management Guidelines

1. *Exercise horses regularly.* Horses are athletes and should be given the opportunity to work. Exercise is necessary to keep the muscles in good condition and prevent the horse from becoming too fat.

2. *Make sure that parasite control is adequate.* The most common cause of thin horses is a heavy load of parasites. To ensure a good feeding program, there must also be adequate control of parasites. A heavy load of parasites can decrease the efficiency of feed utilization and total feed intake and can prevent weight gains.

3. *Examine teeth regularly.* Thin horses often have poor teeth because an animal with poor teeth cannot eat or chew properly. Care of the teeth, including floating (filing or rasping of the sharp edges of the cheek teeth), is important. The diet of older horses with poor or missing teeth can be pelleted to aid digestion.

4. *Feed at regular times.* Horses are creatures of habit. They appear to appreciate being fed at regular times. Feeding at regular times may also help decrease some stable vices (see section 6.5).

5. *Avoid moldy feed.* Horses are quite susceptible to moldy feed toxicosis.

6. *Keep the feed manger clean.* A clean manger decreases feed waste and helps prevent horses from going off feed. Molds might also develop if the manger is not clean.

7. *Give small, frequent feedings.* Small, frequent feedings decrease the chances of gastric distention, founder, or colic. It is recommended that grain be fed at least twice a day if total grain intake exceeds 0.5 percent of the body weight.

8. *Feed by weight, not by volume.* There are considerable differences in density among horse feeds. Therefore, when feeding by volume, severe discrepancies may arise. For example, a quart of wheat bran weighs approximately 1/2 lb, whereas a quart of barley weighs 1 1/2 lb. One quart of corn may provide twice as much digestible energy as one quart of oats because corn weighs more per unit volume and is more digestible.

9. *Make changes in types of feed gradually.* Abrupt changes can cause colic or diarrhea, or can cause the horse to stop eating. The most common problem occurs when a low-energy diet is changed to a high-energy diet.

10. *Do not overfeed.* Remember the Arab proverb, "Fat and rest are two of the horse's greatest enemies." Excessive fat can reduce performance, reproductive efficiency, and perhaps even longevity.

11. *Make sure that water is frequently available, clean, and fresh.* Water should be frequently available except, of course, when the horse is hot. Automatic water bowls can be very useful because water is thus made available at all times and labor costs are decreased. A small heating unit with thermostat controls prevents water from freezing in the bowl. One unit could be located in such a way that it serves 2 box stalls. One large unit may serve 8–10 horses in a lot. One disadvantage of the automatic waterer is the initial expense; another is that certain horses may play with the waterer and cause water spillage. Unfortunately, horsemen often neglect to keep the automatic waterers clean and functioning properly. When using open tanks in a lot, there should be at least one foot of open water per horse. Excessive water intake by a hot horse may cause serious problems such as colic or founder.

Obviously, very cold or very hot water is not desirable. A range of 45°–65°F seems reasonable. Horses with damaged teeth sometimes tolerate warm water better than cold water.

References

Carlson, G. P., and R. A. Mansmann. 1974. Serum electrolyte and plasma protein alterations in horses used in endurance rides. *J.A.V.M.A.* 165: 262.

Davis, G. K., and C. L. Cole. 1943. The relation of ascorbic acid to breeding performance in horses. *J. Animal Sci.* 2:53.

Dimock, W. W., and B. J. Errington. 1942. Nutritional diseases of the equine. *N. Amer. Vet.* 23:152.

Ensminger, E. M. 1969. *Horses and Horsemanship.* Danville, Illinois: The Interstate Printers and Publishers, Inc.

Fallon, E. H. 1971. A veterinarian's viewpoint on horse feeding. *Proc. Cornell Equine Nutrition Conf.,* p. 29.

Fonnesbeck, P. V., and L. D. Symons. 1967. Utilization of the carotene of hay by horses. *J. Animal Sci.* 26:1030.

Harper, F. 1969. *Top Form Book of Horse Care.* New York: Popular Library.

Jordan, R. M., and G. C. Marten. 1975. Effect of three pasture grasses on yearling pony weight gains and pasture carrying capacity. *J. Animal Sci.* 40:86.

Mansmann, R. A., G. P. Carlson, N. A. White, and D. W. Milne. 1974. Synchronus diaphragmatic flutter in horses. *J.A.V.M.A.* 165:265.

Merrit, T. L., J. B. Washko, and R. H. Swain. 1969. *Selection and Management of Forage Species for Horses.* Pennsylvania State University Mimeo. A.S. H-69-1.

Morrison, F. B. 1959. *Feeds and Feeding.* 22d ed. Clinton, Iowa: Morrison.

National Academy of Sciences. 1971. *Atlas of Nutritional Data in United States and Canadian Feed.* Washington, D.C.

National Research Council. 1973. *Nutrient Requirements of Horses.* Publ. No. 6. Washington, D.C.

Ott, E. A. 1972. Feeding the broodmare. Thoroughbred Nutrition Supplement. *The Thoroughbred Record,* p. 14.

Schneider, B. H. 1947. *Feeds of the World.* Morgantown: West Virginia University.

Schryver, H.F., and H. F. Hintz. 1972. Calcium and phosphorus requirements of horses: A review. *Feedstuffs* 44:(28)35.

Stowe, H. D. 1967. Reproductive performance of barren mares following vitamin A and E supplementation. *Proc. Am. Assoc. Equine Pract.,* p. 81.

Tyznik, W. J. 1972. Nutrition and Disease. In: *Equine Medicine and Surgery.* 2d ed. Wheaton, Illinois: American Veterinary Publications.

322

Appendix

See overleaf

Composition of feeds commonly used in horse rations

Feed				
Common Name	Scientific Name		Reference No.	Dry Matter (%)
Alfalfa	*Medicago sativa*	Aerial part, dehy grnd, min 15 percent protein, (1)	1-00-022	93.1
		Aerial part, dehy grnd, min 17 percent protein, (1)	1-00-023	93.0
		Aerial part, dehy grnd, min 20 percent protein, (1)	1-00-024	93.1
		Hay, sun-cured, early bloom, (1)	1-00-059	90.0
		Hay, sun-cured, mid-bloom, (1)	1-00-063	89.2
		Hay, sun-cured, full bloom, (1)	1-00-068	87.7
		Hay, sun-cured, mature, (1)	1-00-071	91.2
		Aerial part, fresh, pre-bloom, (2)	2-00-181	21.1
		Aerial part, fresh, full bloom, (2)	2-00-188	25.3
Animal	——	Bone, steamed dehy grnd, (6)	6-00-400	95.0
Barley	*Hordeum vulgare*	Straw, (1)	1-00-498	88.2
		Grain, (4)	4-00-530	89.0
		Grain, gr 1 US min wt 47 lb per bushel mix 1 percent foreign material, (4)	4-00-535	89.0
		Grain, gr 3 US min wt 43 lb per bushel mix 3 percent foreign material, (4)	4-00-537	88.0
		Grain, gr 5 US min wt 36 lb per bushel mix 6 percent foreign material, (4)	4-00-540	88.0
		Grain, Pacific coast, (4)	4-07-939	89.0
Beet, sugar	*Beta saccharifera*	Molasses, min 48 percent invert sugar min 79.5 degrees brix, (4)	4-00-668	77.0
		Pulp, dehy, (4)	4-00-669	91.0
Bermuda grass	*Cynodon dactylon*	Aerial part, fresh, (2)	2-00-712	36.7
Bermuda grass, coastal	*Cynodon dactylon*	Hay, sun-cured, (1)	1-00-716	91.5
Bluegrass, Kentucky	*Poa pratensis*	Aerial part, fresh, immature, (2)	2-00-778	30.5
		Aerial part, fresh, milk stage, (2)	2-00-782	35.0
Bluestem	*Andropogon* spp.	Aerial part, fresh, immature, (2)	2-00-821	31.6
		Aerial part, fresh, mature, (2)	2-00-825	71.3
Brome, cheatgrass	*Bromus tectorum*	Aerial part, fresh, immature, (2)	2-00-908	21.0
		Aerial part, fresh, dough stage, (2)	2-00-910	30.0
Brome, smooth	*Bromus inermis*	Hay, sun-cured, mid-bloom, (1)	1-00-890	89.7
		Hay, sun-cured, mature, (1)	1-00-944	92.8
		Aerial part, fresh, immature, (2)	2-00-956	32.5
Calcium phosphate	——	Dibasic, commercial, (6)	6-01-080	96.0
Canarygrass, reed	*Phalaris arundinacea*	Hay, sun-cured, (1)	1-01-104	91.3
Cattle	*Bos* ssp.	Milk, skimmed dehy, mix 8 percent moisture, (5)	5-01-175	94.0
Citrus	*Citrus* spp.	Pulp without fines, shredded dehy, (4)	4-01-237	90.0
Clover, alsike	*Trifolium hybridum*	Hay, sun-cured, (1)	1-01-313	87.9
Clover, crimson	*Trifolium incarnatum*	Hay, sun-cured, (1)	1-01-328	87.4
		Aerial part, fresh, (2)	2-01-336	17.7
Clover, red	*Trifolium pratense*	Hay, sun-cured, (1)	1-01-415	90.1
Corn	*Zea mays*	Cobs, grnd, (1)	1-02-782	90.4
		Ears, grnd, (4)	4-02-849	87.0
		Distillers grains, dehy, (5)	5-02-842	92.0
		Gluten, wet milled dehy, (5)	5-02-900	91.0
Corn, dent yellow	*Zea mays indentata*	Grain, gr 2 US min wt 54 lb per bushel, (4)	4-02-931	89.0

DE (Mcal/kg)	TDN (%)	Protein (%)	Digestible Protein (%)	Crude Fiber (%)	Lignin (%)	Calcium (%)	Cobalt (mg/kg)	Copper (mg/kg)	Iron (%)	Magnesium (%)	Manganese (mg/kg)	Phosphorus (%)
2.29	58.	16.3	10.3	28.4	—	1.32	.190	11.2	.033	.31	31.1	.24
2.36	60.	19.2	13.0	26.1	—	1.43	.390	10.6	.049	.31	31.2	.26
2.43	62.	22.1	15.8	—	—	1.63	.344	11.4	.043	.38	36.5	.29
2.33	59.	18.4	12.3	29.8	—	1.25	.090	13.4	.020	.30	31.5	.23
2.25	57.	17.1	11.0	30.9	7.5	1.35	—	15.4	.010	.35	16.5	.22
2.10	53.	15.9	9.9	33.9	—	1.28	—	13.4	.020	.35	33.7	.20
1.94	49.	13.6	7.7	37.5	9.4	.71	—	—	—	.36	—	.16
2.36	60.	20.5	14.3	26.0	—	2.30	—	—	—	.03	—	.31
2.14	64.	16.9	10.9	31.7	—	1.53	—	—	.040	.27	—	.27
.70	16.	12.7	8.6	2.1	—	30.51	.100	17.2	.088	.67	32.0	14.31
1.56	38.	4.1	.5	42.4	12.6	.34	—	—	.030	.19	17.2	.09
3.66	83.	13.0	8.2	5.6	1.9	.09	.100	8.6	.006	.14	18.3	.47
—	—	13.6	8.7	6.7	—	.27	—	—	—	—	—	.41
—	—	13.4	8.5	6.8	—	.06	—	—	—	—	—	.39
—	—	11.7	6.9	11.4	—	—	—	—	—	—	—	—
3.62	82.	10.9	6.2	7.0	—	.07	—	—	—	—	—	.45
3.92	89.	8.7	5.0	—	—	.21	.500	22.9	.010	.30	6.0	.04
3.18	72.	10.0	4.5	20.9	2.9	.75	.100	13.7	.033	.30	38.5	.11
2.22	56.	11.6	6.8	25.9	—	.53	.070	5.7	.110	.23	100.1	.22
1.94	44.	9.5	4.5	30.5	4.5	.46	—	—	—	.17	—	.18
2.44	62.	17.3	12.2	25.1	3.8	.56	—	14.1	.030	.18	80.3	.47
2.18	55.	11.6	6.8	30.3	—	.19	—	13.9	.017	.23	80.3	.27
—	—	11.0	5.6	28.9	—	.63	—	36.8	.070	—	83.3	.17
1.92	48.	4.5	.8	34.0	—	.40	—	16.1	.060	.06	36.8	.11
2.36	60.	15.8	10.9	22.9	—	.64	—	—	—	—	—	.28
1.96	49.	5.3	1.4	34.8	—	.38	—	—	—	—	—	.27
1.91	44.	11.8	6.2	38.5	4.5	.40	—	8.6	.012	.22	58.0	.20
1.85	46.	5.8	1.8	34.2	—	.43	.130	6.8	.010	.19	105.8	.22
2.36	60.	22.1	16.3	22.4	—	.62	—	—	—	—	—	.57
—	—	—	—	—	—	23.13	—	—	—	—	—	18.65
1.94	46.	11.5	6.0	35.2	3.7	.34	—	11.9	.020	.26	92.4	.25
3.79	86.	35.6	—	.2	—	1.34	.117	12.2	.005	.12	2.3	1.10
3.09	70.	7.3	2.9	14.4	1.0	2.18	—	6.3	.018	.18	7.6	.13
2.21	56.	14.7	8.7	29.4	—	1.31	—	6.0	.030	.45	69.0	.25
2.18	55.	16.9	10.9	32.2	—	1.42	—	—	.070	.27	171.3	.18
2.33	59.	16.7	10.7	28.3	—	1.62	—	—	.070	.41	290.6	.35
2.16	55.	14.2	8.3	29.5	6.3	1.45	—	10.7	.011	.52	76.9	.23
1.23	29.	2.8	.0	35.8	—	.12	.130	7.3	.023	.07	6.2	.04
3.44	78.	9.3	4.6	9.2	—	.05	.300	8.8	.008	.17	15.0	.31
3.70	84.	29.5	23.8	13.0	—	.10	.100	48.6	.020	.07	20.5	.40
3.70	84.	47.1	40.5	4.4	—	.18	.100	31.0	.040	.05	8.0	.44
4.01	91.	10.0	5.3	2.2	0.8	.02	—	—	—	—	—	—

325

(Continued on next page)

Composition of feeds commonly used in horse rations

Feed				
Common Name	Scientific Name		Reference No.	Dry Matter (%)
Cotton	*Gossypium* spp.	Seed with some hulls, solv-extd grnd, min 41 percent protein mix 14 percent fiber min 0.5 percent fat, (5)	5-01-621	91.5
Emmer	*Triticum dicoccum*	Grain, (4)	4-01-830	91.0
Fescue, alta	*Festuca arundinacea*	Hay, sun-cured, mid-bloom, (1)	1-05-684	89.0
Fescue, meadow	*Festuca elatior*	Hay, sun-cured, (1)	1-01-912	88.5
		Aerial part, fresh, (2)	2-01-920	27.6
Flax	*Linum usitatissimum*	Seed, mech-extd grnd, mix 0.5 percent acid insoluble ash, (5)	5-02-045	91.0
		Seed, solv-extd grnd, mix 0.5 percent acid insoluble ash, (5)	5-02-048	91.0
Grains	——	Brewers, dehy, mix 3 percent dried spent hops, (5)	5-02-141	92.0
Lespedeza	*Lespedeza* spp.	Hay, sun-cured, pre-bloom, (1)	1-07-954	92.1
		Hay, sun-cured, full bloom, (1)	1-02-512	93.2
Limestone	——	Grnd, min 33 percent calcium, (6)	6-02-632	100.0
Native plants, intermountain	——	Hay, sun-cured, (1)	1-03-181	92.9
Oats	*Avena sativa*	Hay, sun-cured, (1)	1-03-280	88.2
		Grain, (4)	4-03-309	89.0
		Grain, gr 1 US min wt 34 lb per bushel mix 2 percent foreign material, (4)	4-03-313	91.0
		Grain, gr 2 US min wt 32 lb per bushel mix 3 percent foreign material, (4)	4-03-316	89.0
		Grain, gr 4 US min wt 27 lb per bushel mix 5 percent foreign material, (4)	4-03-318	91.2
		Grain, Pacific coast, (4)	4-07-999	91.2
		Groats, (4)	4-03-331	91.0
Oats, white	*Avena sativa*	Grain, Can 2 CW min wt 36 lb per bushel mix 3 percent foreign material, (4)	4-03-378	86.5
Orchard grass	*Dactylis glomerata*	Hay, sun-cured, (1)	1-03-438	88.3
		Aerial part, fresh, immature, (2)	2-03-440	23.8
		Aerial part, fresh, mid-bloom, (2)	2-03-443	30.0
		Aerial part, fresh, milk stage, (2)	2-03-446	30.0
Pea	*Pisum* spp.	Straw, (1)	1-03-577	87.3
Peanut	*Arachis hypogaea*	Kernels, solv-extd grnd, mix 7 percent fiber, (5)	5-03-650	92.0
Phosphate	——	Defluorinated grnd, min 1 part F per 100 parts P, (6)	6-01-780	99.8
Rice	*Oryza sativa*	Bran w germ dry milled mix 13 percent fiber $CaCO_3$ declared above 3 percent min, (4)	4-03-928	91.0
Sodium phosphate	——	Monobasic, $HaH_2PO_4H_2O$, technical, (6)	6-04-288	96.7
Sodium tripolyphosphate	——	Commercial, (6)	6-08-076	96.0
Sorghum, milo	*Sorghum vulgare*	Grain, (4)	4-04-444	89.0
Sorghum, Sudan grass	*Sorghum vulgare*	Aerial part, fresh, mid-bloom, (2)	2-04-485	22.7
Soybean	*Glycine max*	Seed, solv-extd grnd, mix 7 percent fiber, (5)	5-04-604	89.0
		Seed without hulls, solv-extd grnd, mix 3 percent fiber, (5)	5-04-612	89.8

				On a Dry Basis (Moisture Free)								
DE (Mcal/kg)	TDN (%)	Protein (%)	Digestible Protein (%)	Crude Fiber (%)	Lignin (%)	Calcium (%)	Cobalt (mg/kg)	Copper (mg/kg)	Iron (%)	Magnesium (%)	Manganese (mg/kg)	Phosphorus (%)
3.31	75.	44.8	38.4	13.1	8.1	.17	.164	21.3	.033	.61	23.5	1.31
3.09	70.	14.2	9.3	11.0	—	—	—	37.9	.006	—	94.3	.47
1.81	45.	8.4	3.7	37.9	4.4	.36	—	—	—	.24	—	.21
1.96	49.	10.5	5.3	31.2	6.9	.50	—	—	—	.50	24.5	.36
2.00	50.	15.1	10.3	27.1	—	.51	—	4.0	—	.37	—	.38
3.57	81.	38.8	32.6	9.9	—	.48	.500	29.0	.019	.64	43.3	.98
3.35	76.	38.6	32.5	9.9	—	.44	.200	28.2	.036	.66	41.3	.91
2.25	51.	28.1	22.5	16.3	—	.29	.100	22.2	.027	.15	40.9	.54
2.23	56.	17.8	11.7	23.7	—	1.14	—	—	—	—	—	.26
2.07	52.	13.4	7.5	31.0	—	1.04	—	—	.030	.24	151.5	.23
—	—	—	—	—	—	—	—	—	—	—	—	.02
1.63	40.	9.1	4.2	30.1	—	.57	—	—	—	—	—	.17
1.96	49.	9.2	4.3	31.0	—	.26	.070	4.4	.050	.29	74.7	.24
3.09	70.	13.2	8.3	12.4	—	.11	—	—	—	—	—	.39
3.09	70.	13.3	8.4	13.2	—	.09	—	—	—	—	—	.33
3.09	70.	12.7	7.9	12.4	—	.07	—	—	—	—	—	—
2.87	65.	13.2	8.3	16.5	—	—	—	—	—	—	—	—
3.09	70.	9.9	5.2	12.1	—	.10	—	—	—	—	—	.36
3.70	84.	18.4	13.3	3.3	—	.08	—	7.0	—	.10	31.4	.47
3.09	70.	13.2	8.3	12.0	—	—	—	—	—	—	—	—
1.85	46.	9.0	4.2	34.5	4.1	.45	.020	13.7	.010	.22	249.6	.22
2.36	60.	18.4	13.1	23.6	—	.58	—	—	.020	.31	134.3	.55
2.07	52.	9.1	4.2	31.9	—	—	—	—	—	—	—	—
1.92	48.	8.4	3.7	35.2	—	.23	—	—	—	—	—	.22
1.78	44.	7.6	4.0	38.9	—	—	—	—	—	—	—	—
3.40	77.	51.5	44.7	14.1	—	.22	—	—	—	.04	31.5	.71
—	—	—	—	—	—	33.07	—	—	.922	—	—	18.04
2.87	65.	14.8	9.9	12.1	—	.07	—	14.3	.021	1.04	459.2	2.00
—	—	—	—	—	—	—	—	—	—	—	—	22.46
—	—	—	—	—	—	—	—	—	—	—	—	25.98
3.53	80.	12.4	7.6	2.2	—	.04	.100	15.8	—	.22	14.5	.33
1.92	48.	8.7	3.9	36.1	—	—	—	—	—	—	—	—
3.53	80.	51.5	44.7	6.7	1.2	.36	.100	40.8	.013	.30	30.9	.75
3.70	84.	56.7	49.7	3.1	—	.29	—	—	—	—	50.6	.69

327

(*Continued on next page*)

APPENDIX TABLE 9-1 (*Continued*)

Composition of feeds commonly used in horse rations

Feed				
Common Name	Scientific Name		Reference No.	Dry Matter (%)
Sugarcane	*Saccharum officinarum*	Molasses, min 48 percent invert sugar min 79.5 degrees brix, (4)	4-04-696	75.0
Timothy	*Phleum pratense*	Hay, sun-cured, pre-bloom, (1)	1-04-881	88.6
		Hay, sun-cured, mid-bloom, (1)	1-04-883	88.4
		Hay, sun-cured, late bloom, (1)	1-04-885	88.0
Wheat	*Triticum* spp.	Hay, sun-cured, (1)	1-05-172	85.9
		Straw, (1)	1-05-175	90.1
		Bran, dry milled, (4)	4-05-190	89.0
		Flour by-prod. fine sifted, mix 4 percent fiber, (4)	4-05-203	89.0
		Grain, (4)	4-05-211	89.0
		Grain, Pacific coast, (4)	4-08-142	89.2
Wheat, soft	*Triticum aestivum*	Grain, (4)	4-05-284	90.0
Wheatgrass, crested	*Agropyron cristatum*	Aerial part, fresh, immature, (2)	2-05-420	30.8
		Aerial part, fresh, full bloom, (2)	2-05-424	50.0
		Aerial part, fresh, over ripe, (2)	2-05-428	80.0
Yeast	*Saccharomyces cerevisiae*	Dehy grnd, min 40 percent protein, (7)	7-05-527	93.0
		Irradiated, dehy, (7)	7-05-529	94.0

SOURCE: Adapted from National Research Council. 1973.

NOTE: Numbers in "Form" column indicate the following:

(1) Dry forages and roughages.
(2) Pasture, range plants, and forages fed green.
(3) Silages.
(4) Energy feeds.
(5) Protein supplements.
(6) Minerals.
(7) Vitamins.

On a Dry Basis (Moisture Free)

DE (Mcal/kg)	TDN (%)	Protein (%)	Digestible Protein (%)	Crude Fiber (%)	Lignin (%)	Calcium (%)	Cobalt (mg/kg)	Copper (mg/kg)	Iron (%)	Magnesium (%)	Manganese (mg/kg)	Phosphorus (%)
3.18	72.	4.3	.0	—	—	1.19	—	79.4	.025	.47	56.3	.11
2.34	53.	12.3	6.6	32.9	—	.66	—	—	—	—	—	.34
1.94	49.	8.3	3.6	33.5	5.1	.41	.082	—	—	.20	45.0	.19
1.90	44.	8.3	3.6	—	—	.38	—	—	—	—	—	.18
1.91	47.	7.5	3.4	27.8	—	—	—	—	—	—	—	—
1.45	35.	3.6	.2	41.5	13.7	.17	.040	3.3	.020	.12	40.4	.08
2.57	65.	18.0	12.9	11.2	3.4	.16	.044	13.8	.019	.62	130.0	1.32
3.75	85.	20.2	15.0	2.2	—	.09	—	4.9	.007	.33	42.3	.58
3.88	88.	14.3	9.4	—	1.1	—	—	—	—	—	—	.41
3.88	88.	11.1	6.3	3.0	—	.14	—	—	—	—	—	.34
3.88	88.	12.0	7.2	2.6	—	.10	—	10.8	.006	.11	57.0	.33
2.36	60.	23.6	17.5	22.2	5.9	.46	—	—	—	.28	—	.35
1.85	46.	9.8	4.8	30.3	6.2	.39	—	—	—	—	—	.28
1.56	38.	3.1	.0	40.3	—	.27	.240	8.4	—	—	52.9	.07
3.09	70.	47.9	41.3	3.2	—	.14	.200	35.5	.010	.25	6.1	1.54
2.95	67.	51.2	44.4	7.4	—	—	—	—	—	—	—	1.36

CHAPTER TEN

Problems Associated with Feeding

Consarn a hoss anyhow! If they're wuth anythin they're more bother 'n' a teethin baby. Alwas some dun thing ailin' em.

EDWARD NOYES WESCOTT. *David Harum*. 1898

10.1   Fat Horses and Thin Horses

Many horses are either too fat or too thin. Excess fat is usually a result of overfeeding rather than hormonal problems. There are several conditions that result in overfeeding:

1. Many people enjoy feeding horses used as pets.

2. Many horsemen purposely overfeed show horses or sales horses because fat may help mask undesirable traits; Traditionally, fat horses sell for higher prices.

3. Many horsemen think they must greatly increase the feed intake of a mare as soon as she is pronounced in foal. The energy requirement of a pregnant mare increases only during the last third of gestation.

4. Many horses do not receive adequate exercise, including work.

Some of the common causes of thin horses are:

1. Parasites. In order to have a good feeding program, there should also be a good parasite control program.

2. Milk production. Some mares produce large amounts of milk and therefore need a considerable amount of energy.

3. Hard work. Work can greatly increase the energy requirements of horses. A horse that performs one hour of hard work per day may need twice as much energy as a nonworking horse.

4. Poor teeth. Many horses have difficulty eating and chewing. A regular inspection of teeth is a good husbandry practice.

5. Too much competition. In group feeding, some horses may be deprived of access to feed by the more aggressive horses.

6. Malabsorption. There may be a defect in the gastrointestinal tract, such as lack of enzymes or changes in the intestinal wall, that prevents normal uptake of food.

There is some variation in energy requirements among individual horses, and the old law that "the eye of the master fattens the stock" may be the most important rule. Know the unique traits and needs of your horse and feed it accordingly. Monthly weighings are helpful to monitor weight changes. In fact, there are several reasons for knowing the weight of horses. Many feeding recommendations are based on percentages of the horse's weight. The dosages of drugs, antibiotics, and worming compounds are often based on the weight of the horse.

The best method of determining weight is to use a scale, but when a scale is not available weight can be estimated by using formulas based on measurements such as heart girth and length. For example, Milner and Hewitt (1969) have reported that weight can be estimated by the following formula:

$$\text{Estimated weight (lb)} = \frac{\text{Heart girth}^2 \times \text{Length}}{241.3}$$

In this formula, heart girth is measured in inches and length in inches is measured from point of shoulder to point of hip. Milner and Hewitt measured 108 horses ranging in size from Shetland ponies to draft horses and in age from weanling to mature. The average difference between estimated weights and weights obtained with scales was approximately 6 percent. They compared their results with weight estimates obtained by using tapes supplied by feed companies (Figure 10-1). The tapes also

331

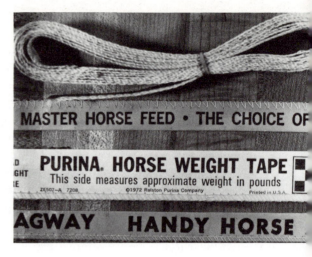

FIGURE 10-1
Tapes can be useful for
estimating the weights of horses.

MASTER HORSE FEED • THE CHOICE OF

PURINA. HORSE WEIGHT TAPE
This side measures approximate weight in pounds
ZE507–A 7208   ©1972 Ralston Purina Company   Printed in U.S.A.

AGWAY   HANDY HORSE

proved to be quite useful; the average difference between estimated and actual weight was less than 10 percent.

10.2 Founder

The word "founder" means to fall in or to fall helplessly and go lame. ("Founder" as a noun can also be a synonym for laminitis.) The acutely foundered horse usually does not fall but rather becomes, as the saying has it, "glued to the floor," and if forced to move, does so with great reluctance, placing his forefeet so carefully in a heel-first manner that he may be appropriately described as "walking on eggs." "Acutely" means that the full-blown symptoms appear quite suddenly—for example, when a pony grazing on lush spring pasture is sound one day and foundered the next; or when a horse finds his way into the grain bin that was not closed at night and by the next night he is foundered; or when a mare foals and develops an infection in her uterus because the afterbirth is not expelled completely, and she is foundered 24–36 hours later.

The acutely foundered horse is suffering from inflammation of the sensitive laminae of its feet. The sensitive laminae are leaflike structures that are lined up vertically around the region between the hoof wall and coffin bone (Figure 10-2). There are approximately 600 of these laminae on each hoof, and secondary and tertiary laminae branch off from the 600 primary laminae. In most cases, only the front feet are affected by founder; however, all 4 feet may be affected.

Acute inflammation of the sensitive laminae beneath the hoof wall is the result of an incompletely understood biological phenomenon in which the sensitive laminae become detached from the insensitive

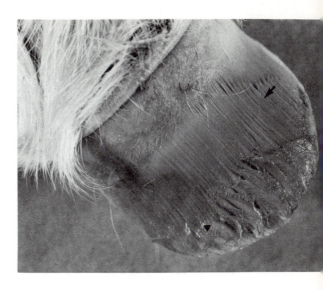

FIGURE 10-2
Foot preparation (hoof removed),
showing sensitive laminae of pony
that has had chronic founder. Arrow
points to normal laminae. Triangle
points to enlarged scarred laminae
in area of chronic founder.

laminae. The insensitive laminae make up the inner part of the hoof wall.
They interlock (dovetail) with the sensitive laminae, the outer part of the
tissue, which cover and are attached to the coffin bone. This interlocking
maintains the suspended nature of the coffin bone within the hoof. When a
horse places its foot on firm ground, especially when wearing shoes, the
hoof wall bears most of the weight and has most contact with the ground.
This force of contact is transferred to the laminae and then to the skeletal
support, starting with the coffin bone and progressing up the limb. The
bones are kept aligned and the force is cushioned by the various ligaments
and attached muscles, all of which are elastic in varying degrees. The
laminae suspend a large portion of the weight of the horse. It is essential
to bear in mind that the laminae are biologically alive and are taking part
in the continual hoof growth process, which starts at the hairline.

Degrees of founder range from very mild to severe, resulting in continual pain. The normal position of the bones in the foot is shown in Fig.
10-3. If founder is severe, the coffin bone may drop away from its normal
position within the hoof. The greatest drop, or "rotation," as it is usually
called, occurs at the toe (Figures 10-4, 10-5). This causes the widened
"white line" and, in many cases, the "seedy toe" associated with founder.
If the coffin bone rotates, the sole has to flatten out also (Figure 10-5). The
sole may even become convex (Figure 10-6), or the tip of the coffin bone
may actually protrude through the sole, and then the sensitive tissue is
exposed to bacterial infection. At the other extreme is the mild "touch"
of founder, in which inflammation is evident but no rotation of the coffin
bone takes place.

Because of the pain within the laminar area, the horse tries to avoid
weight bearing and concussion as much as possible, and thus places its heel
to the ground first in a careful deliberate heel-to-toe movement. When the
initial inflammation subsides, which happens anywhere from one day to
many weeks after the acute founder occurs, the horse is said to be either

333

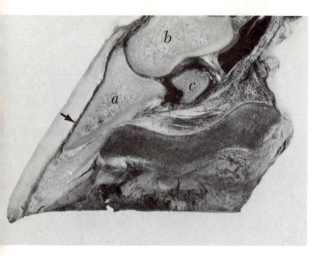

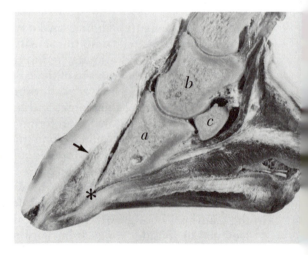

FIGURE 10-3
Vertical cross section of normal horse
foot with long toe in need of
trimming. Arrow points to laminar
area. Note that front of hoof wall and
front of coffin bone (*a*) are parallel.
Photo also shows short pastern
bone (*b*) and navicular bone (*c*).

FIGURE 10-4
Vertical cross section of foot
of chronically foundered pony.
Note rotation of coffin bone: tip
of coffin bone (*asterisk*) should
be where point of arrow is. Area
between star and arrow is filled
with distorted laminae and scar
tissue. *a*, *b*, and *c* are the same
as in Figure 10-3.

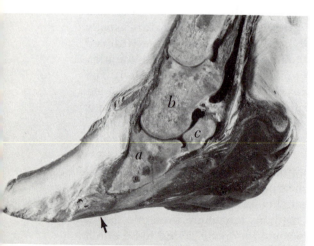

FIGURE 10-5
Vertical cross section of foot of severe
chronically foundered horse. Compare
with Figure 10-3: note complete
distortion of hoof growth and shrivel-
ing up of coffin bone. Arrow points
to flat, nearly convex sole. Specimen
shows more extensive rotation of coffin
bone than is shown in Figure 10-4.

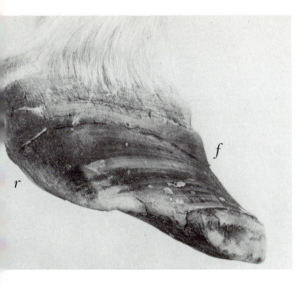

FIGURE 10-6
Outside of hoof of chronically foundered foot shown in Figure 10-5. Note distortion of distance between growth rings: they are close together at front of hoof (*f*) and much wider apart at heel of foot (*r*). Also note the "dished" concave shape of the front of the hoof wall.

cured or to have chronic founder. In all cases of chronic founder, there is some rotation of the coffin bone, widening of the "white line," and evidence of abnormal growth rings on the hoof. The sole is flattened and thinner than normal and the front of the hoof wall may have a "dished" concave shape. The distance between growth rings (Figure 10-5) at the toe is less than the distance between the same growth rings at the quarter or heel. The end result is that the toes will curl upward if they are not trimmed regularly.

The chronically foundered horse may not show pain but usually moves in a heel-to-toe step unless it is correctively shod or trimmed. Apparently, the rotation of the coffin bone does not change the horse's natural inclination to land flat on the coffin bone. A rotated coffin bone landing flat means that the foot lands noticeably heel first. The defect resulting from the ruptured lamina fills in with scar tissue and always leaves some permanent damage and weakened laminar attachment.

For reasons that are not well understood, certain breeds and types of horses founder more often than others. Fat ponies and small fat horses that are "easy keepers" are notorious for being targets of founder. Some breeds have comparatively less founder than others. Table 10-1 shows the total number of cases of all diseases for the breeds listed, the total number of founder cases, and the ratio of total cases to founder cases reported by the New York State Veterinary College, Cornell University, Ithaca, New York, from January 1, 1966, to January 1, 1972.

There is no widely accepted, precise method for treating founder. However, certain principles apply to any treatments used. If founder results secondarily because of overeating of grain or because of indigestion from other causes, treating the horse for the primary condition is essential. The same principle applies to infections of the reproductive tract or lungs. Horses that founder at pasture need to be removed from pasture until they

335

TABLE 10-1
Incidence of founder

Breed	Total Cases, All Diseases	Horses Foundered	Percent Foundered
Appaloosa	565	3	0.5
Thoroughbred	1,253	34	2.7
Quarter Horse	1,584	44	2.8
Arabs	428	14	3.3
Standardbred	2,646	87	3.3
Shetland pony	345	18	5.2
Morgan	251	15	6.0

recover and then should be given only limited access to the pasture while lush growth exists. Injectable antihistamine compounds are widely used because histamine is accepted as an agent of founder. Analgesics (painkillers) are helpful, and some veterinarians have obtained beneficial results by temporarily deadening the nerve supply to the feet and then walking the foundered animal to improve circulation to the injured lamina.

The use of cortisone products is debatable and more information regarding their beneficial or detrimental effects is needed. Methionine, a sulfur containing amino acid, has been administered orally, but its use is not yet widely accepted. Applying pressure on the sole by tying burlap bags to the feet and standing the horse in moist sand are techniques that have been used to help prevent rotation of the coffin bone. Soaking the feet in water is a widely accepted treatment, but there is disagreement concerning whether it should be cold water or warm water. In severe cases of founder that do not respond to treatment, secondary bacterial infection similar to the infection resulting from a puncture wound often occurs in the sole. This infection has to be treated and controlled before substantial progress toward recovery is made.

Corrective trimming and shoeing and reducing the weight of fat horses are primary weapons for treating chronic founder. Lowering the heels, using wide-webbed, beveled shoes to protect the dropped sole and full leather pads to further protect the sole, and rounding off the curling toe help a great deal. Soft acrylic plastics are sometimes applied to the sole to replace the injured hoof area and help realign the rotated coffin bone. The use of plastic requires much more time and expense than corrective trimming. However, the beneficial effects of plastic justifies its use in selected cases.

The fat man often has sore feet and horses are no different. Attainment of a body weight that is in keeping with what the feet can hold up is possible by reducing the feed intake over a period of months. This often means a diet of no grain and limited grass hay or limited amounts of low-nutrient hay. Do not overfeed horses and ponies. Excess feed given either by mistake or by neglect over many months causes a large percentage of founder cases.

Use common sense about riding practices and training practices. Whenever possible, avoid speed on hard surfaces; let animals cool off after exercising them, and continue a parasite control and preventive vaccination program as recommended by your veterinarian.

Learn how to use a rectal thermometer and have one available when needed in order to determine whether the horse has a fever (section 18.1).

10.3 Heaves

Heaves, or pulmonary emphysema, is a condition in which the lungs do not work efficiently (section 18.2). Any management practice that reduces dust may be helpful when horses have heaves. (Horses on pasture seldom have difficulty with heaves.) The use of pelleted feeds, whole clean grains, or wet hay can also be helpful. The hay can be soaked in a water pail 15–30 minutes before feeding. The use of hay substitutes such as beet pulp or citrus pulp may also be beneficial. Dusty bedding should be avoided.

10.4 Colic

The term "colic" is applied to various conditions of the digestive tract of which pain is the chief symptom (section 18.2). It is one of the oldest known disorders of horses—Columella described it in the first century after Christ. It has long been considered the most dangerous and costly equine internal disease. For example, from 1880–1900 there was a 12 percent mortality among the 60,000 horses suffering from colic in the Prussian Army. Parasites are the primary cause of colic and parasite control programs have greatly reduced the incidence of the condition. However, overeating, eating of moldy feed, constipation, rapidly changing to a rich diet, lack of water, and excessive eating of shavings may also cause colic.

10.5 Eating Problems

Depraved Appetite

Chewing wood, eating dirt, sand, and/or gravel, tail biting, and eating the bark of trees are often observed in horses. The craving for unnatural food

337

may result because of a nutrient deficiency. For example, iron deficiency may cause animals to eat dirt (geophagia). Phosphorus deficiency has been reported to produce pica in several species of animals. Reports from Germany have indicated that pica was observed in horses that were reared on pasture deficient in phosphorus. The pica could sometimes be prevented by feeding phosphorus.

However, most horses seem to chew wood, trees and hair for reasons other than a nutrient deficiency. One horseman concluded after several years of study that horses chew wood because they like to. Horses fed a complete pelleted diet frequently chew wood and/or eat dirt. Boredom and lack of exercise may also be causes. Horses may develop the habit by imitating other horses.

Chewing of wood can often be alleviated by using hardwoods such as oak, covering the wood with metal, or treating the wood with materials such as creosote. Exercise and accessibility to hay or minerals free choice can also be helpful. Such vices as wood chewing and dirt or stone eating should be discouraged. Replacing wooden fences and mangers is expensive, and excessive ingestion of foreign material may be harmful to the horse. Eating the bark of trees or shrubs certainly can be harmful to the plants, but whether it is harmful, helpful, or of no consequence to the horse depends on the kind of tree and the extent of chewing. For example, the foliage, bark, and seeds of several types of yews are toxic to horses. The bark of the locust tree may be toxic. Leaves of apricot, peach, almond, and wild cherry trees contain a toxic cyanogentic glycoside. Leaves and sprouts of buckeye and oak trees can be lethal. Although in general, little nutritional benefit is derived from bark chewing, in some cases it apparently can be helpful. For example, it has been reported that horses can obtain calcium from the bark of certain trees in Australia. Plains Indians used the inner bark of the round-leaf or sweet bark cottonwood trees as a supplemental feed for horses during the winter.

Excessive chewing of sand or dirt may result in sand impaction of the cecum and colon. Sand impaction is frequently observed when horses are fed on the ground in such areas as the southwestern United States and Florida. Chewing of hair may result in hair balls. Hair balls, although rare, have been reported in the intestines of horses with a habit of licking themselves when shedding.

Coprophagy (eating of feces) is often observed in young foals. Hence, mares should be treated for parasites during late gestation and early lactation to decrease the chances of infesting the foal. Coprophagy is not likely to cause problems (except that it fosters the growth of parasites); in fact, there is some nutritional benefit. Coprophagy is not as common in mature horses as in young foals, but confined horses fed complete pelleted diets are more apt to practice coprophagy than exercised horses with access to hay. Confined horses fed pelleted diets spent approximately 2 percent of their time eating feces, whereas horses fed hay spent less than 1 percent of their time in that manner (Willard *et al.*, 1973).

Fast Eating

Many horses are extremely greedy, rapid eaters. This practice should be discouraged because it may lead to digestive disorders or choking. Spreading the grain in a thin layer, putting large, smooth stones in the bottom of the manger, or feeding several times a day may be helpful.

Off Feed

What should be done when a horse goes off feed? First of all, try to determine why the horse stopped eating. Is the horse sick? Does it have an elevated temperature? Check the mouth and teeth. A sore tongue or bad teeth are common causes of decreased feed intake. Moldy feed may cause a sudden decrease in feed intake. Perhaps boredom is a cause. Exercise and a change in diet may be helpful. Nutrient deficiencies could also affect intake. Potassium deficiency results in decreased intake, but the probability of potassium deficiency is slight when roughages are fed. It has been suggested that horses that go off feed and become "track sour" may respond to thiamin (Tyznik, 1972). Adding two tablespoonfuls of brewer's yeast to the horse's daily ration may be helpful.

10.6   Metabolic Disorders

Tying-up Disease

Tying-up disease is a muscle disorder that occurs in racehorses and light horses under heavy exercise. It is usually more common in mares than geldings. There is lameness and rigidity of the muscles of the loin. The horse walks as though it has back pain and the muscles feel very hard to the touch. The urine may be coffee-colored because of the myoglobin released from the damaged cells. Some authorities diagnose tying-up as a form of azoturia (Monday morning disease, or black water), a disease that was primarily observed in draft horses not worked on Sunday but given full feed. Azoturia in draft horses also results in rigidity of muscles and release of myoglobin into the urine. In a severe case, the animal will refuse to move, may assume a sitting position, or even fall prostrate on its

339

side. Other authorities suggest that the muscle changes in azoturia are different from those characteristic of tying-up disease.

Reducing the grain intake on days the animals are idle will help prevent azoturia. The relationship of tying-up to nutrition is not clearly defined and much more research needs to be done to clarify it. Many veterinarians feel that injections of vitamin E and selenium are quite helpful in the prevention and cure of tying-up. Others recommend vitamin E, selenium, and thiamin, whereas still others prefer cortisone injections and other methods of treatment. With rest and proper care, most horses will recover unless there has been extensive kidney damage.

Hyperlipemia

Hyperlipemia is a condition in which there is an unusually high level of fat (triglycerides and cholesterol) in the blood. In fact, the blood appears cloudy. Fat ponies are particularly likely to develop the condition. The condition can be produced in healthy animals by withholding food and it has been reported in animals suffering from equine infectious anemia, equine viral arteritis, and other conditions that caused the animals to stop eating (Schotman and Wagenaar, 1969; Baetz and Pearson, 1972). Some of the changes that occur in blood serum as a result of withholding feed are shown in Table 10-2. The hyperlipemia apparently results during inappetence because the animals draw on the body stores of fat for energy; there may also be an impaired utilization of the very low-density lipoproteins (Morris et al., 1972). Feeding will correct the condition, but animals with severe hyperlipemia may not commence eating even after the original cause for inappetence has been corrected. Such ponies have been treated with oral administration of glucose and intramuscular injection of insulin (Wensing et al., 1972). Prolonged fasting is not recommended as a weight-reduction method for horses because of the possibility of hyperlipemia.

TABLE 10-2
Effect of fasting on triglyceride and cholesterol content of blood serum of ponies

Period	Triglycerides (mg/100 ml)		Cholesterol (mg/100 ml)	
Pretrial	25	25	58	67
After 8 days fasting	196	442	108	193

SOURCE: Numbers in columns 1 and 3 from Baetz and Pearson. 1972. Numbers in columns 2 and 4 from Morris et al. 1972.

340

Anemia

Anemia is defined as a deficiency of hemoglobin or number of red blood cells. Hemoglobin is the respiratory pigment of the red blood cells. It combines with and releases oxygen. Thus, the hemoglobin content is of concern to horsemen, particularly racehorse owners, because they feel that the hemoglobin or oxygen-carrying capacity is related to performance. Deficiencies of many nutrients, such as iron, copper, vitamin B_{12}, folic acid, vitamin B_6, vitamin E, and protein, may result in anemia. However, deficiencies of these nutrients are not likely when horses are fed good-quality roughage. The addition of these nutrients to a balanced ration will not significantly increase the hemoglobin content. For example, an injection of 4 mg of vitamin B_{12} in ponies caused a rapid rise in serum B_{12} but the serum level returned to normal within 5–6 days and there was no increase in hemoglobin or hematocrit level. Alexander and Davies (1969) also reported that much of the injected B_{12} was excreted in urine within 1–2 days post-injection and there was no increase in hemoglobin content. Carlson (1970) found that a weekly injection of 20 mg of vitamin B_{12} and 100 mg of folic acid did not increase hemoglobin, hematocrit, or red blood cell count in polo ponies fed a diet of grass hay and oats.

Some reports indicate that heavily parasitized or debilitated animals may respond to vitamin B_{12} therapy but these reports need to be further substantiated (Clifford *et al.*, 1956).

10.7 Stunted Growth and Orphan Foals

If horses are fed a restricted amount of feed during the first year of their life, they might reach full size when mature, but of course, the process will take longer and they cannot be worked as hard or as soon as properly fed horses. Khitenkov (1950) conducted a trial in which groups of foals were fed (1) adequate feed from birth to age 5 years; (2) adequate feed up to 1½ years, insufficient feed from 1½ to 2 years, and then adequate feed; and (3) insufficient feed up to 12 months and then normal feed. The restricted animals grew more slowly, but Khitenkov concluded that under subsequent favorable conditions of feeding and care the horses made up for the delay in growth. Witt and Lohse (1965) conducted a study to determine if poor feeding during winter restricts the growth of horses. The animals were approximately 6 months of age at the start of the trial. One group of horses was fed hay and grain during the winter and the other group was fed only hay. All animals received good feed in the summer.

341

After 3 years the horses that had been fed hay and grain gained an average of 0.5 lb per day during the winter, but horses fed only hay lost 0.51 lb per day during the winter. However, because of the good feed they received during the summer, the horses fed only hay in the winter were able to recover, and after 3 years there were no differences in skeletal size or body measurements between the two groups.

Of course severe diet restriction during the first year of life will result in small, stunted animals.

Orphan Foals

Although the rearing of orphan foals has long been a problem, it is much less so now because of recent advances in nutrition. But it is almost impossible to rear an orphan unless it receives colostrum, the first secretions from the mammary gland after the birth of the foal. Colostrum contains antibodies that give temporary immunity to many of the important foalhood diseases. Most foals that do not receive colostrum die. The foal can absorb the antibodies in colostrum only within the first 36 hours after birth. After that time, the structure of the intestinal tract changes and the antibodies can no longer pass through to the blood stream. Therefore, it is critical that the foal receive at least 1/2 to 1 qt of colostrum the first day. Some farms try to keep a supply of frozen colostrum, obtained from mares with dead foals or high-producing mares, to use if a mare dies or does not produce colostrum. If colostrum is not available, blood can be taken from a mature horse and the serum, which also contains antibodies, separated. Up to 1/2 pint of serum should be fed to the foal several times throughout the day. Because of potential and serious allergic problems of feeding blood to a newborn foal, a veterinarian should be consulted before this procedure is performed.

Once the foal has received colostrum, several different approaches can be taken in rearing the orphan. Of course, a nurse mare may be used, but nurse mares are often difficult to obtain and it may be difficult to get the foal to nurse or to get the mare to accept the foal. There are several commercial milk replacers on the market. Stowe (1967a) suggests that a milk replacer containing 24 percent protein and 10 percent fat was superior to one containing 24 percent protein and 20 percent fat. Ensminger (1969) suggests that orphan foals can be fed a mixture of one pint of cow's milk, one tablespoon of sugar, and 3–5 tablespoonfuls of saturated limewater. He recommends that the foal be fed one-fourth of a pint of this mixture every hour for the first few days of life. Stowe (1967a) reports that bottles and nipple pails are not necessary; the orphan foal can be readily taught to drink from a shallow pan. This is accomplished after a 4- to 6-hour starvation period by offering milk containing an ice cube. The temperature differential between the foal's lips and the cold milk appears to help the foal realize that its lips are in contact with something and he will soon make some sucking or licking movements and readily learn to drink.

10.8 Blood Levels of Nutrients

Analyzing the blood for various nutrients may or may not have value in determining the nutritional status of the animal. For example, a blood sample is not a reliable index of calcium nutrition. As discussed earlier, the body has homeostatic mechanisms that ensure that a normal calcium serum content is maintained. For example, ponies fed diets containing 0.15 percent, 0.4 percent, or 1.50 percent calcium had serum calcium levels of 11.7, 11.5, and 11.3 mg/100 ml, respectively (Schryver *et al.*, 1970).

The state of phosphorus nutrition may be more readily indicated by blood analysis than calcium because high dietary phosphorus intakes may increase the phosphorus blood level and low dietary phosphorus intakes or fasting may decrease blood phosphorus levels. However, even phosphorus blood levels can be misleading. For example, the average blood levels of yearling ponies fed diets containing 0.30, 0.45, and 0.90 percent phosphorus were 4.95, 4.81, and 5.50 mg/100 ml, respectively. Young animals have higher blood phosphorus levels than older animals.

The state of magnesium nutrition can be indicated to some degree by blood analysis. Severe potassium deficiency over time will decrease potassium plasma levels. Although iron absorption is regulated by the horse's need for iron, the diet can influence serum iron levels. However, it has been concluded that the normal range for serum iron concentration is so large that serum iron is of little clinical value (Osbaldiston and Griffith, 1972).

Selenium status may be indicated by serum levels (Stowe, 1967b).

The vitamin A and carotene content of plasma decreases when a diet deficient in these nutrients is fed for prolonged periods. However, the plasma level drops only when the liver stores have been depleted. The blood levels of several nutrients are shown in Table 10-3.

10.9 Poisonous Plants

There are a great many plants that can be poisonous to horses. Fortunately, most of them are not very palatable and the toxic principle is often in a low concentration so that the horse has to eat significant

TABLE 10-3
Blood levels of nutrients

Nutrient	Blood Fraction[a,b]	Value
Protein (g/100 ml)	P	5.3–7.6[1]
Calcium (g/100 ml)	P	12.4 ± 0.58[2]
	S	12.2 ± 0.50[3]
Phosphorus (mg/100 ml)	S	7.1 ± 0.4[3] (less than 3 mo)
	S	5.8 ± 0.7 (6–12 mo)
	S	3.5 ± 0.5 (3–4 yr)
	S	3.1 ± 0.6 (5 yr)
Magnesium (mg/100 ml)	S	2.5 ± .31[2]
Potassium (mEq/l)	P	2.4 − 4.7[1]
Sodium (mEq/1)	P	132 − 146[1]
Chloride (mEq/1)	P	99 − 109[1]
Iron (μg/100 ml)	P	163.1 ± 3.31[4] (Thoroughbred resting)
	P	268.6 ± 6.40 (after exercise)
	S	129 ± 29 (Arab)[5]
	S	154 ± 34 (Quarter Horse)
	S	109 ± 12 (Thoroughbred)
Selenium (μg/100 ml)	S	14.1 ± 2.8[6] (mature Standardbred)
	S	7.9 ± 3.4 (suckling Standardbred)
Zinc (μg/100 ml)	S	140 − 200[7]
	P	64 ± 8[17]
Manganese (μg/100 ml)	P	2.5[8]
	S	1.7[8]
Copper (μg/100 ml)	P	170[9]
Inorganic iodine (μg/100 ml)	P	0.2[10]
Vitamin A (μg/100 ml)	P	15 − 31[11]
Vitamin C (mg/100 ml)	P	0.27 − 0.41[12]
Vitamin B_{12} (μg/ml)	S	6.7 ± 0.42[13]
	S	6.3 ± 0.37[14]
Folic acid (μg/100 ml)	S	1.10[15] (grass-fed)
	S	0.75 (hay-fed)
Vitamin B_6 (μg/100 ml)	P	16.2[16] ± 2.69

SOURCES:
1. Tasker, J. 1966. *Cornell Vet.* 56:70.
2. Jennings, F. W., and W. Mulligan. 1953. *J. Comp. Path. Therap.* 63:286.
3. Craige, A. H., and J. D. Gadd. 1941. *Am. J. Vet. Res.* 2:227
4. Sneter, F. 1959. *Can. J. Biochem. Phys.* 37:273.
5. Osbaldiston, G. W., and P. R. Griffith. 1972. *Can. Vet. J.* 13:105.
6. Stowe, H. D. 1967. *J. Nutr.* 93:60.
7. Harrington, D. D., *et al.* 1973. *Proc. Equine Nutr. Phys. Symp.*, Univ. of Fla., p. 51.
8. Weisen, M., and E. Lucas. 1966. *Nutr. Abs. Rev.* 36:431.
9. Stowe, H. D. 1968. *J. Nutr.* 95:179.
10. Baker, H. J., and J. R. Lindsay. 1968. *J.A.V.M.A.* 152:1618.
11. Fonnesbeck, P. V., and L. D. Symons. 1967. *J. Animal Sci.* 26:1030.
12. Stillions, M. C., *et al.* 1971. *J. Animal Sci.* 32:249.
13. Stillions, M. C., *et al.* 1971. *J. Animal Sci.* 32:252.
14. Alexander, F., and M. E. Davies. 1969. *Brit. Vet. J.* 125:169.
15. Seckington, I. M., *et al.* 1967. *Vet. Rec.* 81:158.
16. Slesinger, F. 1967. *Zentralbl. Vet. Med.* 14A:155.
17. Meyer, H. and U. Lemmer. 1973. *Deut. Tierartz. Woch.* 80:173.

[a]P = Plasma
[b]S = Serum

amounts of the plants before there is any danger. Nevertheless, the danger of plant poisoning is a real one and steps should be taken to minimize it. Never put hungry horses in a strange pasture because they are more apt to eat poisonous plants when they are hungry. Be alert for poisonous plants in the pasture. They can be eliminated by digging or by applying chemical weed killers. Fowler (1963) points out that certain plants

TABLE 10-4
Plants that can be poisonous to horses

Plant	Species	Effect
Bracken fern	*Pteridium aquilinium*	Thiamin deficiency[1]
Castor bean	*Ricinus communis*	Severe irritation to intestinal tract[2]
Fiddleneck	*Ansinckia intermedia*	Liver cirrhosis[3]
Golden weed	*Onopis* spp.	Selenium poisoning[4]
Horsetail	*Equisetum* spp.	Thiamin deficiency[5]
Japanese yew	*Taxus cuspidata*	Nervous system damage[6]
Jimsonweed	*Datura* spp.	Alkaloid poisoning[7]
Locoweed	*Astragalus* spp.	Nervous system damage[8]
Oleander	*Nerium oleander*	Digitalis effect[9]
Prince's plume	*Stanleya* spp.	Selenium poisoning[4]
Rattleweed	*Crotalaria spectabilis*	Liver cirrhosis[10]
Russian knapweed	*Centaurea repens*	Encephalomalacia[11]
Tansy ragwort	*Senecio jacobaea*	Liver cirrhosis[12]
Whitehead	*Sphenosciodium capitallatum*	Photosensitization[13]
Wild cherry	*Prunus* spp.	Cyanide poisoning[14]
Wild onion	*Allium validum*	Hemolytic anemia[15]
Wild tobacco	*Nicotiana trigonophylla*	Paralysis[16]
Woody aster	*Xylorrheza* spp.	Selenium poisoning[4]
Yellow star thistle	*Centaurea solstitialis*	Encephalomalacia[17]

SOURCES:
1. Hadwen, S. 1917. *J.A.V.M.A.* 50:702.
2. McCunn, J. 1947. *Brit. Vet. J.* 103:273.
3. McCulloch, E. C. 1940. *J.A.V.M.A.* 96:5.
4. Trealease, S. F., and O. A. Beath. 1949. *Selenium.* New York: Trealease and Beath.
5. Lott, D. G. 1951. *Can. J. Comp. Med.* 15:274.
6. Lowe, J. E., *et al.* 1970. *Cornell Vet.* 60:36.
7. Hansen, A. A. 1924. *J.A.V.M.A.* 66:351.
8. James, L. F., *et al.* 1970. *Am. J. Vet. Res.* 31:663.
9. Wilson, F. 1909. *Ariz. Agr. Exp. Sta. Bul.* 59:14.
10. Cox, D. N., *et al.* 1958. *J.A.V.M.A.* 133:425.
11. Young, R. *et al.* 1970. *Am. J. Vet. Res.* 31:1393.
12. VanEs, L. 1929. *Nebraska Exp. Sta. Bul.* 43:1.
13. Fowler, M. E., *et al.* 1970. *J.A.V.M.A.* 157:1187.
14. Pijoan, M., 1942. *Am. J. Med. Sci.* 204:550.
15. Pierce, K. R., *et al.* 1972. *J.A.V.M.A.* 160:323.
16. Burgess, P. S. 1934. *Ariz. Exp. Sta. Bul. Rpt.* 45:44.
17. Cordy, D. R. 1956. *J. Neuropath. Exper. Neurol.* 13:330.

are poisonous only during a particular season, and it may be necessary to remove horses from pastures during this time. For example, in California, yellow star thistle is a problem especially during the late summer and fall. When the grass is in short supply, care should be taken to provide animals with supplemental forage or else they may eat the star thistle. Fowler further states that yellow star thistle is one plant for which horses will acquire a taste.

Further information about poisonous plants can be obtained from Kingsbury (1964) and Fowler (1963). Table 10-4 is a partial list of plants that should be avoided.

References

Alexander, F., and M. E. Davies. 1969. Studies on vitamin B_{12} in the horse. *Brit. Vet. J.* 125:169.

Baetz, A. L., and J. E. Pearson. 1972. Blood constituent changes in fasted ponies. *Am. J. Vet. Res.* 33:1941.

Carlson, K. A. 1970. *A study of certain hematinics in the horse.* Senior Research Project. New York State Veterinary College, Cornell University, Ithaca, New York.

Clifford, R. J., G. N. Henderson, and J. H. Wilkins. 1956. The effect of feeding penicillin and vitamin B_{12} to mature debilitated horses. *Vet. Rec.* 68:48.

Ensminger, M. E. 1969. *Horses and Horsemanship.* Danville, Illinois: The Interstate Printers and Publishers, Inc.

Fowler, M. E. 1963. Poisonous Plants. In: *Equine Medicine and Surgery.* 1st ed. Wheaton, Illinois: American Veterinary Publications.

Khitenkov, G. G. 1950. The growth of crossbreds on different feeding levels. *Konevodstvo.* 8:15 [Abstracted in *Nutr. Abs. Rev.* 21:751, 1951.]

Kingsbury, J. 1964. *Poisonous plants of the United States and Canada.* Englewood Cliffs, New Jersey: Prentice-Hall.

Meyer, H., and U. Lemmer. 1973. Mineralstoff- und Spurenelementgehalt in Serum bzw. Plasma des Pferdes. *Dtsch. tierärtzl. Wschr.* 80:173.

Milner, J., and D. Hewitt. 1969. Weight of horses: Improved estimates based on girth and length. *Can. Vet. J.* 10:314.

Morris, M. D., D. B. Zilversmit, and H. F. Hintz. 1972. Hyperlipopro-teinemia in fasting ponies. *J. Lipid Research* 13:383.

Osbaldiston, G. W., and P. R. Griffith. 1972. Serum iron levels in normal and anemic horses. *Can Vet. J.* 13:105.

Schotman, A. J. H., and G. Wagenaar. 1969. Hyperlipemia in ponies. *Zentralb. Vet.-Med.* A16:1–7.

Schryver, H. F., P. H. Craig, and H. F. Hintz. 1970. Calcium metabolism in ponies fed varying levels of calcium. *J. Nutr.* 100:955.

Stowe, H. D. 1967a. Automated Orphan Foal Feeding. *Proc. Am. Assoc. Equine Pract.*, p. 65.

Stowe, H. D. 1967b. Serum selenium and related parameters of naturally and experimentally fed horses. *J. Nutr.* 93:60.

Tyznik, W. J. 1972. Nutrition and Disease. In: *Equine Medicine and Surgery.* 2d ed. Wheaton, Illinois: American Veterinary Publications.

Willard, J., J. C. Willard, and J. P. Baker. 1973. Dietary influence on feeding behavior in ponies. *J. Animal Sci.* 37:227.

Witt, M., and B. Lohse. 1965. Effect of different winter feeding on growth of Fjord horses up to the third year of life. *Zeittschr. Tierzucht. Zucht.* 81:167–199.

Wensing, T., A. J. H. Schotman, and J. Kroneman. 1972. A new treatment of hyperlipemia. *Tydschr. Diergeneesk.* 97:481.

PART FOUR *Reproduction in the Horse*

CHAPTER ELEVEN *Anatomy and*

Physiology of Reproduction in the Mare

Traditionally, the mare has been regarded as having a low reproductive efficiency because many mares that had successful performance records were kept as broodmares without consideration of their existing reproductive problems. Reproduction in the mare is a complex process, and she is unique in several ways, including anatomical site of ovulation, follicular growth patterns, spontaneously prolonged corpora lutea, differentiation of fertile and nonfertile ova in the Fallopian tubes, and serum gonadotropin secretion (in pregnant mares). To be a successful horse breeder and to induce the difficult broodmare to conceive and foal, one must have a working knowledge of the anatomy of the reproductive tract and of the physiology of reproduction in the mare.

11.1 Reproductive Tract

The mare's reproductive tract is shown in Figure 11-1. The tract consists of 2 ovaries, 2 Fallopian tubes, uterus, cervix, vagina, clitoris, and vulva.

Ovaries

The ovaries function as endocrine and exocrine glands and are the essential organs of reproduction. As endocrine glands, they produce the estrogenic and progestational hormones whose functions are described in Chapter 12. As exocrine glands, they produce and release ova. The anatomical structure of the mare's ovaries has been described by Sisson and

351

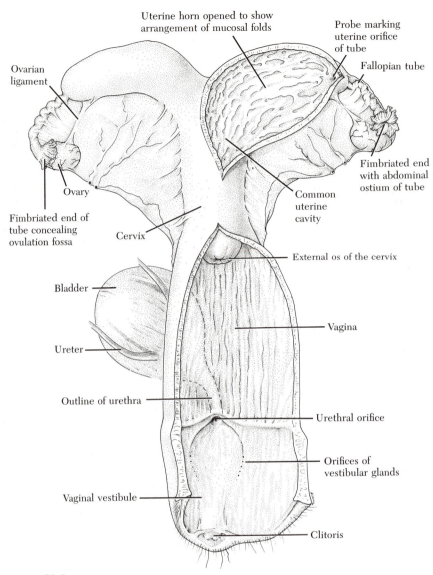

FIGURE 11-1
Reproductive organs of the mare (*posterior view*) showing vagina and right half of uterus opened. From Eckstein and Zuckerman. 1956.

Grossman (1953) as bean- or kidney-shaped because of the presence of a definite *ovulation fossa* (Figure 11-2). The size of the ovaries varies according to the age, breed, size, and reproductive state of the mare. In the mature mare, each ovary weighs approximately 50–75 g and is 6–7 cm long and 3–4 cm wide. Hammond and Wodzicki (1941) have reported that the mature ovary reaches maximum size at 3–4 years of age and then decreases in size. Although one ovary is frequently larger than the other,

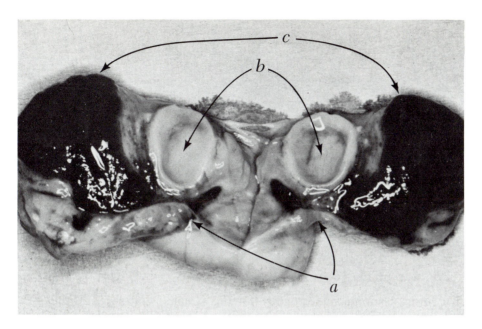

FIGURE 11-2
Cross section of a mare's ovary: *a*, ovulation fossa; *b*, Graafian follicles; *c*, corpus hemorraghicum. Photograph courtesy of John Hughes.

these researchers found that the average weights for each side from several mares were not significantly different. Nishikawa (1959) has studied a Japanese sample and reported that the ovaries of the jenny ass are similar in size and shape to those of the mare, whereas Berliner (1959) has observed that in the United States the ovaries of the jenny ass are larger than mare ovaries.

A *serous coat* that is part of the *peritoneum* covers the outer surface of the ovaries except at the *hilus,* where the blood vessels and nerves enter the ovaries, and at the ovulation fossa, which is covered by a layer of primitive germinal epithelium. The inside of the ovaries is composed of connective tissue and numerous follicles that are in varying stages of development during the breeding season. The *follicles* are not confined to a particular area or outer layer, as they are in other animals, but are distributed throughout the ovary.

The follicles are classified as being either primordial, growing, or Graafian. Primordial follicles consist of an *oocyte* surrounded by a flattened layer of cells known as the *zona pellucida*. As the primordial follicle starts to develop, it becomes surrounded by several layers of granulosa cells and is referred to as the growing follicle. The growing follicle continues to develop and forms the Graafian follicle. The Graafian follicle (Figure 11-3) is surrounded by the granulosa cells and by the *theca folliculi,* which has developed from the connective tissue surrounding the follicle. The theca folliculi differentiates into two layers called the *theca externa* and *theca interna*. The theca externa is a fibrous network

353

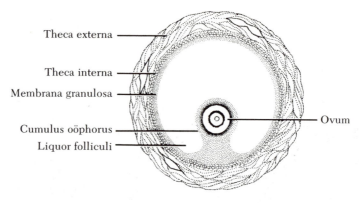

Theca externa

Theca interna

Membrana granulosa

Cumulus oöphorus

Liquor folliculi

Ovum

FIGURE 11-3

A Graafian follicle. Diagram courtesy of M. Morris.

that forms a supporting structure for the Graafian follicle. The theca interna, the inside layer of the theca folliculi, contains the vascular supply, and the cells that compose it are responsible for secreting the estrogenic hormones. The granulosa cells continue to increase in number. A cavity or antrum forms within the granulosa cells. At maturity, the cavity or antrum of the Graafian follicle is surrounded by the granulosa membrane and is filled with follicular fluid. Granulosa cells forming the *cumulus oöphorus* surround the ovum and form a stalk that projects the ovum toward the center of the antrum. As the follicle grows and develops, it migrates toward the ovulation fossa. Ovulation (rupture of the follicle) is spontaneous, and extrusion of the egg occurs in the ovulation fossa.

The development of the *corpus luteum* has been described in detail by Harrison (1946) and by many other investigators. Upon ovulation, the follicle walls collapse and fold inward. A blood clot forms in the cavity as a result of hemorrhage of the thecal capillaries (Figure 11-2). The granulosa cells undergo *lutealization,* and the theca interna cells invade the granulosa wall. The folds of the wall take on the appearance of *trabeculae,* which consist of theca externa cells and degenerating theca interna cells. The theca externa cells and degenerating theca interna cells invade the lutealizing granulosa cells. The trabeculae are extensively vascularized, and thecal capillaries exist between the luteal cells. By the sixth day, the whole corpus luteum is well vascularized, the theca cells are evenly distributed, the trabeculae are decreased in size and serve as a support for blood vessels, and the theca externa cells begin to pass inward. After approximately 14 days, the corpus luteum decreases in size, and its progestin-synthesizing capabilities decline quite rapidly if the mare is not pregnant.

Blood is supplied to the ovaries via the ovarian artery (Figure 11-4). The ovaries are supplied with an extensive arterial network that forms

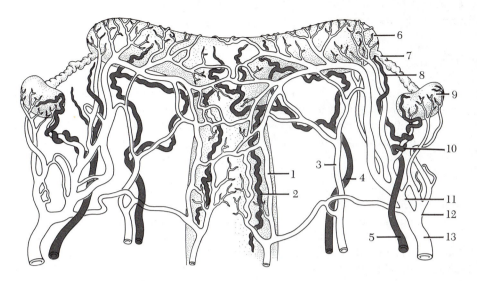

FIGURE 11-4

Composite diagram of dorsal view of arteries (*cross-marked*) and veins (*shaded*) of uterus and ovaries of the mare: (1) uterine branch of vaginal vein; (2) uterine branch of vaginal artery; (3) uterine vein; (4) uterine artery; (5) ovarian artery; (6) uterine horn; (7) uterine tube; (8) uterine branch of ovarian artery; (9) ovary; (10) ovarian branch of ovarian artery; (11) uterine branch of ovarian vein; (12) ovarian branch of ovarian vein; (13) ovarian vein. From Ginther, Garcia, Squires, and Steffenhagen. 1972.

anastomoses with tributaries of the uterine branch of the ovarian artery. Several veins drain the ovaries and then unite to form the ovarian branch of the ovarian vein. The drainage is such that there is an extensive utero-ovarian plexus. The nerve supply is derived from the renal and aortic plexus of the sympathetic system.

Fallopian Tubes

The Fallopian tubes or oviducts conduct the ova from the ovary to the uterus and are the usual site of fertilization. They are approximately 30–70 mm long and 4–8 mm thick and have an inside tubal diameter of 2–3 mm. The end adjacent to the ovaries is expanded to form the *ampulla* and the *infundibulum*, which partially surrounds the ovary and directs the ova into the Fallopian tube. The edge of the infundibulum is split so as to form fingerlike projections, or fimbriae. The opening of the oviduct into the peritoneal cavity is called the *ostium abdominale*, and the uterine opening is called the *ostium uterinum*. Three layers of tissue compose the Fallopian tubes: tunica serosa, muscularis (longitudinal and circular), and mucosa.

Uterus

The uterus of the mare consists of a body and 2 horns. The horns, which are located in the abdominal cavity, are approximately 25 cm in length and cylindrical. The body of the uterus is located partly in the abdominal cavity and partly in the pelvic cavity. The body is approximately 18–20 cm long and 10 cm in diameter. The broad ligament of the uterus attaches it to the abdominal and pelvic walls.

Three coats of tissue similar to the ones forming the oviducts form the uterine wall. The serous coat is continuous with the broad ligament. The muscular coat consists of a muscularis longitudinalis, muscularis vascularis, and muscularis circularis. The muscularis longitudinalis and muscularis vascularis form one inseparable layer of muscle that can be separated from the muscularis circularis. The third layer of the uterus or mucosa is composed of a loose connective-tissue network (tunica propria), a deeper layer containing the long, tubular-shaped uterine glands, and the stratum epithelial.

Uterine blood supply is derived on both sides from 3 arteries: the uterine branch of the vaginal artery, the uterine artery, and the uterine branch of the ovarian artery. Three veins drain the uterus and correspond to the 3 arteries. Nerves derived from the uterine and pelvic plexus provide the nerve supply to the uterus.

Cervix

The cervix separates, anatomically and physiologically, the body of the uterus from the vagina. It is approximately 5–7.5 cm in length and consists of a powerful, well-developed muscular layer. Extensive folding of the muscle layer leaves no well-defined cervical canal. The mucosa of the cervix contains mucosal cells that secrete the mucus found in the vagina. The cervix protrudes into the vagina, forming a well-defined angle between the cervix and vagina known as the fornix.

Vagina

The vagina extends from the cervix to the vulva. It is approximately 15–20 cm in length and 10–12 cm in diameter. The vagina is divided into the vagina proper and the vestibulum vaginae. The hymen separates the two parts and is just anterior to the area where the urethra enters the reproductive tract. The mucous coat contains no glands, is composed of a layer of loose connective tissue, and is covered with a stratified epithelium. Longitudinal and circular muscle fibers are surrounded by a *fibrous adventitia.*

Blood supply to the vagina is via the internal pudic arteries and drainage is via the internal pudic veins. The nerve supply is from the pelvic plexus of the sympathetic nervous system.

Vulva

The vulva is the terminal part of the reproductive tract. It is 10–12 cm in length and the external orifice is a vertical split approximately 12–15 cm long. The external urethral orifice is located 10–12 cm inside the vulva, and the glans clitoris is located approximately 5 cm within the vulva. The clitoris is the homologue of the male penis.

Mammary Gland

The udder is located in the inguinal region and is composed of 2 gland complexes. The 2 teats are broad and flat. Each teat is canalized by at least 2 streak canals that lead from separate teat cisterns. Each teat cistern is connected to a gland cistern that has a system of ducts leading into it from a secretory gland. The udder is served by the external pudendal artery and is drained by the external pudendal and subcutaneous abdominal veins. The nerve supply is derived from the inguinal nerve.

11.2   Physiology of Reproduction

Estrous Cycle

The average age of the filly at puberty is 12–15 months. Russian researchers have reported that crossbred Russian trotter mares reach sexual maturity at 10–11 months. Once puberty is reached, the filly begins to come into estrus (heat) in a rhythmic cycle. The estrous cycle is the interval from the onset of estrus until the onset of the next estrus. In the mare, it is commonly divided into 2 periods for practical purposes. The follicular phase or estrous period of the cycle is the period during which the mare shows behavioral signs of estrus, has rapid follicular growth, and finally ovulates. During the estrous period, the mare is interested in and is receptive to a stallion. Most mares in estrus display several characteristic behavioral signs when teased with a stallion (Figure 11-5). Initially, a mare may be agitated but will respond to the stallion and allow him to bite her on the neck and flank. Her stance is characterized by a raised tail without switching, hind legs spread apart, and pelvis flexed. The labia

357

FIGURE 11-5
Behavioral display of estrus (heat) by
a mare: *a*, elevated tail, flexed pelvis,
and acceptance of stallion; *b*, eversion
of clitoris (winking).

of the vulva contracts and relaxes, and there is eversion of the clitoris,
which is commonly referred to as "winking." Estrual winking, alone,
should not be confused with winking after urination. Mares in estrus
usually urinate quite frequently when teased.

358   Sexual receptivity is influenced by season. The behavioral signs of
mares coming out of anestrus are rather variable, that is, some mares

have a normal estrous period whereas others are in and out of estrus for several days.

The behavioral signs of estrus in the jenny are quite different from those in the mare. Jennies will stand for the jackass with their hind legs spread apart. The head is lowered, the jaws display a chewing motion, and the labia repetitively contracts, exposing the clitoris. Jennies urinate frequently, and quite often a slimy mucus is discharged from the vagina.

In both the mare and jenny, the intensity of estrus manifestations increases from weak signs at the start of estrus to a peak at ovulation and then quickly declines to the diestrous state.

The diestrous period is the luteal phase of the cycle and begins with ovulation. During *diestrus*, the corpus luteum is formed and secretes progestins. The behavioral response of a diestrous mare to teasing with a stallion varies from a passive, noninterested attitude to complete resentment, often manifested by violent attempts to kick and bite the stallion.

The change from behavioral estrus to diestrus occurs quite rapidly after ovulation. Hughes *et al.* (1972b) have reported that approximately 50 percent of the mares they studied were in diestrus within 24 hours after ovulation and 80 percent were in diestrus within 48 hours. This finding emphasizes the close relationship between ovulation and the end of sexual receptivity. Occasionally, a mare will ovulate after she has ceased showing signs of estrus.

Estrous cycles of the mare are usually 21–23 days in length (Table 11-1). A wide range of estrous cycle lengths has been reported in the literature. Cycles vary from 7–175 days, but generally, approximately 50–60 percent of all mares have a cycle of 21, 22, or 23 days.

There are many causes of prolonged estrous cycles. Season of the year is the most common cause of irregularity. In California, the average estrous cycle length is shortest between April and October and longest between November and March. In South Africa, the average estrous cycle is shortest during the summer months of November through February and longest during the winter months of May to August. Winter *anestrus* (period of sexual inactivity) is responsible for the longer average length of time from one estrus to the next between November and March (Figure 11-6) (Hughes *et al.*, 1972b). During the winter months, ovulation often occurs without estrus. The estrous cycles can also be interrupted by spontaneous prolongation of the corpus luteum life-span (Figure 11-7). A spontaneously prolonged corpus luteum is a corpus luteum that continues to secrete enough progestins to maintain plasma levels above 3–5 ng/ml plasma, which suppresses signs of estrus. The spontaneous prolongation may be due to a failure of the uterus to produce or release the "luteolysin" required to lyse the corpus luteum at the proper stage of the cycle. An interruption of regular cyclicity may occur during very hot weather and was observed by Hughes *et al.* (1972a) in a 3-year study of a group of mares. Prolonged cycles are often merely a result of the stud

359

TABLE 11-1
Length of estrous cycle and estrous period of mares with 1 or 2 ovulations per cycle

No. of Ovulations per Estrous Cycle	Length of Estrous Cycle (days)	Length of Estrus (days)	Length of Diestrus (days)	Corpus Luteum Life-span (days)
One	20.7 ± 0.2 (234) (range 13–34)	5.4 ± 3.0 (225) (range 1–24)	15.4 ± 3.1 (201) (range 6–25)	12.6 ± 2.9 (18) (range 8–18)
Two	20.2 ± 4.5 (76) (range 13–27)	6.1 ± 2.7 (69) (range 1–21)	14.6 ± 3.5 (59) (range 8–25)	12.2 ± 3.3 (17) (range 5–17)

SOURCE: Figures in last column from Stabenfeldt, Hughes, and Evans. 1970. All other figures from Hughes, Stabenfeldt, and Evans, 1972b.

NOTE: All deviations are standard deviations. Same 11 mares were studied to obtain data for Tables 11-1 through 11-4.

manager's failure to observe estrus. Another problem that is frequently encountered is that lactating mares that are extremely possessive of their foals may not show estrus.

The seasonal variability of the estrous cycle, excluding anestrus, seems mainly to be due to variability of the estrous period (Table 11-2). The normal length of estrus is usually 5–7 days, but from February to May (late winter and early spring in California), it is 7.6 days. The longest estrous periods are observed when mares are either going into or coming out of anestrus. Throughout the year, the diestrous period seems to average 14–16 days in length when anestrous periods are excluded.

Loy (1970) has classified mares into 3 groups according to seasonal variability. There is considerable overlapping of his classifications because of the variability of mares. In the first category is the polyestrous mare, which cycles regularly throughout the year even though she has seasonal variations that fall within the normal range. The second group includes the seasonally polyestrous mare, which has a definite breeding season and a definite anestrous period (Figure 11-6). The third classification is the seasonally polyestrous mare (Table 11-2), which has erratic reproductive patterns. "Silent heat," the failure to show behavioral signs of estrus, occurs infrequently in some mares, although other mares seldom show behavioral signs (Figure 11-8). Usually these mares ovulate and their plasma progestin profile is normal. Approximately 50 percent of mares ovulate at least once without estrus during a 2-year period. The opposite condition, estrus without ovulation, is less frequently observed— it occurred in approximately 3 percent of estrous periods during a 2-year period (Hughes *et al.*, 1972b). Nonovulatory estrus is usually observed immediately preceding the onset of winter anestrus. Split estrous periods, in which the mare is in estrus for a few days, out of estrus for a few days,

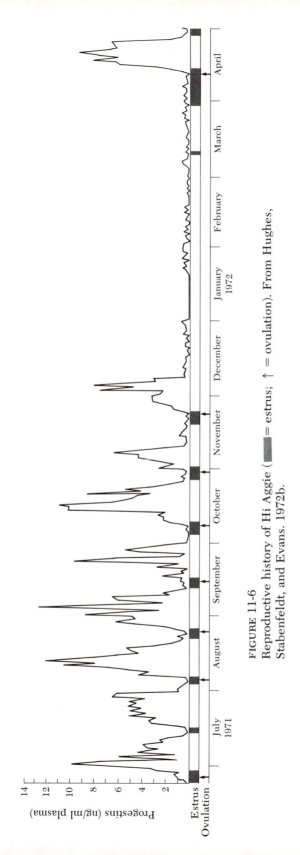

FIGURE 11-6
Reproductive history of Hi Aggie (■ = estrus; ↑ = ovulation). From Hughes, Stabenfeldt, and Evans. 1972b.

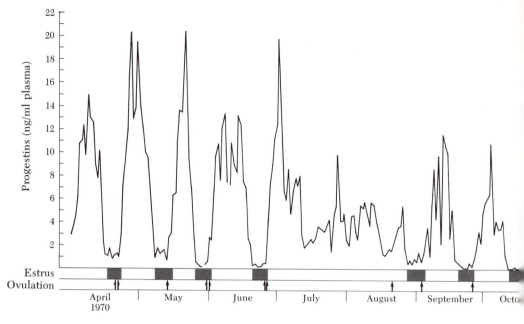

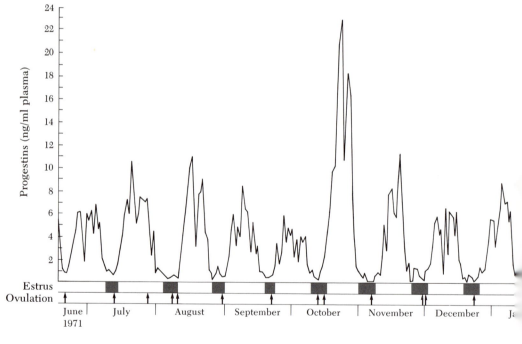

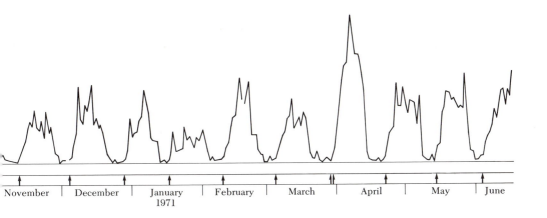

November | December | January 1971 | February | March | April | May | June

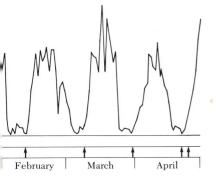

February | March | April

FIGURE 11-7
Reproductive history of Paisley Star
(▧ = estrus; ↑ = ovulation). From
Hughes, Stabenfeldt, and Evans. 1972b.
p. 119.

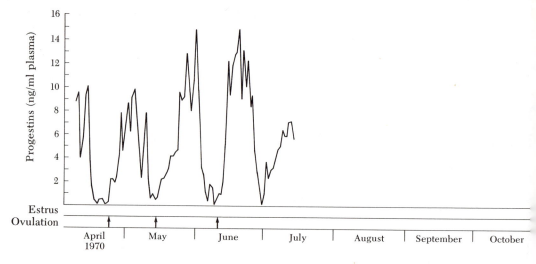

FIGURE 11-8

Reproductive history of Bashful Boots (████ = estrus; ↑ = ovulation). Notice the "silent heat" periods and double ovulations. Graph courtesy of G. H. Stabenfeldt, J. P. Hughes, and J. W. Evans.

and then returns to estrus, are observed during approximately 5 percent of the cycles. Split estrous periods average 12 days in length.

Since most mares are seasonally polyestrus, periods of anestrus are observed in most mares that are observed for approximately 2 years. The winter anestrous period is usually 50–70 days in length but may be 4 or 5 months long. During the anestrous period, approximately 50 percent of mares ovulate at regular cyclic intervals. Other anestrous periods are accompanied by insignificant ovarian activity or the persistent presence of a corpus luteum. Even though anestrus is primarily a winter phenomenon, cyclic ovulation without estrus has been observed at other times of the year.

Diestrous ovulations without signs of estrus occur in most mares some time during a 2-year period (Figure 11-9, Table 11-1). The ovaries are the only part of the reproductive tract that is changed when ovulation occurs during diestrus. If the reproductive history of a mare is not known, the diestrous ovulation may be assumed to occur during a silent heat.

The mare is generally assumed to have one ovulation per estrous period; however, several follicles start to grow during each estrous cycle. Just before estrus, follicles destined to ovulate rapidly increase in size until they are to 35–60 mm long. When a group of Thoroughbred and Quarter Horse mares were observed at the University of California at Davis (Hughes *et al.*, 1972b), twin ovulations occurred approximately 21 percent of the time during a 2-year period (Figures 11-6 and 11-9 and

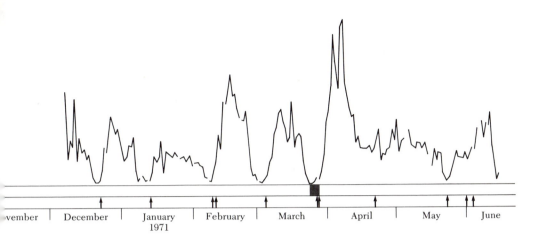

November | December | January 1971 | February | March | April | May | June

Table 11-3), and several other researchers have reported similar percentages. The percentage of twin conception is lower (1–5 percent). The percentage of live foals is 0.5–1.5 percent (Berliner, 1959). Some mares have a tendency to have multiple ovulations, and one mare had 25 twin ovulations in 24 months (Figure 11-9). Multiple ovulations do not appear to affect the duration of estrus, the length of the estrous cycle, or the level of plasma progestins (Table 11-1). A seasonal influence was indicated since few multiple ovulations were observed early in the breeding season (Table 11-4). Double ovulations are rare in pony mares.

Changes in the Reproductive Tract During the Estrous Cycle

The reproductive tract of the mare undergoes several characteristic changes during the estrous cycle. These changes are useful as a guide in determining the optimal time to breed a mare during estrus — especially mares with silent heats. The changes have been discussed by Warszawsky *et al.* (1972) and are summarized in Table 11-5.

During anestrus, the ovaries may be small and inactive, although some mares have considerable ovarian activity. As the mare comes out of anestrus, the ovaries begin to enlarge and soften as the follicles begin to develop. Although several follicles may start to increase in size, usu-

365

TABLE 11-2
Effects of seasonal changes on reproduction in the mare

	Jan	Feb	Mar	Apr	May	Jun	Jul	Aug	Sep	Oct	Nov	Dec
Average estrous cycle length (days)	32.3	34.4	26.1	21.9	19.5	21.1	24.6	20.4	20.6	20.5	24.8	30.4
Number of cycles observed	22	20	25	28	39	31	28	27	32	35	25	21
Number of periods of estrus	18	13	26	29	28	28	20	24	27	31	27	22
Average length of estrus (days)	5.06	6.69	8.38	7.76	5.72	4.47	4.70	4.75	4.44	4.53	5.20	7.23
Total ovulations for each month for all 11 mares	20	23	46	45	44	54	48	41	42	44	43	27
Average number of ovulations per month	0.9	1.1	2.1	2.1	2.0	2.5	2.2	1.9	1.9	2.0	2.0	1.2
Total number of diestrous periods without anestrus	16	13	21	27	24	24	21	21	26	27	22	20
Average length of diestrus without anestrus	16.3	16.3	14.2	11.8	14.0	15.8	16.2	15.4	16.1	15.3	16.0	14.3

SOURCE: Adapted from Hughes, Stabenfeldt, and Evans. 1972b. p. 119.

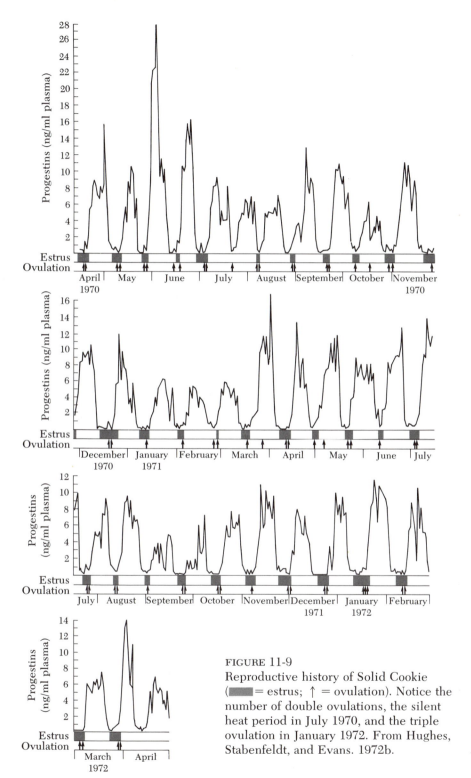

FIGURE 11-9

Reproductive history of Solid Cookie (▨ = estrus; ↑ = ovulation). Notice the number of double ovulations, the silent heat period in July 1970, and the triple ovulation in January 1972. From Hughes, Stabenfeldt, and Evans. 1972b.

TABLE 11-3
Incidence of multiple ovulation by mare and by ovaries, during 2-year period

Mare	No. of Triple Ovulations	No. of Double Ovulations	Ovulations				Average Interval between Ovulations (days)
			No. LL	No. RR	No. LR[a]	No. RL[a]	
Aggie Tess	0	7	1	1	2	3	0.7
Bashful Boots	0	9	2	2	1	3	1.5
Double Dark	0	5	2	2	1	0	1.6
Hi Aggie	0	1	0	0	1	0	0.0
Mr. Bruce's Miss	0	2	1	1	0	0	1.0
Paisley Star	0	6	2	1	3	0	1.2
Psychedelic Miss	0	4	0	2	0	2	1.2
Solid Charm	0	4	2	0	1	1	1.0
Solid Cookie	1	25	3	9	10	3	0.7
Solimistic	0	10	2	2	3	3	1.5
Tule Goose	1	11	1	3	6	1	0.5
Total	2	83	16	23	28	16	1.0

SOURCE: Hughes, Stabenfeldt, and Evans. 1972b. p. 119.

[a]First letter indicates ovary in which first ovulation occurred.

TABLE 11-4
Multiple ovulations, by month

Month	Number per Month	Percentage per Month
January	3	23.5
February	4	22.2
March	10	40.6
April	9	25.7
May	10	32.3
June	10	25.5
July	9	25.0
August	7	21.2
September	8	24.2
October	7	20.0
November	6	17.1
December	4	18.2

SOURCE: Hughes, Stabenfeldt, and Evans. 1972b. p. 119.

TABLE 11-5
Changes in mare's reproductive tract during the estrous cycle

Structure	Day of Estrous Cycle				
	2	4	7	11	17
Anterior portion of vagina (g)	188	216	173	194	230
Cervix (g)	141	168	153	133	164
Uterus (g)	696	674	558	669	849
Uterine horn (left)					
Diameter (mm)	68	55	61	58	62
Length (mm)	151	146	152	154	137
Uterine horn (right)					
Diameter (mm)	58	60	44	61	64
Length (mm)	148	155	144	160	152
Oviduct (left)					
Weight (g)	5.57	5.72	4.85	6.17	5.20
Length (mm)	147	140	149	162	152
Oviduct (right)					
Weight (g)	7.12	6.83	6.02	6.61	6.61
Length (mm)	154	155	147	166	143
Ovaries	136.7	128.4	122.0	111.7	116.4
Extraluteal tissue (g)	71.9	69.6	70.5	69.0	81.8
Extraluteal fluid (g)	62.7	54.4	42.9	25.6	22.4
Follicles 10–30 mm (no.)	6.3	6.1	7.6	4.6	3.8
Follicles 20–30 mm (no.)	3.4	2.0	1.4	1.7	1.3
Follicles > 30 mm (no.)	1.3	0.9	0.5	0.2	0.1

369

SOURCE: Adapted from Warszawsky, L. F., et al. 1972. pp. 19–26, 172.

ally only 1 or 2 reach ovulatory size. The follicle destined to ovulate usually becomes quite prominent just before estrus and starts the rapid growth phase approximately 5 days before ovulation. Generally, maximum follicle size (40–50 mm) is reached the day before ovulation, but it may occur 3–4 days before ovulation. Some follicles soften just before ovulation, whereas others do not. Because of the variations in the occurrence and degree of softening, softening of the follicle cannot be used to predict ovulation accurately. Hughes *et al.* (1972b) observed that follicles that were 25–50 mm in size appeared in addition to the ovulatory follicle in 57.3 percent of the estrous periods of the 11 mares studied. These follicles may continue to increase in size before they regress. Smaller follicles may remain for a couple of cycles and then develop into the ovulatory follicle (Figure 11-10).

Definite changes occur in the cervix during the estrous cycle, and they are quite useful in predicting approaching ovulation. During diestrus, the cervix is covered by a small amount of sticky mucus. The quantity increases during estrus until a considerable amount of slimy mucus is present. During diestrus, the cervix is tightly constricted and pale pink in color. During estrus, the vascularity increases and the cervix becomes

FIGURE 11-10
Curves of growth of follicle and corpus luteum during the estrous cycle. From Hammond and Wodzicki. 1941.

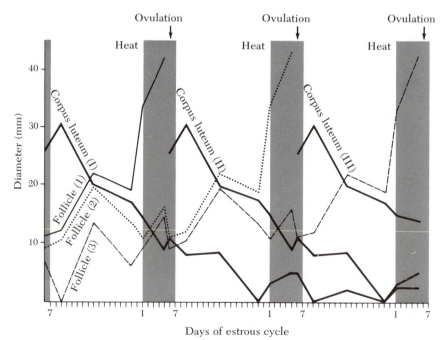

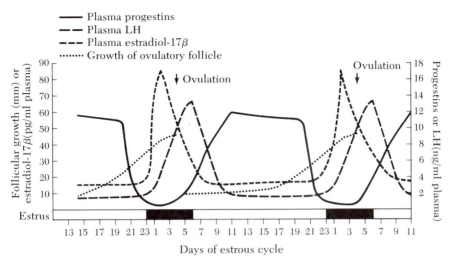

FIGURE 11-11
Endocrine patterns during the estrous cycle of a mare.

reddish in color. A complete relaxation occurs during estrus to the extent that the cervix may lie on the floor of the vagina. Palpation reveals the tactile sensitivity and muscular contractions of the estrual cervix.

The changes that occur in the vagina are more difficult to interpret than the cervical changes. The most obvious changes that occur in the vagina during estrus are an increase in vascularity resulting in a change from a pale to a rosy color and an increase in the size and number of secondary mucosal folds. The walls are dry and sticky during diestrus and become slimy during estrus as a result of changes in cervical mucus secretion.

Hughes *et al.* (1972b) have discussed the changes in uterine form that occur during the estrous cycle. From a practical standpoint, these changes vary in interpretation and their pattern is not sufficiently uniform to be useful in determining the optimal time to breed. The uterus has only slight muscle tone and is turgid during estrus; it may even be termed flaccid. During diestrus, an increase in tone and "tubularity" (contracted state that closely resembles a tube) is observed. However, during late diestrus, tone and tubularity may decrease.

During anestrus, the cervix and uterus lose muscle tone and usually become completely flaccid in most mares that have no follicular activity. In mares that have considerable ovarian activity, the uterus may have some muscle tone and the cervix may be firm and tightly constricted.

Endocrine Control

Endocrine control of the estrous cycle is not completely understood. Figure 11-11 is a generalized diagram of the sequence of events. The hormones known to control the estrous cycle originate in the pituitary gland, the ovaries, and possibly the uterus.

The pituitary hormones are the *follicle stimulating hormone* (FSH) and the *luteinizing hormone* (LH). They are produced in the basophil cells of the medullary area of the anterior pituitary gland. FSH causes ovarian follicles to grow and to produce increasing amounts of estrogenic substances as they grow. FSH has been purified and its properties characterized by Braselton and McShan (1970) and by Nuti *et al.* (1972). It is a glycoprotein consisting of 74.9 percent protein, 9.3 percent hexose, 9.1 percent hexosamine, 4.7 percent sialic acid, and 1.3 percent fucose, and it has a molecular weight of approximately 33,200–47,900. The amino acid composition is characterized by high levels of cysteine (half-cystine), threonine, lysine, and aspartic and glutamic acids, and a low level of methionine. The NH_2-terminal amino acids are phenylalanine and aspartic acids, and the COOH-terminal residues are leucine and glutamic acid. The isoelectric point is pH 4.1.

The luteinizing hormone causes ovulation and initiates the formation of the corpus luteum. Equine LH has a number of LH components and an FSH component. Four LH components have isoelectric points at pH 7.5, 5.9, 6.6, and 7.3, and the FSH component isoelectric point is pH 4.8. The molecular weight is 44,500–63,800. LH concentration starts to increase in the plasma 2–3 days before ovulation, reaches a peak 1–2 days after ovulation, and declines to diestrus levels 6 days after ovulation (Geschwind *et al.*, 1975). FSH and LH work in a synergistic manner in the processes of follicular growth, maturation, and ovulation.

The ovarian hormones that control the estrous cycle are estrogens and progestins. Estradiol-17β is produced by the granulosa cells and by the theca interna of the Graafian follicles. The amount of estradiol-17β in the plasma begins to increase at the onset of estrus, reaches a peak 12–27 hours before ovulation, and declines to diestrus levels 5–8 days after ovulation (Figure 11-11). Because estrogen reaches a peak before LH peaks, it is possible that the estrogen surge may facilitate the ovulatory surge of LH. Within 24 hours after ovulation, the corpus luteum begins to secrete progestins. By the sixth day after ovulation, maximum levels of plasma progestins have been attained. The corpus luteum remains active for approximately 12–14 days, and then rapidly undergoes regression. The roles of the pituitary gland and the uterus in the maintenance and regression of the corpus luteum function are not fully understood. Injection of antibodies against FSH and LH during days 3–7 of diestrus causes a significant decrease in the weight of the corpus luteum, indicating that the mare's pituitary contains a substance that is necessary for maintenance of the corpus luteum. Evidence for a so-called uterine luteolysin has been provided by hysterectomy studies conducted by Stabenfeldt *et al.* (1974), in which functional corpora lutea were maintained for as long as 175 days postovulation after hysterectomy. It is believed that prostaglandin is the luteolysin.

The interval between the cessation of corpus luteum function and estrus is approximately 3 days. Estrus normally does not occur until the progestin concentration is less than 1 ng/ml in the plasma.

11.3 Gestation

Length of Gestation Period

Knowledge of the length of gestation and the ability to predict the mare's foaling date are important to the successful management of the pregnant mare. The average gestation period usually ranges from 335 to 340 days. There is considerable variation in the length of gestation, as evidenced by Paul's (1973) observations of Morgan Horses. The range was 300–385 days, the median was 342.5 days, the mean was 339.6 days.

Sex of the foal, month of conception, and the individual traits of the mare significantly affect the duration of pregnancy, although size of foal, sire of dam, age of sire, age of dam, and year apparently have no effect. Colts are usually carried 2–7 days longer than fillies, indicating that the sire does exert an influence on gestation length through the genotype. Season of the year seems to have an effect, in that the gestation length is shorter for foals born during warm weather. Mares on a high plane of nutrition foal approximately 4 days before mares on a low plane of nutrition. Therefore, the rate of development of the fetus could be affected by the nutritional plane of the mare. Fetal genotype has an effect; the gestation period of mares carrying a mule fetus (jack × mare) is approximately 10 days longer than the gestation period of the same mare when carrying a horse fetus.

The ovum migrates to the uterus 4–6 days after fertilization. Implantation does not occur for approximately 8 weeks. During the first 8 weeks of gestation, fetal fluid pressure holds the chorion (Figure 11-12) next to the uterine mucosa. By the tenth week, penetration of the uterine mucosa by the chorionic villi is quite extensive, and by 14 weeks the attachment is complete. The type of attachment is epitheliochorial, that is, the chorion of the fetus is in contact with the epithelium of the mare's uterus.

In the mare and donkey, the fetal placenta is formed by three membranes (Figure 11-12): chorion, allantois, and amnion. Villi, or fingerlike projections, are scattered over the surface of the chorion (outermost membrane), and for this reason the attachment is frequently said to be

373

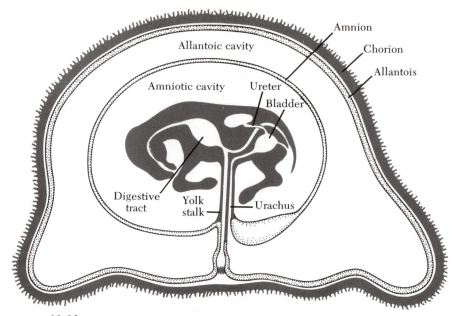

FIGURE 11-12
Fetus of horse within the placenta. The chorion and allantois make up the
chorioallantois, often called the chorion. From Frandson, R. D., ed. 1974.
p. 388. Originally in Witchi. 1956. *Development of Vertebrates*.
Philadelphia: W. B. Saunders.

"diffuse." The allantois (second membrane) lines the inside of the chorion
and is fused with the amnion, thus forming the first water-bag or allantoic
cavity. The allantoic cavity is continuous with the bladder by way of the
urachus, which passes through the umbilical cord. The amnion is the
innermost membrane and forms the second water-bag or amnionic cavity.

The umbilical arteries and veins are located in the connective tissue
between the allantois and chorion. The umbilical arteries and their tributaries carry unoxygenated blood and waste products from the fetus to the
mare. In general, the blood of the fetus does not mix with maternal blood.
However, the two circulations are very close at the junction of the chorion and endometrium. At least 6 layers of tissue separate the maternal
and fetal blood (Figure 11-13): fetal vein, stroma between fetal vein and
cytotrophoblast, cytotrophoblast, uterine epithelium, uterine stroma, and
maternal artery.

The mare has a peculiar specialization, in that *endometrial cups* begin
to form on the thirty-sixth day of pregnancy opposite a transitory, though
well-defined, circumferential thickening of the chorion called the allantochorionic girdle. Allen (1970a) has shown that the endometrial cups of
the mare are composed of fetal cells and are not of maternal origin, as
was thought previously. The endometrial cups are a discrete and densely
packed mass of large, epithelioid, decidual-like cells, that develop before
implantation. Upon development of the cups, a central depressed area

374

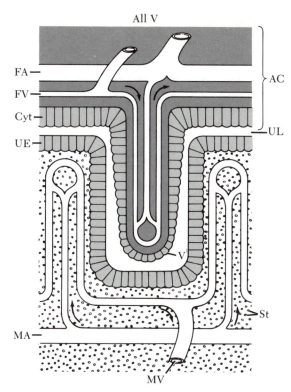

All V

FA —
FV —
Cyt —
UE —

AC

UL

V

St

MA —

MV

FIGURE 11-13
Diagrammatic representation of
relationship between maternal
and fetal tissues in the epitheliochorial type of placenta: FA, fetal
artery; FV, fetal vein; AC, allantochorion; UL, uterine lumen;
MA, maternal artery; MV,
maternal vein; UE, uterine
epithelium; Cyt, cytotrophoblast;
V, villous; St, stroma; All V,
allantoic vesicle. From Harvey,
E. B. 1959, p. 433.

filled with coagulum is formed. The accumulation of coagulum, consisting of degenerate epithelial cells, erythrocytes, polymorphonuclear leuco-
cytes, and pregnant mare's serum gonadotropin, causes a pouch to form
in the allantochorion. The importance of the secretion of gonadotropins is
discussed in the next section on hormonal changes that occur during pregnancy. Figure 11-14 illustrates the growth and development of the fetus.

Hormonal Changes that Occur during Pregnancy

Large quantities of pregnant mare's serum (gonadotropin), or PMSG, are
present in the serum of mares between days 40 and 130 of gestation (Figure 11-15). The rate of secretion and/or absorption is sufficient by 35–40
days for it to be detected in the blood. Maximum levels are attained at
55–60 days, and the concentration declines until, after 130 days, it is
undetectable in the blood. The amount of PMSG produced by the mare
is related to the genotype of the fetus. Mares carrying a mule fetus (jack
× mare) produce less PMSG than mares carrying a horse fetus. A jenny
carrying a hinny fetus (stallion × jenny) produces more PMSG than the
same jenny when carrying a donkey fetus.

375

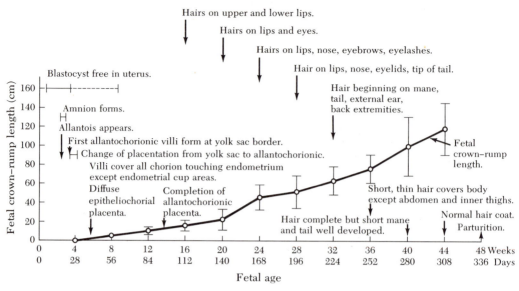

FIGURE 11-14
Fetal growth. From Bitteridge and Laing. 1970. p. 98.

PMSG is predominately follicle-stimulating in effect, but it also possesses a luteinizing fraction. The chemical characterization of PMSG has been reviewed by Papkoff (1969). The molecular weight is approximately 28,000. PMSG has a polypeptide content of 30–40 percent and a carbohydrate content of 45 percent.

Nett *et al.* (1972) have shown that estrogen starts to increase at approximately 45 days of gestation and increases at a rapid rate beginning at 80 days of gestation. Maximum levels are reached at 200–210 days, and then a gradual decline occurs. At parturition, a rapid decline occurs. Lovell *et al.* (1975) have observed that a rapid decline in progesterone levels occurs on the day of parturition.

Ovarian activity, including formation and ovulation of many Graafian follicles and luteinization of follicles, reaches a maximum during the second and third month of pregnancy. It is during this period that accessory corpora lutea are formed and secrete progestins to maintain pregnancy. Between 150 and 200 days, the corpora lutea undergo degeneration and no large follicles are present. By 200 days, the secretion of progesterone by the corpora lutea is insignificant since removal of the ovaries does not result in abortion.

There are several methods to diagnose pregnancy in the mare, although under normal conditions the first indication of pregnancy is failure to come into estrus 16–18 days after being bred. The most popular method is diagnosis by rectal palpation. This method has a decided advantage in that the result is immediately available. A skilled clinician can detect pregnancy in most mares at 25–30 days of gestation and be sure of accuracy after 30 days. After 45 days and until approximately 140 days, the detection of PMSG in the blood is a positive pregnancy diagnosis. Commercially prepared kits to test for PMSG are available to the horse owner who is without veterinary service. The detection of urinary estrogen by chemical means after 120 days of gestation is an accurate method. Fetal movements can often be observed in the mare's flank after the seventh month.

Foal Heat

A mare should come into "foal heat" between 1 and 12 days post-foaling. Even though a wide range of 1–50 days post-foaling has been observed, most mares are in estrus on the seventh to ninth day. The foal heat period may be as long as 12 days, but normally it is approximately 3 days in length.

FIGURE 11-15
Endocrine patterns during gestation of a mare.

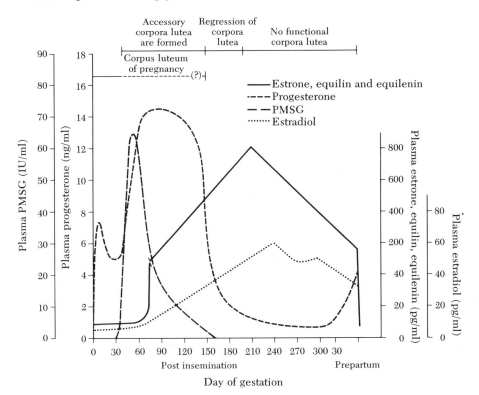

References

Allen, W. R. 1970a. Endocrinology of early pregnancy in the mare. *Equine Vet. J.* 2:64.

Allen, W. R. 1970b. *Equine gonadotrophins.* Ph.D. thesis. University of Cambridge, England.

Amoroso, E. C. 1955. Endocrinology of pregnancy. *Br. Med. Bull.* 11:117.

Arthur, G. H., and W. E. Allen. 1972. Clinical observations on reproduction in a pony stud. *Equine Vet. J.* 4:109.

Berliner, V. R. 1959. The estrous cycle of the mare. In *Reproduction in Domestic Animals.* H. H. Cole and P. T. Cupps, eds. Vol. 1 New York: Academic Press.

Bitteridge, K. J., and J. A. Laing. 1970. "The diagnosis of pregnancy." In *Fertility and Infertility in the Domestic Animals.* J. A. Laing, ed. Baltimore: Williams and Williams.

Braselton, W. E., and W. H. McShan. 1970. Purification and properties of follicle-stimulating and luteinizing hormones from horse pituitary glands. *Arch. Bichem. Biophy.* 139:45.

Clegg, M. T., J. M. Boda, and H. H. Cole. 1954. The endometrial cups and allantochorionic pouches in the mare with emphasis on the source of equine gonadotrophin. *Endocrinol.* 54:448.

Cole, H. H., and P. T. Cupps, eds. 1959. *Reproduction in Domestic Animals.* New York: Academic Press.

Cole, H. H., and H. Goss. 1943. The Source of Equine Gonadotropin. In *Essays in Biology.* No. 107. Berkeley: University of California Press.

Cole, H. H., and G. H. Hart. 1942. Diagnosis of pregnancy in the mare by hormonal means. *J. A. V. M. A.* 101:124.

Eckstein, P., and S. Zuckerman. 1956. Morphology of the Reproductive Tract. In *Marshall's Physiology of Reproduction.* A. S. Parkes, ed. 3rd ed. Boston: Little, Brown.

Frandson, R. D., ed. 1974. *Anatomy and Physiology of Farm Animals.* Philadelphia: Lea & Febiger.

Geschwind, I. I., R. Dewey, J. P. Hughes, J. W. Evans, and G. H. Stabenfeldt. 1975. Circulating luteinizing hormone levels in the mare during oestrous cycle. *J. Reprod. Fert.,* Suppl. 23:207–212.

Ginther, O. J., and N. L. First. 1971. Maintenance of the corpus luteum in hysterectomized mares. *Amer. J. Vet. Res.* 32:1687.

Ginther, O. J., M. C. Garcia, E. L. Squires, and W. P. Steffenhagen. 1972. Anatomy of vasculature of uterus and ovaries in the mare. *Amer. J. Vet. Res.* 33:1561.

Hammond, J., and K. Wodzicki. 1941. Anatomical and histological changes during the oestrous cycle in the mare. *Proc. Royal Soc.* 130(B):1.

Harrison, R. J. 1946. The early development of the corpus luteum in the mare. *J. Anat.* 80:160.

Harvey, E. B. 1959. Implantation, development of the fetus, and fetal membranes. In *Reproduction in Domestic Animals.* H. H. Cole and P. T. Cupps, eds. Vol. 1. New York: Academic Press.

Hughes, J. P., G. H. Stabenfeldt, and J. W. Evans. 1972a. Estrous cycle and ovulation in the mare. *J. A. V. M. A.* 161:1367.

Hughes, J. P., G. H. Stabenfeldt, and J. W. Evans. 1972b. Clinical and endocrine aspects of the estrous cycle of the mare. *Proc. A. A. E. P.*:119.

Jeffcott, L. B., J. G. Atherton, and J. Mingay. 1969. Equine pregnancy diagnosis. *Vet. Record* 84:80.

Jeffcott, L. B., and K. E. Whitwell. 1973. Twinning as a cause of foetal and neonatal loss in the Thoroughbred mare. *J. Comp. Path.* 73:83.

Laing, J. A., ed. 1970. *Fertility and Infertility in the Domestic Animals.* Baltimore: Williams and Wilkins.

Lovell, J. D., G. H. Stabenfeldt, J. P. Hughes, and J. W. Evans. 1975. Endocrine patterns of the mare at term. *J. Reprod. Fert.,* Suppl. 23:449–456.

Loy, R. G. 1970. The reproductive cycle of the mare. *Lectures of Stud Managers Courses*:20.

Nett, T. M., D. W. Holtan, and V. L. Estergreen. 1972. Plasma estrogens in pregnant mares. *Proc. Western Sect. of Amer. Soc. Anim. Sci.* 23:509.

Nishikawa, Y. 1959. *Studies on Reproduction in Horses.* Japan Racing Association, Tokyo.

Nuti, L. C., H. J. Grimek, W. E. Braselton, and W. H. McShan. 1972. Chemical properties of equine pituitary follicle-stimulating hormone. *Endocrinol.* 91:1418.

Papkoff, H. 1969. Chemistry of the gonadotropins. In *Reproduction in Domestic Animals.* H. H. Cole and P. T. Cupps, eds. New York: Academic Press.

Pattison, M. L., C. L. Chen, and S. L. King. 1972. Determination of LH and estradiol-17β surge with reference to the time of ovulation in mares. *Biol. of Reprod.* 7:136.

Paul, R. R. 1973. Foaling date. *The Morgan Horse* 33:40.

Penida, M. H., O. J. Ginther, and W. H. McShan. 1972. Regression of the corpus luteum in mares treated with an antiserum against equine pituitary fraction. *Amer. J. Vet. Res.* 33:1767.

Rollins, W. C., and C. E. Howell. 1951. Genetic sources of variation in the gestation length of the horse. *J. Animal Sci.* 10:797.

Ropiha, R. T., R. G. Matthews, R. M. Butterworth, F. M. Moss, and W. J. McFadden. 1969. The duration of pregnancy in Thoroughbred mares. *Vet. Rec.* 84:552.

Ryan, R. J., and R. V. Short. 1965. Formation of estradiol-17β by granulosa and theca cells of the equine ovarian follicle. *Endocrinol.* 76:108.

Sisson, S., and J. D. Grossman. 1953. *The Anatomy of Domestic Animals.* Philadelphia: W. B. Saunders.

Stabenfeldt, G. H., J. P. Hughes, and J. W. Evans. 1970. Ovarian activity during the estrous cycle of the mare. *Endocrinol.* 90:1379.

Stabenfeldt, G. H., J. P. Hughes, J. D. Wheat, J. W. Evans, P. C. Kennedy, and P. T. Cupps. 1974. The role of the uterus in ovarian control in the mare. *J. Reprod. Fert.* 37:343.

Turner, C. W. 1952. *The Mammary Gland.* Vol. 1. *The Anatomy of the Udder of Cattle and Domestic Animals.* Columbia, Missouri: Lucas Brothers.

Warszawsky, L. F., W. G. Parker, N. L. First, and O. J. Ginther. 1972. Gross changes of internal genitalia during the estrous cycle in the mare. *Amer. J. Vet. Res.* 33:19.

CHAPTER TWELVE *Reproductive Physiology of the Stallion*

The stallion has always been the key to a successful breeding operation and is usually a source of pride for the owner. Today, when stallions are syndicated for $6–$10 million to stand at stud, it is essential that they be managed quite carefully. To develop a management program to ensure continued use of a stallion and to maintain his production of quality semen, the stud manager must have a knowledge of the anatomy and physiology of reproduction in the stallion. This knowledge then serves as the basis for the rest of the management procedures.

12.1   Anatomy of the Reproductive Tract

Figure 12-1 is a diagram of the anatomy of the stallion's reproductive tract. The various parts of the reproductive tract are described in detail in the following sections.

Scrotum

The scrotum of the stallion, a diverticulum of the abdomen, is somewhat asymmetrical, and less pendulous than that of the bull or ram. The scrotum is asymmetrical because one testicle is slightly larger and placed a little further back than the other. (The testicle of a stallion is shown in Figures 12-2 and 12-3.) The testes lie horizontally in the scrotum when the cremaster muscle is relaxed. When in the relaxed state, the scrotum has a smooth appearance and is constricted superiorly next to the abdomen. Upon exposure to cold, the external cremaster muscle and the

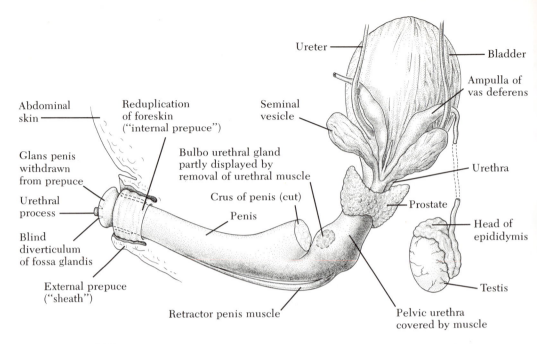

Ureter — — Bladder

Ampulla of
vas deferens

Abdominal   Reduplication   Seminal
skin   of foreskin   vesicle
             ("internal prepuce")

Glans penis   Bulbo urethral gland   Urethra
withdrawn   partly displayed by
from prepuce   removal of urethral muscle

Urethral   Crus of penis (cut)
process   Prostate
                    Penis
Blind   Head of
diverticulum   epididymis
of fossa glandis

External prepuce   Testis
("sheath")

Retractor penis muscle   Pelvic urethra
                               covered by muscle

FIGURE 12-1
Reproductive tract of the stallion (*lateral view*). Bladder and upper urethra are
twisted to expose posterior aspects. From Eckstein and Zuckerman. 1956. p. 43.

tunica dartos muscle contract so that the scrotum becomes drawn up and
wrinkled. The relaxation and contraction of these muscles serve a necessary thermo-regulatory function. The wall of the scrotum is composed of
layers that include the skin, the tunica dartos muscle, the scrotum fascia,
and the parietal layer of the tunica vaginalis propria. The circulatory
system in the scrotum is composed of branches of the external pudic
artery, and vein and lymph drainage passes to the superficial inguinal
lymph node. Innervation of the scrotum is derived from the ventral
branches of the second and third lumbar nerves.

Testes

The testicles (Figures 12-2, 12-3) have been described by Sisson and
Grossman (1953) as being 10–12 cm long, 6–8 cm high, and 5 cm wide;
each approximately weighs 225–300 g; and quite frequently the left one
is larger. The tunica vaginalis propria (Figure 12-2), an extension of the
visceral layer of the serosa, covers the outer surface of the testicle and
envelops the spermatic cord except where the blood vessels and nerves
enter the testicle. The tunica albuginea (Figure 12-2) is immediately beneath the tunica vaginalis propria and forms a strong capsule composed of
dense white fibrous tissue and smooth muscle fibers. Trabeculae septa of

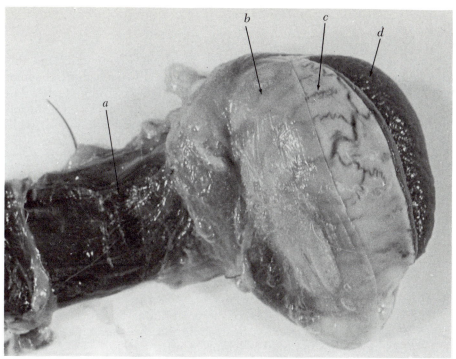

FIGURE 12-2
Testicle of a stallion showing *a*, cremaster muscle; *b*, tunica vaginalis propria; *c*, tunica albuginea; and *d*, gland substance.

FIGURE 12-3
Testicle, epididymis, and vas deferens of the stallion: *a*, testicle; *b*, head of epididymis; *c*, body of epididymis; *d* tail of epididymis; and *e*, vas deferens.

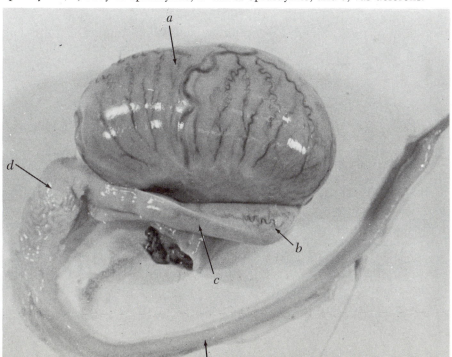

connective tissue project into the gland substance (Figure 12-2) and sub-divide the testicular parenchyma into lobules. However, the trabeculae and intralobular septa do not form a distinct mediastinum testis. The septa are interconnected and contain blood vessels and smooth muscle fibers. Each lobule contains seminiferous tubules, interstitial cells (cells of Leydig), and loose connective tissue. The seminiferous tubule is the functional unit of the testis. The tubule in cross-section is composed of connective tissue and a basement membrane that contains layers of sper-matogenic cells in various stages of development. Sustentacular cells extend from the basement membrane and are distributed between the spermatogenic cells, thus serving as a source of nutrition to the sperma-togenic cells. The seminiferous tubules unite but do not form a rete testis in the center of the testicle as they do in some other species. The semi-niferous tubules, after uniting, converge to the attached border of the testicle, where several efferent ducts pierce the albuginea and enter the head of the epididymis.

The spermatic artery, a branch of the posterior aorta, supplies blood to the testicle. The blood leaves the testicle via the spermatic vein, and lymph is drained into the lumbar lymph glands.

Epididymis

At the tunica albuginea, the seminiferous tubules unite into a single duct to form the head of the epididymis (Figure 12-3). The epididymis re-mains attached to the testicle; the main part of the attached epididymis is known as the body. The tail of the epididymis is located at the lower extremity of the testicle. The epididymis serves a number of functions, such as transporting spermatozoa and other contributions of the testes to semen, concentrating the spermatozoa as a result of water absorption, and providing a place for maturation and storage of spermatozoa.

Vas Deferens

The tail portion of the epididymis gradually merges with the vas deferens (Figure 12-3). Spermatozoa are transported from the tail of the epididymis to the urethra by the vas deferens. A thick muscular wall surrounds a relatively small lumen. Lumen size is constant but the wall thickens considerably to form the ampulla (Figure 12-4) approximately 15–20 cm from the entrance to the urethra. The increased size is caused by the presence of numerous glands in the ampullar region. The size of the vas deferens decreases sharply as the duct disappears under the isthmus of the seminal vesicles (Figure 12-4) and opens into the urethra. The

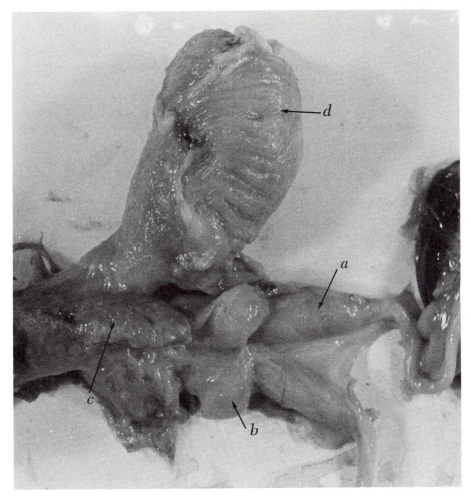

FIGURE 12-4
Accessory sex glands of the stallion: *a*, ampulla; *b*, seminal vesicles; and
c, prostate gland. The bladder is labeled *d*.

opening into the urethra is common with excretory ducts of the seminal
vesicles, but there is no ejaculatory duct in the horse as there is in man.

Penis

The penis of the stallion is approximately 50 cm long in the relaxed state,
approximately 15–20 cm of it lies in the prepuce. During erection, the
size increases about twofold. The penis is somewhat cylindrical in shape,
but compressed laterally. It is roughly divided into the head, body, and
glans. The glans or free end of the penis is bell-shaped, particularly dur-

385

ing erection, and the urethral process extends approximately 2.5 cm from the surface of the deep depression or fossa glandis. The size and shape of the donkey penis are similar to those of the stallion.

Prepuce

The sheath, properly called the prepuce, has been described by Sisson and Grossman (1953) as a "double invagination of the skin which contains and covers the free or prescrotum portion of the penis when not erect." The external prepuce extends from the scrotum to within 5–7 cm of the umbilicus. Before reaching the umbilicus, it is reflected backward and dorsally to form the preputial orifice. The internal prepuce passes backward from the preputal orifice in such a way that it lines the inside of the external prepuce. After passing backward for 15–20 cm, it is then reflected forward until it approaches the orifice, where it is again reflected backward to form a secondary tubular invagination that contains the relaxed penis. The internal layers of skin contain large sebaceous glands and coil glands or preputal glands whose secretions, together with desquamated epithelial cells, form the fatty smegma.

The circulatory system of the penis is formed from branches of the external pudic arteries and veins, whereas the lymph drainage is to the superficial and lumbar lymph glands. Penile innervation is derived from the pudic, ilio-hypogastric, and ilio-inguinal nerves.

Accessory Sex Glands

Seminal Vesicles. The accessory sex glands contribute to stallion semen a fluid of characteristic composition. The seminal vesicles (Figure 12-4) are paired glands, and each one is 15–20 cm long and approximately 5 cm in diameter. The long axes are parallel to the vas deferens, and the excretory duct passes under the prostate before it opens into the urethra.

Bulbourethral Glands. The bulbourethral glands are paired, ovoid-shaped, lobulated glands that lie near the ischial arch. Each gland is approximately 4 × 2.5 cm and has 6–8 excretory ducts opening into the urethra behind the prostatic ducts.

Prostate Gland. The prostate gland (Figure 12-4) consists of two lateral bulbs (each 3 × 1.5 × 0.5 cm) that are connected by a thin isthmus (2 cm wide). The isthmus lies over the junction of the bladder with the urethra. Approximately 15–20 prostatic ducts perforate the urethra.

12.2   Semen Production

Morphology of the Stallion Spermatozoan

The morphology of the mature stallion spermatozoan has the same basic characteristics as that of other mammalian spermatozoa. The spermatozoan is composed of 3 principle regions: the head, the neck, and the tail (Figure 12-5).

The head is 6–8 μm long and 3.3–4.6 μm wide. It is composed chiefly of a nucleus that contains the genetic material, and it is covered anteriorally by the acrosome and posteriorally by the postnuclear cap. The head of horse spermatozoan is small and slender compared with ovine, bovine, and porcine spermatozoa. The locomotor system, the tail, is connected to the head by the neck. The tail of the spermatozoan is composed of 3 regions: the middle piece, the main piece, and the end of the axial filament or endpiece. The middle piece, which is located between the neck and main piece, is 8–10 μm long and 0.5 μm wide. It is a source of energy for the spermatozoan. The main piece is 30–43 μm in length and provides the contraction mechanism that is necessary for motility. The endpiece, which is approximately 3 μm long, is the terminal portion of the tail.

Nishikawa (1959) has described the spermatozoan of the ass as being 64.1 μm long. The head is approximately 6.9 μm long and 4 μm wide.

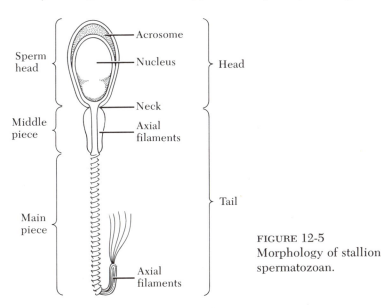

FIGURE 12-5
Morphology of stallion spermatozoan.

387

The middle piece is 9.9 μm (9.4–10.4), and the tail is 47.3 μm long. Therefore, the ass spermatozoan is very similar to the horse spermatozoan except the head is wider and the entire length is longer.

Endocrinology

At present, no detailed studies have been made of the hormone control of the reproductive processes of the stallion. Studies of laboratory animals have developed the following concept of hormone control. Follicle stimulating hormone (FSH) is secreted by the anterior pituitary gland and is responsible for spermatogenesis in the seminiferous tubule of the testis as well as maintenance and repair of the tubular epithelium. Luteinizing hormone, which is also known as the interstitial cell stimulating hormone (ICSH), in the male is primarily responsible for maintenance of the interstitial cells and for androgen production. Since ICSH is responsible for testosterone production, it is secondarily responsible for stimulation of the accessory sex characteristics and accessory sex glands.

Stallion urine contains high levels of estrogen that is produced by the Sertoli cells and interstitial cells. The role of estrogen in the stallion is not presently known.

Puberty

Hauer *et al.* (1970) have defined puberty in the stallion as the age at which an ejaculate contains a minimum of 1×10^8 total sperm with 10 percent progressive motility. They found the mean age of puberty in Quarter Horse stallions to be 67 weeks at a weight of 367 kg. Skinner and Bowen (1968) have observed spermatozoa in the ejaculate of Welsh stallions at the age of 11.5–14.5 months.

Very few stallions are used at stud as 2-year olds. If they are used, the number of services should be restricted to 2 per week. As 3-year olds, they can be used once a day. The number of mares that can be bred to young stallions depends upon the length of the breeding season and whether artificial insemination is used. Approximately 6–7 mares can be "hand bred" by the 2-year-old and 10–12 can be bred by the 3-year-old. Mature stallions can be used twice daily for short periods if they are rested one day per week. When artificial insemination is used, 10 mares per day may be bred by a stallion that produces good-quality semen.

Semen Characteristics

388   The semen of the stallion, greyish-white in appearance, consists of the seminal plasma or fluid medium and spermatozoa. The whole semen is

a series of 8 (range 5–10) seminal jets ejaculated in sequence (Tischner *et al.*, 1974). The first 3 jets are milky in color and consistency and contain 80 percent of the total number of spermatozoa ejaculated. The fluid medium of the first 3 jets has a high level of ergothioneine, indicating that the fluid is derived mainly from the ampular glands of the vas deferens. The later jets (range 4–10) contain very few sperm cells. They are mucinous in appearance and contain a high concentration of citric acid, indicating that the fluid is derived mainly from the seminal vesicles.

Semen Evaluation

At least 4 criteria are used to evaluate stallion semen: the volume of semen and the concentration, motility, and morphology of the spermatozoa. The ejaculate volume is usually 50–75 ml but may be as great as 150–170 ml. At least 2 factors influence semen volume: season and stallion. The volume of semen is larger during the breeding season than during the winter. The absence of or the amount of gel, which is influenced by stallion variability and season, is an important determinant of volume. The concentration of sperm per milliliter of ejaculate ranges between 30 and 800 million. Pickett *et al.* (1970) have reported a large variation between stallions, first and second ejaculates, and months of the year for first ejaculates. The mean concentration of spermatozoa in gel-free seminal fluid for first ejaculates was $347.8 \pm 124.9 \times 10^6$/ml, compared with $211.9 \pm 88.1 \times 10^6$/ml for second ejaculates. Consequently, the total number of spermatozoa was influenced by stallion, ejaculation frequency, and season. A mean total number of spermatozoa of $9.3 \pm 3.9 \times 10^9$ was reported for first ejaculates and $4.6 \pm 1.9 \times 10^9$ for second ejaculates. Other reports have indicated concentrations ranging from 6.3 to 26×10^9 spermatozoa per ejaculate. The seasonal effect on sperm output and total volume of semen is very marked. During the winter months, volume may be decreased by as much as 60 percent, causing a 50 percent reduction in total sperm output. Thus, because of his decreased ability to produce sperm during the early part of the breeding season, it is easy to overuse the stallion. Another reason for lower conception rates and stallion overuse is that most mares require more breedings per estrous cycle because they are not cycling normally. The percentage of motile spermatozoa in an ejaculate is usually 60–100 percent, and 70 percent is considered quite good. The season of the year does not affect the motility of spermatozoa. Therefore, a stallion is just as fertile during the winter months as during the breeding season; however, he cannot be used to breed as many mares because he does not produce as many sperm.

Stallion spermatozoa move in a straight line rather than in a twisting progression. The percentage of deformed sperm cells incapable of fertilization usually varies between 20 percent and 30 percent, but some

389

stallions have less than 20 percent abnormal spermatozoa. Abnormal types of sperm cells include those with deformed heads, such as small, large, isolated, and polycephaly, and those with deformed tails, such as twisted, abnormally curvy, double tails, and acephaly.

Kenny *et al.* (1971) have observed that the one single seminal factor that best predicted pregnancy was sperm concentration; the best combination of two factors was concentration and volume; the best three factors were concentration, volume, and percentage morphologically normal; and the best four factors were these three plus initial progressive motility after washing and dilution.

The semen of the jack, *Equus asinus*, has been described by Nishikawa (1959) as being more milky or brownish yellow than stallion semen. The volume per ejaculate averages 50 ml and ranges from 10 to 115 ml. Very little or no gelatinous material is ejaculated. The concentration varies between 95 and 264 and 10^6/ml and the total number of spermatozoa per ejaculate varies between 8 and 43×10^9. The average total number is 24×10^9.

During the breeding season, most farms make a practice of evaluating the semen every 2 weeks for volume and for the concentration, morphology, and motility of the spermatozoa. If the quality and/or quantity start to decline, the stallion is not used for a few days. The fertility of a stallion is questioned when, upon evaluation of the semen, one or more of the following characteristics exist: the ejaculate volume is below 50 ml, fewer than 50 percent of the sperm cells have normal motility and morphology, and/or concentration of the sperm cells is below 8×10^6 per ml. Before declaring the stallion infertile, several semen collections should be evaluated, because the time interval between semen collections is important. Before a routine semen evaluation is made, the stallion should have one week of sexual rest. Two seminal collections are obtained. A second ejaculate is obtained one hour after the first ejaculate. The second ejaculate should contain approximately one-half of the total number of spermatozoa contained in the first. If the difference between the two ejaculates is not approximately 50 percent, one of three conditions may exist: one of the ejaculates may be incomplete; the stallion has low spermatozoan reserves; or spermatozoa have accumulated in the reproductive tract. In such cases, another ejaculate should be obtained the same day as the first two ejaculates and the evaluation process should be repeated one week later to determine the cause. If a stallion has poor-quality semen that may be the result of ill health (fever) or injury, it is advisable to wait at least 60–90 days before performing a second semen evaluation. This allows time for one complete spermatogenic cycle to occur. To evaluate the ability of a stallion to produce spermatozoa, daily ejaculates should be obtained for 8–10 days after a week of sexual rest. After 6–8 days of collection, the number of spermatozoa per ejaculate becomes relatively stable and is a close approximation of the daily sperm production. The number of mares that a stallion can service per season can be determined from the results of this evaluation. Those with poor ability to produce semen are capable of breeding fewer mares per season. Dismount samples, collected when a stallion is dismounting from the mare, are used by some farms to evaluate semen quality, but they are not really indicative of semen quality. The last ejaculate jets normally contain few if any spermatozoa.

When a stallion is used in an artificial insemination program where fresh semen is used or in an A.I. stud where semen is being frozen, it is important to obtain the maximum number of spermatozoa that that stallion is capable of producing. If the stallion is collected too frequently, the concentration of spermatozoa in the semen will decline, as will his libido. Usually, the maximum number of spermatozoa can be obtained when the stallion is collected 3 to 4 times a week. However, the only true test of semen quality is the conception rate.

Stallion Infertility

There are many possible causes of infertility. A stallion suffering from poor health and/or nutrition, injury, worry, or anxiety will sometimes recover with proper management. Another common problem with the stallion is masturbation. It is difficult to catch some stallions in the act of masturbation, but the presence of dried semen on the abdomen or on the back of the forelegs and a shrinkage of muscles of the loin are good indicators that the stallion has been masturbating. A couple of management practices have been tried to eliminate the vice. Some stallions that are turned outside where they can exercise and see other horses will stop masturbating, but others require that a stallion ring be placed behind the glans penis. The ring is removed before breeding a mare and is subsequently replaced. Care must be taken that a local inflammation does not develop.

Pickett *et al.* (1976) have implicated mismanagement as the most common cause of abnormal sexual behavior leading to infertility. Overuse of a stallion as a 2- or 3-year-old may lead to the development of poor breeding behavior such as a slow reaction time to breed a mare. A slow reaction time may develop in mature stallions because of overuse during the winter and fall months. Often, the overused young stallion will develop a bad habit of savaging (excessively biting) a mare. Unnecessary roughness in handling a stallion may lead to disinterest in breeding a mare. Disinterest may also result from excessive use of the stallion as a teaser to determine which mares are in estrus.

Breeding Soundness Evaluation

In addition to performing a semen evaluation, a breeding soundness evaluation should be completed on the stallion before purchase or before the start of the breeding season. If possible, the stallion's past breeding records should be examined to determine his past ability to "settle" mares. The stallion should be in excellent physical health, as evidenced by a general physical examination and his physical appearance. Regardless of his genetic ability to sire good foals, he must be physically fit and able to perform in the stud. There are several things to consider in a soundness evaluation. Injuries to the hind legs may prevent the stallion from, or cause problems when, breeding mares. Overweight and underweight conditions reduce the potential breeding performance. The condition of the respiratory tract and cardiovascular system may have a direct bearing on the ability of the stallion to survive at stud. Other problems, such as arthritis and melanomas, are common in aged stallions. The digestive tract should be checked for internal parasites. If possible, any history of colic should be ascertained. The reproductive tract should be examined by palpation for any abnormalities. Retention of one or both testicles in the abdominal cavity can be determined by examination of the scrotum. Inguinal hernias are detected by rectal examination.

Libido of the stallion can be evaluated by observing the stallion tease and breed a mare. Ejaculatory disturbances that cause incomplete or inhibited ejaculation resulting from testicular malfunction, physiological inhibition, or psychological inhibition may be observed during the breeding process. Temperament is an important consideration. Stallions that are vicious, stall kickers, or cribbers, or are prone to bite the handler or themselves, are difficult to handle and have a tendency to injure themselves or their handlers. Heritable imperfections, such as overshot and undershot jaws, should be noted.

Artificial Insemination

Artificial insemination (A.I.) has been widely used in the improvement of several species of domestic animals. Even though the mare was reported to be the first animal to be artificially inseminated, the technique has not been used extensively with mares in the United States. However, it has been widely utilized in other countries, such as Japan, China, and Russia. Artificial insemination offers many obvious advantages. It permits disease control. (For example, it was practiced in Romania until 1961 to successfully eradicate dourine, a venereal disease, from the horse.) Injured or crippled stallions that have difficulty mounting a mare may be used in an A.I. program. A.I. may be used to prevent injury to the stallion if the mare is nervous or shy at breeding. One of the major advantages is that more mares per season can be bred to the stallion because the stallion is not overused. Mares with physical disabilities that prevent mounting by the stallion may be bred. Caslicked mares, that is, mares whose vulva are sutured to prevent windsucking of contaminants into the reproductive tract, do not have to have the sutures removed for breeding. Mares that do not show behavioral signs of estrus may be bred without risk of injury to the mare or stallion. One objection to A.I. in horses is that if too many mares are bred to a stallion, the market value of his colts may be lowered.

Collection Equipment.   Stallion semen is collected for artificial insemination or for evaluation of semen quality by the use of a breeder's bag (condom) or artificial vagina. The artificial vagina provides more satisfactory results and consistently less contaminated samples. The Fujihira model (Figure 12-6) has been used quite successfully at the University of California at Davis. The artificial vagina is basically a lightweight, rigid frame with a rubber inner liner. Water (temperature of 42°–44°C at time of collection) is used to fill the space between the liner and the frame and a valve

FIGURE 12-6
Equipment used for artificial insemination: *a*, rubber liner for artificial vagina; *b*, cup to fill artificial vagina with warm water and to keep ejaculate at proper temperature after collection; *c*, glove; *d*, thermometer; *e*, speculum; *f*, chambers catheter; *g*, collection bulb that slips over end of artificial vagina; *h*, lubricating jelly; *i*, artificial vagina; *j*, light; *k*, syringe.

maintains the water pressure during collection. A rubber dam is at the end of the vagina so that pressure can be exerted on the glans penis by the collector. The pressure on the glans penis and the temperature of the water are the two main factors responsible for ejaculation. The opening of the artificial vagina is lubricated with a sterile lubricant, and a rubber collection bag is placed over the end of the vagina.

Collection Procedure. During collection, the stallion mounts a mare that has been properly prepared (see Chapter 13). The penis is directed into the artificial vagina, which is held at a fixed position until the stallion begins vigorous thrusts, at which time the collector maintains firm pressure against the glans penis until ejaculation is complete. Ejaculation can be determined visually by flagging of the tail or manually by feeling the pulsations of the urethra at the opening of the artificial vagina.

Semen-handling Procedures. After it has been collected, the semen can be used raw, although Hansen (1965) has reported that better results are obtained when the semen is extended with a dilutor before use. During handling, the semen is held at 102°–105°F in a water bath. Several extenders are frequently used. Hughes and Loy (1970) have described skimmed milk and cream-gelatin dilutors. Skimmed milk dilutor is prepared by warming skimmed milk in a double boiler to 95°C for 4 minutes. After the milk has cooled, 1,000 units of penicillin, 1 mg of dehyc rostreptomycin, and 200 units of Polymyxin B sulfate are added per milliliter of dilutor. Cream-gelatin dilutor is prepared by warming half-and-half cream in a double boiler to 95°C for 2–4 minutes. Any scum is removed and the hot half-and-half cream is added to 1.3 grams of Knox gelatin that has been autoclaved with 10 ml of distilled water to a volume of 100 ml. When the mixture cools, antibiotics are added as prescribed for the milk dilutor. The dilutors can be frozen and stored until needed. They are warmed to 102°–105°F before use. The semen is diluted 1:1 or 1:4 after collection and removal of the gel fraction. The gel is removed so that the semen can be evenly diluted and handled in a syringe. The gel can be removed by aspiration with a syringe or by straining the semen through 4–5 layers of sterile gauze.

Insemination of Mare. The insemination of the mare has been described by Hughes and Loy (1970). A sterile glass speculum is inserted into the vagina. A sterile Chambers catheter (Figure 12-6) is then passed through the speculum and into the uterus by way of the cervix. A sterile 50-cc syringe filled with semen is then attached to the Chambers catheter and the semen is deposited into the uterus. Hansen (1965) has described an alternate method whereby the operator wears a disposable arm-length glove and guides the catheter through the cervix into the uterus with a finger.

Insemination Problems. One of the major problems that must be solved before artificial insemination can be used successfully in the mare is development of a method to store frozen semen. As evidenced by consistently low percentage of foals produced by frozen semen, more research efforts are needed before the use of frozen semen becomes common in the horse-breeding industry.

12.3   Castration

Age. A castrated horse is referred to as a gelding. Most horses chosen to be castrated are usually castrated between birth and 2 years of age. Several factors usually determine the age when they are gelded. Colts that have poor conformation and/or a poor pedigree are gelded as soon as the testicles descend into the scrotum. The testicles are usually in the scrotum at birth or arrive there before the tenth month after birth, but occasionally they are not fully down until the twelfth or fifteenth month after birth. If a horse has good conformation and a good pedigree and warrants a performance test, he is kept intact until he fails to meet specific performance criteria. Stallions that are able to perform but do not sire good foals should also be castrated. There are too many good stallions available to keep poorly conformed and nonperforming stallions or stallions whose progeny are of poor quality.

Advantages of Castration. Gelding a horse has several advantages. Several geldings may be kept in a paddock, whereas each stallion must be kept by himself. Geldings are easier to care for, less prone to injury, and easier to haul because of their attitude. Many people object to working stallions because they tend to be lazy performers and are not consistent in their performance.

Procedure for Castration. Because of the possible complications that may result from castration and the need to anesthetize many of the colts or stallions to prevent injury, it is customary for a veterinarian to perform the castration. At least 3 methods of castrating a horse have been described. Lowe and Dougherty (1972) have described the *primary closure method.* An incision is made through the skin and vaginal tunic between the scrotum and superficial inguinal ring on each side of the scrotum. The vessels and ductus deferens are tied by transfixation ligatures. The testicles are removed and all dissected planes are closed with chromic gut. With the *closed technique,* each testicle and spermatic cord still contained within the parietal layer of the tunica vaginalis is freed by blunt dissection from the surrounding tissue well into the inguinal canal. The cord struc-

395

tures are divided by means of an emasculator, which is left in position for approximately one minute. When the *open technique* is used, the tunica vaginalis is freed from the surrounding tissue as in the closed method. Then the tunica vaginalis communis is split with scissors so that all structures that are to be removed can be identified. The testicles, epididymis, and part of the cord are then removed as previously indicated. If the horse has been immunized against tetanus, postoperative care consists of exercise to prevent or control swelling and edema. The stallion libido usually subsides in 4–6 months but may last for one year.

Cryptorchids. An animal with one or both testes undescended into the scrotum is a cryptorchid, more commonly referred to as a ridgeling. The testes may be descended at birth and are usually descended by the age of 10 months. Some colts may be 12–15 months of age before descent of the testes. After 15 months of age, colts are considered cryptorchid if the testes are not descended. A positive diagnosis can be made if the vas deferens does not pass through the inguinal canal. These horses are difficult to castrate, and many castrated ridgelings seem to retain their stallion attitude for several months after castration.

12.4   Sexual Behavior

Olfaction is one of the fundamental stimuli of the reproductive responses of the stallion. When the stallion smells the external genitalia of the mare or voided urine, he displays the olfactory or Flehman reflex, in which he extends his neck upward and curls his lip. During exhibition of the reflex he inhales and exhales air in the upper respiratory passages. During the courtship period, the stallion also smells the groin of the mare and bites the mare on the croup and neck. At the first approach to the mare or even upon removal from his paddock to tease mares, the stallion will snort and continues to snort periodically during courtship. Erection in the stallion is usually slow and, in some stallions, may take several minutes. The reaction time for an attempted mount after first visual stimulation is approximately 5 minutes. Upon determination that the mare is in estrus and that erection has occurred, the stallion may mount the mare 2 or 3 times before intromission. Pickett *et al.* (1970) have observed a seasonal influence on mounts per ejaculate. Fewer mounts (1.5) per ejaculate were observed during the breeding season. The time of copulation varies from a few seconds to several minutes and the ejaculatory reflex lasts from 15 seconds to one minute. The number of intravaginal thrusts necessary to evoke ejaculation is 5–10 and their average duration is 11 seconds (Tischner *et al.*, 1974). Ejaculation can usually be determined by "tail flagging," in which the stallion raises and lowers his tail several times.

References

Asbury, A. C., and J. P. Hughes. 1964. Use of the artificial vagina for equine semen collection. *J.A.V.M.A.* 8:879.

Bielanski, W. 1960. Reproduction in horses. Vol. 1. Stallions. *Instytut Bull.* 116. Kracow, Poland: Instytut Zootechniki.

Eckstein, P., and S. Zuckerman. 1956. Morphology of the reproductive tract. In *Marshall's Physiology of Reproduction.* 3rd ed. A. S. Parkes, ed. Boston: Little, Brown.

Fraser, A. F. 1968. *Reproductive Behavior in Ungulates.* New York: Academic Press.

Hafez, E. S. E. 1968. *Reproduction in Farm Animals.* Philadelphia: Lea and Febiger.

Hansen, J. C. 1965. Artificial insemination. *The Blood Horse* 90:3368.

Hauer, E. P., H. C. Dellgren, S. E. McCraine, and C. K. Vincent. 1970. Puberal characteristics of Quarter Horse stallions. *J. Anim. Sci.* 30:321.

Heinze, C. D. 1966. Methods of equine castration. *J.A.V.M.A.* 148:428.

Hughes, J. P., and R. G. Loy. 1970. Artificial insemination in the equine. A comparison of natural breeding and artificial insemination of mares using semen from six stallions. *The Cornell Vet.* 60:463.

Julian, L. M., and W. S. Tyler. 1959. Anatomy of the Male Reproductive Organs. In: *Reproduction in Domestic Animals.* H. H. Cole and P. T. Cupps, eds. Vol. 1. New York: Academic Press.

Kenny, R. M., R. S. Kingston, A. H. Rajamannon, and C. F. Ramberg. 1971. Stallion semen characteristics for predicting fertility. *Proc. Amer. Assoc. Equine Practitioners.* 17:53.

Lowe, J. E., and R. Dougherty. 1972. Castration of horses and ponies by a primary closure method. *J.A.V.M.A.* 160:183.

Nishikawa, Y. 1959. *Studies on Reproduction in Horses.* Tokyo: Japan Racing Association.

Pickett, B. W. 1974. Evaluation of Stallion Semen. In O. R. Adams, *Lameness in Horses.* Philadelphia: Lea and Febiger.

Pickett, B. W. 1976. Stallion management with special reference to semen collection, evaluation and artificial insemination. *Proc. 1st National Horsemen's Seminar,* pp. 37–47.

Pickett, B. W., L. C. Faulkner, and T. M. Sutherland. 1970. Effect of month and stallion on seminal characteristics and sexual behavior. *J. Anim. Sci.* 31:713.

397

Sisson, S., and J. D. Grossman. 1953. *The Anatomy of Domestic Animals.* Philadelphia: W. B. Saunders.

Skinner, J. D., and J. Bowen. 1968. Puberty in the Welsh stallion. *J. Reprod. Fert.* 16:133.

Swierstra, E. E., M. R. Gebauer, and B. W. Pickett. 1974. Reproductive physiology of the stallion. I. Spermatogenesis and testis composition. *J. Reprod. Fert.* 40:113.

Tischner, M., K. Kosiniak, and W. Bielanski. 1974. Analysis of the pattern of ejaculation in stallions. *J. Reprod. Fert.* 41:329–335.

Wierzbowski, S. 1958. Ejaculatory reflexes in stallions following natural stimulation and the use of the artificial vagina. *Anim. Breed. Abstr.* 26:367.

CHAPTER THIRTEEN *Horse-Breeding Problems*

To be successful, a stallion farm requires skilled and knowledgeable personnel to handle the breeding herd and stallions. Personnel need to understand the basic principles of reproductive physiology and to be able to apply them to practical situations. If they do, many mares that would not ordinarily conceive will do so without too many problems.

13.1 Preparation for Breeding

Teasing

One of the main determinants of a successful breeding season is the skill of the stud manager in handling the teaser while teasing mares and in determining when mares are in estrus. He must be able to recognize the characteristic behavioral signs of estrus and all of their variations. Teasing mares at the proper interval, to determine whether they are in the early phase of estrus, is important. For best results, each mare should be teased once a day, although some breeding farms tease every other day.

Methods. Which teasing method is to be used is determined by the number of mares, the physical facilities, and/or the stud manager's preference. If a limited number of mares are to be teased every day, each mare may be brought to the stallion's stall and teased. The stall must be specially constructed so that the stallion can reach the mare with his head and nuzzle her. The retaining wall must be high enough so that he will not attempt to jump out of the stall, and the opening above the wall should be approximately 3½ feet high. The stallion can be taken to each mare in her paddock. The teasing should be done across a specially built teasing wall. Teasing walls permit the stallion and mare to strike at each other without the risk of injuring each other. The teasing wall is approximately 3½ to 4 feet high, approximately 8 foot long, and of solid construction so that there is no opportunity for a foot to get caught between the boards. Many farms tease mares across a regular fence and run a high risk of injury. Some farms take the mare and stallion to a special teasing area that has a teasing wall (Figure 13-1) or rail. The teasing wall is so designed that both the handlers are protected from the mare and stallion but can stay close to the horses to control them. Some farms use a rail made of pipe, but it does not offer protection for the horses and handlers.

When a large number of mares must be teased daily, the teaser stallion may be placed in a "cage" (a specially built stall) inside a large pen. As many as 20 or 30 mares are driven into the pen and teased at one time. Careful records must be kept so that mares that are timid, or are having silent heats, can be removed from the broodmare band and teased individually. To prevent aggressive mares from kicking the other mares or from approaching the stallion, a teasing mill can be used (Figure 13-2). The stallion is in a special pen surrounded by 10 pens that hold individual mares.

Pasture teasing is dangerous to both a good teaser stallion and the handler. The teaser stallion should be protected with padding, particularly on his belly. His penis should be covered with a blanket so that he cannot accidentally service a mare if he escapes from the handler. Ac-

FIGURE 13-1
Teasing a mare with a stallion across a teasing wall. Both handlers are protected from the kicking and striking of the mare and stallion. Illustration by M. Morris.

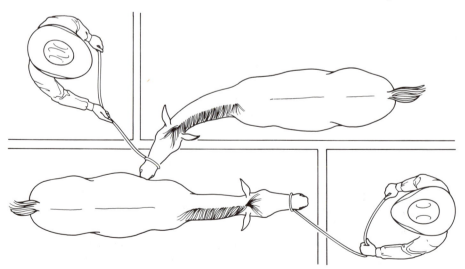

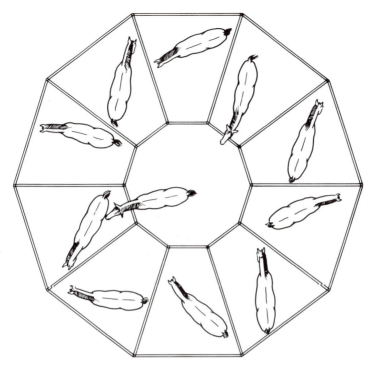

FIGURE 13-2
"Teasing mill" used by Thane Lancaster to tease several mares
simultaneously at the Magic Valley Stallion Station. A stallion
is put in the pen in the center. From *The Quarter Horse Journal*
28 (1975):202.

cidental conceptions can also be prevented by using a vasectomized stallion as a teaser. The handler should carry a whip to protect himself from
aggressive mares that are out of heat. A pony stallion can be turned loose
in a pen or a pasture with mares so long as he is too small to service the
mares. If a long drag rope is connected to his halter, he can easily be
caught when he has finished teasing the mares.

Teaser. The teaser stallion, by his actions, can often determine the success of detecting mares in estrus. An aggressive individual with a lot of
libido that does a lot of squealing seems to work best under most circumstances. Most teaser stallions become disinterested in teasing if they are
used daily. To help maintain his libido, a stallion can be periodically
bred to grade mares. When several mares are teased daily, it usually is
necessary to use 2 or 3 teasers during the breeding season or the stallions
lose interest.

Timid mares seldom show estrus to a very aggressive stallion that does
a lot of kicking and squealing. A timid mare frequently will display estrus
when placed in a stall that is close enough to a stallion so that she can
hear and smell but not see him. Maiden mares should be teased with a

401

quiet stallion the first few times that they are in estrus so that they do not become frightened. A common problem for horse owners who have 1 or 2 mares to be bred is how to detect when the mare is in estrus because they have no stallion to tease the mares. Quite often, the mare is delivered to a stud farm so that the stallions there can tease the mare. Some mares occasionally show estrus to a strange mare or gelding when they are first introduced. Some horse owners have found that it is economical to buy an inexpensive pony stallion and use him as a teaser until the mare is successfully bred.

Hauling Effects. If the owner of a mare keeps the mare at home until she is in estrus and ready to be bred, he sometimes finds that she will not show estrus when she is delivered to the stallion. Some mares are sensitive to strange surroundings and strange people. In such a situation, the stallion owner should call a veterinarian to rectally palpate the mare to determine if she is ready to be bred. If she is, she can be artificially bred without risk of injury because she will not accept the stallion.

Maiden, Barren, and Open Mares

The maiden, barren, and open mares should be properly prepared for the breeding season. Since an increasing amount of daylight stimulates a mare to cycle regularly, artificial lights can be used effectively to encourage mares to cycle regularly early in the breeding season. The ability to breed these mares early will help distribute the "book" of a stallion (the mares to be bred to him) and may prevent overusing him during the latter part of the season. All maiden, open, and barren mares should be placed under 11 hours of artificial light per day around the middle of November. The period of lighting is then increased at the rate of 15 minutes per week until the mares are under 18–19 hours of continuous light per day. The extra 15 minutes per week can be added at the end of the lighted period; some managers prefer to add half of the time in the morning and the other half in the evening. Either fluorescent or regular light bulbs can be used and controlled by an electrical timer. The average size stall requires approximately 200 watts. The mares may be kept on pasture when a lighted shelter is provided.

As the maiden, barren, and open mares come into estrus, they should be given a physical examination by a veterinarian and cultured for uterine infections if warranted. Mares that have uterine infections should be treated. The vulvas of mares that are aspirating air and contaminants into their reproductive tracts should be sutured (Caslick operation) to prevent further aspiration of air. Many of these mares have a deep-set anus and a vulva that forms a shelf instead of being nearly vertical.

Genital Organ Examinations

During the breeding season, all mares are usually teased daily, and as each mare comes into estrus, she is given a genital organ examination by a veterinarian. The examination consists of visual inspection of the cervix and vagina and a palpatation per rectum of the uterus and ovaries. The changes in the cervix, vagina, and ovaries are most significant (see Chapter 11) and are correlated with behavioral signs of estrus to determine whether it is the optimal time to breed. (The optimal time to breed is just before ovulation.) The survival time of the ovum, for breeding purposes, is approximately 24 hours, even though it may be as long as 48 hours. Stallion semen in the reproductive tract of the mare is viable for 48 hours under practical conditions but may be viable for as long as 5 days. If it is not possible to have the mare palpated, breeding should start on day 3 of estrus, and the mare may be bred every other day until she goes out of heat. This method enables viable sperm to be in the tract while the ovum is viable, even if the mare has a short 3-day cycle or a longer-than-usual estrus.

Foal Heat

Care must be taken in order to breed mares successfully during the foal heat. Only those mares that had a normal delivery should be bred. If any of the following conditions exist upon examination by a veterinarian, the mare should not be bred: bruised cervix, lacerations or tears in cervix or vagina, vaginal discharge, placenta retained more than 3 hours, lack of tone in the uterus or vagina, or presence of urine in the vagina. In fact, if there is any question about breeding the mare, it is better to wait. Indiscriminate breeding of mares during the foal heat results in a low (25 percent) conception rate.

Estrous Cycle Manipulations

Several situations commonly occur during the breeding season when the stud manager will need to manipulate the estrous cycle of the mare (the period when the mare comes into heat and ovulates) to increase conception percentages or correct fertility problems. Some of the problems that can be corrected or situations that should be avoided are lactation anestrus, spontaneously prolonged corpus luteum, and overuse of the stallion. Several techniques can be used during the breeding season to manipulate the estrous cycle or some aspect of it.

Human Chorionic Gonadotropin (HCG). One of the most commonly used techniques is to use human chorionic gonadotropin (HCG) to stimu-

403

late follicles to ovulate. This method is particularly useful when a follicle reaches ovulatory size but does not ovulate within a reasonable
period. Some farms are using the technique more extensively in that each
mare receives an HCG injection 24 hours after the beginning of estrus.
The mares are bred 24 hours after the injection, and ovulation usually
occurs before 48 hours post-injection.

Prostaglandins.   One of the prostaglandins, $PGF_{2\alpha}$, can be used to correct several infertility problems and to manipulate the time of ovulation.
Prostaglandins are used because of their luteolytic effect (Figure 13-3).
They cause the corpus luteum to undergo involution and cease producing progesterone when they are administered 4 to 12 or 14 days post-
ovulation. Plasma progesterone concentration will rapidly decline to
below 1 ng/ml and the mare will come into estrus in approximately 2–4
days following treatment (Allen and Roswon, 1973). Most mares will ovulate a fertile ovum by 10–12 days post-treatment and some will ovulate
as soon as 6 days post-treatment. One of the major mare infertility problems is the spontaneously prolonged corpus luteum (Figure 13-4). The
corpus luteum does not cease to produce progesterone at approximately

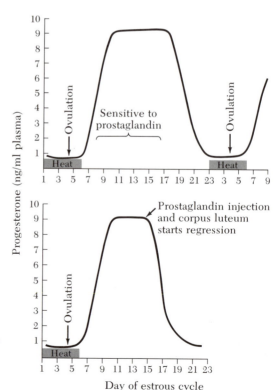

FIGURE 13-3
Graphs showing days during
the estrous cycle when a mare is
most sensitive to prostaglandin.

404

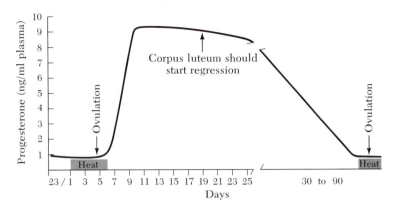

FIGURE 13-4

Effect of spontaneously prolonged corpus luteum on the estrous cycle.

14 days post-ovulation but continues to function for an additional 1–3 months. The mare with the spontaneously prolonged corpus luteum is usually normal in all respects except that she has a high level of progesterone in the blood that keeps her out of estrus and from having estrous cycles. Open, barren, or maiden mares that are not pregnant and are not having estrous cycles during the breeding season should be tested for a spontaneously prolonged corpus luteum by analyzing a blood sample for progesterone concentration. The same problem (spontaneously prolonged corpus luteum) in the "pseudo-pregnant" mare makes detection of continued progesterone secretion more confusing and difficult. The pseudo-pregnant mare shown in Figure 13-5 was bred and ceased having estrous cycles. At 45 days when she was given a pregnancy examination, she was found to be open (not pregnant). The mare either coincidentally developed a spontaneously prolonged corpus luteum, or she may have

FIGURE 13-5

Effect of administering prostaglandin treatment to a pseudo-pregnant mare.

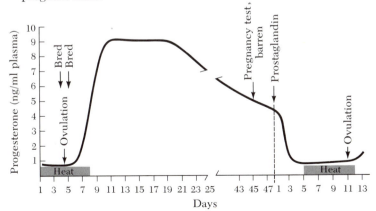

405

conceived and reabsorbed the fetus. In both cases, there is an active corpus luteum producing progesterone, which should not be present. When diagnosed, these problems can be corrected by treatment with prostaglandin. The mare would then come into heat and ovulate as previously discussed (Figure 13-6).

Another practical use of prostaglandins is to control the length of the estrous cycle (Figure 13-7). It is frequently helpful to breed a mare 10–12 days earlier than when she is due to come into heat. This is particularly true during the latter half of the breeding season. It is also advantageous to be able to control the time of ovulation of a group of mares that are to be bred artificially with frozen semen because in such a situation it would be helpful if all the mares came into heat and ovulated at the same time. In a situation where a stallion has a large book of mares and artificial insemination is not permissible, it would be desirable to prevent the stallion's overuse by preventing several mares from ovulating at approximately the same time. To shorten the estrous cycle of an individual mare, prostaglandin administration between days 4 and 12 postovulation will cause the corpus luteum to cease producing progesterone and allow the mare to come into heat 3–4 days post-injection and to ovulate within 10–12 days post-injection. She may ovulate as soon as 6 days post-injection. The ovulation following prostaglandin treatment is as fertile as normal ovulations. All subsequent estrous cycles will be of normal length, and fertility is not decreased.

After foaling, prostaglandin treatment may be of benefit to breed mares before the time of their next normal estrous period. This is particularly true for mares that do not pass the veterinarian's inspection to breed on the foal heat (the first heat period following foaling). Mares are not bred

FIGURE 13-6
Effect of administering prostaglandin treatment to a mare with a prolonged corpus luteum.

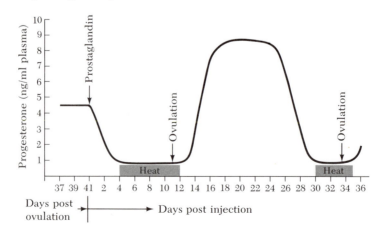

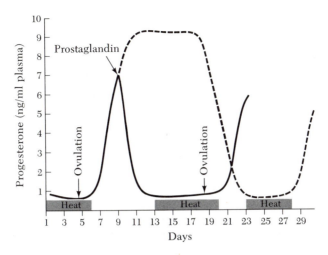

FIGURE 13-7
Effect of administering prostaglandin to shorten the
length of the estrous cycle.

on the foal heat if they have a bruised cervix, lacerations of the cervix or vagina, or a vaginal discharge, or if they retain the placenta more than 3 hours or evidence lack of tone in the uterus or vagina. In addition, there may be other conditions that indicate the inadvisability of breeding on the foal heat. The reproductive tract of the mare may not have had enough time to return to a breedable condition by the time the mare came into heat at 9–11 days after foaling, or the mare may have had a very early foal heat ovulation at 7–9 days post-foaling. In these situations, the mare can be treated with prostaglandins on the fifth day after her foal heat ovulation, and she will ovulate again within 10–12 days or possibly sooner

FIGURE 13-8
Effect of administering prostaglandin to breed the
foaling mare before her normal second estrous period.

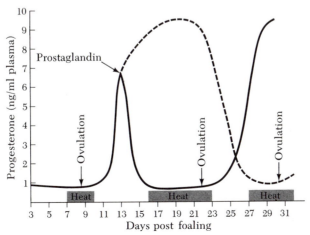

407

(Figure 13-8). The mare can be bred at least 6–8 days sooner than normal and in some cases as many as 10–12 days earlier than her next normal estrous period.

Some mares will not cycle during lactation. Usually, such a mare will have her foal heat and then will not come back into heat for a long period. These mares may have a persistent corpus luteum as a result of the foal heat ovulation, or they may be extremely possessive of their foals and do not want to approach the stallion. Many of these mares will respond to the prostaglandin treatment in the manner previously discussed.

Prostaglandins can be used to induce abortions at 5 days post-breeding. Prostaglandins cause the corpus luteum to cease producing progesterone, which is required for maintenance of pregnancy. This is useful if a mare is bred to the wrong stallion by mistake or if the mare had unexpected twin ovulations after she was bred and the stud manager does not want to take a chance that she conceived twins.

Saline Infusions. The length of the estrous cycle can be shortened by 4 days with an intra-uterine infusion of 250–500 ml of warm 0.9 percent salt solution on days 6 or 7 post-ovulation. The warm saline infusion is also an important technique in another situation. Some mares are bred and do not come back into estrus; however, upon palpation, they are not found to be pregnant. If the mare has a persistent corpus luteum, the saline infusion can cause regression of the corpus luteum. Occasionally, mares that are extremely possessive of their foals will not cycle while lactating, and a saline infusion may start them to cycle.

13.2 Breeding

Hygiene Procedures

After it has been determined that a mare is ready to be bred, the next consideration is breeding hygiene. Breeding hygiene is important because some infections that cause abortions are the result of introduction of bacteria in the mare during breeding.

Mare. The first step is to tease the mare so that she will empty her bladder. The tail should then be wrapped with gauze or some other type of disposable wrapping. The mare's external genitalia and the surrounding area should be cleaned with a mild soap such as Ivory or Phisoderm. After the area is clean, the soap should be thoroughly rinsed off because it is spermicidal and causes irritation.

Stallion. The stallion's penis should also be washed with a mild soap and warm water, rinsed with an abundant amount of water, and dried off with a disposable towel. Water is spermicidal so his penis must be dry before breeding. After breeding the mare, his penis is rinsed with a mild antiseptic solution and dried off. To prevent the spread of bacteria or other deleterious microorganisms from one stallion to another, a separate wash bucket should be kept for each stallion.

Safety

Stallion. Most stallions are valuable and should be protected from injury during the breeding process. A stallion can be protected from mare-induced injuries to some extent by tying up one front leg of the mare, but the mare does not then have a strong base of support. One of the safer methods is to use a set of breeding hobbles and, if necessary, a twitch (Figure 13-9). The mare can still move around when hobbled but

FIGURE 13-9
Mare prepared for breeding. The mare is hobbled with a set of breeding hobbles that prevent her from kicking the stallion. The areas around her genital organs have been washed and her tail has been wrapped with sterile gauze to help prevent transmission of genital diseases.

409

is unable to kick. It is advisable to walk the mare around before the stallion mounts so that she knows she is hobbled. Excessive biting of a mare can be prevented by muzzling the stallion. This is particularly important when the mare is to be shown at halter or performance classes.

Maiden Mares. In breeding young maiden mares, there is a chance of causing injury to the vagina or cervix. Many of the lacerations, tears, or bruises can be prevented by the use of a breeding roll to restrict entry by the stallion (Figure 13-10). The padded roll is 4–6 inches in diameter and approximately 18 inches long. A handle on one end allows easy insertion between the mare's rump and the stallion just above the penis as the stallion mounts. In keeping with strict rules of hygiene, the roll should be covered with a disposable cover, such as a plastic examination glove. The maiden should also be examined by a veterinarian and the hymen opened if necessary.

Size Differences. Wide differences in the physical size of mares and stallions may cause difficulties during breeding. Because of the size difference, the stallion may repeatedly mount and then dismount, thus increasing the chance of injury. Short mares that are being bred to tall stallions can be placed on a slight mound in the breeding shed. In the opposite situation, the mare's hind legs can be placed near the back end of a shallow depression. The stallion can then stand on the edge of the depression and service the mare.

Breeding Area

When mares are hand bred, the area that is used for a breeding shed or paddock should be surfaced with a dust-free material and protected from wind or air drafts. The mare and stallion should be washed outside the breeding area to prevent the surface from becoming slick. Sufficient space is necessary to separate the mare from the stallion if she should "explode" unexpectedly because of the hobbles or the approach of the stallion. A

FIGURE 13-10
Breeding roll used to protect maiden mares from excessive penetration of the stallion during mating. Illustration by M. Morris.

a

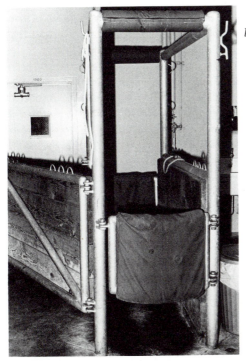

b

FIGURE 13-11
Palpation chute used during female
genital organ examinations – side
(*a*) and front (*b*) views. The chute
is also used to restrain a horse for
other purposes.

palpation chute (Figure 13-11), used to safely restrain mares and/or foals
during breeding preparations, such as genital organ examinations, Caslick
operations, artificial insemination, and hygiene procedures, should be
located adjacent to the breeding area for convenience. A properly designed chute allows a mare to keep her head inside a small foal holding
pen, thus preventing many disturbances among mares with foals at side.
The chute should also be designed so that it can be opened immediately
to free a horse.

411

13.3 Foaling

Pregnant Mare Care

The care of a pregnant mare for several weeks before foaling warrants special consideration. If possible, it is wise to keep the mare in an area where she can get an adequate amount of exercise to keep her muscles in tone. Mares that are used to being ridden can be ridden up until the time that they foal. During the last month, the exercise should not be strenuous. The feet and teeth should also receive proper attention, and good nutritional and health programs should be maintained.

Approximately one month before the expected foaling date, the mare should be checked to determine whether she has been sutured. If so, the sutures should be removed. Early removal will prevent an unexpected parturition in which the vulva is torn.

When the mare approaches her time to foal, she may be brought into a foaling stall or she may be placed in a large, clean, grassy paddock. Many mares foal on grass and seldom have any complications. Because horses are expensive and the expected foal is the result of a carefully planned mating, most mares are kept in a clean 12 ft × 14 ft foaling stall for approximately one week before foaling. The stall should be well lighted and free of any projections, such as nails or broken boards. The choice of bedding is important. Straw that is free of dust and cut in long lengths is preferred. Shavings and similar materials will stick to the wet nostrils of a newborn foal and may suffocate it.

Signs of Parturition

The signs of approaching parturition are not always reliable. Some mares show no signs and merely lie down and have their foal. The general indicators are as follows. Approximately 2–6 weeks before foaling, the udder becomes distended. A marked shrinkage of the muscles in the croup area occurs 7–10 days before foaling as a result of a general relaxation of the muscles and ligaments in the area of the pelvis. There is a tendency for the mare to leave a band of mares and want to be alone just before foaling. The teats fill out their nipples 4–6 days before foaling and wax builds up on the ends of the teats 2–4 days before foaling. Immediately before foaling (less than one day, but the number of hours varies), the wax may fall off and milk starts to drip. Finally, the mare becomes quite nervous, raises her tail and passes small amounts of urine quite frequently, appears to have cramps, breaks out in a sweat, and may walk around the stall in an anxious manner. The first water bag breaks, and 2–5 gallons of water are expelled. When the mare lies down, she may have her foal after a couple of contractions, or she may lie down and get up a couple of times before the foal is delivered (Figure 13-12). The entire process takes 10–20 minutes.

FIGURE 13-12
Delivery of a normal foal. Signs of approaching foaling: *a*, mare rolling; *b*, mare looking at her side; and *c*, mare sweating and kicking at her belly. The delivery: *d*, first appearance of the placenta; *e*, appearance of the forelegs; *f*, body of foal passing through the vulva; *g*, forelegs tearing placenta; *h*, placenta torn; *i*, mare getting up; *j*, mare up and navel cord broken.

a

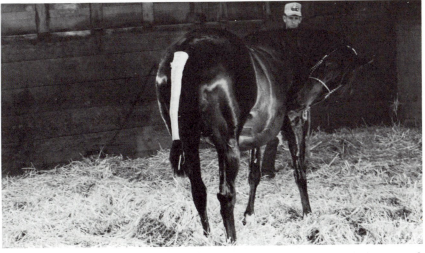

b

413

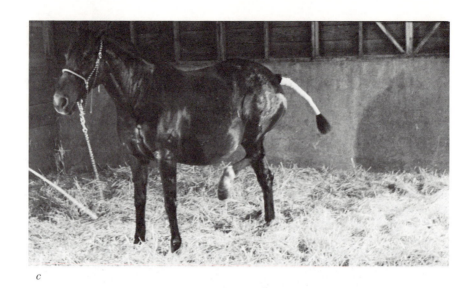

c

d

414

e

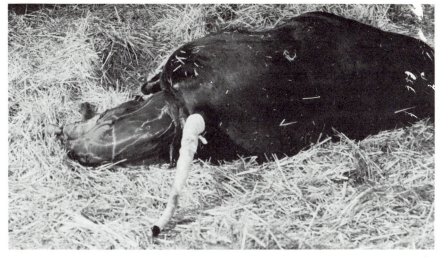

f

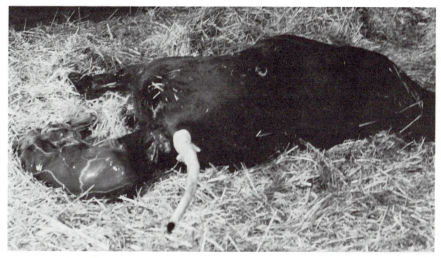

g

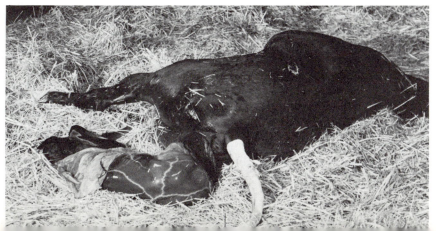

415

h

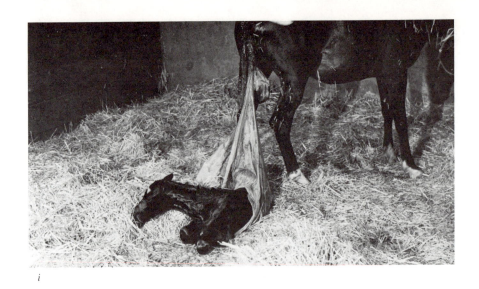

i

j

Foaling Problems

The normal position of the foal during delivery is shown in Figure 13-13. The forelegs are extended and the head and neck rest on them. The forelegs appear first, and the muzzle does not become visible until the legs are out approximately to the knees. The body is passed quite easily until the hips pass the mare's pelvis. As the hips pass, a slight delay in the rate of delivery usually occurs. When the foaling process starts, it is advisable to leave the mare alone unless she has trouble. Some indications

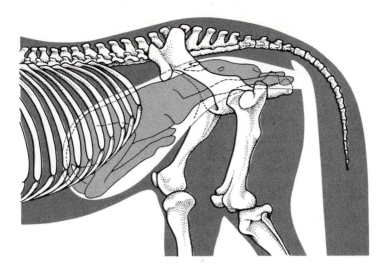

FIGURE 13-13
Normal position of a foal during foaling. The forelegs are
extended and the head and neck rest on the forelegs.

of trouble are: one foreleg out to the knee, two forelegs out but no head,
head out without forelegs, or prolonged labor without any parts visible.
At the first indication of trouble, an experienced person should be notified.
If the foaling attendant does not know what to do, he should not attempt
to correct the difficulty, but he should keep the mare up and moving until
help arrives.

The afterbirth should be passed by the mare within a couple of hours,
and it is usually passed 10–15 minutes post-foaling. If it is not, a veterinarian should be notified so that a treatment can be given to aid in its
passage. Manual removal will damage the uterus, and part of the placenta
may break off. Retention of the placenta or any part of it may lead to
founder. However, some mares will retain a portion of the placenta for
24 hours without ill effects. To be sure that the entire placenta has been
passed, it should be spread out on the floor or ground and visually examined to make sure that no part of it has been retained (Figure 13-14).

As soon as the placenta has passed, the mare that previously had her
vulva sutured should be resutured as soon as possible.

A few mares may display symptoms of colic within a few minutes of
foaling. These symptoms last for only a few minutes. The abdominal pain
is due to contraction of the uterine muscles. A mild sedative used for colic
may be used for severe cases.

Foal Care

Immediate Care. Upon delivery of the foal, it should be examined to
make sure that it is breathing. If necessary, the placenta should be re-

417

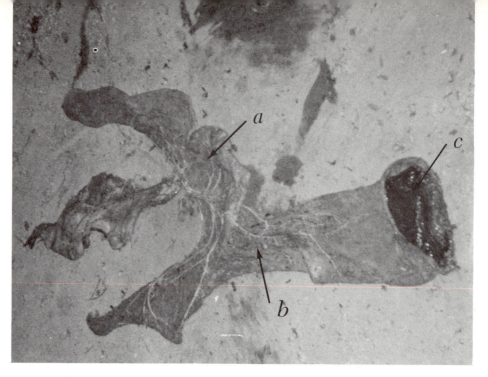

FIGURE 13-14
Placenta has been spread out on the ground to make sure that it is complete and that part of it has not been left in the mare: *a*, pregnant horn; *b*, body; *c*, point of rupture. Photograph courtesy of Patricia Barry.

moved from its nostrils and artificial respiration should be given immediately. Blowing into the foal's mouth or working its ribs as well as vigorously rubbing its body will stimulate respiration. In some cases, lifting up the foal and gently dropping it may start respiration.

Navel. The navel stump should be dipped in a tincture of 10 percent iodine. The navel cord should not be cut during delivery, but the foal should be allowed to break it to prevent excessive bleeding. The stump should be treated and examined for a few days after delivery. Lack of treatment or the presence of urine on the stump may lead to an infection, which in turn leads to navel ill. The urine on the stump is due to a failure of the urachus (Figure 11-12) to close and is referred to as pervious or persistent urachus. Silver nitrate applications usually result in prompt closure.

Tetanus. After treatment of the navel stump, a tetanus antitoxin is administered to the foal and mare. To avoid the antitoxin treatment, the mare can be given a tetanus toxoid booster shot approximately one month before foaling. Sufficient antibodies are formed to protect the mare and the foal (via colostrum). Some farms also administer a prophylactic dose of antibiotics, but the practice is controversial.

418

Nursing. The normal foal should stand and nurse within a few minutes. If the foal is not up and nursing by 2 hours after delivery, it should be helped up and guided to the mare's udder. It is important for the foal to receive the colostrum because it is a laxative and contains antibodies that protect the foal. The foal's digestive tract permits absorption of the colostrum antibodies for approximately 36 hours after birth.

Defecation. Within 4–12 hours after birth, the foal should pass the meconium, which is the fetal excrement. If the foal fails to eliminate the meconium or if constipation is evidenced by persistent straining and elevation of the tail, an enema consisting of 1 or 2 quarts of warm, soapy water should be given. The treatment should be repeated until yellow feces appear.

Eyes. Within 1 or 2 days after birth, some foals' eyes will start to water because the eyelids and lashes are turned in (a condition called entropion). The eyelids should be rolled out and an eye ointment rubbed in the eye.

Diarrhea. Diarrhea is a common problem of foals, particularly when the mare has her foal heat. If it ceases after the mare goes out of heat, no treatment is necessary. Persistent diarrhea should be treated by a veterinarian. Quite often a digestive disturbance occurs as a result of consumption of too much milk. Reducing the feed consumption of the mare or muzzling the foal for a few hours will eliminate the condition. A squirting type of diarrhea can dehydrate a foal and lead to death within a matter of hours.

Orphan Foals

Occasionally, a mare will die during foaling or shortly thereafter. If possible, the foal should be transferred to another mare. This is difficult unless a "nurse mare" is kept for foster mother qualities. Oil of linseed or whiskey poured over the foal will disguise the foal's odor so that another mare will let it suckle. On some farms, the use of a milk goat has been successful. If these methods are unsuccessful, the foal will have to be bottle fed (see section 10.7).

Weaning

The stress of weaning is reduced if the foal is fed grain and hay beginning a few days after birth. At 4–6 months, the foal is receiving a small percentage of its daily nutrient intake from the mare. If possible, it is desirable to wean 2 foals at the same time. By placing them in the same box stall or

419

paddock, they seem to fret less than foals weaned by themselves. The mare and foal should be separated so that they are unable to see or hear each other. After a week, the weaning process should be completed.

Once the mare and foal have been separated, the mare's feed should be reduced for a few days so that the "drying up" process takes less time. The mare should not be milked out because the udder will fill up and get tight. If the mare is too uncomfortable, an oil preparation containing spirits of camphor can be rubbed on the udder a couple of times a day for 4 or 5 days. After approximately one week, the udder should get soft and flabby. Some horsemen milk out the ½ to 1 cup of liquid left in the udder at the end of a week.

13.4   Stallion Contract

Since 1960, light horse production has become a lucrative business. It is not uncommon for mares to be shipped from coast to coast to be bred. Since the two parties who participate in breeding the mare seldom know or live close to each other, stallion owners are using contracts that specifically state the conditions under which the mare will be bred. The purpose of the contract is to prevent misunderstandings and hard feelings, and if it does not, it does not fulfill its intended purpose.

Most people are not familiar with legal terminology and the contract conditions for mating and thus do not fully understand the obligations of the stallion and the mare owners. The contract should be simply worded so that it is easy to understand and so that both parties know their obligations. All the terms and conditions should be clearly spelled out so there is no opportunity for misunderstandings or hard feelings. There are several items that should be included in a basic contract, but a contract should be written for a specific farm since circumstances are different for each farm.

The stallion and the mare should be clearly identified. The identification form should include the stallion's registration number and the name and address of the owner or lessee. The owner of the foal requires this information to complete the registration application. The stallion owner's name and address do not have to appear on the Breeder's Certificate since the manager of the stallion may sign it. If the manager of the stallion signs the Breeder's Certificate, it may be difficult to obtain the stallion owner's name and address at a later time. To complete the Stallion Breeding Report, it is necessary to know the mare's registration number and the recorded owner of the mare at the time of service. Following is a typical example of wording to obtain this information:

"The University of California, Department of Animal Science, Davis, California 95616, is willing to breed your mare, _____, Reg. No. _____, foaled in 19___, during the breeding season of February 1, 1974, to June 15, 1974, to the stallion, Mr. Bruce #97,545, owned by and standing at the Department of Animal Science, University of California, Davis, California, for $500.00 upon the following terms and conditions."

Other significant information is included in the "terms and conditions." The age of the mare is given so that the stallion manager will know if he needs to give the mare any special consideration, particularly if she is barren. A definite breeding season is stated. The limited season is important to the stallion owner so that the horse can be shown or used for other purposes during the remainder of the year. To help prevent overuse of a stallion, some owners will limit the number of times that a mare will be bred. Many mares are problem mares and simply will not conceive regardless of how many times they are bred, even though they appear to be normal. The location of the breeding farm where the stallion will stand for this breeding season is given so that the mare owner knows exactly where to deliver his mare. The stud fee and the terms and conditions of breeding are also stated.

In many instances, payment of a booking fee or deposit is required to validate the contract. The terms of its payment should be outlined in the contract. The fee may be due upon return of the contract at the time the mare is booked, or it may be due at a later date. The wording should clearly state whether the money is refundable. If it is, it is a booking deposit. If the mare does not conceive and the money is not refundable, it is a booking fee. High booking fees are a source of irritation to many mare owners, particularly if the mare goes home barren and the owner has encountered other excessive expenses for board, examination, vanning, trimming, and so on. Sometimes it is difficult for the stallion owner to decide the correct booking deposit or fee for a stallion because he wants to discourage the mare owner from changing his mind, forfeiting the deposit, and breeding his mare to another stallion.

Payment of the amount of the stud fee that is due after the booking fee or deposit has been paid should be outlined in detail. There are as many ways of handling it as there are stallion owners. It is quite common for Quarter Horse stud fees to be paid when the mare is returned home. Other farms are more lenient in obtaining payment. They may specify a given date as October 1 for payment, or the fee may be due when the foal is born. The stallion owner usually makes certain guarantees concerning pregnancy or birth that must be fulfilled before payment is due or a refund is given. A stallion owner's obligations may be considered completely ful-

421

filled if the mare is positively in foal at 45 days. In this author's opinion, the stallion owner has performed his responsibilities when the mare conceives and should not be financially responsible for later events leading to abortion that are beyond his control. A live foal guarantee means different things to different people, so the stallion owner's definition must be fully spelled out. The existence of a previously live foal is verified by a veterinarian if a piece of the dead foal's lung floats in water. With a live foal guarantee, the mare owner may have to make a critical decision at birth if the foal does not breathe immediately after presentation. Before artificial respiration is given or the foal is stimulated to breathe by other means, the owner or attendant must rapidly evaluate the foal for conformation and appearance to see if an attempt to save it is economical. In most cases, other feelings override economic decisions and an attempt is made to save the foal. It is common to see the conditions specified of a live foal that stands and nurses or that stands and nurses without assistance. These conditions usually mean that there is a reasonable chance for a healthy foal. Most farms require notification and/or certification by a licensed veterinarian within a short time of failure of live birth. If this is not forthcoming, the mare owner is held for payment of the stud fee. This is the reason many farms send a bill for the stud fee approximately 11 months after the last service when payment is due if a live foal is guaranteed. Other farms that have previously collected the stud fee require the certification before the fee is refunded. It is to the mare owner's benefit that the stud fee be returned within a given time of certification of live birth failure. Most stallion owners actually reserve an option to refund the fee or rebreed the mare only during the following season. This option allows the stallion to be sold without obligations to breed him with certain mares, to change the breeding fee, and/or to change the location of the stallion.

Another important condition of the contract may be that a Certificate of Service is not to be issued until the stud fee and all other charges that are due under the contract have been paid. This encourages the mare owner to pay his bills, for if he does not he cannot register the foal.

In addition to the stud fee, all other expenses that are to be paid by the mare owner should be specified. The daily rates for boarding the mare, or mare and foal, should be defined. Many breeding farms give the mare owner several options that vary in price so that he may decide whether the mare is to be kept at pasture, receive a certain type of hay, or receive grain. To ensure that the mare owner is aware, a statement should specify who is responsible for payment of examination fees to the veterinarian for determination of ovarian activity, pregnancy, and the presence of infections, as well as other veterinary services essential to the mare's health. One item that is seldom clarified in a contract is which party is responsible for artificial insemination expenses. The A.I. expenses should be paid by the stallion owner if he is using them to increase the number of mares bred to a stallion. The mare owner should expect to pay the fee for crippled mares, mares that are sutured to prevent windsucking, or mares that cannot be serviced naturally, and this is usually understood by the stallion owner when a statement is included to the effect that the stallion owner is authorized to have a veterinarian perform services that are conducive to the pregnancy of the mare. This statement will also include payment for worming and for floating the teeth of mares that are in poor physical condition. It is usually a good policy to state that the mare's feet will be trimmed and to specify the trimming fee.

Stallion owners usually include a clause stating that the mare must be healthy and in sound breeding condition. This is to protect the farm from a disease outbreak and to prevent use of the stallion to breed mares that will not conceive.

Almost all contracts should have a liability clause that releases the stallion owner and his agents from liability for illness, injury, or death, except in the case of negligence. The clause should also release the mare owner from liability if the mare injures the stallion during the breeding procedure.

13.5   Records

Each breed and registry has established a specific set of records that the breeding farm must keep. The information required to complete the forms can be collected from a basic set of farm records. A record of each mare should be maintained, which includes her name, registration number, sire and dam (with their registration numbers), birth date, color, peculiar characteristics, produce names, numbers, sex and date foaled, estrous cycle record (including dates in estrus, of ovulation, and of breeding), and health records. If the mare belongs to someone else and is to be bred to a stallion standing on the farm, the record should include the stallion owner's name, address, and telephone number, and his management procedures. A chronology of each stallion's breeding services should also be maintained. The breeding farm should also keep records to indicate the names and registration numbers of horses gelded, deaths, mares foaling, and barren mares. With each horse's records, a chart of its vaccinations, wormings, shoeing, and so on should be maintained.

13.6   Advertising

Advertising a stallion is important to his success at stud. The scope of the advertising will depend on the horse's record. Horses that bring low stallion fees are advertised on a local scale, whereas others that have displayed exceptional performance are advertised statewide, nationwide, or even worldwide. Breed or trade magazines that are circulated to people interested in the same type of horse as your stallion are utilized by most breeding farms. Horses demanding high stallion fees may be advertised by mailing advertisements to all the members of a particular registry. Inefficient use of the advertising budget results from overadvertising a stallion or placing advertisements in journals that do not circulate to the proper potential customers.

13.7   Training a Young Stallion

Training a young stallion to breed mares must be a carefully planned process. The stallion should be completely trained before the breeding season. The mare that is selected should be gentle and in definite estrus. The stallion's approach to the mare should be the same each time after he learns to mount a mare. During the first session, it may take him 30 minutes to an hour before he realizes that he can mount the mare. After a couple of sessions, most stallions know that they are going to breed the mare, and their behavior and approach to the mare should be controlled. During each session, the stallion should become accustomed to the teasing process, to encourage him to let down his penis, and to the hygiene procedure, so that he will stand and not kick the stud manager. With careful training, the stallion will be calm and less likely to injure the mare or the breeding management personnel.

References

Allen, W. R., and L. E. A. Roswon. 1973. Control of the mare's oestrous cycle by prostaglandins. *J. Reprod. Fert.* 33:539.

Andrist, F. 1962. *Mares, Foals and Foaling.* London: J. A. Allen.

Arthur, G. H. 1970. The induction of oestrus in mares by uterine infusion of saline. *Vet. Rec.* 86:584.

Burkhardt, J. 1947. Transition from anoestrus in the mare and the effects of artificial lighting. *J. Agric. Sci.* 37:64.

Evans, J. W. 1973. Stallion contracts. *Quarter Horse of the Pacific Coast* 10:35.

Jennings, James. 1975. I was born to be a horseman. *The Quarter Horse Journal* 28:194–202.

Laing, J. A. 1943. Observations on the survival of stored spermatozoa in the genital tract of the mare. *J. Agric. Sci.* 33:64.

Loy, R. G., and J. P. Hughes. 1966. The effects of human chorionic gonadotrophin on ovulation, length of estrus and fertility in the mare. *Cornell Vet.* 61:41.

McGee, W. R. *Veterinary Notes for the Standardbred Breeder.* Columbus, Ohio: United States Trotting Association.

Noden, P. A., H. D. Hafs, and W. D. Oxender. 1973. Progesterone, estrus and ovulation after prostaglandin F-2-alpha in horses. *Fed. Proc.* 32:229.

Rosborough, J. P. 1960. Breeding hygiene, procedures and practices. *Proceedings Illinois Short Courses for Horse Breeders,* p. 30.

Rossdale, P. D. 1973. Mares in breeding season. *The Thoroughbred of California* 61:42.

Wood, K. A. 1973. *The Business of Horses.* Chula Vista, California: Wood Publications.

Zemjanis, R. 1970. Examination of the Mare. *Diagnostic and Therapeutic Techniques in Animal Reproduction.* Baltimore: Williams and Wilkins.

PART FIVE *Genetics of the Horse*

CHAPTER FOURTEEN *Principles of Mendelian Inheritance*

An Austrian monk, Gregor Mendel, first worked out the principles of how genetic material is transmitted from one generation to the next. His experiments, reported in 1866, were done with the garden pea and were concerned with what are called simply inherited traits. His discoveries received widespread attention after 1900. Although most horsemen have at one time or another been exposed to these basic principles, a brief review is appropriate.

14.1   Transmission of Genetic Material

Genetic Material

Genetic material is transmitted from parents to their offspring. Each cell of a horse contains in its nucleus a complete copy of the horse's genetic material. The genetic material is contained in *chromosomes*, which are long, slender, threadlike structures that are paired although the pairs are not exact duplicates. Horses and ponies have 32 pairs of chromosomes; asses have 31 pairs. The karyotypes (preparations of the chromosomes) of a stallion and a mare are shown in Figure 14-1. The numbers of chromosomes for some other relatives of the horse are given in Table 14-1; their karyotypes are shown in Figure 14-2. These relatives, including 2 types of zebra (Grant's and Damara) having 44 chromosomes, are pictured in Figure 14-3.

Despite the difference in chromosome numbers, live hybrids have been born from crosses between all these species except for the crosses of Przewalski's horse with Grevy's zebra and with true zebras, and crosses

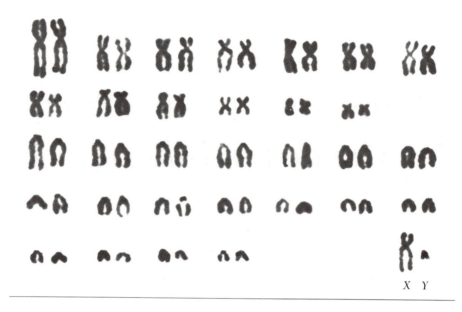

X Y

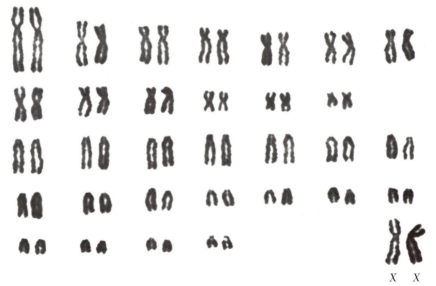

X X

FIGURE 14-1
Karyotypes of the horse: stallion (*top*) and mare (*bottom*). From Hsu and Benirschke. 1967.

430

TABLE 14-1
Numbers of chromosomes for some equine species

Scientific Name	Common Name or Names	Diploid Number of Chromosomes
Equus caballus, przewalskii	Przewalski's horse	66
Equus caballus	Horse	64
Equus asinus	Donkey, ass	62
Equus hemionus	Onager, kiang, Asiatic wild ass	56
Equus grevyi	Grevy's zebra	46
Equus burchelli	Burchell's zebra, Damara zebra, Chapman's zebra, Grant's zebra, Boehm's zebra	44
Equus zebra	Mountain zebra, true zebra, Hartmann's zebra	32

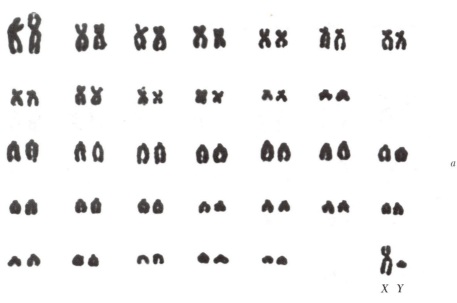

a

X Y

FIGURE 14-2
Karyotypes of some relatives of the horse: *a*, Przewalski's horse; *b*, donkey; *c*, onager; *d*, Grevy's zebra; *e*, Grant's zebra; *f*, mountain zebra. Photographs courtesy of Kurt Benirschke, University of California at San Diego, La Jolla, California.

(Figure 14-2 continued on overleaf)
431

b

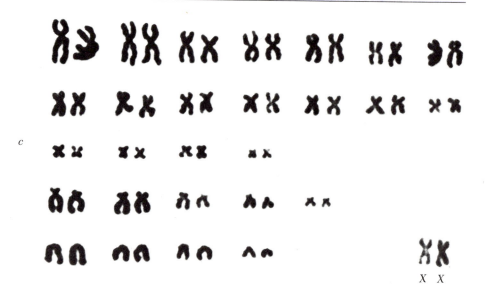

c

FIGURE 14-2 (*Continued*)

d

X Y

e

X Y

f

X Y

433

a

b

c

d

FIGURE 14-3
Some species related to the horse: *a*, Przewalski's horse; *b*, horse (American Paso Fino stallion); *c*, mammoth jack, *d*, onager; *e*, Grevy's zebra; *f*, Grant's zebra; *g*, Damara zebra; *h*, Hartmann's mountain zebra. Photographs *a* and *f* courtesy

f

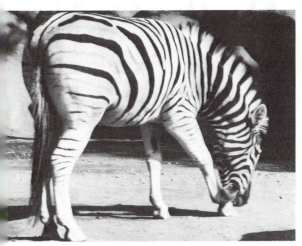

h

of Kurt Benirschke, University of California at San Diego, La Jolla, California; b, courtesy of M. L. Hirsch, Jr., Maryland Heights, Missouri; c, courtesy of American Donkey and Mule Society, Indianapolis, Indiana.

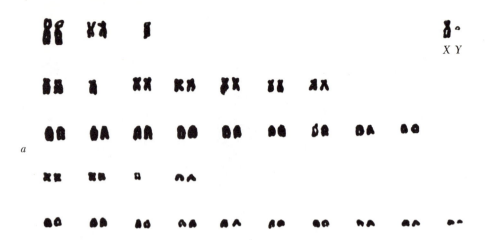

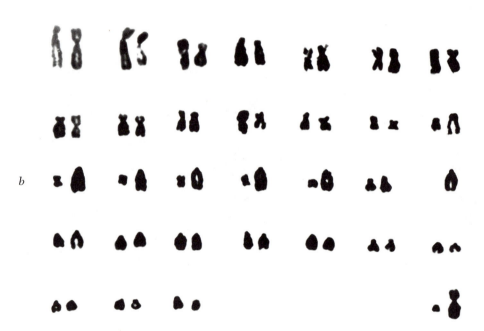

FIGURE 14-4
Karyotypes of hybrids from crosses between the horse and its relatives: *a*, horse and wild horse (Przewalski's horse) (2*n* = 65); *b*, jackass by mare (mule) (2*n* = 63); *c*, stallion by jennet (hinny) (2*n* = 63); *d*, male Grevy's zebra by mare (zebroid) (2*n* = 53); *e*, male Grant's zebra by jennet (zebronkey) (2*n* = 53). Photographs courtesy of Kurt Benirschke, University of California at San Diego, La Jolla, California.

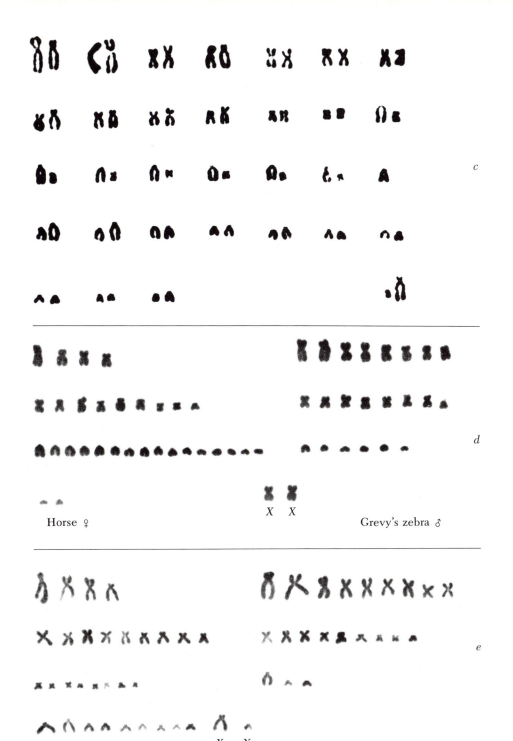

c

d

Horse ♀

X   X

Grevy's zebra ♂

e

Ass ♀

X   Y

Grant's zebra ♂

437

of Grevy's zebra with the onager and with Burchell's zebra (Gray, 1972). Reciprocal crosses have been reported for most of these combinations. Only hybrids between the horse and the Przewalski's horse have definitely been shown to be fertile. Reports of fertile mules have not been positively proved. Hybrids apparently are viable because the chromosome material is similar enough for all species, but the hybrids apparently cannot produce functional gametes because of synaptic failure due to rearrangement of the chromosome sets (Benirschke and Malouf, 1967). The karyotypes of some equid hybrids are shown in Figure 14-4.

A cross between a stallion and a jennet is called a hinny. A male hinny is shown in Figure 14-5a. The reciprocal cross, between a jackass and a mare, is known as a mule. A group of miniature mules from a burro jack and Shetland pony mares is pictured in Figure 14-5b. A cross between a Shetland pony and a zebra is shown in Figure 14-5c.

The *genes* that control the expression of traits of the horse are located along the chromosomes and correspond to chemical structures that determine individual traits. Since the chromosomes are paired, the genes are paired although the two genes that make up each pair may or may not be identical. Nonidentical genes that are located at the same physical position (*locus*) on a chromosome are called *alleles*.

In the transmission of the genetic material, germ cells (sperm in the male and ova in the female) are formed by a process called *reduction division*. These germ cells contain only one member of each chromosome or gene pair.

Assume that the top horse in Figure 14-6 carries as a pair the gene for black hair color, B, and the gene for chestnut (brown) hair color, b. The pair of genes at the location for black or brown color is not identical for this animal. The bottom horse carries two identical genes, BB.

When the paired genes are not identical, the animal is said to be *heterozygous* for that gene pair (horse on left in Figure 14-6). If the paired genes are identical, as in the horse on the right in Figure 14-6, the animal is *homozygous* for the gene pair. For genes at the B or b locus, a homozygous animal could be BB or bb.

Each cell of the heterozygous animal contains both B and b alleles: B on one chromosome and b on the paired chromosome. Thus, the two kinds of sperm or ova will be formed in equal numbers. The same pattern holds for all pairs of genes that control other traits except sex-linked traits, which will be discussed in section 14.2. The homozygous animal can produce only one kind of germ cell with respect to that gene pair.

The parent of the other sex produces germ cells that also contain unpaired chromosomes and genes. When union (fertilization) of a sperm and ovum occurs, the genes are again paired; one gene of each pair is contributed by the stallion and the other gene of the pair is contributed by the mare. As an example, suppose that a stallion that is BB is mated to a

438

a

b

FIGURE 14-5
Crosses between the horse and ass
and between the horse and zebra:
a, hinny from cross between a
Morgan stallion and a jennet;
b, unusual miniature mules from
cross between a burro jack and
Shetland pony mares; *c*, zeony
from cross between a zebra and a
Shetland pony. Photographs *a* and
b courtesy of American Donkey
and Mule Society, Indianapolis,
Indiana.

c

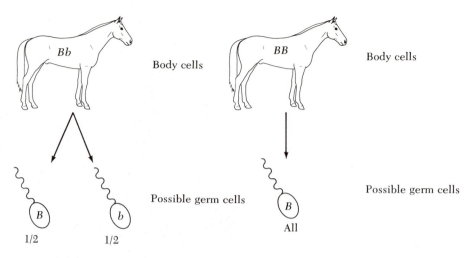

FIGURE 14-6
Formation of germ cells: from a heterozygous horse (*left*), and from a homozygous horse (*right*).

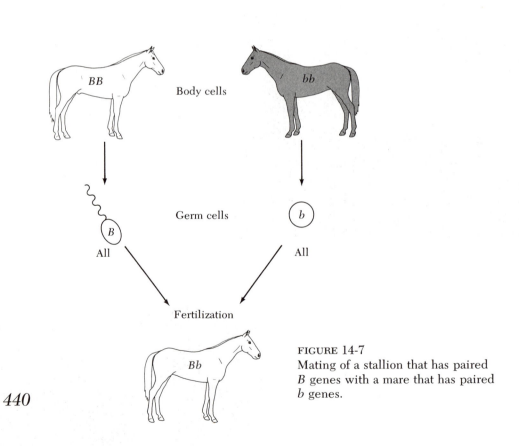

FIGURE 14-7
Mating of a stallion that has paired *B* genes with a mare that has paired *b* genes.

mare that is *bb*, as shown in Figure 14-7. In this example, the sperm produced by the stallion contain only the *B* gene, and all eggs produced by the mare contain only the *b* gene. The body cells of their foal, however, contain both the *B* and *b* genes.

Genotypic Frequencies

If the parents themselves have nonidentical paired genes at some locus, then, as in Figure 14-6, two kinds of germ cells are formed with respect to the different genes, and the genes of the offspring are determined by the chance union of two germ cells, one from each parent. The frequencies of each kind of union depend on the frequencies of the different kinds of germ cells. For example, suppose that two animals that are both heterozygous are mated, as shown in Figure 14-8. Notice that the frequency of the homozygous *BB* foals is $(1/2) \times (1/2) = 1/4$ or the frequency of *B* containing sperm times the frequency of *B* containing ova. Similar calculations can be made for the other three possible unions.

The mating of a homozygous mare (*bb*) with a heterozygous stallion (*Bb*) is shown in Figure 14-9. The expected frequency of *Bb* foals is $(1/2) \times (1) = 1/2$, or the frequency of the *B* containing sperm times the frequency of the *b* containing ova. Similarly, the expected frequency of *bb* foals is also $(1/2) \times (1) = 1/2$, or the frequency of *b* containing sperm times the frequency of *b* containing ova.

The mating between homozygotes was shown in Figure 14-7. Mating of like homozygotes (*BB* × *BB*) or (*bb* × *bb*) will result in progeny that are homozygous, the same as the parents.

When there are two alleles at a locus, there are six possible matings, as shown in Table 14-2. The expected frequencies of foals can be computed using the principles illustrated in Figures 14-7, 14-8, and 14-9.

The proportions of foals from various matings are those that may be expected if many such matings are made. Any particular mating might, however, give considerably different proportions. Suppose that a mating is *Bb* × *Bb* and only two foals are obtained. Some two-foal families would both be *BB*, some would be all *bb*, and others would have various proportions of the three genotypes, all by chance. Nevertheless, average proportions for a large number of offspring would be close to the expected proportions of 1/4 *BB*, 1/2 *Bb*, and 1/4 *bb*.

Phenotypic Expression

What the animals look like (that is, their *phenotypes*) in relation to their genotypes has not yet been described in this chapter. How the phenotype

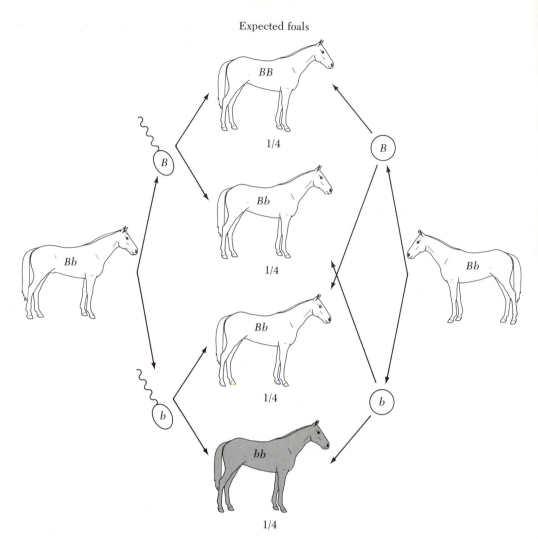

Expected foals

FIGURE 14-8
The frequency of different offspring expected when two heterozygotes are mated.

is related to the genotype can be explained by giving some examples. For two alleles at a locus, there are three usual types of gene action.

Dominance. First consider an example of a dominant gene—the gene for black coat color, *B*. The allelic gene for brown (chestnut) color is *b*. Figure 14-10 shows the three possible genotypes and their corresponding phenotypes. Two "black" genes result in a black horse. Two "chestnut" genes result in a chestnut horse. However, one "black" and one "chestnut" gene also result in a black horse. Thus, the "black" gene is *dominant* over the "chestnut" gene and masks any effect of the "chestnut" gene. The

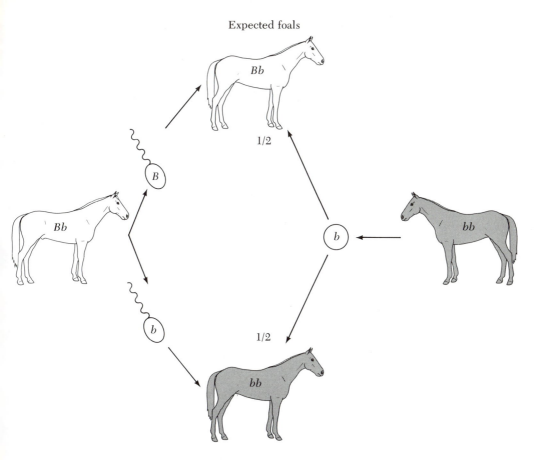

Expected foals

FIGURE 14-9
The frequency of different offspring expected when a homozygote and a
heterozygote are mated.

TABLE 14-2
Expected frequencies of foals from the 6 possible matings for
2 alleles at a single locus

First Parent		Second Parent	Expected Frequencies of Foals
BB	×	BB	All BB
BB	×	Bb	1/2 BB + 1/2 Bb
BB	×	bb	All Bb
Bb	×	Bb	1/4 BB + 1/2 Bb + 1/4 bb
Bb	×	bb	1/2 Bb + 1/2 bb
bb	×	bb	All bb

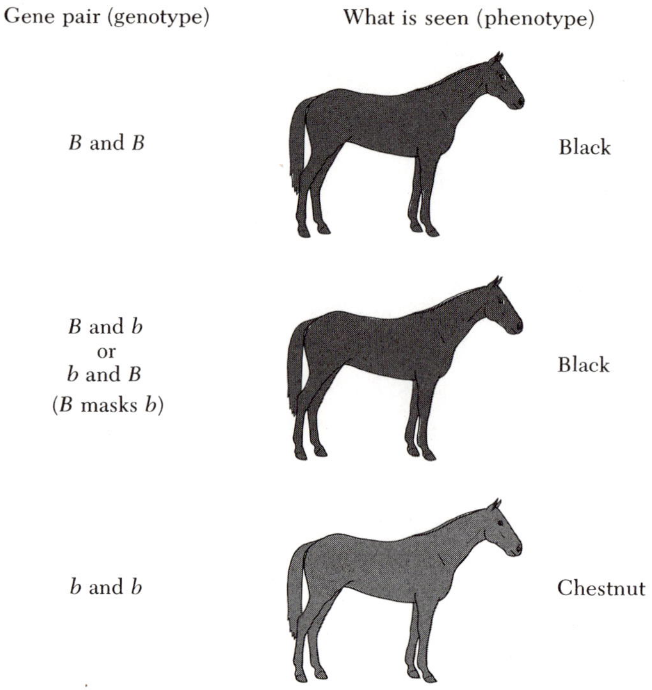

Gene pair (genotype)	What is seen (phenotype)

B and B — Black

B and b
or
b and B
(B masks b) — Black

b and b — Chestnut

FIGURE 14-10
Correspondence of genotype and phenotype for dominant
gene action.

gene that is masked is said to be *recessive*. Many genes that affect simply
inherited traits are dominant or recessive.

Codominance. The type of gene action that causes the phenotype of the
heterozygote to be intermediate between those of either homozygote is
called codominance. In some cases, the heterozygote has features of both
homozygotes. For example, in the horse, two codominant alleles control
the kind of serum albumin found in the blood. Let Alb^A be the gene for
production of albumin Type A and Alb^B be the gene for production of
albumin Type B. The phenotypes for the three genotypes are given in
Table 14-3. Neither Alb^A nor the Alb^B gene is dominant. Both are expressed
if present, so they are called codominant genes.

Partial Dominance. Another form of gene action that is similar to codominance is called partial dominance. The heterozygote is intermediate between the two homozygotes although not necessarily exactly intermediate
as with codominance.

The dilution gene (D) that gives the palomino color pattern is an example. This gene is located at a chromosome location different from the
location for black and chestnut. Figure 14-11 shows the effects of no dilu-

444

TABLE 14-3
Correspondence of genotype and phenotype for codominant
gene action

Genotype	Phenotype
Alb^A and Alb^A	All albumin Type A
Alb^A and Alb^B	Both albumin Type A and albumin Type B
Alb^B and Alb^B	All albumin Type B

tion genes, of one dilution gene, and of two dilution genes when a horse
has the genetic makeup for chestnut, *bb*.

The *dd* genotype causes no change in the chestnut color; that is, it allows
complete expression of the chestnut genotype. One *D* gene causes a dilution of the chestnut color to the newly minted gold dollar color of the
palomino, whereas two *D* genes cause even more dilution to an almost
white color, which is called cremello or, incorrectly, albino.

The dilution gene similarly affects horses that are genetically bays, as
shown in Figure 14-12. The genetics of bay and other color patterns will
be discussed in Chapter 15.

FIGURE 14-11
The effect of the dilution gene on coat color of horses that
are genetically chestnut.

Genotype   Phenotype

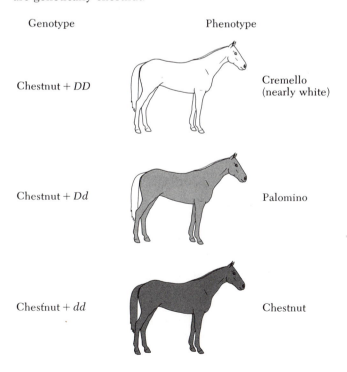

Chestnut + DD   Cremello (nearly white)

Chestnut + Dd   Palomino

Chestnut + dd   Chestnut

445

Genotype   Phenotype

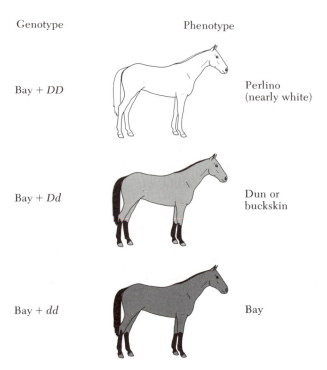

Bay + DD   Perlino
                                            (nearly white)

Bay + Dd   Dun or
                                            buckskin

Bay + dd   Bay

FIGURE 14-12
The effect of the dilution gene on coat color of horses
that are genetically bay.

The dun and buckskin single dilutions of bay occur with the dark manes and tails associated with the bay pattern, whereas the palomino pattern occurs with white or flaxen manes and tails. Again, two D genes cause more than twice the dilution of one D gene.

Multiple Alleles

There are more than 2 alleles possible at many loci. For example, the blood transferrin system contains 6 codominant alleles and the bay-seal brown-black color pattern system contains 3 alleles with an order of dominance. When allelic genes are codominant or partially dominant, each genotype produces a distinctive phenotype. In the transferrin system, there are 21 possible genotypes and 21 corresponding phenotypes. In the bay color system, there are 6 genotypes but only 3 phenotypes because of dominance. The heterozygous genotypes have the same phenotypes as the homozygous genotype containing the most dominant gene.

446

14.2   Sex Determination and Sex Linkage

Sex Determination

One pair of chromosomes is responsible for the sex of the foal. Thus, these chromosomes are referred to as the sex chromosomes. This is the only pair that is not visually identical when karyotyped, as can be seen in Figure 14-1. The pair of chromosomes of the mare is designated XX and the pair of the stallion is designated XY. The stallion has the unmatched pair. The mechanism of transmission of X and Y chromosomes from parent to offspring is exactly the same as for the genes described in section 14.1 and is illustrated in Figure 14-13.

The mare produces ova, all of which contain an X chromosome, although the paired genes on the paired X chromosomes may be different alleles. The sperm are of two kinds and occur in equal numbers—those containing the X chromosome and those containing the Y chromosome. Since very few, if any, genes are known to be carried on the Y chromosome, female offspring will have exact duplicates of the X chromosome of their father.

Some traits are *sex limited*. For example, only females produce milk; only males can be cryptorchid. Other traits are modified by the sex of the animal and are called *sex-influenced* traits. Some color patterns of the Appaloosa, for instance, are much brighter in males than in females although the genotypes for the trait are the same. Still other traits are *sex linked*; that is, they are transmitted on the X chromosome.

Sex Linkage

Hemophilia of the horse is a sex-linked trait and will be used as an example of sex linkage. Hemophilia (bleeders' disease) is the inability of the blood to clot in a normal amount of time; thus, most hemophilic horses do not live to reproduce so that the trait is essentially a sex-linked lethal trait. Other sex-linked traits may not be lethal. The hemophilia gene is a recessive gene in the female, but in the male it is dominant because, being located on the X chromosome, the gene for hemophilia does not have a "normal" paired gene on the Y chromosome. Suppose that X^H is the normal clotting allele. Then males will be of two types, X^HY (nonbleeder) and X^hY (bleeder), where X indicates the chromosome on which the gene is carried. The Y chromosome does not contain an allele for clotting or nonclotting. Mares will have one of three possible genotypes: X^HX^H, X^HX^h, and X^hX^h. Only the X^hX^h type will be hemophilic. Note that for a mare to be hemophilic, each parent must contribute the hemophilia

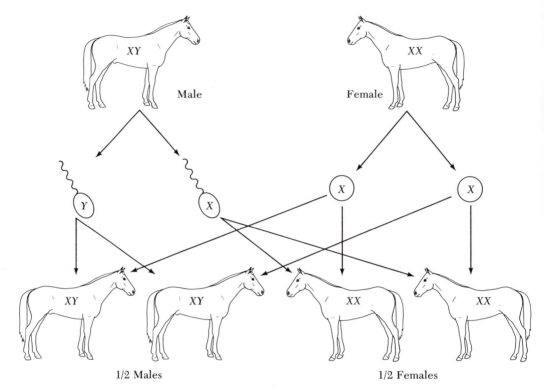

FIGURE 14-13
Sex determination depends on presence of the Y chromosome.

gene, so that the sire of a hemophilic mare would have to be a bleeder. A hemophilic stallion, on the other hand, receives the "bleeder" gene from his dam, which may be heterozygous but exhibits normal clotting of the blood. For all practical purposes, all affected animals die before reproduction; thus, only mating of normal stallions to heterozygous mares can produce hemophilics. Only male offspring will be affected, although heterozygous females also may be produced, as illustrated in Figure 14-14.

Sex-linked traits that are not lethal can be diagrammed similarly. In general, the frequency of the trait will be much higher in stallions than in mares. If q is the frequency of the sex-linked, nonlethal, recessive allele, then a fraction q of the males will have the trait, but the fraction of the females having the trait will be only q^2. These fractions are shown in Table 14-4.

448

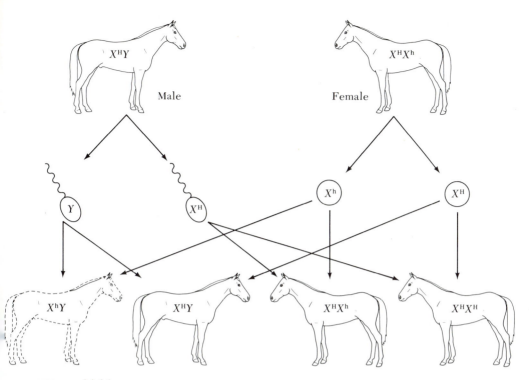

FIGURE 14-14
Transmission of hemophilia from a carrier mare to one-half of her sons. One-half of her daughters will be carriers of the hemophilia gene.

TABLE 14-4
Frequency of nonlethal, sex-linked, recessive traits in males and females

Frequency of Gene q	Frequency of Trait	
	In Males q	In Females q^2
0	0	0
.1	.1	.01
.2	.2	.04
.3	.3	.09
.4	.4	.16
.5	.5	.25
.6	.6	.36
.7	.7	.49
.8	.8	.64
.9	.9	.81
1.0	1.0	1.00

14.3   Combinations of Traits

Independent Loci

Often a combination of loci rather than a single loci is involved in a mating. A simple rule holds for finding the expected results for more than one locus if the genes at one locus are independent of the genes at another locus, that is, carried on different chromosomes or far apart if on the same chromosome. The rule is to multiply the expected results at one locus by the expected results of the other locus, the multiplication continuing for all loci.

As an example, consider the dilution gene, D, and the gene for straight hair, S, which is dominant to the gene for curly hair, s. Assume that the other color loci are homozygous for chestnut, so that those loci can be ignored, and that two Palominos are mated, one of which is heterozygous for the gene for straight hair and one of which is homozygous for curly hair, that is, $DdSs \times Ddss$.

The expected genotypic results for the "color" locus are $[(1/2)(D) + (1/2)(d)] \times [(1/2)(D) + (1/2)(d)] = (1/4)(DD) + (1/2)(Dd) + (1/4)(dd)$. The expected phenotypic results are 1/4 cremello + 1/2 palomino + 1/4 chestnut.

The expected results for the "hair" locus are $[(1/2)(S) + (1/2)(s)] \times [(1)(s)] = (1/2)(Ss) + (1/2)(ss)$. The expected phenotypic results are 1/2 with straight hair and 1/2 with curly hair.

The expected joint frequencies for the 6 genotypes are $[(1/4)(DD) + (1/2)(Dd) + (1/4)(dd)] \times [(1/2)(Ss) + (1/2)(ss)] = (1/8)(DDSs) + (1/8)(DDss) + (1/4)(DdSs) + (1/4)(Ddss) + (1/8)(ddSs) + (1/8)(ddss)$.

The expected frequencies of the joint phenotypes can be found by adding the frequencies of genotypes that look alike. In this example, the phenotypic frequencies are the same as the genotypic frequencies, but in other examples this would not be true. For example, if the second animal were heterozygous for the curly hair gene, there would be 9 possible genotypes but only 6 phenotypes. Another way to find the joint phenotypic frequencies is to multiply the phenotypic results for each locus together. For example, (1/4 cremello + 1/2 palomino + 1/4 chestnut) × (1/2 straight hair + 1/2 curly hair) = 1/8 cremello straight hair + 1/8 cremello curly hair + 1/4 palomino straight hair + 1/4 palomino curly hair + 1/8 chestnut straight hair + 1/8 chestnut curly hair.

Epistasis

The joint phenotypic frequencies will be different if the genes at one locus affect the expression of genes at another locus, a form of gene action called *epistasis*. The rule is to obtain the genotypic frequencies as before, then examine these to determine the phenotypes. An example is the gene for white, W. (There is no true albino gene in horses. Horses with the W gene have colored eyes.) The W gene masks any other colors that may be present. In addition, when homozygous for W, the fetus is reabsorbed before birth so that no WW animals are born, which results in an apparent lowered conception rate. A homozygote for ww will express the color determined by the other loci.

Suppose that a white stallion that is heterozygous for black is mated to a white mare that is also heterozygous for black (both $WwBb$). The results at the "white" locus are, for genotypic frequencies, $[(1/2)(W) + (1/2)(w)] \times [(1/2)(W) + (1/2)(w)] = (1/4)(WW) + (1/2)(Ww) + (1/4(ww)$, and for phenotypic frequencies, 1/4 no foal + 1/2 white + 1/4 color. The results at the "black and chestnut" locus are, for genotypic frequencies, $[(1/2)(B) + (1/2)(b)] \times [(1/2)(B) + (1/2)(b)] = (1/4)(BB) + (1/2)(Bb) + (1/4)(bb)$, and for phenotypic frequencies, 3/4 black + 1/4 chestnut. The joint genotypic results are $[(1/4)(WW) + (1/2)(Ww) + (1/4)(ww)] \times [(1/4)(BB) + (1/2)(Bb) + (1/2)(bb)] = (1/16)(WWBB) + (1/8)(WwBB) + (1/16)(wwBB) + (1/8)(WWBb) + (1/4)(WwBb) + (1/8)(wwBb) + (1/16)(WWbb) + (1/8)(Wwbb) + (1/16)(wwbb)$. The joint phenotypic frequencies are $[(1/16)(WWBB) + (1/8)(WWBb) + (1/16)(WWbb)] = 1/4$ no foal, $[(1/8)(WwBB) + (1/4)(WwBb) + (1/8)(Wwbb)] = 1/2$ white, $[(1/16)(wwBB) + (1/8)(wwBb)] = 3/16$ black, and $(1/16)(wwbb) = 1/16$ chestnut. If only live foals are counted, 2/3 are white, 1/4 are black, and 1/12 are chestnut, since 1/4 of the matings will not produce a live foal to be counted.

A gene that masks the effect of another gene at a different locus is said to be *epistatic* to the masked gene; that is, in the example just described, the gene for white is epistatic to the genes for black and chestnut.

Linked Genes

The simple formula for finding genotypic results with respect to several loci will not work if the loci are linked. Linkage or a tendency for genes at certain loci to be inherited together occurs when the loci are near each other on the same chromosome. The phenomenon of crossing over (exchange of genetic material on corresponding parts) between the members of a pair of paired chromosomes in the production of germ cells does, however, result in some recombination of genes from the linked loci. The frequency of recombination of genes depends on the distance between loci. Since horses have only 32 pairs of chromosomes, many genes must be linked on the same chromsomes. In spite of this, no important linkages have been found. Thus, no further discussion of linkage is warranted here. Any standard genetic text will provide more explanation of linkage maps showing distances between loci on the same chromosome and techniques for determining the map distances.

451

14.4   Selection for Dominant and Recessive Genes

The major problem in selection for simply inherited traits is selection against recessive genes. Dominant genes can obviously be selected against very easily because all animals with the dominant gene can be readily identified.

Sex-linked recessive genes can also be eliminated quite quickly. All males as well as all homozygous females with the gene can be identified and culled. Unless female carriers are preferred to the homozygous normal females, the result is that the frequency of the sex-linked recessive gene will decrease by 1/2 each generation. Similarly, the frequency of affected males drops by 1/2 each generation, and no affected females are born—as long as no affected males are used in the breeding program. The decrease may be a little more rapid if mares that have affected foals are also culled.

Elimination of non-sex-linked recessive genes is more difficult because heterozygous carriers cannot be readily identified. Even then, simply eliminating all affected individuals (those homozygous for the recessive gene) can be quite effective. If q is the frequency of the recessive gene, then the frequency of affected animals is q^2. After n generations of selection, the frequency of the gene is $[q/(1 + nq)]$ and the frequency of affected animals is $[q/(1 + nq)]^2$. This formula works as long as the phenotypically normal carrier animals are not preferred to the homozygous normal animals.

Elimination of recessive genes can be increased by testing for carriers —especially males—and then using only those males that have a high chance of not being a carrier. Testing does require time and effort.

The best method of testing to identify carrier males is through test mating by artificial insemination (A.I.) to a random sample of mares. Because A.I. has not been widely practiced with horses, this method will not be discussed here. A discussion of A.I. testing programs for recessives in dairy cattle populations that would also be applicable for horses may be found in Chapter 9 of *Principles of Dairy Science* by Schmidt and Van Vleck (1974).

The problem of detecting carriers is obvious. There is no way to tell the difference between a "normal" horse with two desirable genes and a "normal" horse that carries one undesirable gene in addition to the one desirable gene. A carrier, however, will transmit the undesirable gene to half of his foals.

A carrier stallion is identified if he sires at least one undesirable foal, since any affected foal must have received one undesirable gene from the stallion as well as one from its dam. If the carrier stallion is mated to a group of mares, the expected proportion of normal and undesirable foals can be determined if the proportion of ova carrying the desirable and un-

TABLE 14-5
Chances of detecting a carrier stallion from various types of matings

Number of Foals n	Detects Only One Recessive		Detects All Recessives
	Mating to Homozygous Recessive Mares $1 - (1/2)^n$	Mating to Known Carrier Mares $1 - (3/4)^n$	Mating to Own Daughters $1 - (7/8)^n$
1	.50	.25	.12
2	.75	.44	.23
3	.88	.58	.33
4	.94	.68	.41
5	.97	.76	.49
6	.98	.82	.55
7	.99	.87	.61
8	~1.00	.90	.66
9		.92	.70
10		.94	.74
15		.99	.87
20		1.00	.93
50			~1.00

desirable genes is known. This proportion can be determined for the testing methods described in the remainder of this section.

Mating to Homozygous Recessive Mares

The chance of obtaining a normal foal by mating a carrier stallion to a homozygous recessive mare is 1/2, as shown in Figure 14-9. Thus, the chance of obtaining all normal foals by mating a carrier stallion to n homozygous recessive mares is $(1/2)^n$, since the type of foal in each birth is independent of the type of foal in other births. This probability is the chance of not obtaining any undesirable foals, and thus is the chance of *not* detecting a carrier from the foals produced by n matings to homozygous recessive mares. The chance of detection plus the chance of nondetection must be 1. Therefore, the chance of detecting a carrier is $1 - (1/2)^n$. See Table 14-5 for a listing of chances of detection for different numbers of matings.

Mating to Known Carrier Mares

Another method is to mate the stallion to known carrier mares—of the type Bb. The chance of obtaining all normal foals out of n foals will be $(3/4)^n$. The chance of detection will be $1 - (3/4)^n$, as indicated in Table 14-5.   *453*

Mating to Own Daughters

A third method is to mate a stallion to his own daughters. This method provides an equal chance of detecting all recessive genes that the stallion may be carrying. For a specific recessive gene, mating a stallion to daughters of a known carrier stallion is equivalent to mating to his own daughters.

In calculating the chance of detection by mating a stallion to his own daughters, both genes of each of his original mates are assumed to be normal. The result, as shown in Figure 14-15, is that half the daughters will be carriers if the stallion is a carrier. The chance of the undesirable trait appearing in a foal when a carrier stallion is mated to a daughter is 1/8, and the chance of obtaining n normal foals from n such matings is $(7/8)^n$. The chance of detecting a carrier stallion from matings to his own daughters is $1 - (7/8)^n$, as shown in Table 14-5.

Noncarrier Cannot Be Proved

A noncarrier stallion can never produce a foal with an undesirable trait caused by a recessive gene. Thus, any stallion with an undesirable foal is immediately labeled a carrier. A stallion, on the other hand, can never be completely proved to be a noncarrier. There will always be some small chance of nondetection no matter how many normal foals he sires.

The principles discussed in this chapter will be applied in Chapter 15 in the discussion of parentage tests and color inheritance and in the listings of simply inherited lethal and semilethal traits.

14.5   Practice Problems

Problem 1

Assume gene action at three loci to be:

WW   Dies early after fertilization
Ww   White, epistatic to all other colors
ww   Allows color

BB   Black
Bb   Black
bb   Chestnut

OO   Solid color
Oo   Solid color
oo   Recessive, causes white spotting on all colors

Step 1: Original mating

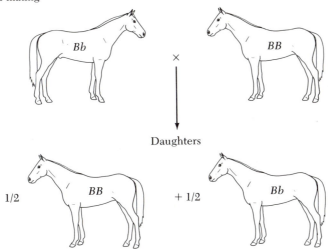

Daughters

Step 2: Mating to daughters from original matings

Daughters

FIGURE 14-15
Detecting a carrier stallion from matings to his own daughters.

Suppose that a white stallion and a white mare are mated and that both are heterozygous for the black gene and the recessive white spotting gene, that is, $WwBbOo \times WwBbOo$. What are the expected frequencies of possible genotypes of live offspring? What are the possible phenotypes and expected frequencies?

Problem 2

Repeat Problem 1, assuming that the stallion is $WwBboo$.

455

Problem 3

The red blood cells of the horse and the donkey carry an enzyme known as glucose-6-phosphate dehydrogenase (G-6-PD). The horse has one kind of G-6-PD and the donkey a distinctly different kind of G-6-PD. The genes that control for G-6-PD are sex linked. The G-6-PD genes of the horse and the donkey are codominant.

What will be the G-6-PD phenotype for a male produced from a cross between a jack and a mare? What will be the phenotype of a female offspring? The phenotype of a male produced from a cross between a stallion and a jennet? The phenotype of a female offspring?

References

Anderson, W. S. 1939. Fertile mare mules. *J. Heredity* 30:549.

Archer, R. K. 1961. True haemophilia (haemophilia A) in a Thoroughbred foal. *Vet. Record* 73:338.

Auerbach, C. 1961. *The Science of Genetics*. New York: Harper & Row.

Baldwin, J. T., Jr. 1957. An early report of a fertile female mule. *J. Heredity* 39:84.

Bartlett, O. 1963. Zeehorses and zebronkeys. *Animals* 2:394.

Benirschke, K., L. E. Brownhill, and M. M. Beath. 1962. Somatic chromosomes of the horse, the donkey, and their hybrids, the mule and hinny. *J. Reprod. Fert.* 4:319.

Benirschke, K., R. J. Low, L. E. Brownhill, L. B. Caday, and J. DeVenecia-Fernandez. 1964. Chromosome studies of a donkey-Grevy zebra hybrid. *Chromosoma* 15:1.

Benirschke, K., R. J. Low, M. M. Sullivan, and R. M. Carter. 1964. Chromosome study of an alleged fertile mare mule. *J. Heredity* 55:31.

Benirschke, K., and N. Malouf. 1957. Chromosome studies of equidae. In *Equus*. H. Dathe, ed. Vol. 1, No. 2. Berlin: Tierpark.

Blakeslee, L. H., R. S. Hudson, and R. H. Hunt. 1943. Curly coat of horses. *J. Heredity* 34:115.

Bonadonna, T. 1966. The interspecific and reciprocal crossing horse-donkey and the fertility of resulting hybrids. *World Review of Animal Production* 3:46.

Cradock-Watson, J. E. 1967. Immunological similarity of horse, donkey, and mule haemoglobins. *Nature* 215:630.

Craft, W. A. 1938. The sex ratio in mules and other hybrid mammals. *Quart. Rev. Biol.* 13:19.

Gray, A. P. 1972. *Mammalian Hybrids.* Slough, England: Commonwealth Agricultural Bureaus, Farnham Royal.

Groth, A. H. 1928. A fertile mare mule. *J. Heredity* 19:413.

Heck, H. 1952. The breeding of the Tarpan. *Oryx* 1:338.

Hsu, T. C., and K. Benirschke. 1967. *An Atlas of Mammalian Chromosomes.* New York: Springer-Verlag.

Hutt, F. B. 1964. *Animal Genetics.* New York: Ronald Press.

Johansson, I., and J. Rendel. 1968. *Genetics and Animal Breeding.* San Francisco: Freeman.

Jones, W. E., and R. Bogart. 1971. *Genetics of the Horse.* East Lansing, Michigan: Caballus.

King, J. M., R. V. Short, O. E. Mutton, and J. L. Hamerton. 1965. The reproductive physiology of male zebra-horse and zebra-donkey hybrids. *J. Reprod. Fert.* 9:391.

Lasley, J. F. 1972. *Genetics of Livestock Improvement.* Englewood Cliffs, New Jersey: Prentice-Hall.

Lloyd-Jones, O. 1916. Mules that breed. *J. Heredity* 7:494.

Lydekker, R. 1912. *The Horse and Its Relatives.* New York: Macmillan.

Makino, S. 1943. Notes on the cytological feature of male sterility in the mule. *Experentia* 11:224.

Martin, G. H., Jr. 1962. The zebronkey: A riddle of science? *Univ. Philippines Vet.* 7:23.

Petzsch, H. 1962. Birth of a zebroid from a ♀ ass mated with a ♂ Grant's zebra. *Saugetierk. Mitt.* 10:61.

Rice, V. A., F. N. Andrews, E. J. Warwick, and J. E. Legates. 1970. *Breeding and Improvement of Farm Animals.* New York: McGraw-Hill.

Roberts, E. 1929. Zebra-horse cross. *J. Heredity* 20:12.

Sangor, V. L., R. E. Mairs, and A. L. Trapp. 1964. Hemophilia in a foal. *J. Am. Vet. Med. Assoc.* 142:259.

Schmidt, G. H., and L. D. Van Vleck. 1974. *Principles of Dairy Science.* San Francisco: Freeman.

Smith, H. H. 1939. Fertile mule from Arizona. *J. Heredity* 30:548.

Trujillo, J. M., C. Stenius, L. Christian, and S. Ohno. 1962. Chromosomes of the horse, the donkey, and the mule. *Chromosoma* 13:243.

Trujillo, J. M., Betty Walden, Peggy O'Neil, and H. B. Anstall. 1965. Sex-linkage of glucose-6-phosphate dehydrogenase in the horse and donkey. *Science* 148:1603.

Trujillo, J. M., Betty Walden, Peggy O'Neil, and H. B. Anstall. 1967. Inheritance and sub-unit composition of haemoglobin in the horse, donkey, and their hybrids. *Nature* 213:88.

CHAPTER FIFTEEN *Some Mendelian Traits: Blood Factors, Colors, Lethals*

Most breeders are usually interested in one or more of three types of genetic effects that are simply inherited. Everyone is concerned about lethal or semilethal traits. If caused by a single gene, these traits can be eliminated by the procedures described in section 14.4. Such traits will be listed in section 15.3. Breeders of the color breeds, such as the Appaloosa, Buckskin, Palomino, Pony of the Americas, Pinto, and Paint, are especially concerned with the color genes to maintain the established breed colors or to breed for more fashionable colors. Many other breeders also have marked preferences for certain colors. Color inheritance will be discussed in section 15.2. The other main area of interest of breeders is tests of parentage. Simply inherited traits can be used successfully in many cases of disputed parentage—not to prove parentage, but to exclude some animals as possible parents. The most useful traits for parentage tests, in addition to the obvious color traits, are the types of blood proteins, enzymes, antigens, and antibodies. The potential and limitations of these traits for parentage testing will be described in the next section, but not from a technical point of view.

15.1 Genetic Tests for Disputed Parentage

Differences in at least 21 physiological characteristics of blood are known to be the result of alleles at as many loci. Eight loci control the blood antigen systems listed in Table 15-1. The details of the laboratory procedures for determining these blood factors are complicated but have been elucidated by many researchers, including Stormont and his colleagues at the University of California at Davis, the location of the only blood typing

458

TABLE 15-1
Genetic loci that control blood antigen systems

Blood Antigen Locus Symbol	Known Alleles	No. of Phenotypes	Comments
A	$a^{A_1}, a^{A'}, a^H, a^{A'H}, a$	8	All are dominant to a; remainder are codominant to each other. $a^{A'H}$ will give the same phenotype as $a^{A'}a^H$.
C	c^C, c	2	Dominant.
D	$d^{Sw10,E}, d^{Sw10}, d^{Sw14,D}$ $d^{Sw10,J}, d^{Sw14,J}, d^{Sw14}$	21	The J, E, and D types are codominant but dominant to their absence. The Sw10 and Sw14 characters are codominant.
K	k^K, k	2	Dominant.
P	$p^{P_1}, p^{P'}, p$	4	All are dominant to p; remainder are codominant.
Q	$q^Q, q^R, q^S, q^{QR}, q^{RS}, q$	8	All are dominant to q; others are codominant but different combinations can give same phenotype—not very useful.
T	t^T, t	2	Dominant.
U	u^U, u	2	Dominant.

laboratory that routinely types the blood of horses in the United States. Blood protein systems controlled by 13 other loci are shown in Table 15-2. The phenotypes of most of these systems are determined by electrophoresis. Many new alleles and systems can be expected to become known as blood analysis techniques become more refined.

Both blood factors and blood proteins can be used for tests of disputed paternity, partial verification of parentage, and as a permanent record of identification.

At most loci that control the blood antigens, the alleles are codominant except for one recessive allele. The alleles at loci for most of the blood proteins are codominant. The dominance relationships for each locus are indicated in Tables 15-1 and 15-2.

If the blood type of the mother is unknown, only codominant systems are useful in determining possible identities of the father because of the difficulty of determining whether a horse with a dominant phenotype is homozygous or heterozygous.

Within a breed, the number of segregating alleles at each locus is also important. If nearly all horses of a breed have a particular allele at a locus, then that locus will not be very useful in parentage tests. Similarly, the larger the number of blood systems that can be used, the greater the chance of excluding an incorrect parent.

TABLE 15-2
Genetic loci controlling electrophoretic markers and other factors in the blood of horses

Genetic System	Locus Symbol	Known Alleles	No. of Phenotypes	Comments
Hemoglobin	Hb	Hb^A, Hb^B	3	Codominant.
Albumen	Alb	Alb^F, Alb^I, Alb^S	6	Codominant; allele Alb^C has been found in donkeys and zebras.
Pre-albumen	Pr	Pr^1, Pr^2, Pr^3, Pr^4 Pr^5, Pr^6, Pr^7	28	Codominant.
Transferrin	Tf	Tf^D, Tf^{F_1}, Tf^{F_2}, Tf^H, Tf^M, Tf^O, Tf^R	28	Codominant.
Esterase	Es	Es^F, Es^I, Es^{X_1}, Es^{X_2}, Es^S, Es^O	15	All are dominant to Es^O (the lack of enzyme); remainder are codominant.
Post-albumen	Pa	Pa^F, Pa^S	3	Codominant.
Carbonic anhydrase	CA	CA^F, CA^I, CA^L, CA^O, CA^S	15	Codominant.
Red cell catalase	CAT	CAT^F, CAT^S	3	Codominant.
Glucose-6-phosphate	G-6-PD			One in horses, one in donkeys; sex linked.
6-phosphogluconate dehydrogenase	6-PGD	PGD^D, PGD^F, PGD^S	6	Codominant.
Autolytic factor	LF	LF^+, LF^-	2	Recessive factor in Arabians that that may prevent blood typing by lysis of red cells.
Cholinesterase	Ch	Ch^A, Ch^B, Ch^C, Ch^D	10	Codominant.
Phosphoglucomatase	PGM	PGM^F, PGM^S	3	Codominant.

TABLE 15-3
Frequencies of blood factor alleles in Shetland
ponies and Thoroughbreds

Locus	Allele	Frequency in	
		Shetlands	Thoroughbreds
A	a^{A_1}	.311	.705
	$a^{A'}$	.285	.029
	a^H	.036	.004
	$a^{A'H}$	.060	.000
	a	.308	.262
C	c^C	.652	.732
D	d^D	.139	.000
	d^J	.122	.150
	d	.739	.850
K	k^K	.180	.064
P	p^P	.342	.206
	$p^{P'}$	.048	.091
	p	.610	.703
Q	q^Q	.152	.508
	q^R	.387	.000
	q^S	.010	.104
	q^{QR}	.131	.076
	q^{RS}	.189	.312
	q	.131	.000
T	t^T	.450	.659
U	u^U	.317	.148

SOURCE: Stormont and Suzuki. 1964.

Some frequencies of different alleles for the blood antigen loci of Shetlands and Thoroughbreds, as determined by Stormont and Suzuki (1964), are given in Table 15-3. Table 15-3 shows that, especially for Thoroughbreds, the frequency of the recessive allele for most of the blood antigen systems is relatively high except in the Q system, where there exists the problem that several genotypes may have the same phenotype. These systems are essentially reduced to a dominant-recessive basis since the frequency of codominant genotypes is relatively low.

The codominant systems, exemplified by the albumen and transferrin loci, are generally more efficient in parentage tests since both genes are identified in the offspring as well as in the disputed parent. Frequencies in this system for some Shetlands, Thoroughbreds, and Arabians are shown in Table 15-4 (see also Figure 15-1). Table 15-4 also shows that a marked similarity exists between Arabians and Thoroughbreds with respect to the transferrin frequencies, which is not surprising because many of the Thoroughbred's ancestors were Arabians or were closely related to Arabians. In fact, frequencies of various genes are used to indicate pathways and similarities in the development of breeds.

TABLE 15-4

Frequencies of albumen and transferrin alleles in American Shetlands, American Thoroughbreds, South African Arabians, and South African Thoroughbreds

Locus	Allele	American Shetlands (n = 273)	American Thoroughbreds (n = 150)	South African Arabians (n = 45)	South African Thoroughbreds (n = 54)
Albumen	Alb^A	.387	.214	.620	.278
	Alb^B	.613	.786	.380	.722
Transferrin	Tf^D	.172	.267	.300	.167
	Tf^{Fa}	.460	.563	.477	.648
	Tf^H	.026	.027	.056	.009
	Tf^M	.031	0	0	0
	Tf^O	.108	.090	.167	.046
	Tf^R	.203	.053	0	.130

SOURCE: Osterhoff, Schmid, and Ward-Cox. 1970. Stormont and Suzuki. 1964.

[a]The frequency of Tf^F would be the sum of the frequencies of alleles for subtypes Tf^{F1} and Tf^{F2}.

a

b

c

FIGURE 15-1

The frequencies of alleles at the blood loci can be used to trace the development of various breeds. For example, Thoroughbreds (*a*) are more closely related to Arabians (*b*) than to Shetlands (*c*). Master Hand, a dark brown Thoroughbred stallion, is shown in *a*; Sx Symphonette, a sandy bay Arabian mare, is shown in *b*; and Luster of Charming Fare, a 7-year-old Shetland pony mare, is shown in *c*. Photo *a* courtesy of Walmac Farm; *b* by Polly J. Knoll, courtesy of Albert G. King, DLK Ranch; *c* courtesy of Harry K. Megson, Chazy River Farms.

TABLE 15-5
Frequencies of esterase alleles in Arabians and Thoroughbreds

Breed	Allele					
	Es^F	Es^I	Es^S	Es^{X_1}	Es^{X_2}	Es^O
Arabian	0	0	.987	.022	0	0
Thoroughbred	.037	0	.926	0	.037	0

SOURCE: Osterhoff, Schmid, and Ward-Cox. 1970.

In a survey taken in the early 1960s (see Table 15-5), 6 alleles were identified in the esterase system, but only 2 alleles were found in Arabians and 3 were found in Thoroughbreds.

Stormont has estimated the efficiency of excluding the wrong stallion from the correct stallion for the 8 blood antigen systems and the albumen and transferrin systems. The efficiency depends, as indicated in Table 15-6, on the number of alleles, their frequencies, and their dominance relationships. The efficiency values for Shetlands and Thoroughbreds are given in Table 15-6. The greater amount of heterozygosity and greater number of alleles in the Shetlands results in more efficient exclusion for them than for Thoroughbreds.

TABLE 15-6
Expected frequencies of excluding the incorrect stallion when the true sire and another sire are possible fathers

Locus	Fraction of Expected Exclusions	
	Shetlands	Thoroughbreds
BLOOD ANTIGEN LOCUS		
A	.220	.038
C	.010	.004
D	.170	.078
K	.081	.049
P	.118	.165
Q	.079	.030
T	.041	.009
U	.069	.078
All above combined	.572	.378
BLOOD PROTEIN LOCUS		
Alb	.181	.138
Tf	.366	.291
Tf and Alb systems combined	.481	.389
ALL SYSTEMS COMBINED	.778	.620

SOURCE: Stormont, Suzuki, and Rendel. 1965.

TABLE 15-7

Phenotypes of foal, dam, and disputed sire as an example of parentage testing

Horse	System							
	A	C	D	K	P	Q	Alb	Tf
Foal	A_1	C	DJ	K	P_1	Q	B	D
Dam	A_1H	C	J	–	–	–	A	DH
Disputed sire	A_1	C	J	K	P_1	Q	A	D

Exclusion Principle

The basic rule in parentage tests is that an animal cannot be proven to be a parent of another but can only be proven *not* to be the parent. There are two rules to keep in mind in dealing with parentage tests. First, a blood group factor cannot be present in a foal unless it is present either in one parent or in both parents. Second, if a parent is homozygous for a particular blood group gene, the foal also must have that allele.

Two examples will help to explain how parentage tests work. Table 15-7 gives the genetic information on a foal and its dam as well as on the supposed sire in this first example. Each locus is examined to see if the results are consistent with genetic principles. At the A and C loci, the genotype of the disputed sire is in agreement with that of the foal and its dam, but at the D locus the dam must contribute either d^J or d since her genotype is not completely known. The foal, however, has d^D and d^J, so the d^J must have come from the dam. Then the d^D gene must come from the foal's sire. The disputed sire does not possess the d^D allele so he is excluded as the sire. The albumen locus provides further proof in exactly the same way.

A more difficult problem in disputed parentage occurs when the dam's phenotype is not known. An example that concerns possible sires of a foal is shown in Table 15-8. The presence of recessive genes at loci A, C, D, and P, as well as the lack of any codominant phenotypes in the foal or dis-

TABLE 15-8

Phenotypes of a foal and 2 possible sires as an example of parentage testing

Horse	System							
	A	C	D	K	P	Q	Alb	Tf
Foal	A_1	–	D	–	P'	RS	A	DH
Sire I	H	C	J	–	P'	R	A	DF
Sire II	A_1	C	D	–	P	S	A	FO

puted sires, makes it impossible to exclude either sire as a possible parent with respect to those loci. The results at the K locus are also in agreement for either sire. From inspection of what is known at the Q locus, it can be seen that if the dam contributed an S allele, sire II would be excluded; if the dam contributed an R allele, sire I would be excluded; and if the dam contributed an RS allele, neither sire would be excluded. Information on the dam is, however, not known. There is no disagreement for either stallion at the albumen locus. At the codominant transferrin locus, however, there are no genes in common between the foal and sire II, and that sire is, therefore, excluded. Sire I is not excluded and, thus, *may be* the sire of the foal.

Parentage tests are obviously useful for ensuring proper identification for registered breeds and especially for stallions used artificially—particularly if the use of frozen semen and artificial insemination becomes more practical and widespread. For example, all dairy bulls used artificially in the United States are required to be blood typed for 10 different blood systems. The cost of blood typing for horses is somewhat higher than for cattle, primarily because fewer horses are blood typed.

15.2   Color Inheritance

Many breeders, such as those breeding Standardbreds or Thoroughbreds or Quarter Horses, have only a slight preference for the color of their horses. Others may strongly desire to obtain certain color patterns, such as a particular type or types of Appaloosa, a Paint or Pinto, a Buckskin, a Palomino, or an American White Horse. In this section the odds for and against the "color" breeders will, in part, be explained, and such information may help others to understand the genetics of certain basic colors.

Color inheritance in the horse is complex and is not completely understood. Many of the inferences in this section are based on studies by Castle and his associates. The basis for the discussion will be Figure 15-2, which summarizes what is known about color inheritance. When disputes or uncertainties exist, a question will be raised and a speculation as to its answer will be given. These fan diagrams begin with the loci for the basic body colors and then show how genes at other loci may modify these colors. Accumulation of minor modifying genes may, however, cause some of these different genotypes to have the same appearance. For example, some dark bays and seal browns may look the same, and some different genotypes of chestnut may look alike. The insert at the back of the book illustrates some of these colors. The pictures do not necessarily capture the true colors of the horses or even the exact color for the supposed

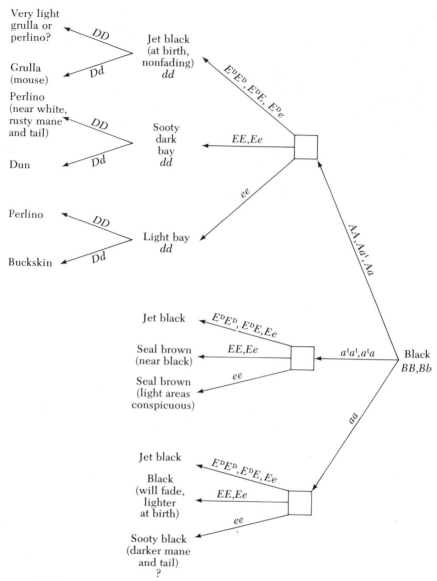

FIGURE 15-2

This chart shows the probable colors that will result from combinations of the 4 major color loci in the horse. The capital letters represent the dominant alleles for 2 alleles at a locus; for 3 alleles at a locus, the alleles are listed in order of dominance from top to bottom. The dilution gene *D* is incompletely dominant; the *dd* genotype will not change the color resulting from the *B*, *A*, and *E* loci.

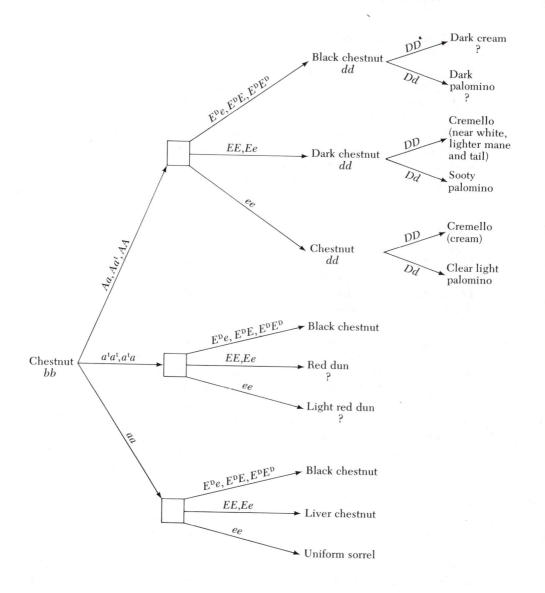

Thus, the probable colors are given in the 2 outermost columns on each side of the chart. A question mark indicates that there is no knowledge of the gene effects, but a probable result is indicated. A single dilution gene is not thought to affect animals with a^t and a genotypes; the effect of the homozygous genotype DD on A^t and a genotypes is unknown. There is uncertainty about the effects of genes at the A and E loci on chestnut colors.

genotype, but they do give a reasonably accurate idea of the colors described. Colors may appear to be different in sunlight than in shade, and
may seem to change at different times of the year; they may also be modified by the diet or other environmental factors.

Another major problem encountered in discussing color inheritance or
analyzing research reports is that colors may be relative to the person
describing them. For example, some people may use the terms sorrel and
chestnut for the same horse, whereas others would call the same color a
medium brown. Nevertheless, these terms will be used and, it is hoped,
described accurately enough to give an idea of the colors being discussed.

Major Color Loci

Genes from 5 loci interact to cause most of the major color patterns. Several
others mask, spot, grey, or roan some of these colors. In addition, modifier
genes that have relatively small effects probably cause much of the variation in the basic colors.

The C Locus.   In nearly all mammals except the horse, there is a recessive
gene for the true pink-eyed and pink-skinned albino. Such a gene has not
been found in the horse. There are, however, several genetic pathways
that result in a white or near-white horse, but none give the true albino.
Thus, all horses are thought to be homozygous for the gene C, which allows
other color genes to express themselves. In the remainder of this book,
the CC designation will be assumed and not written in discussion of color
genotypes. The other 4 major color loci are designated by others of the first
5 letters of the alphabet: A, B, D, and E. Each of these has 2 or more alleles.

The B Locus.   Starting with the B locus seems somewhat logical since the
2 alleles at that locus control whether the basic pigment formation will be
black or chestnut (brown). Chestnut will be used to describe the brown
color that is alternative to black in order to avoid as much as possible the
confusion resulting from the fact that the so-called brown horse actually
results from a modification of the basic black genotype. The gene for black
pigment, B, is dominant to the gene for chestnut pigment, b.

The A Locus.   Most breeders know that bay is dominant to black. The
reason is that genes at another locus, the A locus, determine whether the
black pigment is expressed fully or is restricted to mane, tail, and legs.
There are probably 4 alleles at the A locus. In order of decreasing dominance, they can be named A^+, A, a^t, and a. The A^+ allele creates the wild-
type coat, which resembles the protective coloration of most wild animals,
as exemplified by the Przewalski's horse shown in Figure 15-3. The net
appearance is somewhat bay. There is some dispute about the existence of

FIGURE 15-3
The Przewalski's horse shows the
restrictive effects of the wild-type
allele at the *A* locus of the genotype
for formation of black pigment.

this allele, but the allele really does not concern the modern breeder and is not included in Figure 15-2 or the color insert at the back of the book. The other 3 alleles modify the black pigment, as shown in Figure 15-2. The *A* gene restricts the black areas to the periphery and to the mane and tail. The result is the bay horse, with reddish (bay) body, black legs when not hidden by white stockings, and black mane and tail. The a^t allele, $a^t a^t$ or $a^t a$, does not restrict the black as much, so the result is the dark brown or seal brown horse, which is sometimes mistaken for a black horse. Again the points will be black. The very dark seal brown horse can be distinguished from a true black horse only by the presence of brown hair around the muzzle or on the flanks. The picture in the color insert that illustrates the dark seal brown is somewhat lighter than sometimes would normally be seen, so that some brown can be seen. Lighter seal brown horses show more brown areas, particularly at the flank and behind the shoulder. This brown does not have a reddish appearance, although distinguishing between dark bay and light seal brown may sometimes be difficult due to minor modifier genes that may lighten or darken the basic color. The most recessive allele, *a*, when homozygous, does not affect the distribution of the black pigment, and thus a uniformly black horse will result. Such a black horse may fade from exposure to the sun, and the body color may become blackish-bay.

The effects of the genes of the *A* locus on the chestnut genotype are not as clearly known. The *A* allele, together with the *bb* genotype, may give a chestnut color that is essentially the same color as bay except that the points are not black. The *aa* genotype may be expressed as a deep, liver chestnut color. The effect of the a^t allele is not clear. If the effect parallels that on black pigment, a horse that is a medium shade of brown but with nonblack points would be expected. Castle has suggested that one possibility is the claybank or red dun. The claybank description is

469

somewhat self-explanatory and refers to a reddish-yellow color. The legs are a slightly darker red than the body but are not black. A dark red, but not black, dorsal stripe that carries through the mane and tail often is also part of the red dun pattern. The mane and tail may in some cases be flaxen with the stripe showing in the tail. These possibilities are shown in the color insert at the back of the book.

The E *Locus.* Although some dispute exists concerning the effects of the restriction genes of the *A* locus and the genes of the *E* locus on the extension of dark pigment (Odriozola, 1951), the system proposed by Castle will be discussed here. For a number of years, only the *E* and *e* alleles were hypothesized to exist. According to that hypothesis, the *E* allele extended the dark pigment (black or brown) to more of the body. The basic genotypes at the *B* and *A* loci were thus made darker by the action of the *E* genotype. The *ee* genotype either had no effect or slightly lightened the dark pigment.

According to such a theory, however, all black by black matings should breed true; that is, *aaBB* × *aaBB* will give only *aaBB* or, if heterozygous, *aaBb* × *aaBb* will give, on the average, 3/4 black and 1/4 chestnut offspring. However, in reality, a small number of bay foals always resulted when large numbers of black matings were made. Errors in distinguishing between dark brown and black could not account for the discrepancy. Therefore, Castle postulated that another allele, E^D, extends the dark pigment so much that it actually masks the effect of the bay pattern gene, *A*. He called this the gene for dominant black and described the color as jet black, which does not fade in sunlight as the recessive black may do. The foal coat is also black, whereas the first coat of the recessive black is more of a mouse gray color. The existence of a similar gene in other mammals helped lead him to this conclusion. Thus, E^D is thought to extend the dark color even if *A* or a^t is present (is epistatic to *A* and a^t), whereas *E* allows normal expression and *e* lightens the normal expression of the genes at the *A* locus. The effect of E^D on chestnut horses with any combination of *A* genes is not clear, although the deep liver or black chestnut color may be one result. Black chestnut horses will show brown hairs on the lower legs and face, compared with black and seal brown horses, which have black legs. It is not known whether there is any difference between the effects of E^D in the homozygous and heterozygous forms. In Figure 15-2 and the color insert at the back of the book, complete dominance in order of E^D, *E*, and *e* is assumed.

The D *Locus.* There is some controversy about the naming of the *D* locus. There is a locus controlling dilution of color in many animals that has been named the *D* locus for those species. Because the dilution gene in the horse does not act in the same way, some geneticists have suggested that it is really an allele at the *C* locus, c^{cr}. As the albino gene, *c*, is not present, there is no difference in the genetic results, whether the gene is at a separate locus called D or whether it really belongs to the C series. Since the D nomenclature seems to be more widely used, it will be used here.

The D gene is incompletely dominant. The Dd genotype results in a dilution of the basic coat color. The DD genotype dilutes the color even more, so that such animals are sometimes called albinos although they are not true albinos because they have colored eyes and some pigment. The dd genotype has no effect on the basic color. The dilution acts by causing a portion of the hair shaft to lack pigment (Gremmel, 1939).

Castle (1960) presented evidence that the Dd genotype has no effect if the genotype is aa. Similarly, Singleton and Bond (1966) suggested that Dd has no effect on either a^t genotypes or a genotypes. Thus, Dd causes dilution only if the A allele is present. These researchers did not determine whether the double dilution genotype, DD, has any effect on the a^t and a genotypes. Therefore, the effects of the DD and Dd genotypes are shown in Figure 15-2 and the color insert only for genotypes containing the A allele.

The effect of the dilution gene on the dominant, E^D, black horse probably is a lightening to a smoky black or grulla color for those horses having the A allele as shown in Figure 15-2. Some reports have suggested that the dilution gene operates on the recessive black to cause the grulla color. This result seems unlikely in view of the study by Singleton and Bond. The results are even more speculative for dilution of the black chestnut horse, but such a dilution may result in either a grulla color with lighter points or, more likely, a very dark palomino.

The Dd genotype turns the dark chestnut horse into a sooty (not clear) dark palomino with light mane and tail. The light chestnut horse becomes a clear, light palomino. The DD genotype turns both the dark and light chestnut horses having the A allele into what is called cremello (creamy white, near white, blue-eyed) with light mane and tail. The cremello horse is sometimes incorrectly called an albino. These colors are listed in the outside columns of Figure 15-2.

If the basic color is bay, the heterozygous dilution genotype, Dd, also dilutes the body color—the dark bay to a dun and the lighter bay to a buckskin. The body colors of these horses are similar to palomino, but the manes, tails, and legs are black. Dun is somewhat darker and has less yellow than buckskin. Some duns and buckskins also have the black dorsal stripe and some zebra striping on the legs and shoulders, although these characteristics may be due to the presence of other genes at other loci. The DD genotype dilutes the bay colors to what is called perlino, which also is incorrectly called albino. The tails and manes are darker (a rusty color) than the body color and darker than those of the cremellos. Some aged gray horses also have a white body color and reddish mane and tail but can easily be distinguished by the dark pigment around the muzzle. The effect of the double dilution on the dominant black background is not clear. It may result in either a perlino or a very light grulla, although the body color

471

may be even lighter than light grulla and there may be less black in the points.

Any of the dilutions—dun, buckskin, palomino—can occur with or without a dorsal stripe. A separate gene may be the cause, although dorsal stripes are much rarer with Palominos than with Duns or Buckskins. The red dun color pattern can also occur without the stripe but would usually be called chestnut. (Breed registries would, however, not call this pattern a red dun unless the dorsal stripe was present.)

Major Modifying Loci

Masking, graying, roaning, and spotting loci have major effects that affect coat color. These loci are listed in Table 15-9.

The W Locus. A dominant gene, W, for white color, has mixed merit for breeders of white horses. The gene masks all other color patterns. Many geneticists had suspected that the homozygous genotype, WW, was lethal. In 1969, Pulos and Hutt confirmed this suspicion. They concluded that because no abortions or dead foals were observed, the lethal effect must occur very early in pregnancy. The result is that the apparent conception rate for matings of white horses is reduced, since matings of Ww × Ww result in 1/4 WW, 1/2 Ww, and 1/4 ww genotypes. The WW genotype is not born, so two-thirds of the foals born are white and one-third are colored, rather than the three-to-one ratio that would be expected from crosses of horses heterozygous for a dominant gene. The allele w is recessive and allows expression of other color loci. The dominant white horses have colored eyes (blue, brown, hazel) and usually have small spots of skin pigment, so they are not in any sense true albinos even though they are eligible for registry as American Albino Horses.

Another gene in the W series has been hypothesized by Jones and Bogart (1971) as being responsible for one of the Appaloosa color patterns. The W^{ap} gene may cause the white blanket on the rump. The extent of the blanket may depend on the number of modifier genes. This gene may be similar to that proposed by Miller in his study of Appaloosa inheritance, which will be discussed later in this section.

The G Locus. The gene for progressive graying is designated as G. The g gene when homozygous allows regular color expression. The graying action begins after the first coat, which shows the basic color, is shed. Each succeeding coat has an increasingly larger number of white hairs mingled with hairs of the base color. Homozygous (GG) horses may exhibit graying earlier in life and to a greater degree than heterozygous (Gg) horses, and

472

TABLE 15-9
Loci of genes that mask or cause variation in basic color patterns

Locus and Allele	Effects
W	Dominant clear white; masks all colors; brown, hazel, or blue eyes; lethal before birth when homozygous.
W^{ap}	Dominance for white blanket on rump of Appaloosas; may cause leopard pattern as homozygote with proper modifiers; allele proposed by Jones and Bogart (1971).
w	Recessive for normal color.
G	Dominant gray; frequency of white hairs mingling with basic color increases with age; first coat has no white hairs; may become white when aged; GG may gray faster than Gg.
g	Recessive; no graying.
Rn	Dominant roan; mixing of white hairs with basic color; no change with age; some believe homozygote is lethal since there have been many reports of no roans breeding true. There has been one report, however, of two true-breeding roans.
Rn^{ap}	Intermediate dominance; may cause a roaning over hips in Appaloosas; allele proposed by Jones and Bogart (1971).
rn	Recessive; no roaning.
S	Dominant silver dappling in Shetlands; strong dilution of black to dark cream or light chocolate; red less diluted, almost to dappled chestnut.
s	Recessive; normal allele.
T	Dominant for white spotting (Tobiano pattern); spotting independent of other basic color; homozygote may have more white.
t	Recessive; allows normal expression of genes at other loci.
o	Recessive for white spotting (Overo pattern).
o^{e}	Recessive for Overo spotting, but when homozygous will cause lethal white foal syndrome; allele proposed by Jones and Bogart (1971).
O	Dominant; allows normal expression of genes at other loci.
Sl	Gene for silver or varnish roan; may be at same locus as Rn; modifiers can result in slight silvering to completely white.
Sl^{ap}	Homozygous: may cause leopard pattern with proper modifiers. Heterozygous: frosty hip blanket or overall frosty roan depending on modifiers. Allele proposed by Jones and Bogart (1971).
f	Recessive for kink in tail; may be associated with Appaloosa blanket.
blo	Recessive for blotchiness; may be associated with Appaloosa patterns.

473

both may become white when aged. Most "white" horses are really gray horses whose hair has become completely white. The skin pigment will, however, be dark in places where the hair was originally colored and around the muzzle, in contrast to the dominant white horse, which has a pink muzzle. Although dappling may occur with most colors, it is especially noticeable on gray horses. Figure 15-4 shows progressive graying with and without dappling. Some gray horses retain a dark mane and tail for some time, whereas the mane and tail of others turn white before the body (Figure 15-5). Many gray horses also develop very small brownish or dark spots as they age, which result in a "flea-bitten" appearance. Comments about the effects of the gray gene on colors other than black parallel those in the following section on the roan locus.

The Rn *Locus.* The gene for roaning, *Rn*, is easily confused with the graying gene because it also results in white hairs mingled with the basic color hairs. The white hairs are, however, present in the first coat and do not increase in frequency with age, although horses carrying both the roaning and graying genes would be born with white hairs and would become progressively gray. Roans (and grays also) are of different types depending on the base color (see Figure 15-6). A chestnut base results in a chestnut roan or rose gray. A bay when roan is a red roan. A sorrel may be a strawberry roan. Actually, the most accurate terminology is obtained by combining the base color and roan or gray, that is, bay roan, gray on bay, and so on. The roan gene often detracts from the color pattern when present with genes distinguishing a color breed. Roaning can hide some Appaloosa patterns and can make paint and palomino patterns indistinct. Some breeders believe that the homozygote *RnRn* is lethal because there have been many reports that roans never breed true. However, Singleton (1969) cites a 1918 report of Babcock and Clausen concerning 2 stallions, a bay roan that sired 256 bay roan foals and a red roan that sired 230 bay roan and 24 black roan foals. These stallions were also described by Wentworth in 1913. Since both were listed as red roan stallions and since there is always the chance of confusing roans with grays, it is possible that they were actually gray on a bay background and, if homozygous for *G*, would breed true. Many modifiers must affect the percentage of white hairs in

---

FIGURE 15-4

Progressive graying of Welsh Ponies, from solid color as a foal to almost total white. One pony also shows the distinctive dappling frequently noticeable in gray horses. GlanNant Sonnet (*a*) at weaning; (*b*) at about 2 years; (*c*) as an aged mare. GlanNant Saga (*d*) at 3 months; (*e*) at about 2 years; (*f*) at about 4 years. Photograph *c* by Ernest L. Mauger; photograph *d* by Downhill; photographs *e* and *f* by Tarrance Photos. Photographs courtesy of Mrs. Karl D. Butler, Ithaca, New York.

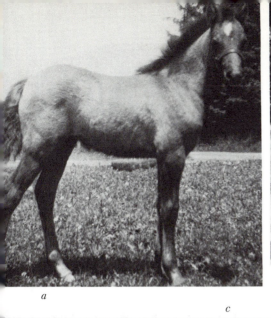

a

b

c

d

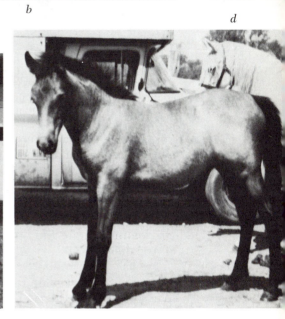

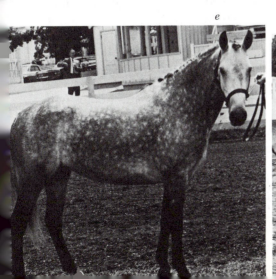

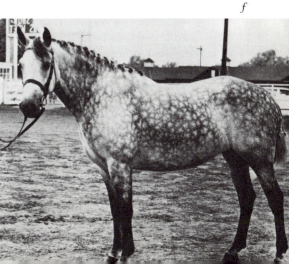

e

f

FIGURE 15-5

The manes and tails of gray horses may turn white earlier or later than the body: *a*, X-Star Special, a 5-year-old Arabian stallion with white mane and tail; *b*, Zane Grey's Silver Tip, a Missouri Fox Trotting stallion with darker mane and tail. Photograph *a* courtesy of Sue Anna Yarborough, Jasper, Arkansas; photograph *b* courtesy of Ed Edwards, West Plains, Missouri.

the roan because the variation in the amount of white is great. Most roans are much darker around the head, neck, and legs than on the body (Figure 15-6), and this characteristic helps distinguish roan from gray. The amount of roan appears to vary in different seasons because of the length of hair and the amount of undercoat that shows.

Jones and Bogart (1971) have speculated also that there is an intermediate dominant gene Rn^{ap} in this series that may cause roaning on the hips of Appaloosas.

The S Locus. Shetlands are reported to have yet another dominant gene that is responsible for silver dappling—diluting black to a dark cream or light chocolate, almost to a dappled chestnut; the mane and tail are white or nearly white (see Figure 15-7). Castle (1953) postulated that the most striking effect is on the E^D dominant black background. Red colors are diluted less than black colors. Homozygotes, SS, may be diluted to a greater extent than heterozygotes. The combination of S and the graying gene produces a white or gray-white pony that turns white by 1 or 2 years of age. The foal coat may even contain white hairs. Such white ponies will show pigment on the nose or around the eyes.

The Sl Locus. There have been some reports of a progressive silvering gene, but the reports do not clearly distinguish between its effects and those of G and Rn genes. The gene is named Sl and results in a silver or varnish roan that varies from slight silvering to complete white. An allele at this locus, Sl^{ap}, is thought by Jones and Bogart to cause, when homozygous, a leopard-spotted Appaloosa if the proper modifiers are present. The heterozygous genotype $Sl^{ap}sl$ may give a frosty hip blanket or overall frosty roan depending on modifiers present, according to Jones and Bogart (1971).

FIGURE 15-6
Roan ponies showing the characteristic darker color (lack of interspersed white hairs) around the head and neck and on the legs. Notice the difference of the intensity of roaning. *a*: Roan on a bay background (*note black points*). *b*: Roan on a chestnut background (*note chestnut points*). *c*: Roan on a light chestnut background. *d*: Roan on a chestnut background with light mane and tail (GlanNant Rhyme, a champion Welsh Pony). Photographs *a*, *b*, and *c* courtesy of Harold A. Willman, Ithaca, New York. Photograph *d* by Tarrance Photos, courtesy of Mrs. Karl D. Butler, Ithaca, New York.

a

b

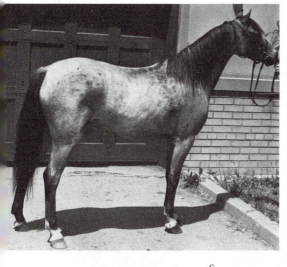

c

d

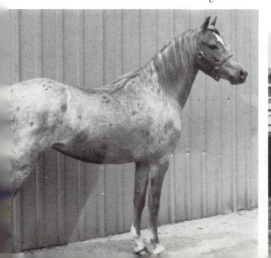

FIGURE 15-7
Hilltop's Little Bummer, a silver dappled chestnut pony. Although the body is dappled, there is a "mask" on the face and the mane and tail are white. Although the color is called chestnut, the genotype is for black but is modified by the silver dappling gene. Photograph by Frank's Photo House, courtesy of Jim and Loretta Murphy, Huron, South Dakota.

The T *Locus.* At least two forms of white spotting are thought to exist. One is dominant or incompletely dominant and the other is recessive. Spotting is independent of other color patterns and presumably may occur on any color except, of course, white. *Piebald spotting* is white and black; spotting of white and shades of red is referred to as *skewbald spotting.* The dominant gene for white spotting is designated *T* for the Tobiano pattern, which was described in Chapter 2. The spotting has been described as similar to that obtained by pouring white paint over a solid-color horse (Figure 15-8). The head is marked similarly to that of a solid-color horse. Horses that are *tt* will not be spotted unless spotting is caused by genes at another locus. The homozygote *TT* may have more white than the heterozygote.

FIGURE 15-8
Tobiano pattern on Cherokee War Chief, a Paint Horse champion. Photograph by Marge Spence, courtesy of the American Paint Horse Association, Fort Worth, Texas.

478

FIGURE 15-9
Overo pattern on Flash Thru Bars, an
International Pinto Horse Halter
Champion. Photograph by Marge
Spence, Courtesy of Dorothy
Lawrence, Sperry, Oklahoma.

The O Locus. The Overo pattern of recessive spotting is due to the *oo* genotype. The Overo pattern is in some respects the complement of the Tobiano pattern. A horse exhibiting this pattern is likely to have a dark back and underside; the spotting is mostly confined to the middle of the body, as shown in Figure 15-9. The dominant allele, *O*, codes for normal coloring. Spotting in horses that carry *O* will be due to genes at another locus. Since these spotting genes are at two different loci, they may in combination account for much variation in spotting patterns, but variation in amount of spotting must also be due to many modifier genes.

Other Loci

The f Locus. The recessive *ff* genotype is said to result in the kink found in the tail of many Appaloosas. Since it is associated with Appaloosas, some geneticists have speculated that it also may be responsible for the Appaloosa blanket when present with the appropriate modifier genes.

The blo Locus. Blotchiness in the color pattern is the result of the homozygous genotype *bloblo* for blotchiness. This gene may act as a major modifier of the Appaloosa patterns.

The Mottled Locus. The mottled or parti-colored skin, which appears particularly on the genitalia and muzzle of the Appaloosa, is apparently due to a dominant gene *M* (Figure 15-10).

479

FIGURE 15-10
Co-Regent, an Appaloosa stallion, showing the effects of the mottling gene around the face. Photograph by DiGinio Photography, courtesy of Lynn and Jack Nankivil, Sahaptin Farm, Winona, Minnesota.

Locus for Flaxen Mane and Tail. There is some confusion as to the reason for the whitish mane and tail of the Palomino. Some speculate that a recessive gene called flaxen is responsible. Others believe that the optical density of the basic brown pigment is diluted so much in the mane and tail that it appears to be lighter than the body color. The flaxen mane and tail also appear on chestnut horses, particularly Belgians and Shetlands. Figure 15-11 shows two chestnut horses with and without the light mane and tail. Wentworth (1913) presented some data that indicate that the gene for flaxen mane and tail is recessive, at least on chestnut backgrounds. Very likely it is not effective on a genetically black horse.

Loci for Markings. There are numerous genes that may cause white stockings, stars on the forehead, the blaze face, and so on. The chin spot is thought to be a recessive character produced by the genotype *chch*. The gene for white snip on the nose is thought to be recessive by some geneticists and dominant by others. Similarly, it is not clear whether the blaze or white stripe on the front of the face or the white forehead star are due to recessive or dominant genes.

Appaloosa Loci

The inheritance of the many color patterns of the Appaloosa is not completely clear. Miller, in an undated report, gives the results of his study of 9,955 parents and progeny of Appaloosa breeding, which led him to propose the following model for the expression of the white blanket over the rump and croup and for the expression of small, dark spots in the area of the blanket. A dominant gene *Ap* is necessary for expression of the Appaloosa blanket and dark spots. This gene seems to correspond to the W^{ap} gene proposed by Jones and Bogart (1971). Another gene *wb* is neces-

480

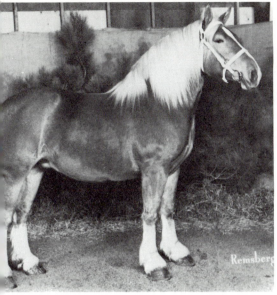

a

b

FIGURE 15-11

Two Belgian mares: *a*, Trixie du Marais, with white mane and tail; *b*, Sunny Lane Nanette, with chestnut mane and tail. Photograph *a* by Remsburg, courtesy of Donald J. Wack, Zelienople, Pennsylvania; photograph *b* courtesy of Leo J. Fox, David City, Nebraska.

sary for the blanket and still another gene *sp* is necessary for the dark spots. The gene effects of these two loci are sex influenced, so that the blanket and dark spots can occur in homozygous and heterozygous males but only in homozygous females, as shown in Table 15-10. Modifiers for both the blanket and spot characteristics determine the extent of the blanket and spots. Enough blanket modifiers may result in what is essentially a white horse. Spots can occur without the blanket, and the blanket can occur without spots (Figures 15-12 and 15-13).

Crew and Buchanan-Smith (1930) proposed that the dalmation or leopard spotting consisting of dark spots on white background (Figure 15-14) is the result of a dominant gene. The leopard mule shown in Figure 2-67 is evidence to support this view since only one gene for spotting could have been inherited from the Appaloosa mother.

Jones and Bogart (1971), however, suggest that leopard spotting can result from the $W^{ap}W^{ap}$ genotype, or from $W^{ap}w^{ap}$ with enough modifiers, or from $Sl^{ap}Sl^{ap}$ with enough modifiers. According to their proposal, $W^{ap}w^{ap}$ would usually result in the blanket pattern, as would $W^{ap}W^{ap}$ with few modifiers. $Sl^{ap}Sl^{ap}$ would result in silver roans or horses with frosty blankets over their hips that might, with the proper modifiers, cover virtually the entire body. Appaloosa roaning, mainly over the hips, is thought by Jones and Bogart to be due to a dominant gene Rn^{ap}. Modifier

481

TABLE 15-10
A genetic model for the inheritance of the
white blanket and dark spots characteristic
of Appaloosas

In the Presence of *Ap* (*ApAp* or *Apap*)		
Genotypes	Male	Female
	Blanket characteristic	
WbWb	Solid	Solid
Wbwb	Blanket	Solid
wbwb	Blanket	Blanket
	Spotting characteristic	
SpSp	No dark spots	No dark spots
Spsp	Dark spots	No dark spots
spsp	Dark spots	Dark spots
In the Absence of *Ap* (*apap*)		

apap results in no blanket and no dark
spots, although *Wb* and *Sp* may be present.

SOURCE: Adapted from Miller, R. W. *Appaloosa Coat Color Inheritance*.

FIGURE 15-12
Appaloosas showing a white blanket without spots (*a*) and with spots (*b*).
a: Lace Hankie, an Appaloosa mare. *b*: Prince Jet Band, an Appaloosa stallion.
Photograph *a* courtesy of Lou and Val Whitson, Livingston, California; photograph *b* courtesy of Joan McGloon, Woodbury, Connecticut.

a

b

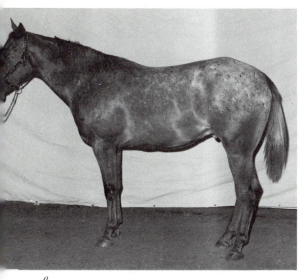

a

FIGURE 15-13
Appaloosas showing dark spots without blanket on a chestnut background (*a*), dark spots on a light background (*b*), and dark and white spots on a chestnut background (*c*). *a*: Joker's Red Baron, an Appaloosa gelding. *b*: Red Hill Coco Bars, an Appaloosa mare. *c*: Jocay's Hi Johnny, an Appaloosa stallion. Photograph *a* by Norman R. Olson, courtesy of Marilyn S. Olson, Libuse, Louisiana; photograph *b* by CORA, courtesy of Cora Morris, Marshall, Arkansas; photograph *c* courtesy of Carolyn Ann Young, Jocay Stables, Indianapolis, Indiana.

b

c

genes cause the expression to vary, but the Rn^{ap} gene is not associated with leopard spotting.

Obviously, there are many unanswered questions about color inheritance in horses. Certainly modifier genes are responsible for differences in shading of the basic colors. Horse breeders apparently will continue to be surprised by the colors of the foals that result from some of their matings. Perhaps color is not very important to breeders of working horses, but it is to "color horse" breeders, and much more knowledge is needed. Examination of Figure 15-2 and the color insert at the back of the book indicates

483

a

b

c

FIGURE 15-14
Appaloosa stallions showing the variation in
size of spots of the leopard or dalmation
spotting pattern. The size and distribution of
the spots depends on modifier genes.
a: Prince's Joker. b: Joker's John E. c: D-R
Joker's Playboy. d: Oxburn's Snafu. Photograph a courtesy of Richard Herrmann,
Theilman, Minnesota; photograph b courtesy
of Mr. and Mrs. E. D. Pollard, Caldwell,
Idaho; photograph c courtesy of Linda
Roberts, South Lyon, Michigan; photograph
d courtesy of Lynn and Jack Nankivil,
Sahaptin Farm, Winona, Minnesota.

d

what can usually be expected; it also indicates that "pure breeding" may not always result in higher frequencies of the desired colors. For example, the frequency of palomino foals to be expected from the mating of palominos is one-half regardless of the number of generations of palomino ancestry.

The basic rules of genetics given in Chapter 14 can be used to calculate the frequencies of possible genotypes that will result from particular matings. These genotypes can then be used, together with Figure 15-2, the color insert, and the information in section 15.2, to predict the frequencies of various colors and color patterns.

15.3 Simply Inherited Lethals

According to Britton (1962), as many as 20 percent of all foals are born with some form of abnormality. Approximately one-half of these are severely handicapped or are born dead. Many other conditions may result in abortion or resorption of the fetus early in gestation, resulting in a lowered foaling rate. Most of these abnormalities either are influenced by the joint action of many genes or are nongenetically controlled accidents in development. Some of the more common lethals and abnormalities will now be discussed, and an indication will be given of whether they may be simply inherited.

Hemolytic Disease of Foals

Neonatal isoerythrolysis and hemolytic icterus are two names for the destruction of red blood cells of the foal by serum antibodies in the first milk of the mare. This condition is somewhat similar to the "blue baby" phenomenon caused by Rh factor incompatibility in humans. The mare may be stimulated to produce antibodies against the red blood cells of the foal if she somehow receives red cells that are antigenically different from hers. These cells may be received by transfusion and antigen vaccination or even by the passage of the foal's blood through an abnormal placenta to maternal tissues. Apparently, the antibodies that result cannot pass back to the fetal blood, so the foal is born with no harmful effect of the incompatibility. The antibodies may, however, build up in the colostrum of the mare. If the newborn foal nurses, the antibodies in the milk pass directly to the foal's blood and destroy the red blood cells. The foal becomes anemic and sluggish within 12–36 hours and generally dies within a few days. A yellowish and continuous discoloration of the urine occurs after 24–48 hours. During late pregnancy, the mare's serum can be tested for the pres-

485

ence of such antibodies. Further confirmation of the diagnosis requires an agglutination test using the dam's serum and red blood cells of the sire. Fortunately, isoerythrolysis is rare, so the passage of the incompatible blood antigens of the foal to the blood of the mare (sensitivization) does not occur often.

Since responsible antigens and antibodies have not been isolated, no genetic selection can be done, although future research may show which blood systems are involved.

When isoerythrolysis is probable, the foal should be kept from nursing its mother for 36 hours and either nursed by a foster mare or bottle fed as shown in Figure 15-15. Transfusion therapy is also used, but the foal cannot be allowed to nurse until its mother's colostrum is gone, or for 36 hours when antibodies of the colostrum are no longer absorbed intact by the foal. Otherwise, the condition is generally lethal. The foal should be kept close to the mother during this period to avoid being rejected by her when her milk becomes safe.

Hemophilia

Another blood-related lethal is the sex-linked recessive factor for bleeders' disease (hemophilia) that was discussed in section 14.2. As was shown in Figure 14-14, the disease is lethal and is transmitted from a normal carrier mare to half of her sons.

The Lethal White Gene, W

As described in section 15.2, the gene for dominant white (Figure 15-16) was shown to be lethal when homozygous by Pulos and Hutt (1969). The breeder may never realize the existence of the problem because the WW fetus dies early in fetal development and is either resorbed or aborted without trace. Only an apparently low conception rate is noted. An earlier report by Wriedt (1924) implied the lethality of the gene for white because of the high degree of sterility in matings of white horses. The name Fredericksborg lethal was originally given to this phenomenon.

Combined Immunodeficiency

Deficiency of B- and T-lymphocytes has been found in Arabian foals, all of which have died because of lack of resistance to disease. Many die specifically as a result of adenoviral infections of the respiratory system. The evidence for a genetic basis for the deficiency is: (1) only Arabian foals have been reported to be affected; (2) full siblings have been affected,

486

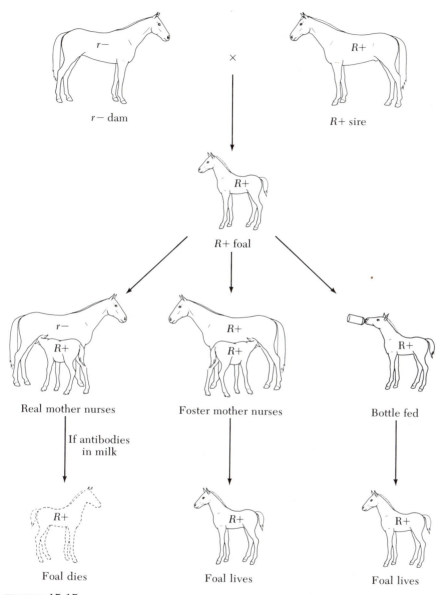

FIGURE 15-15
Hemolytic disease. An r^- mare with an R^+ foal may produce antibodies against R^+ blood cells. If the newborn foal drinks and absorbs these antibodies from the colostrum, they could destroy its blood cells.

FIGURE 15-16
The dominant white horse is hetero-
zygous for a gene causing the white
color, which, when homozygous,
causes early embryonic death.
Photograph courtesy of Ruth White,
American Albino Association,
Crabtree, Oregon.

but the incidence of such an occurrence is low; (3) the syndrome in the horse is similar to that in man, and in man it is known to be genetic; and (4) abnormalities (lymphopenia and immunoglobulin deficiency) have been detected before signs of infection (McGuire, Poppie, and Banks, 1974). This report also suggests that the trait is autosomal, recessive, and lethal, since (1) affected foals come from normal parents, (2) only bone marrow transplants could allow affected foals to live to maturity, and (3) both males and females are affected.

Melanoma

A tumor of the pigment-forming cells (melanocytes) is called a melanoma. Although horses of all colors may be affected, the majority of horses that have melanomas are gray. Thus, the gray gene G apparently predisposes horses to this form of cancer. Older horses are more frequently affected than younger horses. The growths commonly begin near and spread from the anus. Melanomas that spread to the lungs and other organs soon cause death.

White Colt Syndrome

This problem is different from that of dominant white. When two Overo horses with strong modifiers for white are mated, the foal will sometimes have little pigment. In addition, other effects are sometimes present, including atresia coli, which is essentially a closing in the large intestine or a narrowing of the lumen of the large intestine. If the condition is severe enough, the foal usually dies. Jones and Bogart (1971) have proposed that a recessive allele of the Overo series is responsible. The $o^e o^e$ genotype would be affected and could result from matings of overos $o^e o \times o^e o$ or even from nonspotted horses $Oo^e \times Oo^e$.

Atresia Coli (Severed Large Intestine)

This disease appears to result from more than one mechanism because it has been reported in Thoroughbreds as well as in white foals. Surgical correction is usually unsuccessful. A genetic mechanism may be the cause since the trait appeared in many foals of the Percheron stallion Superb when he was used in Japan in about 1886 (Yamane, 1927). Affected foals appear healthy for 8–24 hours until increasingly severe "colic" results in death 3 or 4 days later as a result of failure to eliminate by-products of digestion.

Anal Atresia (Blocked Anus)

Because the anus is lacking, no products of digestion can be passed. Other problems may be caused by this condition since surgical correction is rarely of any benefit. The condition is rare and sporadic, so it may be due to a dominant gene that arises by mutation or to a recessive gene, which is very infrequent. Nutritional excesses or deficiencies or the presence or absence of drugs at the critical stage of development may also be the cause.

Hydrocephalus (Water Head)

In this condition, cerebrospinal fluid accumulates, causing the head to enlarge (as shown in Figure 15-17) and the nervous system to be abnormal. The condition is nearly always lethal within 48 hours but fortunately it is rare, which indicates that the cause may be a dominant mutation or an environmentally caused accident of development.

Shistosoma Reflexum

Fetuses with this abnormal condition, characterized by complete lack of amniotic development, are usually aborted before full term. Inbreeding apparently caused this recessive lethal to become homozygous in a group of horses studied by Weber (1947).

Stiff Forelegs

Menzin, a Polish Anglo-Arabian, sired foals affected with flexed, stiff, or contracted forelegs according to a report by Prawochenski (1936). Seven of

489

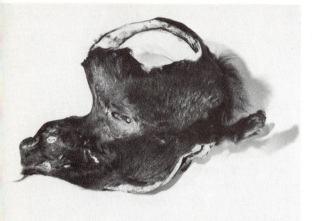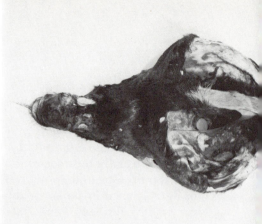

a   *b*

FIGURE 15-17
Hydrocephalus, shown in a section of the head, causes death within 48 hours
of birth. *a*: Side view. *b*: Top View.

the 22 foals sired by Menzin in 1934 and 1935 were affected. The hind legs
and bodies were normal. Since the foal cannot stand to nurse, the condition
is lethal. The mares were not closely related to the sire, but all had a
common sire, Shagya, in their pedigrees. This may be a recessive characteristic affected by modifier genes or other environmental factors. An
affected Appaloosa foal is shown in Figure 15-18.

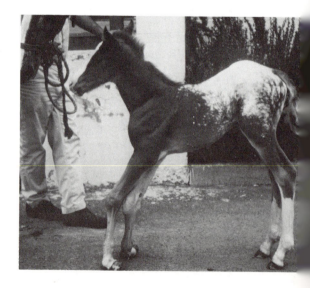

FIGURE 15-18
Flexed or contracted tendons,
which prevent normal extension
of the pasterns, is a lethal
characteristic in nature because
it prevents the foal from nursing.

Epitheliogenesis Imperfecta (Missing Patches of Skin)

Either hair or large pieces of skin on the lower limbs is lacking at birth. Occasionally a hoof is also absent. Foals are subject to infection, which usually kills them in a few days. Cases of the condition have been reported sporadically. Pedigree examination has suggested that a recessive gene is the cause.

Sex-Linked Lethal

Evidence has been found that a sex-linked lethal results in a sex ratio of two females for each male foal born. Presumably, the male that carries the factor dies early in pregnancy. Similar non-sex-linked lethals may also occur with no outward sign other than reduced fertility (Kislovsky (1932) as cited by Stormont (1958)).

Wobbles (Jinxed Back, Weak Loin)

The symptoms of wobbles, also called equine spinal ataxia, are bilateral incoordination and paddling of the hind feet. It usually occurs in young horses and rarely is reported in older horses. The cause is degeneration of the spinal column due to overgrowth of the atricular processes. Severity of the disease depends on the location of the bony lesions along the spinal column. Overgrowth close to the head is most severe. The symptoms often occur suddenly and advance rapidly. In many cases, the horse bends the neck to one side, indicating the presence of neck pain. The mode of inheritance is not clear, but 43 percent of the cases of wobbles in Thoroughbreds were traced to one of the 3 foundation sires. Some mares have had more than one foal with wobbles.

The symptoms of the nerve disorder described in the following section resemble superficially the symptoms of wobbles, but whereas wobbles affects the spinal cord, this disease affects the brain directly.

Cerebellar Hypoplasia and Degeneration

The part of the brain called the cerebellum controls coordination of movement. Foals afflicted with cerebellar hypoplasia either have none of the cells responsible for coordination or are deficient in such cells so that normal motor function is prevented. The abnormal function is manifested in incoordination, overreaching, paddling, and head tremor. The tremor is more noticeable when the horse is excited. The disease is often confused with wobbles but occurs at an even younger age (by 4 months), and the

491

horse suffering from this disease has less difficulty in backing and walking when blindfolded than the horse suffering from wobbles. All reported cases involved Arabians: 20 pure Arabians and a Welsh-Arabian cross. Sponseller (1967) has reported cases in which several mares foaled more than one affected foal. Inbreeding had occurred, and the names of 2 stallions appeared frequently in the pedigrees of 19 of the affected foals.

Fibular Enlargement

In the condition of fibular enlargement, the ponies are normal except that the hind legs splay outward from the hock joint. The fibula is reduced in modern horses, but in the affected ponies the fibula is a full-length shaft that matches improperly with the tibia. The mechanical pressures that are exerted cause lameness, which does not improve with time. Speed (1958) reported observing this condition in some families of Shetlands and suggested that it may be related to dwarfism. Affected ponies have been foaled by normal parents.

Hereditary Multiple Exostosis

This name is given to numerous bony protrusions that extend from the normal contour of the affected bones. A similar condition occurs in humans and is hereditary. It may affect most long bones as well as the ribs and pelvis of horses. Some horses are barely affected and severe lameness seldom results. Although there is no clear-cut genetic implication except for the similarity to human multiple exostosis, afflicted horses should not be used for breeding as a precaution.

Hip Dysplasia

When the upper hind leg fits into a flattened, shallow hip joint rather than a normal joint, hip dysplasia may result. A mincing gait and severe lameness are often the first symptoms. The condition does not appear very frequently, but it has been reported in Standardbreds by Jogi and Norberg (1962) and in Shetlands by Manning (1963). The trait is partially determined by genetics in some breeds of dogs.

Umbilical Hernia

492 Since this commonly occurring condition usually persists for only a few months and then disappears, it is not a serious problem (Figure 15-19).

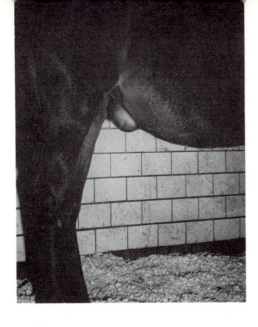

FIGURE 15-19
Umbilical hernia, as shown by a
2-year-old colt, is usually not a serious
problem. Photograph by John E.
Lowe, courtesy of Robert H. Whitlock,
Ithaca, New York.

Surgery is usually successful for those hernias that persist. The inheritance
pattern is not known, although Aurich (1959) and Schlaak (1942) have
postulated that a recessive gene is the predisposing cause.

Cryptorchidism

The failure of one or both testes to descend completely into the scrotum
is called cryptorchidism. If only one testis fails to descend (unilateral
cryptorchidism), the affected stallion is usually fertile. However, if both
testes fail to descend (bilateral cryptorchidism), the stallion is sterile.
Stanic (1960) presented the unusual data that appear in Table 15-11. These
data indicate a surprisingly greater incidence of cryptorchidism on the left
side than on the right, particularly in abdominal cryptorchids. The influence of heredity is not clear, but as a precaution, monorchid horses should
not be used for breeding.

TABLE 15-11
Incidence of bilateral and unilateral cryptorchidism ($n = 417$)

Location	Left Side	Right Side	Both	Percentage
Abdominal	158/417	77/417	16/417	60.2
Inguinal	75/417	78/417	10/417	39.1
Both	0	0	3	.7
Percentage	55.8	37.2	7.0	

SOURCE: Stanic, M. N. 1960.

Equine Periodic Ophthalmia (Moon Blindness)

Equine periodic ophthalmia (EPO) is an infection of the eye that was originally observed to reoccur approximately as often as a new moon. As the disease progresses, cataract formation and eventual blindness occur. There are many theories as to the cause of EPO, such as vitamin deficiency or excess, other nutritional factors, and genetics. There is some evidence that a leptospiral infection is involved. A recent theory (Lowe, personal communication, 1975) is that EPO is the result of an autoimmune reaction. Cross (1966) found no evidence for quantitative inheritance. He did estimate a frequency of 10–20 percent in the northeastern United States. The British, however, reduced the incidence from 20–30 percent in 1840 to nearly 7 percent by 1900. Whether or not selection was the cause, stallions with symptoms of EPO (that is, cataract) were not allowed to breed as a result of the recommendations of the Royal Commission for Horse Breeding. This evidence supports at least a genetic predisposition to the disease, although some environmental factors may also have changed during such a long period.

Other Characters

Some other abnormalities not discussed here are mentioned by Jones and Bogart (1971), Stormont (1958), and Lerner (1944).

The relative brevity of the foregoing discussion and the repeated lack of solid facts concerning inheritance patterns emphasize the fact that not much is known about the inheritance of most lethals and abnormalities in horses. Fortunately, few of such abnormalities are major problems that are beyond the control of the horse breeder.

References

Blood Systems

Bengtsson, S., B. Gahne, and J. Rendel. 1968. Genetic studies on transferrins, albumins, prealbumins, and esterases in Swedish horses. *Acta. Agric. Scand.* 18:60.

Bengtsson, S., and K. Sandberg. 1972. Phosphoglucomutase polymorphism in Swedish horses. *Anim. Blood Groups and Biochem. Genetics* 3:115.

Braend, M. 1964. Serum types of Norwegian horses. *Nord. Vet. Med.* 16:363.

Braend, M. 1967. Genetic variation of horse hemoglobin. *Hereditas* 58:385.

Braend, M. 1970. Genetics of horse acidic prealbumins. *Genetics* 65:495.

Braend, M., and G. Efremov. 1965. Hemoglobins, haptoglobins, and albumins of horses. *Proceedings of 9th European Conference on Animal Blood Groups and Biochemical Polymorphism, Prague, 1964*:253.

Braend, M., and C. Stormont. 1964. Studies on hemoglobin and transferrin types of horses. *Nord. Vet. Med.* 16:31.

Cradock-Watson, J. E. 1967. Immunological similarity of horse, donkey, and mule haemoglobins. *Nature* 215:630.

Franks, D. 1962a. Differences in red-cell antigen strength in the horse due to gene interaction. *Nature* 195:580.

Franks, D. 1962b. Horse blood groups and hemolytic disease of the newborn foal. *Ann. N.Y. Acad. Sci.* 97:235.

Gahne, B. 1961. Studies of transferrins in serum and milk of Swedish cattle. *Anim. Prod.* 3:135.

Gahne, B. 1966. Studies of the inheritance of electrophoretic forms of transferrins, albumins, prealbumins, and plasma esterases of horses. *Genetics* 53:681.

Gahne, B., S. Bengtsson, and K. Sandberg. 1970. Genetic control of cholinesterase activity in horse serum. *Anim. Blood Groups and Biochem. Genetics* 1:207.

Jamieson, A. 1965. The genetics of transferrins in cattle. *Heredity* 20:419.

Kelly, E. P., C. Stormont, and Y. Suzuki. 1971. Catalase polymorphism in the red cells of horses. *Anim. Blood Groups and Biochem. Genetics* 2:135.

Mathai, C. K., S. Ohno, and E. Beutler. 1966. Sex-linkage of the glucose-6-phosphate dehydrogenase gene in *Equidae*. *Nature* 210:115.

Niece, R. L., and D. W. Kracht. 1967. Genetics of transferrins in burros (*Equus asinus*). *Genetics* 57:837.

Osterhoff, D. R. 1967. Haemoglobin, transferrin, and albumin types in equidae (horses, mules, donkeys, and zebras). *Proceedings of 10th European Conference on Animal Blood Groups and Biochemical Polymorphism, Paris, 1966*:345.

Osterhoff, D. R., D. O. Schmid, and I. S. Ward-Cox. 1970. Blood group and serum type studies in Basuto ponies. *Proceedings of 11th European Conference on Animal Blood Groups and Biochemical Polymorphism, Warsaw, 1968*:453.

Osterhoff, D. R., and I. S. Ward-Cox. 1972. Quantitative studies on horse hemoglobins. *Proceedings of 12th European Conference on Animal Blood Groups and Biochemical Polymorphism, 1970*:541.

Sandberg, K. 1968. Genetic polymorphism in carbonic anhydrase from horse erythrocytes. *Hereditas* 60:411.

Sandberg, K. 1970. Blood group factors and erythrocytic protein polymorphism in Swedish horses. *Proceedings of 11th European Conference on Animal Blood Groups and Biochemical Polymorphism, Warsaw, 1968:447.*

Sandberg, K. 1972. A third allele in the horse albumin system. *Anim. Blood Groups and Biochem. Genetics* 3:207.

Sandberg, K. 1974. Blood typing of horses: Current status and application to identification problems. *1st World Congress on Genetics Applied to Livestock Production* 1:253.

Sandberg, K., and S. Bengtsson. 1972. Polymorphism of hemoglobin and 6-phosphogluconate dehydrogenase in horse erythrocytes. *Proceedings of 12th European Conference on Animal Blood Groups and Biochemical Polymorphism, 1970:527.*

Schmid, D. O. 1966. Further progress in serogenetics in horses. *Proceedings of 10th European Conference on Animal Blood Groups and Biochemical Polymorphism, Paris, 1966:339.*

Scott, A. M. 1972. Improved separation of polymorphic esterases in horses. *Proceedings of 12th European Conference on Animal Blood Groups and Biochemical Polymorphism, 1970:551.*

Stormont, C. 1972. Genetic markers in the blood of horses. *Proc. Horse Identification Seminar, December 8–9.* Washington State University, Pullman, p. 76.

Stormont, C., and Y. Suzuki. 1963. Genetic control of albumin phenotypes in horses. *Proc. Soc. Exper. Biol. Med.* 114:673.

Stormont, C., and Y. Suzuki. 1964. Genetic systems of blood groups in horses. *Genetics* 50:915.

Stormont, C., and Y. Suzuki. 1965. Paternity tests in horses. *Cornell Vet.* 55:365.

Stormont, C., Y. Suzuki, and J. Rendel. 1965. Application of blood typing and protein tests in horses. *Proceedings of 9th European Conference on Animal Blood Groups and Biochemical Polymorphism, Prague, 1964:221.*

Stormont, C., Y. Suzuki, and E. A. Rhode. 1964. Serology of horse blood groups. *Cornell Vet.* 54:439.

Suzuki, Y., and C. Stormont. 1972. Genetic control of an *in vitro* autolytic factor in horse red cells. *Proceedings of 12th European Conference on Animal Blood Groups and Biochemical Polymorphism, 1970:525.*

Vandeplassche, M., and L. Podliachouk. 1970. Chimerism in horses. *Proceedings of 11th European Conference on Animal Blood Groups and Biochemical Polymorphism, Warsaw, 1968:459.*

Coat Color

Anderson, W. S. 1913. The inheritance of coat color in horses. *American Nat.* 47:615.

Anderson, W. S. 1914. The inheritance of coat colors in horses. *Kentucky Agr. Expt. Sta. Bull. 180.*

Anderson, W. S. 1926. The inheritance of coat colour in domestic livestock. *Am. Vet. Med Asso.* 23:338.

Babcock, E. B., and R. E. Clausen. 1918. *Genetics in Relation to Agriculture.* New York: McGraw-Hill.

Berge, S. 1963. Hestefargenes genetikk. *Tidsskr. Det Norske Landbruk.* 70:359.

Blakeslee, L. H., R. S. Hudson, and H. R. Hunt. 1943. Curly coat in horses. *J. Heredity* 34:115.

Blanchard, N. 1902. Inheritance of coat color in Thoroughbred horses. *Biometrika* 1:361.

Blunn, C. T., and C. E. Howell. 1936. The inheritance of white facial markings in Arabian horses. *J. Heredity* 27:293.

Briquet, R., Jr. 1957. So-called "albino horses." *Boletim Indus. Anim.* 16:243.

Briquet, R., Jr. 1959a. Investigations on the relationship between markings on face and limbs in horses. *Rev. Remonta Vet.* 19.

Briquet, R., Jr. 1959b. *Genetica da Pelagem do Cavalo.* Rio de Janeiro: Instituto de Zootechnia.

Bunsow, R. 1911. Inheritance in race horses: Coat color. *Mendel. Jour.* 2:74.

Castle, W. E. 1940. The genetics of coat color in horses. *J. Heredity* 31:127.

Castle, W. E. 1946. Genetics of the Palomino horse. *J. Heredity* 37:35.

Castle, W. E. 1948. The ABC of color inheritance in horses. *Genetics* 33:22.

Castle, W. E. 1951a. Dominant and recessive black in mammals. *J. Heredity* 42:48.

Castle, W. E. 1951b. Genetics of the color varieties of horses. *J. Heredity* 42:297.

Castle, W. E. 1953. Note on the silver dapple mutation of Shetland ponies. *J. Heredity* 44:224.

Castle, W. E. 1954. Coat color inheritance in horses and other mammals. *Genetics* 39:35.

Castle, W. E. 1960. Fashion in the color of Shetland ponies and its genetic basis. *J. Heredity* 51:247.

Castle, W. E. 1961. Genetics of the Claybank dun horse. *J. Heredity* 51:121.

497

Castle, W. E., and F. L. King. 1951. New evidence on the genetics of the Palomino horse. *J. Heredity* 42:61.

Castle, W. E., and W. R. Singleton. 1960. Genetics of the "brown" horse. *J. Heredity* 51:127.

Castle, W. E., and W. R. Singleton. 1961. The Palomino horse. *Genetics* 46:1143.

Castle, W. E., and W. H. Smith. 1953. Silver dapple, a unique color variety among Shetland ponies. *J. Heredity* 44:139.

Charles, D. R. 1938. Studies on spotting patterns. *Genetics* 23:523.

Colombani, B. 1964. A case of total albinism in a Sardinian ass. *Ann. Fac. Med. Vet. Pisa* 16:76.

Comfort, A. 1958. Coat-colour and longevity in Thoroughbred mares. *Nature* 182:1531.

Crew, F. A. E., and A. D. Buchanan-Smith. 1930. The genetics of the horse. *Bibliographica Genetica* 6:123.

Domanski, A. J., and R. T. Prawochenski. 1948. Dun coat color in horses. *J. Heredity* 39:267.

Dreux, P. 1970. The degree of expression on limited piebaldness in the domestic horse. *Ann. Genet. Sel. Anim.* 2:119.

Estes, B. W. 1948. Lack of correlation between coat color and temperament. *J. Heredity* 39:84.

Gibbon, Helen. 1941. Leopard spotting and color alteration in that recently established breed of horses, the Colorado Ranger. *J. Colorado-Wyoming Acad. Sci.* 3:48.

Gilbey, Sir Walter. 1912. *Horses Breeding to Color.* London: Vinton and Co.

Gregory, W. K. 1926. The horse in the tiger's skin. *Bull. Zool. Soc.* 29:111.

Gremmel, F. 1939. Coat colors in horses. *J. Heredity* 30:437.

Hadwen, S. 1931. The melanomata of gray and white horses. *Canad. Med. Asso. J.* 21:519.

Harper, C. H. 1905. Studies in the inheritance of color in Percheron horses. *Biol. Bull.* 9:265.

Hatley, George. 1962. Crosses that will kill your color. *Appaloosa News* (February).

Heizer, E. E. 1931. Color inheritance in horses. *Proceedings of 24th Congress of American Society of Animal Production:*184.

Huitema, H. 1904. Archaic pattern in the horse and its relation to colour genes. *Z. Saugetierk.* 29:42.

Hurst, C. C. 1906. Inheritance of coat colour in horses. *Proc. Royal Soc.* 77(B):388.

Jones, W. E., and R. Bogart. 1971. *Genetics of the Horse.* East Lansing, Michigan: Caballus.

Keeler, C. F. 1947. Coat color and physique and temperament. *J. Heredity* 38:271.

Klemola, V. 1933. The "pied" and "splashed white" patterns in horses and ponies. *J. Heredity* 24:65.

Lehmann-Mathildenhoh, E. von. 1941. Beitrag zur Vererbungweissgeborener Pferde. *Zeit. Tierz. Zuchtungsbiol.* 49:191.

Lusis, J. A. 1942. Striping patterns in domestic horses. *Genetica* 23:31.

McCann, L. P. 1916. Sorrel color in horses. *J. Heredity* 7:370.

Miller, R. W. *Appaloosa Coat Color Inheritance.* Moscow, Idaho: Montana State University, Bozeman and Appaloosa Horse Club, Inc.

Odriozola, M. 1940. Where are the Thoroughbred "Palominos"? *J. Heredity* 31:128.

Odriozola, M. 1948. Agouti color in horses: Change of dominance in equine hybrids. *Proceedings of 8th International Congress on Genetics:*635.

Odriozola, M. 1951. *A los Colores del Caballo.* Madrid: National Syndicate of Livestock.

Odriozola, M. 1952. The eumelanin horse: Black or brown? *J. Heredity* 43:76.

Pearson, K. 1901. Mathematical contributions to the theory of evolution. Vol. 8. On the inheritance of coat colour in horses. *Philosophical Transactions of the Royal Society.* 195:79.

Pocock, R. I. 1903. The coloration of Quaggas. *Nature* 68:356.

Pocock, R. I. 1909. On the colours of horses, zebras, and Tapirs. *Ann. Mag. Nat. Hist.* 4:404.

Pulos, W. L., and F. B. Hutt. 1969. Lethal dominant white in horses. *J. Heredity* 60:59.

Richardson, T. C. 1924. The "pinto" burro. *J. Heredity* 15:73.

Ridgeway, W. 1919. The colour of race horses. *Nature* 104:334.

Salisbury, G. W. 1941. The inheritance of equine coat color. *J. Heredity* 32:235.

Salisbury, G. W., and J. W. Britton. 1941. The inheritance of equine coat color. Vol. 2. The dilutes with special reference to the Palomino. *J. Heredity* 32:255.

Searle, A. G. 1968. *Comparative Genetics of Coat Colour in Mammals.* London: Logo Press, Ltd.

Singleton, W. R., and Q. C. Bond. 1966. An allele necessary for dilute coat color in horses. *J. Heredity* 57:75.

Singleton, W. R., and J. N. Dent. 1964. Coat color in small horses of the Philippines. *J. Heredity* 55:220.

Smith, A. T. 1972. Inheritance of chin spot markings in horses. *J. Heredity* 63:100.

Stirling, H. B. 1925. Colour heredity in horses. *Scot. Jour. Agric.* 8:32.

Sturtevant, A. H. 1910. On the inheritance of coat color in American Harness horses. *Biol. Bull.* 19:204.

Sturtevant, A. H. 1912. A critical examination of recent studies of colour inheritance in horses. *J. Genetics* 2:41.

Tuff, P. 1933. Genetiske undersokelser over hestefarver. *Nord. Vet.* 6:28.

Wentworth, E. N. 1913. Color inheritance in the horse. *Zeit. Induktive Abst. Vererbungslehre* 11:10.

Wilson, J. 1910. The inheritance of coat color in horses. *Proceedings of Royal Dublin Society* 12:331.

Wilson, J. 1912. The inheritance of the dun coat color in horses. *Proceedings of Royal Dublin Society* 13:184.

Wright, S. 1917. Color inheritance in mammals. Vol. 7. Horse. *J. Heredity* 8:561.

Lethals and Defects

Archer, R. K. 1961. True haemophilia (haemophilia A) in a Thoroughbred foal. *Vet. Record* 75:338.

Archer, R. K. 1972. True haemophilia in horses. *Vet. Record* 91:665.

Aurich, R. 1959. A contribution to the inheritance of umbilical hernia in the horse. *Berl. Münch. tierärtzl. Wschr.* 72:420.

Bain, A. M. 1969. Foetal losses during pregnancy in the Thoroughbred mare: A record of 2,562 pregnancies. *New Zealand Vet. J.* 17:155.

Basrur, P. K., H. Kanagawa, and J. P. W. Gilman. 1969. An equine intersex with unilateral gonadal agenesis. *Canad. J. Comp. Med.* 33:297.

Basrur, P. K., H. Kanagawa, and L. Podliachouk. 1970. Further studies on the cell populations of an intersex horse. *Canad. J. Comp. Med.* 34:294.

Bekschner, H. G. 1969. *Horses' Diseases.* Sydney: Angus and Robertson.

Bielanski, W. 1946. The inheritance of shortening of the lower jaw (brachygnathia inferior) in the horse. *Przegl. hodowl.* 14:24.

Blakeslee, L. H., and R. S. Hudson. 1942. Twinning in horses. *J. Animal Sci.* 1:118.

Bornstein, S. 1967. The genetic sex of two intersexual horses and some notes on the karyotypes of normal horses. *Acta. Vet. Scand.* 8:291.

Bouters, R., M. Vandeplassche, and A. de Moor. 1972. An intersex (male pseudohermaphrodite) horse with 64,XX/65,XXY mosaicism. *Equine Vet. J.* 4:150.

Britton, J. W. 1945. An equine hermaphrodite. *Cornell Vet.* 35:373.

Britton, J. W. 1962. Birth defects in foals. *Thoroughbred* 34:288.

Bruner, D. W., E. R. Doll, F. E. Hull, and A. S. Kinkaid. 1950. Further studies on hemolytic icterus in foals. *Am. J. Vet. Res.* 11:22.

Bruner, D. W., F. E. Hull, and E. R. Doll. 1948. The relationship of blood factors to icteric foals. *Am. J. Vet. Res.* 9:237.

Bruner, D. W., F. E. Hull, P. R. Edwards, and E. R. Doll. 1948. Icteric foals. *J. Am. Vet. Med. Asso.* 122:440.

Buckingham, J. 1936. Hermaphrodite horses. *Vet. Record* 48:218.

Butz, H., and H. Meyer. 1957. Epitheliogenesis imperfecta neonatorium equi (Incomplete skin formation in the foal). *Dtsch. tierärztl. Wschr.* 64:555.

Comfort, A. 1952. Coat colour and longevity in Thoroughbred mares. *Nature* 182:1531.

Cronin, N. T. I. 1956. Hemolytic disease of newborn foals. *Vet. Rec.* 67:474.

Cross, R. S. N. 1966. Equine periodic ophthalmia. *Vet. Rec.* 78:8.

Dimock, W. W. 1950. "Wobbles"—an hereditary disease in horses. *J. Heredity* 41:319.

Doll, E. R. 1953. Evidence of production of anti-isoantibodies by foals with hemolytic icterus. *Cornell Vet.* 43:44.

Doll, E. R., and F. E. Hull. 1951. Observations on hemolytic icterus in newborn foals. *Cornell Vet.* 41:14.

Donahue, M. 1935. Navicular disease in horses. *Vet. Med.* 30:244.

Dungsworth, D. I., and M. E. Fowler. 1966. Cerebellar hypoplasia and degeneration in a foal. *Cornell Vet.* 56:17.

Dunn, H. O., J. T. Vaughan, and K. McEntee. 1974. Bilaterally cryptorchid stallion with female karyotype. *Cornell Vet.* 64:265.

Eaton, O. H. 1937. A summary of lethal characters in animals and man. *J. Heredity* 28:320.

Eriksson, K. 1955. Hereditary aniridia with secondary cataract in horses. *Nord. Vet.* 7:773.

Eriksson, K., and H. Sandstedt. 1938. Hereditary malformation of the iris and ciliary body with secondary cataract in the horse. *Svensk Vettidskr.* 43:11.

Fischer, H., and K. Helbig. 1951. A contribution to the question of the inheritance of patella dislocation in the horse. *Tierzucht.* 5:105.

Flechsig, J. 1950. Hereditary cryptorchism in a depot stallion. *Tierzucht.* 4:208.

Franks, David. 1962. Horse blood groups and hemolytic disease of the newborn foal. *Ann. N.Y. Acad. Sci.* 97:235.

Fraser, W. 1966. Two dissimilar types of cerebellar disorders in the horse. *Vet. Rec.* 78:608.

Gilman, J. P. W. 1956. Congenital hydrocephalus in domestic animals. *Cornell Vet.* 46:482.

Gluhovski, N., H. Bistriceanu, A. Sucui, and M. Bratu. 1970. A case of intersexuality in the horse with type 2A + XXXY chromosome formula. *Brit. Vet. J.* 126:522.

Gonzalez, B. M., and V. Villegas. 1928. "Bighead" of horses: A heritable disease. *J. Heredity* 19:159.

Hadorn, E. 1961. *Developmental Genetics and Lethal Factors.* New York: Wiley.

Hadwen, S. 1931. The melanomata of gray and white horses. *Canad. Med. Asso. J.* 25:519.

Hamori, D. 1940a. Genetical notes. Congenital patella subluxation in horses. *Allatorv. Lapok* 63:141.

Hamori, D. 1940b. Inheritance of the tendency to hernia in horses. *Allatorv. Lapok* 63:136.

Hamori, D. 1941a. Genetical notes. Myopia. *Allatorv. Lapok* 64:101.

Hamori, D. 1941b. Parrot mouth and hog mouth as inherited deformities. *Allatorv. Lapok* 64:57.

Hitenkov, G. G. 1941. Stringhalt in horses and its inheritance. *Vestn. Seljskohoz. Nauki Zivotn.* 2:64.

Hosoda, T. 1950. On the heritability of susceptibility to wind-sucking in horses. *Jap. J. Zootech. Sci.* 21:25.

Hutchins, D. R., E. E. Lepherd, and I. G. Crook. 1967. A case of equine haemophilia. *Aust. Vet. J.* 43:83.

Jogi, O., and I. Norberg. 1962. Malformation of the hip joint in a Standardbred horse. *Vet. Record* 74:421.

Jones, T. C., and F. D. Maurer. 1942. Heredity in periodic ophthalmia. *J. Am. Vet. Med. Asso.* 101:248.

Kaleff, B. 1935. Inheritance of flat-hoof in the horse. *Z. Zucht.* 33:153.

Kieffer, N. M., N. Judge, and S. Burns. 1971. Some cytogenetic aspects of an *Equus caballus* intersex. *Mammalian Chromosome News Letter* 12:18.

Koch, P. 1957. The heritability of chronic pulmonary emphysema in the horse. *Dtsch. tierärztl. Wschr.* 64:485.

Koch, P., and H. Fischer. 1950. Hereditary ataxia in Oldenburg foals. *Tierärztl. Umsch.* 5:317.

Koch, P., and H. Fischer. 1951. Oldenburg foal ataxia as a hereditary disease. *Tierärztl. Umsch.* 6:158.

502

Koch, W. 1936. Some hereditary diseases in the horse and their practical significance. *Münch. tierärztl. Wschr.* 87:181.

Lambert, W. V., S. R. Speelman, and E. P. Osborn. 1939. Differences in incidence of encephalomyelitis in horses. *J. Heredity* 30:349.

Lauprecht. E. 1935. Inheritance of twinning tendency in the horse. *Zuchtungskunde* 10:433.

Lerner, I. M. 1944. Lethal and sublethal characters in farm animals. *J. Heredity* 35:219.

McChesney, A. E., J. J. England, J. L. Adcock, L. L. Stackhouse, and T. L. Chow. 1970. Adenoviral infection in suckling Arabian foals. *Path. Vet.* 7:547.

McChesney, A. E., J. J. England, and L. J. Rich. 1973. Adenoviral infections in foals. *J. Am. Vet. Med. Asso.* 162:545.

McFeely, R. A., W. C. D. Hare, and J. D. Biggers. 1967. Chromosome studies in 14 cases of intersex in domestic animals. *Cytogenetics* 6:242.

McGuire, T. C., and M. J. Poppie. 1973. Hypogammaglobulinemia and thymic hypoplasia in horses: A primary combined immunodeficiency disorder. *Infect. Immun.* 8:272.

McGuire, T. C., and M. J. Poppie. 1973. Primary hypogammaglobulinemia and thymic hypoplasia in horses. *Fed. Proc.* 32:821.

McGuire, T. C., Marinel J. Poppie, and K. L. Banks. 1974. Combined (B- and T-lymphocyte) immunodeficiency: A fatal genetic disease in Arabian foals. *J. Am. Vet. Med. Asso.* 164:70.

Mackay-Smith, M. P. 1963. Discussion of pathogenesis and pathology of equine osteoarthritis. *Am. Vet. Med. J.* 141:1248.

Mahaffey, Leo W. 1968. Abortion in mares. *Vet. Rec.* 82:681.

Manning, J. P. 1963. Equine hip dysplasia-osteoarthritis. *Mod. Vet. Prac.* 44:44.

Mauderer, H. 1938. Hereditary defects in the horse. *Dtsch. tierärztl. Wschr.* 46:469.

Mauderer, H. 1942. Abrachia and torticollis: Lethal factors in horse breeding. *Zeit. tierärztl. Zucht.* 51:215.

Meacham, T., and C. Hutton. 1968. Reproductive efficiency on 14 horse farms. *J. Anim. Sci.* 27:434.

Miller, J. E. 1917. Horned horses. *J. Heredity* 8:303.

Morgan, J. P., W. D. Carlson, and O. R. Adams. 1962. Hereditary multiple exostosis in the horse. *J. Am. Vet. Med. Asso.* 140:1320.

Plank, G. M. van der. 1936. Pathology and inheritance. *Neue Forsch. Tierz. Abstammungsl.*:233–237.

Prawochenski, R. T. 1936. A case of lethal genes in the horse. *Nature* 137:869.

Prawochenski, R. 1941. *Proceedings of 7th International Genetics Congress, Edinburgh*:241.

Pulos, W., and F. B. Hutt. 1969. Lethal dominant white in horses. *J. Heredity* 60:59.

Roberts, Stephen J. 1956. *Veterinary Obstetrics and Genital Disease.* Author's publication, Ithaca, New York.

Rooney, F. R. 1963. Equine incoordination. *Cornell Vet.* 53:411.

Rooney, F. R. 1966. Contracted foals. *Cornell Vet.* 56:172.

Rooney, F. R., and M. E. Prickett. 1966. Foreleg splints in horses. *Cornell Vet.* 56:259.

Rooney, F. R., and M. E. Prickett. 1967. Congenital lordosis of the horse. *Cornell Vet.* 57:417.

Rooney, F. R., C. W. Raker, and K. J. Harmany. 1971. Congenital lateral luxation of the patella in the horse. *Cornell Vet.* 61:670.

Rossdale, P. D. 1968. Abnormal perinatal behavior in the Thoroughbred horse. *Brit. Vet. J.* 124:540.

Runciman, B. 1940. Roaring and whistling in Thoroughbred horses. *Vet. Record* 53:37.

Sangor, V. L., R. E. Mairs, and A. L. Trapp. 1964. Hemophilia in a foal. *J. Am. Vet. Med. Asso.* 142:259.

Scekin, V. A. 1973. The inheritance of stringhalt (cock gait) in the horse. *Konevodstru* 2:20.

Schlaak, F. 1942. Investigations on the inheritance of umbilical hernias in a horse breeding region. *Z. Tierz. Zuchtbiol.* 52:198.

Schlotthauer, C. F., and P. E. Zollman. 1956. The occurrence of so-called "white heifer" disease in a white Shetland Pony mare. *J. Am. Vet. Med. Asso.* 129:309.

Severson, B. D. 1917. Cloven hoof in Percherons. *J. Heredity* 8:466.

Severson, B. D. 1918. Extra toes in horse and steer. *J. Heredity* 9:39.

Shupe, J. L., A. E. Olson, and R. P. Sharma. 1970. Multiple exostosis in horses. *Mod. Vet. Pract.* 51:34.

Smith, G. A. 1968. A case of consulsive syndrome in a newborn hunter foal. *Vet. Record* 83:588.

Speed, J. G. 1958. A cause of malformation of the limbs of Shetland Ponies with a note on its phylogenic significance. *Brit. Vet. J.* 114:18.

Sponseller, M. L. 1967. Equine cerebellar hypoplasia and degeneration. *Proceedings of 12th Annual Meeting of American Association of Equine Practitioners.*

Spurrell, F. A., L. V. Baudin, and W. J. L. Felts. 1965. Radiography of the forelimb of the horse. *Proceedings of 11th Annual Meeting of American Association of Equine Practitioners.*

Stanic, M. N. 1960. *Mod. Vet. Pract.* 41:30.

Stormont, Clyde. 1958. Genetics and disease. In *Advances in Veterinary Science*. C. A. Brandly and E. L. Jungheer, eds. Vol. 4, New York: Academic Press, p. 137.

Stormont, Clyde, and Y. Suzuki. 1964. Genetics systems of blood groups in horses. *Genetics* 50:915.

Theile, H. 1958. Polydactyly in a foal. *Monatshefte Vet. Med.* 13:342.

Tuff, P. 1945. Inheritance of inguinal hernia in domestic animals. *Norsk. Veterinaertidsskrift* 57:332.

Tuff, P. 1948. The inheritance of a number of defects in the joints, bones, and ligaments of the foot of the horse. *Norsk. Veterinaertidsskrift* 60:385.

Vandeplassche, M., Luba Podliachouk, and R. Beaud. 1970. Some aspects of twin gestation in the mare. *Canad. J. Comp. Med.* 34:218.

Van Der May, G. J. W., E. F. Kleyn, and C. C. Van De Watering. 1967. Investigation of hereditary predisposition to navicular disease. *Tijdschr. Diergenessk.* 92:1261.

Weber, W. 1947a. Congenital cataract, a recessive mutation in the horse. *Schweiz. Arch. Tierheilk.* 89:397.

Weber, W. 1947b. Schistosoma reflexum in the horse, with a contribution on its origin. *Schweiz. Arch. Tierheilk.* 89:244.

Weischer, F. 1949. Clarifying the hereditary and environmental relationships in equine mallenders. *Tierärztl. Umsch.* 4:318.

Weisner, E. 1955. The importance of inherited eye defects in horse breeding. *Tierzucht.* 4:310.

Wheat, J. D., and P. C. Kennedy. 1953. Cerebellar hypoplasia and its sequilae in a horse. *J. Am. Vet. Med. Asso.* 131:241.

White, D. J., and D. A. Farebrother. 1969. A case of intersexuality in the horse. *Vet. Rec.* 85:203.

Wille, H. 1945. Is inguinal hernia hereditary in the horse? *Norsk. Veterinaertidsskrift* 57:332.

Wriedt, C. 1924. Vererbungsfaktoren bei weissen Pferden im Gestüt Fredriksborg. *Zeit. Tierz. Zuchtungsbiol.* 1:231.

Wriedt, C. 1930. *Heredity in Livestock*. London: Macmillan.

Wussow, W., and W. Hartwig. 1955. Genetic investigations on mallenders in cold-blood horses. *Tierzucht.* 9:195.

Yamane, J. 1927. Atresia coli in the horse. *Zeit. Induktive Abst. Vererbungslehre* 46:188.

CHAPTER SIXTEEN *Relationships and Inbreeding*

Horses are often said to have so much of the blood of one horse and so much of the blood of another. Naturally this is not literally true, but these estimates may actually apply to the fraction of genes that come from some common ancestor.

For example, the foal in Figure 16-1 received a sample half of the genes of its Appaloosa sire. The relationship between a parent and its offspring is said to be 50 percent. An animal (noninbred) is related to itself by 100 percent. This halving of relationships and genes in common occurs with each generation. The relationship to each parent is 50 percent, to each grandparent is 25 percent, to each great-grandparent is 12.5 percent, and so on. Thus, after only a few generations, any ancestor is likely to be the source of only a small fraction of the genes of its descendants. These rules hold when all the ancestors are unrelated. When some are related, inbreeding results, and the problem of determining relationships is more complex.

Relationships between individuals not in direct line of descent but with a common ancestor can also be determined essentially by a halving for each intervening animal in the pedigree. For example, colts by the same stallion but different mares (paternal half-sibs, Figure 16-2) have an average relationship of 25 percent. Maternal half-sibs are also 25 percent related to each other. Fraternal twins have the same sire and dam as do full brothers or sisters (Figure 16-3). They are related by 50 percent to each other (25 percent through the sire and 25 percent through the dam), as are full sibs born at different times. Identical twins are genetically alike, so they are 100 percent related to each other. The frequency of all twinning (fraternal and identical) in horses, however, is low, so not many of the even less frequent identical twins are encountered.

FIGURE 16-3
A Belgian mare and her full brother-sister progeny. Photograph courtesy of John Briggs, Cornell University, Ithaca, New York.

Some samples of common relationships are given in Figure 16-4. Pedigrees are indicated by arrows to increase the reader's understanding of the nomenclature of relationships.

16.1   Importance of Relationships

There are two important reasons to calculate additive relationships between relatives. First, the *additive relationship* is a measure of the fraction of like genes shared by two animals and thus shows how reliable one of the relative's records will be in predicting the genetic value of the other. Second, the *inbreeding coefficient* of an animal, which, if high, is usually undesirable, is calculated as half the additive relationship between the parents. For example, if the non-inbred son in Figure 16-5 is mated to his dam, what will be the inbreeding of the resulting foals? The dam and son additive relationship is 50 percent. Since the relationship of the parents is halved, the foals will be 25 percent inbred.

Linebreeding is closely related to inbreeding. Actually, it is a form of inbreeding aimed at trying to maintain a close relationship to a particular animal. Thus, lines usually trace to or are named after the animal that is

Pair	Relatives	Relationship (percent)
B,C	parent-progeny	50
C,D	full brothers or sisters	50
A,G	grandparent–grandprogeny	25
A,K	great–grandparent–great-grandprogeny	12.5
C,H	full aunt–niece	25
G,H	full cousins	12.5

Pair	Relatives	Relationship (percent)
E,F	half–brothers or sisters	25
E,J	half–aunt–niece	12.5
I,J	half–cousins	6.25

Pair	Relatives	Relationship (percent)
C,C′	if identical twins	100
C,C	non–inbred animal to itself	100

FIGURE 16-4
Examples of common relationships.

FIGURE 16-5
Leeward Bodick, a perlino-colored Gotland colt, and his buckskin-colored dam, Honung. Photograph courtesy of John R. Price, Shady Trail Ranch, Bonner Springs, Kansas.

GENETICS OF THE HORSE

used as a base. For example, the King Ranch breeding program for Quarter Horses was based on linebreeding to what they considered the ideal Quarter Horse, Old Sorrel. An example of matings to Wimpy, a double grandson of Old Sorrel, is shown in Figure 16-6. A 1945 study of King Ranch Quarter Horses showed an average relationship of 40 percent to Old Sorrel.

Thus, knowledge of relationships can be helpful in selecting animals on the basis of relatives' records or in arranging matings to avoid high levels of inbreeding.

16.2   Computing Relationships

Unfortunately, there is no very easy way to compute the relationships and inbreeding of horses in a herd, but anyone can do the computations by following a few simple rules. The procedure appears to be quite complicated, but working two or three examples will show that many relationships can be calculated more simply and more quickly by using these rules than by any other method.

The next few paragraphs describe a procedure for calculating the relationships among all the animals in a herd. The procedure takes quite a lot of time and a large sheet (or sheets) of paper but is relatively easy. The method is based on the fact that if two animals are related, then one or both of the parents of the younger of the two must also be related to the older animal of the pair. In fact, if C and D are the two animals and A and B are the parents of D, the additive relationship between animals C and D is one-half the relationship between A and C plus one-half the relationship between B and C. [$a_{CD} = (1/2)a_{AC} + (1/2)a_{BC}$, where a stands for the additive relationship and the subscripts refer to the animals that are related.] The basis for this method is illustrated in Figure 16-7. Similarly, the coefficient of inbreeding of an animal is calculated as one-half the additive relationship between its parents, as diagrammed in Figure 16-8.

Tabular Method

The procedure is called the tabular method because it requires construction of a table that, when finished, will give the additive relationship of any animal to any other in the herd. For example, in Table 16-1, A and B are parents of D, while C has as one parent animal A. The other parent of C is not related to A or B so it is ignored. The table gives the additive relationships among all pairs of the 4 animals. To find the additive relationship between C and D, go to row C and then across to column D. The additive relationship is 1/4 or 25 percent.

510

Foal No.

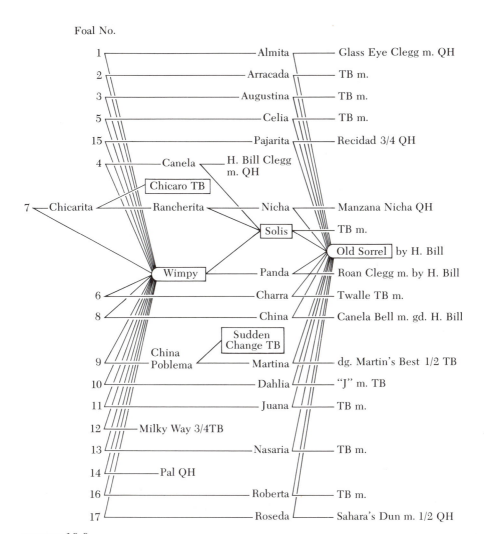

FIGURE 16-6

Matings to Wimpy, a Quarter Horse stallion. Wimpy, a double grandson of Old Sorrel, was mated to mares whose average relationship to him was equivalent to their being his half-sisters. Wimpy's foals derived nearly half (44.9 percent) of their genes from Old Sorrel. They derived 67 percent of their genes from the Quarter Horse breed and the remaining 33 percent from the Thoroughbred. All sires are boxed in. All horizontal lines trace female lines of descent; all diagonal lines trace male lines of descent. The foals are numbered consecutively in an alphabetical listing of their dams. For example, foal number one is out of Almita by Wimpy; Almita is out of the Glass Eye Clegg mare by Old Sorrel. Adapted from Rhoad and Kleberg. 1946.

511

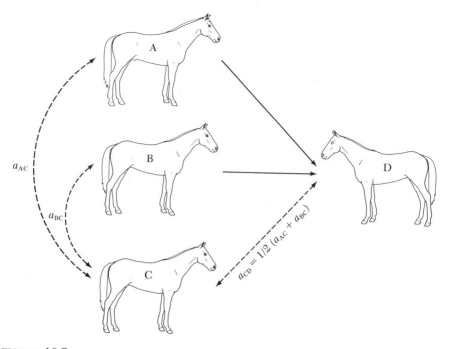

FIGURE 16-7

Basis for tabular method of computing relationships is that the relationship between C and D is one-half the relationship between C and the sire of D plus one-half the relationship between C and the dam of D.

FIGURE 16-8

The inbreeding coefficient for an animal (F_Z for animal Z) is one-half the relationship between the parents (a_{XY} for X and Y).

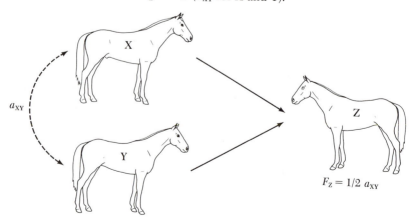

$$F_Z = 1/2\ a_{XY}$$

TABLE 16-1
Relationship table

		Animals (columns)			
				A-?	A-B
		A	B	C	D
	A	1	0	1/2	1/2
	B	0	1	0	1/2
Animals (rows)	C	1/2	0	1	1/4
	D	1/2	1/2	1/4	1

The rules for computing additive relationships and inbreeding are:

1. First, determine which animals are to be included. Put them in order by date of birth, oldest first. This step is very important.

2. Write the names or numbers of the animals in order of birth across the top of the table (the columns) and down the left side of the table (the rows) as shown in Table 16-1.

3. Write above the numbers of the animals the names or numbers of their parents, if known.

4. Put a 1 in each of the diagonal cells of the table, such as row 1, column 1; row 2, column 2. This is the animal's basic additive relationship of 100 percent to itself unless the animal is inbred. If the inbreeding coefficient of any of the first or base animals is known, add that to the diagonal for that animal. All other inbreeding coefficients will be computed in this manner.

5. Compute entries for each off-diagonal cell of row 1 according to the rule of 1/2 the entry for the first parent in this row plus 1/2 the entry for the second parent in the row. When the first row is finished, write the same values down the first column. If this step is not correctly followed, difficulty will almost always result.

6. Go to the next row and begin at the diagonal, which now has a 1 in it. Add to that 1, one-half of the relationship between the animal's parents, which can be found from an earlier entry in the table — or perhaps the parents are known or assumed to be unrelated. This is the inbreeding coefficient described in rule 4. Often the inbreeding coefficient is zero. Continue across the row as before, computing the off-diagonal entries according to rule 5. Put the values for this row down the corresponding column.

7. Continue in this manner until the table is complete, always remembering to do a row at a time and to put the same values down the corresponding column before going to the next row.

513

In summary, the first basic step is to add to the 1 in the diagonal the inbreeding coefficient, which is one-half the relationship between the animal's parents. This value is found at the intersection of the row and column of the parents, as shown in Figure 16-8. The second basic step is to compute the off-diagonal relationships. In Figure 16-7, the relationship is one-half the sum of the two relationships that appear to the left in the same row.

Because these rules may seem complicated, the following example is given to clarify the procedure.

Example

Suppose that a stallion, sire A, is mated to his own daughter, C, as in Figure 16-9. Note that the only individuals in an animal's pedigree that must be recorded are its parents. The animals, in order by age, are A, B, C, and D, and should be written as described in step 1. Write the parents, if known, above the letters as shown in Table 16-2. The parents of A and B can be ignored unless they are known to be related to each other. Write 1's in all 4 diagonal cells [where the (A,A), (B,B), (C,C), and (D,D) rows and columns meet].

Now begin on row 1, that is, the row for A. B is assumed not to be related to A so enter zero under the column labeled B. If the relationship of A and B is known and it is not zero, enter that instead.

The entry for row A, column C is determined according to rule 5 (1/2 the entry for row A, column A plus 1/2 the entry for row A, column B) since A and B are the parents of C. Thus, $(1/2)(1) + (1/2)(0) = 1/2$.

The entry for row A, column D will be 1/2 the (A,A) entry plus 1/2 the (A,C) entry, which is $(1/2)(1) + (1/2)(1/2) = 3/4$. The first row is now finished.

The last part of rule 5 is to write the values in row A down column A. Column A will be 1, 0, 1/2, and 3/4. The additive relationships of animal A to the other 3 animals have now been computed.

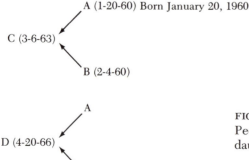

A (1-20-60) Born January 20, 1960

C (3-6-63)

B (2-4-60)

A

D (4-20-66)

C

FIGURE 16-9
Pedigree for a stallion, A, mated to his daughter, C.

TABLE 16-2
Relationship table for the sample pedigree in Figure 16-9 (The relationships are given in fractions; to obtain percentages, multiply by 100.)

Birthdate:	1-20-60	2-4-60	3-6-63	4-20-66
Parents:	—	—	A-B	A-C
Animal	A	B	C	D
A	1	0	1/2	3/4
B	0	1	1/2	1/4
C	1/2	1/2	$1 + (1/2)(0) = 1$	3/4
D	3/4	1/4	3/4	$1 + (1/2)(1/2) = 1 + 1/4$

The second row, row B, is done similarly, beginning at row B, column B. The parents of B were not related so B is not inbred. Therefore, do not add anything to the 1 already in the (B,B) cell.

The entry for row B, column C is $(1/2)(0) + (1/2)(1) = 1/2$. The value for row B, column D is $(1/2)(0) + (1/2)(1/2) = 1/4$. Now write the values for row B down column B: 0, 1, 1/2, and 1/4. The 0 and 1 were already there.

Next, row C. The row C, column C entry is the 1 already there plus 1/2 the additive relationship between the parents of C, which are A and B. Look at the entry for row A, column B, and find zero for the additive relationship between A and B. The entry is then $1 + (1/2)(0) = 1$.

The row C, column D entry is $(1/2)(1/2) + (1/2)(1) = 3/4$. Write this value also into row D, column C, according to step 5.

The last entry is row D, column D. Add to the 1 already there, 1/2 the additive relationship between the parents, A and C. A and C are found to be related by 1/2 from the row A, column C entry. The row D, column D entry is then $1 + (1/2)(1/2) = 1 + 1/4$. Thus, D is 1/4 or 25 percent inbred.

Note from this special kind of mating that animal D is related to A, her father, by 75 percent and also by 75 percent to her mother, C, but is related to her grandmother only by 25 percent. The only way that two animals can be related by more than 50 percent is if one or both the animals is inbred. This was true with D and C and also with D and A. D is inbred.

For a herd of any size, the amount of paper required will be large and the amount of time to complete the table will be great. The labor involved, however, is simple and straightforward. Before starting a large herd, it would be a good idea to practice on a small segment of the herd and to work through the examples given here, or to take a particular horse family and find the relationships among the members of the family. Many breeders might be surprised by the results.

Reading the Table

To review, the relationship of any animal to any other animal is obtained by finding the row of the first animal and then going over to the column of the second animal. The value at the intersection of the row and column is the relationship between the first animal and the second animal. The entries in the diagonal (for example, row A and column A) give the relationship of an animal to itself. If the value is greater than 1, the excess over 1 is the inbreeding coefficient for that animal. For example, the value for animal D is found in row D, column D to be $1 + 1/4$. The excess over 1 is $1/4$, so the inbreeding coefficient of D is $1/4$ or 25 percent.

Since an inbred animal will have an additive relationship with itself (diagonal in the table) of greater than 1, the question may arise as to how relationships can be greater than 1. Actually, the additive relationship can be as small as zero and as large as 2. The additive relationship is twice the probability of identical genes occurring in the 2 animals. The maximum of such a probability for identical twins is 1; thus, doubling gives a maximum additive relationship of 2. The additive relationship is, however, the one that gives the fraction of gene effects alike and, thus, is the one used in devising weighting factors for records of relatives in genetic evaluation. The additive relationship between the parents of an animal is also used in computing the inbreeding coefficient for an animal. Even if the additive relationship seems somewhat illogical, it is the most useful measure of relationships. The *coefficient of relationship* is often used to compute a relationship that can have a minimum value of zero and a maximum value of 1. For non-inbred animals, the coefficient of relationship is the same as the additive relationship. For inbred animals (say, A and B), the coefficient of relationship can be computed as $r_{AB} = (a_{AB})/(\sqrt{a_{AA}a_{BB}})$. For example, suppose that we want to find the coefficient of relationship between animals C and D in Table 16-2: $a_{CD} = 3/4$, $a_{CC} = 1$, and $a_{DD} = 1\frac{1}{4}$. Thus, $r_{CD} = (3/4)/[\sqrt{(1)(1\frac{1}{4})}] = .67$ rather than $a_{CD} = .75$. The coefficient of relationship between non-inbred animals A and C (Table 16-2) is $r_{AC} = (1/2)/[\sqrt{(1)(1)}] = .5$, which is the same as a_{AC}.

A Real Example

A more realistic example would be to compute the relationship between one of the foundation sires of the Tennessee Walking Horse breed, Allan F-1, and his great-great-grandson, Hound Allen. The pedigree is shown in Figure 16-10. The horses have been labeled A, B, . . . , J for the purpose of computing the relationships in Table 16-3. The completed table shows all relationships among the 10 animals and their inbreeding coefficients. J. Lane Fletcher computed relationships and inbreeding coefficients for a sample of the Tennessee Walking Horse breed and found average inbreeding to be low: 1.24 percent for foundation animals and 3.62 percent for those born in 1940.

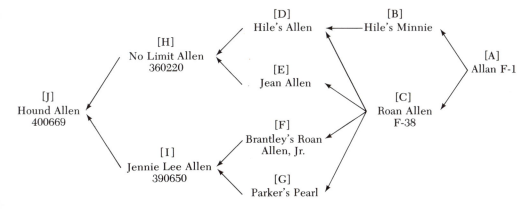

FIGURE 16-10
Pedigree of Hound Allen, A Tennessee Walking Horse. This pedigree shows the extent of inbreeding to Allan F-1 and to his prominent sons, among whom the most important is Roan Allen. The coefficient of inbreeding of Hound Allen is 14.05 percent (12.5 percent from Roan Allen and 1.56 percent from Allan F-1). Adapted from Fletcher. 1946.

Inbreeding appears to have little value in horse-breeding programs because of its many detrimental effects, especially the increase in mortality with increasing inbreeding and the increase in fertility problems. However, few systematic studies have been made of the effects of inbreeding. Although the King Ranch followed a linebreeding program in attempting to fix the characteristics of Old Sorrel in the Quarter Horse breed, they also avoided inbreeding as much as possible. The study by Fletcher (1945) showed a higher inbreeding (4.9 percent) for King Ranch horses than for a sample of other Quarter Horses (1.7 percent). The average relationship among the King Ranch Quarter Horses, however, was 20.1 percent, so that random mating of them would have resulted in an average inbreeding coefficient of 10 percent.

Some breeders have stressed crosses between varying sire or dam lines. The amount of inbreeding in the lines, however, has usually been low. Lasley (1972) has suggested that development of inbred lines for crossing may be advantageous. There is no evidence to support or refute such a view.

TABLE 16-3
Relationships in pedigree of Hound Allen (J) show a high relationship of Allan F-1 (A) to his great-great-grandson, Hound Allen (J), as a result of linebreeding, and an even higher relationship of Roan Allen F-38 (C) to his great-grandson (J)

	A	A-? B	A-? C	B-C D	C-? E	C-? F	C-? G	D-E H	F-G I	H-I J
A	1	1/2	1/2	1/2	1/4	1/4	1/4	3/8	1/4	5/16
B	1/2	1	1/4	5/8	1/8	1/8	1/8	3/8	1/8	1/4
C	1/2	1/4	1	5/8	1/2	1/2	1/2	9/16	1/2	17/32
D	1/2	5/8	5/8	1+1/8	5/16	5/16	5/16	23/32	5/16	33/64
E	1/4	1/8	1/2	5/16	1	1/4	1/4	21/32	1/4	29/64
F	1/4	1/8	1/2	5/16	1/4	1	1/4	9/32	5/8	29/64
G	1/4	1/8	1/2	5/16	1/4	1/4	1	9/32	5/8	29/64
H	3/8	3/8	9/16	23/32	21/32	9/32	9/32	1+5/32	9/32	23/32
I	1/4	1/8	1/2	5/16	1/4	5/8	5/8	9/32	1+1/8	45/64
J	5/16	1/4	17/32	33/64	29/64	29/64	29/64	23/32	45/64	1+9/64

16.3   Practice Problems in Computing Relationships and Inbreeding

Practice Problem One

Following is an example of systematic inbreeding where a sire, A, is mated back to his daughters in each succeeding generation.

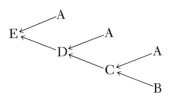

Compute the relationships among the 5 animals as well as the inbreeding coefficients of D and E. Assume that the parents of A and B are unrelated.

Parents		—	—	A–B	A–C	A–D
Animal		A	B	C	D	E
A		1	0			
B		0	1			
C						
D						
E						

Solution to Practice Problem

Parents		—	—	A–B	A–C	A–D
Animal		A	B	C	D	E
A		1	0	1/2	3/4	7/8
B		0	1	1/2	1/4	1/8
C		1/2	1/2	1	3/4	5/8
D		3/4	1/4	3/4	1 + 1/4	1
E		7/8	1/8	5/8	1	1 + 3/8

(See computations on pp. 520–521)   519

TABLE 16-4

Relationships in the pedigree of 4 King Ranch stallions: Solis, Old Sorrel, Hickory Bill, and Peter McCue, as computed for Figure 16-11

	— A	A-? B	B-? C	B-? D	B-? E	D-? F	C-? G	D-? H
A	1	1/2	1/4	1/4	1/4	1/8	1/8	1/8
B	1/2	1	1/2	1/2	1/2	1/4	1/4	1/4
C	1/4	1/2	1	1/4	1/4	1/8	1/2	1/8
D	1/4	1/2	1/4	1	1/4	1/2	1/8	1/2
E	1/4	1/2	1/4	1/4	1	1/8	1/8	1/8
F	1/8	1/4	1/8	1/2	1/8	1	1/16	1/4
G	1/8	1/4	1/2	1/8	1/8	1/16	1	1/16
H	1/8	1/4	1/8	1/2	1/8	1/4	1/16	1
I	1/8	1/4	1/8	1/2	1/8	1/4	1/16	1/4
J	1/4	1/2	1/4	5/8	5/8	5/16	1/8	5/16
K	1/8	1/4	1/8	1/2	1/8	1/4	1/16	1/4
L	1/16	1/8	1/16	1/4	1/16	1/2	1/32	1/8
M	3/16	3/8	3/8	9/16	3/16	9/32	9/16	9/32
N	1/8	1/4	1/8	1/2	1/8	1/4	1/16	5/8
O	3/16	3/8	3/16	9/16	3/8	9/32	3/32	9/32
P	3/32	3/16	3/32	3/8	3/32	3/8	3/64	3/16

Computations:

(row, column)

$(A,C) = (1/2)(1) + (1/2)(0) = 1/2$
$(A,D) = (1/2)(1) + (1/2)(1/2) = 3/4$
$(A,E) = (1/2)(1) + (1/2)(3/4) = 7/8$

$(B,C) = (1/2)(0) + (1/2)(1) = 1/2$
$(B,D) = (1/2)(0) + (1/2)(1/2) = 1/4$
$(B,E) = (1/2)(0) + (1/2)(1/4) = 1/8$

$(C,C) = 1 + (1/2)(A,B) = 1 + (1/2)(0) = 1$
$(C,D) = (1/2)(1/2) + (1/2)(1) = 3/4$
$(C,E) = (1/2)(1/2) + (1/2)(3/4) = 5/8$

(row, column)

$(C,A) = 1/2$
$(D,A) = 3/4$
$(E,A) = 7/8$

$(C,B) = 1/2$
$(D,B) = 1/4$
$(E,B) = 1/8$

$(D,C) = 3/4$
$(E,C) = 5/8$

D-? I	D-E J	D-? K	F-? L	D-G M	H-I N	I-J O	K-L P
1/8	1/4	1/8	1/16	3/16	1/8	3/16	3/32
1/4	1/2	1/4	1/8	3/8	1/4	3/8	3/16
1/8	1/4	1/8	1/16	3/8	1/8	3/16	3/32
1/2	5/8	1/2	1/4	9/16	1/2	9/16	3/8
1/8	5/8	1/8	1/16	3/16	1/8	3/8	3/32
1/4	5/16	1/4	1/2	9/32	1/4	9/32	3/8
1/16	1/8	1/16	1/32	9/16	1/16	3/32	3/64
1/4	5/16	1/4	1/8	9/32	5/8	9/32	3/16
1	5/16	1/4	1/8	9/32	5/8	21/32	3/16
5/16	1 + 1/8	5/16	5/32	3/8	5/16	23/32	15/64
1/4	5/16	1	1/8	9/32	1/4	9/32	9/16
1/8	5/32	1/8	1	9/64	1/8	9/64	9/16
9/32	3/8	9/32	9/64	1 + 1/16	9/32	21/64	27/128
5/8	5/16	1/4	1/8	9/32	1 + 1/8	15/32	3/16
21/32	23/32	9/32	9/64	21/64	15/32	1 + 5/32	27/128
3/16	15/64	9/16	9/16	27/128	3/16	27/128	1 + 1/16

$$(D,D) = 1 + (1/2)(A,C) = 1 + (1/2)(1/2) = 1 + 1/4$$
$$(D,E) = (1/2)(3/4) + (1/2)(1 + 1/4) = 1 \qquad\qquad (E,D) = 1$$

$$(E,E) = 1 + (1/2)(A,D) = 1 + (1/2)(3/4) = 1 + 3/8$$

Practice Problem Two: A Real Practice Problem

A more complicated practice problem is to work out the relationships in the pedigree of the 4 King Ranch stallions shown in Figure 16-11. Again, letters have replaced the names for ease of setting up the relationship table. The solution is given in Table 16-4.

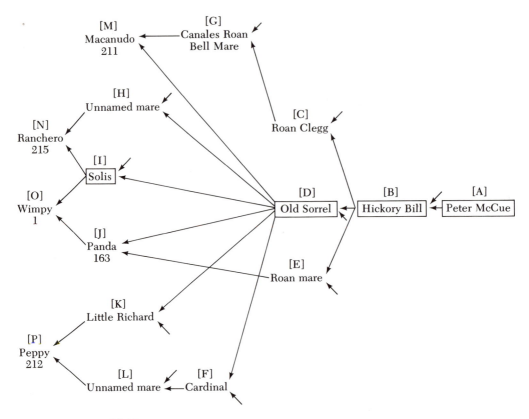

FIGURE 16-11
Lines of descent of 4 King Ranch Quarter Horse stallions, showing relationship to Old Sorrel, Hickory Bill, and Peter McCue. Adapted from Fletcher. 1945.

References

Cruden, Dorothy. 1949. The computation of inbreeding coefficients. *J. Heredity* 40:248.

Dusek, J. 1966. Inbreeding in Thoroughbreds in relation to performance. *Zivoc. Vyroba* 11:121.

Emik, L. O., and C. E. Terrill. 1949. Systematic procedures for calculating inbreeding coefficients. *J. Heredity* 40:51.

Fletcher, J. Lane. 1945. A genetic analysis of the American Quarter Horse. *J. Heredity* 36:346.

Fletcher, J. Lane. 1946. A study of the first fifty years of Tennessee Walking Horse breeding. *J. Heredity* 37:369.

Fomin, A. B. 1966. Heterosis obtained by the pure breeding of Orlov Trotters. *Genetika, Mosk.* 11:131.

Gazder, P. J. 1954. The genetic history of the Arabian horse in the United States. *J. Heredity* 45:95.

Lasley, J. F. 1972. *Genetics of Livestock Improvement.* Englewood Cliffs, New Jersey: Prentice-Hall.

Rhoad, A. O., and R. J. Kleberg, Jr. 1946. The development of a superior family in the modern Quarter Horse. *J. Heredity* 37:226.

Steele, D. G. 1944. A genetic analysis of the recent Thoroughbreds, Standardbreds, and American Saddle Horses. *Kentucky Agr. Exp. Sta. Bull.* 462.

Wright, Sewall. 1922. Coefficients of inbreeding and relationships. *Amer. Naturalist* 56:330.

Wright, Sewall. 1923. Mendelian analysis of the pure breeds of livestock. *J. Heredity* 14:339.

Zaher, A. 1948. *A genetic history of the Arabian horse in America.* Ph.D. thesis. Michigan State University, East Lansing.

CHAPTER SEVENTEEN

Principles of
Selection for
Quantitative Traits

Most of the traits of the horse are influenced by many genes, each of which has a relatively small effect; that is, the traits are not influenced primarily by genes at a single locus. Such traits are called quantitative traits. Many such traits can also be measured quantitatively, as, for example, the speed of a Standardbred for one mile, the speed of the Thoroughbred for a mile and a half or other distances (Figure 17-1), and the speed of a Quarter Horse for a quarter-mile. Measurement is more difficult for certain other traits, such as temperament or cow sense. Nevertheless, if a measurement scale can be devised, possible measurements will be continuous over a wide range. The measurement can be thought of as a result of both the genetic value of the horse and the influence of environmental factors. A shorthand model is $P_i = G_i + E_i$, where P_i is the measurement of a trait of a horse named i; G_i is the combined effect of all the genes of horse i on the trait; and E_i is the combined effect of all environmental factors on the horse.

Stating the problem of selection for such a trait is not difficult. Horses are to be selected that have the greatest possible average G. The complication, of course, is that only P is measured. The environmental effects, which can be plus or minus, mask the genetic effects. This makes prediction (estimation) of G from a measurement, P, less than perfect. Improving the accuracy of prediction by using records on relatives will be discussed in section 17.3. In the following section the key factors that determine progress in improving quantitative traits by selection will be discussed.

FIGURE 17-1
The imported Thoroughbred *Nasrullah, at Claiborne, Paris, Kentucky, was the leading sire of stakes and purse winners for many years. Photograph credit to J. C. Skeets Meadors, courtesy of Keeneland Library, Lexington, Kentucky.

17.1 The Key Factors in Selection

Genetic variation is of prime importance. This means simply that there are differences in the genetic values of horses. Obviously, if the genetic values of all horses in the population are all the same, selection cannot improve the average genetic value. Some must be better and others worse than average so that selection has a chance to improve the average genetic value. The measure of variation that is used is called the genetic standard deviation, which will be discussed later in this section.

525

The *accuracy of prediction* is determined by the method of prediction and by the number and kind of records on a horse and its relatives. Increasing the number of records and relatives will increase accuracy if the best method of predicting genetic value is used.

The method that most accurately predicts which animals are superior is called the selection index. The selection index maximizes accuracy of prediction (the correlation between the predicted genetic value and the true genetic value), maximizes genetic progress by selection, minimizes errors of predicting genetic value, and maximizes the probability of correctly ranking horses with respect to their genetic value.

The amount of progress to be expected from selection also depends on the *intensity of selection*. Even if genetic value were predicted perfectly, there would be no genetic improvement unless the inferior animals were culled. The average genetic value of selected horses increases as more inferior horses are culled. For example, selecting the best 10 percent for breeding instead of the best 20 percent halves the fraction selected and increases the intensity of selection.

These three factors—genetic variation, accuracy of prediction, and selection intensity—determine genetic progress per generation. A fourth factor, *generation interval*, is important in determining rate of genetic improvement per year. Generation interval is the average time between birth of animals and birth of their replacements. Genetic progress per generation divided by the generation interval measured in years gives genetic progress per year.

The equation that summarizes the relationship of these factors to expected genetic progress is:

Genetic Progress per Year

$$= \frac{\text{Accuracy} \times \text{Intensity Factor} \times \text{Genetic Standard Deviation}}{\text{Generation Interval}}$$

An obvious way to maximize genetic progress is to make the numerator parts as large as possible and the generation interval as small as possible. That, indeed, is what to do, but often a change in one factor may cause an undesirable change in another factor. An understanding of the 4 ingredients of yearly genetic progress will be valuable to the person who must decide how to balance these key factors to increase genetic progress to the optimum for a particular breeding program.

Accuracy

Accuracy of predicting the true genetic value of a mare or stallion can often be increased by using records on relatives. This correlation between true and predicted genetic value can range from 0 percent when genetic value is guessed to 100 percent when genetic value is known exactly, and may even be negative if the predicted genetic value is determined by incorrect procedures. Genetic value is difficult to predict exactly, especially for mares, but for stallions prediction can be nearly perfect if there are enough progeny.

Accuracy depends also on the fraction of differences due to genetic effects and the fraction due to environmental effects. The fraction due to genetic differences is called *heritability*. The symbol σ_G^2 (read as genetic variance) is used for the usual measure of genetic variation. The square root of σ_G^2, σ_G, is the genetic standard deviation that appeared in the genetic progress equation. The symbol for total variance is σ_P^2 (read as phenotypic or total variance). Total or phenotypic variance is the sum of the genetic variance and the environmental variance: $\sigma_G^2 + \sigma_E^2$. Thus, heritability $= \sigma_G^2/(\sigma_G^2 + \sigma_E^2)$.

As can be seen, if none of the differences are due to genetic differences, heritability is zero, and of course, genetic progress is impossible. If all differences are genetic, heritability is 100 percent. Then, an animal's record is a perfect measure of its genetic value (accuracy is 100 percent from an animal's record), and genetic progress will be as rapid as the genetic standard deviation, selection intensity, and generation interval will allow.

Accuracy of prediction is greater for traits with high heritability than for traits with low heritability. Figure 17-2 shows the effect of heritability on accuracy of prediction from an animal's own record for traits with different heritability values.

As heritability increases, accuracy becomes nearly perfect, even when based solely on an animal's own record. Most quantitative traits, however, have heritabilities in the range of .1 to .5. Within that range, accuracy certainly is not perfect, ranging approximately from 32 percent to 71 percent.

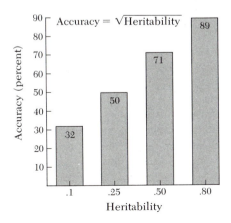

FIGURE 17-2
Accuracy of predicting genetic value depends on heritability of the trait. The graph shows the accuracy that results when selecting on the basis of a single record of the animal.

527

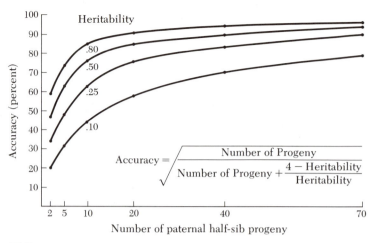

FIGURE 17-3
Accuracy of predicting genetic value from half-sib progeny
depends on heritability of the trait and the number of progeny.

Figure 17-3 shows the differences in accuracy of predicting genetic value that result from using different numbers of half-sib progeny for traits with different heritabilities. Prediction of a stallion's genetic value from his progeny can be nearly 100 percent accurate if a sufficiently large group of his progeny is used in the prediction, no matter what the heritability of the trait, if the heritability is greater than zero. Accuracy is quite high, however, when only the first few progeny are used in cases of traits with high heritabilities. Three Bars, shown in Figure 17-4, is an example of a stallion that was proved to be great through a progeny proof.

Figures 17-2 and 17-3 can be used to compare the accuracy of prediction from own records and from progeny records. Generally, for traits with

FIGURE 17-4
Three Bars, a Thoroughbred, was proved by his progeny to be an outstanding sire of racing Quarter Horses. Photograph courtesy of American Quarter Horse Association and owner Sidney H. Vail, Douglas, Arizona.

528

TABLE 17-1
Heritability estimates for some traits

Trait	Heritability
Speed	.25–.50
Wither height	.25–.60
Body weight	.25–.30
Pulling power	.25
Walking speed	.40
Trotting speed	.40
Points for movement	.40
Points for temperament	.25
Reproductive traits	Low ?
Cow sense	?
Conformation characteristics	?

high heritabilities, progeny records have little advantage over an animal's own record. The result is different for traits with low heritabilities. For example, with a heritability of .1, accuracy of prediction is only 32 percent when based on own records alone, which is equivalent to the accuracy of prediction based on 4 or 5 progeny records. The use of 30 progeny records will give an accuracy of prediction more than twice as great, 66 percent.

Estimates of heritabilities of quantitative traits of horses are based on very little research. Some representative values are given in Table 17-1.

For traits with higher heritabilities, accuracy of prediction increases very little when relatives' records are used, in comparison with the accuracy obtained when a record of the animal is used. Records on closer relatives, of course, add more to accuracy than do those of relatives 2 or more generations removed. As shown in Table 17-2, adding one parent record increases accuracy as much as adding all 4 grandparents even if

TABLE 17-2
Accuracy of predicting genetic value from own and ancestor records (percent)

Records Used	Heritability		
	.1	.25	.50
Own	32%	50%	71%
Own + 1 parent or progeny	35	53	73
Only 1 parent or progeny	16	25	35
Own + 2 parents	38	57	76
Only 2 parents	23	35	50
Own + 1 grandparent	32	51	71
Only 1 grandparent	8	12	18
Own + 4 grandparents	35	53	73
Only 4 grandparents	16	25	35

heritability is low. For traits with low heritabilities, adding progeny records when an animal's record is known can increase accuracy substantially, as shown in Figure 17-5.

Intensity of Selection

The factor for intensity of selection is not quite proportional to the fraction culled. The intensity factor increases at an increasing rate as the fraction selected declines. Intensity factors for various fractions of selection are given in Table 17-3. These factors are a relative measure of how much the selected group will exceed the average of the population from which selected animals are taken. For the intensity factors to apply, selection must be based entirely on predicted genetic value. That is, selection of a random 10 out of the top 50 of 100 horses is not 10 percent selection but is equivalent to selection of the best 50 percent—the same as selecting the best 50 of 100—since selection is random out of the best 50.

Intensity of selection can have an important effect on genetic progress, particularly in selection of stallions, since fewer stallions than mares are needed for breeding. Bret Hanover, pictured in Figure 17-6, has had a large influence on the Standardbred breed. His individual performances were outstanding as are those of his progeny. In addition, the accuracy of evaluating stallions may be greater than that for mares because a record is

FIGURE 17-5
Accuracy of prediction that results from using a single record of an animal and the records of several half-sib progeny.

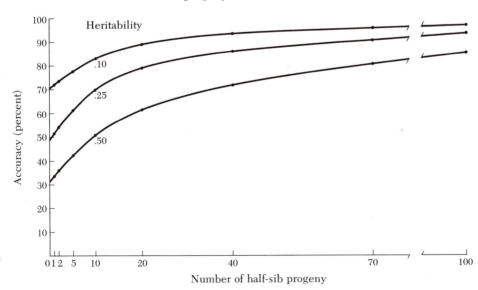

TABLE 17-3
Selection intensity factor

Select Top Percentage	Selection Intensity Factor	Comments
100	.00	No culling
90	.20	Usual level for selection of mares
85	.27	
75	.42	
70	.50	
60	.64	
50	.80	
40	.97	
30	1.16	Range for selecting dams of stud stallions
20	1.40	
10	1.75	
5	2.06	
4	2.15	
3	2.27	Possible range for selecting stallions
2	2.42	
1	2.67	

available or because progeny records are available. Mares without records must be evaluated from records of their paternal sibs or their sire. This one generation gap in records reduces accuracy considerably, as shown in Table 17-2.

Genetic Standard Deviation

Genetic variation must exist if selection is to be effective. Lack of genetic differences among animals will result in no genetic progress, whether prediction is accurate or selection is intense. Some traits have little genetic variation and others express considerable genetic variation. Variation in traits of horses has been measured neither very often nor for many traits. Quite likely, there is little genetic variation in fertility, but there is a great

FIGURE 17-6
Bret Hanover, a champion pacer, shown with trainer-driver Frank Ervin winning the final heat for the 1964 Goshen Cup. He won 62 of 68 starts, was undefeated in 24 starts as a 2-year-old, and was the first 3-time winner of "Harness Horse of the Year" award (1964, 1965, and 1966). Photograph courtesy of *The Horseman and Fair World*, Lexington, Kentucky.

531

deal in performance traits such as speed and agility and in size traits such as height at the withers and weight at maturity.

The genetic standard deviation is related to heritability and total or phenotypic variation. Since heritability is defined as the ratio of genetic variance to total variance, the genetic variance is the product of heritability and total variance: $\sigma_G^2 =$ heritability $\times$ phenotypic variance.

The genetic standard deviation is the square root of the genetic variance. Since heritability must have a value between 0 and 1 depending on the trait, the genetic variance is less than or no greater than the phenotypic variance.

Variance is a standard way of describing variation. For example, many traits have a distribution that is very similar to the normal or bell-shaped distribution. The variance describes how close or how far the individual values are likely to be from the overall average. The best time for one mile for a group of Standardbreds is plotted in Figure 17-7, which shows the distribution of times. The frequency of horses in each time class was plotted as a vertical bar, and if the midpoints of the tops of the bars were connected, a curve similar to the normal distribution would result.

FIGURE 17-7
An approximation of the normal distribution from the best times (to the nearest second) at trot or pace for the mile on half-mile tracks for 2,498 Standardbred dams of progeny with standard times. The standard deviation was 3.45 seconds, and the average was 129.7 seconds. Data courtesy of Richard Hintz, Cornell University, Ithaca, New York.

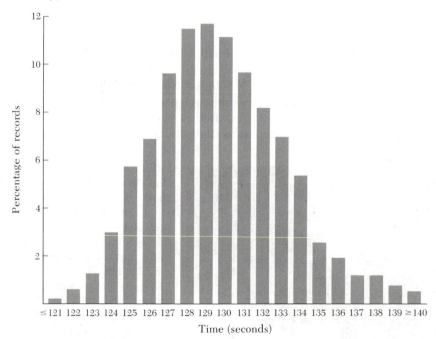

TABLE 17-4

Fraction of measurements expected to be between the average and the average plus a stated number of standard deviations

Standard Deviation (n)	Fraction[a]
.1	.04
.2	.08
.3	.12
.4	.16
.5	.19
.6	.23
.7	.26
.8	.29
.9	.32
1.0	.34
1.5	.43
2.05	.48
2.33	.49

[a]Since the normal curve is symmetrical, this is also the fraction between the average and the average minus that number of standard deviations.

How spread out or how closely bunched the records are determines the phenotypic variance. In fact, the square root of the variance gives the standard deviation, which is the standard measure for determining what size of an interval above or below the average will contain a specified fraction of all measurements. Tables are available that give the fraction of measurements expected within a certain number of standard deviations from the average. Table 17-4 gives some of these values.

For example, 34 percent of the measurements are expected to be between the average and the average plus one standard deviation. Similarly, 34 percent are expected to be between the average and the average minus one standard deviation. Thus, 68 percent are in the range of one standard deviation on either side of the average.

Suppose, for example, that the distribution of Standardbred times for one mile is really normal and that the standard deviation of speed for the mile (not just the best times) for a random sample of Standardbreds is 10 seconds and the average is 140 seconds. Then, 68 percent of the times would be expected to be between 140 ± 10 — or 130 and 150 — seconds. Similarly, 96 percent would be between 140 ± 2.05 (10) — or 119.5 and 160.5 — seconds. The actual distribution for Standardbred times is not quite normal since the lower limit is approximately 115 seconds. Yet this approximation works quite well.

The phenotypic variance and, hence, the phenotypic standard deviation can be computed directly from records. The procedure is not too complicated and can be found in any elementary statistics text.

The genetic values cannot be observed directly, so the genetic variance can be computed only indirectly from the correlation between relatives

533

according to quantitative genetic theory. These techniques are also not difficult and can be found in most animal breeding textbooks.

Generation Interval

A general statement of the influence of generation interval on genetic progress is that the shorter the generation interval, the more genetic progress per year. One reason for relatively slow progress in breeding horses is the long generation interval compared with that of other farm animals. Generally, low fertility, a longer gestation period, and lack of financial incentive may be some of the reasons. The generation interval, however, commonly becomes shorter when a breed is expanding rapidly. Studies made in the early 1940s of the Tennessee Walking Horse, the Quarter Horse, the Standardbred, and the Thoroughbred showed a range in generation intervals from approximately 9 years for the Quarter Horse to 12 years for the Thoroughbred. The interval for sires was longer than that for dams. Since then, the Quarter Horse breed has expanded rapidly, so their average generation interval may have become even less.

When males and females have different generation intervals, different accuracies of prediction, and different selection intensities, overall genetic progress per year can be written as:

Genetic Progress per Year

$$= \frac{\text{Selected Male Superiority} + \text{Selected Female Superiority}}{\text{Generation Interval for Males} + \text{Generation Interval for Females}}$$

where

Selected Male Superiority

= Accuracy for Males × Intensity Factor for Males × Genetic Standard Deviation

and

Selected Female Superiority

= Accuracy for Females × Intensity Factor for Females × Genetic Standard Deviation

As mentioned earlier in this section, changes in some of the key factors for genetic progress may affect other factors. For example, decreasing generation interval will probably decrease accuracy since fewer records would be available to use in selection. Often, accuracy needs to be balanced against intensity of selection, particularly if stallions are being progeny-tested on a fixed number of mares. The genetic standard deviation is a fixed part of the equation; that is, it is a constant value for a particular trait in a specified population and thus is not affected by changes in the other key factors.

17.2   Traits to Measure and Use in Selection

Records are essential in any effective selection program. Performance records, of course, are obviously of interest, but other information is also needed to adjust performance records to a common base. For example, age influences racing speed, and the post position affects the chance of winning, particularly for trotters and pacers.

The essential trait for racehorses is speed for a desired distance (Figure 17-8). Conformation and temperament are important to the extent that they influence racing ability, but racing ability is a composite measure of all such factors. There are fast horses of varying conformation and temperament, which implies that no one ideal standard for conformation and temperament is best.

The average earnings index (AEI) is used as a performance measure for Thoroughbreds. Each year the average earnings of a horse are divided

FIGURE 17-8
Man O' War, winner of 21 of 22 races (second by ½ length) from 1919 to 1920 and still holder of Thoroughbred record for 1⅜ miles (2:14 1/5), was the holder in 1920 of records for 1, 1⅛, 1⅜, 1½, and 1⅝ miles. Shown with groom, Will Harbut. Photograph credit to J. C. Skeets Meadors, courtesy of Keeneland Library, Lexington, Kentucky.

FIGURE 17-9

Tropical Gale, a Pinto being ridden by Michelle MacFarlane, shows the typical action and flashiness in a parade horse class. Photograph by Jack Holvoet, Fort Madison, Iowa, courtesy of Ellen S. Davis, San Diego, California.

by the average earnings for all starters that year. For example, a horse that earned $12,000 in 1970 when the average horse earned $4,000 would have an AEI of 3. The heritability of this measure appears to be lower than that for speed. Performance rates and handicap weights are also measures of racing performance.

Some factors that may influence performance are age, nutrition, skill of the trainer, starting position, condition of the track, handicap weight, sex, and of course, level of competition. Adjustments for these factors generally have not been developed, but such adjustments are needed to apply accurately the basic principles of selection. Biases may result from the use of unadjusted records and may slow the rate of progress.

Jumpers, cutting horses, and polo ponies, for example, all can be measured in the same manner as racehorses for the performance that is required of them. Horses shown in harness and riding classes are judged on action and style, which are difficult to score on a quantitative basis. Winnings or some type of score card measure may be used as traits for selection. Figure 17-9 shows Tropical Gale in typical parade horse action. The Hackney Pony, Fernwick's Brown Jet, is shown in a Cob-Tail harness class in Figure 17-10.

Horses in halter classes constitute another category (Figure 17-11).

FIGURE 17-10
An international champion, Cob-Tail
Hackney Pony, Fernwick's Brown
Jet, driven by Mrs. David LaSalle,
showing the action and animation
selected for by Hackney breeders.
Photograph courtesy of David LaSalle,
Harness Makers, North Scituate,
Rhode Island.

Their conformation and temperament traits are many and varied. Winnings may be a reasonable measure of composite ability to place well. The general rule of thumb is that if selection is for n traits simultaneously, the progress for any one is only $1/\sqrt{n}$ as much as if selection were for that trait alone. Of course, if all n traits are important, then selection for only one trait is less preferable than simultaneous selection for all of them. The important point is to place the proper emphasis on each trait—more on valuable traits and less on fine points that have little value.

FIGURE 17-11
The Quarter Horse stallion Poco Bueno appears in the pedigree of many breed champions. Photograph courtesy of United States Department of Agriculture.

537

Horses used for pleasure should have traits that actually make riding them a pleasure — even temperament, smoothness of gait, and endurance. Freedom from abnormalities is also essential.

Draft horses need to have pulling power and endurance. If actually used commercially, they also need a pleasant disposition. A team of Percherons is shown in action in Figure 17-12.

The coat color and pattern of the coat color of the color breeds must be recorded. Color horses used for racing or pleasure should have the same traits as racers or pleasure horses. Breeders of the color breeds are thus handicapped somewhat because they must select for color patterns, which is quite difficult, in addition to selecting for the other traits of economic value.

Some breeders have attempted to breed for the small or miniature horses that were in demand in the 1970s. Size is easy to select for because of the high heritability and because of the wide range of sizes of various breeds, as illustrated in Figure 17-13.

FIGURE 17-12
A hitch of Percheron horses pulling a load of hay at the Meyring Livestock Company Ranch, Walden, Colorado. Draft horses have been selected for their ability to start and pull heavy loads. Photograph courtesy of Oliver Meyring, Walden, Colorado.

FIGURE 17-13
Size and weight are traits that can be increased or decreased by selection. The wide differences in size among breeds are illustrated by (a) Drake Farms Leonet, an imported Percheron stallion weighing more than one ton; and (b) Little Bummer, an American Miniature Horse stallion that weighs 190 pounds, contrasted with Elai, a yearling Arabian filly. Photograph a courtesy of Glenn Burns, Meadville, Pennsylvania; photograph b by Franks Photo House, courtesy of Jim and Loretta Murphy, Hilltop Farm, Huron, South Dakota.

17.3 Application of Relatives' Records to Selection

Records of relatives can be used for selection, although their importance varies according to the heritability of the trait, the closeness of relationship of the relatives to the animal being evaluated, and which other relatives' records are also used.

In selection of mares, relatives' records, in general, have value in the following order: (1) own record, (2) progeny average, (3) average of progeny of animal's sire, (4) parent's or parents' records, and (5) average of progeny of a grandsire.

539

In the evaluation of a stallion, his own record or his progeny average is most valuable; his relatives' records rank in importance in the same order as those for mares. Usually, no more than two of these kinds of records need to be used in an evaluation. Additional records will add only a little to the accuracy of the prediction.

The general selection index procedure for finding the best weights for records on any number of relatives is given in Box 17-1. Some specific weights and accuracy values are given in Table 17-5. A few combinations will now be discussed.

Box 17-1

General Selection Index Procedure
for Use of Records of Relatives

The selection index weights for records of relatives are obtained by minimizing the average squared error of prediction of genetic value; that is, the average of $(\hat{G} - G)^2$, where G is the true genetic value and $\hat{G}$ is the prediction of genetic value, or $\hat{G} = b_1(X_1 - \bar{X}) + \cdots + b_n(X_n - \bar{X})$. The b's are the best weighting factors for the average of records (X_i) on relatives $1, 2, \ldots, n$. For example, X_1 may be the average of records on the animal itself; X_2 may be a record of the dam; X_3 may be the average of p_3 paternal half-sibs of the animal; and so on.

The general equations to solve to find the b's to predict genetic value for some symbolic animal α can be simplified to the form:

$$d_1 b_1 + a_{12} b_2 + a_{13} b_3 + \cdots + a_{1n} b_n = a_{1\alpha}$$

$$a_{21} b_1 + d_2 b_2 + a_{23} b_3 + \cdots + a_{2n} b_n = a_{2\alpha}$$

$$a_{31} b_1 + a_{32} b_2 + d_3 b_3 + \cdots + a_{3n} b_n = a_{3\alpha}$$

$$\cdot \qquad \cdot \qquad \cdot \qquad \qquad \cdot \qquad \cdot$$
$$\cdot \qquad \cdot \qquad \cdot \qquad \qquad \cdot \qquad \cdot$$
$$\cdot \qquad \cdot \qquad \cdot \qquad \qquad \cdot \qquad \cdot$$

$$a_{n1} b_1 + a_{n2} b_2 + a_{n3} b_3 + \cdots + d_n b_n = a_{n\alpha}$$

There will be one equation for each kind of record (X_i) available for use in the index. If there is only one, let it be X_1, and the equation to find b_1 is $d_1 b_1 = a_{1\alpha}$. If there are two, X_1 and X_2, the equations are:

$$d_1 b_1 + a_{12} b_2 = a_{1\alpha}$$

$$a_{21} b_1 + d_2 b_2 = a_{2\alpha}$$

Evaluation Using Own Record Only

When only a record on the animal is available, genetic value can best be predicted as $\hat{G} = h^2(\text{record} - \bar{X})$, where $\hat{G}$ is the estimate of genetic value as a difference from the population average, $\bar{X}$ is the average of the population with which the horse is being compared, and h^2 is the symbol for heritability. The prediction, including the population average, is $\bar{X} + \hat{G}$. The accuracy of the prediction is $\sqrt{h^2}$, as given in Table 17-5.

For some traits, an animal can have several records. (For example,

---

When more X's are available, the pattern continues.

The a's are the additive relationships among the animals: a_{12} between relative type 1 and relative type 2, $a_{1\alpha}$ between relative type 1 and the animal to be evaluated, α.

The d's are the diagonal coefficients; $d_i = \left[\{[1 + (n_i - 1)r]/n_i h^2\} + \{[p_i - 1]a_{ii'}\} \right]/p_i$.

This procedure assumes that X_i is the average of exactly n_i records on each of p_i animals in the group, all related to each other by the additive relationship, $a_{ii'}$, and all related to the animal being evaluated, α, by $a_{i\alpha}$. As in Table 17-5, h^2 is heritability and r is repeatability of the trait.

Note that when each animal in the group has only one record, $n_i = 1$ and $d_i = [(1/h^2) + (p_i - 1)a_{ii'}]/p_i$, and that when there is only one animal in the group with n_i records (for example, the dam's records), then $p_i = 1$ and $d_i = [1 + (n_i - 1)r]/n_i h^2$. The accuracy (correlation between G and $\hat{G}$) of the index, $r_{G\hat{G}}$, can be found by using the equation $r_{G\hat{G}} = \sqrt{b_1 a_{1\alpha} + b_2 a_{2\alpha} + \cdots + b_n a_{n\alpha}}$.

If a future record of animal α, rather than the genetic value of the animal, is to be predicted, the equations to find the b's are the same except that if the animal already has a record, or several records (for example, X_1), the corresponding part of the right-hand side of the equation changes from $a_{1\alpha} = 1$ to $a_{1\alpha} = r/h^2$. If the animal has no previous records, the equations are the same as those for predicting genetic value and the index is also the same.

The accuracy, however, changes since, in addition to predicting G_α, the index is trying to predict $P_\alpha = G_\alpha + E_\alpha$, and the E_α is random and essentially nonpredictable. In this case, the accuracy is $r_{P\hat{P}} = \sqrt{h^2(b_1 a_{1\alpha} + b_2 a_{2\alpha} + \cdots + b_n a_{n\alpha})} = r_{G\hat{G}} \sqrt{h^2}$. Specific examples using these general equations to find the b's and accuracy values for predicting G are given in the text.

TABLE 17-5

Weights and accuracy values for predicting additive genetic value from records of various relatives (h^2 = heritability; r = repeatability.)

Records		Weights	Accuracy
Individual	(1)	h^2	$\sqrt{h^2}$
	(n)	$nh^2/[1 + (n-1)r]$	$\sqrt{nh^2/[1 + (n-1)r]}$
Dam or sire or progeny	(1)	$h^2/2$	$\sqrt{h^2}/2$
	(n)	$nh^2/2[1 + (n-1)r]$	$\sqrt{nh^2/[1 + (n-1)r]}/2$
Sire and dam	(1)	$h^2/2; h^2/2$	$.71\sqrt{h^2}$
	(n)	$nh^2/2[1 + (n-1)r];$ $nh^2/2[1 + (n-1)r]$	$.71\sqrt{nh^2/[1 + (n-1)r]}$
One grandparent		$h^2/4$	$\sqrt{h^2}/4$
Four grandparents		All $h^2/4$	$\sqrt{h^2}/2$
One great-grandparent		$h^2/8$	$\sqrt{h^2}/8$
Eight great-grandparents		All $h^2/8$	$.35\sqrt{h^2}$
Individual and one parent or progeny		$[h^2 - (h^2/2)^2]/[1 \quad (h^2/2)^2];$ $[h^2(1 - h^2)/2]/[1 - (h^2/2)^2]$	$\sqrt{(5h^2 - 2h^4)/(4 - h^4)}$
Individual and both parents		$h^2(h^2 - 2)/(h^4 - 2);$ $h^2(h^2 - 1)/(h^4 - 2) \ldots$	$\sqrt{h^2(2h^2 - 3)/(h^4 - 2)}$
Individual and one grandparent or grandprogeny		$h^2(h^2 - 16)/(h^4 - 16);$ $4h^2(h^2 - 1)/(h^4 - 16)$	$\sqrt{h^2(2h^2 - 17)/(h^4 - 16)}$
Individual and four grandparents		$h^2(h^2 - 4)/(h^4 - 4);$ $h^2(h^2 - 1)/(h^4 - 4) \ldots$	$\sqrt{h^2(2h^2 - 5)/(h^4 - 4)}$
Parent and progeny		$2h^2/(4 + h^2); 2h^2/(4 + h^2)$	$\sqrt{2h^2/(4 + h^2)}$
Progeny (p half-sibs)		$2ph^2/[4 + (p-1)h^2]$	$\sqrt{ph^2/[4 + (p-1)h^2]}$

Let $A = [1 + (n-1)r]/n$, $D = \{1 + [(p-1)h^2/4]\}/p$, and $C = AD - (h^4/16)$

Records		Weights	Accuracy
Individual (n) and paternal half-sibs (p)		$[h^2D - (h^2/4)^2]/C;$ $h^2(A - h^2)/4C$	$\sqrt{b_1 + (b_2/4)}$
Individual (n) and his paternal half-sib progeny (p)		$[h^2D - (h^2/2)]/[C - (3h^4/16)];$ $h^2(A - h^2)/2[C - (3h^4/16)]$	$\sqrt{b_1 + (b_2/2)}$
Dam (n) and paternal half-sibs (p)		$nh^2/2[1 + (n-1)r];$ $ph^2/[4 + (p-1)h^2]$	$\sqrt{(b_1/2) + (b_1/4)}$
Dam (1), sire (1), and progeny (1)		$[h^2 - (h^4/16)]/[2 - (h^4/64)];$ $[h^2 - (h^4/16)]/[2 - (h^4/64)];$ $[h^2 - (h^4/8)]/[2 - (h^4/64)]$	$\sqrt{(b_1 + b_2 + b_3)/2}$
Paternal half-sibs (m), dam (n), and paternal half-sibs (p)		$mh^2/[4 + (m-1)h^2];$ $h^2[D - (h^2/16)]/2C$ $h^2(A - h^2)/8C$	$\sqrt{(b_1/4) + (b_2/2) + (b_3/8)}$

542

several times can be recorded for a certain length of race). Then, repeatability is needed in addition to heritability. The symbol used is r, and it represents the correlation between records of the same animal. Repeatability is as large as or larger than heritability, and like heritability, is a fixed value for a particular trait in a specified population.

The prediction of genetic value for an animal with n records is $\hat{G} = \{nh^2/[1 + (n-1)r]\}\{$average of n records $- \bar{X}\}$. The accuracy of prediction is $\sqrt{nh^2/[1 + (n-1)r]}$, as given in Table 17-5.

As an example, assume that heritability, h^2, for birth weight of foals as a trait of the mare is .20 and repeatability is .40. The genetic value for foal weight is to be predicted for 3 mares. (Assume that the foal weights have already been adjusted for age of the mare.) Mare A has 3 foals that at birth weighed 70, 60, and 80 pounds. Mare B has one foal that weighed 75 pounds. Mare C has 2 foals that weighed 65 and 75 pounds. Assume that the farm average for foal birth weight is 60 pounds. Then,

$$\hat{G}_A = (3)(.20)/[1 + (3 - 1)(.40)]\{[(70 + 60 + 80)/3] - 60\}$$

$$= .3333(70 - 60) = 3.33 \text{ pounds}$$

$$\hat{G}_B = (.20)(75 - 60) = 3.00 \text{ pounds}$$

$$\hat{G}_C = (2)(.20)/[1 + (2 - 1)(.40)] [(65 + 75)/2] - 60$$

$$= .2875(70 - 60) = 2.88 \text{ pounds}$$

Note that this is not a prediction of the genetic value of birth weight of the mares but of their genetic value for birth weight of their foals as a difference from the farm average. Adding the farm average gives the predicted foal weights, $\bar{X} + \hat{G}$: 63.33 for A, 63.00 for B, and 62.88 for C.

This procedure allows comparison of animals with different numbers of records.

Evaluation from Progeny Average Alone

Prediction of a stallion's genetic value from his progeny average is simple if each of the paternal half-sib progeny has only one record: $\hat{G} = [2p/\{p + [(4 - h^2)/h^2]\}] [$average of his p progeny $- \bar{X}]$.

Even when the progeny have more than one record, the above prediction is a good approximation. The accuracy of prediction is $\sqrt{p/\{p + [(4 - h^2)/h^2]\}}$. The weights and accuracy in Table 17-5 are algebraically the same but are written differently.

If the average of future progeny of a stallion is being predicted from his present progeny, the weighting factor is half that for predicting the stallion's genetic value: predicted future progeny $= [p/\{p + [(4-h^2)/h^2]\}]$ [average of his p progeny $- \bar{X}$].

For example, assume that racing speed for the quarter-mile has a heritability of .50 and that the appropriate average is 25 seconds. Two stallions are to be evaluated for racing speed from age-adjusted records of their paternal half-sib progeny. Stallion A has 25 progeny that averaged 24.50 seconds. Stallion B has 5 progeny that averaged 24.25 seconds. Then,

$$\hat{G}_A = [(2)(25)/\{25 + [(4-.50)/.50]\}][24.5 - 25]$$

$$= 1.5625(-.5) = -.78 \text{ seconds}$$

$$\hat{G}_B = [(2)(5)/(5+7)][24.25 - 25]$$

$$= .8333(-.75) = -.62 \text{ seconds}$$

The prediction of averages of future progeny would be

$$A: .78125(-.5) = -.39 \text{ seconds}$$

$$B: .4167(-.75) = -.31 \text{ seconds}$$

After adding the population average of 25 seconds, the progeny predictions are 24.61 and 24.69 seconds, respectively.

Evaluation from the Sire's and Dam's Predicted Genetic Values

The equation for prediction of the genetic value of the progeny from the sire's and dam's predicted genetic values is $\hat{G}_{\text{progeny}} = (\hat{G}_{\text{sire}} + \hat{G}_{\text{dam}})/2$. The accuracy is $\sqrt{(\text{accuracy for sire})^2 + (\text{accuracy for dam})^2/2}$ when the sire and dam are not related.

Other Combinations

Table 17-5 gives weights for predicting genetic value from most of the possible combinations of relatives. The procedure is to find the weights for each relative or group of relatives, (b_1 for relative 1, b_2 for relative 2, and so on) and to use the equation, $\hat{G}_{\text{animal}} = b_1(\text{average for first relative} - \bar{X}) + b_2(\text{average for second relative} - \bar{X}) + \cdots + b_n(\text{average for } n\text{th relative} - \bar{X})$. To avoid using the predictions as differences (some positive and some negative), the population average, $\bar{X}$, can be added to $\hat{G}$.

17.4   Selection for Several Traits

The preceding section gave methods of predicting genetic value for a single trait by using records for that trait on the animal and its relatives. These methods ignore other traits; in fact, they assume that other traits have no economic value. Yet, many horse breeders must select to improve more than one trait because each of several traits may contribute to the economic value of the animal.

The problem of predicting total economic value by considering all economically important traits is complicated for several reasons. The genetic value for each trait is unknown and can only be predicted. Economic values are difficult to determine for many traits (for example, temperament and cow sense). The correlations between genetic values and between environmental effects for the economically important traits are also necessary for accurate prediction of total economic value but are difficult to estimate. The problem is especially difficult in horse breeding because so little research has been devoted to estimating these relationships—the correlations between genetic values for different traits and the correlations between phenotypic values for different traits.

Method of Selection for Total Economic Value

The method of selection for more than one trait is similar to that for selection for a single trait. The result is an index of economic value made up of records on traits of the animal and its relatives. The weight for each of the records depends on the relationships among the relatives, economic values of the traits, genetic and environmental correlations among the traits, and heritabilities of the traits. A full explanation of this procedure is beyond the scope of this book and also depends on correlations that are probably not accurately estimated. Box 17-2 does, however, illustrate the procedure for those who have the patience and interest to investigate selection for overall economic value further.

Some research has suggested that when genetic and environmental correlations are likely to be poorly estimated, a simpler procedure may be appropriate. The genetic value of each trait is predicted from records for that trait as described in the preceding section. Those predicted genetic values are then weighted by their economic values, which in many cases will have to be "educated guesses" based on the good sense of the breeder. For example, suppose that a one-second decrease in time to run a quarter-mile is worth $400 and that cow sense is scored on a point scale of 1–20 with a one-point increase worth $50. Suppose also that the genetic values for speed and cow sense for two horses have been predicted as shown in

Box 17-2

Computation of an Index
of Economic Value

Overall economic value can be defined as $G = v_1G_1 + v_2G_2 + \cdots + v_nG_n$, where G_i ($i = 1, \ldots, n$) are the genetic values for the n economically important traits and v_i is the net economic value for a one unit increase in trait i. The procedure described here is based on minimizing the average of squared errors of prediction by the same method that was used when records of relatives were used to predict the genetic value for a single trait.

First, estimate the genetic value of the animal for each trait that is considered economically important. The availability of one record on each of n traits will be assumed. All records should be adjusted for fixed factors and should be expressed as differences from the appropriate herd or population average if necessary.

For trait 1, the equations used to find the weights (b's) for the records are:

$$V_{11}b_{11} + V_{12}b_{21} + V_{13}b_{31} + \cdots + V_{1n}b_{n1} - h_1^2V_{11}$$

$$V_{21}b_{11} + V_{22}b_{21} + V_{23}b_{31} + \cdots + V_{2n}b_{n1} = r_{g_{12}}\sqrt{h_1^2V_{11}(h_2^2V_{22})}$$

$$V_{31}b_{11} + V_{32}b_{21} + V_{33}b_{31} + \cdots + V_{3n}b_{n1} = r_{g_{13}}\sqrt{h_1^2V_{11}(h_3^2V_{33})}$$

$$\vdots$$

$$V_{n1}b_{11} + V_{n2}b_{21} + V_{n3}b_{31} + \cdots + V_{nn}b_{n1} = r_{g_{1n}}\sqrt{h_1^2V_{11}(h_n^2V_{nn})}$$

where V_{ii} is the phenotypic (total) variance of trait i; V_{ij} is the phenotypic covariance between traits i and j, and $V_{ij} = r_{p_{ij}}\sqrt{V_{ii}V_{jj}}$ where $r_{p_{ij}}$ is the phenotypic correlation between traits i and j; b_{11} is the weight for the record on trait 1 in predicting the genetic value for trait 1, b_{21} is the weight for the record on trait 2 in predicting trait 1, $\ldots$, and b_{n1} is the weight for the record on trait n in predicting trait 1; h_i^2 is the heritability for trait i; and $r_{g_{ij}}$ is the genetic correlation between traits i and j.

The second subscript of the weights refers to the trait being predicted; the first subscript refers to the trait being used. The index for genetic value for trait 1 is thus $I_1 = b_{11}X_1 + b_{21}X_2 + b_{31}X_3 + \cdots + b_{n1}X_n$, where the X's are records on the n traits. This will also be the index for trait 1 when all traits are used if selection is for trait 1 alone.

The equations are the same for trait 2 except that b_{i2} ($i = 1, \ldots, n$) are substituted for the b_{i1}'s, and the right sides of the equations become

$$r_{g_{21}} \sqrt{h_2^2 V_{22}(h_1^2 V_{11})}$$

$$h_2^2 V_{22}$$

$$r_{g_{23}} \sqrt{h_2^2 V_{22}(h_3^2 V_{33})}$$

.

.

.

$$r_{g_{2n}} \sqrt{h_2^2 V_{22}(h_n^2 V_{nn})}$$

The index for trait 2 is $I_2 = b_{12}X_1 + b_{22}X_2 + b_{32}X_3 + \cdots + b_{n2}X_n$.

Use similar substitutions for the other traits—new b's and new right sides of the equations—so that the general term on the right side of the equation is $r_{g_{ki}} \sqrt{h_k^2 V_{kk}(h_i^2 V_{ii})}$ for equation i when selecting for trait k. Note that when $k = i$ (selecting for trait i and for equation k), $r_{g_{kk}} = 1$, and the right side of the equation becomes $h_k^2 V_{kk}$.

After the indexes for each trait have been computed ($I_1, I_2, \ldots, I_n$), they can be combined by weighting by the appropriate economic value per unit for each trait. If v_1 is the economic value for trait 1, v_2 is the value for trait 2, . . . , and v_n is the value for trait n, then the overall index for total economic value is $I = v_1 I_1 + v_2 I_2 + \cdots + v_n I_n$.

By substitution, the overall index can be written as $I = \beta_1 X_1 + \beta_2 X_2 + \cdots + \beta_n X_n$, where

$$\beta_1 = v_1 b_{11} + v_2 b_{12} + v_3 b_{13} + \cdots + v_n b_{1n}$$

$$\beta_2 = v_1 b_{21} + v_2 b_{22} + v_3 b_{23} + \cdots + v_n b_{2n}$$

$$\beta_3 = v_1 b_{31} + v_2 b_{32} + v_3 b_{33} + \cdots + v_n b_{3n}$$

.   .   .   .   .

.   .   .   .   .

.   .   .   .   .

$$\beta_n = v_1 b_{n1} + v_2 b_{n2} + v_3 b_{n3} + \cdots + v_n b_{nn}$$

The correlated genetic response for the genetic value of trait c, G_c, can be predicted from the following expression: change in G_c = selection intensity factor × [covariance (G_c,I)]/standard deviation of I.

The formula for variance of I is $\beta_1^2 V_{11} + \beta_2^2 V_{22} + \cdots + \beta_n^2 V_{nn} + 2\beta_1\beta_2 V_{12} + 2\beta_1\beta_3 V_{13} + \cdots + 2\beta_1\beta_n V_{1n} + 2\beta_2\beta_3 V_{23} + \cdots + 2\beta_{n-1}\beta_n V_{n-1,n}$, which is the sum of the products of the overall index weights squared and the corresponding variances plus the sum of twice the product of all covariances and the corresponding weights. The square root of the variance of the index gives the standard deviation of the index. The expected superiority in overall economic value by selection is the standard deviation of I times the selection intensity factor.

The formula for the covariance between the genetic value for trait c and the index I is $\beta_1 r_{g_{1c}} \sqrt{h_1^2 V_{11}(h_c^2 V_{cc})} + \beta_2 r_{g_{2c}} \sqrt{h_2^2 V_{22}(h_c^2 V_{cc})} + \cdots + \beta_n r_{g_{nc}} \sqrt{h_n^2 V_{nn}(h_c^2 V_{cc})}$.

TABLE 17-6
Example of selecting for overall genetic value using 2 traits

Horse	Predicted Genetic Value	
	Speed (seconds)	Cow Sense (points)
A	−.5	−1
B	1.0	+2
Economic value of one-unit increase in the trait	−$400	$50

Table 17-6. These predictions are differences from the population averages.

The economic value for a longer time is negative because a lower time is desirable. The predicted overall economic values are, for A: $(-\$400)(-.5) + (\$50)(-1) = \$150$, and, for B: $(-\$400)(1.0) + (\$50)(2) = -\$300$. There is a difference of $450 in predicted genetic value of the two horses after the value of two economically important traits is considered.

This example illustrates two points. First, the procedure predicts the difference between two horses or their differences from an average horse. Second, economic values are difficult to assign. Whether the economic values used in this example make sense is debatable.

This method of predicting overall genetic value can, in general, be summarized as $I = v_1\hat{G}_1 + v_2\hat{G}_2 + \cdots + v_n\hat{G}_n$, where I is the overall index of economic value, $\hat{G}_1$ is the prediction of genetic value for trait 1, $\hat{G}_2$ is the prediction of genetic value for trait 2, . . . , $\hat{G}_n$ is the prediction of economic value for trait n, and the v's are corresponding economic values.

Relative Progress

The usual rule of thumb is that if selection is jointly for n traits, the progress for one of them is $1/\sqrt{n}$ of the progress from selection for that trait alone. This approximation applies exactly when the traits have equal economic values per standard deviation, equal heritabilities, and zero genetic and phenotypic correlations. Such assumptions are not likely to be exactly true, but the rule does provide a rough guideline. The rule is illustrated in Figure 17-14, where racing speed is the trait for which progress is being compared.

17.5   Practice Problems

1. Assume that the heritability for an overall conformation score is .30 for scores ranging from 1 to 10 that have a population average of 6. Predict

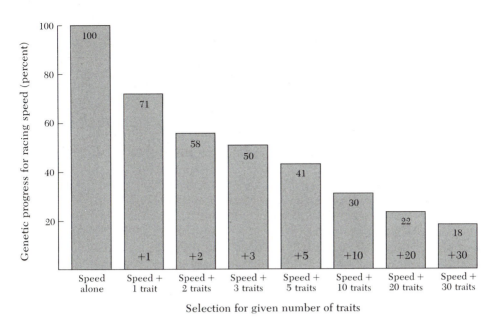

FIGURE 17-14
Relative progress in breeding for racing speed if selection emphasis is equal for several traits.

the genetic value for this trait for 5 horses that have the following records:

Horse A: A's own record is 7.
Horse B: The record of B's sire is 8 and the record of B's dam is 5.
Horse C: The records of C's 4 grandparents are 7, 6, 5, and 8.
Horse D: The average of 20 of D's half-sib progeny is 6.5.
Horse E: The record of E's dam is 8 and the average of 10 of E's paternal half-sibs (half-brothers and half-sisters through the sire) is 7.

Rank the animals with regard to predicted genetic value.

2. Compute the accuracy of predictions for horses with information similar to that in Problem 1. Try to explain why some accuracies of prediction are larger or smaller than others; for example, compare the accuracy of prediction for A with that for B and C.

3. Assume that "horse sense" has been measured for the same animals for which conformation was measured in Problem 1 and that heritability is .40 for these measures, which range between 6 and 16 with a population average of 12. The following records are available:

Horse A: A's own record is 15.
Horse B: The record of B's sire is 11 and the record of B's dam is 13.

Horse C: The records of C's 4 grandparents are 12, 12, 14, and 16.

Horse D: The average of 20 of D's half-sib progeny is 13.

Horse E: The record of E's dam is 10 and the average of 10 of E's paternal half-sibs is 14.

Rank the animals for predicted genetic value for "horse sense."

4. Use the approximate procedure to predict the overall genetic value for horses A, B, C, D, and E of Problems 1 and 3 if the economic value of a one-unit increase in conformation score is $50.00 and the economic value of a one-unit increase in "horse sense" is $100.00. Rank the horses for predicted overall economic genetic value.

5. Repeat Problem 4, but assume that the economic values are $100.00 for conformation score and $50.00 for "horse sense."

References

Baumohl, A., and J. A. Estes. 1960. Racing class and sire success. *The Blood-Horse* 80:48.

Bormann, P. 1960. A comparison between handicap weight and timing as measures of selection in Thoroughbred breeding. *Zuchtungskunde* 38:301.

Clark, David. 1970. Are they better race horses? *Hoofbeats* (October):32.

Dusek, J. 1965. The heritability of some characters in the horse. *Zivoc. Vyroba* 10:449.

Dusek, J. 1970. Heritability of conformation and gait in the horse. *Z. Tierzucht. Zuchtbiol.* 87:14.

Dusek, J. 1971. Some biological factors and factors of performance in the study of heredity in horse breeding. *Sci. Agric. Bohemoslov* 3:199.

Estes, B. W. 1952. A study of the relationship between temperament of Thoroughbred mares and performance of offspring. *J. Gen. Psy.* 81:273.

Estes, J. A. 1959. Probabilities based on two parents. *The Blood-Horse* (April 12):1068.

Foye, D. B., H. C. Dickey, and C. J. Sniffen. 1972. Heritability of racing performance and a selection index for breeding potential in the Thoroughbred horse. *J. Animal Sci.* 35:1141.

Gillespie, R. H. 1971. Performance rates. *The Thoroughbred Record* (April 17):961.

Green, D. A. 1969. A study of growth rate in Thoroughbred foals. *Brit. Vet. J.* 125:539.

Hamori, D. 1963. The inheritance of performance in Thoroughbreds. *Acta. Agron.* 12:19.

Hartwig, W., and U. Reichardt. 1958. The heritability of fertility in horse breeding. *Zuchtungskunde* 30:205.

Hazel, L. N. 1943. The genetic basis for constructing selection indexes. *Genetics* 28:476.

Hildebrand, M. 1959. Motions of the running cheetah and horse. *J. Mammals* 40:481.

Hollingsworth, K. 1967. Conclusion: The greater a colt's earnings on the track, the greater his chance of success as a stallion. *The Blood-Horse* (November 4):3267.

Kieffer, Nat. 1973. Inheritance of racing ability in the Thoroughbred. *Thoroughbred Rec.* (July 7):50.

Kownacki, M., M. Fabiani, and K. J. Jaszczak. 1971. Genetical parameters of some traits of Thoroughbred horses. *Genetica Pol.* 12:431.

Lasley, J. F. 1972. *Genetics of Livestock Improvement*. Englewood Cliffs, New Jersey: Prentice-Hall.

Laughlin, H. H. 1934. Racing capacity in the Thoroughbred horse. *Sci. Monthly* 38:210.

More O'Ferral, G. J., and E. P. Cunningham. 1974. Heritability of racing performance in Thoroughbred horses. *Livest. Prod. Sci.* 1:87.

Ocsage, J. 1963. Which methods are suitable for evaluating the inheritance of speed potential in stud stallions of racing breeds? *Acta. Agron.* 12:181.

Pern, E. M. 1970. The heritability of speed in Thoroughbred horses. *Genetika Mosk.* 6:110.

Pirri, J., and D. G. Steele. 1952. The heritability of racing capacity. *The Blood-Horse* 63:976.

Pirchner, F. 1969. *Population Genetics in Animal Breeding*. San Francisco: Freeman.

Rollins, W. C., and C. E. Howell. 1951. Genetic sources of variation in the gestation length of the horse. *J. Animal Sci.* 10:797.

Schwark, H. J., and E. Neisser. 1971. Breeding of English Thoroughbred horses in the G.D.R. Vol. 2. Results of estimates of heritability and breeding value. *Arch. Tierz.* 14:69.

Sloan, F. 1949. Color and temperament in horses. *J. Heredity* 40:12.

Solá, Gloria A. 1969. *Environmental factors affecting the speed of pacing horses*. M.S. thesis. Ohio State University, Columbus.

Steele, D. G. 1942. Are pedigrees important? *The Blood-Horse* 38 (November 7):574.

Stevens, R. W. C. 1969. Artificial insemination in horses: Genetic potential and control. *Canad. Vet. J.* 10:203.

Varo, M. 1965. On the relationship between characters for selection in horses. *Ann. Agr. Fenn.* 4:38.

Varo, M. 1965. Some coefficients of heritability in horses. *Ann. Agr. Fenn.* 4:223.

Walton, A., and J. Hammond. 1938. The maternal effects on growth and conformation in Shire Horse-Shetland Pony crosses. *Proc. Royal Soc.* 125(B):311.

Watanabe, Y. 1969. Timing as a measure of selection in Thoroughbred breeding. *Jap. J. Zootech. Sci.* 40:271.

PART SIX *Health of the Horse*

CHAPTER EIGHTEEN *Diseases of the Horse*

"Give my roan horse a drench," says he.

Henry IV, Part I, Act 2, Scene 4

A good health program is one of the most important components of horse management. To maintain an effective health care program, a horse owner must

1. have the ability to identify problems;

2. keep accurate records;

3. have knowledge of equine diseases and recent research results;

4. organize a vaccination program;

5. avoid conditions or situations that make the animal a high risk for disease or injury.

18.1   Identification of Problems

A physical examination and an accurate history of the horse are necessary if the horse owner is to decide whether his horse is sick, and if so, whether to call the veterinarian, treat the horse himself, or simply assume that the horse will recover without treatment.

The general impression and appearance of the animal are important indicators of its state of health. Does the animal appear to be active? How does he respond to normal stimuli such as noise? Is he alert or depressed? Excessive excitability may also indicate a problem. The posture should be noted. For example, continual shifting of weight from limb to limb may indicate laminitis. "Saw horse position" or straddling of legs is characteristic of severe abdominal pain or tetanus.

What is the body condition of the animal? Has there been a recent significant loss of weight? Does the hair coat shine? Did the winter coat shed late or fail to shed?

Behavior may also indicate the state of health. An animal that remains away from its group is often ill. What are its eating habits? Inappetence indicates that something is wrong. Routine examination of the teeth is important. Is there any pain, swelling, heat, or inflammation? Chewing may be slow or one-sided when teeth are affected. Swallowing may be painful with strangles. Does the animal defecate and urinate normally? Is the animal's respiration rate normal, or does it have trouble breathing?

After the general impression is noted, a more detailed examination should be made. For example, are the eyelids swollen? Is there any discharge from the eyes or nose?

These criteria are often subjective, and a certain amount of experience is required to interpret them properly. However, there are some objective measurements that even the novice can readily use.

Body temperature is usually taken with a rectal thermometer. The normal temperature for a horse is 100.5°F (99–101°F). Low readings may result if the temperature is taken immediately after defecation or if the thermometer is stuck into a fecal ball. Temperature may be low in the morning and peak in the afternoon. High environmental temperature and humidity may increase the body temperature as much as 2°F. Working may increase the temperature up to 3°F, and up to 2 hours may be required to return it to normal. A body temperature above 101°F in a resting horse should be considered abnormal.

The pulse can be taken from the external mandibular (lingual facial) artery. The external mandibular artery is felt in a shallow grove on the lower border of the jaw beneath the last cheek tooth. You can practice feeling the pulse by using your own mandibular artery. Pulse rate is dependent on the heart, and normally the rate is 30–40 waves per minute. The rate may be much greater in the newborn foal (see Table 5-1). Tachycardia (rapid heart rate) occurs most often when the animal is in pain or excited, or suffering from toxemia (toxic substances in the blood) or septicemia (virulent microorganisms in the blood). Bradycardia (slow heart rate) is unusual. The respiration rate can be determined by observing the rise and fall of the flank or rib cage. The normal rate is 8–16 respirations per minute. Pain or fever will increase the rate, as will exercise, poor ventilation in buildings, hot weather, or excitement.

18.2   Accurate Records

Records should include the age of animals, as well as a health history including vaccination and worming schedule. Weights of the animals should be taken periodically, either by scales or by heart girth measurement tapes. The breeding history of mares should be recorded (see section 13.5).

18.3   Infectious Diseases

Foalhood Septicemias

The foal is very susceptible to infection. Septicemia, frequently localized in the joints, is often caused by *Escherichia coli, Actinobacillus equuli, Salmonella abortivoequina, Streptococcus pyogenes equi,* or *Salmonella typhimurium. Clostridium perfringens* may cause enteritis (inflammation of the intestine). Bacteria may enter the foal's blood system via the umbilical cord and thus the navel should be disinfected at birth.

(The umbilical cord should not be cut too soon after birth because if it is, the foal will be deprived of substantial quantities of blood. The cord will usually break without any help from the attendant.)

Strangles

Strangles is an acute contagious disease caused by infection with *Streptococcus equi.* The upper respiratory tract is inflamed and the adjacent lymph nodes become enlarged and abscessed. The swelling of the nodes may take 3–4 days to develop. If not effectively treated, the nodes may rupture after about 10 days and discharge a thick, cream-colored pus. When the infection is severe, many other nodes may also abscess. Local abscesses may even occur on the body surface. In the first stage of the disease, the horse usually goes off feed, has a high temperature (103–105°F), and emits a watery nasal discharge that rapidly becomes purulent. The larynx and pharynx become inflamed and swallowing may be difficult. Body temperature may decrease to normal after 2–3 days but increases again when abscesses develop in the lymph nodes.

Strangles usually affects horses of 1–5 years of age, although the condition may develop in horses of any age. Outbreaks are most likely to occur after horses are moved, particularly during inclement weather.

557

The disease is spread when the nasal discharge of the infected animals contaminates pasture, feed troughs, or water troughs. Infected horses may spread the disease for at least 4 weeks, and the organisms may survive in the environment for a month or more after the infected animals are removed.

Thus, infected animals should be isolated as soon as possible. The stall, feed troughs, water buckets, brushes, and so on, should be disinfected. If animals can be treated before an abscess is formed, penicillin is effective. Inadequate treatment may result in recurrence of the infection. Horses that have recovered from natural infection are usually immune, but the condition may repeat itself after approximately 6 months.

Preventive measures include isolating new animals for 2–3 weeks. A vaccine made from killed bacteria is also available for animals 12 weeks of age or older. The vaccine is given 2 or 3 times at 8-week intervals. Annual booster injections are usually recommended. Vaccination does not prevent outbreaks of the disease but may decrease its severity. The effectiveness of the vaccine is controversial, and it is not uniformly accepted by the veterinary profession.

Pneumonia

The term "pneumonia" refers to any inflammatory disease of the lungs. There are several types of pneumonia, which can be caused by a bacteria or a virus or a combination of the two. There is often a predisposing factor, such as chilling or previous infection with influenza or strangles. Affected horses usually have a temperature of 102°–105°F, have difficulty breathing, have a nasal discharge, go off feed, and suffer from chest pains and lung congestion. Prompt treatment with antibiotics is usually effective if the infection is of bacterial origin.

Inhalation pneumonia is caused by improper oral administration of liquids. For example, a stomach tube might be wrongly placed in the lungs rather than in the stomach, and materials such as worm medicine or mineral oil may be poured into the lungs — a fatal mistake. Therefore, stomach tubes should be inserted only by experienced individuals.

Arabian foals may develop adenoviral pneumonia. The condition is acute or progressively chronic and frequently fatal in an animal with an inherited combined immunodeficiency (McGuire et al., 1974; Thompson et al., 1975). Foals with this immune deficiency have a small or hypoplastic thymus, a very low number of lymphocytes in the blood, and low levels of gamma globulin in the blood. Foals that do not receive protective antibodies in the colostrum and therefore lack gamma globulin may also suffer from adenoviral pneumonia (McChesney et al., 1974). These latter animals will respond to treatment.

558

Influenza

Influenza is caused by myxoviruses and has many of the characteristics of influenza in man. The horse develops a high temperature (101–106°F), has a depressed appetite, and emits a watery nasal discharge. The condition is usually not fatal, but diseased horses that are worked, shipped, or exposed to bad weather may develop fatal complications. Young foals are particularly susceptible and may develop pneumonia and die.

Some strains of human influenza virus have produced influenza in horses, but the most common viruses in the United States are myxovirus influenza A/Equi 1 and myxovirus influenza A/Equi 2. The incidence of the disease varies greatly from year to year. It has been estimated that in 1963, 50–90 percent of the horses in some areas of the United States suffered from the disease (Blood and Henderson, 1972). Influenza is spread by droplet inhalation, and the aerosol form of the virus can survive from 24 to 36 hours. Fortunately, the virus is usually transmitted only short distances, and isolation of new animals prevents spreading of the condition. An effective vaccine made from killed virus is now available. It contains both types of equine influenza viruses. Young horses should be vaccinated twice at intervals of 6–12 weeks before they come in contact with new horses and then given an annual booster shot. If they are frequently exposed to large groups of strange horses, a booster shot every 6 months is advisable. All animals on a farm or in a stable should be vaccinated.

Equine Viral Rhinopneumonitis (EVR)

This disease is caused by a herpes virus, although secondary bacterial infection is often a complicating factor. A fever of up to 106°F may last 2–5 days, and may be accompanied by a clear nasal discharge and coughing. Coughing may persist up to 3 weeks. EVR is not fatal to mature horses but may cause abortion. Abortions may occur up to 4 months after the respiratory signs are noted, although in some cases the latter are so mild that they may escape observation. Abortions occur most frequently during the last third of the gestation period. If one abortion occurs, a high percentage of the mares on the farm may also have abortions (that is, there may be an abortion storm).

Although there is no treatment, antibiotics are often given to control secondary bacterial infections. Recovered animals are immune for several months but may be reinfected.

A planned infection program has been effective on large farms with fixed breeding seasons. All animals are infected in June and October with live virus vaccine. The farm must be under quarantine for 3 weeks follow-

559

ing infection. This practice may result in an occasional abortion but will prevent a "storm." Owners with small numbers of mares are not advised to use such a procedure. Recently a modified live virus vaccine has been used extensively and appears to afford adequate protection (Stear, 1976). Booster shots at 6-month intervals are recommended.

Viral Arteritis

This is an acute upper-respiratory tract infection caused by a specific herpes virus that also causes abortion. Viral arteritis is similar to influenza and rhinopneumonitis in that there is a fever (102–106°F) and a nasal discharge, but is more serious to the mature horse than either, because horses of all age groups are susceptible. Although the disease is severe, the mortality rate is usually low. However, under certain conditions mortality may be as high as 33 percent and the abortion rate is approximately 50 percent. Laboratory examinations using complement-fixation or serum neutralization tests may be necessary to diagnose the disease. The disease spreads rapidly and is probably transmitted by inhalation of droplets from infected horses or from ingestion of contaminated material. An infected animal can transmit the virus for 8–10 days. Outbreaks of viral arteritis are reported infrequently today but antibody titers are common, indicating that subclinical infection is occurring. This natural immunity is probably responsible for the decrease of reported cases.

Equine Encephalomyelitis

Of all the equine diseases, this disease has received the greatest public attention in the past few years because of an outbreak in 1971 and because the disease can be transmitted to humans. The disease at present is restricted to the American continents. Several different viruses cause equine encephalomyelitis and are usually designated by geographical terms; Venezuelan (VEE), Eastern (EEE), and Western (WEE) are the three most common types. The disease is transmitted primarily by mosquitoes (especially *Culex* spp.) from infected horses to susceptible horses or to man. Other insects, such as ticks, bloodsucking bugs, mites, and lice, may also occasionally transmit the disease. The Venezuelan type can also be spread by aerosol when animals are in close contact. The viruses have been isolated from many species of animals, such as horses, mules, donkeys, man, monkeys, snakes, and frogs, in natural conditions and calves, dogs, mice, and guinea pigs under experimental conditions. Wild birds, however, are the principal reservoir of the virus.

560   The Western strain usually has the lowest mortality rate: 20–30 percent of the infected animals die. The Eastern and Venezuelan strains have mor-

tality rates of 70–90 percent. Young horses are most susceptible. Immunity can last for approximately 2 years after infection, but recovered animals often have suffered permanent brain damage that makes them useless.

The incubation period may last from 1 to 3 weeks. One of the earliest signs is a fever that may reach 106°F. The fever usually lasts for no more then 24–48 hours and may not be detected. Nervous signs that appear during the period of peak fever include hypersensitivity to sound, a transitory period of excitement, and restlessness. Shortly thereafter, the signs associated with brain lesions, such as drowsiness, drooping ears, abnormal gait, and circling, appear. The horse may stand with head held low and food hanging from the lips.

The next stage is paralysis. The horse loses the ability to raise its head, the lower lip drops, and the tongue may hang out. The horse also has difficulty walking. Defecation and urination are difficult. The final stage — complete paralysis and death — may occur 2–4 days after the first signs appear.

Encephalitis can be prevented by vaccination. A combination of killed Eastern and Western viruses given in two doses provides protection for about one year. A modified live virus product from the Venezuelan strain gives protection for several years. A killed Venezuelan virus vaccine has only recently become available.

Equine Infectious Anemia (EIA) (Swamp Fever)

This viral disease has received considerable attention in recent years. Incidences of it have been reported in many parts of the world and in all of the contiguous United States. Equine species are the only known natural hosts.

The acute form of the disease is characterized by the sudden onset of a high fever of 104–108°F, severe depression, depressed appetite, and loss of weight. The animal usually becomes weak and loses coordination. Jaundice and edema of the ventral abdomen, sheath, scrotum, and limbs may develop. The spleen becomes enlarged, as can sometimes be verified by rectal examination. There is rapid destruction of red blood cells. The anemia is characterized by low hematocrit and low hemoglobin levels, low red blood cell count, and a high sedimentation rate. In severe cases the mortality rate is high.

The subacute form is reported to be the most common form. The signs are similar to the acute form but are not severe and death seldom occurs.

Horses with a chronic form of the disease usually appear to be unthrifty and lack stamina. They may have acute or subacute attacks. Anemia may develop periodically. Such animals are usually not satisfactory for work or breeding. Some horses may appear to recover after 7–20 days but may have another attack weeks, months, or even years later, usually during

561

periods of stress. These animals are dangerous to the welfare of other horses because they are carriers of the virus but may not be recognized as such.

EIA is transmitted in the blood from infected horses. Bloodsucking flies are probably the most common vectors but mosquitoes, hypodermic needles, surgical instruments, dental floats, and bridle bits may also transmit the virus.

No vaccine is available but recently a reliable diagnostic method has become available. The Coggins test, named after Dr. Leroy Coggins of Cornell University, is an agar gel-immuno-diffusion test that is now the official USDA-approved test. Only 10 cc of the animal's blood is needed to conduct the test and the results can be available within 48 hours. Previously, it was necessary to take blood from a suspected animal and inject it into a horse or pony that had been in isolation. Thirty to sixty days were then required to detect evidence of infection in the test animal. Presently, horses with a positive Coggins test do not have to be destroyed but must be identified and isolated. Regulations and testing intervals vary from state to state.

Tetanus (Lockjaw)

Tetanus is caused by *Clostridium tetani*. The bacteria can be found in the feces of horses and in soil contaminated by horse feces throughout the world. The bacteria, which enter the body through a wound or the naval cord, are anaerobic, and thus deep puncture wounds are more likely to result in tetanus than are surface lacerations. A neurotoxin is produced, which reaches the central nervous system by traveling up peripheral nerve trunks rather than by passing through the blood stream. The exact mode of action of the toxin is not known, but it brings about overreaction to reflex and motor stimuli, resulting in spasmodic or constant muscular rigidity. Thus the animal has great difficulty walking and may develop a "saw-horse" posture. The prolapse of the third eyelid is a characteristic sign of tetanus. Death usually occurs by asphyxiation because of rigidity of the muscles of respiration.

Mortality is almost 100 percent in untreated animals and 75–80 percent in treated animals. Treatment includes relaxation of muscles by frequent injections of muscle-relaxing drugs. Tranquilizers have also been used. Slinging and stomach tubing or intravenous feeding are necessary in some cases because the animals cannot eat. Enemas may also be useful because the animal cannot defecate properly.

The best approach is prevention. Active immunity is best achieved by injection of tetanus toxoid with annual boosters. Any horse, not immunized, that has suffered a puncture wound or deep laceration should be given tetanus antitoxin immediately. Antitoxin affords temporary protection that lasts approximately 2 weeks.

Glanders

Glanders was once quite prevalent but has been eradicated from North America. It still occurs in Eastern Europe, Asia Minor, Asia, and North Africa. Caused by the bacillus *Actinobacillus mallei,* the disease most commonly affects horses, mules, and donkeys, but man may also contract the disease. Signs include a high fever, nasal discharge, ulcers on the nasal mucosa, and nodules on the lower legs and abdomen. Septicemia occurs in a few days and death usually follows shortly thereafter. If the animal recovers, the ulcers leave a star-shaped scar.

No successful vaccination programs are available. The disease was eradicated from the United States by quarantine and destruction of infected animals.

Anthrax

Anthrax is caused by *Bacillus anthracis* and is always an acute disease in the horse, but the clinical signs may vary according to the route of infection. Ingestion of the anthrax spores causes septicemia, enteritis, and colic. Infection caused by a biting insect results in a high fever and hot, painful, edematous swelling of the throat, lower chest, abdomen, prepuce, and mammary gland. The condition lasts 48–96 hours and the mortality rate is high.

Anthrax is often transmitted by ingestion of spores from infected material—contaminated animal products such as bone meal, contaminated grains or forages, and fecal material from infected animals. Biting flies and other insects may also transmit the disease.

Treatment includes injections of antibiotics (penicillin or oxytetracycline) and anti-anthrax serum. The disease can be controlled by immunization. Many types of serums, bacterins, and vaccines are available. In areas where there is a history of anthrax, vaccination should be done annually.

Infected carcasses should be buried at least 6 feet deep. All suspected cases should be isolated and the farm placed in quarantine.

Scratches (Grease Heel)

Scratches is an eczema that affects the fetlock and heel areas. Repeated exposure to sweat, mud, and filth predisposes the development of the

563

condition. There may be complications caused by secondary bacterial or fungal infection. The affected area should be thoroughly cleaned, long hair clipped, and skin debris removed. Application of ointments and topical antibiotics is helpful.

Thrush

Thrush is a degenerative condition of the frog. A black discharge, the offensive odor of which identifies the condition, is emitted from the frog. In severe cases most of the frog may be eroded and lameness may occur. The frog is normally resistant to bacterial infection, but continued exposure to bacteria (such as standing in manure) overcomes the resistance. The foot should be thoroughly cleaned with soap and water, the rotting frog trimmed away, and an antiseptic applied.

18.4 Vaccination Program

Start this program at 3 months of age or at any age thereafter.

All Animals

Tetanus (Lockjaw). Initially requires 2 doses 4–8 weeks apart, with yearly booster dose thereafter. If vaccination status is unknown, tetanus antitoxin can be administered. It gives approximately 2 weeks' protection.

Selected Animals

Equine Influenza. Vaccine is recommended for weanlings, yearlings, and horses that are shown, raced, or, in general, brought in direct contact with groups of strange horses. Initially requires 2 doses 4–12 weeks apart with 1 to 4 booster injections annually depending on exposure to outbreaks.

Eastern and Western Equine Encephalomyelitis (EEE, WEE). Requires 2 doses each spring before mosquito season. (The dose of one type of commonly used vaccine is repeated in 7–14 days; the dose of the other type is repeated in 4–8 weeks.)

564 *Venezuelan Equine Encephalomyelitis (VEE).* Requires one dose only, good for 3 years or longer. Venezuelan encephalitis vaccine is no longer

recommended except in those states bordering Mexico. If an outbreak occurs again in the United States, widespread vaccination will be utilized. Protection is afforded within 14 days or less after initial vaccination.

A combined Eastern, Western, and Venezuelan equine encephalitis vaccine is also available.

Equine Viral Rhinopneumonitis (Viral Abortion). One form of protection is an intranasal "planned infection program." It should be carried out only on those farms presently on the program or where specifically recommended by the local veterinarian. The owner must understand that there is an attendant abortion risk whenever this "planned infection program" is initiated for the first time on a given farm. An injectable vaccine is also available. Two doses are required, 4–8 weeks apart with a yearly booster. The vaccine can be used on any horse at any age over 3 months.

Strangles (Streptococcus Equi *Infection*). An injectable vaccine is available. Three doses are required, 2 months apart with a yearly booster.

Anthrax. A number of vaccines are available. They are for use only under federal control in an epidemic area.

18.5 *Metabolic and Miscellaneous Diseases*

Colic

Colic is a general term indicating abdominal pain. The pain may cause the horse to become restless, paw, kick at its belly or get up and down frequently. The horse may roll, lie on its back or sit like a dog. The saw horse posture is often observed. Geldings may exhibit the penis without urinating. The pain may be intermittent but, in severe cases, is constant and unrelenting. The pulse rate is increased but temperature may be normal or elevated from 101–103° as a result of physical activity.

There are many types and many causes of colic. Digestive colic may be caused by overfeeding, sudden change in type of feed, moldy feed, or feed that was not properly chewed because of poor teeth or bolting. Heavy work after a large meal may also produce digestive colic. Spasmodic colic is caused by severe contraction of the intestines. The condition is so named because there are intervals between the spasms of pain. The noise caused by the severe contractions can be heard by putting your ear to the flank of the horse.

Intestinal obstruction or blocking of the bowel, although a less frequent cause of colic, is a severe condition that causes extreme pain and is a threat to the life of the horse.

565

Intestinal obstruction can be caused by eating foreign objects. A technical term for eating unnatural material is *allotriophagy*. Large objects may directly block the intestine, causing a very acute, extremely painful, and usually fatal illness.

S. M. Getty and co-workers at Michigan State University recently reported such a case of intestinal obstruction (Getty *et al.*, 1976). A 5-month-old filly was presented to the university clinic because her feed intake was greatly reduced and she was losing weight, was lethargic, and suffered from recurring attacks of colic. She died shortly after admission. At autopsy, large masses of cord from a rubber fence were found in the stomach, small intestine, and large intestine. The researchers concluded,

> Because of this case, it is our opinion that persons who contemplate the use of rubberized fencing should either consider constructing an inner strand of electric wire between the horse and the fencing to prevent direct contact, or apply a sealer to the fencing material to reduce the potential for consumption. Horses, especially the young, frequently exhibit allotriophagy and will consume strands of cord unravelled from rubberized fencing. Although rubber fencing may have the distinct advantage of confining horses atraumatically, one disadvantage might be its potential as a source of intestinal obstruction.

Small objects might become the center of balls of ingesta called fecaliths. The fecaliths "grow" by accumulating material on their surfaces. Several fecaliths each approximately 2 inches in diameter were recently surgically removed from the intestine of a horse with chronic colic. A piece of wood the size of $\frac{1}{3}$ of a toothpick was found in the center of each of the fecaliths. (The horse was a habitual wood chewer.) Fecaliths composed primarily of minerals may also be found, but for unknown reasons the incidence of this type of fecalith has decreased.

Horses that are fed on the ground may develop sand colic because they ingest so much sand that the intestine becomes obstructed. This condition is common in the Southwestern United States, Texas, and Florida. Gravel or small stones are also eaten by horses and may cause intestinal obstruction.

Parasites are the most common cause of colic. Migrating strongyle larvae damage the blood vessels by producing aneurisms, that is, by weakening the walls. Hence the blood supply to the intestines is decreased and the cells become anoxic, resulting in decreased motility and pain. Roundworms in large numbers can cause impaction or obstruction of the intestine and may even cause intussesception (telescoping of the intestine). A good parasite control program is essential for the prevention of colic.

Twisted intestines also result in obstruction and colic. The causes of the twisting are not clearly defined. Although it is often suggested that violent rolling may result in twisting, further studies are needed to verify this suggestion.

A horse with colic should be walked to help relieve the anxiety that accompanies colic and to prevent injury during rolling. If after one-half hour of walking, the horse acts as if the pain is unrelenting or increasing and he makes repeated attempts to lie down or breaks out in a cold sweat, a veterinarian should be called. The treatment for colic varies with the type of colic. For example, recovery may be spontaneous. Analgesics (pain-relieving drugs) may be adequate in some cases, but in other cases, such as a horse with a twisted intestine or foreign material obstruction, surgery may be necessary.

Pulmonary Emphysema (Heaves)

In pulmonary emphysema, air is trapped in the lungs and the lungs become distended, although the effective air space is reduced because the elastic recoil of the lungs is reduced and the air cannot be efficiently forced out. The disease develops gradually and the clinical signs are most commonly seen in horses 5 years old or older. At first the animal has a cough or wheeze that may be more pronounced after exercise. As the disease progresses, the coughing becomes more frequent and a nasal discharge may be present. With chronic heaves, a "heave line" may develop because of the extra effort needed to compensate for the failure of elastic recoil. The heave line is a prominent ridge of abdominal muscle that is seen as a nearly straight line from high in the flank diagonally forward and down. It appears with each expiration following normal relaxation of the rib cage because the abdominal muscles give an extra squeeze to force the intestines against the diaphragm, which in turn forces air out of the affected lungs.

Horses with clinical emphysema are of little use for performing work because of the reduced capacity for oxygen uptake. Horses with mild emphysema, however, can be used as pleasure horses if they are not pushed too hard and, with proper care can lead a long and useful life.

The causes of emphysema are not well defined. Some reports indicate that it is an allergic response that is perhaps due to molds. Dusty feeds greatly aggrevate the condition. Emphysema is seldom seen in horses pastured the year round.

No treatment is known that will result in complete recovery. The condition is alleviated by resting the animal, providing fresh air, and eliminating dust. Pasturing the horse is often the best solution. Wetting the hay and grain or using a complete pelleted ration may be helpful in reducing dust. The bedding should not be dusty. Shavings might be substituted for straw. The animal should be protected against extreme environments such as high humidity or high temperature. Antihistamine drugs may be

567

of value in some situations. But, to repeat, the most important remedies are rest, elimination of dust, and provision of fresh air.

Roaring (Laryngeal Hemiplegia)

Roaring is caused by damage to the recurrent laryngeal nerve and results in lack of muscular control of the vocal cords. The affected vocal cords vibrate with inspiration, causing a roaring sound. The severity of the condition varies but the symptoms are usually most noticeable after exercise. Roaring greatly impairs the use of working horses, such as racehorses, cow ponies, hunters, and jumpers. If the horse is used only for light pleasure riding, roaring might not impair its serviceability, but the roaring sound may be annoying to the rider. Roaring can usually be corrected by surgery. The etiology of the damage to the nerve remains obscure, although the left nerve is almost always damaged, probably because it travels around the arch of the aorta and along the deep face of that vessel, where it receives pressure from the strong aortic pulsations. Many cases of roaring follow attacks of pneumonia. Infrequently, pressure damage to the nerve is caused by enlarged lymph nodes, tumors, abscesses, or aneurisms. (See sections 10.2 and 10.6 for a discussion of other diseases, such as recurrent uveitis, founder, and azoturia.)

References

Belschner, H. G. 1969. *Horse Diseases.* London: Angus and Robertson.

Blood, D. C., and J. A. Henderson. 1972. *Veterinary Medicine.* London: Bailliure, Tindall and Cassel.

Bryans, J. T., and H. Gerber, eds. 1973. Equine Infectious Diseases. In *Proc. 3rd International Conf. Equine Infectious Diseases*, Basel, Switzerland. New York: Karger.

Catcott, E. J., and J. F. Smithcors. 1972. *Equine Medicine and Surgery.* Wheaton, Illinois: Am. Vet. Publ.

Getty, S. M., D. J. Ellis, J. D. Krehbiel, and D. L. Whitenak. 1976. Rubberized fencing as a gastrointestinal obstruction in a young horse. *Vet. Med. Small Animal Clin.* 71:221.

McChesney, A. E., J. J. England, C. E. Whiteman, and J. L. Adcock. 1974. Experimental transmission of equine adenovirus in Arabian and non-Arabian foals. *Amer. J. Vet. Res.* 35:1015–1023.

McGuire, T. C., M. J. Poppie, and K. L. Banks. 1974. Combined (B- and T-lymphocyte) immunodeficiency: A fatal genetic disease in Arabian foals. *J. Amer. Vet. Med. Assn.* 164:70.

Rossdale, P. D., and S. M. Wreford. 1974. *The Horse's Health from A to Z.* London: David and Charles.

Stear, R. L. 1976. Diagnosis and control of equine rhinopneumonitis. *Proc. 1st National Horsemen's Seminar.* Virginia Horse Council, Fredericksburg, Virginia. p. 175.

Thompson, D. B., M. J. Studdert, R. G. Beilharz, and I. R. Littlejohns. 1975. Inheritance of a lethal immunodeficiency disease of Arabian foals. *Austr. Vet. J.* 51:109.

(See overleaf for disease tables)

TABLE 18-1
Summary of infectious diseases

Disease	Cause	Primary Characteristics	Prevention	Treatment
Influenza	Myxovirus	Fever of 101–105°F, watery nasal discharge.	Vaccination. Isolation of new animals.	Good nursing care
Strangles	*Streptococcus equi*	Enlarged lymph nodes, nasal discharge — watery at first, then purulent. Fever of 103–105°F.	Isolation of new animals. Vaccinate all animals with killed vaccine.	Antibiotics
Pneumonia	Virus; bacteria	Fever of 102–105°F. Chest pains, lung congestion, difficulty in breathing.	Good management. Avoid chills and stress. Provide proper ventilation.	Antibiotics when cause is bacterial.
Rhinopneu-monitis	Herpes virus	Fever of 102–106°F, coughing, clear nasal discharge. Abortion primarily in last third of gestation.	Modified live virus vaccine.	No treatment
Viral arteritis	Herpes virus	Fever of 102–106°F. Abortion.	No vaccine available.	Good nursing care

Disease	Cause	Symptoms	Prevention	Treatment
Equine encephalomyelitis	Virus	brain lesions, drowsiness, fever. Lower lip drops. Difficulty in walking.	Vaccination.	Good nursing care
Equine infectious anemia	Virus transmitted in blood of infected horses	Fever of 104–108°F. Weakness, jaundice, edema of ventral abdomen.	Use of Coggins test to detect carriers.	No treatment
Tetanus	Clostridium tetani	Muscular rigidity. Prolapse of third eyelid.	Tetanus toxoid or antitoxin.	(Mortality rate is high)
Anthrax	Bacillus anthracis	High fever, edema about throat, lower neck, and chest. Lasts approximately 48–96 hours.	Vaccines—use only in an epidemic area.	Antibiotics, anti-anthrax serum
Glanders	Bacteria	High fever; ulcers of nasal mucosa; septicemia.	Isolation. (No vaccine available; disease no longer present in United States.)	

TABLE 18-2
Summary of metabolic and miscellaneous diseases of the horse

Condition	Cause	Primary Characteristics	Prevention	Treatment
Colic	Parasites; overfeeding; moldy feed; twisted intestines.	Abdominal pain; kicking at belly; rolling; saw horse posture.	Parasite control; proper feeding methods.	Walking; laxatives; analgesics; surgery in some cases.
Pulmonary emphysema	Not well defined — perhaps allergic response.	Coughing; heave line.	Prevent and treat respiratory infections; control stable dust.	Control dust; provide fresh air; give antihistamine drugs.
Roaring	Damage to recurrent laryngeal nerve.	Noise during inspiration.	Prevent and treat respiratory infections.	Surgery.
Recurrent uveitis	Immunological response, particularly to infection with leptospirosis.	Eye is periodically cloudy. After several attacks, permanent blindness may result.	Recommendations cannot be made for adequate prevention because of insufficient knowledge concerning the condition.	Steroid therapy may be helpful.
Azoturia	Unknown, but condition occurs when animal is exercised after being full fed during period of inactivity.	Stiff gait; reluctance to move; dark-colored urine.	Reduce feed intake when animal is not working.	Injections of thiamin, vitamin E, and selenium are frequently used. Further studies are needed to determine their value.
Founder	Overeating; retained placenta.	Lameness; heat in hoof; "seedy toe"; drop of coffin bone.	Maintain a sound feeding program; do not keep horses too fat.	Acute: obtain immediate veterinary attention. Chronic: perform corrective trimming and shoeing.

CHAPTER NINETEEN *Parasites of the Horse*

19.1 Parasites and Parasitism

A *parasite* is a small organism that lives on or in and at the expense of a larger organism called the host. Parasites that attack the skin and body openings of the host are called external parasites or *ectoparasites*, and those that live in the internal organs, body cavities, and tissues are called internal parasites or *endoparasites*.

Parasitic adaptation is a product of evolution, and parasite species have evolved special anatomical and physiological modifications that render them capable of exploiting the energy source embodied in their host species. These special modifications have no alternative applications, so most parasites rely entirely upon their hosts and perish without them. For example, *Gasterophilus* species, the stomach botflies, have evolved intricate mechanisms for gaining access to the stomach of a horse and for resisting digestion there for up to 9 months, but they are completely incapable of making a living in any other way. The adult botflies do not even have mouthparts and so cannot eat anything; they must mate and lay their eggs using energy that they stored when they were parasitic larvae (stomach bots). Most of the parasites of horses are equally committed to the parasitic way of life, although many have so-called *free-living stages* that represent a period of development outside the host. This period of development invariably culminates in an *infective stage*, a stage that is anatomically and physiologically adapted to gaining access to and taking up residence in (that is, infecting) the host.

Certain parasites of horses also utilize other species of hosts as sources of energy. Examples of these include the "horseflies," mosquitoes, certain ticks, faceflies, and one species of stomach worm called *Trichostrongylus axei*. Other parasites are entirely faithful to the horse, and the most important among these are the strongyle and ascarid intestinal worms and the stomach bots. This chapter is devoted mainly to the biology of this latter group.

19.2   The Nematodes or Roundworms

Nematodes have slender, unsegmented, cylindrical bodies that taper toward each end (Figure 19-1). With a single exception (*Strongyloides westeri*), both male and female sexes are represented in all species of nematodes that parasitize the horse. Male nematodes are smaller than the females of their species. The posterior ends of the males of many species expand to form a *copulatory bursa* (Figure 19-2) for grasping the female and are equipped with somewhat rigid rod-shaped *spicules* for dilating the vulva. The female reproductive tract consists of two ovaries, oviducts, and uteri connected to a single vagina and vulva (Figure 19-1). The uteri of female worms contain enormous numbers of eggs that, in most cases, leave the host with the feces to undergo a period of development in the outside world or in the body of an *intermediate host* before becoming infective. A tiny worm, or first-stage larva as it is called, develops within the egg (Figure 19-3). Depending on the species of worm, this larva may hatch out of the egg, as do the strongyles, or it may remain within the egg to undergo further development and await ingestion by a horse, as do the ascarids (Figure 19-4). All nematodes, however, undergo a series of 4 molts characterized by a *lethargus* or resting stage, *metamorphosis* or restructuring, *ecdysis* or casting of the old larval skin, and, finally, emergence as a new worm adapted anatomically and physiologically to overcome the obstacles that are to be encountered and to achieve the goals that must be achieved if that individual is to play a role in the perpetuation of its species. For example, in the first and second stages of the development of *Strongylus vulgaris*, these nematodes feed on the bacteria that abound in the feces that constitute their environment. In the third, infective stage, they no longer feed on bacteria but, consuming stored energy, move in water films on the surface of vegetation until they are ingested by a horse, whereupon they burrow into the mucous membrane of the intestinal tract, curl up, and molt to the fourth stage. In the fourth stage, *Strongylus vulgaris* larvae have great powers of penetration and rapidly bore through tissue, enter the small arterioles in the wall of the gut, and, crawling along the lining of the arteries, migrate at random for several months. Finally, they return to the wall of the large intestine, molt to the fifth or adult stage, and enter the lumen of the large intestine to mate and reproduce. Thus, each stage in the life history of this nematode is peculiarly and uniquely adapted to overcome the particular obstacles that confront that stage, and a major

574

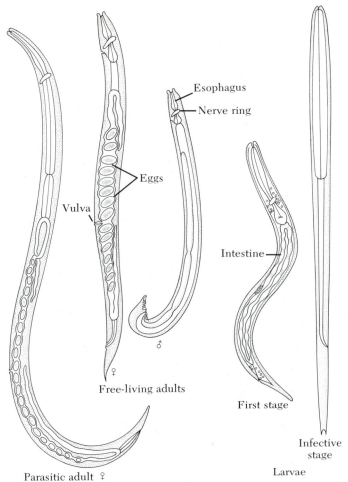

Esophagus

Nerve ring

Eggs

Vulva

Intestine

Free-living adults

First stage

Parasitic adult ♀

Infective stage

Larvae

FIGURE 19-1

General structure of male, female, and larval stages of a nematode worm, *Strongyloides*. *Strongyloides* is unique among nematode parasites because it has both parasitic and free-living generations. *Strongyloides westeri*, a species that parasitizes the horse, is capable of causing illness in nursing foals. Adapted from Craig and Faust. 1945.

"overhaul" or "retooling" is accomplished by each metamorphosis. The life cycle of *Strongylus vulgaris* is summarized diagrammatically in Figure 19-5.

Strongyles

The horse is host to the approximately 54 species that belong to the family Strongylidae. The most important of these are the "big three," *Strongylus*

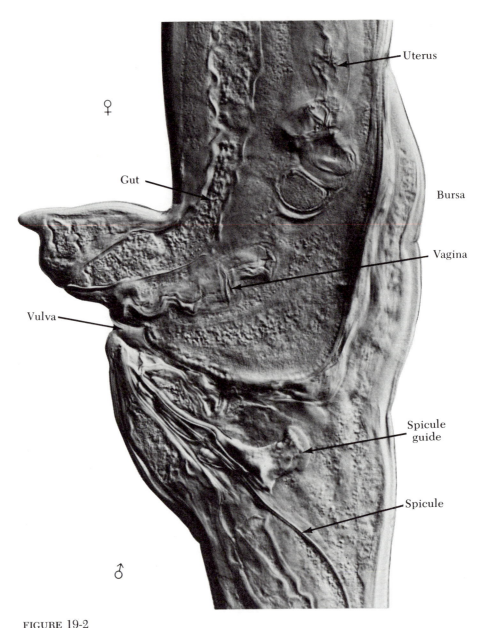

FIGURE 19-2
Male and female nematodes copulating. The bursa is a special male organ used
for clasping the female. Only the dorsal ray of the bursa is visible in the optical
plane of this photomicrograph, but there are also lateral rays that are applied to
each side of the female. The spicules of the male worm have not yet entered the
vagina of the female. The worms shown here are *Cylicocerus catinatus*, a species
of small strongyle that parasitizes the large intestine of the horse.

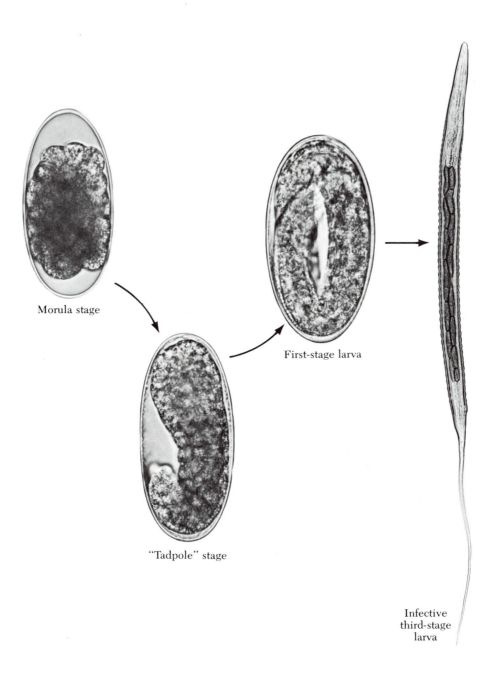

Morula stage

"Tadpole" stage

First-stage larva

Infective
third-stage
larva

FIGURE 19-3
Development of a strongyle from egg to infective larva.

577

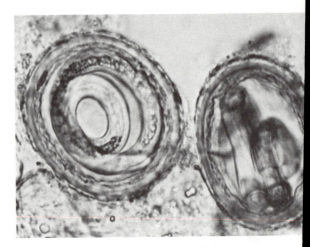

FIGURE 19-4
Two infective eggs of the ascarid *Parascaris equorum*. The infective second-stage larva does not hatch until the egg is ingested by a horse. Thus, in the infective stage, *P. equorum* is less mobile than the strongyle larva, but, encased in its sticky and protective shell, it may remain alive and stuck to a surface for years.

FIGURE 19-5
Life cycle of *Strongylus vulgaris*. From Georgi. 1974.

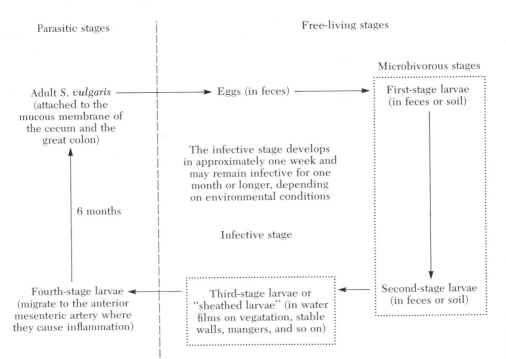

Parasitic stages   Free-living stages

Microbivorous stages

Adult *S. vulgaris* ⟶ Eggs (in feces) ⟶ First-stage larvae
(attached to the (in feces or soil)
mucous membrane of
the cecum and the
great colon)

The infective stage develops
in approximately one week and
may remain infective for one
month or longer, depending
on environmental conditions

6 months

Infective stage

Fourth-stage larvae ⟵ Third-stage larvae or ⟵ Second-stage larvae
(migrate to the anterior "sheathed larvae" (in water (in feces or soil)
mesenteric artery where films on vegatation, stable
they cause inflammation) walls, mangers, and so on)

vulgaris, S. edentatus, and *S. equinus,* which, along with several species of *Triodontophorus* and a few rare species, constitute the "large strongyles." The rest of the species, collectively called small strongyles, are usually dismissed as having little or no pathological significance, although invasion of the intestinal mucous membrane by large numbers of them in their immature stages can cause severe diarrhea.

As adult worms, all of the "big three" are bloodsucking parasites of the large intestine (Figure 19-6) and are capable of causing various degrees of anemia, depending upon the number of worms present and the constitutional vigor and state of nutrition of the horse. As immature or larval worms, however, each of these three species undergoes a characteristic, prolonged, and destructive migration through the organs and tissues of its host that may prove even more harmful to the health of the horse than the bloodsucking activities of the adult worms.

Strongylus vulgaris.   When ingested by a horse, the infective third-stage larvae of *Strongylus vulgaris* cast off their sheaths in the stomach and small intestine and enter the wall of the cecum and ventral colon. Here the larvae curl up under the mucous membrane, become encapsulated by the inflammation of the surrounding tissues, and prepare to molt. After 8 days, the molt is completed and the fourth-stage larvae resume their migrations, leaving behind only a few host inflammatory cells and their third-stage

FIGURE 19-6
The "big three" strongyle nematodes of the horse, *Strongylus vulgaris,*
S. equinus, and *S. edentatus.* Note the large mouths, by which they attach themselves to the lining of the large intestine.

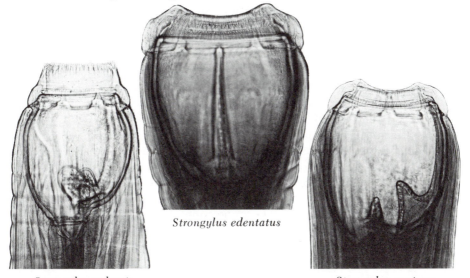

Strongylus edentatus

Strongylus vulgaris

Strongylus equinus

579

cuticles. The fourth-stage larvae now penetrate the walls of small arterioles lying in the submucosa and wander upstream into progressively larger arteries by crawling along the intima or innermost layer of the arterial wall. Inflammation and a slight deposit of fibrin trace the course of each larva, and wherever many such paths cross, summation of the individual reactions leads to gross thrombosis that may even occlude the vessel lumen. Because the cranial mesenteric artery is the stem trunk connecting the abdominal aorta with all of the branch arteries that supply blood to the intestines, all possible migration routes converge upon this inch-long vessel. In almost every horse, the cranial mesenteric artery bears some mark of the effect of the larvae of *Strongylus vulgaris*. A few larvae excite a superficial inflammatory reaction that results in the formation of a *thrombus* (an intravascular clot). Continued invasion of the inflamed area by larvae causes progressive growth of the thrombus and extension of the inflammatory process into the deeper layers of the arterial wall. Pieces of thrombus called *emboli* (singular, *embolus*) may break away and be carried by the bloodstream until they enter a branch that is too small to accommodate them. Obstruction of various branches of the anterior mesenteric artery by emboli is probably a common occurrence; its effect on the maintenance of arterial circulation to the intestinal tract is discussed in the following paragraphs of this discussion of *Strongylus vulgaris*. Deep inflammation weakens the arterial wall and causes it to yield to the pressure of the blood within, leading to the formation of a sac-like dilatation called an aneurysm. Finally, the larvae leave the thrombi, return to the wall of the intestine, molt to the fifth (adult) stage, and enter the lumen of the intestine to mate and reproduce. This final molt may occur as early as 90 days after invasion but may occur much later. Larvae that are enmeshed and detained in thrombi may molt even before returning to the intestinal wall. Thus, there is much variation in the generation time of *S. vulgaris* from egg to egg; the minimum is approximately 6 months. These *S. vulgaris* larval migrations were demonstrated experimentally in 1950 and 1951 by Karl Enigk of the Tierärztliche Hochschule, Hanover. An English translation of Enigk's brilliant work has recently been published (Georgi, 1973).

Before we further consider the effects of thrombosis and embolism of the arteries that supply the wall of the bowel with blood, we must first define the familiar but frequently misunderstood term "colic."

Colic is acute abdominal pain characterized by restlessness (see section 18.5). Anything capable of distending or obstructing the lumen of the intestinal tract is capable of causing colic. In 1870, Otto Bollinger hypothesized that occlusion of the intestinal arteries by worm thrombi or emboli could account for the majority of equine colic cases, both fatal and nonfatal. Occlusion of intestinal arteries would, according to Bollinger, always lead to partial or complete paralysis of the musculature of the bowel wall with consequent slowing or stoppage of the flow of intestinal ingesta and gases. The accumulation of gas, aggravated by accelerated fermentation, would then painfully distend the affected portions of the intestine. Unless the circulatory impairment were overcome and intestinal motility restored, the horse would die an excruciatingly painful death. Bollinger interpreted a variety of postmortem lesions as direct manifestations of the thromboembolism of the intestinal arteries and pointed out that many cases of fatal displacements and obstructions of the bowel were probably the result rather than the cause of the colic victim's agonized rolling and thrashing about. Thus, Bollinger believed that virtually all pathological changes observed at a postmortem examination of fatal colic cases had their origins in verminous thrombosis or embolism of the intestinal arteries. However, his views were challenged on two counts.

First, the classical morbid anatomists (pathologists) argued that mere occlusion of an artery, even a large one, is not proof that the blood supply has been completely cut off. They insisted that evidence of infarction or massive death of the affected region of the bowel wall must be present to justify a diagnosis of thrombo-embolic colic. Second, experimental efforts to induce such changes by surgical ligation of major arterial branches also failed to produce fatal infarction of the bowel wall. The reason that occlusion of intestinal arteries either by verminous thrombo-embolism or by surgical ligation infrequently leads to complete cessation of blood flow is that there exists in the intestinal arterial tree of the horse a truly amazing network of interconnections called *anastomoses*. These anastomoses afford rapid development of *collateral circulation* by means of which blood is "detoured" around the obstruction, and nutrition of the deprived area is thereby restored. Figures 19-7 and 19-8 show several kinds of anastomoses. The larger the caliber of the anastomotic connection, the more rapidly will collateral circulation be established. Thus, obstruction of either the dorsal or the vental colic artery will be rapidly overcome via the anastomosis of these two arteries at the pelvic flexure (Figure 19-7). On the other hand, the establishment of collateral circulation to the area of bowel wall deprived of circulation by double embolism of either the dorsal or the ventral colic artery would necessitate great dilation of the small-caliber perivenous network (Figure 19-8) and cross-anastomoses, and consequently would require more time.

Of all domestic animals, the horse has by far the most highly developed system of anastomoses in the arterial tree serving the intestine. In an evolutionary context, this may be interpreted as evidence that *Strongylus vulgaris*, which has no direct counterpart in other domestic animals, has probably been making a mess of horses' arteries for millions of years. In other words, the extraordinary network of anastomoses in the arterial supply to the intestines of the horse may logically be interpreted as an evolutionary adaptation to a selection pressure imposed by this parasite whose larval migrations tend to cause the occlusion of these particular vessels.

The arteries that supply certain portions of the bowel wall are less well supplied with anastomoses, and occlusion of these branches is more likely

581

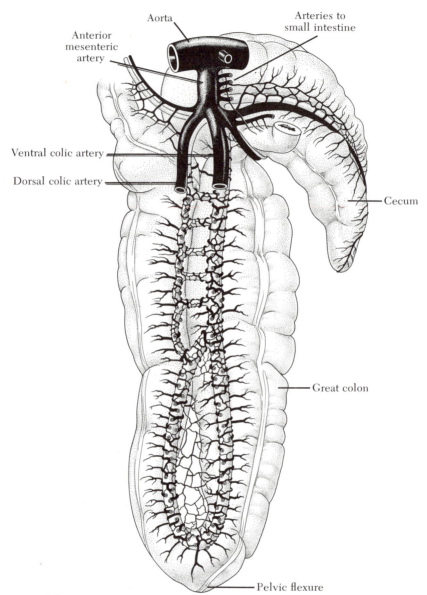

Aorta

Arteries to
small intestine

Anterior
mesenteric
artery

Ventral colic artery

Dorsal colic artery

Cecum

Great colon

Pelvic flexure

FIGURE 19-7
The large intestine of the horse and its principal arteries. The anterior
mesenteric artery, frequently the site of verminous thrombosis and aneurysm
formation, supplies virtually all of the arterial blood to the small intestine, great
colon, and cecum. Examples of anastomoses depicted here include (1) the fusion
of dorsal and ventral colic vessels at the pelvic flexure, and (2) the cross-
anastomoses connecting the dorsal and ventral colic arteries along most of their
lengths. Adapted from Dobberstein and Hartmann. 1932.

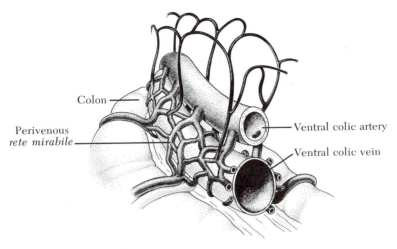

Colon

Perivenous
rete mirabile

Ventral colic artery

Ventral colic vein

FIGURE 19-8
Arterial network (*rete mirabile*) encasing the ventral colic vein.
Dilation of this arterial network can establish a detour (collateral
circulation) around an obstructed region in the parent artery (that is,
the ventral colic artery) and thus maintain the blood supply to the
wall of the colon. Adapted from Dobberstein and Hartmann. 1932.

to lead to severe circulatory disturbances. For example, the medial and
lateral arteries of the cecum do not join at the tip of the cecum, and thus
obstruction of either cecal artery is far more serious than obstruction of
either the dorsal or ventral colic artery. Fortunately, verminous embolism
of the cecal arteries happens much less frequently than does embolism of
the colic arteries. It has been claimed that this is because the cecal artery
leaves its parent vessel at a right angle, whereas the colic arteries represent more or less direct continuation of the parent trunk, and that solid
emboli are less likely to negotiate sharp turns than the liquid blood transporting them (Figure 19-7). Whatever the reason for the relative infre-
quency of verminous embolism of the cecal arteries, the corresponding lack
of extensive anastomoses of these vessels may be considered further evidence of the important role that *Strongylus vulgaris* has played in the
evolution of the horse.

Although it is probably true that obstruction of intestinal arteries by
worm thrombi or emboli leads to infarction and death of the intestinal
wall in only a small proportion of cases, it appears equally likely that
temporary curtailment of blood flow pending establishment of collateral
circulation could very well produce the sequence of morbid events hypothesized by Bollinger and expressed clinically as colic. Further, the
fatal intestinal displacements often interpreted at postmortem examination
to be the cause of colic symptoms are more likely to be the *result* of abnormalities of intestinal tone and motility brought about by overeating
or verminous thrombo-embolism and of the horses' violent efforts to
obtain relief.

Karl Enigk (1950, 1951) showed that as few as several hundred infective *S. vulgaris* larvae could cause widespread and fatal thrombosis of the very fine branches (arterioles) of the intestinal arteries of young foals that were reared parasite free. Thrombosis of these small vessels occurred very early in the course of infection, even before a single larva had reached the anterior mesenteric stem artery. In such cases, infarction of the bowel wall is present at postmortem examination, but no thromboses or emboli can be demonstrated by gross dissection.

These are some of the reasons that *Strongylus vulgaris* is the most important parasite of the horse.

Strongylus edentatus *and* Strongylus equinus. Adult *Strongylus edentatus* and *S. equinus* worms are twice as large as adult *S. vulgaris*, and are usually more difficult to remove with anthelmintic drugs. There is no doubt that the prolonged migrations of these parasites are destructive and capable of producing disease, but their pathogenic importance is overshadowed by that of *S. vulgaris*. The migration routes followed by *Strongylus edentatus* and *S. equinus* were the subject of years of patient research by Rudolph Wetzel and his co-workers (1942) at the University of Berlin. The exsheathed third-stage larvae of *S. edentatus* migrate to the liver, where they become encapsulated and molt to the fourth stage in approximately 2 weeks. After molting, the fourth-stage larvae wander about aimlessly in the liver tissue for approximately 2 months, during which they continue to grow. Leaving the liver by way of the ligaments that hold this organ in position, the larvae wander for months in the connective tissue layer that lies immediately beneath the peritoneal lining of the abdominal cavity. Eleven months after infection, the mature *S. edentatus* worms may be found attached by means of their enormous suction cuplike mouths to the lining of the cecum and colon.

Third-stage *Strongylus equinus* larvae, like those of *S. vulgaris*, encyst and undergo their third molt in the wall of the large intestine, principally the cecum. Many of these larvae appear as nodules under the serosa or peritoneal covering of the intestinal wall. After molting, they bore through the intestinal wall and enter the right half of the liver, which, in the living horse, lies in contact with this portion of the large intestine. The larvae tunnel about in the liver tissue for 6–7 weeks or more before emerging and entering the pancreas and the abdominal cavity in which locations they complete their development into adult male and female worms. Finally, these adult worms penetrate the wall of the intestine and re-enter the lumen of the large intestine to mate and produce eggs.

The wounds inflicted by the migrating "big three" larvae heal but seldom without the formation of scar tissue and a consequent reduction in the functional capacity of this tissue. Because there is no cure for such damage once it has occurred, every effort must be made to prevent it.

The Small Strongyles. The small strongyles or *Cyathostominae,* of which there are approximately 40 species, do not migrate far beyond the mucous membrane of the intestinal tract and are, therefore, far less harmful to the health of the horse. They are important mainly because of the similarity of their eggs to those of the "big three" and their ability to cause diarrhea when they are present in overwhelming numbers. Massive numbers of the bright-red larvae of one species of small strongyle, *Cylicocyclus insigne* tend to invade and riddle the mucosa of the large intestine.

The Ascarid, *Parascaris equorum*

Parascaris equorum is a very large (5–15 inches long), yellowish-white nematode parasite of the small intestine. Extraordinarily severe infections caused by adult worms may result in perforation of the bowel wall and fatal peritonitis, but such accidents are fortunately rare. More moderate degrees of infection may cause chronic enteritis and result in subnormal growth by interfering with digestion and absorption of nutrients, notably protein. A foal with heavy ascarid burdens is smaller than it would have been, its haircoat is dull, its skin dry and leathery, and its abdomen distended. In short, it is a victim of malnutrition. A major portion of the blame, however, can be ascribed to the ascarid larvae, whose destructive migrations through the liver and lungs are discussed in the following two paragraphs.

The life cycle of *Parascaris equorum* (Figure 19-9) is described as follows. When infective eggs are swallowed, they hatch and liberate second-stage larvae, which burrow into the wall of the small intestine and are carried to the liver by the portal vein. After migrating through the liver tissue, these larvae enter the hepatic veins and are carried by the posterior vena cava to the lungs, where they break into the alveoli, molt twice, and are coughed up and swallowed, thus returning to the small intestine where they mature. The first waves of larvae mainly inflict mechanical injury that appears to the unaided eye to be tiny hemorrhages. However, as the host becomes immunized to *Parascaris,* the immunity is expressed, in part at least, as allergic inflammation, which increases the damage inflicted by subsequent waves of migrating larvae. The damage done to the liver and lungs eventually heals, but the chronic reduction in functional capacity suffered during what is normally a period of rapid growth leaves a permanent mark on the yearling; it will never be what it could have been.

As indicated in Figure 19-9, only 1–2 weeks are required for the *P. equorum* eggs shed in the feces of an infected horse to develop to the infective stage. The outer, proteinaceous layer of the *P. equorum* eggshell is very sticky and causes the eggs to adhere to stall walls, mangers, water buckets, and the like. For these reasons, stall sanitation for the control of ascarids must, in order to prove effective, include weekly removal of all

585

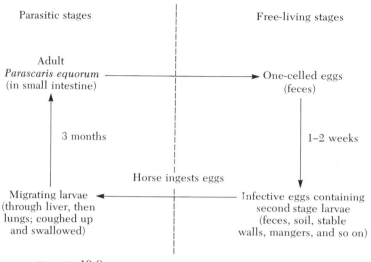

Parasitic stages   Free-living stages

Adult
Parascaris equorum ─────────────────────→ One-celled eggs
(in small intestine)   (feces)

3 months   1–2 weeks

Horse ingests eggs

Migrating larvae ←───────────── Infective eggs containing
(through liver, then   second stage larvae
lungs; coughed up   (feces, soil, stable
and swallowed)   walls, mangers, and so on)

FIGURE 19-9
Life cycle of *Parascaris equorum.* From Georgi. 1974.

manure and bedding and thorough cleaning of all surfaces with a high-pressure sprayer of the sort used in car wash stalls or with a steam jenny. Most chemical disinfectants have no effect on ascarid eggs, and therefore thorough cleansing with very hot water or live steam (steam under pressure) is necessary. The removal of manure before its burden of parasite eggs has had time to develop to the infective stage is particularly important when foals are being raised because foals deliberately eat substantial amounts of manure. This phenomenon, termed *coprophagia,* is considered in greater detail in section 19.4.

A Peculiar Parasite, *Strongyloides westeri*

Strongyloides literally means "strongyle-like," but this worm is really not at all like a strongyle. Members of this genus are unique among parasites of domestic animals in that they have both parasitic and free-living generations. The larvae stemming from parasitic females develop from unfertilized eggs. Parasitic males do not exist and parasitic females contain no male gonads. The tiny (less than 1 cm long) parasitic females are thus partheno-genetic, not hermaphroditic, and their progeny are termed homogonic (arising from one gonad) to distinguish them from the heterogonic offspring of the sexual generation. A homogonic *Strongyloides* larva may develop into either a male or a female free-living (nonparasitic) worm or, in some species, directly into an infective larva. The heterogonic larvae of the free-living generation develop into an infective larva. These somewhat complex relationships are summarized diagrammatically in Figure 19-10. Because the complete *S. westeri* life cycle can be completed in less than 2 weeks and

586

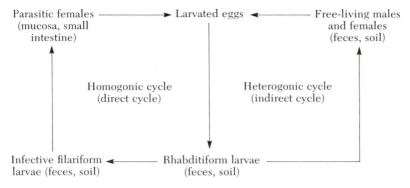

FIGURE 19-10
Life cycle of *Strongyloides*. The terms *filariform* (threadlike) and *rhabditiform* (rodlike) refer to the shape of the esophagus of the parasitic and free-living generations, respectively.

because there is multiplication in the free-living stage, populations of this species can grow to gigantic proportions in a relatively short time, especially in stables. Foals are particularly susceptible to *S. westeri* infection, which can occur both by penetration of the foal's skin by infective larvae in the bedding and by ingestion of larvae in their dam's milk. These larvae migrate through the lungs on their way to the mucous membrane of the small intestine and, especially when they invade in large numbers, inflict significant injury in passing. Control of an outbreak of *S. westeri* is a matter of daily removal of all manure and bedding from stalls and professional treatment of infected individuals. E. T. Lyons and his co-workers at the University of Kentucky consider the passage of larvae from dam to foal via the milk to be the more important route of infection. If so, it may prove difficult to cope with.

19.3 Stomach Bots

Bots are the larvae of botflies of the genus *Gasterophilus*. The adult flies have vestigial mouth parts and never feed; they are propelled by stored energy and the instinctive urge to mate and deposit their eggs on the hairs of a horse. The three principal North American species, *Gasterophilus nasalis*, *G. hemorrhoidalis*, and *G. intestinalis*, differ importantly in the area of the skin selected for egg laying and in the tactics adopted by the larvae that hatch from these eggs to gain entry to the stomach of the horse.

  Gasterophilus nasalis female flies deposit their yellowish-white eggs (Figure 19-11) on the hairs of the space between the jawbones. First-stage larvae (Figure 19-12) develop within 5 or 6 days and hatch in the absence of any external stimulus. The larvae crawl downward toward the chin, pro-

587

FIGURE 19-11
Eggs of *Gasterophilus* species.
Each species of *Gasterophilus*
lays its eggs on the hairs of a
particular region of the horse's
body. Adapted from Wells and
Knipling. 1938.

*Gasterophilus
nasalis* *Gasterophilus
intestinalis* *Gasterophilus
hemorrhoidalis*

FIGURE 19-12
First-stage larvae of *Gasterophilus*
species. Adapted from Wells and
Knipling. 1938.

*Gasterophilus
nasalis* *Gasterophilus
intestinalis* *Gasterophilus
hemorrhoidalis*

ceed from there directly toward the mouth, and pass between the lips. In
the mouth, the larvae burrow into pockets between the molar teeth and
develop for a period of several weeks, after which they molt to the second
stage, are swallowed, and attach themselves to the lining of the stomach.
Following further development and a final molt, the fully developed third-
stage larvae (Figure 19-13) may be found attached by means of their for-
midable mouth hooks to the glandular portion of the stomach and to the
mucous membrane of the duodenum. Bots spend approximately 9 months
clinging to the insides of a horse waiting for spring and storing the energy
needed for the metamorphosis into adult flies, the mating flight, and finally
588 the laying of eggs. When the time comes, the bots let go, pass out with the

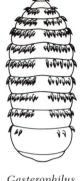

FIGURE 19-13
Third-stage larvae of botfly of
Gasterophilus species. Adapted
from Wells and Knipling. 1938.

| *Gasterophilus* | *Gasterophilus* | *Gasterophilus* |
| nasalis | intestinalis | hemorrhoidalis |

manure, and burrow into the ground to pupate. How the bots know when the right time has arrived is a mystery. During these months they remain in total darkness, immersed in gastric juice with hydrogen ion concentration of approximately 0.1 moles per liter and a temperature of 38°C. Either some signal of spring must get through to them (perhaps the horse eats something that gives them a clue), or they have some sort of intrinsic "fuse" that tells them when it is time to leave. We do know that no adult fly survives killing frost and that each species of *Gasterophilus* is dependent on its parasitic larvae to overwinter and perpetuate its kind. Is it not remarkable that, in spite of the obvious vulnerability of such a life history to annihilation and in spite of a long list of extraordinarily effective antiparasitic drugs, almost every horse is host to at least a few bots every winter?

The *Gasterophilus hemorrhoidalis* female deposits her black eggs on the short hairs that adjoin the lips. After 2–4 days of incubation, these eggs hatch on contact with moisture and penetrate the epidermis of the lips, then burrow in the mucous membrane of the mouth. Thereafter, the life cycle of *G. hemorrhoidalis* is much like that of *G. nasalis*, just described.

The most common botfly, *Gasterophilus intestinalis*, deposits its eggs on the hairs of the forelimbs and shoulders. After an incubation period of 5 days, these eggs are prepared to hatch rapidly in response to the sudden rise in temperature that occurs when the horse brings its warm lips and breath in contact with them. Then the larvae pop out of their egg cases, enter the horse's mouth, and bore into the upper surface of the tongue near its tip. For the next month or so, these bot larvae bore their way toward the root of the tongue, stopping occasionally to make breathing holes and rest. At last they emerge from the back of the tongue, attach for a while to the mucous membrane of the pharynx, and are finally swallowed. Except that they prefer the nonglandular portion of the gastric mucous membrane, these *G. intestinalis* bots behave like *G. nasalis* for the balance of their parasitic careers. The life cycle of *Gasterophilus* species is summarized diagrammatically in Figure 19-14.

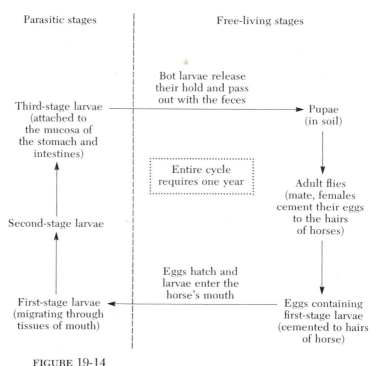

Parasitic stages | Free-living stages

Bot larvae release
their hold and pass
out with the feces

Third-stage larvae
(attached to
the mucosa of
the stomach and
intestines) ⟶ Pupae
(in soil)

Entire cycle
requires one year

Adult flies
(mate, females
cement their eggs
to the hairs
of horses)

Second-stage larvae

First-stage larvae
(migrating through
tissues of mouth) ⟵ Eggs hatch and
larvae enter the
horse's mouth ⟵ Eggs containing
first-stage larvae
(cemented to hairs
of horse)

FIGURE 19-14
Life cycle of *Gasterophilus* species. From Georgi. 1974.

19.4 Development of Worm Infections in Foals

Ann F. Russell, a research fellow of the Ministry of Agriculture and Fisheries, Weybridge, England, has written a remarkable account of the development of strongyle and other helminth infections in Thoroughbred foals reared "under the ordinary conditions of stud management." Her report, brilliant enough in its own right, is invaluable to us now for the unique picture it presents of the natural sequence of changes in the composition of parasite species that invade the foal during its first year of life. Today, the almost universal application of periodic or continuous anthelmintic medication on stud farms precludes duplication of her work.

Figure 19-15 shows the 5 kinds of worm eggs existing in the manure of horses that can be distinguished on the basis of their microscopic structure. Unfortunately, there are approximately 54 species of worms that lay indistinguishable "strongyle" eggs. Some of these (the "big three," for example) are extremely destructive; others, the smaller representatives of the Cyathostominae, are relatively harmless, but they all lay "strongyle" eggs. The only way of determining which species of strongyles are infecting a living horse is to incubate the manure for 7–12 days in order to allow

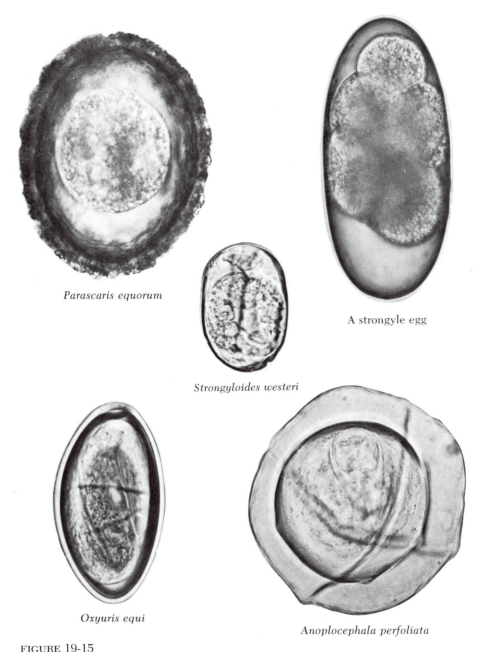

Parascaris equorum

Strongyloides westeri

A strongyle egg

Oxyuris equi

Anoplocephala perfoliata

FIGURE 19-15
Eggs of worm parasites of the horse. *Parascaris equorum* eggs have a sticky
surface layer that causes them to adhere to stall walls, mangers, and the like.
These eggs are extremely difficult to destroy. Strongyle eggs present a problem.
There are approximately 54 species of strongyle worms. They vary greatly in
pathogenicity, but their eggs cannot be told apart. *Strongyloides westeri* eggs
contain a larva when deposited in the manure. *Oxyuris equi* eggs are not usually
found in the manure; they adhere to the skin of the anus. *Anoplocephala
perfoliata* is a tapeworm; all of the others shown in this figure are nematodes.

591

the eggs to hatch and develop to the third or infective stage. An expert can identify these third-stage larvae, and this is how Russell determined the sequential changes in the composition of worm populations in 26 foals from 7 different studs. She made observations on foals every week from the age of 4 weeks to at least 6 months of age and in a few cases to more than one year of age.

In Figure 19-16, the number of eggs per gram of manure is plotted against time for *Strongyloides westeri*, for *Parascaris equorum*, and for the "strongyles" collectively. Note that the *Strongyloides westeri* infection was at a maximum during the early weeks of life, rapidly dropped to a low level, and finally disappeared at approximately 5 months of age. Infection with *Strongyloides* occurs soon after birth by ingestion of larvae shed in the dam's milk and progresses until the foal develops sufficient immunity to reject these parasites.

Parascaris equorum behaved similarly except that evidence of infection did not appear until the twelfth week, and the infection persisted indefinitely at a low level after the main peak had been reached. The 12-week delay in the appearance of *P. equorum* eggs in the feces corresponds exactly to the period during which this parasite is migrating through the liver and lungs, and we may deduce from this that significant infection of the foals

FIGURE 19-16

Average number of eggs of *Parascaris equorum*, "strongyles," and *Strongyloides westeri* counted per gram of manure. Data obtained from weekly observations of 26 foals. Adapted from Russell. 1948. p. 112.

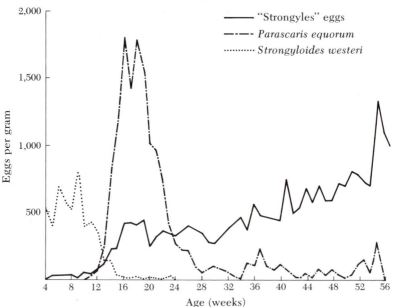

was acquired immediately after birth. Anthelmintic medication of the pregnant mare with piperazine compounds, careful bathing of her udder and teats, and thorough cleaning of her stall at foaling time are thus logical measures for the prevention of significant infection of foals with *Parascaris equorum*. The persistence of infection at a low level after the peak has passed and the extreme resistance of the infective egg to the rigors of the external environment make *Parascaris equorum* a difficult parasite to control.

The third and most important curve shown in Figure 19-16 represents a gradual increase in the number of strongyle eggs per gram of manure during the first year of life. In order to make sense out of this curve, we must be aware of the species of strongyles being considered. This was determined by culture of these eggs and identification of the resulting larvae. The findings are summarized in Figure 19-17. It is immediately obvious from Figure 19-17 that the eggs of small strongyles (Cyathostominae) always predominate in the feces of foals that are less than one year of age. This is what might be expected in view of the 6–11 month period required for development of the "big three" to the egg-laying stage. It is interest-

FIGURE 19-17
Percentage of larvae of different species of strongyles in fecal cultures. Data obtained from monthly observations of 26 foals. Adapted from Russell. 1948. p. 112.

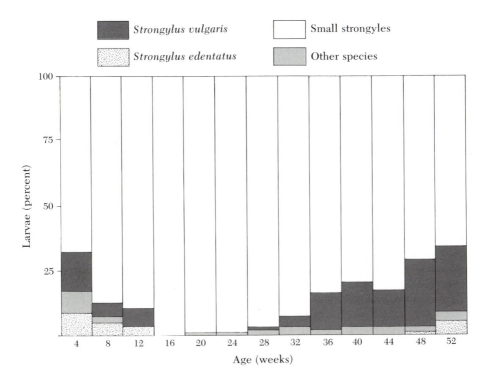

ing, therefore, that small numbers of strongyle eggs are already being shed at 4–12 weeks of age and that some of these are eggs of *Strongylus vulgaris* and *S. edentatus*. Russell observed this phenomenon in every one of her 26 foals and interpreted it as a confirmation of Wetzel's (1942) suggestion that the appearance of strongyle eggs in the manure of foals less than 6 weeks old results from a foal's proclivity for nibbling at its dam's manure (coprophagia). Russell even calculated the amount of manure ingested by a particular foal: "For example, the egg count of foal 11 at five weeks was 100 e.p.g., while that of its dam for the same week was 1,200 e.p.g. If the foal was passing per day 2 lb. of feces with a total of approximately 98,800 eggs it must have eaten about 2½ oz. of the dam's feces in order to produce the count of 100 e.p.g." This ingestion of feces (coprophagia) by foals may be related to the normal "seeding" of the cecum and great colon with the proper species of microorganisms essential for digestion of forage, but it is also a clear opportunity for parasites to invade virgin territory. Only eggs that are undeveloped when ingested will pass through the foal's digestive tract undamaged; infective eggs and larvae from similar sources will have found their goal in life — a susceptible host.

As Figures 19-16 and 19-17 show, strongyle eggs are passed in ever increasing numbers, and *Strongylus vulgaris* and *S. edentatus* make their appearances on schedule at 6 and 11 months, respectively. This information clearly indicates that worm infection of foals starts at birth and proceeds without interruption. Because young foals are much more susceptible to the pathogenic effects of these parasites than older horses, it follows that the greatest efforts should be directed toward preventing excessive exposure, especially during the first months of life.

19.5   Other Parasites

Pinworms

The horse is host to two species of pinworm, so called because their tails are slender and terminate in a point. The small pinworm, *Probstmayria vivipara*, measures less than 3 mm in length. Although it is capable of completing all stages of its life cycle within the confines of its host's large intestine and thus developing enormous infections, this pinworm is apparently quite harmless. The large white pinworm, *Oxyuris equi*, is 50 times as large as *P. vivipara* but of only slightly greater importance to the health of the horse. It has been reported that severe infections of third- and fourth-stage larvae may produce significant inflammation of the cecum and colon manifested by vague signs of abdominal discomfort. However, the most common complaint attributable to *Oxyuris* is *pruritus ani*, or itching of the anus caused by the adhesive egg masses that are deposited on the skin

of the anus and surrounding area by the female worm. In its efforts to relieve the itching the horse will habitually rub its tail against posts, mangers,
and the like until the tail head becomes disheveled, bare of hair, and even
scarified or lacerated. Disfigurement and discomfort are thus the principal
undesirable effects of *Oxyuris* infection.

Adult male and female *Oxyuris equi* live in the large intestine. When
ready to deposit eggs, the female does not simply discharge them into the
intestinal contents of the host in the same manner as do the strongyles,
ascardis, and other intestinal nematodes. Instead, the gravid female *Oxyuris*
migrates down the intestine and out through the anal opening to cement
her egg masses to the skin of the anus and its immediate surroundings.
These egg masses consist of a tenacious, yellowish-gray fluid containing
8,000–60,000 eggs. The eggs develop to the infective stage in the course
of 4 or 5 days, during which the cementing fluid dries, cracks, and detaches
from the skin in flakes containing large numbers of infective eggs. These
flakes are still sticky enough to adhere to mangers, pails, walls, and the
like, thus contaminating the environment of the horse and increasing the
likelihood of reinfection or the spread of infection to other horses (see
Figure 19-18). It should be obvious from these considerations that the same
cloth or sponge should never be applied to the area under a horse's tail

FIGURE 19-18
Life cycle of *Oxyuris equi*, the large pinworm of the horse. From Georgi. 1974.

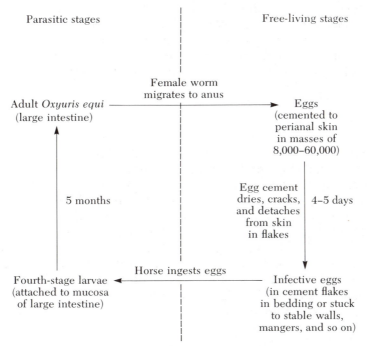

Parasitic stages | Free-living stages

Female worm
migrates to anus

Adult *Oxyuris equi* ⟶ Eggs
(large intestine) (cemented to
perianal skin
in masses of
8,000–60,000)

Egg cement
5 months dries, cracks, 4–5 days
and detaches
from skin
in flakes

Horse ingests eggs

Fourth-stage larvae ⟵ Infective eggs
(attached to mucosa (in cement flakes
of large intestine) in bedding or stuck
to stable walls,
mangers, and so on)

595

and then to the muzzle and nostrils. Any effort to eliminate or control pinworms should certainly include regular cleansing of the anal area with warm water and mild soap to remove the egg masses before they have an opportunity to develop and scale off. However, paper towels or disposable cloths are to be preferred for this purpose because any nonexpendable object, such as a sponge or terrycloth, will inevitably become heavily contaminated with eggs and thus become a source of infection.

Another cause of *pruritus ani* to be differentiated from that caused by pinworms is infestation with the tail mange mite *Chorioptes equi* or the biting louse *Damalinia equi* (see the following sections on lice and mites).

Neither pinworm of the horse has anything to do with pinworm infection in children. The human pinworm, *Enterobius vermicularis*, is a distinct species that does not occur in any domestic animal, including the dog, although many people are misinformed on this point.

Tapeworms

Horses are hosts to three species of tapeworm: *Anoplocephala magna*, *A. perfoliata*, and *Paranoplocephala mamillana*. Infection is acquired at pasture where the horse accidentally ingests free-living mites that are infected with tapeworm larvae. Ordinarily, tapeworm infections have no measurable deleterious effects on horses and tapeworms are infrequently considered in the planning of worming programs. Exceptionally, however, severe infections of *A. perfoliata*, which have a remarkable tendency to group together in clusters near the ileo-cecal junction, may cause chronic diarrhea, and have sometimes been accused of precipitating intersusception, a telescoping of the intestine that has fatal consequences.

Lice

Two species of lice infest the horse, the bloodsucking louse, *Haematopinus asini* (Figure 19-19), and the biting louse, *Damalinia equi* (Figure 19-20). These lice spend their entire life from egg to adult clinging to the hairs of a horse. Without a hair to grasp a louse is relatively helpless. It passes from host to host most efficiently when the hosts' haircoats are in direct contact with one another. The practical consequence of this is that louse infestation is usually transmitted by direct contact between horses, although the blanket of a lousy horse could conceivably transmit the infestation if it were placed on another horse within a matter of hours. Lice of other domestic animals, such as chickens and cattle, do not remain long on a horse, nor is there any hazard of an exchange of lice between humans and horses in either direction.

596

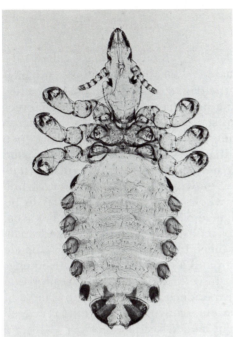

FIGURE 19-19
The bloodsucking louse, *Haematopinus asini*. From Georgi. 1974.

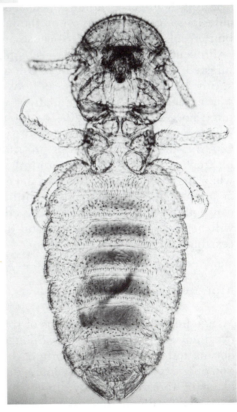

FIGURE 19-20
The biting louse, *Damalinia equi*.
From Georgi. 1974.

The life cycle of a louse is simple. The rather large eggs, called *nits*, develop in the abdomen of the female. When the female lays an egg, a sticky secretion is passed that glues the egg to the shaft of a hair. In a few days a tiny nymph, closely resembling its parents in appearance, emerges through a lid or *operculum* at the distal end of the egg. As the nymph grows in size, its rigid skin becomes too small. The louse inside then becomes quiescent (undergoes a lethargus), reorganizes its tissues, and develops a new, more pliable skin. When ready, the nymph splits open its old skin and emerges, now capable of growing and expanding for a while until its new skin hardens and the whole process of molting has to be repeated. Because no remarkable change occurs from one nymphal stage or *instar* to the next, the sequence of molts culminating in an adult male or female louse is termed gradual or incomplete metamorphosis. A female louse lives for approximately a month and a half and may lay 20–30 eggs at intervals of 1½ days. This contrasts with the extraordinary alteration in form (complete metamorphosis) experienced by the pupating larva of *Gasterophilus* that culminates in the emergence of a winged, six-legged fly from the barrel-shaped puparium or tanned last larval skin.

Biting lice cause rather severe itching that may result in self-inflicted abrasions and lacerations when the horse attempts to scratch itself. Heavy burdens of bloodsucking lice cause anemia.

Prevention of lousiness is accomplished by avoidance of contact with infested horses. Sunshine and fresh air are inimical to lice, and therefore severe louse infestation is rarely observed in pastured horses during the warmer months. Louse populations sometimes increase rapidly on pastured horses late in the fall. Treatment is available in the form of various powders and sprays containing organophosphorus compounds (Vapona, Ciodrin, and so on). Powders are satisfactory if only a few horses are to be treated and are to be preferred for use during cold winter weather when the thorough saturation of the coat required for effective application of sprays would surely result in chilling of the horse, perhaps with serious consequences. If the horse can be clipped, much of the louse population will be removed with the hair and the lice that remain will be more accessible to treatment.

Mange Mites

Mange mites are distant cousins of spiders. Barely visible to a person with excellent eyesight, these tiny 8-legged nuisances live on or in the epidermis and cause mange, a form of dermatitis characterized by the formation of crusts or scabs, and by intense itching. As is true of louse infestation, mange is spread mainly by direct contact with infested individuals. Diagnosis and treatment are tasks for the veterinarian.

Habronemiasis

Habronema species are of little consequence as nematode parasites of the stomach. One species, *Habronema megastoma* (often called *Draschia megastoma*), stimulates the formation by the host of fibrous nodules that project from the wall into the lumen of the stomach. These nodules are riddled with intercommunicating galleries filled with pus and with the rather small (approximately 1 cm) worms. Although impressive when described, these nodules and their occupants usually do not affect the health of the horse in any observable way. Larvae of *Habronema* species, on the other hand, are incriminated in the production of persistent, disfiguring, and intensely itching skin lesions called swamp cancer, summer sores, and a variety of other colloquial names. Houseflies and stableflies serve as intermediate hosts for *Habronema* species. When these infected insects visit fresh wounds or areas of skin that are subjected to somewhat continuous moisture, *Habronema* larvae enter the tissues and cause an inflammatory reaction characterized by severe itching and the production of "proud flesh," or "exuberant" granulation tissue, as it is sometimes called. When infected flies feed in the corner of a horse's eyes, *Habronema* larvae may enter the conjunctival membranes and engender a chronic conjunctivitis.

Cutaneous and conjunctival habronemiasis are chronic, persistent and very difficult to cure, especially during summer and early fall. Professional veterinary treatment for the patient and extreme patience on the part of the owner are essential.

19.6 Anthelmintic Medication

An important point with regard to worming is frequently overlooked or simply misunderstood: worm remedies as routinely administered are effective only against the adult parasites living in the lumen or attached to the mucous membrane lining the intestinal tract. This means that the main damage inflicted by strongyles and ascarids to the horse has already been done, and instead of treating a disease we are, in a sense, merely exacting retribution. What benefit, then, can the drug bestow beyond relieving the horse of the comparatively less serious physiological burden imposed by the lumen-dwelling adult parasites? The anthelmintic drug helps to reduce the contamination of the environment with eggs by reducing the numbers of adult parasites (not even the best anthelmintics remove them all) and by depressing the reproductive functions of the worms that happen to survive. Thus, the principal objective of worming horses is

599

really to prevent environmental contamination and thereby reduce the degree of reinfection and the transmission of infection to young, highly susceptible horses. In the cavalry and on rich estates of old, this contamination was dealt with by an unremitting sweeping and raking of horse droppings into bushel baskets by squads of troopers or grooms. The bottle of anthelmintic drug thus represents a relatively inexpensive substitute for a laborer with broom and bushel basket. With the true objective of anthelmintic medication thus defined, two strategies for the control of parasites suggest themselves.

Routine Worming of All Horses

Either sustained administration of low levels of medication (for example, phenothiazine mixed with the grain ration at the rate of 2.0 g per day, 21 days per month every month) or the administration of full therapeutic doses at specified intervals usually suppress strongyle egg production sufficiently to achieve satisfactory control. Current practice favors periodic administration of full doses. Empirical observation indicates that strongyle eggs tend to reappear in a horse's feces approximately 6–8 weeks after administration of an effective anthelmintic drug. The adult worms that survived the attack have regained their reproductive powers, and larvae that were migrating through the tissues at the time, thus protected from the effects of the drug, have arrived in the lumen of the bowel and are now starting to lay eggs. Therefore, if a full dose of an effective anthelmintic drug is administered at 2-month intervals (6 times a year) to *all* horses on a premises, the rate of contamination of the environment will be greatly reduced and serious infection of susceptible foals will, it is hoped, be forestalled. The advantage of this strategy is that laboratory examination of fecal specimens is not required to determine the extent of infection. The disadvantages of this strategy are that (1) *all* horses on the premises must be treated no less than 6 times a year, thus multiplying the expense and hazard of toxic reaction inherent in anthelmintic medication, and that (2) persistent application of antiparasitic chemicals inevitably leads to the selection of strains of parasites possessing resistance to those chemicals and thus ultimately ceases to be effective.

Quantitative Fecal Examination and Individual Treatment

Recognizing that the objective of any worming program is to reduce the contamination of the environment with eggs, a reasonable strategy would be to determine what the output of eggs from each horse actually is and to administer an anthelmintic drug only to those individuals with more than some specified number of eggs per gram of feces. The number of eggs tol-

600

erated depends on the stocking rate. For example, 500 eggs per gram would perhaps be acceptable when a few horses occupy a relatively large pasture, but the limit should be lowered to 100 eggs per gram when many horses are confined to a small paddock because of the consequent concentration and accumulation of manure. The limit, in fact, need not be an arbitrary constant but might be adjusted periodically in response to trends observed in the egg count data. The advantage of this plan is that it minimizes the expense and hazards of treatment; the disadvantage is that it requires expert analysis of the feces of all horses on the premises as well as maintenance of accurate records and interpretation of trends in the data. The choice of strategies depends on the relative costs of anthelmintic medication on the one hand and of expert fecal analysis on the other.

A practical qualitative test for the presence of strongyle eggs in horse manure consists of the following. Put a ball of manure in a quart jar, set the lid loosely on top, and place the jar in a dark place at room temperature for approximately one week. Each day examine the inner walls of the jar for the presence of droplets of condensed moisture (evidence that a suitable degree of humidity exists in the culture). If the walls of the jar are dry, add 10–20 drops of water directly to the mass of manure, cover the jar, and return it to the dark. At the end of the week, examine the walls of the jar with a hand lens in bright daylight. Unless the horse that provided the culture medium had very few strongyles, infective larvae will be easily visible as they writhe and thrash about in the droplets of condensed moisture. Cultures from heavily infected horses contain so many larvae that the walls of the jar will appear to be frosted. A subjective impression of the degree of infection can thus be gained by comparing cultures from a number of different horses. If a compound microscope is available, transfer some larvae to a microslide with an eyedropper and kill them by gentle warming. Hold a lighted match below the slide, view the cessation of motion and extension of the larvae from above, and remove the match as soon as motion ceases; otherwise, the larvae will be cooked. Now add a coverslip and examine the specimen with the lower powers of the microscope. With experience, a stable manager can use this simple culture procedure, requiring only quart jars, eyedroppers, a hand lens, and water, as a practical means of monitoring strongyle infection in horses.

Some Thoughts about Management. In 1965, Karl Enigk, of the Tierärztliche Hochschule in Hanover, asserted without qualification that the practice of keeping horses in box stalls rather than tie stalls is to blame for the high degree of worm infection observed in riding horses. For this reason, claimed Enigk, those kinds of worm infection that are almost exclusively acquired in the stable (for example, ascarids, pinworms, and *Strongyloides*) are particularly common. He pointed out that strongyles (especially the pathogenic large strongyles) are the most important parasites of the horse, ascribed their great prevalence to a combination of box stall stabling and

601

exposure at pasture, and prescribed tie stalls, zero grazing, and exclusive feeding of hay for control of these parasites. Strongyle larvae do not survive for longer than 8 months in well-cured hay, and the halter and shank assure that all manure will be deposited several feet from the manger and water bucket. Because the pasture, especially on stud farms, is the greatest source of strongyle infection, zero grazing is a logical measure in strongyle control. These measures advocated by Enigk might appear extreme to the modern pleasure horse owner, but they correspond exactly to the routine husbandry practices employed for draft and cavalry animals a few decades ago. In the days before phenothiazine, there was no really effective drug for removing strongyles; yet civilization depended on horsepower for transportation and agriculture, and great horses performed great feats. Then, any system of horse husbandry that did not, either intentionally or unintentionally, keep strongyles in check could not compete with those that did in producing healthy, useful horses. The same is true today except that in general, anthelmintic chemicals are substituted for rigorous sanitation and for husbandry devices (such as tie stalls) that, by their nature, interfere with the strongyle life cycle.

In arid regions, scattering of droppings on pasture with a tractor and harrow every few days should theoretically reduce strongyle larva populations by breaking up the manure and causing it to dry out before the larvae have achieved the dessication-resistant third stage. However, in the more humid regions that prevail over much of North America, the interior even of scattered manure will remain sufficiently moist long enough for completion of this development. The infective larvae will be capable of withstanding dessication for several weeks if they are large strongyles and for up to 8 months if they are small strongyles. It follows from this that hay harvested from meadows in which horses have been allowed to graze or meadows that have recently been fertilized with horse manure should be aged for at least 8 months before being fed to horses. Alternate grazing of pastures by horses and either cattle or sheep is also of theoretical value in parasite control because, except for *Trichostrongylus axei*, horses and ruminants share no parasites. Therefore, grazing cattle remove larvae from the pasture that are infective for the horse (and vice versa) while time and environmental stresses wear away at the larvae that remain. Of course, advantage can be taken of this principle only when both horses and ruminants are kept, when the terrain and fence construction are suitable for both, and when the pasture actually recovers sufficiently after the first grazing to be of further use that season. (There are many pastures that do not.)

As J. H. Drudge and E. T. Lyons (1966) of the Department of Veterinary Science of the University of Kentucky have pointed out, "An effective parasite control program must be regarded as a long-term undertaking before desired results are achieved and maintained." The extreme hardiness of infective ascarid eggs and the prolonged tissue migrations of the "big three" strongyles introduce an element of inertia that can be overcome by perseverance in the use of effective measures. The beneficial effect of a dose of thiabendazole on a wormy colt is certainly prompt and dramatic, but it is just as certainly temporary.

A knowledge of the life cycles of parasites and of the nature and habits of their infective stages provides a sound basis for parasite control. Anti-parasitic chemicals form an integral part of any practicable program, but their application to the exclusion of appropriate measures of sanitation and management leads to the emergence of resistant parasites and to ultimate failure. As a general rule, a parasite control program, to be effective, must be tailor-made to the farm or stable in question—that is, properly suited to its objectives, landscape, physical resources, horses, and the people managing it.

References

Bollinger, O. 1870. *Sitzungsb. k.-Bayer. Akad. Wissensch. München* 1:539.

Craig, E. F., and E. C. Faust. 1945. *Clinical Parasitology.* Philadelphia: Lea & Febiger.

Dobberstein, J., and H. Hartmann. 1932. *Über die Anastomosenbildung* im Bereich der Blind- und Grimmdarmarterien des Pferdes und ihre Bedeutung für die Entstehung der embolischen Kolik. *Berliner tierärztliche Wochenschrift* 48:399.

Drudge, J. H., and E. T. Lyons, 1966. Control of internal parasites of the horse. *J. Am. Vet. Med. Assoc.* 148 (4):378–383.

Enigk, K. 1950. Zur Entwicklung von *Strongylus vulgaris* [Nematodes] im *Wirtstier. Z. Tropenmed. Parasitol.* 2 (2):287–306.

Enigk, K. 1951. Weitere Untersuchungen zur Biologie von *Strongylus vulgaris* (Nematodes) im *Wirtstier. Z. Tropenmed. Parasitol.* 2:523–535.

Enigk, K. 1965. Behandlung und Vorbeuge des Parasitenbefalles der Pferde. *Deutsch. tierarztl. Wochenschrift* 72:493.

Georgi, J. R. 1973. The Kikuchi-Enigk model of *Strongylus vulgaris* migrations in the horse. *Cornell Vet.* 63 (2):220–263. [English translation of Enigk's articles listed above].

Georgi, J. R. 1974. *Parasitology for Veterinarians.* 2d ed. Philadelphia: W. B. Saunders.

603

Lyons, E. T., J. H. Drudge, and S. C. Tolliver. 1973. On the life cycle of *Strongyloides westeri* in the equine. *Jour. of Parasit.* 59 (October): 780–787.

Russell, Ann F. 1948. The development of helminthiasis in Thoroughbred foals. *J. Comp. Path.* 58:107–127.

Wells, R. W., and E. F. Knipling. 1938. A report of some recent studies of *Gasterophilus* occurring in horses in the United States. *Iowa State College Journal of Science* 12:201.

Wetzel, R. 1940. Zur Entwicklung des grossen Palisadenwormes (*Strongylus equinus*) im Pferd. *Arch. wissensch. u. prakt. Tierh.* 76:81.

Wetzel, R., and W. Kersten. 1956. Die Leberphase der Entwicklung von *Strongylus edentatus. Wien. tierärztl. Monatsschrift.* 11:664.

PART SEVEN *Management of the Horse*

CHAPTER TWENTY *Behavioral Principles of Training and Management*

At least two people always point to a champion performance horse with pride. One is the breeder, who would suggest that he selectively bred this animal to be a superior performance horse. The other is the trainer, who maintains that his influence was what made the horse a champion. Both are partially correct. Behavior in a performing horse is the result of both hereditary and environmental influences. Nature *vs.* nurture is an old controversy that has been studied with regard to several species by proponents of both views, and effects of both genetics and environment have been observed to affect performance.

20.1   Heritability of Performance

Psychologists have been more concerned with environmental effects on behavior than with genetics because of the human application, which lends itself more to environmental manipulation than to genetic control. However, the animal breeder has the opportunity through selective breeding to breed for superior genetic effects on behavior. Therefore, horse breeders are interested in improving performance in their horses through selection for desirable behavioral characteristics. The problem lies in the ability to separate genetic from environmental effects in the performance of a given horse. This leads to difficulty in recognizing animals with superior genotypes for a given type of performance. If a real difference in learning ability in horses does exist, one of the prime goals of horse breeding should be selection for this learning ability. This is because horses are unique among domestic livestock in that the value of horses can be greatly increased with training. Obviously, learning ability is one of the most significant factors in the final performance achieved by any horse.

There is considerable evidence that performance behavior is heritable in several species. Some of the classic experiments demonstrated a difference in the maze-running ability of selected strains of rats. Strains of "bright" and "dull" rats have been developed experimentally, which strongly suggests that behavior has a heritable component. Other types of behavior that have been shown to be partially controlled by genetic influence include (1) level of activity of rats in a rotating cage, (2) emotionality in rats, (3) maze-running ability in mice, (4) sex drive in guinea pigs, (5) nest-building instinct in rabbits, (6) aggression in rabbits, (7) behavior during conditioning in dogs, and (8) avoidance learning in pigs. There have even been reports of hybrid vigor for some of these behavioral characteristics.

Even though little research information is available on the heritability of performance in horses, data obtained with other species strongly suggest that performance in horses is likely to be heritable to some degree. Heritability of racing ability in Thoroughbreds is quite high, but in racehorses, psychological training is not as important as physical training, physiology, conformation, and so on. On the other hand, heritability of performance in cutting horses has been reported to be quite low. This is to be expected since environmental input (ability of the trainer) may vary widely and subsequent performance is likely to be reflective of the trainer and not heredity. Superior trainers can make horses with average ability reach a high level of performance. Other trainers have difficulty getting any horse to reach its potential. All cutting horse trainers believe that there is a heritable component in cutting horses. For example, trainers of cutting horses like to ride sons and daughters of the Quarter Horse stallion Doc Bar because these sons and daughters have done well in the cutting arena.

Every time a mare is bred to a stallion with superior performance records, it is assumed that the foal will inherit some of the characteristics of the stallion. The notion is accepted that part of the stallion's performance is due to inheritance and that this can be transmitted to the foal. Unfortunately, it is difficult at best to separate that portion of the stallion's performance and behavior which is due to genetics from that which is due to the trainer. Most of the criteria available to horsemen to measure performance is biased because the effects of the environment or trainer cannot be held constant between horses. A stallion whose offspring are trained by the best trainers will show an advantage over another stallion whose offspring have average trainers. Choice of trainer is often determined by the financial or other position of the stallion owner. If a given stallion's offspring appear to be superior performance horses, there is always a clamor among trainers to get one of these horses. This only biases further the use

FIGURE 20-1

Colonel Alois Podhajsky of the Vienna Spanish Riding School mounted on one of the school's Lippizaner stallions. The Lippizaners are among the most highly trained horses in the world, but their amenability to training has been influenced to some extent by breeding. Photograph courtesy of The Bettmann Archive.

of performance records as selection criteria because the best trainers usually have the best performing horses.

There is a real need for methods of measuring learning ability in horses that are unbiased, objective, inexpensive, easy to use, and useable at an early age. Until such techniques are available, the breeder must make the best possible use of existing performance information when selecting for learning ability in horses. The breeder must try hard to ascertain the relative contribution of genetics and environment to each horse's performance. Limited research with horses and many studies of other species indicate that there is considerable genetic variance in behavioral characteristics of horses and that the potential for improving learning ability in horses through selection may be substantial.

609

20.2 *Early Experiences*

An animal's ability to learn, to solve problems, or to survive the effects of severe stress has been shown to be greatly influenced by the environment in which that animal was raised. Since these effects precede training, they affect trainability in much the same manner as does heredity.

The effects of early experience have been shown to influence behavior in many animals. Early stimulation may occur before birth, after birth, before weaning, and after weaning. Continuous stimulation, such as radical changes in environment (enriched, deprived, or isolated), and discontinuous stimulation, such as varying periods of daily handling, have both been found to affect behavior. Rats that were raised in an environment where discrete circles and triangles were painted on the walls were superior to rats that were exposed to no designs when both groups were later tested on circle-triangle discrimination tests. Similar tests with diffuse stimuli have shown that such stimuli increase emotionality. Emotionality is also affected by early handling. Rats that were handled daily were less emotional when subjected to stress than a control group of rats that received no handling. Chimps that were raised in darkness and thus suffered perceptual deprivation had problems later in perceiving stimulus movement, form, and direction.

In the period from before weaning through part of the yearling year, the horseman has ample opportunity to influence a horse's learning ability by varying its environment (Figure 20-2). However, the early experience of the horse has not been studied to any extent. Such variables as critical time to stimulate, most effective method of stimulation, and how to manipulate this stimulation effectively to affect the adult performance have not been analyzed. There has been a general observation that the horses of today are more docile, more trainable, and more tractable than were horses

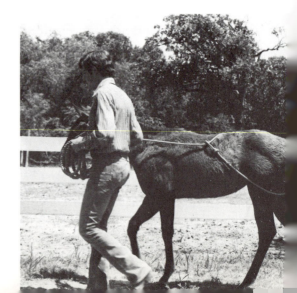

FIGURE 20-2
Desirable early experiences
enhance learning and trainability
in later stages of development.

30 years ago. Some of this change may be due to heredity, but it can easily be attributed to increased handling of horses at earlier ages. Horses that have been trained only as adults are wilder and much less dependable than those with which human contacts have been established early in life. Docility enhances learning in that the horse is less easily distracted. A social relationship between horse and handler can be established much more easily at an early age. Most authorities on the breaking and training of horses recommend that the handling and preparation for riding begin as early as possible. Halter breaking can start before weaning, followed by longeing, saddling, driving, and other activities limited only by the horse's physical capabilities.

20.3   Environmental Influences: Training

There is an abundance of research information on the effects of the environment on laboratory animals that is directly applicable to horse training. Horse training deals with the modification of behavior, and almost all of the principles of learning that apply to other species also apply to horses. When training begins, the horse has a certain operant level of performance. The trainer must determine this level and then progressively modify the behavior in such a manner as to achieve a desired level of performance. At this point the genetic potential of the horse has already been determined, and the hope is that the horse will be capable of reaching the desired level of performance. What the trainer has to manipulate is the environment. He divides this environment into stimuli and reinforcement and then uses them to obtain the response he desires. Stimuli, responses, and reinforcement and their relationships to each other are the basis of the psychology of horse training. The aspiring trainer must develop a clear understanding of each.

Responses

The term "response" is used to refer to specific types of behavior. Responses are the acts or movements of the horse, and the goal of training is to teach the horse to make the desired response. On occasion, the term "response" is used to refer to major maneuvers such as stopping or jumping. However, for the most part, responses should be thought of as smaller segments of these major maneuvers, which are composed of many responses chained together. The trainer must learn to identify the smaller units of the maneuvers (Figure 20-3). For example, the initial reaction of a horse to bit pressure is a response that, properly reinforced, will eventually be part of a stop, which is a major maneuver (Figure 20-4).

611

FIGURE 20-3
Learning to cross the front legs is
the first step in the process of
learning to do the spin or roll-back.

Stimuli

Stimuli can be divided into conditioned and unconditioned categories,
depending upon their natural effect on the horse. If a stimulus can naturally
cause a response with no prior practice, it is said to be unconditioned. Few
of these stimuli are used in horse training. A stimulus that has been learned
through practice is called a conditioned stimulus. These stimuli are frequently used in horse training and are known to horsemen as cues (Figure 20-5). Remember, most *cues are learned;* very few natural stimuli will
cause the response sought in the trained horse.

FIGURE 20-4
Learning to flex at the poll when
pressure is applied on the bit
is a first step in learning to stop
or back correctly.

FIGURE 20-5
Taking a lead as the result of a leg cue must be learned by the horse. Any cue can be used if the trainer is specific and consistent in teaching the cue to the horse.

Basic Cues. Since few of the cues used in training are natural and for the most part must be learned, where does the trainer start? He starts with those basic cues that are closest to being natural. These are cues that practically show the horse what to do. They are very obvious and readily learned. For example, direct rein pressure response is obvious because the horse is shown the direction in which it is supposed to go, and it can learn this quickly. If these obvious cues were all that the horse ever acquired, it would not be considered a very highly trained horse.

Presenting New Cues. The trainer will use these basic cues to advance the horse to new cues. This advancement is accomplished by pairing the new cue with the basic one in the daily training routine. The rate at which the horse learns is affected by the manner in which these two cues are paired.

The new cue should always be presented first, followed by the old cue, which the horse already knows. For best results, there should be only a very slight time lapse between the two cues, but they must not be presented exactly at the same time. The old cue should be paired closely enough with the new one that the two slightly overlap. In teaching a horse the neck rein, the basic cue of the direct rein is introduced first. Once the horse has learned to respond to this cue, the bearing rein is introduced. The bearing rein means nothing to the horse in the beginning, but if the trainer follows its presentation with the direct rein, the horse soon learns to make the desired response to the bearing rein. Assuming that from early training the

613

horse knows that the cue "whoa" means stop, the command "whoa" can enhance learning to stop in response to bit pressure — pull on the bit (new cue) and, while pressure is still intact, say "whoa" (old cue). The horse should learn to stop from the bit pressure faster and more efficiently if this method is used. The trainer continually uses this method to teach the horse less obvious cues, but the method is successful only if the horse has learned the old cue well. The old cue must reliably cause the response before it can be used to encourage the horse to acquire a new cue. In the preceding example, if the bit is getting the correct response, then leg pressures may be introduced to teach stopping from leg cues.

Teaching a horse to make a response to a combination of cues using different sensory modalities is also a common practice. This method has the advantage of presenting a stronger total stimulus to the horse and helps to ensure that the horse gets the message.

Specificity of Cues. The horse can receive stimuli through its sensory systems in many ways, but man's most effective method of communication with the horse seems to be through the horse's senses of touch and hearing. Voice commands and pressures are common stimuli (cues) used in horse training. Pressures are used on the horse's nose by the hackamore, in the mouth by the bit, on the neck by the reins, and on various parts of the body by the rider's feet and legs. Unpublished results of a recent study at Texas A & M University indicated that a horse makes greater use of hearing than touch or sight. Therefore, the use of voice commands should be utilized whenever possible.

Indiscriminate presentation of cues only confuses the horse. Cues must be specific so that the horse can identify them and separate them from other things that are happening to it at the same time that the cues are presented. It takes ability and skill to deliver specific identifiable cues to the horse. This helps to explain why some horsemen are better trainers than others. Good horsemanship is a must. A rider cannot use poor, inconsistent technique with a horse and yet apply discriminate and specific cues that the horse is expected to identify.

It is important to remember that horses must be taught to respond to cues. The trainer should start with the most basic cues, present new cues to be learned just before the old cues are learned, and be very specific in presenting a cue. A trainer can use any cue he wants for a given response if he is specific and consistent in presenting that cue. The horse learns and responds from truth, not confusion.

Reinforcement

614 The principle of reinforcement means that certain events are capable of strengthening responses to certain stimuli. It is doubtful that any learning

can be accomplished without reinforcement. Reinforcement can be divided into the broad categories of primary and secondary reinforcement. Primary reinforcers have natural reinforcing properties. Feed is a primary reinforcer in that the horse naturally appreciates feed, and it can be used to strengthen certain behavior. Only a few primary reinforcers are used directly in training.

Secondary reinforcers are learned by the horse and are acquired over a longer period. General acts of kindness to the horse can acquire secondary reinforcing properties. Learning that the training period will end if the horse performs well is secondary reinforcement for the horse. There are many more examples, but they are all distinguished from primary reinforcements in that they are *learned*. A horse trainer who can condition his horse for secondary reinforcement has another tool with which to work.

Positive Reinforcement. Reinforcers, regardless of whether they are primary or secondary, can be divided further into two general types; positive and negative reinforcers. Positive reinforcement has often been referred to as reward training. The mechanics of using positive reinforcement are not always readily apparent in horse training. What rewards can be bestowed upon the horse during the training process other than a pat on the neck or a spoken word, and how rewarding are they? Any rewarding effects that these positive reinforcements have are of an acquired or learned nature (Figure 20-6). An untrained horse does not appreciate them until they are associated with primary reinforcers such as food and water. Therefore, it is hard for trainers to implement positive reinforcement that is contingent upon desired responses.

Many experienced horsemen report having obtained results from reward training. It is nearly always secondary or acquired reinforcement and some-

FIGURE 20-6
A horse must learn to appreciate secondary positive reinforcement. It is not effective unless the horse learns to appreciate it.

615

times is so vague that it is difficult to describe. The presence of the trainer or the sight of a working ring or a riding trail may acquire reinforcing properties to the horse. Positive reinforcement can be a valuable asset for the horseman if it can be implemented. There is too much evidence of successful results obtained from reward training in other species for the horse trainer to ignore its use.

Negative Reinforcement. These are aversive stimuli that the horse will work to avoid or get rid of if given a choice. There are at least three different methods of training by using negative reinforcement or aversive stimuli:

1. Punishment. In this type of negative reinforcement, the horse makes a response in the absence of a cue and then is punished immediately upon making the response. The aim of this method is not the acquisition of a new response but rather the weakening or elimination of a response that is already in the horse's repertoire. Traditionally, horsemen use this method to break bad habits or to correct vices. The intensity of punishment is critical. It has been shown that light punishment does not break a habit but merely suppresses it. This is why horsemen do not recommend that horses be pecked gently for correction. If the horse must be corrected, it should be punished sharply and quickly. There is much variation among individual horses concerning punishment. A light tap with a bat may mean practically nothing to one horse and be fairly severe punishment for another. To be most effective, punishment must cause the horse to select a desirable alternate response that leads to reward.

2. Escape. In this type of negative reinforcement, the aversive stimulus is applied with little or no cue and independently of what the horse is doing. The execution of a specific response by the horse is necessary for the termination of the stimulus. When a spur is pushed into a horse's ribs to get it to move, the horse makes an escape response that will result in the spur being removed. When a direct rein is applied to the right, the horse turns to the right to escape the right rein pull.

3. Avoidance. In this method the horse is first given a cue to which to respond. If the response is correct, there is no punishment. If the response is incorrect or latent, then aversive stimuli or negative reinforcement is applied (Figure 20-7). This method constitutes the bulk of the negative reinforcement used in horse training. Sharp and precisely trained horses performing with almost imperceptible cues are actually making avoidance responses. The threat of aversive stimuli is what keeps them alert. A well-trained horse will require very little negative reinforcement because it has learned to make the correct response on cue. For example, the response to neck reining is actually an avoidance response. The horse moves as a result of the bearing rein pressure because the threat of the direct rein is always there. Backing when light bit pressure is applied is also avoidance conditioning because the threat of hard pressure on the mouth is always

FIGURE 20-7
Negative reinforcement applied at the correct time and with the proper intensity is very effective in increasing both the effort that a horse will put into a performance and the speed of the performance.

present. This is an example of a stimulus that is a cue at one intensity and negative reinforcement at an increased intensity. Many stimuli fit this description, and are used by horsemen quite frequently. A horse moves when slight heel pressure is applied because failure to do so in the past has been followed by a hard kick.

Contingent Reinforcement-Alternative Response. For any reinforcement to have maximum effectivness, it must be contingent upon the response; that is, it must be given immediately following the response. Contingency between response and reinforcement is limited in reward training. However, in negative reinforcement there are many more possibilities, as was shown in the previously discussed examples. Contingent punishment enables a horse to know what response is being punished, whereas non-contingent punishment causes the horse to have a general fear, and all its behavior will be abnormal.

The availability of alternative responses is also important when negative reinforcement is used as a training tool. This means that when a horse is punished for making a wrong response, the trainer should make sure that the response desired is available to the horse. If alternative responses are not available, it is difficult to change behavior permanently with any kind of aversive stimuli. When alternative responses are available and the punishment is contingent on the behavior being reinforced, negative reinforcement is more effective than any other type of training in causing one response to be abandoned and another adopted.

The effects of contingent reinforcement and alternative response are very evident in the training of cutting horses. A cutting horse must be trained to move with a cow and to make hard stops and turns on its own with only the cow as its cue. When the cutting horse makes a bad turn, the

617

horse should be corrected immediately. This is usually done with the kick of a spur or a sharp pull on the bit. The more contingent this punishment is on the bad turn, the more quickly the horse learns to make the correct maneuver. However, it should be noted that the alternative response (correct turn) is available. The cutting horse may also exhibit abnormal behavior as a result of overly severe and noncontingent punishment. Punishment of this kind will cause the horse to watch the rider much more than the cow and the horse will thus be more likely to make mistakes. Many cutting horse trainers are relying more on reward training and less on severe punishment. Also, they have learned that any punishment used must be contingent and that alternative responses must always be available.

A good trainer is, by necessity, also a good rider because he must be skillful enough to administer contingent negative reinforcement. Realization of the significance of contingent negative reinforcement, combined with the skill to administer it, is one of the key differences between good trainers and mediocre ones. Many novice horsemen do not realize that punishment must be contingent. For example, a barrel-racing horse will frequently be punished after a run is over because it failed to turn the first barrel correctly. The horse does not know why the punishment is being administered, and certainly at this point it cannot make the alternative response—turning the barrel correctly. Punishment of this kind will only make the horse dread the entire ordeal. The correct way to administer the punishment would be to work the horse several times at home, beginning slowly and gradually increasing the speed, and administer punishment when the horse first makes the wrong move around the barrel. It would be more effective to administer no punishment at all than for the punishment to be noncontingent. A wise trainer will let a mistake pass but will be alert for its future occurrences and will then try to administer negative reinforcement contingent upon the mistake.

Punishment must be administered with care so that it will not become a stimulus for bad behavior. If the trainer inflicts punishment on a horse that causes him to become so unmanageable that the punishment must cease, the unmanageable behavior is then reinforced by cessation of the punishment. Every time this particular punishment is initiated the unmanageable condition will reappear. No punishment should be given until all consequences have been considered and there is assurance that control of the horse can be maintained and the desired response is obtained.

Schedules of Reinforcement

Schedules refer to when and how often a response is reinforced. These schedules of reinforcement have a direct effect both on horses being trained and on previously trained horses that are being ridden. Early training, when all behavior is being taught for the first time, is called the acquisition phase. During acquisition, most desirable responses are re-inforced. This is referred to as continuous reinforcement and results in faster learning by the horse. During this phase, the trainer continually either rewards or punishes the horse for every response it makes to cues given it. If cues are presented without any reinforcement, the learned responses will gradually diminish to the pretraining level. Eventually the horse will make no correct responses. This is referred to as extinction.

Continuous reinforcement during acquisition and no reinforcement resulting in extinction represent the two extremes in reinforcement sched-ules. Most older trained horses are reinforced between these two extremes, on some intermittent schedule, to keep them performing correctly. Inter-mittent schedules of reinforcement mean that the horse is reinforced not after each response, but at irregular intervals. This change from continu-ous to intermittent reinforcement usually occurs gradually as the horse progresses in its training. As the horse progresses, the trainer applies less reinforcement, which means he is not reinforcing every response and is moving toward an intermittent schedule.

It is important that a horse be trained with intermittent reinforcement because this will result in resistance to extinction. A horse trained on an intermittent schedule will perform longer with no reinforcement than a horse trained completely on continuous reinforcement. This is what is referred to as a "finished" or fully trained horse. The finished horse is frequently presented as a horse that requires no reinforcement. The impli-cation is that this horse will perform indefinitely in accordance with his cues and that all that is necessary is to present the cues to it. This is not true. If there is no reinforcement, the horse will cease to perform as it was trained regardless of the cues given it. However, this horse can be ridden longer, still responding to cues by a novice rider who lacks reinforcing ability, than a horse trained on continuous reinforcement. Eventually, the novice rider must learn the reinforcement for the horse or a more experi-enced rider will have to ride it again. Horsemen refer to this situation when they talk about getting a horse "tuned up."

A horse that requires continuous reinforcement is not a very well-trained horse. In fact, it is still in the acquisition phase. Horsemen should try to advance the horse to intermittent reinforcement by applying no more reinforcement than is necessary after the initial acquisition phase. This horse should appear to perform repeatedly with only the presentation of cues. The amount of reinforcement necessary should be so minimal that it goes unnoticed by the average horseman.

The principle of extinction is also used to a good advantage in horse training. Horsemen recognize this principle and ignore certain acts of the horse, knowing that the horse will cease doing them. If these acts are not reinforced, they will extinguish themselves. A similar problem arises when a horse is first being reinforced for responses. Very seldom are responses so accurate that there are not some undesirable actions being made at the same time. In some situations, the horse is not sure which response was reinforced. Several trials of contingent reinforcement may be required for this undesirable behavior to extinguish itself as the desirable behavior becomes stronger. The trainer should be aware of what is happening to the horse and be tolerant during these stages. It is important to be sure that some undesired response or behavior is not unknowingly reinforced.

Shaping

A term used by behaviorists that is analogous to horse training is shaping. In the initial stages, behavior is shaped by reinforcing each successive approximation of the desired response. Trainers use different techniques, but each will try to get a horse first to do something similar to the desired response; they will then progressively reinforce only the more desired behavior. The importance of recognizing small responses is paramount at this point. The trainer must recognize and be able to apply reinforcement to these small responses as he progresses to advanced performance. That first step taken backward, properly reinforced, will eventually lead to a good backing horse.

A rollback is a difficult maneuver to teach a horse. It includes a series of movements that must be learned one at a time. The trainer usually starts by teaching a stop. Then he teaches another maneuver designed to get the horse moving laterally, especially in the front. Then the horse is taught some short pivots. Finally, the horse combines all these movements and does a rollback. Throughout, the trainer applies reinforcement to any behavior that approximates that which is desired; however, he must expect more from the horse during each series of trials before reinforcing him or else no progress will be made. As learning progresses, only desired responses will be reinforced. Other undesired responses will drop out because of lack of reinforcement.

Effects of Effort on Learning

The more effort that is required of a horse to make a particular response, the harder it will be for the horse to learn the response. The time and number of trials (amount of practice) required to learn a response will increase as the amount of effort required increases. Less time is usually required to train a pleasure horse for a horse show performance than a reining or jumping horse. The amount of effort required to perform the tasks is the main reason for this time difference. Extinction of the responses is also faster when the response is difficult. To horsemen this means that

620

a reining horse will come untrained more easily than a pleasure horse.

Many of the tasks for which horses are trained require great effort. Horses that have athletic ability should learn faster than those with little or no athletic ability because the former require less effort to perform the tasks. The trainer should be aware of the effort required to do a task and realize that some horses with little athletic ability will learn slowly and may never learn to perform the task well. Apparently, behavior that must be learned is sometimes learned less readily by the horse than by other animals. Because the porpoise has been trained to perform many feats that are quite remarkable, that animal appears to be very intelligent. However, much of the behavior required for these tasks is easily learned by this animal.

Many of the maneuvers and tasks that horses are asked to do are far removed from its natural behavior in the wild state. We do not see untrained horses in pastures doing sliding stops, performing difficult rollbacks, jumping high obstacles, or backing. One real natural behavioral characteristic of the horse is ease of locomotion or, more specifically, an instinctive tendency to run. Consequently, it is not hard to teach a horse to run. It may be difficult to condition it to run well, but any novice can get a horse to run. That this is a natural instinct should be borne in mind when training timed-event horses. Teaching a horse to run will not be difficult, but it will be difficult to teach hard turns, flying lead changes, and stops. For this reason, the training of timed-event horses should concentrate on the hard-to-teach maneuvers.

Massing of Trials

Massing of trials, or prolonged practice, has been proven to be an inefficient method of training. Students who cram for exams are inefficient, as is the football kicker who kicks 12 hours one day and then does not practice again for a week. Fatigue is related to inefficient learning and is thought to have much the same effect as effort. Horses that have been overworked to the point of fatigue will learn, but at an inefficient rate.

During the very early stages of training, it may be necessary to bring about light fatigue in order to gain control of the horse. After this initial period, the trainer will enforce learning by using shorter training periods. This is not to say that the horse cannot be ridden for longer periods, but rather that the time devoted to practice for certain maneuvers should be shortened. For example, the horse may be ridden for one hour but practice rollbacks or jumps for only a few minutes. There might be one or more short practice sessions during each ride, broken by periods of relaxation or simple riding.

621

Inhibition

One intervening variable between a stimulus and a response, often seen with repeated practice, is inhibition. Such a variable is inferred from observed behavior and is used in a theoretical sense only, with no physiological reference. Suppose that animals were allowed 100 free-choice trials down a T maze. We would probably record 50 to the left and 50 to the right. If we close the right side and run left only for 100 additional trials, then open up both sides again, we would expect all choices to be left because of the extra practice in this direction. What we would probably get is all right choices because of the theoretical proposition of inhibition. Eventually, we would again get an equally distributed choice of one-half each way. The influences of inhibition can be seen in horse training. What a horse has learned on one side he must also learn on the other. Consequently, training must be directed at both sides or in both directions. Repeated trials to one side only may actually inhibit the horse from going that direction. To balance the effects of this phenomenon and still train both sides, the trainer should periodically work both sides of the horse and should concentrate on the problem side.

20.4   Intelligence

There are many different kinds of intelligence, and there is no one general measure of intelligence. Not all animals excel in all tests of intelligence, which indicates that some have different abilities for different kinds of activities.

Intelligence includes the ability to reason, and in this category the horse makes a very poor showing. In problem-solving intelligence tests, the horse places low, but so does the dog. Rats, cats, monkeys, and birds commonly score higher in these tests. The donkey possesses much more reasoning power than the horse (although some horsemen would be hard to convince of the validity of this finding).

This apparent lack of reasoning ability does not necessarily condemn the horse to a state of helplessness because it has other talents. The horse learns quite readily. The animal is merely not very adept at integrating a lot of different information to obtain a common solution. The horse can best be evaluated on problems that require skills of locomotion. New tasks are not difficult to learn if the cues affect the stronger senses (tactile, sight, hearing). The great performance horses are examples of the high degree to which these senses can be developed. As early as the nineteenth century, famous cases were recorded in the history of animal psychology that were proof of the horse's ability to respond to stimuli that were almost too weak to be perceived.

The successful horse trainer must be aware of these limitations in the horse's intellect and must concentrate training on the positive assets of the horse. The horse's greatest asset is its ability to learn and discriminate between the slightest of cues. Regardless of how intelligent a horse may appear when working, the trainer should remember that somewhere behind the performance are cues that the horse has learned. In general, the horse does not logically decide what is desired of him; he responds to stimuli or cues.

20.5 Training Summary

All of the principles of horse training have not been presented here; however, those presented are encountered daily in training routines. On occasion, the trainer may apply all of the principles that have been mentioned almost simultaneously. Horse trainers may not recognize some of these principles by the terms used here. However, if the trainer is successful, he is using most of these principles.

Most of this information has been presented to support the following concept. A cue is presented to signal a desired response, and this association is strengthened by reinforcement. The following guidelines are based on this concept and are suggested for training horses.

1. Learn to recognize and appreciate small responses or segments of the final performance during the learning phase.

2. Learn how to start with basic cues and advance to new ones.

3. Be specific and consistent in the presentation of all cues.

4. Be contingent with all reinforcement.

5. Provide alternative responses when using punishment.

6. Learn to shape behavior by reinforcing approximations of the desired response.

7. Advance to intermittent schedules of reinforcement.

8. Do not try to train with negative reinforcement only; it has too many pitfalls and can cause too many undesirable effects.

9. Learn how to use positive reinforcement; try to develop secondary positive reinforcement.

10. Do not expect the horse to have reasoning powers that are not common to horses.

20.6   Behavior and Management

Because of the close social relationship that exists between man and his horse, and because horse behavior is usually modified to some extent during training, an understanding of horse behavior is essential to effective management. There is also a "generation gap" in the transmission of knowledge about horses, and thus many people who are currently part of the horse industry have only a limited notion of the difference between normal and abnormal horse behavior. Management of horses in close confinement (as opposed to open ranges) also necessitates an awareness of how horses react to each other.

Categories of Behavior

Although the research that has been conducted on horse behavior is limited, several reports of research on the behavior of other species of animals have made possible the organization of information into concepts that are applicable to horses. Social behavior in animals has been considered by several researchers, and some have classified this behavior into 9 categories. These categories will be convenient for the following discussion of horse behavior.

Contactual Behavior.   This type of behavior is generally considered the result of seeking affection or protection, although horses sometimes exhibit contactual behavior for other reasons. Contactual behavior is also seen in many other animals. Horses will huddle together during inclement weather or at times of suspected danger. Although contactual behavior is not as highly developed in the horse as in some other species, horses do exhibit variations of this type of behavior.

Ingestive Behavior.   Ingestive behavior is the taking of food or water into the digestive tract. Ingestion of solid food by the horse begins at a very young age. Foals will start nibbling grass and will begin to eat grain within the first week of life if given the opportunity. Such behavior as chewing the bark of trees and tail chewing is not considered normal ingestive behavior and is generally a result of deprivation of roughage or nutrients, boredom, lack of exercise, or a combination of these. Horses vary tremendously in their rate of feed consumption. Some horses eat very fast, even to the extent that feed is not thoroughly masticated, whereas others eat very slowly.

The anatomy and physiology of the digestive system are such that horses will, if given a chance, take in small amounts of food at one time and eat at frequent intervals. Grazing horses prefer to cover a large area, taking small bites of grass at one time and seldom taking more than one or two bites before taking a step. Consequently, horses will usually bite the top of a bunch of grass and leave the bottom portion if the pasture is not contaminated with large amounts of feces. In pastures where stocking rate is high and in pastures that are not routinely harrowed, horses will graze portions of the pasture very close and will leave defecation areas to grow tall.

Horses are very apt to overeat, particularly if given access to feed after periods of low feed intake. Consequently, horses are very susceptible to digestive disorders caused by overeating.

Eliminative Behavior. In general, horses will interrupt any activity to urinate or defecate. Usually they will not urinate or defecate while walking, eating, or drinking.

Horses are likely to establish an elimination area in the pasture or paddocks and will not graze that area until there is no other source of feed (Figure 20-8). Horses will generally walk some distance to the elimination area to urinate or defecate.

Many horses will defecate in the same place when being moved. For example, some horses will routinely defecate when going through a particular gate between pastures or paddocks. This may be a result of an attempt at territorial marking by the horse.

Some horses will readily urinate in a stall or trailer whereas others will urinate immediately after being let out of a trailer or stall. Almost all horses will defecate when approaching a trailer or immediately after they are inside it. This is probably because of the nervous action resulting from anticipation.

Elimination patterns often differ between the sexes. Characteristically, stallions will smell the elimination area and walk up on it or back down on it before defecating or urinating. As a result, the elimination area of stallions usually does not become appreciably larger in diameter. Mares and geldings will usually smell the spot and urinate or defecate without

FIGURE 20-8
Horses will establish an elimination area in a paddock or pasture. In this area the grass grows tall, and horses will not readily graze it.

625

walking upon the spot. Therefore, the elimination area of mares and geldings usually becomes larger.

Adult horses will generally reject feces of their own kind, but foals will repeatedly eat feces of mares, especially when kept in dry lots. Coprophagy in adult horses is not believed to be a normal phenomenon.

Sexual Behavior. Sexual behavior includes all acts associated with the ultimate fertilization process, including courtship and copulation. Sexual behavior is not confined to mares and stallions. Geldings will definitely show signs of sexual behavior, particularly if castrated after puberty, because sexual behavior is controlled by both hormonal and neural influences. Many geldings will tease mares in estrus and will even mount. Also, many geldings are very possessive of mares that are pastured with them and will fight for a particular mare. Horsemen should not assume that geldings will not cause trouble around mares. Usually they will not. However, putting a gelding in the presence of mares in estrus or vice versa can cause serious behavioral problems and upset management of horses.

Discussion of normal sexual behavior in mares and stallions is omitted here since it is discussed in the chapters on reproductive physiology.

Epimeletic Behavior. The giving of care and attention is common between mare and foal, but other behavioral acts of this nature are also observed among horses. Such behavior is not common in mature stallions but is commonly seen in mares, geldings, and young horses. For example, horses will routinely stand in the shade head-to-tail and mutually fight flies for each other. Licking another animal is not very common in horses, but many horses will simultaneously scratch each other on the neck and over the withers and back.

Et-Epimeletic Behavior. Both young and adult horses signal for care and attention by calling or movement. This behavior is commonly seen when horses are separated from each other. Foals will call very excitedly for their dams when accidently separated or when weaned. Even adult horses that are accustomed to being together will call repeatedly for their companion.

Strong pair-bonding relationships exist between horses, and breaking of these relationships can complicate management. Horses will often go through or over fences that they normally would not bother with to get together. Some horses, when separated at a show, will become excited and call for their companion to the extent that such action interferes with their performance.

As a result of conditioning, many horses will call for the handler at feeding time. It is common for horses to call on sight of the manager when feeding time is near. Horses being supplementally fed in pastures are likely to go to the feeding place at or near feeding time.

Allelomimetic Behavior (Mimicry). This type of behavior is also referred to as contagious or infectious behavior. Horses are not thought to be likely to copy the behavior of another horse to the extent that other animal species copy each other. There are, however, some examples of this kind of behavior in horses. Horses in a group are likely to run simply because another horse is running. This may be mimicry, or it may be the result of fright. Some horses seem to run and play because other horses run and play. Having a horse that is hard to catch in a group will likely result in other horses in that group becoming hard to catch. Horses stalled adjacent to another horse that chews wood have a tendency to copy this behavior. Suckling foals will chew on a feed trough after being exposed to this behavior in their dams.

Investigative Behavior. Sensory inspection of the environment is very highly developed in horses and generally involves movement and one or all of the horse's senses — sight, touch, smell, hearing, and sometimes taste. Horses are very curious, particularly of new surroundings or objects, and will use all necessary senses to investigate them (Figure 20-9). Horses do not see detail very efficiently and therefore are seldom satisfied to investigate something new by sight alone. They cannot resist smelling, listening, touching, and sometimes tasting a new object. This investigation apparently must be completed before a horse will accept something new without sustained apprehension. Even strange horses are investigated. During the investigative processes, horses are very excitable and are likely to overreact to sudden movement or sounds. Horses have frequently injured themselves as a result of running into a fence or other object after being excited by a new object. Horses put into a new paddock or pasture next to strange horses may run into the fence in their attempt to investigate these new horses. It is not uncommon for a horse to fear being caught or trapped as a result of investigating a strange object.

Agonistic Behavior. This type of behavior includes all actions that are a result of or associated with conflict or fighting and includes aggression, submission, and attempts to escape. Agonistic behavior in horses is very

FIGURE 20-9
Horses are very curious and investigative of new objects. During the investigative process, horses are very excitable and may run into fences or other objects as a result of a sudden movement or sound.

627

pronounced and highly variable. It causes many problems for horsemen, but when carefully observed it can be managed. Awareness of agonistic behavior in horses and implementation of management practices to minimize its adverse effects are essential to successful horse management.

Dominance. Agonistic behavior in horses is the result of highly developed dominance hierarchies. Dominance hierarchies or "pecking orders" are seen in many species of animals and are definitely a significant part of the normal behavior of horses (Figure 20-10). Dominance in horses is established through aggression, but for the purpose of preventing severe fighting. Once the dominance hierarchy is established and so long as all horses in a group stay together, only the threat of aggression is needed to maintain the dominance hierarchy (Figure 20-11). Seldom will the dominant horse have to do more than pin its ears, bare its teeth, or make a sudden move toward the other horse to maintain the dominant position. The submissive horse will seldom challenge the dominant horse for position. Horses learn to live together without serious conflict as a result of their recognition of the dominance hierarchy. The dominance hierarchy is thought to be linear—from the most dominant down to the most submissive animal in the group. However, there are instances in which an animal that is low in the order may appear dominant over some animal at the top of the order. Most researchers believe this to be an example of a dominance hierarchy that has not been completely explained.

In establishing dominance, animals may have very traumatic experiences, or they may fight little or not at all. For example, stallions in the wild state often fought to the death of one or until crippling injury resulted. Putting two "boss" mares together may result in severe fighting. Many groups of horses can resolve the dominance problem without serious consequence *if* the submissive animal is allowed plenty of room for retreat and is not

FIGURE 20-10
In every group of horses there is a "boss" horse.

FIGURE 20-11
When the dominant horse makes a
threat, submissive horses will retreat
if possible.

forced to stand and fight. Therefore, when grouping strange horses it is
very important that they have plenty of room and are watched closely.

There are many considerations that affect the degree of aggression in
horses and that may influence the expression of dominance. Hormone levels
in males obviously affect the degree of aggression since stallions are normally more difficult to manage than geldings. However, blood estrogen
levels in mares do not appear to cause changes in dominance. Even in
deep estrus, the timid mare is not likely to challenge the dominant mare
for position, feed, or presence near the stallion. Some authorities believe
that dominant mares are more aggressive when in estrus, but there is no
clear evidence to support or refute this belief. Some geldings that are
normally very tolerant when in a group of other geldings become very
dominant and aggressive in the presence of a mare. Other variables such
as size, maturity, home territory, old age, and injury affect dominance to
some degree and may mask the real dominance hierarchy. Some horses
that appear dominant in a stall may actually be submissive when outside
and vice versa.

The presence of the manager will often cause a false expression of the
dominance hierarchy. Many horses that are actually in the lower end of
the order will appear aggressive and dominant in the presence of the
manager. On the other hand, some horses that are very dominant in the
herd will not express their dominance in the presence of the manager. It
is important to realize that dominance between horses must be established
by the horses themselves. There is little the manager can do to change or
reduce dominance in his absence. Therefore, the manager should group
horses according to compatibility and closely observe their behavior. Horses
should be grouped to allow orderly establishment of the dominance hierarchy and to minimize fighting and injury.

629

Management Suggestions

The following management practices are suggested to help the perceptive manager who is aware of social and other behavior in horses conduct his operation so that any adverse effects of this behavior are kept to a minimum.

1. Use fences that prevent injury in horses that huddle across the fence from each other.

2. Feed in individual feeders whenever possible. Space feeders well apart and provide at least one feeder for each horse in paddock or pasture.

3. Keep feed rooms locked, and use entrances outside the paddock or stall area.

4. Feed balanced rations according to requirements and include either hay or pasture.

5. Make provision for horses that eat very slowly.

6. Discourage rapid eating.

7. Routinely clean stalls and paddocks, and compost manure before spreading.

8. Mow and harrow pastures to scatter feces and keep grass young and growing.

9. Use rotational grazing whenever possible. Graze heavily for short periods and then change pastures.

10. Provide a mechanism for teasing timid mares.

11. Keep foals in a safe place and in sight of the mare during breeding.

12. Be careful when separating horses that are accustomed to being together.

13. Never turn horses in a new area late in the afternoon or at night. Observe closely when putting a horse in a new area.

14. Never attempt to catch a horse until it can be done. Never let a group of horses start to run when trying to catch them. Stop and pen them.

15. Use only treated wood or metal when building stalls, feeders, fences, and so on, that horses may chew on. Prevention is easier than cure.

16. Keep pastures, pens, and other facilities free of foreign objects. Avoid exposing horses to new objects that may be dangerous.

17. Be careful when turning horses out to pasture with halters on them.

18. Gates should be well secured and hard to open. Horses will investigate them.

19. Group horses by age and sex whenever possible.

20. Observe closely for aggressive behavior when changing groups.

21. Use box stalls with solid partitions between horses to prevent aggression.

22. Be aware of changes in dominance when horses are changed from one type of horse management to another.

23. Keep fences in good repair and avoid using barbed wire.

References

Bingham, W. E., and W. J. Griffiths. 1952. The effect of different environments during infancy on adult behavior in the rat. *J. Comp. Physiol. Psychol.* 45:307.

Collins, R. A. 1970. Aggression in mice selectively bred for brain weight. *Behavior Gen.* 2:169.

Denenberg, V. H., P. B. Sawin, G. P. Frommer, and S. Ross. 1958. Genetic, physiological and behavioral background of reproduction in the rabbit. IV. An analysis of maternal behavior at successive parturitions. *Behavior* 13:131.

Fox, M. W. 1968. *Abnormal Behavior in Animals.* Philadelphia: W. B. Saunders.

Hafez, E. S. E. 1969. *The Behavior of Domestic Animals.* 2d ed. Baltimore: Williams and Wilkins.

Heron, W. T. 1941. The inheritance of brightness and dullness in maze learning ability in the rat. *J. Genet. Psychol.* 59:41.

James, W. T. 1941. Morphological form and its relation to behavior. In *The Genetic and Endocrine Basis for Differences in Form and Behavior.* C. R. Stockard, ed. Philadelphia: Wisar Institute.

Kieffer, N. M. 1968. Heritability of cutting in horses. *Proc. Horse Short Course.* Texas A & M University. p. 46.

Kieffer, N. M. 1974. Methods of estimating the breeding values of potential sires and dams. *Proc. Horse Prod. Short Course.* Texas A & M University. p. 95.

Klinghammer, E., and M. W. Fox. 1971. Ethology and its place in animal science. *J. Animal Sci.* 32:1278.

Kratzer, D. D. 1971. Learning in farm animals. *J. Anim. Sci.* 32:1268.

Miller, R. W. 1974. *Horse Behavior and Training.* Bozeman, Montana: Big Sky Books.

Rundquist, E. A. 1933. Inheritance of spontaneous activity in rats. *J. Comp. Psychol.* 16:415.

Sawin, P. B., and D. D. Crary. 1953. Genetic and physiological background of reproduction in the rabbit. II. Some racial differences in the pattern of maternal behavior. *Behavior* 6:128.

Scott, J. P. 1956. The analysis of social organization in animals. *Ecol.* 37:213.

Scott, J. P. 1962. Introduction to animal behavior. In *Behavior of Domestic Animals.* E.S.E. Hafez, ed. Baltimore: Wilkins and Wilkins.

Tolman, E. C. 1924. The inheritance of maze-learning ability in rats. *J. Comp. Psychol.* 4:1.

Tyler, P. A., and T. E. McClean. 1970. A quantitative genetic analysis of runway learning in mice. *Behavior Gen.* 1:1.

Vicari, E. M. 1921. Heredity of behavior in mice. Washington, D.C.: Carnegie Inst. p. 132.

Wieckert, D. A. 1971. Social behavior in farm animals. *J. Animal Sci.* 32:1274.

Willham, R. L., D. F. Cox, and G. E. Karas. 1953. Genetic variations in a measure of avoidance learning in swine. *J. Comp. and Physiol. Psychol.* 56:294.

Yeates, B. F. 1974a. Applying principles of psychology to horse training. *Proc. Horse Prod. Short Course.* Texas A & M University. p. 77.

Yeates, B. F. 1974b. Recognition and use of social order in horse management. *Proc. Horse Prod. Short Course.* Texas A & M University. p. 71.

CHAPTER TWENTY-ONE *Basic Horsemanship*

The term "horsemanship" means knowledge of the skills necessary for the riding and care of horses. As a result of mechanization, very few skilled horsemen were available to meet the demand for knowledge when the horse population began to increase in the early 1960s. Even today, there is a lack of competent riding masters. Most riding instructors have learned only a few of the basic principles of equitation. Equitation, particularly advanced equitation, is a difficult subject to teach because the individual horse and rider, and a wide selection of equipment, must be taken into account. Also, there are many schools of thought regarding the proper way to teach equitation. The fundamentals of riding must be closely correlated with the proper way of caring for a horse. Only the basic fundamentals of care and equitation are within the scope of this chapter. They are to be used as a basis for further thought and research because each horse and rider needs a different type of training at each stage of development.

21.1 Training the Young Horse

Basic horsemanship begins with a knowledge of the procedures for breaking and training an untrained horse. Four basic errors are made by horsemen during the training of a horse and these four errors are usually the cause of most problems encountered during the training process. The first error is lack of a definite training program. A definite program does not have to be extremely rigid and should be flexible enough to fit individual horses, to the extent that such flexibility does not interfere with the basic

633

principles of the program. Second, inconsistency in the use of training aids and cues by the trainer causes a horse to be confused, hence slowing the rate of accomplishment. Third, there is a tendency on the part of the trainer to expect a horse to progress too rapidly, but if trained slowly, the horse will retain what it learns and will always be a well-trained horse. Horses that are trained too fast are usually trained by rough methods, and such horses respond out of fear. Anyone can beat a horse, but not everyone can train one. Finally, each training session should not demand excessive work. Most horses in training are immature, and excessive strain placed on their bones, ligaments, and muscles leads to unsoundnesses.

Leading

The initial step in training is to teach the horse to accept the halter and to lead. This part of the training should occur before weaning or just after weaning, before the horse gets too large to handle.

One of the most common ways to break foals to lead, before weaning, is to have someone lead the mare approximately 10 feet in front of the foal. The person training the foal pulls on the foal's lead shank, and if the foal does not step forward, a butt rope that winds around the foal's butt just above the hocks is pulled. Weanlings and older horses can easily be taught to lead if they are tied to an 8-foot rope that is anchored 10–11 feet above the ground. This method also teaches a horse not to pull back when tied because it will lose its balance. After the horse learns that it cannot free itself, it should be led around for a few minutes each day until it leads freely.

During the later stages of teaching the horse to lead, the animal should be gentled. This is accomplished by rubbing the foal all over its body. Actually, it can be made accustomed to grooming at this time. As soon as the horse is gentle (not afraid of the trainer) and leads quite well, it can be longed (exercised with a long rope). This exercise is the initial step in the horse's physical training program and is aimed at strengthening the horse's muscles before the animal is ridden. During the longeing phase of training, the horse is taught the voice commands of walk, trot, canter, and whoa. Longeing also teaches a horse to use the correct lead.

Longeing

Equipment.   When teaching the horse to longe, it is helpful to use a round corral of solid construction. The equipment consists of a halter, a light 20-foot longe line, and a longeing whip.

Method of Training. In teaching a horse to longe, you must have the horse's full attention. The initial step is to get the horse to circle you on the end of an ordinary lead shank. Hold the lead shank in one hand while standing next to the horse's flank area and hold the longeing whip in the other hand. To make the horse move, say "walk" and then cluck to it while tapping it from behind with the whip. To teach the horse to stop, say "whoa" and give a quick jerk on the lead shank. After the horse will circle both ways readily, it is then longed on the longe line. The horse is taught to trot by saying "trot" and tap it from behind with the whip. It is taught to canter in the same way.

Carrying Weight

The next step in a horse's training is to accustom the colt to carrying something on its back while being longed. A flat saddle is excellent regardless of whether the horse will be used for western riding or forward-style riding. At this stage of training the horse should be taught to stand quietly. Take a saddle blanket or sack, wave it all around the horse, and gently slap the horse with it. This is referred to as "sacking out." After a few lessons with a saddle on its back, the horse is taught to drive. The purpose of driving the colt is to teach it the basics of turning. If available, a training surcingle should be used; alternatively, the stirrups of a western saddle can be tied together with a rope under the horse's belly. Use of the training surcingle or passing the driving line through the stirrups prevents the horse from getting tangled in the rope and maintains the proper direction of pull. The driving line is attached to each side of the halter and is used to teach the horse to turn and back up. As the horse progresses in this stage, a snaffle bit is attached to the halter and placed in its mouth. By varying the position of the snaffle, the horse is taught to relax with the bit in its mouth. When the colt responds to driving so that it will execute all the turns, and stops and backs up with little pressure applied to the drive lines, the drive line is attached to the snaffle bit. All of the schooling with the drive line is repeated until the colt responds quickly and smoothly to the trainer's cues with the drive line.

Mounting

The colt is now ready to be trained while mounted. At this point, the schooling becomes quite specific according to the proposed use of the horse. The reader is referred to the bibliography at the end of this chapter

635

for the remaining training techniques since they are detailed and beyond the scope of the book.

21.2   Handling the Trained Horse

Haltering

Approach the horse in a deliberate manner to instill confidence in it. A horse kept in a box stall should be allowed to smell you for a moment and then be patted on the neck before you enter the stall, if the animal is standing at the door. Speaking to the horse not kept in a box stall will make the animal aware of your presence, so it will not be startled when it is touched. The horse should be approached from the left side and rubbed on the shoulder and neck for a moment before being haltered. This may not be possible, depending on the horse's position. The animal may also be approached from the right side or head on, but never from the rear. A nervous horse can be calmed by using an appropriate tone of voice, touching and rubbing, and using calm deliberate movements. After the halter is slipped on, the horse can be led out of the stall. The horse should be led from the left side and the distance between your hand and the halter should be approximately 18 inches.

Some horses have stall vices or are difficult to catch. Those that like to kick can be trained with a whip to stand in a corner with their heads facing you. Most horses in the large remudas of ranches were trained to face the ranch foreman when he held a whip. The horse is trained by striking it below the hocks with the whip if the animal faces away from you. Horses that go to a corner of a pen, extend their head out over the rail, and wheel away from you as you try to halter them will respond to this type of training. Others like to lean on the person catching them so that the person is pinned against the wall. You may wish to carry a short, sharp stick with you as you enter the stall so that it can be placed against the wall. The horse will lean against it and soon learn not to play that game.

Restraint

Tying.   Properly tying up a horse can prevent injuries; and tying prevents the horse from learning that it can escape. Horses that learn to escape are difficult to break of the habit. Many horsemen cross-tie a horse when they are working with it in the stable area. The two tie ropes should be firmly anchored at approximately shoulder height and snapped onto the halter. The ends anchored to the walls or posts should be tied with a slip knot so

636

that the horse can be quickly released. When the horse is tied with the lead shank on the halter, the rope should be tied at the height of the withers and should be long enough so that the horse's nose just touches the ground. If tied too loosely, the horse can step over the rope and get tangled. When the horse is tied without a halter, a bowline knot should be used on the end around the horse's neck so that the rope cannot slip and choke the horse (Figure 21-1).

Other Methods of Restraint

When attempting to restrain a horse, the safety of both the horse and the handler must be considered. One of the simplest methods of diverting a horse's attention so that less-painful work can be performed is to twitch the horse. The twitch applies pressure to the sensory nerve of the lip (Figure 21-2). Commercial twitches are available but one can be made simply out of a stick and rope loop. Another old method of restraint to prevent a horse from traveling too fast or too far away is to strap a hobble around the pasterns. The first couple of times a horse is hobbled it may fall over backward, so it must be handled carefully until it is accustomed to the hobble. To prevent a horse from striking, a belt can be strapped around the front leg so that the pastern is brought up close to the arm (Figure 21-3). A back leg can be prevented from kicking by using a hock hobble (Figure 21-4) or by tying up the hind leg (Figure 21-5).

Horses that must be kept under control while being led can be restrained with a war bridle. The simplest war bridle is a loop of rope placed over the poll and across the gum of the upper incisor teeth. If a leather halter is available, the lead shank chain can be run across the horse's nose or through its mouth. With either method, a quick pull will cause pain.

Grasping and twisting a horse's ear is a means of restraint that usually leads to head shyness. This method should be avoided if possible.

After a horse is restrained and is being groomed or worked with, a good horseman lets the horse know his position by keeping one hand on the horse as he moves around the horse. A horse that is unaware that its leg is to be picked up will be startled and may kick the horseman when its leg is touched.

A newborn foal should be held with one arm wrapped around its chest and the other arm held just above the hocks. They cannot escape when held this way and can be examined without difficulty.

Grooming

The horse should be groomed daily if possible and should always be groomed before it is ridden. Dirt on a horse's back will cause saddle sores.

637

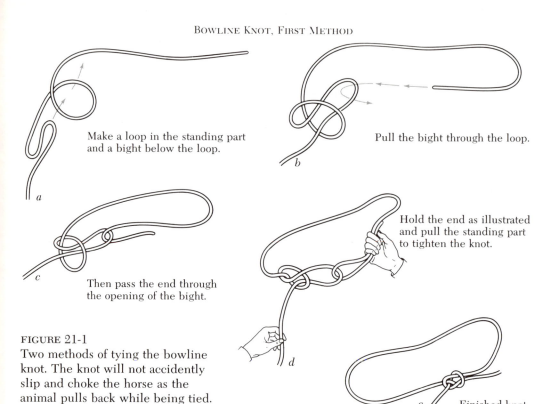

BOWLINE KNOT, FIRST METHOD

Make a loop in the standing part and a bight below the loop.

a

Pull the bight through the loop.

b

Then pass the end through the opening of the bight.

c

Hold the end as illustrated and pull the standing part to tighten the knot.

d

FIGURE 21-1
Two methods of tying the bowline knot. The knot will not accidently slip and choke the horse as the animal pulls back while being tied.

e Finished knot.

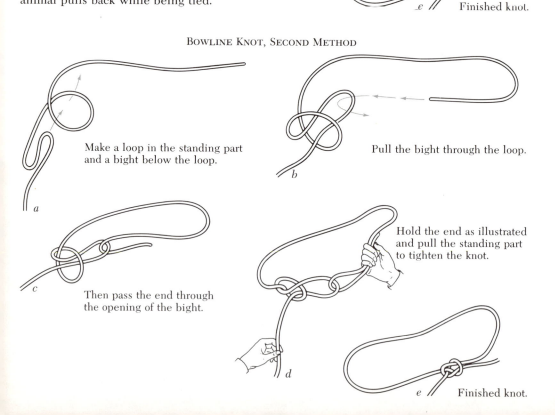

BOWLINE KNOT, SECOND METHOD

Make a loop in the standing part and a bight below the loop.

a

Pull the bight through the loop.

b

Then pass the end through the opening of the bight.

c

Hold the end as illustrated and pull the standing part to tighten the knot.

d

e Finished knot.

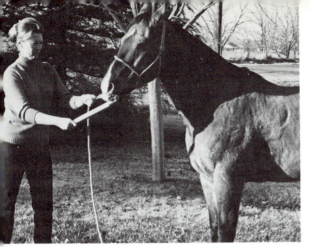

FIGURE 21-2
Lip twitch applied to a horse
as a means of restraint.

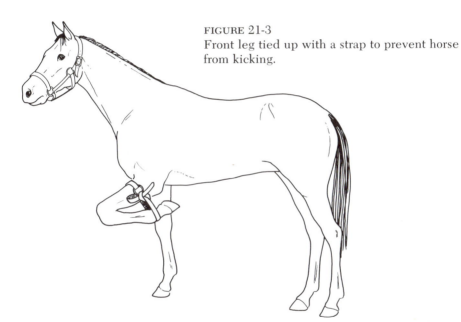

FIGURE 21-3
Front leg tied up with a strap to prevent horse
from kicking.

FIGURE 21-4
Use of hock hobble to prevent kicking.

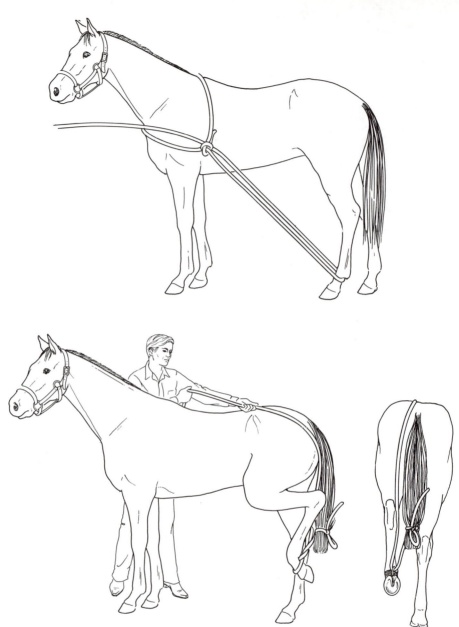

FIGURE 21-5

Two methods of tying up a hind leg to prevent a horse from kicking.

Irritation from dirt under a cinch may cause a horse to buck, or may form a raw spot. In either case, the horse cannot be ridden until the sore heals. Proper grooming equipment is shown in Figure 21-6. A rubber curry comb is used in a circular or back-and-forth motion over the horse's body above the hocks to loosen the dirt. It is used against the lay of the hair. A soft body brush is then used to remove the loose dirt and straighten the hairs so that they all lie in the proper direction. A dandy brush may be used

640

Pure linen
rub rag

English dandy brush

Body brush

Sweat
scraper

Washer-groomer comb

Sponge

Mane comb

Hoof pick

Hoof dressing brush

Roaching shears

Rubber curry comb

Electric clipper

FIGURE 21-6
A basic set of grooming equipment consists of at least the following: hoof pick,
dandy brush, body brush, mane comb, washer-groomer comb, sponges, sweat
scraper, rub rags, hoof dressing brush, shears, hard rubber curry comb, clippers.

instead of the rubber curry comb to loosen and remove dirt. The face and the legs below the knees and hocks are cleaned with a rag. The mane and tail can be combed with a mane comb. The feet are always cleaned, with a hoof pick, before and after the horse is ridden.

Sweat is irritating to horses, so the horse should be cooled and brushed off after being exercised. Otherwise, the horse may injure itself by scratching itself on something, or rolling to relieve the itching.

Horses can be bathed with a mild shampoo. A hose is usually used to squirt water on the body to remove the soap, but avoid getting water in the ears. A wash rag or sponge is usually used on the head. After a thorough rinsing to remove all the soap, the excess water can be removed with a sweat scraper (Figure 21-6). The horse should be dried off by being rubbed with a turkish towel, or by standing in the sun before being returned to its stall. If the horse is returned to its stall before it is dry, it may develop a cold.

Saddling

Before the saddle is placed on a horse, the horse's back and cinch areas should be inspected to make sure that they are clean and that all the hairs are lying in their natural direction.

In the forward saddle (hunt seat) (Figure 21-7), the girth (leather strap

FIGURE 21-7
Forward (hunt seat) saddle.

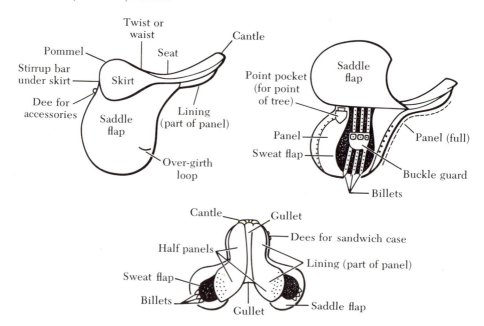

that goes under the belly) is lying across the seat and the stirrups are pulled up high before the saddle is placed on the horse's back. A saddle pad is not necessary, but if it is used, it is connected to the saddle before saddling up. The saddle and pad are placed gently on the horse's back from the near (left) side and just behind the shoulder blades. The saddle is then moved back approximately 1½ inches so that the hairs are straightened. The saddle is never moved forward because if it is, the hairs become ruffled and will cause saddle sores. Next the girth is attached to the off (right) side billets (Figure 21-7). The girth is pulled up and buckled to the near (left) side billets. Before the girth is tightened enough to ride, all skin wrinkled under it is smoothed out and the horse is led around briefly. The girth is then tightened enough to keep the saddle in position during the ride. The stirrup leathers on a hunt seat saddle should be adjusted for proper length and the stirrups pulled up high again until the horse is to be mounted. The stirrup length should be such that the stirrup iron reaches the armpit when the arm is extended with the fingertips touching the stirrup buckles. Some people adjust (shorten or lengthen) their stirrups to a position in which the iron hits just below the ankle bone. A riding instructor may suggest changing the standard stirrup length to improve the rider's position.

To saddle a horse for western riding, the saddle pad is placed on the horse's back forward of the horse's withers. If a saddle blanket is used, the fold should be placed forward of the withers. Then, the western saddle (Figure 21-8) is prepared for saddling by placing the cinches and right stirrup across the seat. The saddle is gripped by the pommel and cantle and placed gently on the horse's back and saddle pad just behind the shoulder blades. The saddle and pad are moved backward to a position where the bars will not rub the shoulder blades. After the cinches and right stirrup are lowered, the saddle is cinched up, but not too tight. If the saddle has front and back cinches, the front cinch is tightened first to prevent the horse from bucking the saddle off. After the horse is walked around, the cinches are tightened. The saddle gullet should be checked to make sure that it is not exerting pressure on the horse's withers. Severe bruising of the withers can result in fistulous withers (see Chapter 7). There should be a distance of at least 2 finger lengths between the gullet and pads.

Bridling

When bridling a horse, the crown (Figure 21-9) is held in the right hand. As the right hand pulls the bridle upward, the left hand guides the bit into the horse's mouth. If the teeth are banged with the bit during a few bridlings, the horse usually becomes head shy and hard to bridle. If the horse does not open its mouth for the bit, the thumb and forefinger can be inserted between the bars and the horse will usually open its mouth. After

643

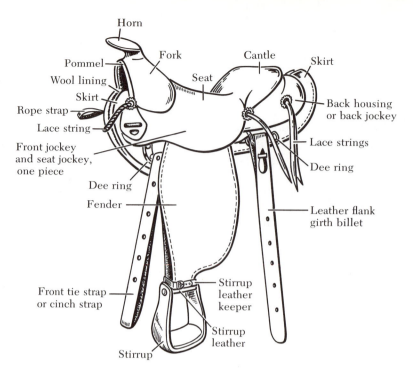

FIGURE 21-8
Basic western saddle.

the bridle is adjusted to allow insertion of the bit in the mouth so that there are 1 or 2 wrinkles at the corners of the mouth, the throatlatch strap, if present, is adjusted so that 3 or 4 fingers can be inserted between it and the horse's jaws. The noseband (English bridle) and curb strap must also be properly adjusted for the horse (see next section, "bitting"). When removing the bridle, the left hand is placed on the horse's face to keep its nose down. If the head is held in this position, the bit will not hit the teeth when it is removed.

21.3   Tack

Bitting

Bitting a horse has traditionally been by trial and error, and probably will continue to be. Each person has a different feel for a given horse's mouth with a particular bit and may have to use a different bit on the horse to obtain a maximum performance. Similarly, each horse may require a different bit for maximum performance because of differences in jaw width,

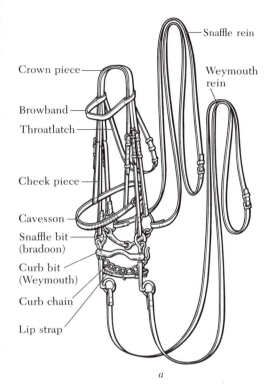

Snaffle rein

Weymouth rein

Crown piece

Browband

Throatlatch

Cheek piece

Cavesson

Snaffle bit (bradoon)

Curb bit (Weymouth)

Curb chain

Lip strap

a

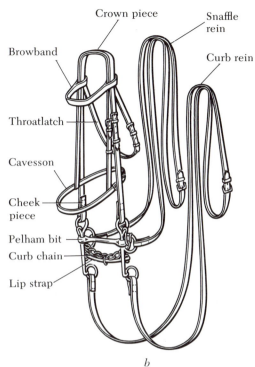

Crown piece

Snaffle rein

Browband

Curb rein

Throatlatch

Cavesson

Cheek piece

Pelham bit

Curb chain

Lip strap

b

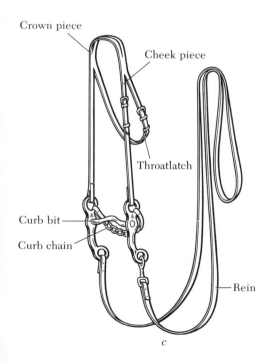

Crown piece

Cheek piece

Throatlatch

Curb bit

Curb chain

Rein

c

FIGURE 21-9
Three types of bridles. *a*: The
Weymouth bridle, composed of
snaffle and curb bits with double
reins, is used in showing three- and
five-gaited horses. *b*: The Pelham
bridle, a single-bitted, double-reined
bridle, is used on hunters, polo
ponies, and pleasure horses. *c*: The
one-ear, or split-ear bridle is used on
working stock horses (horses that
work livestock); the type shown
has a roping rein and a curb bit.

645

tongue thickness, head length, and amount of pressure applied by the bit to specific areas.

A bit must fit the horse's mouth so that the horse is comfortable. Bit selection also depends upon the horse's training and temperament and the kinds of riding the owner does. Selecting the wrong bit can cause control problems or delay training. Proper selection requires an understanding of the types and uses of bits.

Classification. Bits are classified as hackamore, curb, and snaffle (Figure 21-10). English and western riders are acquainted with the many types and uses of snaffle bits. Western riders use curb bits that have many variations, whereas English riders use kimblewicks (commonly called kimberwickes), curbs, and pelhams. The snaffle bit comes in a wide variety of forms (Figure 21-11) and is used for many purposes. The common feature of all snaffle bits is that the mouthpiece is jointed or straight with rings for the reins at both ends. The rings on the ends of the mouthpiece may be of 4 types: round, egg butt, racing dee, or full cheek. The snaffle is a mild bit

FIGURE 21-10
Three basic types of bits.

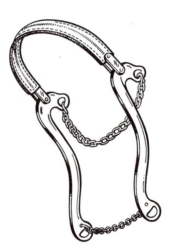

Hackamore bit

Curb bit

Snaffle bit

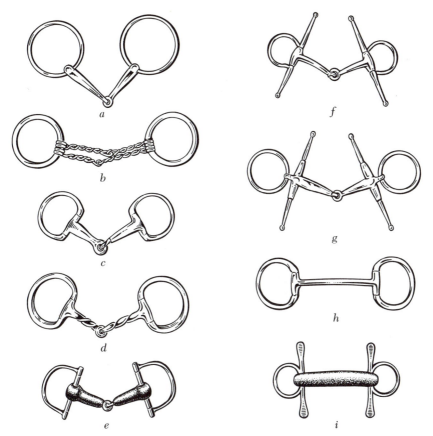

FIGURE 21-11

Types of snaffle bits: *a*, jointed mouth; *b*, flat ring, Y or W twisted wire snaffle; *c*, jointed mouth, German egg butt snaffle; *d*, jointed mouth, twisted egg butt snaffle; *e*, rubber-covered racing dee snaffle; *f*, egg butt full cheek snaffle; *g*, Australian loose-ring or Fulmer snaffle; *h*, metal mullen mouth egg butt snaffle; *i*, soft rubber mullen mouth full-spoon cheek snaffle. From duPont. 1973.

and the severity is regulated by the circumference of the mouthpiece, that is, the smaller the circumference, the more severe the bit. Mouthpieces that are twisted also increase the severity of the bit and if used improperly can ruin the bars of a horse's mouth. The pull of the rein exerts a direct pull on the horse's mouth equal to the force exerted by the rider. Therefore, lowering a snaffle in a horse's mouth from the correct position of 1 or 2 wrinkles at the corners of the mouth will increase its severity. The round rings must be large enough not to pull through the mouth. Quite often, the lips will be pinched by the rings. To prevent this, the racing dee and egg butt snaffles have metal casing around the joints. The full cheek snaffle has 2 small bars inside the rings that prevent the rings from sliding into the mouth and serve as a steering aid for the young horse.

647

The hackamore bit (Figure 21-10) is often confused with a hackamore (Figure 21-12). Hackamore bits are bits that do not have a mouthpiece. They are used on horses that will not accept a bit or have mouth injuries that would be irritated by a mouthpiece. Many hackamore bits have long shanks, and thus a lot of pressure can be applied to the nose and chin groove without much pull on the reins.

A true hackamore (Figure 21-12), derived from the Spanish word *jáquima*, is used to start colts in training. The hackamore is used to apply a direct pressure on the nose and chin with the bosal. Bosals can be made of any of several materials such as rope, horsehair, or leather, but a braided rawhide bosal with a rawhide core is preferred. It is essential that the bosal fit closely around the horse's nose and low near the soft cartilage. The bosal is held in place with a headstall and a fiador. The fiador (Figure 21-12), which is a small double rope attached to the heel knot, passes over the poll and serves as a throatlatch. The mecate (Figure 21-12) is a soft, large-diameter rope that is easy to grip and is long enough to form a lead rope after the continuous rein is adjusted so that it reaches the saddle horn. Attachment of the mecate to the bosal forms the lead rope knot. The size of the bosal is adjusted by the hackamore knot (Figure 21-13) so that a slight lift to the heel knot will cause the cheeks of the bosal to apply pressure to the chin. The heel knot should be heavy enough so that chin

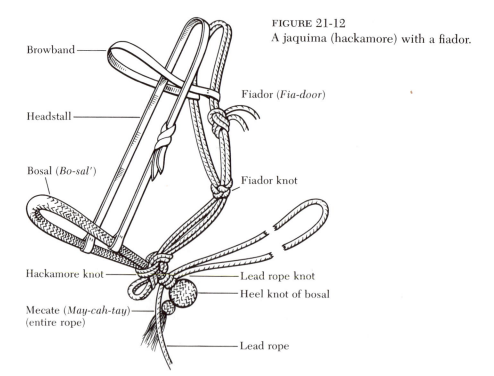

FIGURE 21-12
A jaquima (hackamore) with a fiador.

Browband

Fiador (*Fia-door*)

Headstall

Bosal (*Bo-sal'*)

Fiador knot

Hackamore knot

Lead rope knot

Heel knot of bosal

Mecate (*May-cah-tay*)
(entire rope)

Lead rope

pressure is relieved as soon as rein pressure is decreased. Both reins of a hackamore are used simultaneously in the early stages of training so that the horse learns to respond to a direct rein and a bearing rein. The direct rein applies lateral pressure to the horse's head and the bearing rein applies pressure to the side of the neck.

The kimblewick bit (Figure 21-14) is similar to a snaffle bit except that there are loops or slots at the top of the rings for attachment of the bridle and a curb chain. The kimblewick uses single reins that exert light pressure on the mouthpiece. Increasing the pull on the reins causes the D-rings to act as short shanks and apply curb chain pressure. The curb pressure is not severe because of the short lever action of the D-rings and because the rider does not have much control over the amount of curb action.

To have greater control than snaffle and curb pressure, English riders use the double-reined pelham bit (Figure 21-14). One set of reins attaches to rings that exert a pull on the mouthpiece and the other set is attached to rein loops on the ends of shanks. By pulling on both reins simultaneously or on the snaffle rein, snaffle action is obtained. Pulling only on the curb rein activates the curb action, which also applies pressure to the curb chain groove and on the poll. The pelham bit is popular because it is easy for a rider to learn to use.

The double bridle allows the English rider to use snaffle and curb action either simultaneously or separately. The two bits, called a Weymouth set (Figure 21-15), are composed of a bradoon (small ring snaffle) and a curb. They are used primarily on dressage and gaited horses and sometimes on hunters.

Curb bits for western riders come in thousands of shapes and combinations of mouthpieces and shanks. The basic curb bit is shown in Figure 21-16. The distance between the center of the mouthpiece and the center of the bridle loop should be $1\frac{7}{8}$ inches to 2 inches for proper action of the bit. The distance between the center of the mouthpiece and the center of the rein loop (shank length) determines the leverage or amount of pull from the reins that will be exerted on the bit. The shanks of most curbs are $5-5\frac{1}{2}$ inches long. Mouthpieces are $4\frac{1}{2}-5$ inches long. Solid mouthpieces usually have a rise (port) in the middle that relieves part of the tongue pressure and applies pressure to the roof of the mouth. The "half-breed" has a high port ($1\frac{1}{2}$ inches maximum) with a roller in it. The curb chain must be kept fairly tight to prevent the port from injuring the roof of the mouth. Most horses play with the roller with their tongues and in so doing, keep their mouths moist. Quite often, rollers and the ports of bits are covered with copper, which increases the flow of saliva to keep a horse's mouth moist. The spade bit (Figure 21-17) is a very severe bit ($3\frac{1}{2}$ inch port) that must be used with a tight curb chain and very light rein pull. The spade bit also has a roller (cricket) and springs.

A bit and bridle can exert pressure on one location or on a combination of several different locations on a horse's head. The shape, weight, and size

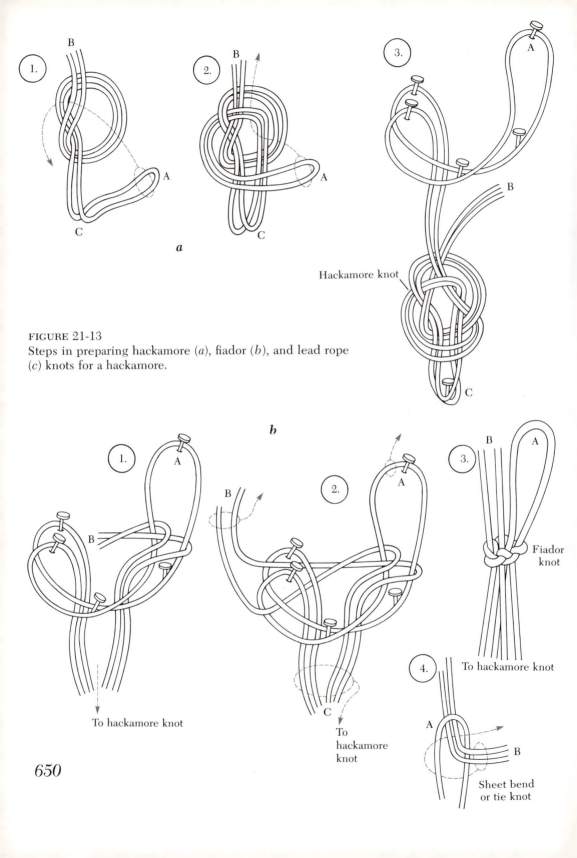

FIGURE 21-13
Steps in preparing hackamore (*a*), fiador (*b*), and lead rope
(*c*) knots for a hackamore.

650

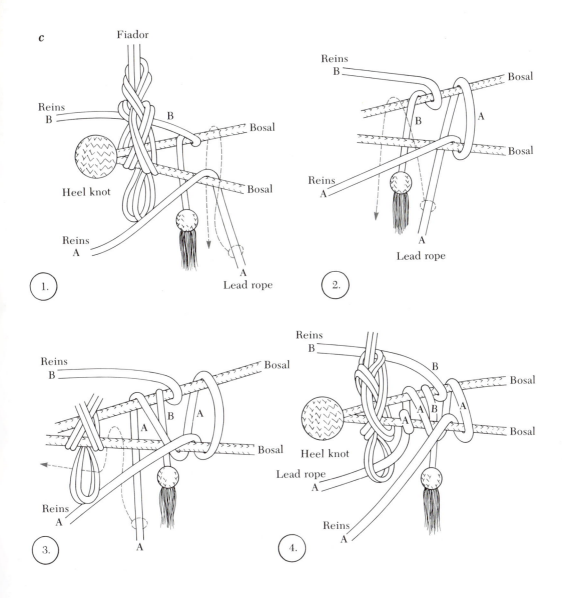

_c_

1. Fiador · Reins B · B · Bosal · Heel knot · Bosal · Reins A · A Lead rope

2. Reins B · Bosal · B · A · Bosal · Reins A · A · Lead rope

3. Reins B · Bosal · A · B · A · Bosal · A · Reins A

4. Reins B · B · Bosal · A B · A · Bosal · Heel knot · Lead rope A · A · Reins A

of the mouthpiece and the thickness of the horse's tongue determine the amount of pressure exerted on the tongue. A common mistake is to use a thick mouthpiece on a thick-tongued horse so that the animal cannot comfortably close its mouth. When the mouth is closed, too much pressure is applied on the tongue by the mouthpiece so that the horse wants to keep his mouth open. The curb chain applies pressure to the curb chain groove. Proper adjustment for different types of bits is necessary for proper action. A "half-breed" bit with a roller or a spade bit requires a tighter curb chain than does a curb bit. This limits the rise of the port, avoiding possible injury to the roof of the mouth. Curb chains that are too loose will pinch the corners of the mouth when the reins are pulled tight and will not give the

651

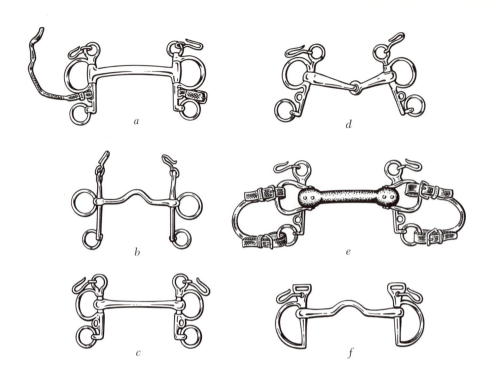

FIGURE 21-14
Pelham and kimblewick (or kimberwicke) bits: *a*, Mullen mouth egg butt steel
pelham with lip strap; *b*, loose ring, fixed port mouth steel pelham; *c*, Mullen
mouth, sliding cheek, Tom Thumb pelham; *d*, jointed mouth steel pelham;
e, hard nylon Tom Thumb pelham with converter straps; *f*, steel kimblewick.
From duPont. 1973.

desired pressure on the chin groove. A general rule is that 2 fingers should
be able to be inserted between the curb chain and the chin groove.

The bars carry the weight of a snaffle bit primarily when the bit is passive unless the horse properly flexes its head at the poll to relieve the
pressures. The curb bit places pressure on the bars when the curb chain
becomes tight. Because of the fulcrum action of the mouthpiece, most
curb bits exert some pressure on the poll right behind the ears when the
reins are pulled. The pressure results from movement of the curb strap
loop forward and downward. Bridle adjustment will vary the amount of
pressure that is applied by a curb bit to the poll. (A loose bridle will apply
less pressure.) The lips receive pressure at the corners of the mouth and
over the bars, which they cover until heavy pressure is applied to a curb
or snaffle bit. The amount of pressure applied to the roof of the mouth is
controlled by the type and movement of the curb bit port. As previously
discussed, the curb chain adjustment will limit the rise of the port. Certain
types of bits, such as the hackamore bit (Figure 21-10), apply pressure to
the nose.

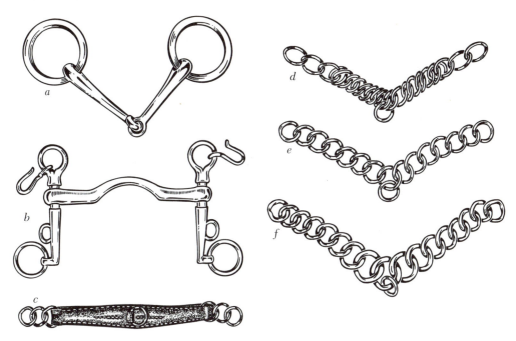

FIGURE 21-15
Weymouth set: *a*, flat ring bradoon; *b*, sliding cheek curb; *c*, leather curb strap; *d*, double link curb chain; *e*, single link curb chain; *f*, wide, single flat link curb chain. From duPont. 1973.

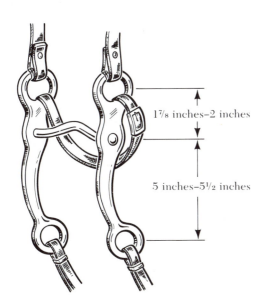

1⅞ inches–2 inches

5 inches–5½ inches

FIGURE 21-16
Curb bit.

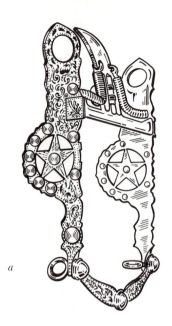

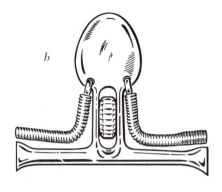

FIGURE 21-17
Santa Barbara silver mounted spade bit (*a*)
and spoon spade mouthpiece (*b*).

The balance or collection of a horse can be controlled to a certain extent by the bit it carries. With curb bits, the ratio of the distance from the curb strap loop to the mouthpiece, compared with the distance from the rein loop to the mouthpiece (Figure 21-16), controls the horse's balance. A horse that is heavy on the forehand (that is, its center of balance is too far forward) will pick its head up, bring in its nose, and flex at the poll so that the center of gravity is shifted backward when the ratio is decreased (that is, 1:1 to 1:3). In contrast, a horse with a sensitive mouth will perform much better for a heavy-handed rider when the ratio is increased and less pressure is applied for a given pull on the reins.

In addition to bits and bridles, two other aids are used for control. A noseband (cavesson) can be used to prevent the horse from evading bit action by opening its mouth (Figure 21-9). The effectiveness of the noseband can be increased by dropping the chin portion forward and under the mouthpiece of the bit and moving it across the chin groove. A standing martingale is used to keep a horse from carrying its head too high (Figure 21-18). It attaches to the noseband, is supported by a neck strap, and is connected to the girth. A running martingale (Figure 21-18) works on the mouth to keep the head low. The reins are run through the rings on the end of the straps, which change the direction of the rein pull. The Irish martingale (Figure 21-18) is a leather strap with rings at each end. It is used to link the reins together in front of the horse's neck to prevent them from being flipped over onto the same side of the neck during a stumble or other sudden unexpected movement of the horse's head. It is merely a safety device and does not affect a horse's performance.

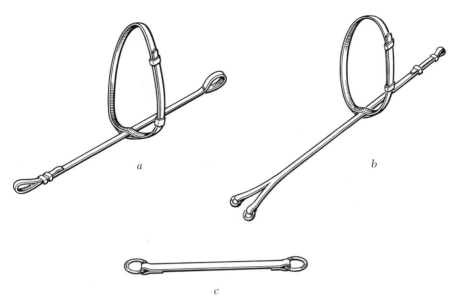

FIGURE 21-18
Martingales: *a*, standing; *b*, running; *c*, Irish.

Bridles

Western. Western riders use a bridle composed of a set of reins, a bit, and a headstall (Figure 21-9c). The type of reins varies with the use of the horse. Braided rawhide reins with a romal are quite popular with many riders. Rope horses are usually ridden with a single closed rein. The split reins are an old standby that are used on ranch, pleasure, and show horses. Many variations of headstalls are used. The simplest headstall consists of a leather strap that goes over the poll and is split so it encircles one ear. Other types of headstalls have a browband and/or throatlatch to keep the headstall in the proper position on the horse's head.

Forward. English bridles (Figure 21-9) come in a variety of types depending upon the use of the horse and type of bit it needs. The so-called pelham bridle is composed of a double set of reins, the pelham bit, cavesson, headstall, browband, and throatlatch. It is commonly used on hunters, polo ponies, and pleasure horses. The Weymouth or double bridle is similar to the pelham bridle except that it has an extra set of straps to support the bradoon. The Weymouth bridle is used to develop flexion while maintaining the head carriage induced by riding the horse into the bradoon. Consequently, it is used on pleasure, three-gaited, and five-gaited horses.

FIGURE 21-19
The western saddle in use: A Pony Express rider enroute from the Missouri
River to San Francisco. From a drawing by G. H. Andrews. 1861. Photograph
courtesy of The Mansell Collection, London.

Saddles

Western.   The western saddle developed as a result of a need by horsemen
who spent long hours riding to have a comfortable saddle for the horse and
for themselves and to have a strong saddle that could hold a steer after it was
roped. The basic western saddle is shown in Figure 21-8. In selecting a
western saddle, one of the main considerations is the seat. The seat should
be flat and not built up in front. A seat that is built up in front prevents
the rider from getting forward over the center of gravity of the horse. The
rider then sits too far back on the loins of the horse and causes the horse
to become fatigued too quickly. The placement of the stirrup leathers will
determine the position (forward or backward) of the legs and feet and
thus, balance, when riding. Many saddles are made with the stirrups too
far forward.

The tree is the basic unit of the saddle. Saddle trees (Figure 21-21) are
made of fiberglass or wood covered with rawhide. The way that a saddle
fits on a horse's back is determined by the width and height of the gullet
and the flare of the bars. Gullet height and width are important in determining what type of horse the saddle tree will fit. A low, wide gullet will
probably rub against the withers of a narrow, high-withered horse, whereas
a narrow or regular-width gullet will not fit down on a wide-backed horse.

FIGURE 21-20
The western saddle in use: *The Cowboy,* a painting by the American cowboy artist Frederic Remington. The Museum of Fine Arts, Houston (Hogg Brothers Collection).

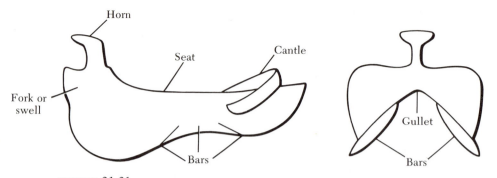

FIGURE 21-21
Side (*top*) and front (*bottom*) views of a saddle tree around which the rest of the western saddle is built. From Hyland. 1971.

The bars of a saddle tree must have the proper angle and "twist" to fit a horse. The bars must be long enough so that they do not irritate the back over the loin. Longer bars give more bearing space on the horse's back and distribute the rider's weight more evenly. These factors often determine the difference between a low-cost saddle that causes saddle sores on the shoulders and back, and a good, useable saddle. The size of the tree determines the size of the finished saddle. The average size of a tree is 15 or 15½ inches measured from where the seat joins the fork to the inside of the cantle after the saddle is completed. The saddle is rigged as center-fire, 5/8, 3/4, 7/8, or full depending on the position of the front cinch ring (Figure 21-22). The centerfire rigged saddle is rigged with a single cinch. Cowboys found that it tended to tip and slip forward when they roped cattle so the front cinch was moved forward and a flank cinch was added (Figure 21-8). Today, most saddles are rigged double—full or 3/4. Western saddles weigh approximately 40 pounds but may be lighter or heavier. The saddles used by single-steer ropers take a lot of strain and weigh 43–45 pounds.

Western saddles require a pad between the saddle and the horse's back.

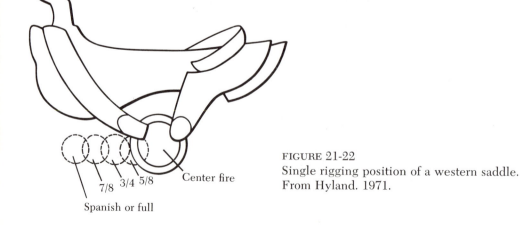

FIGURE 21-22
Single rigging position of a western saddle. From Hyland. 1971.

Saddle pads are made of a variety of materials. Pads made of synthetic material can be washed and kept clean quite easily. The "hair pad" has been a standby over the years. It does cake with dirt when it is wet with sweat, but the dirt can be brushed out. Failure to clean a hair pad will result in a bruised or irritated area on the horse's back. Wool blankets are used on horses that are not worked very hard and are ridden for short periods.

Forward. Three general types of saddles are used for English-style riding. The different parts of the forward seat saddle are shown in Figure 21-7. The so-called flat or hacking saddle is used for general-purpose riding. Recently, its popularity has declined in favor of the forward seat saddle. The forward seat saddle differs from the flat saddle in that the flaps are cut in such a way that they are well forward and have padded knee rolls incorporated into them. The seat is deeper and has a rather high cantle. The front of the forward seat saddle may be cut back. The third type, the show saddle, has a flat seat that causes the rider to sit back toward the cantle. The flaps are straight down. Usually, the pommel is cut back. Show saddles are used in saddle seat classes, and for saddle-bred and gaited horses that are ridden with long stirrups.

The girths that hold the English-type saddle on the horse are made of several types of material. Those made of a sturdy washable cotton webbing or folded leather are the most popular. When chafing problems arise, a tubular, sheep-wool girth cover can be slipped over the girth to prevent the chafing.

If the girth is not sufficient to hold the saddle in position, a breastplate is attached to the sides of the pommel and to the girth. It is frequently used on hunters. Many plump-bellied ponies require the use of a crupper under the tail to prevent the saddle from slipping forward.

Saddle pads or "nunnals" are not necessary for English-type saddles but are used by many horsemen, particularly during ordinary riding. The pad is attached to the saddle by running the billets through 2 straps. Pads are usually made of sponge rubber, sheepskin, or felt. They absorb sweat (thus protecting the saddle) and protect the horse's back and withers.

Stirrup leathers for English-type saddles are a separate item. To keep the stirrups adjusted to the same length, it is essential that the holes be punched at exactly the same length on both stirrups. They should be switched from one side of the saddle to the other quite regularly because mounting tends to stretch the stirrup leathers.

Stirrup irons must be properly sized so that they are approximately 1 inch wider than the rider's foot. Safety stirrups (Figure 21-24) are used by many novice riders because they automatically open if the rider falls. Rubber stirrup treads are quite popular, but are dangerous to use because the rider's foot does not slip out of the stirrup as easily when an accident occurs.

659

FIGURE 21-23
Two engravings from the late nineteenth century showing women mounted sidesaddle. The sidesaddle is a variation of the forward saddle that allows women to ride with both feet on one side of the horse. Both engravings courtesy of The Bettmann Archive.

661

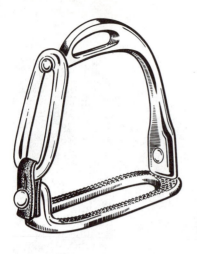

FIGURE 21-24
Safety stirrup for forward seat saddle. The pressure from a fall disengages the heavy rubber band from the hook, thus releasing the rider's foot.

21.4   Western Riding

Mounting

When mounting a western horse, it is customary to mount from the near (left) side. However, all horses should be accustomed to being mounted from the off (right) side because conditions may preclude mounting from the near side. The reins are properly gripped in the left hand, which also grips the mane in front of the saddle. When mounting, the rider faces the rear of the horse and the left foot is placed securely in the left stirrup. The right hand grips the saddle horn and the right leg is swung over the saddle. The right leg swing should be close to the saddle, the left toe should not hit the horse, and the left knee should not exert excess pressure on the horse's side. The right foot is then placed in the right stirrup. On cold, frosty mornings or when mounting horses that may buck, the rider can pull the head toward him with his left hand to prevent the horse from bucking until it is mounted. The procedure for dismounting is opposite from the procedure for mounting.

Before the horse is ridden, the stirrups should be properly adjusted for length. Each individual needs a different length of stirrup to maintain the proper position, but a general rule is to adjust the stirrup so that it strikes 1 inch above the ankle bone.

Position

After learning to mount and dismount, the rider's next consideration is position. The rider must have good position to have control of the horse and be able to use the aids. A rider with good position is graceful and relaxed when the horse is in motion. The basic position is usually modified slightly by each rider, and the positions that are popular in the show ring are different in different parts of the country. The American Association for Health, Physical Education and Recreation, Division for Girl's and Women's Sports and the Division for Men's Athletics, has prepared a description of the basic position. Their description lists 4 elements of good position. Good position allows unity of horse and rider, is nonabusive to the horse, ensures security for the rider, and permits the effective use of aids or controls. Proper riding position is shown in Figure 21-25. The ankles are flexed, the toes turned outward approximately 30 degrees. When the ankles are flexed so that the heels are down, the ankles are able to act as shock absorbers. The weight of the body is dropped into the heels and the inside area of the ball of the foot is slightly lower. With a good position that allows the rider to be balanced, the ball of the foot rests on the stirrup treads and the inside of the ball of the foot is lower than the outside (Figure 21-26). This foot position, with the toes turned out slightly, keeps the inner side of the calf in close contact with the saddle fender for good frictional grip. To aid in shock absorption, the ankles are flexed so that the

FIGURE 21-25
Basic position for western riding. From Shannon. 1970.

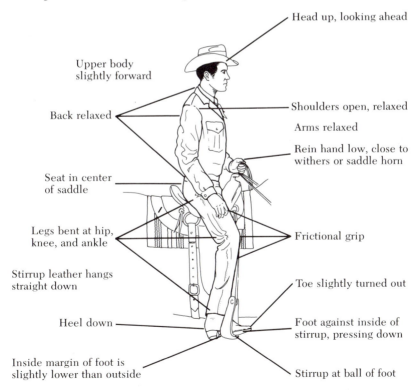

663

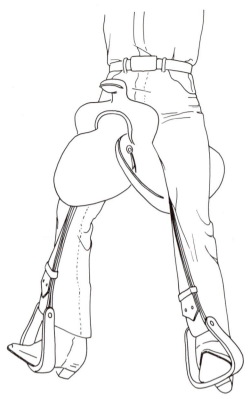

FIGURE 21-26
Frictional grip: thighs, knees, and calves held in contact with horse by weight flowing into heels. The rider's weight is supported by the crotch and seat bones. The inner surface of the thigh is held flat against the saddle and the knee and lower thigh are positioned against the fender of the saddle barrel of the horse. The inner surface of the upper calf is in contact with the barrel of the horse; the lower part of the leg does not grip the horse. The lower leg is used to give signals to the horse to indicate the movements the rider desires. The ball of the foot is positioned in the stirrup in such a way that the inside margin is lower than the outside margin, and the foot is positioned against the inner curve of the stirrup. From Shannon. 1970.

heels are dropped downward. Because the body weight is carried in the heels, the stability of the lower leg is increased. The position of the lower leg is completed by keeping the inside of the calf in contact with the saddle so that the leg from the knee down allows the stirrup to hang vertically. The lower leg can thus be used efficiently and effectively to give signals to the horse.

One of the most common mistakes of beginning riders is to keep a stiff ankle. The concussion, rather than being absorbed by the ankle, is transferred upward and the rider bounces in the saddle. Bouncing around on the saddle is irritating and tiring to the horse as well as to the rider. The knee is flexed to help absorb concussion and aids in slightly gripping the saddle. The inner surface of the thigh is kept flat against the saddle to complete the leg-gripping action.

If the rider is to keep his balance with the horse, the hip joints should be relaxed and mobile. Relaxed and mobile hip joints allow the upper part of the body to make adjustments for changes in speed and direction of travel. Three-point contact should be maintained between the rider's seat and saddle (that is, between the 2 seat bones and the crotch).

The back is kept straight except for a slight arch in the small of the back. The upper body is inclined slightly forward to maintain balance and to align with the horse's center of gravity. The shoulders should be kept open and even. The rider's head is held erect and he looks straight forward.

The left arm is allowed to drop in a natural position adjacent to the body. The left hand holds the reins (Figure 21-27) just above the saddle horn. Wrist and finger motion and carriage are important to obtain proper response from the horse. The wrist is held straight but relaxed. To feel the horse's mouth, the fingers must be kept relaxed and "soft." A rider's lack of self confidence or nervousness is quickly transmitted to the horse via a rider's hands. The style of holding the reins varies from locality to locality and under different conditions. Some of the styles are shown in Figure 21-27.

The right arm is carried in a relaxed position, and can rest on the thigh or be used to hold the romal (Figure 21-28).

As the speed of the horse increases, the frictional grip of the thighs, knees, and calves is increased and the upper body is inclined forward to maintain balance. If the upper body gets behind the center of gravity of the horse, and more weight is not shifted into the lower leg, the rider's balance, control of the horse, and effective and efficient use of the aids are lost. Most riders also feel that, with speed, it is easier to carry the free forearm parallel to the belt.

FIGURE 21-27
Proper way to hold reins during western riding. From Shannon. 1970.

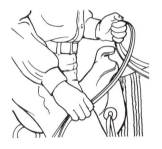

Free hand holding split
ends of reins or romal.

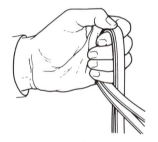

Reins in one hand.

Reins in one hand passing
down through the thumb and
index finger.

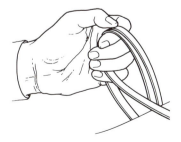

Reins in one hand separated
by the little finger.

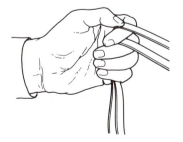

Reins separated by the
index finger.

Free hand holding
split reins or romal
(juniors).

Free hand on thigh.

Free hand at belt.

FIGURE 21-28
Positions for free hand during western riding. From Shannon. 1970.

21.5 Forward Riding

Mounting

The sequence of mounting the horse for forward riding is shown in Figure 21-29. The reins are addressed and then held with the bight on the right side. As the rider stands facing the rear of the horse and just forward of his shoulder, the left hand is held on the withers. The right hand is used to position the left foot in the stirrup. After positioning the stirrup, the offside of the cantle is gripped with the right hand. To aid in obtaining momentum to swing up, one or two hops may be taken on the right foot. The right leg is swung over the horse's hips and the rider eases into the seat. The right foot is positioned in the stirrup. In general, dismounting is a reversal of mounting. After the right leg is swung over the horse's hips, the rider may step down or slide down, depending upon the size of the rider and the horse.

Position

The basic position (Figure 21-29) has been described as follows by George H. Morris, former United States Equestrian Team member. The ball of the foot is placed in the middle of the stirrup with the heel down and just behind the girth. When the toe is turned out (to a maximum of 15 degrees), the calf and inner knee bones establish equal contact with the horse. Thighs grip the saddle with the same pressure as the calves and knees. The seat is placed forward in the saddle as close to the pommel as possible and as far from the cantle as possible. The upper body is carried erect but relaxed. A plumb line will fall from the rider's ear, to his shoulder down through the hip bone to the back of the heel. The head should be carried so that the rider is looking directly ahead. Shoulders are not carried forward or backward. Hands are positioned so that there is a direct line between the rider's elbow and the horse's mouth. "Flexible" hands should be above and slightly in front of the withers. The thumbs are 2 or 3 inches apart and are just inside a vertical line drawn through the hand. Wrists are kept as straight as possible. The correct position of the reins is illustrated in Figure 21-30.

When the horse is in motion, the rider's body is farther forward so that the center of gravity is shifted forward. This allows the rider to be with the motion of the horse. The faster the motion, the farther forward the body is shifted.

21.6 Tack Care

Tack is expensive and requires adequate care if it is to have a long and useful life. By spending a few minutes after each ride, tack can be kept in excellent condition. Leather can be kept soft, pliable, and strong. Soft, pliable leather is comfortable to the horse as well as to the rider.

Cleaning

Daily cleaning of tack that is exposed to sweat, moisture, and dirt will prolong its usefulness. Leather tack can be cleaned with saddle soap. Bits can be cleaned with a damp cloth. If a bit is removed from a sick horse, it should be boiled in water before it is used again. This will help prevent the spread of disease. Daily cleaning also allows an opportunity to inspect the tack for damage and excessive wear.

Every 3–6 months, all tack should be stripped, thoroughly cleaned with saddle soap, and preserved with pure neats-foot oil. There are commercial preparations that combine neats-foot oil with other compounds to form an excellent preservative and waterproofing compound. During these 2–4 cleanings each year, all of the tack components should be given a thorough safety inspection. The sheepskin of western saddles should be cleaned with a brush. Dirty and lumpy sheepskin will cause saddle sores.

Excessive dirt can be removed from tack by soaking in warm water and

FIGURE 21-29

English equitation: mounting, correct seat, and dismounting. *a*, Preparing to lead. *b*, Standing at horse's head. *c*, Mounting, first step. *d*, Mounting, second step.

e, Positioning right foot. *f*, Addressing the reins. *g*, Position of hands. *h*, Basic position in saddle. *i*, Ready to ride. *j*, Preparation to dismount. *k*, Dismounting. *l*, Stepping down. From Bradley and Hardwicke. 1971.

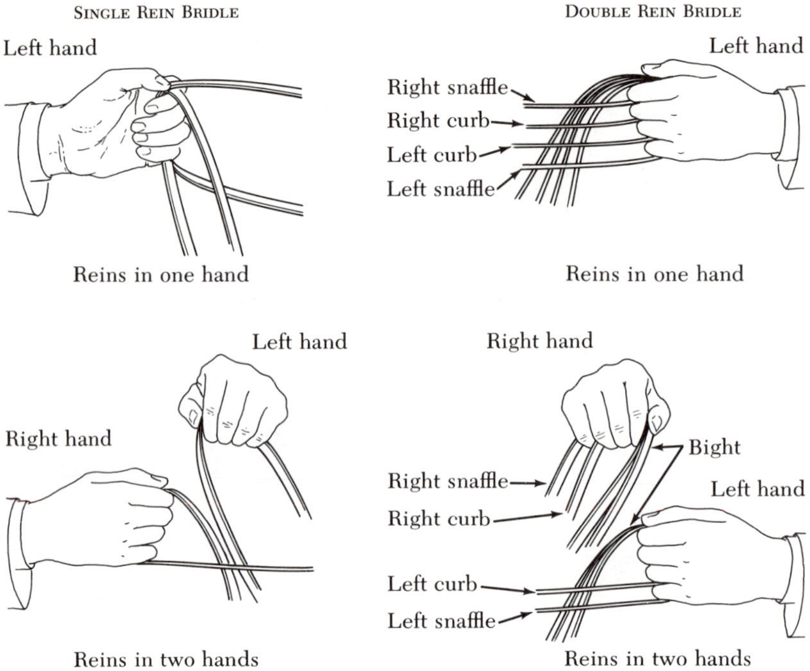

Single Rein Bridle
Double Rein Bridle
Left hand
Left hand
Right snaffle
Right curb
Left curb
Left snaffle
Reins in one hand
Reins in one hand
Left hand
Right hand
Right hand
Bight
Right snaffle
Left hand
Right curb
Left curb
Left snaffle
Reins in two hands
Reins in two hands

FIGURE 21-30
Methods of holding the reins for forward-style riding.

castile soap. After the dirt is soft, it can be removed with a stiff brush. The leather should be allowed to partially dry in the sun, but while still damp, it should be wiped with neats-foot oil. Usually 2 or 3 coats of neats-foot oil are needed to restore it to a useable condition. Old, dried, and cracked leather can be rejuvenated by applying warm neats-foot oil at least once a day over a period of several days.

Saddle pads and blankets should be cleaned with a brush after drying. Dirty blankets are frequent causes of saddle sores. The new synthetic pads are machine washable and are easy to keep clean.

Storage

Tack should be stored in a dry room because moisture and mildew cause rapid deterioration. To keep tack clean, the room should be free from dust, or a dust cover can be placed on the saddle. The room should be free of rodents and insects. Rodents chew on tack to obtain salt and can ruin a lot of tack in a short time.

Saddles are stored on saddle racks to prevent the tree from being damaged and to keep the sheepskin clean. The cinch straps and cinch should be placed across the seat or hung from the saddle horn. English saddles are stored on a rack with the irons slid up the stirrup leathers next to the saddle flap. The girth is placed over the seat so that the saddle is ready to be placed on a horse.

It is important to hang the bridle over a round rack that is approximately 4 inches in diameter and similar to a coffee can, to keep the headstall in the proper shape. Bridles and reins that are hung over nails tend to crack and develop a weak spot. Bits that are not made of stainless steel can be prevented from rusting with Vaseline. Other types of oils leave a bad taste in the horse's mouth even after they are wiped off.

21.7 Horse Safety

The importance of observing safety precautions when in the presence of a horse cannot be stressed enough. When horsemen become overconfident around a horse and fail to observe safety procedures, they usually receive an injury "sooner or later." The Extension Service of the United States Department of Agriculture, in cooperation with the National Horse and Pony Youth Activities Council, The American Horse Council, and the National Safety Council, has published the following horse safety guidelines.

Approaching

A horse's vision is restricted directly in front and to the rear, but its hearing is acute. Always speak to a horse as you are approaching it. Failure to do so may startle the horse and incite it to kick.

Always approach the horse at an angle, never directly from the front or rear. This is possible even in single stalls or other confined areas.

Pet a horse by first placing a hand on its shoulder or neck. The touch should be a rubbing action. Do not "dab" at the end of a horse's nose.

Always stay out of kicking range when walking around a horse. Never walk under or step over the tie rope.

Handling

A person's actions around a horse reflect his ability and confidence in handling a horse.

While working around horses, stay close to the horse so that if it kicks, the full impact is not received. Stay out of kicking range whenever possible. When necessary to go to the opposite side of a horse, move away and go around it out of kicking range.

Know the horse, its temperament, and its reactions. The horseman must

671

control his temper at all times, but he must let the horse know that he is its firm and kind master.

The good horseman always lets a horse know what he intends to do. When picking up the horse's feet, for example, do not grab the foot hurriedly. This will startle the horse and may cause it to kick. Learn the proper way to lift the feet.

Learn and use simple methods of restraint.

Tying or holding the head is the safest method when working around a horse.

Work around a horse from a position as near the shoulder as possible.

Never stand directly behind a horse to work with its tail. Stand off to the side, near the point of the buttock, facing to the rear. Grasp the tail and draw it around to you.

Be calm and confident around horses. A nervous handler will have a nervous, unsafe horse.

A good horseman keeps his balance at all times. An accidental slip or stumble can result in unintentional injury by the horse.

Do not drop grooming tools underfoot while grooming. Place them where they will not cause you to trip and where the horse will not step on them.

Know the horse's peculiarities. If someone who is unfamiliar with a horse is riding it, they should ask what to expect from the horse.

Teasing a horse may cause it to develop dangerous habits for the rest of its life. If so, the public safety is in serious jeopardy.

If a horse must be punished, do so only at the instant of its disobedience. If you wait, even for a minute, the horse will not understand why it is being punished. Punish without anger, lest the punishment be too severe. Never strike a horse around its head.

It is not safe to leave a halter on a loose horse. When necessary to do so, the halter should be checked daily. Some halter materials will shrink, so be certain to check the fit. There is a possibility that the horse may catch a foot in the halter strap. A halter might catch on posts or other objects.

Most horsemen wear footgear that protect their feet from being stepped on and from being injured by nails and other small objects around the stables and barnyard. Boots or hard-toed shoes are preferable. Never wear tennis shoes or moccasins or go barefooted.

Leading

The horse should walk beside the horseman when it is led. It should not run ahead or lag behind. A position that is even with the horse's head or halfway between the horse's head and its shoulder is considered safest. Always turn the horse to the right and walk with it.

Use a long lead strap, with the excess strap folded in a figure eight style in your left hand, when leading. It is customary to lead from the left (near) side, using the right hand to hold the lead near the halter. The right elbow should be extended slightly toward the horse. If the horse makes contact with the person leading it, the horse's shoulder will hit the horseman's elbow first and move him away from it. The elbow can also be used in the horse's neck to keep the head and neck straight for control, as well as to prevent the horse from crowding.

A horse should be trained to be workable from both sides, even for dismounting and mounting.

A horse is larger and stronger than a person. If it resists, do not get in front and try to pull.

Never wrap the lead strap, halter shank, or reins around a hand, wrist, or body. A knot at the end of the lead shank aids in maintaining a secure grip when needed for control.

When leading, tying, or untying a horse, avoid getting hands or fingers entangled. Use caution to prevent catching a finger in dangerous positions in halter and bridle hardware, including snaps, bits, rings, and loops.

Be extremely cautious when leading a horse through narrow openings, such as a door. Be certain of firm control and step through first. Step through quickly and get to one side to avoid being crowded.

Any time you dismount or lead the horse, the stirrup irons on an English saddle should be run up, or "dressed." Also, be cautious that the stirrups do not catch on objects when using a western saddle.

Use judgment when turning a horse loose. It is generally safest to lead completely through the gate or door and turn the horse around, facing the direction of entry. Then release the lead strap or remove the halter or bridle. Make the horse stand quietly while it is rubbed at the sweaty spot on the poll where the crown piece has rested. Avoid letting a horse bolt away when released. Good habits prevent accidents.

To prevent becoming accidentally entangled, do not use excessively long lead ropes. Watch the coils when using lariats or longe lines.

Tying

Know and use the proper knots for tying and restraining a horse.

Tie the horse far enough away from strange horses so that they cannot fight.

Always untie the horse before removing the halter.

Avoid using excessively long lead ropes in order to prevent becoming accidentally entangled. When using lariats or longe lines, watch the coils.

Always tie a horse in a place that is safe for it and for other people. Use the halter rope—not the bridle reins.

673

Tie the horse a safe distance from other horses and from tree limbs or brush where the horse may become entangled.

Be certain to tie the horse to something strong and secure to avoid danger that the rope may break or come loose if the horse pulls back. Always tie at a level above the horse's withers.

Bridling

The horseman's head must be protected from the horse's head when bridling. Stand in close just behind and to one side (preferably on the left side) of the horse's head. Use caution when handling the horse's ears.

Maintain control of the horse when bridling by refastening the halter around the neck.

Be certain the bridle is adjusted to fit the horse before it is ridden. Three points to check are the placement of the bit, the adjustment of the curb strap, and the adjustment of the throatlatch.

Saddling

Check the saddle blanket and all other equipment for foreign objects. Be certain the horse's back and the cinch or girth areas are clean.

When using a double-rigged western saddle, remember to fasten the front cinch first and the rear cinch last when saddling. Unfasten the rear cinch first and the front cinch last when unsaddling. Be certain that the strap connecting the front and back cinches (along the horse's belly) is secure.

Fasten accessory straps (tie-downs, breast collars, martingales, and so on) after the saddle is cinched on. Unfasten them first before loosening the cinch.

When using English equipment, it is sometimes necessary to thread the girth through the martingale loop before the girth is secured.

The back cinch should not be so loose that the horse can get a hind leg caught between the cinch and its belly.

When saddling, it is safest to keep the off-cinches and stirrup secured over the saddle seats and ease them down when the saddle is on. Do not let them swing wide and hit the horse on the off-knee or belly—this hurts the horse and causes him to shy.

Swing the western saddle into position easily, not suddenly. Dropping the saddle down too quickly or hard may scare the horse. An English saddle is much lighter than a stock saddle. You do not need to, and should not, swing the saddle into position. Lift it and place it into position.

Pull up slowly to tighten the cinch. Check the cinch three times: (1) after

674

saddling; (2) after walking a few steps (untracking); and (3) after mounting and riding a short distance.

Mounting and Dismounting

Never mount or dismount a horse in a barn or near fences, trees, or over-hanging projections. Side-stepping and rearing mounts have injured riders who failed to take these precautions.

A horse should stand quietly for mounting and dismounting. To be certain of this, you must have light control of its head through the reins.

Using English Equipment

Immediately upon dismounting, the rider should "run-up" the stirrups. The dangling stirrup may startle or annoy the horse. It is possible for the horse to catch a cheek of the bit or even a hind foot in a dangling stirrup iron when it is fighting flies. The dangling stirrup can also catch on doorways and other projections while you are leading the horse.

After running-up the stirrups, immediately bring the reins forward over the horse's head. In this position they can be used for leading.

Using Western Equipment

Closed reins or a romal should be brought forward over the horse's head after dismounting.

Riding

Keep the horse under control and maintain a secure seat at all times. Horses are easily frightened by unusual objects and noises.

Until the horseman knows his horse, riding should be confined to an arena or other enclosed area. Riders should ride in open spaces or un-confined areas only after they are familiar with their horse.

If a horse becomes frightened, remain calm, speak to it quietly, steady it, and give it time to overcome its fear. Then ride or lead the horse past the obstacle.

Hold the horse to a walk when going up or down a hill.

Allow a horse to pick its way at a walk when riding on rough ground, or in sand, mud, ice, or snow where there is danger of slipping or falling.

675

Do not fool around. Horseplay is dangerous.

Be cautious when riding bareback.

Always bridle the horse — riding with just a halter does not give control.

Use judgment when riding in pairs or in groups. Be certain there is sufficient space.

Select a location with care. Choose controlled bridle paths or familiar, safe open areas. Try to avoid paved or other hard-surfaced roads. Walk the horse when crossing such roads.

In heavy traffic, it is safest to dismount and lead across.

If necessary to ride on roads or highways, ride on the side required by law. State laws vary as to which side of the road you should ride on. Ride on the shoulders of roads or in ditches, but watch for junk. Riding at night can be a pleasure, but must be recognized as being more hazardous than daytime riding. Walk the horse; fast gaits are dangerous. Wear light-colored clothing and carry a flashlight and reflectors when riding at night. Check your state's regulations for details.

Never rush past riders who are proceeding at a slower gait, because to do so startles both horses and riders, and often causes accidents. Instead, approach slowly, indicate a desire to pass, and proceed cautiously on the left side.

Never ride off until all riders in a group are mounted.

Ride abreast or stay a full horse's length from the horse in front to avoid the possibility of a rider being kicked, or the rider's horse being kicked.

Walk the horse when approaching and going through underpasses and over bridges.

When the horse is full of energy, exercise it on a longe line or ride it in an enclosed area until it is settled.

Do not let a horse run to and from the stables. Walk the horse the last mile home.

Know the proper use of and the purpose of spurs before wearing them. Dogs and horses are not always good companions. If you have a dog, keep it under control at all times around horses.

Wear protective headgear appropriate to the activity in which you are engaged, especially in any form of jumping.

Trail Riding

If you plan to ride alone, tell someone where you are going and approximately when you expect to return.

Ride a well-mannered horse.

Do not play practical jokes or indulge in horseplay.

Watch where the horse is traveling — avoid dangerous ground. Note landmarks. The rider should study the country and view behind himself so he will know how it looks.

Courtesy is the best safety on the trail.

Think of the horse first. Watch its condition, avoid injuries, and care for it properly.

Carry a good pocket knife to cut ropes and so on, in the event of entanglement.

Do not tie the reins together.

Ride balanced and erect to avoid tiring the horse and creating sore backs and legs.

Check the equipment:

1. Have a halter and rope. Hobbles are fine if the horse is accustomed to them.

2. Have clean saddle blankets or pads.

3. Be certain that the equipment is in good repair and fits the horse.

4. Include bad-weather clothing.

5. A pair of wire cutters is handy to use should the horse become entangled in wire.

6. A lariat is handy for many needs, but know how to use one and be certain the horse is accustomed to a rope.

7. Extras should include pieces of leather or rawhide for repairs, a few spare horseshoe nails, and a few matches.

If the horse is unsaddled, store the gear properly and place the saddle blanket where it will dry.

Keep the gear covered overnight.

Do not water a horse when it is hot. Cool it first.

Always tie a horse in a safe place. Use the halter rope—not the bridle reins.

Tie the horse a safe distance from other horses and from tree limbs or brush where the horse may become entangled.

Never tie below the level of the horse's withers. Be certain to tie the horse to an object that is strong and secure to avoid the danger that the rope may break or come loose if the horse pulls back.

Be extremely cautious of cigarettes, matches, and fires. Make sure they are out before discarding them or leaving the area.

Obtain current, accurate maps and information on the area. Become familiar with the terrain and climate.

When riding on federal or state lands, seek advice from the forest or park officials. Know their rules concerning use of the trails and their fire regulations.

Be certain the horse is in good physical condition and that its hooves and shoes are ready for the trail.

Use extreme caution at wet spots or boggy places.

Speed on the trail is unsafe. Ride at safe gaits.

Avoid overhanging limbs. Warn the rider behind you if you encounter one. Watch the rider ahead so that a limb pushed aside does not snap back and slap the next horse in the face.

Equipment and Clothing

Learn to handle a rope before carrying one on a horse. Always use caution when working with a rope if the horse is not "rope-broken." Never tie the rope "hard and fast" to a saddle horn while roping from a "green" horse.

Bridle reins, stirrup leathers, headstalls, curb straps, and cinch straps should be kept in the best possible condition; the rider's safety depends on these straps. Replace any of the straps when they begin to show signs of wear (cracking or checking).

Be sure all tack fits the horse. Adjust the tie-downs and similar equipment to a safe length that will not hinder the horse's balance.

Spurs can trip the person wearing them when he is working on the ground. Take them off when not mounted.

Wear neat, well-fitted clothing that will not snag on equipment. Belts, jackets, and front chap straps can become hooked over the saddle horn.

Wear boots or shoes with heels to keep the foot from slipping through the stirrup.

Keep the horse's feet properly trimmed and/or shod.

Infectious organisms such as tetanus are prevalent around barns, corrals, and fences. Gloves are a safeguard against cuts, scratches, splinters, and rope burns.

Trailering or Other Hauling

Loading a horse on a trailer should be done by two persons if possible.

Always stand to one side, never directly behind, when loading or unloading a horse from a trailer or truck.

The circumstances of loading a horse vary, but the following methods are given in order of preference.

Train the horse so that it can be sent into the trailer.

When loading a two-horse trailer, the handler leads the horse into the left side while he enters the trailer on the right side of the center divider, or vice versa.

It is least desirable to get in front and lead the horse in. Never do this if there is no escape door or front exit. Even if there is a door, use caution — most are awkward to get through; also, horses have been known to follow the handler out.

678   Be certain that the ground area behind and around the truck or trailer affords safe footing before loading or unloading.

It is safest to remove all equipment (such as bridles and saddles) before loading. Use a halter.

Always speak before handling a horse in a truck or trailer.

If you have trouble loading or unloading, get experienced help.

Secure the butt bar or chain before tying the horse. Use care when reaching for it. Ease it down after it is unfastened to avoid bumping the horse's legs.

When unloading, always untie a horse before opening the gate or door.

Avoid slick trailer floors. Use matting or some type of bedding for secure footing.

Check your trailer regularly for (1) rotting or weakened floor boards; (2) rusted and weakened door hinges; (3) broken hitch welds; (4) worn or broken spring shackles and wheel bearings. Have a competent mechanic check these when the trailer is serviced.

Make sure the trailer is properly constructed. You may need to ask an expert about this.

Be certain the trailer meets state requirements for brakes and lights.

The trailer should be high enough to give a horse ample neck and head room. Remove or cover any protruding objects.

When driving always:

1. Double-check all connections (lights, brakes, hitch, and safety chains).

2. Be certain that all doors are closed and secured.

3. Drive carefully. Make turns slowly. Start and stop slowly and steadily.

4. Look far ahead to avoid emergencies. Drive in a defensive manner.

When hauling a stallion with other horses, it is safer to load the stallion first and to unload it last.

Distribute the weight of the load evenly. When hauling one horse, the safest method is to load it on the left side of the trailer.

Never throw lighted cigarettes or matches from a car or truck window. You might start a fire in the area or the wind might suck them into the trailer.

Check the horse and trailer hitch at every stop.

Opinions vary on whether a horse should be hauled tied or loose. If you tie, allow sufficient length of rope so the horse can move its head for balance. Use a safety release or a quick-release knot.

If hauling in a truck or other open carrier, protect the horse's eyes from wind and foreign objects by using goggles or some type of wind shield.

Horses are like people—some get sick from motion. Adjust the feeding schedule to avoid traveling when the horse is full of feed and water. Feed smaller amounts more often if necessary.

679

References

Abby, H. C. 1970. *Show Your Horse.* New York: A. S. Barnes.

Bauer, J. J. *Riding for Rehabilitation.* Toronto: Canadian Stage and Arts Publications.

Bradley, M. 1973. *Intermediate Trail Riding.* Science and Technology Guide 2883. Columbia: University of Missouri Cooperative Extension.

Bradley, M. 1973. *Western Equitation: Mounting, Correct Seat, Dismounting.* Science and Technology Guide 2876. Columbia: University of Missouri Cooperative Extension.

Bradley, M., and S. D. Hardwicke. 1971. *English Equitation: Mounting, Correct Seat, Dismounting.* Science and Technology Guide 2875. Columbia: University of Missouri Cooperative Extension.

Chamberlain, H. D. 1937. *Training Hunters, Jumpers, and Hacks.* New York: Surrydale Press.

Davis, J. A. *The Reins of Life.* Plant City, Florida: Ken Kimbal Horse Books.

deRomasskan, G. 1964. *Fundamentals of Riding.* New York: Doubleday.

deRomasskan, G. 1968. *Riding Problems.* Brattleboro, Vermont: Stephen Greene Press.

Dillon, J. 1960. *A School for Young Riders.* New York: ARCO.

Dillon, J. 1961. *Form over Fences.* New York: ARCO.

duPont, J. 1973. From Egg Butt to Billet Strap. *The Quarter Horse Journal* 25:84.

Edwards, R. H. 1965. *Saddlery.* New York: A. S. Barnes.

Ensminger, M. E. 1972. *Breeding and Raising Horses.* United States Department of Agriculture Handbook No. 394. Washington, D.C.: Agricultural Research Service.

Felton, S. W. 1967. *The Literature of Equitation.* London: J. A. Allen.

Ferguson, B. 1971. An Explanation of the Aids as Used at the Walk, Trot, and Canter. *The Morgan Horse* 31:32.

Forbes, J. 1972. *So Your Kids Want a Pony.* Battleboro, Vermont: Stephen Greene Press.

Foreman, M. *Horse Handling Science.* Vols. 1, 2, and 3. Fort Worth, Texas: Horse Handling Science, P. O. Box 9371.

Gianoli, L. 1969. *Horses and Horsemanship Through the Ages.* New York: Crown.

Gorman, J. A. 1967. *The Western Horse: Its Types and Training.* Danville, Illinois: The Interstate Printers & Publishers, Inc.

Hyland, A. 1971. *Beginner's Guide to Western Riding*. London: Pelham Books.

Jones, S. N. 1966. *The Art of Western Riding*. Portales, New Mexico: Bishop Printing and Litho Co.

Kiser, J. J. 1972. *What the Judge Looks for in Equitation Classes*. Science and Technology Guide 2838. Columbia: University of Missouri Cooperative Extension.

Kulesza, S. 1965. *Modern Riding*. New York: A. S. Barnes.

Levings, N. P. 1968. *Training the Quarter Horse Jumper*. New York: A. S. Barnes.

Littauer, V. S. 1973. *How the Horse Jumps*. London: J. A. Allen.

Littauer, V. S. 1967. *The Development of Modern Riding*. London: J. A. Allen.

Littauer, V. S. 1963. *Common Sense Horsemanship*. Rev. ed. New York: ARCO.

Littauer, V. S. 1956. *Schooling Your Horse*. New York: ARCO.

Mason, B. S. 1940. *Roping*. New York: Ronald Press.

McCowan, L. L. *It is Ability that Counts*. Augusta, Michigan: Cheff Center for the Handicapped. Rural Route 1, P. O. Box 171.

Morris, G. 1971. *Hunter Seat Equitation*. New York: Doubleday.

Powell, M. D. 1970. Who owns horses? *Arabian Horse World* 11:66.

Santini, P. 1967. *The Caprilli Papers*. London: J. A. Allen.

Saunders, G. C. 1966. *Your Horse*. Rev. ed. New York: Van Nostrand Reinhold.

Shannon, E. 1970. *Manual for Teaching Western Riding*. Washington, D.C.: American Association for Health, Physical Education, and Recreation.

Stoneridge, M. A. 1968. *A Horse of Your Own*. New York: Doubleday.

Trench, C. C. 1970. *A History of Horsemanship*. Norwich, England: Jarrold and Sons.

Tuke, D. 1965. *Bit by Bit*. New York: A. S. Barnes.

Williamson, C. O. 1965. *Breaking and Training for Stock Horses*. 5th ed. Hamilton, Nebraska: Williamson School of Horsemanship, P. O. Box 506.

Wright, G. 1966. *Learning to Ride, Hunt and Show*. New York: Doubleday.

Yeates, B. V., and M. Bradley. 1972. *Pre-Bit Hackamore Training*. Science and Technology Guide 2864. Columbia: University of Missouri Cooperative Extension.

Young, J. R. 1954. *The Schooling of the Western Horse*. Norman: University of Oklahoma Press.

No author. 1973. About bits. *Practical Horseman*. pp. 30–33, 50–51.

No author. 1969. Tree Talk. *Appaloosa News*. 26:8–9.

CHAPTER TWENTY-TWO *Anatomy and Care of the Foot*

If the horseman is to obtain maximum performance and prolong the useful life of a horse, it is essential that he understand the anatomy, physiology, and care of the horse's feet.

22.1 *Anatomy and Physiology*

Anatomy

The external structures of the foot are illustrated in Figure 22-1, and the internal structures are illustrated in Figure 22-2.

Hoof Wall and Laminae. The bulk of the hoof wall is composed of epithelia cells that have been keratinized. The cells are arranged in tubules that run perpendicular to the ground surface. This part of the hoof wall also contains the pigment. The outer surface of the wall is covered by the periople and the stratum tectorium. The periople extends below the coronary band for approximately three-quarters of an inch. At the heels, it covers the bulbs. The stratum tectorium covers the rest of the hoof wall and helps to protect the wall from moisture evaporation. Removal of the stratum tectorium with the rasp during trimming or shoeing of the hoof should be avoided.

The inner layer of the hoof wall is the insensitive laminar layer. The insensitive laminar layer intermeshes with the sensitive laminae. The sensitive laminae are attached to the top surface of the third phalanx. Therefore, the weight of the horse is not exerted on the sole surface, but is borne by the hoof wall. The third phalanx (major bone in the foot) is suspended from

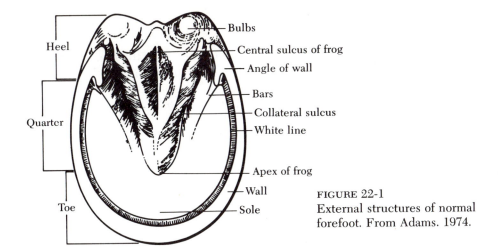

Heel

Quarter

Toe

Bulbs

Central sulcus of frog

Angle of wall

Bars

Collateral sulcus

White line

Apex of frog

Wall

Sole

FIGURE 22-1
External structures of normal
forefoot. From Adams. 1974.

FIGURE 22-2
Sagittal section of digit and distal part of metacarpus of horse. *a*, metacarpal bone;
b, first phalanx; *c*, second phalanx; *d*, third phalanx; *e*, distal sesamoid bone.
1, volar pouch of capsule of fetlock joint; 2, intersesamoidean ligament;
3,4, proximal end of digital synovial sheath; 5, ring formed by superficial flexor
tendon; 6, fibrous tissue underlying ergot; 7, ergot; 8,9, branches of digital
vessels; 10, distal ligament of distal sesamoid bone; 11, suspensory ligament of
distal sesamoid bone; 12, proximal end of navicular bursa; 12', distal end of
navicular bursa. The superficial flexor tendon (*behind 4*) is not shown. From Sisson
and Grossman. 1953.

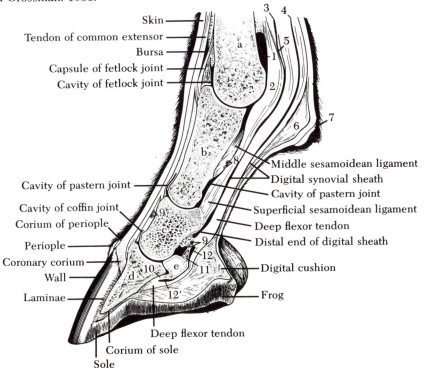

Skin

Tendon of common extensor

Bursa

Capsule of fetlock joint

Cavity of fetlock joint

Cavity of pastern joint

Cavity of coffin joint

Corium of periople

Periople

Coronary corium

Wall

Laminae

Deep flexor tendon

Corium of sole

Sole

Middle sesamoidean ligament

Digital synovial sheath

Cavity of pastern joint

Superficial sesamoidean ligament

Deep flexor tendon

Distal end of digital sheath

Digital cushion

Frog

683

the inside of the hoof wall. The hoof wall is thickest at the toe. At the angle of the wall, the wall is reflected forward to form the bars of the foot. The bars serve as a brace structure to prevent overexpansion of the hoof wall. The white line separates the hoof wall from the sole.

Sole. The composition of the sole is similar to that of the hoof wall. The sole tubules curl near the ground in such a way that after they curl, the ground surface part is dead. This is the reason for the self-limiting growth of the sole. The sole is concave on the ground surface.

Frog. The frog is the elastic, wedge-shaped mass that occupies the area between the bars. The bottom surface is marked by a depression called the central sulcus or cleft. Internally, the frog stay is formed as a result of the wedge shape. The point of the frog toward the toe is referred to as the apex.

Coriums. There are five coriums of modified vascular tissue that furnish nutrition to the hoof. The perioplic corium lies within the perioplic groove in the coronary band and serves the periople. The coronary corium, responsible for the growth and nutrition of the bulk of the hoof wall, lies within the coronary band. Because the coronary band is responsible for wall growth, injury to the coronary band is quite serious and usually leads to a defect in wall growth and structure. The laminar corium is attached to the top of the third phalanx and bears the insensitive laminae. Consequently, it transports the blood supply and nutrition to the sensitive and insensitive laminae as well as to the white line. The sole corium, on the lower surface of the third phalanx, nourishes the sole. The frog is nourished by the frog corium.

Digital Cushion. The back half of the foot contains the digital, or plantar cushion. This fibro-elastic, fatty cushion acts as a shock absorber for the foot.

Bones. Three bones are located in the horse's foot: the second phalanx (or short pastern), the third phalanx (or coffin bone), and the navicular bone. The third phalanx is located mainly to the front of the hoof and slightly to the outer side of the hoof. It is the largest bone in the foot, is quite porous, and resembles a miniature foot in shape. The second phalanx is partly in the hoof and partly above it. The navicular bone is the smallest bone of the foot and serves to increase the articulatory surface and movement of the distal interphalangeal (foot or coffin) joint.

Lateral Cartilage. The lateral cartilages are attached to the wings of the third phalanx (Figure 22-2). They rise above the coronary band and extend approximately one-third of the way around each side of the hoof from the heel.

Physiology

The structures of the foot work together to absorb concussion when the foot strikes the ground. As the foot strikes the ground, the heels are expanded by frog action. The frog is pushed upward and, because of its wedge shape, the frog stay forces the digital cushion upward and outward on both sides of the foot. Movement of the digital cushion exerts pressure on the lateral cartilages, which in turn move outward. The lateral cartilages compress the blood veins draining the foot. Compression of the blood veins forces blood toward the heart and also causes blood to pool in the foot. The pooled blood then acts as a hydraulic cushion that absorbs concussion. To aid further in concussion absorption, the third phalanx descends slightly and the sole yields slightly. The laminae also help absorb shock. In addition, the navicular bone helps absorb concussion as a result of its placement in the joint. As the weight is transferred from the second phalanx to the navicular bone, the navicular bone yields slightly before the weight is transferred to the third phalanx. The deep flexor tendon supports the navicular bone. The remainder of the concussion is absorbed at the pasterns, knee, and shoulder.

The shape of the hind foot is slightly different from that of the forefoot. The toe of the hind foot is more pointed and the sole is more concave.

22.2   Hoof Care

Proper foot care is one of the most important aspects of horsemanship. Lameness of the feet and legs is the cause of most incapacitations of horses. Neglect of a horse's feet can lead to lameness and improper foot action, and good foot care can hasten recovery from lameness or prevent it from occurring.

Cleaning

Horses that are kept in confinement—in stalls and small paddocks—should have their feet cleaned daily. A hoof pick is used to clean out the dirt and debris. The pick should be run from the heels toward the toe. If the pick is being run the opposite way and the horse jerks its foot away from you, it may bruise or puncture the frog or sole when the foot strikes the ground. The cleft and commissures of the frog should be carefully cleaned. Failure to clean these areas thoroughly is one of the main causes of thrush.

685

Daily Inspection

After the feet are clean, they should be inspected for rocks, nails, bruises, loose shoes (if shod), abnormal growth, uneven wear, and hoof condition (that is, cracks, splitting, and inadequate moisture). Rocks and other foreign matter are usually removed during the cleaning process. Close visual inspection may reveal a nail in the foot or a puncture wound. The nail should be removed and the depth of the puncture wound determined. If a veterinarian is not available, the wound should be cleaned out and packed with iodine. If the horse has not had a tetanus toxoid series and yearly boosters, it should be given a tetanus antitoxin shot. Adequate hoof moisture is important because dry hooves tend to contract and lose their physiological function. Moisture, to get into a dry hoof, must travel from the ground surface upward because the fibrous tubules that form the hoof wall and sole run perpendicular to the ground. To provide such moisture, horsemen sometimes allow the water trough to overflow so there is moist ground around the trough. Other means include packing the feet with mud or wet clay or wrapping the feet in wet burlap sacks. To retain the moisture once it is regained or to prevent the evaporation of moisture, a hoof dressing or oil can be applied to the wall, frog, and sole.

Trimming

Mature Horses. The hoof wall grows at the rate of $1/4$ to $1/2$ inch per month. Therefore, the hooves should be trimmed or shod every 6–8 weeks. They may need to be trimmed more frequently if they are growing abnormally fast, such as after founder, or if they show uneven wear. Horses that wear the hoof wall unevenly usually have crooked feet or legs. The uneven wear of the hoof wall accentuates the faulty conformation and way of going. Keeping the hoof wall level will not correct the fault in conformation of mature horses, but it may prevent leg interference. Quite often corrective trimming only requires one side of the hoof wall to be rasped down until it is level with the opposite wall.

The outside wall is worn down at a faster rate than the inside wall of horses that are base-narrow and toe-in or toe-out. Consequently, the inside wall needs to be rasped level with the outside wall. Additional hoof wall should be removed if the wall is too long after it is leveled. Horses that are base-wide and toe-out or toe-in wear the inside wall at a faster rate. If the horse only toes out, the inside wall is worn at a faster rate, and if it toes in, the outside wall is worn at a faster rate.

The toe of the hoof wall grows at a faster rate than the heels. A long toe decreases the expansion of the wall when the hoof strikes the ground. Since the contraction forces in a hoof wall are greater than the expansion forces, the walls start to contract inward. Contracted heels cause excess pressure on the third phalanx and thus pain. Failure to trim the hooves when they become too long leads to contracted heels, faulty gaits, and limb interference. Long toes and low heels inhibit the rolling over of the foot during forward motion and may cause forging, overreaching, and scalping.

Foals.   Many faulty positions of stance or incorrect ways of going in young foals can be helped or corrected by proper trimming of the feet. Corrective trimming of young foals is based on three principles.

First, adequate exercise is important if the foal is to be "straight legged" when it matures. Support muscles increase in size and strength as the body size increases. However, when foals are kept in close confinement, the muscles required for shoulder propulsion and rotation are not used as much as they should be to stimulate normal development. Consequently, these muscles shrink and weaken as the foal grows, allowing the legs to become base-wide. Then, the feet become toed-out and the inside hoof wall is worn off because the foot rolls over the inside wall. To prevent this sequence of events, foals should be kept where they have room to run and play, or they should be vigorously exercised for a few minutes every day.

Second, pressure across the growth plate or epiphysis of the leg bones influences the rate of bone growth. Uneven distribution of pressure across the epiphyseal plate will cause improper bone growth. The objective of corrective trimming of a young foal's feet is to maintain an even distribution of pressure across the epiphysis and, when necessary, to change the distribution of pressure to stimulate and depress bone growth on the appropriate sides of the bone to straighten the leg. In the toe-wide stance, excess pressure is being applied to the lateral (toward the outside) side of the epiphysis and less pressure is applied to the medial (toward the center of the horse) side. Excess pressure decreases and less pressure increases bone growth so that the medial side of the bone grows at a faster rate than the lateral side. Consequently, the condition worsens if the feet are not correctively trimmed.

Third, corrective trimming must begin when the foal is a few days old and the hoof wall is hard enough to trim. All corrections must be accomplished before the epiphyseal plate closes for a particular bone. Radiographic data indicate that the epiphyses of the first and second phalanges are closed at approximately 9 months (Figure 22-3). The epiphysis at the distal end of the cannon bone closes at 9–12 months. Most of the remaining bones' epiphyses are closed at 1–2½ years.

Trimming Procedure.   Trimming the feet requires a minimum set of tools. In addition to the hoof pick, a farrier's knife, rasp, and nippers (Figure 22-4) are required. (These tools are discussed in the next section on horseshoeing equipment.) After the foot is cleaned, the excess dead sole is removed with the hoof knife. It is necessary to remove more sole from the toe area than from the quarter or heel areas. Removal of too much sole, to

687

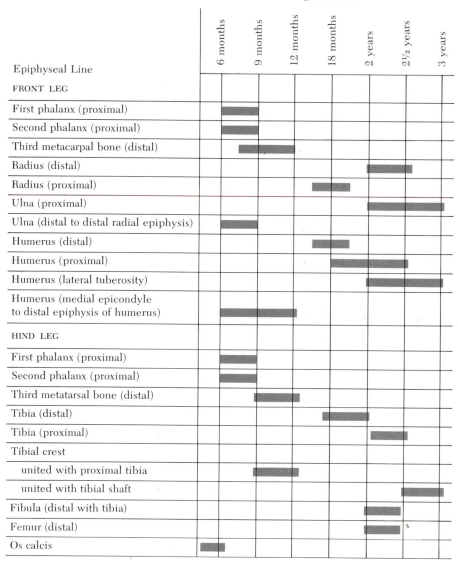

Age of epiphyseal closure based on Quarter Horse and Thoroughbred breeds, both male and female. The age of epiphyseal closure given here is based on radiographic determination, which will be earlier than actual closure determined histologically.

Age during which closure usually takes place.

FIGURE 22-3
Closure of epiphyseal plates. From Adams. 1974.

the thickness where it can be flexed by pressing on it with your thumbs, does not allow sufficient protection for the ground surface. If trimmed too close, the sole is quite sensitive, and stepping on small rocks or dirt clods causes bruises and pain and thus lameness. After sufficient dead sole is removed, the hoof wall is cut with the nippers. The wall should be cut to within ¼ inch of the sole and should never be cut below the level of the sole. The wall is then rasped level with the coarse side of the rasp. After the wall is level, the outside edge of the wall is rounded to prevent splitting and chipping. The frog is taken care of in the same way as when the horse is shod. The proper angle of the hoof wall (50–55 degrees) should be maintained and is best determined by the angle of the shoulder. The angle of the forefeet should be the same as the angle of the shoulder; the angle of the hind feet is usually 2–3 degrees greater.

Shoeing

Horses are shod for various reasons: to increase traction of the feet; to protect the foot from breaking and wearing away at a rate greater than growth of horn when the horse is kept or worked under circumstances that cause excessive wear of the hoof wall; to modify the action of the feet and legs in order to improve the execution of the gaits; and to improve or correct faults in gaits, such as scalping and overreaching. Shoeing has been termed a necessary evil because it does interfere with proper physiological functioning of the foot structure. Also, each nail destroys a number of horn fibers, thus weakening the hoof wall. In order to keep the interference of physiological function and damage to the hoof wall to a minimum, the farrier must have a working knowledge of the anatomy and physiology of the equine leg and foot and must know how to use his tools properly.

Horseshoeing is almost a lost art, but since about 1960 it has been revived as a result of the increase in the light horse population. Proper horseshoeing requires considerable knowledge and manual dexterity. Each horse requires its shoes to be shaped or manufactured and fitted to each foot. The farrier must understand each movement of the feet and legs for the various gaits and how to influence foot and leg movement, and must have a knowledge of the therapeutic shoeing required by the various pathological conditions of the feet and legs. Shoeing is not a simple task that can be acquired during a short training period but requires continuing education by experience.

Equipment and Shoeing Aids. The basic horseshoeing tools are shown in Figure 22-4. The anvil is the farrier's workbench, and is used in many ways to prepare the shoe properly. Normally, the anvil weighs 80–125 pounds. The farrier's anvil has a thinner heel and a longer, more tapered horn than the blacksmith's anvil. The horn may have a chipping block to

689

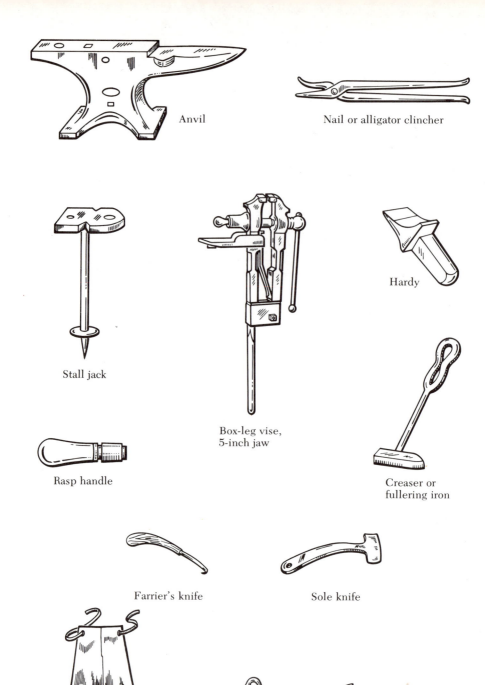

Anvil

Nail or alligator clincher

Stall jack

Box-leg vise,
5-inch jaw

Hardy

Rasp handle

Creaser or
fullering iron

Farrier's knife

Sole knife

Apron

Hoof pick

Clinch cutter

FIGURE 22-4
Horseshoeing tools.

Rounding hammer   Driving hammer

Nipper   Hoof parer   Pincers

Farrier's tong

Divider   Clinch block

Pritchel

Shoeing box

Hoof hook

Shoe spreader

Hoof leveler

691

Tang rasp 14 inches long

draw out clips. The face or flat area has a hole for the hardy and one or two pritchel holes. The hardy is used for cutting hot metals, such as the heels of the shoe. It is also used to cut blank bars to the proper length to be made into shoes. A pritchel is used to expand the nail holes in a shoe or to remove nails that are broken or cut off even with the web of the shoe. The stall jack is a handy tool used by farriers to shape aluminum plates when shoeing racehorses so that the foot does not have to be put down during the shoeing process.

The leather apron (Figure 22-4) protects the farrier against nail cuts and against heat when he is working at the forge. The tie strings of the apron should be long enough to be crossed behind and tucked under at the sides. When secured in this manner, the farrier may quickly free himself by pulling on the strings if a horse hooks a nail in the apron and starts kicking. Many farriers sew a pocket on the apron to hold the hoof knife where it can be reached and to keep the blade from being damaged. The hoof knife, or farrier's knife, is used for removing dead sole scales, "tagging-up" the frog, and cutting out corns. During hot, dry weather, the sole may be too hard to cut with the farrier's knife, and a sole knife must be used. The sole knife is used in the same manner as a chisel. To protect the blade of the farrier's knife or chisel, the sole of the foot is cleaned of all rocks and dirt with a hoof pick.

The blade end of a clinch cutter or buffer is used to cut or straighten the clinches before removing a shoe from the foot. After the shoe is removed, the pritchel-shaped end is used to remove seated nails from the shoe after they are cut off.

Many types of hammers are used by farriers, but the rounding and driving hammers are essential. The rounding hammer is used for making and shaping shoes. The driving hammer is used for driving nails and forming and finishing the clinches. The claws of the driving hammer are used for wringing off the nails.

Cutting nippers have 2 sharp edges and are used for removing excess hoof wall. Some farriers prefer a hoof parer, which is similar to the nippers but has a blunt edge and a sharp edge. The farrier's pincers, commonly called the "pullers," are similar in shape to the cutting nippers but are used to pull shoes or nails from the foot and may be used to clinch the nails. Usually, a clinch block or an alligator clincher is used to set the clinches. If the pincers are used as a clinch block, they are closed, and the backside of the jaw is held against the nail.

The tang rasp, fitted with a wooden handle, is used to level the bearing surface of the foot and finish the clinches. The rough side is used for rasping the hoof and the smoother side is used for final leveling and for finishing the clinches. In the final leveling process, a hoof leveler is used to determine the angle of the wall and to determine if the foot is level. The length of the wall is usually checked with hoof calipers or a divider to make sure both feet are the same and are of the proper length.

A 5-inch vise is quite useful, particularly when filing the heels or turning calks.

Shoes

Many types, sizes, and weights of manufactured horseshoes are available, or the farrier may elect to make the shoe from an iron bar. A typical shoe and its parts are shown in Figure 22-5. The kind and weight of the shoe selected for a horse depends on the type of work to be performed. The size of the shoe to be used is determined by the size of the hoof, the position of the nail holes, and length of the heels of the shoe. The last nail hole on a front shoe should not be behind the widest part of the foot. If the nail is placed too far back, expansion of the heels will be inhibited. In the hind foot, the last nail may be a little further back. The branches (Figure 22-5) must be long enough to support the entire hoof wall. If they are too long on the front feet, a hind foot may overreach and pull the front shoe. If too short, the heels of the horse will grow and the heels of the shoe will rest on the sole. This will produce corns.

The most commonly used shoes are keg shoes. Keg shoes are pre-sized and often are fitted "cold." There are several types of keg shoes. The saddle horse, western, or cowboy shoe (Figure 22-6) is used on most pleasure horses and on working cow horses. The cowboy shoe is available in several sizes (Table 22-1) to cover the range of light horse hoof shapes. Standard Diamond brand shoe sizes range from the No. 000, which is 4^{7}/$_{16}$ inches long and 3^{11}/$_{16}$ inches wide, to the No. 3, which is 6^{3}/$_{16}$ inches long and 5^{9}/$_{16}$ inches wide. The No. 1 shoe fits the average horse. Another size system is used by the Multi-Products Company. In this system the No. 3 is equivalent to the standard No. 00, the No. 6 is equivalent to the standard

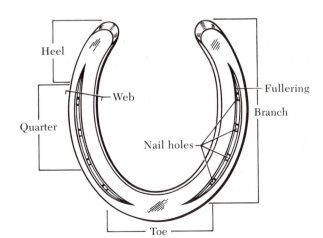

FIGURE 22-5
Ground surface view of a horseshoe.

693

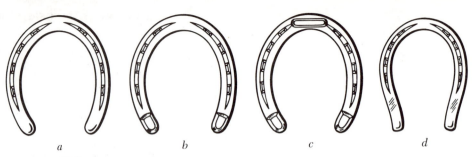

FIGURE 22-6
Cowboy shoes: *a*, plain; *b*, heeled (with heel calks); *c*, heeled and toed (with heel and toe calks); *d*, extra extra light (hot shoe).

No. 1, and the No. 9 is equivalent to the standard No. 3. The No. 4 is slightly smaller than the standard No. 0 and the No. 5 is slightly larger than the standard No. 0. The No. 7 is slightly smaller and the No. 8 is slightly larger then the standard No. 2. These so-called half-sizes almost completely eliminate the necessity to shape standard shoes to obtain a good fit. Pony shoes come in 2 sizes (Table 22-2). A No. 2 pony size is equivalent to the standard No. 000.

Cowboy shoes are made in several weights for each size (Table 22-1). They are classified as light, extra light, and extra extra light. Weight of the shoe decreases speed and agility and increases fatigue of the leg. Therefore, most pleasure horses wear the extra light or extra extra light. Keg shoes that are fitted "cold" are extra light and the extra extra light are fitted "hot." The heels of the extra extra light keg shoes must be turned inward.

Light and extra light cowboy shoes are also classified as plain, heeled, or toed and heeled (Figure 22-6). The heeled shoes have heel calks, and the heel and toed shoes have heel and toe calks. Calks increase the traction on slick or soft surfaces, and in rough terrain. The extra extra light shoes' heels are long enough so that heel calks can be formed without cutting off the heels. To form the calks, it is necessary to heat the shoe with a forge. If toe calks, or "toe-grabs," are required, they must be welded to the toe.

Mule shoes are a variation of keg shoes and are similar to cowboy shoes. However, their sizes (Table 22-2) are slightly different, and they are shaped to fit a mule's feet (Figure 22-7).

Plates are a type of keg shoe that is used on racehorses. Very seldom are steel plates used on running horses because the aluminum racing plate is lighter. The sizes and weights of steel plates are given in Table 22-3. They are available in two sizes, light or heavy, and can be obtained with a variety of combinations for toe and heel calks (Figure 22-8). Aluminum racing plates (Figures 22-9, 22-10) weigh 2–3 ounces. The front plates can be obtained plain, which means that there are no calks on the plate. A regular toe has a toe calk. If the toe calk is lower than the regular height, it is a low toe plate. Heel calks on the front plates are referred to as jar calks. The hind aluminum racing plates are also available with various toe and

TABLE 22-1
Specifications for Diamond brand cowboy shoes

Size No.	Length (inches)	Width (inches)	Approx. Weight (ounces)	Approx. No. in 50-lb Carton
		Light, Plain		
000	$4^7/_{16}$	$3^{11}/_{16}$	$7^1/_2$	107
00	$4^3/_4$	$4^9/_{32}$	9	90
0	$4^{31}/_{32}$	$4^5/_8$	$10^3/_4$	78
1	$5^5/_{16}$	$4^{13}/_{16}$	12	66
2	$5^{21}/_{32}$	$5^1/_8$	$14^1/_4$	53
3	$6^3/_{16}$	$5^9/_{16}$	$18^1/_4$	44
		Light, Heeled Only		
000	$4^7/_{16}$	$3^{11}/_{16}$	$7^3/_4$	103
00	$4^3/_4$	$4^9/_{32}$	$9^3/_4$	82
0	$4^{31}/_{32}$	$4^5/_8$	11	73
1	$5^5/_{16}$	$4^{13}/_{16}$	$12^1/_2$	62
2	$5^{21}/_{32}$	$5^1/_8$	15	53
3	$6^3/_{16}$	$5^9/_{16}$	19	42
4	$6^{21}/_{32}$	6	$22^1/_2$	35
		Light, Toed and Heeled		
00	$4^3/_4$	$4^9/_{32}$	$9^3/_4$	79
0	$4^{31}/_{32}$	$4^5/_8$	$11^1/_2$	71
1	$5^5/_{16}$	$4^{13}/_{16}$	$13^3/_4$	61
2	$5^{21}/_{32}$	$5^1/_8$	16	49
3	$6^3/_{16}$	$5^9/_{16}$	$19^1/_2$	42
4	$6^{21}/_{32}$	6	$22^3/_4$	34
		Extra Light, Plain or Heeled		
S00	$4^1/_2$	$4^1/_8$	$6^1/_4$	128
S0	$4^3/_4$	$4^9/_{32}$	7	114
S1	5	$4^{21}/_{32}$	$8^1/_4$	97
S2	$5^3/_8$	$4^{13}/_{16}$	9	89
		Extra Extra Light (Hot Shoe)		
0	$5^9/_{16}$	$4^9/_{32}$	8	100
1	$5^{13}/_{16}$	$4^5/_8$	9	82
2	$6^1/_{16}$	$4^{25}/_{32}$	11	79
Size No.	Length (inches)	Width (inches)	Approx. Weight (ounces)	Approx. No. in 50-lb Carton

TABLE 22-2
Specifications for Diamond brand pony and mule shoes

Size No.	Length (inches)	Width (inches)	Approx. Weight (ounces)	Approx. No. in 50-lb Carton
Pony Shoe				
0	$3\frac{3}{4}$	$3\frac{5}{16}$	$5\frac{3}{4}$	139
1	$4\frac{1}{16}$	$3\frac{7}{16}$	$6\frac{1}{4}$	128
Plain Mule Shoe				
2	$5\frac{1}{8}$	4	$10\frac{1}{2}$	75
3	$5\frac{1}{2}$	$4\frac{1}{4}$	$12\frac{3}{4}$	62
4	6	$4\frac{1}{2}$	$15\frac{3}{4}$	49
Heeled Mule Shoe				
2	$5\frac{1}{8}$	4	$11\frac{1}{4}$	70
3	$5\frac{1}{2}$	$4\frac{1}{4}$	$13\frac{1}{2}$	58
4	6	$4\frac{1}{2}$	$16\frac{1}{2}$	46

Plain mule shoes　　Heeled mule shoes　　Plain pony shoes　　Plain　　Block heels toed

FIGURE 22-7
Shapes of pony and mule shoes (Diamond brand).

FIGURE 22-8
Shape of steel racing (running) plates.

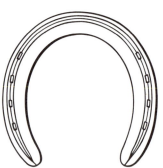 

Plain　　　　　　　　　　　　Block heels toed

TABLE 22-3
Sizes and weights of Phoenix brand steel racing plates

Type	Size	Weight (oz)
Plain, light	00	3¾
	0	4
	1	4¼
	2	4½
	3	4¾
	4	5
Plain, heavy	00	4
	0	4¾
	1	5
	2	5¼
	3	5½
	4	5¾
Hind, toed, and block heels	00	5¼
	0	5½
	1	5¾
	2	6
	3	6¼
	4	6½

FIGURE 22-9
Aluminum racing plates for front feet.

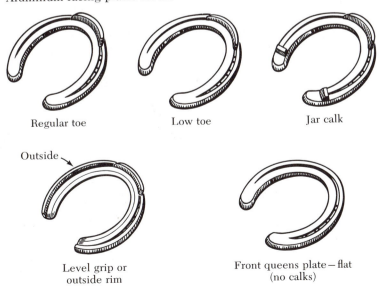

Regular toe   Low toe   Jar calk

Outside

Level grip or   Front queens plate—flat
outside rim   (no calks)

697

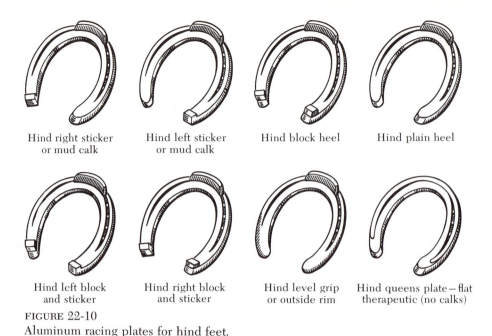

Hind right sticker or mud calk   Hind left sticker or mud calk   Hind block heel   Hind plain heel

Hind left block and sticker   Hind right block and sticker   Hind level grip or outside rim   Hind queens plate—flat therapeutic (no calks)

FIGURE 22-10
Aluminum racing plates for hind feet.

heel calk combinations. The heel calk on a hind plate is referred to as a block, or sticker, depending on its shape. The sticker, or "mud-calk," is set on the heel in such a way that it goes across the heel, whereas the block is set lengthwise on the heel. Blocks are used to cause a horse's hind feet to break over faster, thus preventing the track surface from burning the ergot area. Stickers are used to increase the traction on a muddy track surface.

Polo shoes (Figure 22-11) differ from cowboy shoes in that the inside rim on the web is raised above the outside rim. This shape increases traction, prevents sliding, and enables the foot to roll over faster. Polo horses and western barrel-racing horses make a lot of turns at high speeds. The polo shoe allows the horse to pivot on the shoe and maintain a toe grip regardless of where the foot breaks over. The sizes and weights of polo shoes are given in Table 22-4.

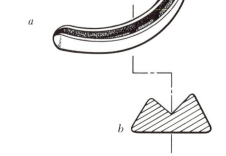

FIGURE 22-11
Polo shoe (a). Cross section (b) shows that inside rim is higher than outside rim.

TABLE 22-4
Specifications of Phoenix brand polo shoes

Size	Weight (oz)	Width (in)	Height (in)
0	$6\frac{1}{2}$	$4\frac{1}{4}$	$4\frac{5}{8}$
1	7	$4\frac{5}{8}$	5
2	$7\frac{3}{4}$	$4\frac{3}{4}$	$5\frac{1}{2}$
3	$8\frac{1}{2}$	$5\frac{1}{4}$	$5\frac{3}{4}$
4	$9\frac{1}{4}$	$5\frac{3}{8}$	$6\frac{1}{4}$

Toe and/or heel clips (Figure 22-12) can be drawn on shoes to help hold the shoe in position. They are essential for horses that have weak hoof walls and whose hoofs do not hold a nail very well. Gaited and walking horses need toe and heel clips to aid in holding the extra heavy shoes. Horses that are required to make sudden stops and turns are difficult to keep shod unless toe and heel clips are added to prevent the hoof wall from sliding off the shoe and tearing out the nail holes. They are also used to support the hoof wall in the areas of cracks.

Borium is applied to horseshoes with an oxy-acetylene torch to improve the gripping properties and life of the shoe. The roughened surface of the applied borium increases the gripping properties of the shoe on ice, pavement, and dry grass. Borium (a metal alloy) is harder than any substance except diamonds, so it doubles or even triples the life of the shoe. Application of borium is particularly important before long trail rides over rough terrain; borium should also be applied to the shoes of pack horses and mules.

Horseshoe nails (Figure 22-13) are made so that one side of the shank is flat and the other side is concave, with a bevel near the point. The head of the nail is tapered and roughened on the same side as the bevel. Horseshoe nails differ according to size and according to shape of the head. The most commonly used sizes are 4, 5, and 6, but sizes range from $2\frac{1}{2}$ to 12 (small to large). After being driven, a regular head does not fit completely into the fullering. The city head fits into the fullering and is used for racing plates. In some areas, sharp beveled heads, called frostheads, are used to increase traction on icy surfaces. A pritchel is used to open the nail holes in a shoe before driving the nails (Figure 22-4).

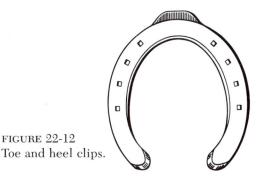

FIGURE 22-12
Toe and heel clips.

Toe clips

Heel clips

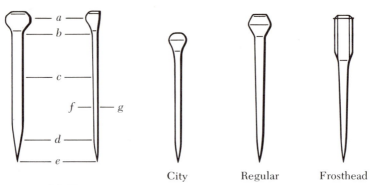

City   Regular   Frosthead

FIGURE 22-13

Horseshoe nails: parts (*top*) and shapes (*bottom*). Parts shown are:
a, head; *b*, neck; *c*, shank; *d*, bevel; *e*, point; *f*, inner face;
g, outer face.

A shoeing box (Figure 22-4) is used by most farriers to keep their tools organized and handy while working on the horse's feet.

Most competent farriers are skilled in the use of a forge to make and shape shoes. The coal-burning forge (Figure 22-14) is the most common and can be carried in the back of a pickup truck. Gas forges are being used in some farrier's shops. The gas forge has an advantage in that the temperature is constant and will not burn up a shoe that is left in the forge too long. Coal-burning forges require the use of a fire shovel to add coal, and a fire rake to remove clinkers (melting metal particles that bind burned coal into larger masses). Farrier's tongs (Figure 22-4) are used to handle the shoes in the forge and during shaping. A fullering iron (Figure 22-4) is necessary to make a crease in a hand-forged shoe or to repair damaged creases during shaping. If a forge is not available to shape shoes, a shoe spreader is used to spread the heels of the shoe (Figure 22-4).

In addition to the shoeing tools, some other equipment facilitates the shoeing of certain horses. It is essential that the farrier carry a halter and lead rope to use on horses when the owner is not present. In some areas where horses are kept together in large numbers and are not handled regularly, a catch rope is necessary. A 2-foot-long knee strap is handy to hold up a front foot of a problem horse. Often, a horse will stand if a twitch is applied to the muzzle. A couple of long soft ropes may be used to tie up a hind foot or tie down a vicious horse. If it is necessary to tie up a hind foot, a 12-inch strap with D-rings in each end will prevent a rope burn around the pastern (Figure 22-15). Some horses will kick, thus requiring the use of a hoof hook (Figure 22-4) to pick up a hind foot.

If a person shoes horses all day, a 14-inch-high foot stand will prevent excessive back strain. However, such stands are not safe to use when shoeing a nervous horse and will teach a young horse to lean on the farrier. A foot stand is seldom used by a farrier who can properly handle a horse's foot.

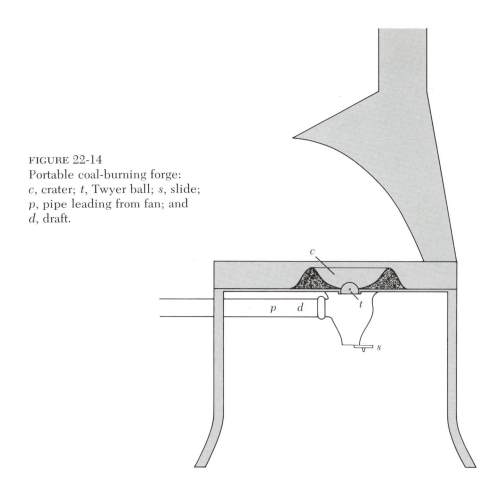

FIGURE 22-14
Portable coal-burning forge:
c, crater; *t*, Twyer ball; *s*, slide;
p, pipe leading from fan; and
d, draft.

Holding the Foot

Often, the difference between a successful, highly skilled farrier and a mediocre one is the ability to handle a horse's feet correctly. A farrier must be able to hold the foot solidly enough to work on it, yet not cause the discomfort of either himself or the horse.

FIGURE 22-15
A small strap with 2 D-rings is placed around the pastern to prevent rope burns.

701

When the horse is approached, it should not be frightened or excited by any unnecessary noise or quick movements. A confident and deliberate approach usually gives confidence to the horse. Before picking up a foot, the farrier should make sure the horse is standing on all 4 feet and is aware of his intention to lift the foot.

When picking up the left front leg (near side) (Figure 22-16), the farrier stands facing the horse's rear quarters and places the left hand on the horse's shoulder. The hand is moved to the fetlock area while remaining in contact with the horse. By pushing the horse with the left shoulder, the horse's weight is shifted to its right foot. The horse will lift its foot when the tendon is pinched just above the fetlock. The foot is then straddled and held just above the farrier's knee. If the farrier's toes are turned inward and the knees are flexed, the horse's foot will be held solid.

The left hind leg is picked up (Figure 22-17) as follows. The left hand is placed on the horse's hip and the right hand is run down the horse's hindquarters and leg to the pastern. When pressure is applied with the left hand, the horse will shift its weight to the right hind leg and his left hind leg can be picked up by pulling on the pastern. The leg is lifted up and the farrier steps toward, and under, the leg. The farrier places his hip under the horse's hock so that the hoof can be supported just above the farrier's knees. If the farrier's knees are bent, the toes turned in, and the left arm placed over the hock, the horse's leg is locked into a steady position. The opposite procedure is used to lift the right hind leg.

To hold up a horse's foot, the farrier must crouch (Figure 22-18). If the farrier straightens up, the foot is raised too high and the horse is uncomfortable and takes its foot away. Injured horses feel increased pain when their feet are held too high. Recognition of each horse's personality makes it easier to hold their feet. Some horses tire easily so their feet cannot be held too long before they start repeatedly to take them away from the farrier. Others must have a stablemate nearby. Flies are irritating to most horses. Horses that will not stand while being tied must be held or merely "ground tied." It is much safer for the farrier to have someone hold the horse while it is being shod. Horses are unpredictable and may fall back against the lead shank.

Shoeing the Normal Foot

The first step in the shoeing process (Figure 22-19) is to remove the shoes, if the horse is shod. The clinches are cut or straightened with a clinch cutter. Some farriers prefer to file the clinches off. The farrier's pincers, commonly called pullers, are inserted under one branch of the shoe toward the heel. The shoe is loosened slightly, and then the pullers are placed under the opposite branch. After the shoe is loose, it is worked from side to side by applying pressure to the toe and medial until the toe nails come

FIGURE 22-16
Picking up the left front leg.

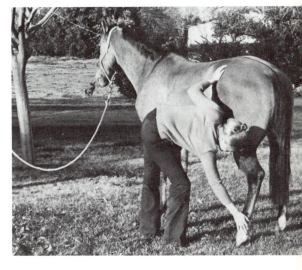

FIGURE 22-17
Picking up the left hind leg.

FIGURE 22-18
Proper way to hold a hind foot.

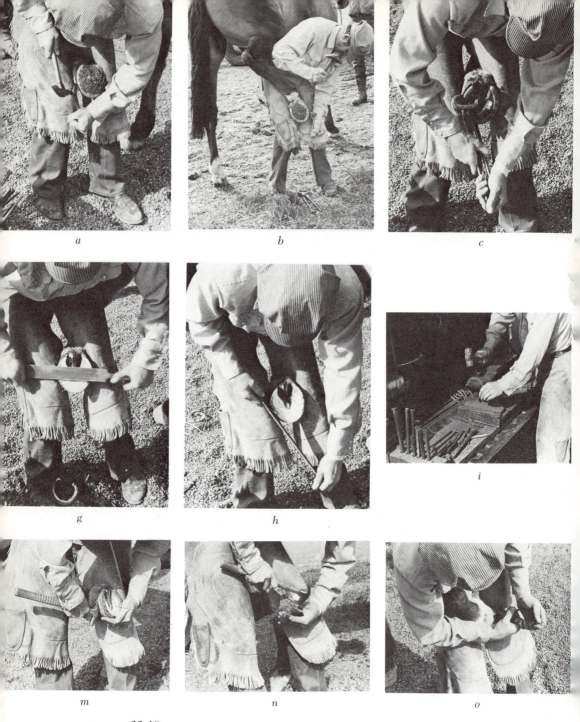

FIGURE 22-19

Shoeing the normal foot. Cutting the clinches of the forefoot (*a*) or hind foot (*b*). Removing the shoe with the pullers (*c* and *d*). Removing the dead sole with the farrier's knife (*e*). Trimming the hoof wall with the nippers (*f*). Rasping the hoof wall level (*g*). Removing the "burrs" around edge of hoof wall (*h*). Shaping the

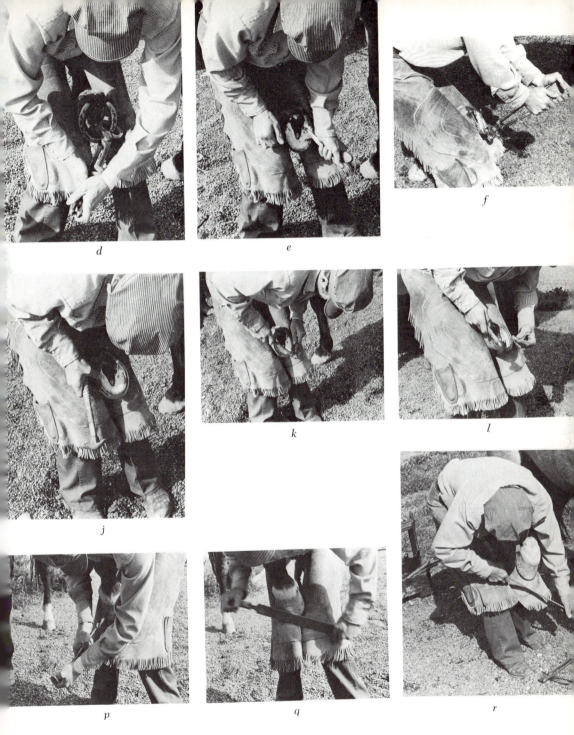

d

e

f

j

k

l

p

q

r

shoe to fit the foot (*i*). Making sure that shoe fits foot (*j*). Starting the first nail (*k*). Driving remainder of nails (*l*). Wringing off nails (*m*) with hammer. Sitting clinches with clinch block (*n*). Cutting off clinches with wire cutters (*o*). Clinches may be set with an alligator clincher (*p*). Dressing off the forefoot (*q*) and hind foot (*r*).

705

out and the shoe can be removed. Any nails or stubs remaining in the hoof wall are removed. It is important for the horseman to know how to remove shoes. If a horse pulls a shoe part of the way off, the horseman must remove it to prevent further damage to the hoof wall. Shoes that work loose should be removed or the clinches tightened to prevent the horse from "throwing the shoe" and damaging the hoof wall.

Frequently, a horse's hooves have been permitted to grow too long and are then shod. Hoof wall growth is $1/4$–$1/2$ inch per month at the toe. The toe of the hoof grows at a faster rate than the heel area. The horse should be shod about every 6–8 weeks. Failure to trim the hoof wall or reshoe the horse allows the heels of the shoe to slip inside the hoof wall. Because the sole is a non-weight-bearing structure, the heels cause a bruise (corn) in the sole area between the bars and hoof wall. The horse is lame for a few days until it heals. Because the toe grows faster, the angle of the hoof wall decreases, and after 7–9 weeks, the change in the angle is sufficient to affect the gaits (see Chapter 6). Long toes retard the breaking over of the hoof, strain the deep flexor tendon (which may result in a "bowed tendon"), and may cause forging and overreaching.

After removal, the shoes are inspected for abnormal wear. Abnormal wear at specific points indicates that the foot is breaking over at a point other than at the toe, or that the foot is landing out of balance. The horse to be reshod or newly shod is then observed to see if it stands straight or crooked, and if the opposite feet are the same size. The angle of the foot should be the same as the angles of the pastern and the shoulder. The horse must also be observed in action to detect lameness (see Chapter 6), faults in gaits, and improper foot action and flight. The overall body conformation should be observed to see if the horse has a short back, long legs, and a tendency to strike the forefeet with the hind feet. Based upon these observations, the farrier prepares the foot and selects the proper shoe.

To prepare the foot, the farrier thoroughly cleans it with a hoof pick and examines it for pathological conditions, such as corns or thrush. The frog is "tagged-up" with the knife to remove loose ends. To function properly, the frog must touch the ground after the horse is shod; therefore, it should never be trimmed out. The sole is trimmed with the hoof knife to remove the horn that is flaking away. Usually, it is necessary to remove more sole in the toe area than in the quarter or heel areas because the toe grows faster. The excess wall is removed with the cutting nippers. It is customary to begin trimming the excess wall at one heel and to work around toward the other heel. Care must be taken so that the proper amount is removed and the wall remains level. The wall should never be cut lower than the sole. Since the bottom of the foot is concave, more wall will be left projecting above the sole at the quarter of the hoof wall. A common beginner's mistake is to remove too much wall at the quarters, or to trim the wall irregularly. To cut the wall as flat as possible, it is essential that the angle of the nippers to the wall be correct. The bars should be trimmed to the same level as the wall. If the bars are trimmed out, the heels tend to contract. The tang rasp is then used to rasp the bearing surface of the wall flat (to ensure uniform contact of the wall with the shoe), to smooth the bearing surface of the wall, and to make the final adjustment of the angle and length. The foot is then shaped to remove any excess outward flare of the hoof wall. After the foot is balanced and rounded off, the rasp is run around the edge of the wall to remove any burrs. The sole adjacent to the white line must be lowered slightly with the knife so that the shoe does not put pressure on it. If thrush or other diseases are present (see Chapter 18), the foot should be treated before applying the shoe. All cracks should also be treated to prevent further development or to eliminate hoof expansion in that area of the hoof wall (see Chapter 18) before the shoe is applied.

Fitting the shoe is a critical step in shoeing. The shoe must be shaped to fit the hoof and not the reverse. The guideline for the fitting process is actually the "white line," since the hoof wall may be distorted from a previous shoeing. The shoe may be fitted hot or cold, but if it is fitted hot, it should not be burned into place. The burned areas that appear on the wall after the hot shoe has been briefly applied indicate the high spots. It is then necessary to rasp the wall to remove them and level the wall. The shoe is centered on a normal foot by using the apex of the frog as a guide. When the shoe is centered, it fits the foot if the branches are approximately $1/16$ inch wider than the wall on both sides, the heels are the proper length to extend $1/4$ inch beyond the wall, and the toe of the shoe is flush with the toe of the foot.

After the shoe has been shaped to the foot and centered, it is nailed. When driving the nails, the point of entry and direction of the nail are important (Figure 22-20). The nail should enter the outer edge of the white line, travel parallel with the horn fibers, and emerge approximately $3/4$ inch above the ground surface. The nail is started with the flat side outside. Light blows with the hammer will allow the nail to travel parallel with the fibers. At the desired depth, a hard blow will force the nail to emerge because of the inside bevel. When the nail is secure, the end is cut off or wrung off with the hammer claws. The nail head should extend approximately $1/16$ inch above the crease. If the nail head is too small and fits down into the crease, the shoe will become loose in a few days. If the horse is pricked or the nails are driven too close to the sensitive laminae, as evidenced by flinching, the horse will be lame. The nail should be taken out; if the horse was pricked, iodine should be poured into the opening and a tetanus antitoxin shot should be given.

There is a difference of opinion as to which nail should be driven first. It does not matter as long as the shoe remains centered on the foot. If the shoe moves slightly when the first nail is driven, it can be moved back by tapping it with the hammer. Ordinarily, 3 nails on each side are sufficient

707

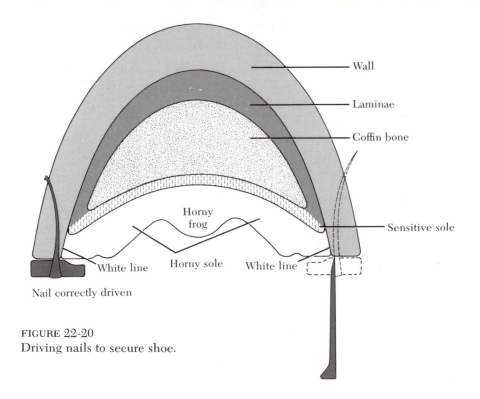

Wall

Laminae

Coffin bone

Horny frog

Sensitive sole

White line　　Horny sole　　White line

Nail correctly driven

FIGURE 22-20
Driving nails to secure shoe.

to hold the shoe. If the horse makes a lot of sudden stops and turns, 4 nails on each side are used.

After all the nails are in, the nail heads must be seated in the crease, and the clinches formed. Either the farrier's pincers or a clinch block is held against the end of the nail, and the head of the nail is struck with the driving hammer. Finishing and smoothing is accomplished by filing a small groove under each clinch and then seating the clinch with the driving hammer. Some farriers prefer to use clinchers (alligator or gooseneck styles) to form and set the clinches. The foot receives a final dressing or is finished off by a light rasping below the clinches if necessary. The hoof wall should not be rasped above the clinches, because if it is, the stratum tectorium (the outer layer of cells, which give the wall a glossy appearance) will be removed. Removal of the stratum tectorium will result in loss of moisture from the hoof.

Final Inspection

After the horse is shod, the farrier and the owner or handler should inspect the work to ensure proper health and condition of the feet and legs. The following points should be noted:

1. The opposite feet should be the same size; the toes should be the same length and the heels should be the same height. The toes should not be dubbed (rasped perpendicular to the ground).

2. The foot should be balanced in relation to the leg and directly under the leg; that is, an excessive amount of wall should not be removed from one side of the foot because this will result in an uneven distribution of weight in the foot.

3. The angle of the hoof should be an elongation of the angle of the pastern. This angle is usually the same as the angle of the shoulder. The most common angle is 50–55 degrees but depends upon the breed and use of the horse.

4. The nails and clinches should be evenly spaced and placed at the proper height. The clinches should be smooth and not project from the hoof surface. The last nail should not be too far back.

5. The shoe should be fitted to the foot so that excessive rasping on the wall is not necessary. Rasping above the clinches is not necessary. The shoe branches should be the proper length and set for heel expansions.

6. The frog and bars should not be trimmed out. The nail should be in contact with the shoe so that there are no air spaces.

22.3   Corrective Trimming and Shoeing

To do corrective trimming and shoeing, a thorough understanding of the anatomy and physiology of the horse's foot and leg, as well as a knowledge of the flight of the foot and leg, is necessary. Several horses may have the same defect in their way of going, but each horse may require different corrective measures. If he has a basic knowledge of the proper functioning of a foot and leg, the farrier is able to observe the horse in action and then determine the best corrective measure. At best, the farrier is only able to modify or improve a faulty gait in a mature animal. He is not able to correct it permanently.

Principles

The basic principle of corrective shoeing is to trim the foot level and then apply corrective shoes to improve the faulty gait. Drastic changes in the flight of the foot and leg can cause excess strain or pressure to be applied to other areas on the foot and leg (bones and structures). The new stresses can lead to pathological changes; thus, the least severe corrective measure should be utilized.

Procedure

Visual Inspection. During the visual inspection of the horse's way of traveling, any "break-over" and "landing" areas of the hoof wall are noted. In the base-narrow, toe-in fault in foreleg conformation, the foot breaks over and lands on the outside wall, and if the horse is unshod, the outside wall will be worn down. It is necessary to lower the inside wall to level the foot, and then several corrective measures can be used to force the foot to break over the center of the hoof. One of the simplest and mildest methods of correction is a square toe shoe (Figure 22-21b). Other measures, such as an outside half rim (outside rim) shoe (Figure 22-21a), calks (Figure 22-21d), and a calk at first outside nailhole (Figure 22-21c), or a lateral toe extension (Figure 22-21e), encourage the foot to break over the toe. If the horse is base-narrow but toes out, the foot will break over the outside toe, wing inward, and land on the outside wall. Successful correction methods to encourage the foot to break over the toe include: outside half rim shoe (Figure 22-21a), square toe shoe (Figure 22-21b), outside toe extension (Figure 22-21e), and half shoe on outside wall (Figure 22-21g).

Horses with a base-wide, toe-out conformation tend to break over and land on the inside toe. The fault is corrected by modifying the shoe to make it difficult for the foot to break over the inside toe but easier to break over the center of the toe. One of several modifications, such as heel calks (Figure 22-21d), square toe (Figure 22-21b), or a bar across the break-over point (Figure 22-21h), will force the foot to break over the center of the toe. Base-wide horses that have their toes pointing the opposite way (that is, toe-in) land on the inside wall. To improve their way of going, the inside branch of the shoe must be raised (Figure 22-21a).

Cow-hocked horses tend to break over the inside toe and thus place a strain on the inside of the hock. This fault in conformation is particularly straining when the horse makes a sliding stop. The main objective in correcting the fault is to force the hind foot to break over the center of the toe by braking the inside of the hoof when it lands and rotating the toe inward. A lateral toe extension (Figure 22-21e) or a short inside trailer (Figure 22-21f) will usually accomplish the objective.

The stance of a sickle-hocked or camped-under horse can be improved by shortening the hind toes if they are too long. This correction will cause the hind legs to move backward. The opposite effect can be accomplished for the camped-behind horse by lowering its hind heels if they are too long.

Other less obvious faults in conformation may lead to faulty gaits. Forging and overreaching result when the hind foot breaks over faster than the forefoot in such a way that the toe of the hind foot strikes the sole of the

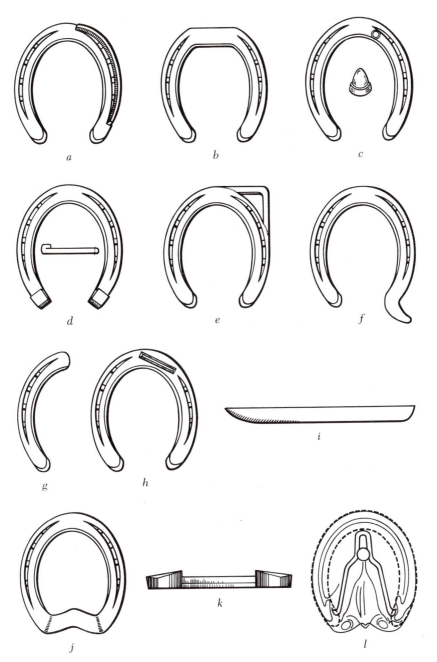

FIGURE 22-21
Corrective and therapeutic shoes: *a*, half-rim shoe; *b*, square toe; *c*, calk at first outside nail hole; *d*, heel calks; *e*, lateral toe extension; *f*, shoe with trailer; *g*, half shoe; *h*, bar across break-over point; *i*, rolled toe; *j*, bar shoe; *k*, slippered heels; *l*, Chadwick spring.

heels of the forefoot. Horses that have short backs and long legs or short forelegs and long hind legs, or that stand under in front or behind have a tendency to forge and overreach. The corrective measure is to speed up the breaking over of the forefoot and to retard the breaking over of the hind foot and/or to increase the height of the forefoot flight. A variety of corrective measures can be used. The fault can be corrected in some horses by rolling the toes (and shoes, as in Figure 22-21i) of the forefeet and leaving the toe of the hind foot slightly longer than usual or placing heel calks (Figure 22-21c) on the hind shoes. In an extreme case, a ½-inch bar can be welded across the heel of the front shoes and across the toe of the hind shoes.

When the toe of the forefoot is striking the hairline of the hind foot ("scalping"), rolling the toe will enable the forefoot to break over faster and may prevent contact. The same corrective principle and objectives apply to horses that are scalping and/or shin-hitting as to those that forge and overreach.

Pacers that toe-out in front and toe-in behind have a tendency to cross fire. To prevent the hind foot from hitting the opposite forefoot, all feet must be shod to encourage breaking over the toe. Corrective measures include those previously discussed for correcting the front toed-out and hind toed-in conditions.

Interference usually results when a horse is base-wide or base-narrow and has a toed-out conformation in the forelimbs or is cowhocked in the hind limbs. Correction of these conditions has been previously discussed and applied also to interference.

22.4 Therapeutic Shoeing

Often, a farrier encounters horses with pathological conditions that require therapeutic shoeing. The most common conditions are contracted heels, ringbone, sidebone, navicular disease, and toe or quarter cracks.

There are several ways, or combinations of ways, to re-establish proper foot function in a horse with contracted heels. Frog pressure can be increased with a bar shoe so that the bar maintains constant pressure on the frog (Figure 22-21j). Other types of shoes include shoes with slippered (beveled) heels (Figure 22-21k) or a Chadwick spring (Figure 22-21l) to force the wall outward. The expansion process should be gradual, but additional expansion aids can be used; for example, cutting a horizontal groove below the coronary band, or cutting several vertical grooves in the quarter area, or thinning the wall at the quarters with a rasp.

Horses with ringbone have impaired or no action of the pastern and/or coffin joints. The objective of a corrective measure is to enable the foot to break over more easily so that the required action of the joint or joints is reduced. The simplest corrective measure is to roll the toe (Figure 22-21*i*). When sidebone is the problem, the action of the coffin joint needs to be decreased, so rolling the toe is helpful. To restore the ability of the foot to expand, and relieve pain if the horse is lame, the quarters of the wall are thinned.

The objective of corrective shoeing of a horse with navicular disease is to make it easier for the foot to break over and to reduce the anticoncussive activity of the deep flexor tendon against the navicular bone. By raising the heels (Figure 22-21*c*) and rolling the toe (Figure 22-21*i*), the foot will break over faster and concussion to the navicular bone will be reduced. To further reduce trauma to the area, a bar shoe (Figure 22-21*j*) or pads are used. This type of correction tends to contract the heels because frog pressure is reduced. The tendency for the heels to contract can be reduced by slippering the heels of the shoe (Figure 22-21*k*) so that they slope to the outside. This causes the wall to slide outward as the foot strikes the ground. The expansion of the wall can be further aided by thinning the quarters with a rasp.

When shoeing a horse with flat feet, the sole is trimmed slightly but the frog is not trimmed. The sole is prevented from dropping further by making sure that the shoe covers the entire wall and white line and covers only a small part of the outside edge of the sole. Pads are usually necessary to prevent sole bruising.

Toe, quarter, and heel cracks are encountered quite often. Each crack requires individual analysis with regard to the corrective treatment and shoeing. The general principle is to use a toe clip on each side of the crack to prevent wall expansion and to lower the wall under the crack so the wall will not bear weight. Plastics may be used to seal the crack and prevent expansion and contraction of the crack during foot action.

References

Adams, O. R. 1974. *Lameness in Horses.* 3rd ed. Philadelphia: Lea and Febiger.

Canfield, D. M. *Elements of Farrier Science.* Albert Lea, Minnesota: Enderes Tool Co., Inc.

Evans, L. H., J. Jenny, and C. W. Raker. 1966. The repair of hoof cracks with acrylic. *J.A.V.M.A.* 148:355–359.

Greeley, R. G. 1970. *The Art and Science of Horseshoeing.* Philadelphia: Lippincott.

713

Kays, D. J. 1969. *How to Shoe a Horse.* New York: A. S. Barnes.

O'Connor, J. T., and J. C. Briggs. 1971. Feet, conformation and motion. *The Morgan Horse* 364:27–32.

Sisson, S., and J. D. Grossman. 1953. *Anatomy of the Domestic Animals.* 4th ed. Philadelphia: W. B. Saunders.

Springhall, J. A. 1964. *Elements of Horseshoeing.* Brisbane: University of Queensland Press.

Technical Manual TMA-220. 1941. *The Horseshoer.* Washington, D.C.: War Department. March 11.

Wiseman, R. F. 1968. *The Complete Horshoeing Guide.* Norman: University of Oklahoma Press.

CHAPTER TWENTY-THREE *Fences,*

Buildings, and Equipment

for Horses

The usefulness of the horse lies in its athletic ability, and therefore facilities must be provided that enhance the performance of the animal. Any design of buildings, fences, and facilities must keep in mind the basic nature of the horse. For example, fences or stalls that are adequate for cattle may be hazardous or otherwise unsatisfactory for horses. Because the purchase of a horse represents a considerable economic and emotional investment, the primary consideration for any horse facility should be *safety*. There are, of course, other important considerations, such as cost, durability, usefulness, flexibility, accessibility, and suitability for purpose. The intent of this chapter is not to provide specific recommendations concerning construction, for no such recommendations can be absolute, but rather to describe various ideas and plans that have been successful.

23.1 General Considerations for the Design of Horse Facilities

Safety

Facilities must be designed to protect the horse, which, as an active, alert athlete is often injured accidentally because of its inherent reaction to flee from danger whether real or imagined. Many horses are injured as a result of neglect, that is, by protruding nails, sharp edges, unscreened glass, exposed electric wires, sagging fences, broken gates, and barbed wire. Other injuries result from poor planning. Horses have gone through misplaced windows, through fences that could not be seen, and over gates that were too low or poorly designed. O'Dea's survey (1966) of injuries treated by a

715

New York State equine clinic revealed that 29.2 percent were caused by buildings and appointments, 16.2 percent were caused by fences and gates, and 6.3 percent were caused by soil, ground conditions, or pasture hazards. Thus, more than one-half (51.9 percent) of the injuries treated by these veterinarians were the result of the facilities in which the horses were kept. Loading, shipping, teasing, and breeding accounted for only 3.5 percent of the injuries, whereas the use of the horse in such activities as training, racing, hunting, showing, and trail riding accounted for the remaining 44.9 percent of treated injuries. Undoubtedly, there were additional facility-caused injuries that were treated without veterinary assistance or that went undetected by the owners.

Thus, safety to the horse and handler should be the major consideration in planning horse facilities. There is no excuse for injuries that are caused by human negligence. Many facility-induced injuries can be eliminated by proper design, careful construction, and diligent maintenance. Many Thoroughbred and Standardbred breeding farms are models of safety because of the value of the animals that are bred. The book published by *The Blood-Horse* magazine, *A Barn Well Filled,* and Harry M. Harvey's chapter in *Care and Training of the Trotter and Pacer* provide excellent information on horse facilities whose design has stressed safety.

Cost

The most limiting factor in the construction of new horse facilities is cost. Elaborate, well-planned, and well-maintained horse farms are a pleasure to visit, but such facilities are beyond the economic means of the average horseman. On the other hand, rugged, durable, well-constructed, labor-saving facilities may be less expensive in the long run because they are less expensive to operate.

Durability. Horses are particularly hard on facilities. They can chew stalls, fences, and gates; break up stalls; and tear down fences at an alarming rate. A farm should be so designed and constructed that repairs will be minimal. The common denominator of all poorly managed stables is lack of maintenance. Sagging fences, broken stall doors, and poor gate latches result in wasted labor and, unfortunately, frequently cause serious animal injuries.

Efficient Use of Labor. Labor is the most expensive and variable item on a horse farm. The facilities should be so designed that efficient use is made of labor and an attractive and desirable atmosphere is provided in which to work. Too many horse facilities are designed with little thought for the personnel who will work there. Gates that fail to latch, muddy, inaccessible pastures, and inconveniently located barns will discourage most workers.

Flexibility

Planning should include consideration of possible future use. Permanent structures should be so designed that expansion or conversion can be readily accomplished with a minimum of cost and disruption of the farm operation. Clear-span structures (buildings without interior supporting posts) have the advantage of enabling interior modification without alteration of the structural soundness.

Accessibility

Driveways and lanes should be so designed that pastures, paddocks, and buildings are readily accessible and useable in all types of weather. Plan the facilities so they will not be isolated or destroyed by blizzards, thawing ground, or floods. Barns should have all-weather roads with wide entrance gates for fire protection as well as for ease in the day-to-day management of the stable.

23.2   The Land

Fertile land that will grow an abundance of nutritious grass for grazing and hay is a key to a successful, economical horse farm. Traditional horse-breeding areas of the United States, such as the bluegrass region of Kentucky and Virginia and the great Standardbred regions of Pennsylvania, Maryland, and Ohio, are blessed with well-drained loam soil, fertile, gently rolling land, numerous large shade trees, and an adequate supply of fresh water. The soil of the rapidly growing horse-breeding regions of Florida, California, the Southeast, and the south central states may not be as fertile, but the climate of these areas is ideally suited to raising horses.

Nevertheless, topography and soil are important considerations in selecting a site for raising horses. Horses are particularly hard on the land, and the types of soil that produce abundant pastures and withstand wear and tear from horses are the most desirable. Well-drained loam or sandy loam soils are best. Such soils do not pack or become excessively muddy and they support plant growth well. Clay soils are slippery when wet and become rough and hard when dry. However, clay soils withstand drought well. Gravel and sandy soils do not hold nutrients and are unsatisfactory in dry weather. Sand colic may be a problem with sandy soils (see section 18.5).

The topography can be hilly or flat, but low land with boggy areas is not desirable for horses. There must be plenty of clean water available

717

on a horse farm—either from natural ponds or streams, or from drilled wells, or from the municipal water supply. The water supply should be free from agricultural, industrial, and residential pollutants.

Climate is also important in choosing the location of a horse farm. Extremes in weather increase management problems. The major increase in the number of horse-breeding farms in the United States has occurred in the South and mid-South rather than in the North, where there is less pasture and breeding seasons are greatly reduced.

Finally, horse farms should be located in rural areas where land is plentiful. Urban sprawl creates additional management problems, and, in fact, zoning laws in some regions limit or prohibit horses. On the other hand, to be successful, riding stables generally must be located near population centers.

23.3   Pastures

Pastures are an important part of the farm's feeding program. They supply a nutritious feed at low cost while saving labor and improving the health and disposition of the horses. Pasture forage provides an excellent source of protein, vitamins, and minerals. Horses on pasture receive exercise and sunshine and thus have fewer respiratory and breeding problems (see sections 10.4 and 24.4 for a discussion of pasture management).

Pastures should have shade for horses. Trees are ideal but they must be fenced off, covered with protective wire, or painted with creosote or similar material to protect them from horses that may attempt to chew them. Any corner of a pasture is hazardous and should be rounded and fenced off. A lane between pastures is another safety precaution that should be taken when two groups of horses are running side by side. Some type of corral or catch pen is helpful in handling horses. High-traffic areas such as gates and around waterers should be graveled. Waterers should be safely placed and free from sharp edges or corners. Guy wires on electric poles should be guarded or fenced off, as should fence and gate brace wires. Corral, paddock, stallion, and perimeter fences should be higher and of sturdier construction than fences around large pastures or dividing fences.

23.4   Fences

718   There is no such thing as a good fence for horses because all are designed to restrict their wandering nature and thereby create a potential hazard to

the horse. However, horses can be safely contained by a variety of satis-factory fences. Board fences are traditional, but excellent fences can also be made of wire, pipe, concrete, split rails, cable, and even rubber, so long as they are properly designed and constructed for horses.

The secret of a successful horse fence is strength, height, and tightness, and this is accomplished by correctly setting the posts — particularly the corner, gate, and brace posts. Wood fence posts are still the most popular and should be 7½–8 feet long and set 3 feet in the ground. Corner posts should be at least 10 inches in diameter and set 4 feet in the ground with adjacent posts to which braces are attached. Locust and cedar make the best wood posts, but softer-pressure treated posts also resist rot although they may not hold staples or nails as well. Some builders prefer to set corner and adjacent brace posts in concrete for greater strength.

Detailed pamphlets on building fences can be obtained from agricul-tural colleges and fence suppliers. Anyone contemplating building a fence should read Charles Sone's article, "Good Fences Make Good Neighbors and Good Horse Farms," and Harry M. Harvey's chapter entitled "Stock Farm Management." The experience and philosophy of these two men are revealed in these excellent practical discussions of horse fencing.

Board Fences

Board fences are rugged and have the advantage of being easily seen by the horse. However, they are expensive to build and maintain, are chewed by horses, will splinter or break, and eventually rot. The boards must be painted or treated in some way to preserve them, and they require contin-uous maintenance. On the other hand, board fences are attractive and are among the strongest and safest fences for horses.

Board fences should be made of 1 × 6 inch boards and the centers of the posts should be no more than 8 feet apart. Oak boards are strongest and will resist chewing, but pine is more readily available and less likely to warp. A 4-board fence with a top board that is 48–53 inches high is adequate for horses. The bottom board should be 5–6 inches above the ground, and there should be 8 inches between the remaining boards. The wood board fence should be painted with lead-free white paint or treated with liquid asphalt, creosote, or some other wood preserver that will discourage chewing.

Post and Rail Fences

These types of wood fence add beauty to a farm but are expensive to in-stall. The split chestnut rails are excellent because they are strong and long lived and they resist chewing, but they are difficult to obtain. Pres-sure-treated and chemically treated rails that inhibit chewing are also

719

available. A post and rail fence does not last as long as a board fence because the posts tend to split and the rails break. Post and rail fences are also set on 8-foot centers.

Wire Fences

Several types of wire fence are available for horses. Wire fences are less expensive and faster to erect than board fences but are not as safe. Wire fences can be built with posts on 12-foot centers or with metal drive posts, thus resulting in considerable saving. Woven wire or stock fence is the most common wire fence, but a 2 × 4 inch V-mesh horse fence is safer and is gaining in popularity. A woven wire fence with a board at the top (and sometimes at the bottom) keeps the wire taut and provides a good visual barrier for horses. A single twisted wire or barbed wire at the top of a woven wire fence will also prevent horses from leaning on the fence, thus causing it to loosen and sag. Barbed wire is inexpensive but should *never* be used as the only wire with horses. A twisted barbless wire has been used successfully with horses. This type of fence should contain at least 4 strands of wire. It is inexpensive to build but can be difficult for the horse to see.

Pipe Fences

Pipe fences are strong and safe for horses but prohibitively expensive in many parts of the country. Pipe fences are excellent for corrals, paddocks, and heavily used areas but require welding and painting and the posts must be set in concrete. Pipe fences are most popular in the oil-producing regions where surplus pipe is available.

Chain Link Fences

This type of fence is particularly good for stallion pens or other small paddocks because it is extremely strong and safe. The top of the fence should be smooth or protected in some manner because sharp twisted ends are sometimes exposed at the top. A chain link fence will stretch from kicking, cannot be tightened, and is expensive to install.

Post and Cable Fences

720

This combination makes another satisfactory horse fence. The cable is usually threaded through the middle of wooden posts and attached by a turn buckle or spring to the corner posts. Cable fences are initially expensive but are strong, safe, and long lasting.

Precast Concrete Fences

These fences, made to resemble post and rail, are quite attractive. They are white, never need painting, withstand weather, and are virtually indestructible. However, a concrete fence is difficult to obtain and expensive to ship and install because of its weight.

Rubber-Nylon Fencing

This material has recently been made available for use as a horse fence and, when properly erected, is taut, attractive, and safe. The rubber-nylon belting is 2–4 inches wide and, from a distance, gives the appearance of a black board fence. This fence requires a minimum of maintenance, is easy to erect, and is relatively inexpensive.

Electric Fences

These fences can be used either alone or in conjunction with another type of fence. Electric fences have been used with some success but have not been universally accepted. When used alone, a 3- or 4-strand electric fence is effective and inexpensive, but it is difficult for the horse to see, and the light-gauge straight wire can cut. The electric fences will short out easily, particularly in wet weather. An electric fence is particularly effective when located on top of a woven wire fence or inside another fence. It keeps the horses "off the fences" and thereby reduces maintenance and the chance of injury. Two strands of electric fences supported on cross arms in a dividing fence will reduce "horse play."

23.5 Gates

Gates should be easy to use and should be as strong and safe as possible. They should be placed on high ground, and the gate area should be filled with sand or gravel to prevent the development of a mud hole at the gate entrance.

Wood gates are satisfactory but should be made of oak, or the top of the boards should be covered with metal to prevent chewing. Such gates are quite heavy but are long lasting. Welded iron and pipe gates are excellent but must be designed in such a manner that the horse cannot get a foot caught in them. Galvanized iron and aluminum gates are available commercially. The latter are light but also bend and break easily. Wire gates are difficult for a horse to see and are not very satisfactory unless the wire is attached to a stout frame.

Gate latches should be durable and easy to use but not easily opened by the horse or the wind. A chain and snap combination that goes through the gate and around the post is simple and works well.

23.6   Buildings for Horses

Horse barns should be located on sites that are well drained and easily accessible in all types of weather. They should take maximum advantage of prevailing winds in warm weather and be sheltered from winter storms. They should be placed so that the surrounding community is not annoyed by odor, noise, or flies. The barns should be surrounded by pastures or paddocks so that a loose horse cannot get out onto a main road. The barn area should be readily serviced by a hard-surfaced road and by public utilities (water, electricity, and telephone).

Stables should be pleasant places in which to work and should be designed for ease in feeding and cleaning. Construction considerations include attractiveness, ventilation, and fire resistance, as well as safety, cost, durability, and flexibility of design. Many barns are constructed of wood, but concrete, steel, aluminum, masonry, and other durable, fireproof construction materials can be used. The *Horse Handbook: Housing and Equipment* provides details on the construction of proper ventilation, and barn layout. This excellent study is inexpensive and is available from the extension agricultural engineer at your state university.

The type of barn depends upon the climatic conditions and the intended use. The requirements of a breeding farm differ from those of a small pleasure stable or a professional training stable. The type of shelter can range from a simple, open-front building to an elaborate show stable with large box stalls and fancy tackroom and lounge.

Open-front Shelters

Horses do well in free-access barns. These open-front sheds have become popular in all parts of the country in all phases of the horse industry because of the advantages they offer. They are inexpensive to build and maintain and alleviate the major problems associated with stabling horses: labor,

722

ventilation, and fire. There is no daily stall cleaning. Open-front sheds are well ventilated and horses housed in them have fewer respiratory and digestive problems. They also seem to have better mental attitude and improved muscle tone. Some managers believe that injuries may be reduced because the horses get more relaxed exercise and seem less apt to run wildly or fight. Fires, a dread of all horsemen, are not likely to occur in sheds, and if they do start, the horses are not trapped.

The biggest disadvantage of shed housing is that because of lack of surveillance, it is much easier to overlook an injury or illness. (When horses are maintained in stables, they must be examined carefully every day.) Horses kept in loose housing also grow shaggier hair coats and look rougher and dirtier than stabled horses, particularly during the mud season. Open sheds are not a good place to "show off" sale horses or show, race, and other performing horses.

Horses can withstand the elements so long as they are sheltered from the extremes. Flies, hot weather, cold rains, and strong, cold winds seem to bother horses, and run-in sheds provide adequate protection from these conditions. Charlie Kenney, manager of Stone Creek Stud near Paris, Kentucky, thinks that the horses prefer free-access housing. He notes that horses "rarely go into sheds except for food. They will go under a shed in sleeting weather or to get out of a cold rain, but do not seem to be bothered by ordinary snow or rain or wind unless the weather is really bitter. It makes a fellow wonder whether horses are kept up too much" (Hollingsworth, 1971).

Open-front buildings should face away from the prevailing winds. If it is located in the northern half of this country, the shed should face to the south to take advantage of the low winter sun. The opening should be at least 10 feet high and wide enough for all the horses to run out safely. Unless a clear-span structure is used, the supporting posts are set on 16-foot centers and padded in some manner. Sheds provide flexibility as to the number of horses that can be housed, but a minimum of 75 square feet per horse should be maintained. There must be no sharp edges, and the corners of sheds should be designed so that a horse cannot get trapped by a "kicker."

The roof should slope away from the opening or should be designed in such a way that rain water or snow will not collect at the entrance to the shed. The sheds should be located on high ground or graded so that water drains away from the building. Because steel and aluminum roofs are noisy in sleet storms and driving rainstorms, they should be insulated to reduce the noise so that it does not drive the horses out in bad weather.

Hay, mineral, salt, and grain feeders can be built into the back wall of the shed, but many managers prefer to feed hay outside—either on the ground or in separate field mangers. Waterers are best placed in the field away from the shed. In paddocks, waterers are located most successfully in the fence lines.

Barns with Stalls

For many horse enterprises, conventional stables with stalls are more satisfactory than open sheds. Horses kept in stalls can receive more individual attention and can be kept cleaner and more presentable, and the feed and exercise program can be controlled. Foaling mares, mares during the breeding season, and young horses can be closely observed. Horses kept in stalls are generally cared for daily, and this consideration is important for young horses and stallions.

Inadequate ventilation is probably the biggest mistake made in the construction of horse facilities. The heat and moisture produced by horses must be removed from the barn to prevent condensation and odor buildup. Horses did not evolve in stuffy, heated barns, but many well-intentioned owners provide low ceilings, small windows, and insufficient ventilation, thereby creating a perfect atmosphere for pneumonia and other respiratory problems. Old, porous buildings with no ceilings or with haylofts overhead provide a better environment than some of the newer, tight, draft-free barns. H. H. Sutton (1963), giving a veterinarian's view of farm management, states that "more respiratory infection is associated with confinement in small, tight, poorly ventilated stalls than in horses confined by gates in drafty barns."

Because ventilation is such a critical problem in raising horses, many outstanding breeding farms in the bluegrass region continue to use the old, converted, airy tobacco barns that have served them well for many years. Edward Fallon (1967) notes that "the healthiest barn I can imagine is one that we frequently see, and that is a tobacco barn which contains stalls for horses. They furnish adequate shelter and probably the best ventilation."

23.7 Stalls

The structure of the stall walls should be considered carefully. Wood is the most popular building material but may be chewed by idle, bored horses. Oak and other hard woods will withstand chewing longer than the soft woods. A beautiful new barn of pine was literally devoured by horses during one winter. Wood can be treated with creosote, liquid asphalt, or other commercial anti-chew products, but covering exposed edges with steel angle iron or sheet metal is a more satisfactory solution. No sharp corners or nail heads should be left exposed. Some stables use an electric fence wire to prevent chewing (and tail rubbing) in the stall, but such use is not recommended because it creates a fire hazard and the charged wire can be a nuisance to the handlers.

Stall Walls

Concrete, cinderblock, steel, and chain link fences are used for stall walls. Chain link fences are used especially in hot climates where maximum air circulation is desired. Concrete and cinderblock are very durable and can be covered with epoxy paint to achieve smoothness and to improve their appearance. Concrete walls are excessively hard if you have a "stall kicker," and cinderblock will break and crack from kicking.

The size of the box stall depends on its use. The most popular size is 12 feet × 12 feet. The more time the horse spends in the stall, the larger it should be. A box stall 10 feet × 10 feet is adequate for young horses and for some of the smaller breeds if the horses are turned out regularly. A larger stall is better for a foaling stall (see section 23.8).

Stall partitions should be solid to a height of 5 feet with some sort of divider to the ceiling. If there is no ceiling the stall walls should be 8 feet high. Air circulation may be more important than solid partitions in hot climates. Horses, especially stallions, that can see each other are usually calmer and happier. Thus, a light, airy barn with chain link, welded wire, or pipe dividers at the top of the stall partitions is preferred. However, there are instances when a completely solid stall wall is desirable (that is, for some stallions, for foaling stalls, and for many performing horses). In either case the walls should be smooth—the fewer projections (mangers, feeders, waterers) into the stall, the better.

The fronts of the stalls can be open above 5 feet but many owners prefer some sort of screening to keep the horse's head out of the aisle. Doors should slide or open outward. For convenience and safety, never have a stall door open into the stall. The stall doors should be at least 4 feet wide and 8 feet high. Dutch doors are popular: the bottom panel is usually 5 feet high and 4 feet wide and the top panel is 4 feet wide and 3 feet high. Some horsemen insist on having 2 doors for each stall, one into the aisle and the other outside into a paddock to provide fire safety. Aisles should be at least 10 feet wide and should be designed to accommodate a pickup truck or tractor. The aisle floors should be durable and easy to clean, and should provide good footing.

Windows

The windows should never be lower than 4 feet from the floor and should slide or open outward. They should *always* be screened in some manner to protect the horse from the glass. Some windows are designed to hinge at the bottom and to open inward so that they deflect the air upward to avoid direct drafts. These windows must be mounted at least 8 feet above the floor. The ceilings in stalls should be a minimum of 8 feet high, but

725

10-foot ceilings or no ceilings are safer and provide better ventilation. Electrical wires and fixtures should be covered and should be safely out of the reach of the horse.

Feeders, Waterers, and Mangers

The use and location of feeders, waterers, and hay mangers is a controversial topic among farm managers. A number of commercial models are available, but care should be used in choosing equipment to make sure that it is safe and designed specifically for horses. Feeders and waterers are usually placed "out of the way" in the corners. Some stable managers prefer to feed hay directly on the floor, a more natural location. Since horses often pull hay out of the mangers and eat it off the ground anyway, these managers consider the manger an unnecessary hazard in the stall. Rubber and plastic feed tubs are rapidly replacing cast iron tubs because they are less expensive, easier to clean, safe, light, and quite durable.

The type of watering facilities in the stall is also controversial. Automatic waterers save labor but must be cleaned and checked *regularly* because a plugged float can leave a horse without water for several days before detection. Freezing and flooding are also potential problems. Some excellent commercial stall waterers are available, but they must be mounted safely in the stall. Some horsemen prefer to water with a bucket because it is easily cleaned, water consumption can be observed, and the water can be easily withheld when necessary. On the other hand, bucket watering is time-consuming, and horses are often left without water, particularly overnight. Rubber buckets are safer than galvanized pails and can be hung in the corner of the stall with a snap.

Stall Floors

A variety of flooring surfaces have been used successfully in stables. The most popular stall flooring material is hard-packed clay, which is relatively warm and resilient but tends to be slippery when wet, and holes or pockets may develop. A concrete or asphalt apron at the stall door discourages "digging." Clay should be placed over a well-drained subfloor of crushed rock or gravel. Stone dust and sand also make excellent stall floors but are not as durable as clay. Sand requires no additional bedding but must be cleaned regularly and changed occasionally.

Wooden planks are often used to cover concrete or in elevated floors, but they tend to be slippery when wet, they are difficult to clean completely, and they harbor odors. Wood block floors were popular in many older barns but are now prohibitively expensive. Concrete, even when roughened, is potentially slippery, cold, and hard, even when plenty of bedding is used, but it is easy to clean and long lasting. Asphalt (macadam or blacktop) is very satisfactory. It provides better traction than concrete, is durable, resilient, and easy to clean. It has been used successfully to cover existing concrete, dirt, clay, and even wood floors but is cold and hard. New composition materials, such as Tartan surfacing, carpeting, and even astroturf, provide fine surfaces but are expensive to install and maintain.

Ease of cleaning and of manure disposal are important considerations in planning stalls. Mechanical cleaners are used in some stables but the majority of barns are still cleaned by manual labor. The alley in front should be large enough to accommodate cleaning equipment.

23.8   Specialized Structures

Tie Stalls

Straight stalls or tie stalls are not as widely used for light horses as they were for draft or carriage horses. However, straight stalls provide stabling for more horses in a given area than box stalls and require less bedding and labor. The construction details and flooring of tie stalls are similar to those of box stalls except that a manger is usually built into the front of the stall, provision is made for tying the horse, and a tail chain is often put across the back of the stall. Straight stalls should be 9 feet in length, including the manger, and 5 feet in width. Tie stalls are popular in riding stables.

Foaling Stalls

Foaling facilities should be light, dry, and secluded. The stall is often isolated from the rest of the stalls. On large farms, a separate barn is used as the foaling barn. Foaling stalls should be roomy (12 feet × 16 feet or 16 feet × 20 feet), well ventilated, and designed so that the mare can be observed without disruption. An attendant should always be present during foaling because of potential problems that may arise during the foaling process. Consequently, many foaling stalls have windows facing into adjoining heated "waiting rooms" where the attendant can quietly observe the activities of the expectant mare. Closed circuit television provides another effective method of surveillance of foaling mares. Adequate lighting is essential in the foaling area because most mares foal after dark.

Broodmare Barns

Broodmares often foal early in the year, so it may be necessary to have facilities for the mare before foaling as well as for the mare and her foal after foaling. Broodmare barns should have large (16 feet × 16 feet) stalls and be located near paddocks or pastures.

Foal Creep

Many farms provide a foal creep where the nursing foal can have free access to grain while on pasture with its dam. The creep is so designed that foals can enter but mares cannot. A creep may be set up in a part of a shed, a stall, a separate portable building, or a fence line. A pasture creep should provide shade and should be located near an area where mares tend to congregate. The creep should have at least two entrances; the mares are restricted by the height (approximately 46 inches) or width (approximately 16 inches) of the opening of the entrances.

Stallion Facilities

Stallions can be kept in the main barn, but they should have their own large, secure stall. Stud farms have separate stallion barns, often with adjacent stud paddocks. There is an increasing interest among horsemen in keeping stallions in individual sheds in stud paddocks. The paddocks should have strong fences. Most managers prefer that the stud fences be 5 feet high and that the paddocks be separated by at least a 10-foot lane to prevent fighting among the stallions.

Breeding Shed

Farms that stand a stallion must have a designated enclosed area to breed mares. A breeding shed should be large enough (at least 20 feet × 20 feet) and high enough (12–15-foot ceiling) to be safe for horses and handlers (see section 13.2). The safety of horses can be further ensured by padding the walls and installing a dust-free, slip-proof floor. Crushed stone or washed gravel is the floor surface most commonly used in sheds, but other materials, including rubber, asphalt, carpeting, and synthetic turf, are also used. The stone floor can be dug up to provide a hole or mound for the mare to stand on depending on her size. The breeding sheds usually include a teasing board that can be folded out of the way. Sometimes provision is made for an observation area for the mare owner or his representative. The breeding shed should have facilities for examining mares and a laboratory equipped with the necessary sterilizing and sanitizing equipment.

Hay, Bedding, and Other Storage

Hay and bedding are conveniently stored in lofts over the stalls, but they are a fire hazard, and overhead storage is expensive to construct. Consequently, separate hay and bedding sheds provide a better solution to the problem of storage. Hay and bedding should be kept dry and free of birds and rodents, protected from fire, and located conveniently to the horses.

A clean, dry storage area should be available for show buggies, training carts, extra tack, and other equipment.

Feed Room

A feed room in which to formulate and store feed can be located within the stable area. It must be tight, dry, and conveniently located, and must keep out insects, birds, and rodents. The door should be so designed that it cannot be accidently opened by a horse. The feed room may be equipped with metal-lined storage bins, grain crimper, feed cart, and scales. Steel, rodent-proof bulk grain tanks provide good storage and should be so located that the feed grains are augered into the feedroom. On small farms, galvanized cans provide adequate storage.

Barn Office

A stable that serves the public should have a central office where visitors can be greeted, records kept, and business transacted. The office should be comfortable and should be convenient to clean restrooms for the public and employees.

Tack Room

A barn must have a dry, clean room where tack such as bridles, halters, and saddles can be stored. Many tack rooms are show areas where winnings are displayed, but they are also working areas that provide storage for grooming materials, blankets, clippers, farrier's tools, and medications, as well as tack. There should be a refrigerator for storage of pharmaceuticals (see section 21.6).

Wash Rack

Show, training, and sale stables often have specific areas in which horses can be washed. The area must ensure good footing when wet, and must have adequate drains and hot and cold running water. Most wash racks have provisions for crosstying the horses, and some have overhead heaters.

Swimming Pool

Swimming pools have become popular for conditioning horses, particularly those with leg problems. Swimming increases stamina, wind, and muscle tone while preventing trauma to the feet and legs caused by concussion.

Hot Walker

The hot walker, a mechanical device that leads horses in a circle at a slow walk in order to cool them after training, is another labor-saving device now seen on many farms. The walker has recently gained popularity in show stables for use with performing horses and as a means of developing and conditioning halter horses.

Arena

An indoor arena enables a horse farm to operate regardless of the weather and is indispensable for many operations. The minimum size for a training arena is 60 feet × 100 feet; an arena twice that size is needed for shows and public events.

In planning an arena, special attention must be given to ventilation, the riding surface, insulation, heat, lights, entrances, and location. If the arena is to serve the public, consideration must be given to such items as parking, seating, rest rooms, and food services.

References

Blickle, J. D., R. L. Maddex, L. T. Windling, and J. H. Pedersen. 1971. *Horse Handbook: Housing and Equipment.* One in a series developed by the Midwest Plan Service. Iowa State University, Ames.

Dunn, Norman. 1972. Horse handling facilities. *Stud Managers Handbook.* Vol. 8. Clovis, California: Agriservices Foundation.

Ensminger, M. E. 1969. *Horses and Horsemanship.* Danville, Indiana: The Interstate Printers & Publishers, Inc.

Fallon, Edward. 1967. Breeding farm hygiene. *Lectures Stud Managers Course.* Grayson Foundation, Lexington, Kentucky.

Harvey, Harry M. 1968. Stock Farm Management. Chapter 18. *Care and Training of the Trotter and Pacer.* Columbus, Ohio: United States Trotting Association.

Hollingsworth, Kent. 1971. New-design Sheds Serve Well. In *A Barn Well Filled.* Lexington, Kentucky: *The Blood-Horse.*

O'Dea, Joseph C. 1966. Veterinarian's view of farm layout. Lexington, Kentucky: *The Blood-Horse* (December): 3790–3791.

Smith, Peter C. 1967. *The Design and Construction of Stables.* London: J. A. Allen.

Stone, Charles H. 1971. Good Fences Make Good Neighbors and Good Horse Farms. In *A Barn Well Filled.* Lexington, Kentucky: *The Blood-Horse.*

Sutton, H. H. 1963. The Veterinarian and Horse Farm Management. In *Equine Medicine and Surgery.* 1st ed. Wheaton, Illinois: American Veterinary Publications.

Valliere, Donald, W. 1971. A Barn for All Seasons. In *A Barn Well Filled.* Lexington, Kentucky: *The Blood-Horse.*

Willis, Larryann C. 1973. *The Horse Breeding Farm.* Cranbury, New Jersey: A. S. Barnes.

CHAPTER TWENTY-FOUR

Management of a Horse Farm

24.1   Care of the Herd

Successful management of a horse operation requires attention to many details and the application of considerable knowledge and skill. Without proper planning of the year's activities and a sufficient labor force, the job can be overwhelming. The major tasks should be distributed throughout the year to ensure that they are completed at the proper time. Although it is impossible to consider all the necessary details of management, a suggested schedule is discussed here.

Midwinter

December and January (midwinter) are good months for inside maintenance and repair work. When the barns and stables are inspected for necessary repairs, they should also be inspected for fire safety.

Stallions are prepared for the breeding season, which usually starts on February 15. In localities with severe winters, the breeding season may start later. Regardless of when the season begins, the stallion's feed must be regulated so that the stallion is in good breeding condition. Overweight stallions should be placed on a reducing diet so that the weight is lost before the breeding season. Thin stallions should be gaining weight at the onset of the breeding season. Stallions that will be worked and also bred to mares may need to be a little overweight at the start of the breeding season because they will lose weight as the season progresses. Stallions seem to have a better mental attitude toward breeding mares if they are exercised daily and their muscles have good tone. They should be given a physical examination for breeding soundness and semen quality (see Chapter 12). Unsound horses can be treated, and the book (the mares that are to be bred to a particular stallion) of stallions with poor semen quality can be reduced. Poor semen quality also requires that special attention be given to the number of services per week and that frequent semen evaluations be performed. Stallions that are standing at stud for the first time should be trained to breed mares. If they are returning from performance training, they may need to "let down," as discussed for replacement fillies (below).

The stallion's feet should be trimmed every 6–8 weeks. Unsoundness resulting from negligent foot care, particularly of the hind feet, can prevent the use of the stallion if he is unable to mount mares. The stallion's teeth should be checked for "hooks" (Chapter 5) and floated if necessary. A regular worming schedule should be established according to local conditions. As previously discussed (Chapter 20), stallions should be wormed at least every 6 months, and it is suggested that they be wormed every 4 months.

Pregnant mares should be fed so that they are gaining weight. During the last 90 days before foaling, they should gain approximately 5 percent of their normal body weight. Their feet should be trimmed or shod every 6–8 weeks. Their teeth should be checked for hooks and other disorders, such as a long tooth growing into the area left by a broken off or lost tooth.

Pregnant mares should be visually checked at least once and preferably twice a day if they are in the last 90 days of pregnancy. Abortions during this period may be complicated and may lead to the mare's death unless she receives veterinary assistance.

Replacement fillies that have been selected to enter the broodmare band are often returning from performance training. After a horse has been in keen competition such as racing, competitive trail riding, or roping for a year or more, it should be given time to relax or let down for 2–6 months. This vacation allows the horse sufficient time to relax and readjust its mental attitude, and allows its body structures to recover. Most of the horses are keyed up and quite nervous when they are returned to the farm to let down; therefore, the early stages of the let-down period require time and patience. The ideal situation is to have a box stall with an outside paddock and a small pasture. During the first week or the first few weeks (the time depending on the extent of the nervous condition and the temperament of the horse), it will have to be led out to the pasture and grazed at the end of a lead shank. A couple of weeks may be required before the horse will hold its head down to the ground long enough to graze. The horse will require extra grooming time and frequent washings during the early part of the let-down period. The feet should be shod for normal activities rather than for competition. After the horse stops pacing the fence in its paddock and will graze quietly for a few minutes, it can be released in the pasture. For the first few times, the horse should be released for only an hour or so until it no longer wants to run and is relaxed. Because of its taut muscle

733

tone, the horse should be exercised each day in a relaxing manner until it is sufficiently let down to stay in the pasture all day. The horse's diet is a critical part of the letting-down process. Concentrated feeds must be replaced with hay to prevent digestive disturbances and to prevent the horse from becoming overweight. Because a longer time is required to eat hay, the horse will have something to do and will not get bored. As forage is consumed during the grazing period, the amount of hay can be reduced.

During November, a breeding preparation program should be started for the open and barren mares and replacement fillies. They should be exposed to an artificial light regime (see Chapter 13) and teased at least 3 times a week. When each mare has her first estrous period, she should be given a female genital examination. If the need is indicated from visual inspection, she should be cultured for genital tract infections. Treatment for reproductive disorders should be started during the breeding preparatory period of November, December, and January. The mares' feet should be trimmed or shod every 6–8 weeks, and their teeth should be examined and any imperfections corrected.

Two-year-olds, yearlings, and weanlings should be fed so that they continue to grow and develop at an optimal rate, and their feet must be trimmed every 4–6 weeks. Young horses that require corrective trimming may have their feet trimmed at more frequent intervals. The yearlings and 2-year-olds are wormed every 3 months, and the weanlings are wormed every 2 months. If necessary, some weanlings should be worked with to continue their gentling process. Yearlings that will be raced as 2-year-olds may be placed in light training; if they have finished their preliminary training, they are given a rest period for further development. Two-year-olds returning from the racetrack may be given a rest period before training for their 3-year-old year. Two-year-olds that are to be ridden under the saddle may be placed in light training.

Late Winter

The months of February and March are the beginning of the breeding season for horses. The stallion must be fed properly to maintain good condition. He should be exercised daily. Semen evaluations should be performed weekly if the stallion is breeding several mares each week. During the early part of the season, it may not be necessary to check semen quality as frequently because breeding activity is minimal.

Pregnant mares are cared for in February and March as they were during November, December, and January. At least 2 weeks before foaling, they should be housed in their foaling area. Approximately 30 days before their foaling due date, they should be checked to see if their vulva was sutured (Caslicks operation, see Chapter 13). If so, the vulva should be opened up. After the mare foals, her feed should be gradually increased to meet her needs for milk production, and she should gain .25 to .5 pounds of body weight per day. If the mare is to be rebred, she should be teased on a regular schedule; teasing should begin approximately 7 days after foaling.

Barren, open, and maiden mares should be teased daily or at least on alternate days. As the mares come into estrus, their ovaries should be palpated per rectum on a daily or alternate-day basis to determine the optimal time to breed. All mares should be checked for pregnancy 30–40 days after their last breeding if they have not returned to estrus.

The 2-year-olds and yearlings are managed as they were in November, December, and January. The young foals should be handled so that they become gentle. Some horsemen prefer to halterbreak them at an early age, but others prefer to wait until just before or after weaning.

Spring

Stallions, mares about to foal, and mares still being bred are managed as previously indicated for February and March. Open, barren, and maiden mares that have conceived should be turned out to pasture after they have been wormed. They should be vaccinated for sleeping sickness and rhinopneumonitis and given their booster shots for tetanus.

Foals should be wormed when 6–8 weeks old and then every 2 months until they are yearlings. Foals will start eating grain or a grain-supplement mixture. To prevent consumption by the mare, it is necessary to creep-feed the foals. Their feet require trimming at 4-week intervals. Those requiring corrective trimming should be slightly trimmed more frequently. The foals should be immunized against tetanus, sleeping sickness, rhino-pneumonitis, and influenza when they are 2–4 months of age.

Stallions are immunized against tetanus and sleeping sickness and wormed. They are fed to maintain proper body condition and exercised on a regular schedule. At the end of the breeding season, it is wise to evaluate the stallion's semen and give him a soundness check. Any disorders can then be treated.

Lactating mares should be fed to maintain body condition and milk production. They should be wormed on a regular schedule. The schedule will depend upon the degree of internal parasite load as determined by fecal counts of parasite eggs. Dry mares that are open (not bred the previous year) or pregnant should be kept on a maintenance diet and wormed on a regular schedule with the lactating mares. All mares should have their feet trimmed at 6- to 8-week intervals.

Yearlings are managed as for the late winter period. Those that are to be trained are given their basic handling preparatory to their specific training. They should be immunized with the rest of the horses.

Foals should be weaned at 4–5 months of age. Many considerations

735

determine the exact time to wean the foals (feed conditions, condition of mare, mare's milk production, and availability of physical facilities). Foals should be on a full ration by the time they are weaned. Registration applications must be completed and sent to the breed registry.

Decisions should be made concerning to which stallion each mare will be bred the following year. All necessary breeding records for the year must be completed and sent to the breed organization.

24.2   Record Keeping, Identification, and Contracts

Records

A set of records should be kept for each horse regardless of whether it is owned by a one-horse owner or a large breeding farm. An up-to-date and accurate inventory of all horses should be kept and should include name, registration number, date of birth, sire and dam, registration numbers of sire and dam, date acquired, value of horse and depreciation rate. These records are essential for federal, state, and local tax purposes. It is easy to forget the dates of various activities regarding each horse, so other records must also be kept. To ensure that information concerning the horse's health is accurate, a clinical record of all vaccinations, treatments, wormings, shoeings, and trimmings must be kept. This information is important to someone who buys a horse and aids the veterinarian in treating the horse. Other records that must be kept by breeding farms for their stallion(s) and/or mare(s) include stallion contracts (see Chapter 13), breeding records, breeding certificates, and lease contracts.

Lease Agreements

Many stallions and mares are leased for one or more breeding seasons. All terms regarding use of the animals should be clear to both parties and spelled out in the lease agreement.

The terms concerning stallions should include any restrictions on the horse's use (the number of mares that may be bred, and whether the stallion can be used for purposes other than breeding). The date of arrival and departure and the conditions under which the stallion is kept should be considered. Signature authority for registration of the foals must be decided.

When mares are leased, it must be clearly understood who owns the foal in utero and how long the mare is to be kept by the lessee after she is bred. Warranties concerning the mare's breeding condition as well as the payment are important to both parties.

Breeding Records

Mare owners and breeding farms must keep a very accurate set of records. For example, Tartan Farms, home of Dr. Fager, the 1968 Thoroughbred Horse of the Year, uses forms carefully designed by John Hartigan, the manager, to keep an accurate account of all arrivals (Figure 24-1) and departures (Figure 24-2). If part of the information that is needed to enhance the breeding of the mare is not known, a new arrival report (Figure 24-3) is sent to the mare owner to be returned with the pertinent information.

During the breeding season, accurate records are kept of the sexual activities of all the mares. The Broodmare Stud Record contains daily information about such items as the cervical condition, follicular growth patterns, teasing response, uterine and cervical cultures, pregnancy status, and foaling process. To follow the health status and to maintain an accurate record of preventative medical procedures, a clinical record and a log of procedural activities are kept for each mare (Figure 24-4). These records will be useful, should veterinary services be required, and they contain information that will increase the efficiency of breeding and managing the mare.

FIGURE 24-1
Arrival record for mare brought to farm to be bred. Form is in triplicate:
1 for farm, 1 for main office, and 1 for owner. Form courtesy of Tartan
Farms, Ocala, Florida.

RT. 2, BOX 39-C
OCALA, FLORIDA 32670
PHONE (904) 237-2151

Tartan Farms

ARRIVAL

Fee $...............

Barn ....

Time........................ Date..........................

HORSE ....Color .... Sex .... Age ....

OWNER ....Address ....

....

Method of arrival ....From ....

....

Appearance of Horse ....Tatoo Number..................................

Equipment ....

Instructions ....

....

Remarks ....

....

Signed ....

Tartan Farms

Phone (904) ~~237-2536~~
237-2151

NEW ARRIVAL REPORT

Rt. 2, Box 39-C
Ocala, Florida 32670

TO: _____   Date _____

We have received _____, a _____ _____.
                                                    (Color)   (Sex)

To facilitate our records, please fill out applicable information below and return promptly.

Age _____ Breeding: Sire/Dam _____

Sire of Foal _____ Foaling Date _____

Date of Last Service _____ Booked to _____

Shots	Yes	No	Date
Ensephalo	☐	☐	_____
Virus Abortion	☐	☐	_____
Tetanus Toxoid	☐	☐	_____
Flu Vaccine	☐	☐	_____

Date Last Wormed _____

Date Last Cultured _____

_____

Insurance _____ (Yes/No) Who to contact? _____

Bills & reports should be mailed to: _____

_____ Phone No. _____

Manager's or trainer's instructions _____

_____

All due precautions will be taken, but under no circumstances will Tartan Farms accept any responsibility for accident or disease.

FIGURE 24-2

Notice of new arrival form that is sent to a horse owner. Form courtesy of Tartan Farms, Ocala, Florida.

FIGURE 24-3

Departure notice that is sent to horse owner. Form is in triplicate: 1 for barn, 1 for main office, and 1 for owner. Form courtesy of Tartan Farms, Ocala, Florida.

RT. 2, BOX 39-C
OCALA, FLORIDA 32670
PHONE (904) 237-2151

Tartan Farms Corp.

DEPARTURE

Time ....   Date ....

HORSE ....Color .... Sex .... Age ....

OWNER ....Address ....

....

Shots	Yes	No	Date
Ensephalo	☐	☐	....
Virus Abortion	☐	☐	....
Tetanus Toxoid	☐	☐	....
Flu Vaccine	☐	☐	....
....	☐	☐	....

Date Last Wormed..

Oiled for trip .... (Yes/No)

Tranquilized for trip .... (Yes/No)

Veterinarian ....

Method of Departure .... To ....

....

Appearance of Horse .... Tatoo Number.................

Equipment ....

Instructions ....

Remarks ....

Signed ....

738

TARTAN FARMS
Ocala, Florida

BROOD MARE STUD RECORD
BREEDING SEASON 19___

Name _____
Age _____ Color _____
Tatoo No _____
Jockey Club Cert. No. _____

Sire _____ Dam _____ Sire of Dam _____

Owner of Mare _____ Date of Arrival _____

In Foal To _____ Date Due _____

Approximate Markings _____

Physical Examination (Date and Result) _____

Parasite Count (Date and Result) _____

Parasite Control Program _____

Booked to _____ Genital Examination _____

TEASING CHART — JAN. TO JUNE

	1	2	3	4	5	6	7	8	9	10	11	12	13	14	15	16	17	18	19	20	21	22	23	24	25	26	27	28	29	30	31
JAN																															
FEB																															
MAR																															
APR																															
MAY																															
JUN																															

B—Bred
Cl—Cultured
F—Follicle
H—Horn

I—Inseminate
L or R—Left or Right
N—Barren
O—Showing

P—Pregnant
PN—Pregnant Negative
T—Treated
X—Out

CERVICAL CONDITION
1—Closed
2—Starting to open
3—Open to Breeding
4—Closing

a—No Color
b—Light Pink
c—Breeding Red
d—Infected Red

FOLLICLE
1—None
2—Coming
3—Breeding ready
4—Ovulated

BREEDING DATES _____

TESTS & TREATMENT _____

PREGNANCY TEST DATE _____ RESULT _____

Mare Name _____ Tatoo No. _____

In Foal to _____

GENITAL ORGANS AND FOALING

Udder _____ Vulva _____

Vulva Opened _____ Stitched and or Clamped _____

Delivery _____ Date and Time _____

Placenta Passed _____ Foal Nursed _____ Meconium _____

Condition at Birth _____ Up _____ 1st-3rd Day _____

Foal Description Sex _____ Color _____ Approx. Markings _____

Mare Behavior Before and After Foaling _____

Mare Condition _____

Injections Foal _____

Mare _____

FIGURE 24-4

Broodmare Stud Record form used to record daily estrous cycle
activity. Form courtesy of Tartan Farms, Ocala, Florida.

739

Tartan Farms Corp.

JOHN H. HARTIGAN
FARM MANAGER

TIME .... — BREEDING RECORD — DATE ....

MARE NAME .... AGE........... TATOO # ....

SIRE .... DAM ....

CONDITION OF MARE AT TIME OF BREEDING:
MAIDEN ☐   BARREN ☐   FOALING ☐   FOAL HEAT ☐   27 DAY ☐   OTHER ☐

STABLED AT ....
(Farm Name)

MARE OWNER ....

MARE BRED TO ....

STANDING AT .... BOOKED BY ....

REMARKS ....

ATTENDANT...

FIGURE 24-5
Breeding record form. Stallion attendant fills out the form and sends
it to the farm office. Form courtesy of Tartan Farms, Ocala, Florida.

After each mare is bred, the stud manager or attendant fills out a breeding
record or report (Figure 24-5) that is sent to the farm manager. When the
mare is pronounced in foal, the mare owner is notified (Figure 24-6).

The birth of new foals is reported to the farm manager on a form similar
to that shown in Figure 24-7. The owner of the foal is then notified. The
information on the form will be needed when the mare is rebred and when
registration forms are filled out.

The breeding activity of each stallion is recorded on a stallion record

FIGURE 24-6
Form on one side of postage card used to notify mare owner of pregnancy status of mare. Form courtesy of Tartan Farms, Ocala, Florida.

Date_____, 19____.

GENTLEMEN:

The mare_____ bred to_____

last service date_____ was examined for

pregnancy on_____and has been pronounced:

( ) IN FOAL   ( ) BARREN

Signed:_____

Phone (904) 237-2151

Tartan Farms

Rt. 2, Box 39-C
OCALA, FLORIDA 32670

FOAL REPORT

TIME FOALED ________________ DATE ____________________

☐ Bay ☐ Black ☐ Chestnut ☐ Dk. Bay or Br. ☐ Gray ☐ Colt ☐ Filly

Sire/Dam ____________________

Owner ____________________

Address ____________________

Condition After Foaling ____________________

Approximate Markings ____________________

____

____

Medical Treatment ____________________

____

Equipment ____________________

Signed ____________________

FIGURE 24-7
Foal report form to notify owner of birth of a foal. The form is in triplicate: 1 for foaling barn, 1 for office, and 1 for owner. Form courtesy of Tartan Farms, Ocala, Florida.

FIGURE 24-8
Stallion record of mares bred on a daily basis. Form courtesy of the Animal Science Department, University of California at Davis, Davis, California.

STALLION RECORD

Page________

Name____________________ Breed ____________________ Markings____________________

No. ____________________ Date Foaled ____________________

DATE	MARE	Reg. No. of Mare	BREED	COMMENTS

(Figure 24-8). The form should allow space for the date; the mare's name, registration number, and breed; and a comments section. This form enables the stud manager quickly to determine if the stallion is being used excessively. Semen evaluation data should also be recorded on the same form.

The departure card, a copy of which is sent to the owner, provides the mare owner with the latest information about the mare, including the standard medical procedures that have been performed. Many managers take Polaroid snapshots of the incoming and outgoing horses to avoid owner misunderstandings of any change in the horse's physical condition.

Boarding Stables

Because of the booming horse population, an increasing percentage of horses are being kept in boarding stables. The manager of the boarding stable should require the horse owner to sign a contract. These contracts should clarify for the owner what is to be done in emergencies and who is to be responsible for certain aspects of the horse's care. It is important for the stable personnel to have the authority to call a veterinarian in an emergency and to be assured that the owner will pay for the services. The responsibility for shoeing, grooming, exercising, and training must be determined between the stable and owner. Both the board rate and the due date should be set. To prevent misunderstandings, the feeding program should be outlined and the type of housing facilities for the horse should be specified. A liability clause is usually included in the contract. The owner usually agrees to abide by the rules and regulations of the stable. At some stables, insurance is provided for tack, equipment, and the horse if the owner desires it. A clear understanding of these points can prevent hard feelings between owner and stable personnel.

Identification

Identification of horses and other livestock has always been a problem for livestock owners. If an identification system is to be successful, the marks used in the system must be visible from a distance, permanent, painless, inexpensive, easy to apply, nondamaging, unalterable, and adaptable to data retrieval.

Branding

Hot Iron. The hot iron brand is one of the oldest means of identification. It is a permanent brand, but it can be altered. In addition, hair grows over the scar and identification of the brand from a distance becomes difficult.

742

Another problem with hot iron branding is the stress and pain that must be endured by the horse. Acid brands were introduced but were not successful for similar reasons. Since 1947, Thoroughbred racehorses have been lip-tattooed as a means of identification to prevent the running of "ringers" (look-alikes).

Freeze Branding. In 1965 freeze branding, a new method of identification of livestock, was discovered. The procedure is painless. The intense cold of branding irons kept in liquid nitrogen or dry ice and alcohol destroys the pigment cells of the skin. Regrowth of hair on the frozen area is white. Approximately 6–8 weeks are required for the white hair to grow sufficiently to make the brand legible, but the brand is permanent and easy to read. Several numerical or code systems have been devised so that several billion horses can be branded, each with a different brand. One system utilizes the 26 letters of the alphabet and the digits 0–9. The 36 characters are uniquely designed to prevent alteration of one character to another character (Figure 24-9). Each of the symbols can be arranged in 8 different positions and placed in a quadrant to produce more than 6 billion combinations.

The Y-Tex Corporation has combined freeze branding, a patented angle system, and a computerized data retrieval system to produce an identification system. Using a single iron and a set of alpha characters (Figure 24-10), it is possible to produce more than 20 billion combinations. The angle system makes the brand unalterable. It consists of an alpha character, 2 stacked angles and 6 angles, side by side. The last 6 angles are underscored by a ⅛-inch line. The line is used as a reference line to read the angles and to provide an unalterable mark. The alpha character is used to identify the breed of the horse, that is, "A" represents Appaloosa Horse Club registry and "E" represents unregistered (grade) horses. The stacked angles represent the year of birth. The top angle designates the decade and the bottom angle designates the year. The last angle designates the identification or serial number of the horse. Registration numbers are used for registered horses and a number that is recorded in this program is given to grade horses.

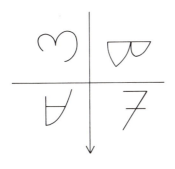

FIGURE 24-9
The brand for 1A132B473. The number one position of the arrow on the crossbars is for 1; position one for letter A is A1; position two for number 3 is for 32; position four for letter B is for B4; and position three for number 7 is for 73.

GRADE HORSE

TIM HARRIS   FREEZE MARKING DEPT.

FIGURE 24-10
The Y-Tex Corporation's system of alpha characters for freeze branding horses.

24.3 Producing and Selling Yearlings

Buying and Selling

When horses are 2 years old, most people make a decision to either keep them or sell them. The most common way of selling horses is by private treaty. The parties involved merely reach an agreement regarding the terms and conditions. Horse auctions are also a popular way to buy and sell horses. Buyers and sellers must understand the conditions of sale as they are printed in the sale catalogue. Horses of higher quality are advertised in other publications, in addition to the sale catalogue. Sellers should have their horses in excellent condition and well mannered for a sale. The stall area assigned to the seller should be kept clean and attractive. Quite often signs or advertising calling attention to the horse are used in the stall area. Public relations at the sale are important, so a place for buyers to relax and have a cup of coffee with the seller is important. Before buying a horse at auction, it is wise to inspect the horse carefully before it enters the sale ring.

744

Cost Considerations in Producing Yearlings

Regardless of whether foals are raised as a hobby or as a commercial enterprise, many costs must be taken into account when agreeing upon a sale price. It is difficult to construct a general cost figure because foals are raised under many different circumstances and in various localities. At least the following factors must be considered.

The purchase price of the mare must be allocated among the expected number of saleable foals she will produce. If it is assumed that the average number of foals produced per mare is 5 and that approximately 70 percent of live foals are saleable because of deaths, injuries, illness, or poor quality, 28.5 percent of the cost of the mare is allocated to each foal's cost.

Several costs must be borne to keep the mare for the period necessary, on the average, to produce a saleable foal. Approximately 70 percent of the mares bred will conceive, and then approximately 80 percent of the pregnant mares will bear a live foal. Therefore, the chance that a live foal will be born is approximately 56 percent. The average mare will have a foal every 2 years, but only 70 percent of live foals are saleable, so the average mare has a 39 percent chance of producing a saleable yearling. This means that the average mare must be kept 2.6 years per saleable yearling. The average cost of boarding a mare is approximately $80 per month or $2,496 for 2.6 years. Veterinary bills will average approximately $75 per year or $195 for 2.6 years. Farrier's charges for 2.6 years will be $94, assuming it costs $6 to trim the mare's feet every 2 months. The total cost for mare care for 2.6 years will be approximately $2,785.

Breeding expenses include the stallion fee, the cost of female genital examinations, and the cost of transportation and board when the mare is away from home. Transportation to and from the stallion will cost approximately $100 on the average. The veterinary examination usually costs approximately $35 per breeding season and the extra cost of boarding the mare is approximately $90 for 60 days. These costs total $225, and since 2.6 breeding seasons are required to obtain a saleable yearling, the cost is $585 per saleable yearling. If the stallion fee is $500, the breeding fee per saleable yearling will be $714 because only 70 percent of live foals are saleable as yearlings.

The cost of raising the foal to the age at which it can be sold will include the cost of boarding, veterinary fees, and farrier's fees. If board cost is $80 per month and the average age at sale is 10 months, the board cost will be $800. Only 70 percent of live foals are saleable, but 85 percent live and must be fed. Therefore, the board cost per saleable yearling is $941. Farrier's fees will be approximately $30 and veterinary fees will approximate $50. These costs total $1,021.

Sale costs vary from nothing for the sale of some yearlings to as much as $1,000 or more for those sold at auctions. The sale costs include entry fees, vanning, advertising, extra help at sale, and sale commissions. On the average, it costs approximately $250 to sell a yearling.

Assuming a $3,000 purchase price for a mare, the cost per saleable yearling is broken down as follows:

Cost of mare (28.5 percent)	$ 855
Mare care	2,785
Breeding cost	1,300
Cost of raising foal	1,021
Selling	250
	$6,211

The total cost is $6,211 per saleable yearling, and this figure does not include such expenses as insurance, taxes, depreciation of buildings and equipment, interest on investments, and cost of equipment.

Advertising

The quality and scope of the advertising of a horse for sale or a stallion standing at stud can often determine whether there will be a profit or a loss. There are many things to consider, but one of the most important is the photograph of the horse. Peter Winants (1971) has outlined 9 hints for a successful photograph:

1. An attractive head is essential. It should be turned to an angle where the off eye is barely visible.

2. A clean, well fitting halter helps to create a favorable impression of both the horse and the farm.

3. A still day helps to insure orderly appearance of the mane and tail, but hair setting gel may be necessary.

4. A bright day and side lighting help to provide brilliant highlights in the horse's coat and more attractive detail.

5. A relatively simple, uncluttered background helps to focus attention on the horse and not the scenery.

6. A straight line from the point of the hock to the ground shows the favorable points of the hind leg.

7. Freshly mowed grass helps to expose the feet and creates a neat appearance for the farm and horse.

8. Forelegs should be slightly separated with the near in front to allow prospective buyers to view both legs. "Daylight to the knees" is a thumb rule.

9. A straight line from the shoulder to the ground is attractive and shows the way a horse should be built.

Another consideration is which trade magazines should be chosen for advertising. Obviously, magazines that reach appropriate interested parties should be utilized. The value of the horse determines the scope of coverage. Inexpensive horses do not require nationwide coverage, which is quite expensive. With regard to stallions, mailing lists for breeders' associations are available, so that a personal advertisement may be sent.

Other, indirect means of advertising are just as important. Neat, well-appointed, and functional facilities are indicative of good management. Attractive horses that are well formed, healthy, in good condition, well mannered, sound, well groomed, and adapted to the purposes desired create buyer demand. Field days and tours for interested groups including 4-H and Future Farmers of America groups, create potential buyers. Appearance at and participation in breeders' association meetings, acceptance of speaking engagements at service clubs, and appearance on television or radio shows are good means of subtle advertising. Horsemen that follow up on horses they have sold create the impression that they are interested in their product.

Loading and Hauling

Before a horse is sold, the animal should be taught to be loaded into a trailer. When problems arise in the loading of a horse, the buyer usually knows he is loading a green horse or a problem horse. This situation is poor advertisement for the farm. The green horse is reluctant to enter a trailer because it is afraid. Confidence must be instilled in the horse through patience. If the green horse is gently urged up the ramp, it will usually load. The gentle urging requires the use of 2 ropes attached to each side of the trailer. The horse is kept directly behind the trailer with its head forward while one person pulls on each rope and a third person leads the horse into the trailer (Figure 24-11). After several practice sessions, the horse should enter the trailer without hesitation. Problem horses can be handled in the same way, but a broom or whip can be used to let the horse know that the horseman is in command of the situation.

If the horse is to be hauled a long distance, it is wise to give the animal a rest every 3 or 4 hours. Some stallions or geldings will not urinate in a trailer. It is advisable to haul a water bucket with which the horse is familiar because many horses will not drink strange water or from strange water troughs. If a stallion must be hauled next to a mare or if two horses that fight must be hauled together, Vicks Vaporub rubbed into their nostrils prevents them from smelling each other. Before going on a long trip, it is advisable to check the trailer for tire damage, rotted floorboards, safety

747

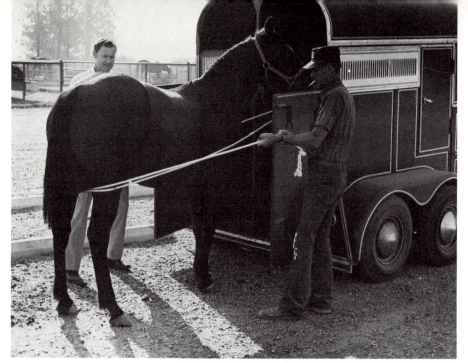

FIGURE 24-11
Use of butt ropes to load a reluctant horse into a trailer.

chains, lights, brakes, and wheel bearings. The driver should drive at an even rate of speed, avoid weaving in and out of traffic, and avoid sudden stops, starts, and turns.

Health Care

The 2-year-olds that will be kept or sold and the yearlings should be vaccinated for tetanus, sleeping sickness, rhinopneumonitis, and influenza, and wormed regularly. The 2-year-olds that will be kept should be marked for permanent identification.

24.4 Pasture Management

Good pastures can be an important part of the horse care program on many horse farms. However, pastures mean different things to different farms. On some farms, pastures are used as exercise and exhibition paddocks and play no role in the nutrition program. On other farms, high-quality pastures supply most or all of the nutrient requirements during most of the year. High-quality pastures offer several advantages. The forage is high in digestible nutrients, is perennial, is harvested by the horses, requires no storage, provides exercise, and requires limited labor. The forage produced by pastures is usually less expensive and provides more nutrients than hay and other purchased feed.

The pasture should have good shade (either trees or artificial shelter) for the horses. A source of fresh, clean water must be available. Salt should also be available, and it may be necessary to have a source of minerals. The pasture should be clean, that is, free from all sharp obstacles and holes. It should be fenced with one of the types of fence mentioned in section 23.4.

The amount of pasture required for a horse farm can be calculated from the number of horses kept on the farm and the expected forage production from the pasture. The average mature horse will consume approximately 25 pounds of dry matter per day or 750 pounds per month. Forage production per acre varies according to the type of pasture and its location. In many counties of the United States, county extension agents have conducted pasture demonstrations. These results are available and can be used as guidelines for calculating forage production. Pastures grow irregularly throughout the year and this must be taken into account. During the period of maximum growth, the excess forage can be made into hay, which can be used to supplement the horses' feed during the period of minimum forage production.

Horse owners are somewhat limited as to the kinds of pasture grasses and legumes that can be grown in each geographical area and that are suitable for horses. Certain species of forage grow profusely while others grow little or not at all. There are warm-season perennials, such as Bermuda grass, Johnson grass, bluestems, and native grasses. There are also warm-season annuals, which include sorghum-Sudan hybrids, Sudans, and millets. The sorghum-Sudan hybrids and Sudans have been known to cause a disorder known as cystitis syndrome, so the county extension agent or local veterinarian should be consulted before they are used as pasture. The cool-season perennials include fescue, orchard grass, Timothy, smooth bromegrass, perennial ryegrass, and bluegrass. The cool-season annuals include oats, barley, wheat, rye, and annual ryegrass. Legumes that are suitable for horses are alfalfa, clover, and birdsfoot trefoil.

Productive grasses, such as orchard grass, which is a bunch grass that produces regrowth rapidly following grazing, should be chosen for irrigated or subirrigated pastures. Smooth bromegrass forms a sod that has a distinct value in the prevention of compaction due to trampling. On wet areas or areas that are subject to heavy travel, tall fescue is quite productive though less palatable than orchard grass or smooth bromegrass. Where a high water table is present, reed canary grass or creeping meadow foxtail are both well adapted. Kentucky bluegrass will usually invade an irrigated grass pasture, so it may not be necessary to include the seed in a seedling mixture. Ladino clover is a selection of white clover that is pro-

749

ductive and quite palatable to horses. It requires frequent irrigation and does not withstand shading by tall grass growth. Alsike clover is adapted to wet, poorly drained sites and is short-lived. Birdsfoot trefoil is difficult to establish when competition from other plants is intense. It does withstand close grazing and is not as exacting in its water requirements as Ladino clover. Trefoil is not winter hardy in areas with extremely cold temperatures and little snow cover. Alfalfa can be maintained as a pasture if grazing is followed by long rest periods. The rambler or rhizoma varieties have low creeping growth and are more suitable for grazing than the hay varieties.

Dryland pastures are usually seeded to crested wheat grass, intermediate wheat grass, or Russian wild rye. Russian wild rye is leafy and palatable throughout the grazing season. Crested wheat grass is best during the spring and after fall regrowth, whereas intermediate wheat grass provides good grazing in the early part of the summer. Often, the dryland pasture will be more productive if Ladak or Orenberg alfalfa are seeded with the grass.

The specific seed mixture should be chosen in consultation with the local county extension agent. He can help the horseman select a legume-grass mixture on the basis of adaptation to soil and climate. The legumes and grasses must be compatible. An aggressive legume cannot be planted with a slow-growing grass and vice versa. Horses are selective grazers, so a highly palatable plant should not be planted with one that is unpalatable.

All necessary land leveling, grading, and shaping should be completed before seedbed preparation. The field should be plowed, deseeded, harrowed, and packed with a roller if necessary to make a firm seedbed. The seedbed should be free from old sod and weeds. If old plants are not completely removed, they will aggressively compete with new seedlings. A firm seedbed is one that allows a mare's foot to sink no deeper than 1/2 inch. Seeds germinate when they absorb soil moisture. This moisture usually comes from below the seed and moves upward through a well-packed seedbed. Packing the seedbed will prevent early drying of the soil and death of the seedlings. The soil should be tested to determine the plant nutrient needs for optimal production. Such a test is inexpensive and allows the horseman to make meaningful decisions about fertilizers.

Proper fertilization will improve protein content, increase tolerance to dry weather, increase regrowth after grazing, and increase resistance to disease. Grass and legume seeds should be planted between 1/4 and 3/4 inches deep. If planted deeper, the seedlings do not have the vigor to emerge and establish themselves. Seeding rates vary with the geographical area, but 6–8 pounds of grass seed plus 1–3 pounds of legume seed per acre are common rates.

After the pasture is established and is being grazed, several important management practices should be followed. The dung piles should be scattered periodically or removed. This will help reduce the parasite population. The pasture should be mowed periodically to remove weeds and rank vegetation around manure and urine spots. A new pasture should not be grazed until it is at least 6 inches high. At no time should the pasture be overgrazed to the point where not enough leaf material is left to permit rapid regrowth. A new pasture should be irrigated frequently so that the soil is not dry near the seed. After emergence, the seedling should not be allowed to become stressed. The roots of established pastures are usually in the upper 3 feet of soil. After this depth is watered, excessive water is wasteful. The pasture should not be irrigated when the horses are on it. The wet soil will compact, water penetration will be restricted, and plant growth will be reduced. If possible, pastures should be grazed on a rotational basis. They should be grazed for one week and rested for 2 weeks. During the rest period, manure is scattered, and the pasture is mowed to a height of 4–5 inches and irrigated. Horses tend to selectively overgraze portions of a pasture and undergraze others. Alternate grazing with cattle will result in better forage utilization. Cattle and horses tend to avoid grazing grass that grows around their own droppings, but will graze around each other's droppings. Grazing with cattle will also tend to reduce the parasite problem. The parasite problem will be minimized if all horses are wormed before they are turned out to pasture and then wormed on a regular basis. Fertilization rates should be established in consultation with the local county extension agent.

Horses establish a hierarchy, so the horseman must be certain that adequate pasture area is available to prevent aggressive horses from injuring the less aggressive ones. If insects become a problem, the horses should be sprayed or dusted.

24.5   Selection of Bedding

Bedding for horses should absorb urine, be free from dust, be readily available, be inexpensive, provide a comfortable bed, and be easy to handle. Several materials are commonly used, but the straws from barley and oats are the most common. The straw should be left in long lengths to keep it free from dust, even though the absorptive capacity of chopped straw is much higher. If it is left long, the stable personnel can quickly separate the clean areas from the dirty areas in the stall and thus less straw is used each day. Wood shavings are preferred by many horsemen. It is essential that such shavings be free from sawdust to prevent respiratory problems. The shavings from the softer woods have a greater absorption capacity. Shavings offer a definite advantage for people traveling to horse shows or sales in that they can be purchased in bales. Rice hulls and peanut hulls provide excellent bedding when they are available. However, they do not absorb water and the stall floor soon becomes saturated with urine.

751

Sand is a poor bedding. It absorbs very little urine, and horses that pick around in it for hay may develop sand colic. It is also quite heavy to handle.

24.6 Fire Safety

The problem of stable fires is acute, but the attitude of most people toward them is similar to their attitude toward fatal wrecks: they always seem to happen to someone else—always, that is, until they happen to you. Between 1960 and 1970, there were at least 140 reported stable fires in the United States. A total of 1,400 horses were burned to death, and property damage amounted to $30 million. The prevention of stable fires is of concern to all horsemen.

Protecting a horse in a stall from the danger of fire is a totally different problem than fire prevention in a person's home. The horse is usually standing in some type of bedding that is kept dry. Oat straw will develop a temperature of approximately 300 degrees at the head of the fire approximately one minute after it starts. Barley straw takes approximately 5 minutes to develop to 300 degrees. The point is that horses are standing in material that develops as much heat at the same rate as gasoline. All that is required to start a stable fire is a match or a spark.

A common problem is that there is usually only one door to the stall and the horse cannot escape into a paddock. The size of the stall is approximately 10 feet × 10 feet or 12 feet × 12 feet. Approximately 2 or 3 minutes are required for a straw fire in a stall to burn an area 10 feet in diameter. By the time the fire covers an area 4 feet in diameter, most horses have been injured. Their lungs are seared when the fire has covered an area 6 feet in diameter. They start to suffocate when the area is 8 feet in diameter and are dead by the time an area 10 feet in diameter has burned.

If a horse is to survive, the fire must be extinguished in the stall within approximately 30 seconds. How does the horseman cope with this special problem?

The most common answer is proper stable construction. Cement-block barns or similar types of construction are meant to save the building and not the horse in an individual stall. If the internal spread of fire through a barn is to be prevented, some construction features are mandatory. Fire-retardant paints are effective in delaying the combustion of wood framework inside the barn. Every 3 or 4 stalls should have partition walls that extend to the ceiling to help delay the spread of fire through the barn.

Sprinkler systems can also be used but most sprinklers were not designed to put out a fire under the circumstances that exist in a stall.

Automatic fire-extinguishing systems must meet at least 2 requirements to be used in a stable. They must not suffocate the horses when they are activated, and they must react within seconds after a fire starts. Most automatic sprinklers were designed to throw a circular pattern instead of a square pattern. The spray must be strong enough to reach the corners of the stall. If a fog-type system is used, the fog must suffocate the fire to extinguish it, otherwise the horse will suffocate along with the fire. Water can cause extensive smoke formation, which in turn will suffocate the horse or at least cause lung damage. This can be prevented if the sprinkler is activated before the fire covers an area 1 foot in diameter. A thermal lag system with sensors located above the stalls takes 4–5 minutes to activate, but this is too long. Recent developments have resulted in sprinkler systems that begin to operate approximately 5 seconds after a fire starts.

Of course, not all fires start inside a stall. A layer of chaff and dust covers the floor of the loft of many barns. The chaff and dust is like gasoline when it starts to burn. The loft and other storage areas of a barn should be swept on a regular schedule. Periodically, the inside of a barn should be hosed down with water to remove all the dust and cobwebs. This is just as important as keeping the alleyways clean.

An adequate number of exits from the barn are necessary so that fire will not block the only exit. All exits should open into enclosed areas. In case of fire, the horses can be turned loose but they must not flee the stable area. The fleeing horses may be killed by automobiles when they cross or travel down roads. They may also ruin other property such as lawns and crops.

The doors on the stalls should open outward into the alley. When horses flee through an emergency exit, their hips and other parts can be caught on doors that open into a stall. When the doors open into the alleyway, there is a possibility that someone may run through the stable, opening all the doors and letting the horses out. If a door accidentally closes and remains unlocked, the horse will open it if it runs into it trying to flee.

Because time is important in emergencies, the stall door latches should be strong and easy for people but not for horses to open.

If a barn is constructed in this manner, all the stall doors can be opened by the rescuer on his first trip through the alley. The horses that leave by themselves will be caught in the outside enclosed area. However, someone should prevent them from returning inside the barn because a scared horse likes to return to its familiar stall. Because of this trait, many horses will not leave their stall unless they are led out. It may be necessary to cover their head with a sack or something similar to prevent them from seeing the fire and smoke. They are easier to lead this way, and if led any other way, they try to climb the back wall of their stalls.

All electricity in a barn should be turned off at night, but the master switch should be located close to an entrance. Then the lights can be

753

turned on and one can see what is taking place inside during an emergency. Flashlights and the bouncing, moving shadows and lighted areas they cause are frightening to a horse. Do not use flashlights unless absolutely essential. The electrical wire in a barn must be protected from mice and rats. They will chew the insulation off, leaving 2 bare wires that can easily start an electrical fire. At the same location as the electrical switch, which should be at an exit, a fire extinguisher should be available in case of a small fire. At this location, there should also be a water hose that will reach the length of the barn. This hose should remain attached to a water hydrant so that one can quickly get water to all parts of a barn.

As another protective measure, each stall should have a hook beside it with a halter and lead rope attached. Then it is not necessary to waste time taking a halter off one horse and putting it on another while rescuing horses. Time is of the essence and a halter is thus waiting at the next stall door.

Personnel working at the stables should obey a strict set of fire prevention rules. Smoking should not be allowed in or adjacent to buildings. For convenience, large receptacles should be placed at building entrances. All electrical equipment should be in safe working condition and inspected regularly. Such appliances as hot plates, coffee pots, and radios should not be left unattended when in use. If they are used they should be used only in a special area. Inflammable materials such as lighter fluid, solvents, or cleaning fluids should not be used in the stable area. The owner or manager should not tolerate rule infractions by his employees or visitors. The rules must be rigidly enforced at all times.

References

Breuer, L. H., T. L. Bullard, and B. F. Yeates. 1970. A suggested schedule for management for a horse breeding farm. *Proc. Tenth Annual Horse Short Course*. Texas A & M University.

Davies, J. 1971. Fire protection for horses is different. *Thoroughbred Record* 193:556–557, 560.

Farrell, R. K., G. A. Laisner, and T. S. Russell. 1969. An international freezemark animal identification system. *J.A.V.M.A.* 154:1561–1572.

Guenthner, H. R. 1974. *Horse Pastures*. Horse Science Series. Cooperative Extension Service C151. Reno: University of Nevada.

Jeffries, N. W. 1970. *Better Pastures for Horses and Ponies.* Montana Cooperative Extension Circular 294 [May]. Bozeman: Montana State University.

Platt, J. N. 1974. Let's grow better pastures. *The Quarter Horse Journal* 26(9):162, 192.

Trimmer, L. 1974. Successful horse photography. *American Horseman* 4:20–22.

Vance, J. D. 1969. Cost factors in commercial thoroughbred breeding. *The Washington Horse* 23(8):940–942.

Vasiloff, M. J. 1970. Letting down. *The Chronicle of the Horse* 33:36 [January 9].

Walding, M. 1974. Horse photography. *The Quarter Horse Journal* 26:178–180.

Winants, P. 1971. Photographing your horse. *The Canadian Horse* 11(6):18–20.

Weight-unit conversion factors

Units Given	Units Wanted	For Conversion Multiply by	Units Given	Units Wanted	For Conversion Multiply by
lb	g	453.6	μg/kg	μg/lb	0.4536
lb	kg	0.4536	Mcal	kcal	1,000.
oz	g	28.35	kcal/kg	kcal/lb	0.4536
kg	lb	2.2046	kcal/lb	kcal/kg	2.2046
kg	mg	1,000,000.	ppm	μg/g	1.
kg	g	1,000.	ppm	mg/kg	1.
g	mg	1,000.	ppm	mg/lb	0.4536
g	μg	1,000,000.	mg/kg	%	0.0001
mg	μg	1,000.	ppm	%	0.0001
mg/g	mg/lb	453.6	mg/g	%	0.1
mg/kg	mg/lb	0.4536	g/kg	%	0.1

SOURCE: National Research Council. 1973.

Weight equivalents

1 lb = 453.6 g = 0.4536 kg = 16 oz
1 oz = 28.35 g
1 kg = 1,000 g = 2.2046 lb
1 g   = 1,000 mg
1 mg = 1,000 μg = 0.001 g
1 μg = 0.001 mg = 0.000001 g
1 μg per g or 1 mg per kg is the same as ppm

SOURCE: National Research Council. 1973.

Index